Public Places - Urban Spaces
The Dimensions of Urban Design

Public Places - Urban Spaces
The Dimensions of Urban Design

Second Edition

Mathew Carmona

Steve Tiesdell

Tim Heath

Taner Oc

ELSEVIER

AMSTERDAM ● BOSTON ● HEIDELBERG ● LONDON ● NEW YORK ● OXFORD
PARIS ● SAN DIEGO ● SAN FRANCISCO ● SINGAPORE ● SYDNEY ● TOKYO

Architectural Press is an Imprint of Elsevier

Architectural Press is an imprint of Elsevier
The Boulevard, Langford Lane, Kidlington, Oxford OX5 1GB, UK
30 Corporate Drive, Suite 400, Burlington, MA 01803, USA

First edition 2003
Second edition 2010

Notice
No responsibility is assumed by the publisher for any injury and/or damage to persons or property as a matter of products liability, negligence or otherwise, or from any use or operation of any methods, products, instructions or ideas contained in the material herein. Because of rapid advances in the medical sciences, in particular, independent verification of diagnoses and drug dosages should be made

British Library Cataloguing in Publication Data
A catalogue record for this book is available from the British Library

Library of Congress Cataloging-in-Publication Data
A catalog record for this book is availabe from the Library of Congress

ISBN—13: 978-1-85617-827-3

For information on all Elsevier publications
visit our web site at books.elsevier.com

Printed and bound in Italy

10 11 12 13 14   10 9 8 7 6 5 4 3 2 1

Working together to grow
libraries in developing countries

www.elsevier.com | www.bookaid.org | www.sabre.org

ELSEVIER   BOOK AID International   Sabre Foundation

Contents

An exposition of the different, but intimately related, dimensions of urban design, this book is an updated and revised version of a book originally published in 2003. Focusing neither on a limited checklist of urban design qualities nor, it is hoped, excluding important areas, it takes a holistic approach to urban design and place-making and thus provides a comprehensive overview of the subject both for those new to the subject and for those requiring a general guide. To facilitate this, it has an easily accessible structure, with self-contained and cross-referenced sections and chapters, enabling readers to dip in for specific information. The incremental layering of concepts aids those reading the book cover to cover.

Urban design is seen here as a design process, in which, as in any design process, there are no 'right' or 'wrong' answers, only 'better' and 'worse' answers, the quality of which may only be known in time. It is, thus, necessary to have a continually questioning and inquisitive approach to urban design rather than a dogmatic view. The book does not seek to produce a 'new' theory of urban design in a prescriptive fashion. Instead it expounds a broad belief in — and attitude to — urban design and place-making as important parts of urban development, renewal, management, planning and conservation processes.

Synthesising and integrating ideas and theories from a wide range of sources, the book derives from a comprehensive review and reading of existing literature and research. It also draws on the authors' experience teaching, researching and writing about urban design in schools of planning, urban studies, architecture and surveying.

Motivation

This book comes from two distinct sources. First, from a period during the 1990s when the authors worked together at the University of Nottingham on an innovative undergraduate urban planning programme. Its primary motivation was a belief that teaching urban design at the core of an interdisciplinary, creative, problem-solving discipline, planning (and other) professionals would have a more valuable learning experience and a better foundation for their future careers. Although in many schools of planning urban design is still figuratively put into a 'box' and taught by the school's single urban design 'specialist',

our contention was that an urban design awareness and sensibility should inform all parts of the curriculum. The same is true of schools of architecture, property, real estate and landscape.

Second, from a need to prepare undergraduate lecture modules presenting ideas, principles and concepts of urban design to support the programme's design studio teaching. Although many excellent urban design books existed, it soon became apparent that none drew from the full range of urban design thought. The writing of these modules generated the idea for the book and provided its overall structure.

The Book's Structure

The book is in three main parts. It begins with a broad exposition of what is meant by 'urban design'. In Chapter 1, the challenge for 'urban design' and for the 'urban designer' is made explicit.

The chapter deliberately adopts a broad understanding of urban design, which sees urban design as more than simply the physical or visual appearance of development, and an integrative (i.e. joined-up) and integrating activity. While urban design's scope may be broad and its boundaries often fuzzy, the heart of its concern is about making places for people — this idea forms the kernel of this book.

More precisely, it is about making *better* places than would otherwise be produced. This is — unashamedly and unapologetically — a normative contention about what we believe urban design *should* be about rather than necessarily what at any point in time it *is* about. We therefore regard urban design as an ethical activity — first, in an axiological sense (because it is intimately concerned with issues of values) and, second, because it is, or should be, concerned with particular values such as social justice, equity and environmental sustainability.

Chapter 2 outlines and discusses issues of change in the contemporary urban context. Chapter 3 presents a number of overarching contexts that provide the background for urban design action — the local, global, market and regulatory. These contexts underpin and inform the discussions of the individual dimensions of urban design principles and practice in Part II.

Part II consists of Chapters 4–9, each of which reviews a substantive dimension of urban design — 'morphological', 'perceptual', 'social', 'visual', 'functional' and 'temporal'. As urban design is a joined-up activity, this separation is for the purpose of clarity in exposition and analysis only. These six overlapping dimensions of urban design are the everyday substance of urban design, while the cross-cutting contexts outlined in Chapter 3 relate to and inform all the dimensions. The six dimensions and four contexts are linked and related by the conception of design as a process of problem solving. The chapters are not intended to delimit boundaries around particular areas of urban design and, instead, highlight the breadth of the subject area, with the connections between the different broad areas being made explicit. Urban design is only holistic if all areas of action — morphological, perceptual, social, visual, functional and temporal — are considered together.

In Part III — Chapters 10–12 — implementation and delivery mechanisms for urban design are explored — that is, how urban design is procured, controlled and communicated, thereby stressing the nature of urban design as a process moving from theory to action. Aspiring urban designers, especially those still in education, can often produce exciting visions and design proposals for the development of urban areas and the creation of (seemingly)

wonderful public places. The qualities of such visions may seem entirely self-evident and the case for their immediate implementation overwhelming. But this is a romantic, perhaps naïve, view of urban design and place-making. We live in the 'real world' and what appears entirely rational on paper is much more difficult to achieve on the ground. Furthermore, the reality is that implementation often fails in some way. Policies and proposals drift off course. Seen differently, however, they also evolve and develop through the implementation process. Stressing that places matter most, the final chapter brings together the various dimensions of the subject to emphasise the holistic and sustainable nature of urban design.

It is important to appreciate how urban designers (primarily those in or working for the public sector, but also others) can encourage, enable and sometimes compel better quality urban design in the form of higher quality development and/or better places for people. Rather than what urban design is or should be, the focus is *how* decisions become outcomes ('ends'), and the processes ('means') by which this happens.

An Emerging and Evolving Activity

It is only recently in the UK that urban design has been recognised as an important area of practice by the existing built environment professions, and even more recently that it has been recognised by central and local governments. This has been marked by central government through urban design and place-making becoming more central elements of the planning remit.

In the USA — in certain states at least — urban design has often been more fully conceptualised and better integrated into the activities of the established built environment professionals. Examining the planning history of cities such as San Francisco and Portland clearly demonstrates this. More generally, as in the UK, recent initiatives at both public and professional levels have combined to give urban design a new prominence — in the public sector, through the spread of design review as a means to promote better design through planning action and through the professions with the emergence of, for example, the Congress for the New Urbanism. In addition, urban design is the focus of well-developed grassroots activity, with local communities participating in the design, management and reshaping of their own local environments.

Urban design is a growing discipline. There is increasing demand for urban design practitioners — or, more simply, for those with urban design expertise and place-making sensibilities — from the public and private sectors around the world. This growth has been matched by a range of new urban design courses at both graduate and undergraduate levels; by greater recognition in planning,

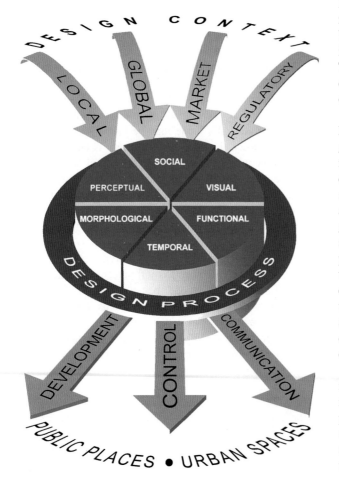

architectural and surveying (real estate) education; by a number of new urban design journals; and by a new demand from both private and public practitioners wanting to develop appropriate skills and knowledge.

All urban designers, whether 'knowing' or 'unknowing' (see Chapter 1), need a clear understanding of how their various actions and interventions in the built environment combine to create high quality, people-friendly, vital and viable environments or, conversely, poor quality, alienating, or simply monotonous environments. As a field of activity, urban design has been the subject of much recent attention and has secured its place among established built environment professions as a key means to address interdisciplinary concerns. In this position, it is a policy and practice-based subject, which, like architecture and planning, benefits from an extensive and legitimising theoretical underpinning. This book draws on that now extensive conceptual underpinning to present many of the key contributions aimed at beneficially influencing the overall quality and liveability of urban environments.

Urban design has developed quickly and continues to evolve, even in the seven or so years since the first edition of this book was written. It is hoped that the structure adopted by this book will continue to stand the test of time and that, over time, it will be able to incorporate other advances in thinking on the practice and process of urban design, and any omissions that — through our ignorance or lack of appreciation — we have not included. Hence, by contributing to the better understanding of good urban design, it is intended that this book will enable the design, development, enhancement and preservation of successful, sustainable and cherished places.

Defining Urban Design

Chapter 1

Urban Design Today

This book adopts a broad understanding of urban design as *the process* of making *better* places for people *than would otherwise be produced* (Figures 1.1–1.3). Four themes are emphasised in this definition: first, that urban design is for people; second, the significance of 'place'; third, that urban design operates in the 'real' world, with its field of opportunity constrained by economic (market) and political (regulatory) forces; and fourth, the importance of design as a process. That urban design is about making better places than would otherwise be produced is, of course, a normative contention about what urban design should be rather than what it is at any point in time.

Introducing and defining urban design, this chapter is organised into three main parts. The first part develops an understanding of the subject. The second part discusses the contemporary need for urban design. The third part discusses urban designers and urban design practice.

UNDERSTANDING URBAN DESIGN

From the early 1960s, a clutch of writers and designers — notably Jane Jacobs, Kevin Lynch, Gordon Cullen, Christopher Alexander, Aldo Rossi, Ian McHarg, Jan Gehl and others — became influential in shaping what would increasingly become known as urban design. The term itself had been coined in North America in the late 1950s and is often associated with Jose Luis Sert, Dean of Harvard's Graduate School of Design, convening an 'urban design' conference at Harvard in 1956 and subsequently setting up the first American urban design programme at that university (see Krieger & Saunders 2009).

As a term for the activity, it replaced the more traditional and narrower term 'civic design'. Typified by the City Beautiful Movement, civic design focused on the siting and design of major civic buildings — city halls, opera houses and museums — and their relationship to open spaces. Evolving from an initial, predominantly aesthetic, concern with the distribution of building masses and the space between buildings, contemporary urban design denotes a more expansive approach and, reflecting the title of this book, has become primarily concerned with shaping urban space as a means to make, or re-make, the 'public' places that people can use and enjoy.

Defining Urban Design

Containing two problematical words, urban design can be an ambiguous term. Taken separately, 'urban' and 'design' have clear meanings: urban describes the characteristics of towns or cities, while design refers to such activities as sketching, planning, arranging, colouring and pattern-making. As used generally within the field, 'urban' has a wide and inclusive meaning, embracing not only the city and town but also the village and hamlet, while 'design', is as much about effective problem solving and/or the processes of delivering or organising development, as about narrow aesthetics or particular physical outcomes.

FIGURE 1.1   Gammel Strand, Copenhagen (*Image: Steve Tiesdell*)

FIGURE 1.2   St Andrews Square, Edinburgh (*Image: Steve Tiesdell*)

Public Places – Urban Spaces. DOI: 10.1016/B978-1-85617-827-3.10001-X

FIGURE 1.3 Chicago (*Image: Matthew Carmona*)

Discussing definitions of urban design, Madanipour (1996: 93–117) identified seven areas of ambiguity:

- Should it be focused at particular scales or levels?
- Should it focus only on the visual qualities of the urban environment or, more broadly, address the organisation and management of urban space?
- Should it simply be about transforming spatial arrangements or should it be about more deeply seated social and cultural relations between spaces and society?
- Should its focus be its product (the urban environment) or the process by which it is produced?
- Should it be the province of architects, planners or landscape architects?
- Should it be a public or private sector activity?
- Should it be an objective–rational process (a science) or an expressive–subjective process (an art)?

The first three are concerned with the 'product' of urban design, the last three concern urban design as a 'process', while the fourth concerns the product–process dilemma. Although Mandanipour's ambiguities are deliberately presented as oppositional and mutually exclusive, it is often a matter of and/both rather than either/or. As we '*consciously shape and manage our built environments*' (Madanipour 1996: 117), urban designers are interested in and engaged with both process and its products. While, in practice, urban design is used to refer to all the products and processes of development, in a more restricted sense it means *adding quality* to both product and process.

Another distinction that can be confusing is that between its use in a descriptive manner and its use in a normative manner. In the former, all urban development is *ipso facto* urban design; in the latter, only urban development of sufficient merit or quality is urban design. Thus, seen analytically, urban design is the process by which the urban

environment comes about; seen normatively, it is – or should be – the process by which *better* urban environments come about. Confusion comes because those 'in-the-know' (designers) will often skip between these forms of use, but others (often social scientists) fail to make this distinction.

Urban design's scope is broad. Indicating the potential scope and diversity of urban design, and attempting to sum up the remit of urban design in simple terms, Tibbalds (1988a) suggested it was '*Everything you can see out of the window.*' While this statement has a basic truth and logic, if 'everything' can be considered to be urban design, then equally perhaps 'nothing' is urban design (see Dagenhart & Sawicki 1994). There is, however, little value in putting boundaries around the subject. The real need is for definitions encapsulating its heart or core rather than prescribing its edge or boundary – that is, for the identification, clarification and debate of its central beliefs and activities.

To explore the source of some of this confusion, urban design can be considered in terms of discipline and geographical scale.

(i) Discipline

In terms of discipline, it is frequently easier to say what urban design is not than precisely what it is. It is not, for example, big architecture, small-scale planning, civic beautification, urban engineering, a pattern-book subject, just visual/aesthetic in its scope, only a public sector concern, nor a narrow self-contained discipline. Despite this, relational definitions – those defining something in relation to something else – can help us to get closer to what it is. Urban design, for example, is typically defined in terms of architecture and town planning – Gosling & Maitland (1984) described it as the 'common ground' between these disciplines, while the UK's former Social Science Research Council located it at

'… the interface between architecture, landscape architecture and town planning, drawing on the design tradition of architecture and landscape architecture, and the environmental management and social science tradition of contemporary planning.'

(Bentley & Butina 1991)

Urban design, however, is not simply an interface. It encompasses and sometimes subsumes a number of disciplines and activities: architecture, town planning, landscape architecture, surveying, property development, environmental management and protection, etc. As Cuthbert (2007: 185) observes, professions are always territorial, and, furthermore, frequently at the behest of professions, academic institutions offering education in professional areas inevitably also become territorial (see Table 1.1). Urban design is not, or should not be, a particular professional territory (see below).

TABLE 1.1 A Systems View of Professional Boundaries

	Architecture	Urban Design	Urban Planning
Definition	The design of individual buildings, which are conceived primarily in terms of the design parameters of artificially controlled environments.	An open system that uses individual architectural elements and ambient space as its basic vocabulary, and that is focused on social interaction and communication in the public realm.	The agent of the state in controlling the production of land for the purposes of capital accumulation and social reproduction; in allocating sites for the collective consumption of social goods such as hospitals, schools and religious buildings; and in providing space for the production, circulation and eventual consumption of commodities.
Element			
(i) Structure	Static + human activity	Morphology of space and form (history + human activity)	Government bureaucracy
(ii) Environment	Three-dimensional (closed system)	Four-dimensional (open system)	The political economy of the state
(iii) Resources	Materials + energy + design theory	Architecture + ambient space + social theory	Systems of legitimation and communication
(iv) Objectives	Social closure/physical protection	Social communication and interaction	To implement the prevailing ideology of power
(v) Behaviour	Design parameters: artificially controlled environments	Dynamics of urban land markets	Dynamics of advanced capitalist societies

Source: Adapted from Cuthbert 2007: 189–90.

Despite some professions periodically making imperialist claims on the field, urban design is typically collaborative and inter-disciplinary, involving an integrated approach and the skills and expertise of a wide range of actors. Some urban design practitioners argue that 'place' is not — or should not be — a professional territory and that, rather than imbuing the creative task of designing urban places in the hands of a single 'all-knowing' designer, it should be shared among many actors. Cowan (2001a: 9), for example, has asked:

'… which profession is best at interpreting policy; assessing the local economy and property market; appraising a site or area in terms of land use, ecology, landscape, ground conditions, social factors, history, archaeology, urban form and transport; managing and facilitating a participative process; drafting and illustrating design principles; and programming the development process?'

He contends that, while all these skills are likely to be needed in, say, producing an urban design framework or masterplan, they are rarely all embodied by a single professional. The best frameworks and masterplans are drawn up by a number of people with different skills working in collaboration. Urban designers typically work within a context of multiple clients, often with conflicting interests and objectives, developing as a consequence of multiple solutions to a problem, rather than a single solution.

Indeed, many consider that the very term 'urban design' places it too much within the purview of professional design experts engaging in self-conscious, knowing design, and prefer the more inclusive term 'place-making' and, at a larger scale, city-making: terms suggesting it is more than just (professional) 'designers' who create places and cities. Described as urban design many non-professionals struggle to see their role; described as place-making they can more easily envision their role and contribution. Urban design can thus be considered the self-conscious practice of knowing urban designers; place-making is the self-conscious and unself-conscious practice of everyone.

An important distinction is between urban design (or place-making) as direct design (place-design) and urban design as indirect design or, more grandly, as political economy. In the latter, actors are involved in shaping the nature of place (place-shaping), through establishing policy, making investment decisions, managing space, etc., but may not themselves be involved in any conscious design process. Urban design encompasses both. George (1997) makes a similar distinction between first-order design and second-order design. First-order design involves direct design of a component of the built environment, such as a building or building complex, or environmental improvements — in short, a project of some sort and usually confined within a single site. Second-order (indirect) design involves 'designing' the 'decision environments' of development actors (e.g. developers, investors, designers, etc.). Urban design may be concerned with first-order design processes (e.g. the design of a new public square), but is often concerned with coordinating the component parts of the urban environment through strategies, frameworks and plans, and is thus commonly a second-order design activity.

(ii) Scale

Scale has also been used as a means of defining urban design, with urban design being commonly considered as the intermediate scale between planning (the settlement) and architecture (individual buildings). In 1976, Reyner Banham defined its field of concern as '... *urban situations about half a mile square.*' This definition is useful only if urban design is seen as mediating between architecture and planning. Lynch (1981: 291) defined urban design more broadly as encompassing a wide range of concerns across different spatial scales, arguing that urban designers may be engaged in preparing a comprehensive regional access study, a new town, or a regional park system and, equally,

'... *may seek to protect neighbourhood streets, revitalise a public square, ... set regulations for conservation or development, build a participatory process, write an interpretative guide or plan a city celebration.*'

Urban design typically operates at *and* across a variety of spatial scales. Considering urban design at particular scales might often be a convenient device, but it detracts from the notion of places as vertically integrated 'wholes'. Urban designers need to be constantly aware of scales above and below the scale at which they are working, and also of the relationships of the parts to the whole, and of the whole to the parts.

Christopher Alexander's pattern language illustrates the range of scales at which urban design operates, with the patterns being broadly ordered in terms of scale, beginning with patterns for strategic (city-wide) design and ending with 'interior design'. While identifying the multi-layered complexities of urban design through the book's 253 patterns, Alexander *et al* (1977: xiii) stressed no pattern was an 'isolated entity':

'*Each pattern can exist in the world only to the extent that it is supported by other patterns: the larger patterns in which it is embedded, the patterns of the same size that surround it, and the smaller patterns which are embedded in it.*'

Urging the built environment professions to see the whole as well as the parts, Tibbalds (1992: 9) argued that 'places matter most':

'*We seem to be losing the ability to stand back and look at what we are producing as a whole. ... We need to stop worrying quite so much about individual buildings and other physical artefacts and think instead about places in their entirety.*'

Traditions of Thought

Two broad traditions of urban design thought stem from different ways of appreciating design and the products of the design process — as aesthetic objects or displays (for looking at) and as environments (for using or living in). Jarvis (1980) discussed this distinction in terms of a visual-artistic tradition emphasising visual form ('buildings-and-space') and a social usage tradition primarily concerned with the public use and experience of urban environments ('people-and-activities'). These traditions have been synthesised into a third — 'making places' — tradition that focuses on process as well as product. More recently, a new tradition of sustainable urban design/place-making is increasingly coming to the fore.

(i) The visual-artistic tradition

The visual-artistic tradition reflects an earlier, more architectural and narrower understanding of urban design. Predominantly product-oriented, it tended to concentrate on the visual qualities and aesthetic experience of urban spaces, rather than the myriad cultural, social, economic, political, and spatial factors and processes contributing to successful urban places.

Jarvis saw it as emanating from Sitte's *City Planning According to Artistic Principles* (1889). He also saw Le Corbusier as a key proponent of this tradition — albeit as Sitte's 'aesthetic antithesis'. The visual-artistic tradition was clearly expressed in Unwin's *Town Planning in Practice* (1909) and subsequently by the various contributions to *Design in Town and Village* (MHLG 1953). Commenting on Gibberd's contribution to the latter on designing residential areas, Jarvis (1980: 53) noted both the absence of explicit references to people's activities in housing areas and the tradition being exemplified by the treatment of front gardens, where, rather than considering privacy and opportunities for personalisation, pictorial composition predominated.

An especially prominent strand of thought in this tradition was that of 'townscape', developed by Gordon Cullen and others in the late 1940s and the 1950s. Cullen's (1961) subsequent book *Townscape*, for example, appeared to emphasise the visual dimension to the virtual exclusion of all others. As Punter &

Carmona (1997: 72) note, although the book developed Cullen's own personal and expressive response to urban environments, it largely failed to acknowledge public perceptions of townscapes and places, in direct contrast to Lynch's contemporaneous *The Image of the City*.

(ii) The social usage tradition

Jarvis contrasts the visual-artistic tradition with the social usage tradition, which emphasises the way in which people use space and encompasses issues of perceptions and sense-of-place. Identifying Kevin Lynch as a key proponent of this approach, Jarvis (1980: 58) highlights how Lynch shifted the focus of urban design in two ways: first, in terms of *the appreciation of the urban environment* — rejecting the notion that this was an exclusive and elitist concern, Lynch emphasised that pleasure in urban places was a commonplace experience — and, second, in terms of *the object of study* — instead of examining the physical and material form of urban places, Lynch (1960: 3) suggested examining people's perceptions and mental images.

Another key proponent was Jane Jacobs, whose book *The Death and Life of Great American Cities* (1961) attacked many of the fundamental concepts of 'modernist' urban planning, heralding many aspects of contemporary urban design (see Chapter 2). Jacobs (1961: 386) argued the city could never be a work of art because art was made by 'selection from life', while a city was '... *life at its most vital, complex and intense.*' Concentrating on the socio-functional aspects of streets, sidewalks and parks, Jacobs' close observations of human behaviour emphasised their role as sites of human activity and places of social interaction. Similar detailed observations informed subsequent studies in this tradition, notably Jan Gehl's studies of public space in Scandinavia (Gehl 1971) and Whyte's *The Social Life of Small Urban Spaces* (1980).

Alexander's work also epitomises the social usage tradition. In *Notes on the Synthesis of Form* (1964) and *A City is Not a Tree* (1965), Alexander identified both the failings of design philosophies that considered 'form without context' and the dangers of approaching urban design in ways that fail to allow for a rich diversity of cross-connections between activities and places (Jarvis 1980: 59). Alexander's ideas were developed further in *A Pattern Language* (Alexander *et al* 1977) and *The Timeless Way of Building* (Alexander *et al* 1979), in which he set out a range of 'patterns'. Rather than 'complete designs', each pattern was a 'sketched minimum framework of essentials', a 'few basic instructions' and 'rough freehand sketches' to be shaped and refined (Jarvis

FIGURE 1.4   Federation Square, Melbourne *(Image: Steve Tiesdell)*

1980: 59). For Alexander, the patterns provide designers with a useable — but not predetermined — series of relationships between activities and spaces. Even those patterns closest to the traditional visual or spatial concerns of urban design — in which Alexander frequently cites Camillo Sitte — are grounded in and justified by research and/or observation of people's use of places.

(iii) The place-making tradition

Over the past 20 years, a place-making tradition of urban design has emerged — a tradition rooted in large part in the work of the urban design pioneers. Synthesising the two earlier traditions, contemporary urban design is simultaneously concerned with the design of urban places as physical/aesthetic entities and as behavioural settings — that is, with the 'hard

FIGURE 1.5   Borough Market, London *(Image: Matthew Carmona)*. Contemporary urban design is concerned with the diversity and activity that helps to create successful urban places and, in particular, how well the physical milieu supports the functions and activities that take place there and how such spaces interact with everyday life.

city' of buildings and spaces and the 'soft city' of people and activities (Figures 1.4 and 1.5)

(iv) **An emerging tradition — sustainable urbanism**

The quest for more sustainable development is an increasingly explicit concern in urban design and place-making, perhaps even the focus of a new, emerging tradition of thought and practice in its own right. Brown *et al* (2009) identify four convergent lines of thinking moving the activity on in the 2000s: (i) the work of Richard Florida (2004) and the arguments he makes that vibrant, walkable neighbourhoods attract the creative classes; (ii) a parallel transformation in the fortunes of America's downtowns as demand for urban living has increased; (iii) an awareness of the growing obesity crisis in the USA (and elsewhere), which has been linked to the spread of car-dependent urbanism; and (iv) a growing interest in the potential of urban form to reduce the carbon footprint of mankind.

The first three reinforce the making-places tradition, while the final trend suggests new thinking may be required. A manifesto celebrating the 50th anniversary of the influential 1958 Penn-Rockefeller Conference on Urban Design argued that:

'The new urban designer will need to feel comfortable operating under conditions of ambiguity, appreciating the fact that the science and art of integrating sustainability into urban design is an evolving challenge requiring the adaptation and advancement of ideas as they emerge. … The ultimate agency for the urban designer is as someone who is able to describe potential futures for the city in visual, technical, and narrative terms that foster social involvement, political action, and economic investment to make reality the post-carbon city.'

(Abramson *et al* 2008: 4—5).

A body of high-quality technical information and case studies is emerging that will assist the achievement of low- and zero-energy developments (see, for example, Dunster *et al* 2008). Thus, just as technology delivered high-rise living and high-speed travel, so — if the will is there — can it also deliver carbon-free living and, in the process, rein back the carbon impact of the building stock. However, as urban design transcends both these very tangible technical questions, and the far less tangible place-making questions discussed above, the challenge for urban designers will be to integrate them. In this way, sustainability is a further dimension in urban design's long quest for a more human-centred environment — one not only delivering quality of life locally, but also mitigating against unwanted consequences globally.

Urban Design and Place-Making Frameworks

As part of the making-places tradition, a number of theorists and practitioners have sought to identify desirable qualities of successful urban places and/or 'good' urban form. It is useful to note the key content of six such attempts.

Kevin Lynch

Lynch (1981: 118—9) identified five performance dimensions of urban design:

- *Vitality* — the degree to which the form of places supports the functions, biological requirements and capabilities of human beings.
- *Sense* — the degree to which places can be clearly perceived and structured in time and space by users.
- *Fit* — the degree to which the form and capacity of spaces matches the pattern of behaviours that people engage in or want to engage in.
- *Access* — the ability to reach other persons, activities, resources, services, information or places, including the quantity and diversity of elements that can be reached.
- *Control* — the degree to which those who use, work or reside in places can create and manage access to spaces and activities.

Two meta-criteria — 'efficiency' and 'justice' — underpinned the basic dimensions. Efficiency related to the relative costs of creating and maintaining a place for any given level of attainment of the above environmental dimensions, while justice related to the way in which environmental benefits were distributed. Thus, for Lynch (1981: 119) the key questions were (i) what is the relative cost of achieving a particular degree of vitality, sense, fit, access or control and (ii) who is getting how much of it?

Allan Jacobs and Donald Appleyard

In 'Towards an Urban Design Manifesto', Jacobs & Appleyard (1987) suggested seven goals 'essential for the future of a good urban environment':

- *Liveability* — a city should be a place where everyone can live in relative comfort.
- *Identity and control* — people should feel that some part of the environment belongs to them, individually and collectively — some part for which they care and are responsible, whether they own it or not.
- *Access to opportunities, imagination and joy* — people should find the city a place where they can break from traditional moulds, extend their experience, meet new people, learn other viewpoints, and have fun.

- *Authenticity and meaning* – people should be able to understand their city (or other people's cities), its basic layout, public functions and institutions; they should be aware of its opportunities.
- *Community and public life* – cities should encourage participation of their citizens in community and public life.
- *Urban self-reliance* – increasingly, cities will have to become more self-sustaining in their uses of energy and other scarce resources.
- *An environment for all* – good environments should be accessible to all. Every citizen is entitled to some minimal level of environmental liveability and minimal levels of identity, control and opportunity (Jacobs & Appleyard 1987: 115–6).

To achieve these goals, five prerequisites of a 'sound' urban environment were identified:

- Liveable streets and neighbourhoods.
- Some minimum density of residential development as well as intensity of land use.
- An integration of activities – living, working, shopping – in some reasonable proximity to each other.
- A manmade environment, particularly buildings, that defines public space (as opposed to buildings sitting in space).
- Many separate, distinct buildings with complex arrangements and relationships (as opposed to a few, large buildings) (Jacobs & Appleyard 1987: 117).

Responsive Environments

During the late 1970s and early 1980s, a team at what was then Oxford Polytechnic formulated an approach to urban design, subsequently published as *Responsive Environments: A Manual for Urban Designers* (Bentley *et al* 1985). Their approach stressed the need for more democratic, enriching environments, which maximise the degree of choice available to users. The core idea was that '… *the built environment should provide its users with an essentially democratic setting, enriching their opportunities by maximising the degree of choice available to them.*' (Bentley *et al* 1985: 9).

The design of a place affects the choices people can make:

- Where they can and can not go (permeability).
- The range of uses available (variety).
- How easily they can understand what opportunities it offers (legibility).
- The degree to which they can use a given place for different purposes (robustness).
- Whether the detailed appearance of the place makes them aware of the choice available (visual appropriateness).

- Their choice of sensory experience (richness).
- The extent to which they can put their own stamp on a place (personalisation).

Places with these qualities were responsive. In 1990, Ian Bentley suggested an additional set of qualities – resource efficiency, cleanliness and biotic support – relating to the ecological impact of urban forms and patterns of activity. Later he developed his ideas into a 'responsive city typology' consisting of six types: the deformed grid (interconnected street pattern); the complex use pattern (mixed use); the robust plot development; the positive privacy gradient (active frontages); the perimeter block; and the native biotic network (Bentley 1999: 215–7). By contrast, two of the other team members – McGlynn & Murrain (1994) – stated that their experience in practice and teaching had reduced the original list to just four fundamental qualities: permeability; variety (vitality, proximity and concentration); legibility; and robustness (resilience).

Francis Tibbalds

In 1989, His Royal Highness Prince Charles had offered a framework for architectural design, comprising the place; hierarchy; scale; harmony; enclosure; materials; decoration; art; signs and lights; and community. Firmly entrenched in the visual-artistic tradition, the Prince's ideas sparked an important debate. In response, the then-president of the Royal Town Planning Institute and founder of the UK-based Urban Design Group, Francis Tibbalds (1988a,b, 1992), suggested a more sophisticated (urban design) framework comprising 10 principles:

- Places matter most
- Learn the lessons of the past
- Encourage mixing of uses and activities
- Design on a human scale
- Encourage pedestrian freedom
- Provide access for all
- Build legible environments
- Build lasting environments
- Control change (incrementally)
- Join it all together.

The Congress for New Urbanism

During the 1990s in the United States, New Urbanism (see chapter 2) developed from two earlier sets of ideas:

- 'Neo-traditional neighbourhoods' (NTDs) and 'traditional neighbourhood development' (TNDs), where the central idea was to design complete new neighbourhoods that would be similar to traditional neighbourhoods (e.g. Duany & Plater-Zyberk 1991).

- 'Pedestrian pockets' and 'transit-oriented development' (TOD), where the central idea was to design neighbourhoods explicitly related to transport connections and of a sufficient density to make public transport viable (e.g. Calthorpe 1989, 1993).

Formalised through the creation of the Congress for New Urbanism (CNU) in 1993, a Charter for New Urbanism (www.cnu.org) was published advocating restructuring public policy and development practices to support the following:

- Neighbourhoods diverse in use and population.
- Communities designed for the pedestrian and transit as well as the car.
- Cities and towns shaped by physically defined and universally accessible public spaces and community institutions.
- Urban places framed by architecture and landscape design that celebrate local history, climate, ecology and building practice.

The charter also asserts a detailed set of principles to guide public policy, development practice, urban planning and design at three spatial scales: (i) the region — the metropolis, city and town; (ii) the neighbourhood, the district and the corridor; and (iii) the block, the street and the building (see www.cnu.org).

Nan Ellin

More recently, Nan Ellin set out a manifesto for what she called 'Integral Urbanism', published as the frontispiece of her 2006 book of the same name. Integral Urbanism demonstrates five qualities: hybridity, connectivity, porosity, authenticity and vulnerability:

- Rather than isolate objects and separate functions, *hybridity* and *connectivity* bring activities and people together, treating people and nature as symbiotic — as well as buildings and landscapes — rather than oppositional.
- *Porosity* preserves the integrity of what is brought together while allowing mutual access through permeable membrane.
- *Authenticity* involves

    'actively engaging and drawing inspiration from actual social and physical conditions with an ethic of care, respect and honesty. Like all healthy organisms, the authenti-City is always growing and evolving according to new needs that arise thanks to a self-adjusting feedback loop that measures and monitors success and failure.' (2006: xiv).

- *Vulnerability* requires *'us to relinquish control, listen deeply, value process as well as product, and re-integrate space with time.' (2006: xiv).*

The Frameworks

Many such frameworks exist, and each has a different degree of prescription regarding desirable physical and spatial forms. Lynch's framework is the least prescriptive and is essentially a series of criteria to guide and evaluate urban design, leaving others to determine physical form. Jacobs and Appleyard's framework is more prescriptive, their criteria suggesting the vibrant, lively and well-integrated urban form of cities such as San Francisco and Paris. The CNU's criteria are also highly prescriptive about physical and spatial forms.

As is discussed later (see Chapters 4 and 8), definitions of urban design should not be too prescriptive about urban form because form depends in particular on issues of local climate and culture. Spatial forms that are appropriate in one climate and one culture may not be in another. Kaliski (2008a: 94—5), for example, acknowledges Jane Jacobs' prioritising of the small scale of daily life as the generative component of good urbanism, but complains that she had:

'… too quickly associated specific forms with good urbanism and defined those forms as good. With hindsight, this type of insular recursion too quickly devalues alternate urbanisms that inevitably are as dearly loved by residents as the routines and forms of Greenwich Village were admired by Jacobs.'

In recent years, 'official' definitions of urban design have expressly embraced place-making and have set down these official positions in similar frameworks to those discussed above. Taking England as an example, the Government first defined urban design in policy in 1997 as:

'… the relationship between different buildings; the relationship between buildings and the streets, squares, parks and other spaces which make up the public domain itself; the relationship of one part of a village, town or city with the other parts; and the patterns of movement and activity which are thereby established. In short, the complex relationships between all the elements of built and unbuilt space.'

(DoE 1997: para 14).

A subsequent government publication — *By Design: Urban Design in the Planning System: Towards Better Practice* (DETR/CABE 2000a: 8) — gave a more rounded and complete definition, stating that urban design was the 'art of making places for people':

'It includes the way places work and matters such as community safety, as well as how they look. It concerns the connections between people and places, movement and urban form, nature and the built fabric, and the processes for ensuring successful villages, towns and cities.'

Seven objectives were identified — each relating to the concept of place:

- *Character* — a place with its own identity.

- *Continuity and enclosure* – a place where public and private spaces are clearly distinguished.
- *Quality of the public realm* – a place with attractive and successful outdoor areas.
- *Ease of movement* – a place that is easy to get to and move through.
- *Legibility* – a place that has a clear image and is easy to understand.
- *Adaptability* – a place that can change easily.
- *Diversity* – a place with variety and choice (DETR/ CABE 2000).

A 2005 update in policy (ODPM 2005) emphasised sustainability's increasing importance within the national urban design agenda: *'Good design ensures attractive, usable, durable and adaptable places and is a key element in achieving sustainable development.'* England is not exceptional in this regard and, demonstrating the spread and acceptance of the place-making canon, such high-level policy is replicated at national/state level around the world (see, for example, New Zealand's Urban Design Protocol – Ministry for the Environment 2005).

While the theoretical frameworks and the qualities of good places given in policy often contain much similarity, the danger of generally desirable design principles becoming inflexible dogma, and of design and place-making being reduced to a formula, is inherent in these frameworks. This would negate the active process of design that relates general principles to specific situations through the application of design intelligence: design principles should be used with the flexibility derived from a deeper understanding and appreciation of their bases, justifications and interrelations. In any design process there are no wholly 'right' or 'wrong' answers – substantially because design involves relating general, and generally desirable, principles to specific sites, where the totality of the outcome is what matters.

Furthermore, as presented here, these frameworks stress the outcomes or products of urban design, rather the process dimensions: they indicate the qualities of 'good' places, but not how such places can or should be delivered or achieved. Effective place-making demands sensitivity to, and cognisance of, power dynamics in and across urban space and its production. Urban designers thus need to understand the contexts within which they operate (see Chapter 3) and the processes by which places and developments come about (see Chapters 10 and 11). As in many spheres, there is often an implementation gap between theory and practice and, in the case of policy, between high-level, aspirational principles and local delivery.

THE NEED FOR URBAN DESIGN

Arguing in 1976 that urban design was still in its 'prehistoric stage', Bentley (1976) saw the emergence of express

concerns for urban design originating in critiques of the urban environmental product, the process by which the built environment was brought about, and the professional role involved in controlling its production. Each critique detected various kinds of fragmentation, a lack of concern for the totality and overall quality of the urban environment. These problems remain today.

Product and Process

There have been many critiques of the quality of the built environment. The poor quality of much of the contemporary built environment and the lack of concern for overall quality is a function of both the processes by which it comes about and the forces that act on and within those processes. Much of this is attributed – rightly or wrongly – to the development industry. The UK's *Urban Design Compendium* (Llewelyn-Davies 2000: 12), for example, argued that the development process and the actors within it had become 'entangled' in a system producing 'developments' not 'places'. Among the constraints on making places of quality, Llewelyn-Davies (2000: 12) identified the *'... predominantly conservative, short-term and supply-driven characteristics of the development industry.'*

Focusing on product rather than process but in a similar vein, Loukaitou-Sideris (1996: 91) discussed place quality in terms of 'cracks', seeing the cracks as:

- The gaps in the urban form, where overall continuity is disrupted.
- The residual spaces left undeveloped, underused or deteriorating.
- The physical divides that purposefully or accidentally separate social worlds.
- The spaces that development has passed by or where new development has fragmentation and interruption.

Examples of such cracks were given for a range of locations, including the urban core:

'... where corporate towers assert their dominance over the skies, but turn their back onto the city; where sunken or elevated plazas, skyways and roof gardens disrupt pedestrian activity; and where the asphalt deserts of parking lots fragment the continuity of the street.'

(Loukaitou-Sideris 1996: 91) (Figure 1.6).

Elsewhere the cracks include car-oriented, commercial strips, lacking sidewalks and pedestrian amenities, and walled or gated developments that *'... assert their privateness by defying any connection with the surrounding landscape.'* (Loukaitou-Sideris 1996: 91–2). Many cracks are the consequence of self-conscious design, but, as well as express design, environmental degradation also results from the cumulative effect of decisions made by unknowing urban designers (see below).

FIGURE 1.6   A crack in the city *(Image: Matthew Carmona)*

Poor quality urban environments also arise through various social and economic trends — such as those of homogenisation and standardisation; the trend towards individualism rather than collectivism; the privatisation of life and culture; and a retreat from and decline of the public realm. More than 20 years ago, Jacobs & Appleyard (1987: 113) commented on how cities, especially American cities, had become privatised due to consumer society's emphasis on the individual and private sector. Escalated greatly by the spread of the car, these trends had resulted in a 'new form of city':

'… one of closed, defended islands with blank and windowless facades surrounded by wastelands of parking lots and fast-moving traffic. … The public environment of many American cities has become an empty desert, leaving public life dependent for its survival solely on planned formal occasions, mostly in protected internal locations.'

(Jacobs & Appleyard 1987: 113).

These processes have intensified over the last 20 years (see Low & Smith 2006).

The Built Environment Professions

Contemporary concern for urban design, and for self-conscious place-making, is also located in critiques of the role of various environmental professionals. The period from the late 1960s onwards — continuing through to today — saw a series of crises of confidence in the main environmental professions about what they were doing and how they were doing it. Lang (1994: 3), for example, attributes urban design's (re-)birth to recognition that

'… the sterile urban environments achieved by applying the ideas of the Modern Movement to both policy-making and to architectural design at the urban scale were a failure in terms of the lives of the people who inhabited them.'

Similarly, McGlynn (1993: 3) argued that, as people lived in and experienced

'… the simplified, fragmented and frequently alienating forms of post-war redevelopment, they began to challenge the values and assumptions of architects and planners and to distrust their ability to improve upon the spatial and physical forms of pre-modernist urbanism.'.

The lack of quality in contemporary development has also been attributed to well-intentioned but ill-conceived public regulation (Ben-Joseph & Szold 2004; Duany & Brain 2005). Drawing inspiration from John Ruskin, Rouse (1998) outlined 'The Seven Clamps of Urban Design' — the reasons '… *why we are consistently failing to achieve high standards of … urban design*' (see Table 1.2 and Chapter 11).

Similarly, discussing planning and development controls in the USA, Duany *et al* (2000: 19) highlight how many development codes have a negative effect on the quality of the built environment:

'Their size and their result are symptoms of the same problem: they are hollow at the core. They do not emanate from any physical vision. They have no images, no diagrams, no recommended models, only numbers and words. Their authors, it seems, have no clear picture of what they want their communities to be. They are not imagining a place that they admire, or buildings that they hope to emulate. Rather, all they seem to imagine is what they don't want: no mixed uses, no slow-moving cars, no parking shortages, no overcrowding.'

They observe that

'… one cannot easily build Charleston anymore, because it is against the law. Similarly, Boston's Beacon Hill, Nantucket, Sante Fe, Carmel — all of these well-known places, many of which have become tourist destinations, exist in direct violation of current zoning ordinance.'

(Duany *et al* 2000: xi).

The problem is particularly pronounced with regard to highway and traffic design standards — rigid application of which effectively determines the layout of many areas. This is, in part, a consequence of fragmentation: the ability to focus on a part — and frequently to measure it against a technical and immutable standard — while failing to see the whole. Urban design, by contrast, is a process of creating 'wholes' from the parts, reflecting how the totality matters most (see Chapters 3 and 9).

While planning, architecture and highway engineering endured considerable public criticism from the 1960s and 1970s onwards, the division of issues and responsibilities concerning the urban environment among the established built environment professions enabled them to blame each other. As McGlynn (1993: 3) argues, architecture's concern was the design of a building

TABLE 1.2 The Seven Clamps of Urban Design

(i) *The Clamp of Strategic Vacuum*
The lack of sufficient national, regional and local policy apparatus to ensure urban design is placed at the heart of political and administrative decision-making.

(ii) *The Clamp of Reactivity*
The failure of the planning system to adopt a strategic approach to urban design process, substituting reactive and negative regulation for proactive and positive intervention.

(iii) *The Clamp of Over-Regulation*
Regulation in the wrong place and time can kill innovation, creativity and risk taking, but that greater flexibility in the processes of development needs to be balanced by stronger control on the quality of design.

(iv) *The Clamp of Meanness*
As we emerge from an age where we learnt the price of everything but forgot the value of so many things, design in general and urban design in particular suffered. Design may cost money, but creates lasting value.

(v) *The Clamp of Illiteracy*
Virtually no one is properly equipped with the skills to demand, create and interpret excellence in urban design – we have become illiterate and we need, collectively, to re-educate ourselves.

(vi) *The Clamp of Small-Mindedness*
Contemporary development is characterised by introspection, low ambition, a tendency to revert to the lowest common denominator and an unhealthy obsession with the successes and failures of the past.

(vii) *The Clamp of Short-Termism*
The systemic, myopic condition that means the shape of new development is dictated not by the projected 100-year life of buildings and the need for aftercare, but by the five-year funding programme, four-year political cycle, three-year public expenditure agreement and by the spectre of annuity.

Source: Rouse (1998).

(or buildings) on a defined site, while planning was responsible for

'… *the general disposition of land uses through policy formulation and plan making and for the detailed and necessarily piecemeal regulation of individual building projects through the operation of the development control system.*'

More generally, planners had become primarily concerned with socio-economic processes and political systems at the expense of considerations of place and people. Relph (1976: 24) argues that, during this period, the concept of 'place' in urban planning meant little more than a location where certain specified interactions occurred and certain limited functions were served: '… *a notion of place that clearly owes little to spatial experience.*'

Carmona (2009a) characterises the divergent cultures as professional 'tyrannies' with the potential to impact negatively on the design quality of development proposals. The first tyranny results from the fetishising of design, where image, rather than inherent value – economic, social or environmental – is of paramount concern, and where the freedom to pursue the creative process is valued above all. Such agendas are most closely associated with the architectural profession. The second reflects the argument that the market knows best, and that what sells counts. Thus, design quality is perceived by developers as a complex mix of factors that includes dominant economic aspects of supply and demand revolving around costs and sales potential – buildability, standardisation, market assessment and customer feedback. Lang (2005: 381), for example, asks 'Who leads?', concluding that, in capitalist countries, private corporations drive urban development. The third, that of regulation, can be analysed (and challenged) in terms of the political economy it represents, namely as an attempt to correct market failure. As Van Doren (2005: 45, 64) argues, regulation is inherently costly and inefficient, but difficult to change because of political support for it from what he describes as 'bootleggers' (special interests who gain economically from the existence of regulation) and 'Baptists' (those who do not like the behaviour of others and want government to restrict it).

Representing extremes, perhaps even caricatures, the tyrannies also reflect realities that practitioners repeatedly face during the development process. They result from profoundly different motivations – respectively peer approval, profit and a narrowly defined view of public interest – but also from very different modes of working and associated professional knowledge fields – respectively design, management/finance and social/technical expertise. They have often led to substandard development solutions, based on conflict, compromise and delay, rather than on what would enhance place quality.

Urban Design as Joining-Up

From the late 1960s onwards, the hard-edged, silo-based and divisive separation of professional responsibilities was seen as contributing to widespread poor-quality environments, development and places. Bentley (1998: 15) argues that the professional practice of urban design arose due to the gaps created by the boundaries set up and institutionalised around the various environmental and development disciplines. Seeing the problem of gaps as linked to the relationship between designers and market processes, and the associated economic rationalisation that results in ever-increasing specialisation, he contended that the inevitable result is a 'fragmented set of professions', with 'tight boundaries around' and 'gaps between them'. As the gaps between the professions became hardened and institution-alised, what increasingly fell through the gaps was concern for '... *the public realm itself — the void between buildings, the streets and spaces which constitute our everyday experiences of urban spaces.*' (McGlynn 1993: 3). This, in turn, suggested a need to focus on integrating professional activity, but, more importantly, a concern for place quality.

The above discussion gives rise to two particular and related notions of urban design — first as a means of restoring or giving qualities of continuity and synergy to otherwise individual, often inward-focused, urban developments (i.e. to improve overall place quality), and second as a means of joining up a fragmented (and sometimes a somewhat estranged) set of professions.

Joining Up the Urban Environment

Sternberg (2000) argues that urban design's primary role is to reassert the 'cohesiveness of the urban experience'. Drawing upon the 'organicist' school of thought — a school that had influenced Patrick Geddes, Lewis Mumford and, more recently, Alexander (1987, 1979) and Alexander *et al* (1977) — he notes how the organicists observed that

'... *modern society (especially its central dynamic mechanism, the market) atomised community, nature and city. Inspired by biological metaphors and philosophical concepts of vitalism, the organicists set out to reassert the natural growth and wholeness that a 'mechanical' market society would tend to undermine.*'

(Sternberg 2000: 267) (see Chapter 9).

Sternberg suggests the ideas informing urban design share an intellectual foundation in implicitly acknowledging the 'non-commodifiability' of the human experience across property boundaries — that it is impossible to separate the parts from the whole. He thus contends that the leading urban design theorists share '... *the view that good design seeks to reintegrate the human experience of urban form in the face of real estate markets that would treat land and buildings as discrete commodities.*' (Sternberg 2000: 265). Thus, he argues that, without conscious concern for urban design as a process of restoring or giving qualities of coherence and continuity to individual, often inward-focused developments, overall place quality is inevitably neglected.

Christopher Alexander's notion of 'things' and 'relationships' also helps to put this idea into a design context. In *The Timeless Way of Building* (Alexander 1979), Alexander argued that what we perceive to be 'things' in our everyday surroundings — buildings, walls, streets, fences — are better understood as 'patterns' intersecting with other patterns (i.e. as relationships). As Kunstler (1996: 83) explains:

'*A window in a house is a relationship between the inside of the house and the outside world. It transmits light and air, and it*

allows glimpses between the public and private realms. When it fails to operate in these ways, it becomes a mere hole in the wall.'

When they cease to be 'relationships' and become 'things' (i.e. isolated or removed from their context), patterns lose the quality Alexander calls 'aliveness'. Thus, just as Alexander *et al* (1977) argued that no pattern is an isolated entity (see above), urban design is, in large part, about joining up the patterns that others (architects, developers, highway engineers, etc.) are primarily concerned with providing.

Explaining Integral Urbanism, Ellin (2006: 91) asserts that 'nothing exists in isolation, only in relation' and cites Jorge Luis Borge: '*The taste of the apple ... lies in the contact of the fruit with the palate, not in the fruit itself; in a similar way (I would say) poetry lies in the meeting of the poem and the reader, not in the lines of symbols printed on the pages of a book.*'

She further asserts that: '*In contrast to the master-planned functionally-zoned city which separates, isolates, alienates, and retreats, Integral Urbanism emphasises connection, communication and celebration*' (Ellin 2006: xv) and thus explains that Integral Urbanism focuses on:

- Networks *not* boundaries
- Relationships and connections *not* isolated objects
- Interdependence *not* independence or dependence
- Natural and social communities *not* just individuals
- Transparency or translucency *not* opacity
- Permeability *not* walls
- Flux or flow *not* stasis
- Connections with nature and relinquishing control, *not* controlling nature
- Catalysts, armatures, frameworks, punctuation marks, *not* final products, masterplans or utopias (Ellin 2006: xxiii).

Joining Up the Built Environment Professions

Problems of place quality are 'wicked problems', which typically have a number of common characteristics, including interconnectivity, complexity, uncertainty, ambiguity and conflict. Inherently multi-dimensional, the dimensions are interdependent, do not fit easily within structures based on separate functional divisions and, hence, require a comprehensive and holistic, 'joined-up' response. Furthermore, unlike tamed problems that have complete solutions, wicked problems can only have partial solutions because they relate to open systems where the 'problem' is continuously changing and evolving. It is, thus, naïve to consider any design proposal, intervention or action as producing an end state or finite solution.

Noting how architectural and, to a lesser degree, land-scape design often place emphasis 'on the solution to the problem rather than on the problem itself', Dobbins (2009: 182) argues that urban design

'... happens in fluid, interactive and ever-changing circumstances. The process of making places that work and satisfy doesn't have a beginning and an end in the way that building projects or other time- and budget-specific projects might have.'

He argues that urban design needs to beware of 'solutionism':

'Some designers rely on the 'big idea', or three of four big ideas, as a way of synthesising an urban design process into an actionable vision. If the big idea reflects a full vetting of the problem, a fully inclusive and citizen-guided process, or the flexibility to do so, there's a good chance the method might work – and it certainly assists in reaching an imageable and comprehendible vision. If, on the other hand, the big ideas simply come out of a consultant's medicine bag labelled 'big ideas', then watch out. However persuasive and compelling, however unconsciously misleading, there's a fair chance that the purveyor of the big idea doesn't know why it has emerged as a generic solution in the first place, or whether its application to the particulars of a problem will make things better or worse.'

(Dobbins 2009: 182–3).

For Dobbins, the urban design field is littered with solutions that have presumed rather than investigated and understood the problem.

Urban design is thus necessarily always open-ended and ongoing – and, furthermore, is an intervention in, or contribution to, other dynamic systems. But, given the speed of contemporary change, the dangers of disjointed incrementalism should not be underestimated, and it may be important that some overall vision is available to guide developments towards agreed objectives – at least (on an evolutionary timescale) in the short-term – both giving the confidence necessary to attract investment and ensuring individual increments result in a synergistic whole (see Chapter 9).

Rigid 'silo-based' professional demarcations reinforce the tendency for professions to see things from their own narrow disciplinary perspective. Brain (2005: 229), for example, laments how

'... disintegrated choices are allowed to aggregate into forms that are largely the result of the technical and administrative problem-solving efforts of a variety of specialists, and in which the ordering logic is dictated primarily by the technical considerations of engineers and administrators and the interest of lending institutions in comparable and predictable investment.'

He argues that effective place-making often involves cracking the 'silo-effect' of disintegrated problem solving by specialists (2005: 234). As different strands of expertise often need to be drawn together, rather than professional specialisation per se, the problem is often one of fragmentation, and lack of integrated holistic consideration.

Specialisation and specialist expertise are often both desirable and necessary (we need brain surgeons as well as general practitioners), but, in making good places, the need is for soft-edged rather than hard-edged professionalism, and collaborative and inclusive working practices.

Rather than perpetuating the culture of blame and buck-passing, from the 1970s onwards some professionals sought to address aspects of professional practice detrimental to place quality, arguing for greater consideration of place and issues of environmental quality in planning and greater appreciation and respect for issues of context in architecture (i.e. including seeing 'site' as something beyond the immediate ownership boundary).

Recognising a need to join up a fragmented set of professions and professionals, certain key individuals – and subsequently organisations – set out to build bridges and create dialogue and common cause among the established built environment professions. In the United Kingdom, the first umbrella organisation was the Urban Design Group (UDG), founded in 1978. The UDG was deliberately inclusive, considering everyone acting in the built environment an urban designer '... *because the decisions they made affected the quality of urban spaces.*' (Linden & Billingham 1998: 40).

Urban design's inter-professional nature was further emphasised in the United Kingdom by the launch of the Urban Design Alliance (UDAL) in 1997. Founded by the Civic Trust, the Landscape Institute, the Institution of Civil Engineers, the Royal Institute of British Architects (RIBA), the Royal Institution of Chartered Surveyors (RICS), the Royal Town Planning Institute (RTPI) and the UDG, UDAL (1997) aims to '... *foster greater awareness of urban design and to promote higher standards of urban design.*'

The campaigning work of these organisations contributed to shifting the UK government's approach to urban design over the following decade (see Chapter 11). Elsewhere, in continental European countries, for example, the boundaries between professions do not exist to the same degree, with planning often seen as a sub-discipline of architecture or engineering, and 'urbanism' as the common intermediate focus for their activities (see Hebbert 2006). Almost everywhere, often within very different professional structures, progress has been made in establishing the activities of urban design and place-making.

During this period, the notion of urban design as a formal profession has nonetheless been a consistent theme. Observing the absence of a formal profession of urban designers in the United States, for example, Peter Calthorpe (in Fishman 2005: 68) argued:

'There is a profession and license for landscape design, for planners, for civil engineers, for structural engineers, for traffic engineers but not for the most important profession, urban design. There is a huge void there ... There is a profession waiting to be

born … Sometimes people slip out of architecture and become urban designers, but that's pretty rare because they are so fascinated with the building. Sometimes good landscape designers become urban designers, but they are not trained to. There is a lot of empathy in the planning field, but very little talent or skill for it because they have no design training … We don't have a profession to address these problems in the way they need to be addressed.'

In the United Kingdom, some interest groups are also pushing for an urban design profession. The UDG, for example, has launched a scheme whereby professionals of any background working in urban design can apply for recognition of their skills and ability, through a new, though artless, designation of 'Recognised Practitioner in Urban Design'.

A common argument for the existence of professions is to steward a set of public goods that would not adequately be produced by unconstrained markets and, furthermore, professions are charged not only with serving clients' needs but also advocating the common good (see Friedson 1994; Childs 2009). And yet, creation of a formal urban design profession would seem to negate the very notion of urban design as a process of joining up and of place-making as an inclusive activity, and, following Ian Bentley's earlier argument, would institutionalise urban design as an inevitably exclusive professional territory.

THE URBAN DESIGNERS

Given a need for urban design, this part discusses 'Who are the urban designers?' An inclusive response is all those who take decisions that shape the urban environment. This includes not just architects, landscape architects, planners, engineers and surveyors, but also developers, investors, occupiers, civil/public servants, politicians, events organisers, crime and fire prevention officers, environmental health officials and many others. In this view, everyday users are as important as designers. As Kaliski (2008b: 105) asserts:

'The person who chooses a different commuting route, posts a sign over an existing sign, sells from a corner cart, or volunteers to organise a community meeting is as much a city designer as the developer and architect who construct a skyscraper or the city official who suggest an ordinance. The city is as much a consequence of these fluid everyday actions of the overarching visions of urban designers who conceptualise fixed-in-time masterplans.'

Individuals and groups are thus engaged in the process of urban design and place-making in different capacities and with different objectives. Their involvement with and influence on express design decisions may also be direct or indirect and, furthermore, they may or may not appreciate how their decisions affect place quality.

There is thus a continuum from 'knowing' (self-conscious) urban design (i.e. what people who see themselves as urban designers create and do) to 'unknowing' (unself-conscious) urban design (i.e. that resulting from the decisions and actions of those who do not see themselves as urban designers) (see Beckley 1979, in Rowley 1994: 187). This is not a distinction in terms of the quality of the outcome — the outcomes of each can be 'good' and 'bad'. Unself-conscious urban design is thus not a 'bad thing' per se but — because overall place quality is not an explicit consideration — the likelihood of good places being created may be lessened. As Barnett (1982: 9) has argued:

'Today's city is not an accident. Its form is usually unintentional, but it is not accidental. It is the product of decisions made for single, separate purposes, whose interrelationships and side effects have not been fully considered. The design of cities has been determined by engineers, surveyors, lawyers, and investors, each making individual, rational decisions for rational reasons.'

Knowing/self-conscious urban designers are typically professionals employed or retained on account of their urban design expertise — that is, urban design practitioners. Many of these often have post-graduate qualifications in urban design, but many others have had no specific urban design education and have often learnt from experience and practice following an initial professional training in architecture, planning and/or landscape architecture.

Further along the continuum is a group consisting of built environment professionals who — despite having an influence on decisions affecting place quality — do not consider themselves to be urban designers. They nevertheless acknowledge and appreciate their role and influence in seeking to maintain and improve place quality. This group may also include those property developers who recognise the potential of design to add value and facilitate long-term commercial success (University of Reading 2000).

'Unknowing' and unself-conscious urban designers are those who make urban design and place-making decisions without appreciating what they are doing (Figures 1.7 and 1.8), such as:

- *Politicians in central/state government*, who set the strategic framework for design as part of the national economic strategy and the policy context for sustainability.
- *Politicians in local or regional government*, who implement the strategy from above, while interpreting and developing it in the light of local circumstances.
- *The business community and civil/public servants*, who make investment decisions, including those relating to the physical infrastructure.
- *Accountants*, who advise the public and private sectors about their investments.
- *Engineers*, who design the roads and public transport infrastructure and integrate it into the public realm.

FIGURE 1.7 Greenwich, London *(Image: Matthew Carmona)*. Introducing wheelie bins in Greenwich, London had an unexpected disruptive impact on the urban scene and represents an example of unknowing urban design.

- *Investors*, who assess short-, medium- and long-term investment opportunities and make decisions about which developments and which developers to support.
- *Urban regeneration agencies*, who invest public funds in regeneration projects and balance environmental, social and economic objectives.
- *Providers of infrastructure* (e.g. electric, gas and telecommunications companies), who invest in the hidden infrastructure and in maintaining the public realm.
- *Community groups*, who support or oppose developments, campaign for improvements, and otherwise involve themselves in the development process.
- *Householders* and *occupiers*, who maintain and/or personalise their property.

FIGURE 1.8 Rome, Italy *(Image: Matthew Carmona)*. Public standards for parking applied by different developers — surface-level on one side of the road and underground on the other — have had an unintended deadening effect on the street for which no one is knowingly responsible. The regulations had no positive vision of the desired place.

This group may also include built environment professionals who do not appreciate how their decisions affect overall place quality.

Without recognition of the qualities and additional value of good design, the creation and production of places often occurs by omission rather than commission. The challenge for knowing urban designers, and especially for urban design practitioners, is to demonstrate the importance and value of urban design and to ensure concern for place is not absent through ignorance or neglect, or omitted for misguided or short-sighted convenience. Part of this role involves educating unknowing urban designers — place-makers — about the important role they play.

Urban Design Practice

Mainstream practice customarily affords urban designers two basic roles: those of 'architect/urban designer' and 'planner/urban designer'— a distinction that broadly accords with that between direct and indirect urban design outlined earlier. The former is typically directly involved with the design of development, usually in the form of a specific building or a series of buildings. The latter typically guides, enables, coordinates and controls the activities of others, and is increasingly being called upon to establish the long-term spatial or physical 'vision' for localities. Such control is typically, but not exclusively, exercised by the public sector over private interests where the public/collective interest is deemed sufficient to justify control, protection or guidance.

Contemporary urban design practice is, nonetheless, much broader than this. The UK's DETR (2000), for example, identified four types of contemporary urban design practice — urban development design; design policies, guidance and control; public realm design; and community urban design (see Table 1.3). Lang (2005) also outlines four key types of urban design action:

- *Total urban design* — complete control by a single design team over the design of a large area — buildings, public space and implementation.
- *All-of-a-piece urban design* — where schemes are parcelled out to different development/design teams following an overall masterplan that acts to coordinate the pieces.
- *Piece-by-piece urban design* — the process of single uncoordinated developments coming forward as and when opportunities or the market allow, although guided by area objectives and policies.
- *Plug-in urban design* — where infrastructure is designed and built in new or existing areas, into which individual development projects can be plugged in later.

Lang (1994: 78–94) had previously discussed these, and other important variants in terms of types of urban designer — Table 1.4 lists 10 types. The roles are not mutually exclusive and, within the same project, urban designers may be involved in a number of them.

Clients and Consumers of Urban Design

If urban design is about making places for people, we must also consider who those 'people' are. In the narrow sense, this can be considered in terms of identifying the clients for urban design. Given their role and relationship to the urban environment, urban design practitioners serve a wide range of client interests. The processes and outcomes of urban design involve and affect many people and interests in different ways: as individuals, members of local groups, communities, and society as a whole; as occupiers and users; and as members of present and future generations.

Lang (1994: 459–62) makes an important distinction between 'paying' and non-paying clients of urban design. Whether in the public or private sector, the paying clients include 'entrepreneurs' and their financial backers. In the public sector, the entrepreneurs are government agencies and politicians; their financial backers are taxpayers, although increasingly also the private sector. In the private sector, the entrepreneurs are developers and their financial backers are bankers and other lending institutions, and, increasingly, through forms of public–private partnership (in the United Kingdom, for example, through the Private Finance Initiative — PFI), governments and their agencies. As Lang notes, these actors often act as surrogates for the people who ultimately pay — purchasers, tenants and users — for the buildings and environments produced.

Lang (1994: 459–62) identifies various types of non-paying client, the main two groups being:

● *Occupiers and users* — Users of developments are non-paying to the degree that they do not hire nor have much contact with the professionals involved in designing for them. The result is an administrative gap between the professional and user–client and perhaps a more

TABLE 1.3 Types of Urban Design Practice

	Professional Domain	Characteristics	Activities
Urban Development Design (place-design)	Traditionally the domain of architects supported by land-scape architects and other designers.	Rooted in the development process. Typically applicable at site and neigh-bourhood scales.	Includes: ● *all-of-a-piece* design situations ● some *total* design situations.
Public Realm Design (place-design)	Engineers, planners, architects, landscape architects and others. But frequently the unintentional result of uncoordinated deci-sions and actions taken by many different parties.	Encompasses design of the 'capital web' (e.g. roads and streets, footpaths and pavements, car parks, public transport interchanges, parks and other urban spaces). Relevant over a range of scales.	Includes: ● design and implementation of specific projects ● production and application of guidelines for design and improvement of a locality ● ongoing management and maintenance of places, including programming of activities and events.
Design Policies, Guidance and Control (place-shaping)	Traditionally the domain of planners supported by archi-tects, landscape architects, conservation officers and others.	The design dimension of the planning process (e.g. primarily a response to anticipated effects of urban change on urban design quality, whereby guidance and control are typically applied from outside development process). The range of considerations is usually wider than the concerns of urban development design. Applicable at all scales of urban design.	Includes: ● area appraisals, design strategy and policy formulation ● preparation of supplemen-tary design guidance and briefs ● exercise of design control.
Community Urban Design (place-shaping and/or place-design)	No particular profession.	Works *with* and *in* communities devel-oping proposals from the grassroots level. Particularly applicable to the neighbour-hood scale.	Employs a range of approaches and techniques to engage with those who will use the environment.

Source: Adapted from University of Reading (2001).

TABLE 1.4 Lang's 10 Types of Urban Designer

(i)	Total designer	An urban designer is a 'total designer' when a single person or team carries a complete project design from inception to completion on site. An urban designer may be a central figure in the design process for a particular project, but, given urban design's multi-disciplinary nature and the many actors involved, it is unlikely that the total designer will be a single individual.
(ii)	'All-of-a-piece' urban designer	This is when an overall illustrative design (e.g. a detailed masterplan) is prepared by a single urban designer (or firm) with detailed guidelines for individual developers and architects to follow in the design of buildings. The distinction between all-of-a-piece urban design and urban design as infrastructure design and guideline-writing is a fine but important one: Lang's basic point is that in the former '... *the urban design team acts as the reviewer of each sub-proposal and implicitly, the elements of the whole project are built within a short period of time of each other, if not simultaneously.*' (1994: 79)
(iii)	Vision-maker (concept provider)	The vision-maker is responsible for providing the vision, concept or idea of how to organise the spatial pattern of a city or urban area. The vision is typically communicated in the form of a framework or a set of guidelines, after which other actors develop and complete individual phases or parts.
(iv)	Infrastructure designer	The infrastructure designer is most closely associated with the civil engineering and, to a lesser degree, the town planning professions. As much of the character and functionality of an urban environment stem from its streets, parks, public spaces and other public facilities, this role should not be underestimated. The culture and objectives of highway engineers and transportation planners have often not been focused on achieving overall place quality.
(v)	Policy-maker	As a policy-maker the urban designer has a close involvement with politicians and other decision-makers. This is a facilitating role, which involves shaping a future, both physically and functionally. Such urban designers also provide guidance and advice to decision-makers regarding the nature of desired change. The policy-maker establishes goals for development, and guidelines within which others operate, and coordinates, monitors and evaluates the work being implemented within those guidelines and policies.
(vi)	Guideline designer	Preparing guidelines involves establishing detailed design principles in policy form. Design guidelines are mechanisms for defining and designing public space, specifying certain uses, encouraging and stimulating development, and conserving existing environments. In the public sector — and increasingly in the private sector — urban designers are responsible for preparing such guidelines, which link policy and practice and set the parameters for design.
(vii)	Urban manager	City centre or urban managers promote, develop and undertake the day-to-day management of the urban core. Initially employed to sustain older retail centres against the economic threat of out-of-town retail centres and new 'edge cities', their role has evolved into a concern for the whole urban environment and often encompasses many of the activities listed under 'facilitator of urban events' below. Other important activities include starting small-scale initiatives through assembling a coalition of interest groups and managing the servicing and maintenance of the public realm.
(viii)	Facilitator of urban events	While successful urban places have natural animation (the coming and going of people), others may not have sufficient animation. The facilitator of urban events is responsible for stimulating additional activity through initiating and/or administering planned programmes of cultural animation with social events and spectacles that encourage a diverse range of people in terms of age, ethnicity and gender to visit, use and linger in urban places. Initiatives require local enthusiasm and usually official recognition, partnership and sponsorship.
(ix)	Community motivator/ catalyst	Urban designers involved at the community level are responsible for enabling community participation and involvement in the development process at the local level. The role entails facilitating public participation and involvement in urban design, planning and the management of their built environment. The community motivator ensures the process and any action plan is planned 'with' and 'by' the local community to suit local circumstances, timescales and resources (see Chapter 12).
(x)	Urban conservationist	Requiring sensitive appreciation of the dynamics and processes of urban change, the urban conservationist influences decision-making by exercising influence over the delicate balance between preservation and change. The scale and level of interest varies from the individual building to large areas of townscape, neighbourhoods or quarters of the city and — in some instances — the whole city. The role is also concerned with promoting change that enhances the existing townscape and area.

Source: Adapted from Lang (1994).

fundamental user—producer gap (see Chapters 10 and 11). The users in the process are often represented in the development process by others, such as public agencies or marketing experts, who claim to know what users' needs are and how they should be met.

- *The public/collective interest* — While it is easy to assert that urban designers should serve the public interest, defining what the public interest is in any particular situation — or even designing a method to ascertain it — is difficult (see Campbell & Marshall 2002). Different participants in the development process typically have competing goals and concepts of the public interest, while built environment professionals' assumptions about the public interest are often based on narrow professional, class and/or social origin factors. In practice, defining the public interest involves bargaining and negotiation among vying parties.

In discussing clients for and consumers of urban design, it is important to note the existence of 'gaps', such as those between the producers and the users or consumers of the urban environment (see Chapter 10), and the communication and social gaps between the designer and the user and the professional and the layperson (see Chapter 12). If their desire is to make places for people, urban designers must narrow these gaps. Noting that actual clients always have some sectional interest, Sir Terry Farrell (2008) argues that the real client for urban design is the place itself.

CONCLUSION

Over the past 50 years, urban design has become a recognised field of activity. Although its scope is broad and its boundaries often fuzzy and sometimes contested, this chapter has argued that it should be seen an as integrative activity, at the heart of which should be concern for making places for people. While it is probably inevitable that different groups, including those with urban design qualifications, will continue to lay claim to it as an exclusive professional territory — perhaps even a discrete profession — urban design is a shared rather than a particular responsibility, not least because the problems posed and challenges presented may often be too complex to be handled by a single individual or profession, and, more importantly, because overall place quality is always much broader than the inevitably specialised expertise of the established built environment professions.

Moreover, creating good places is not the prerogative of professional designers and their patrons: urban design cannot be abstracted from the day-to-day life of urban areas, and all those involved in the creation and functioning of such areas have a role to play in ensuring their success. Many other parties are thus concerned with creating and managing good places — central and local government, local communities, the business community, property developers and investors, occupiers and users, passers-by, future generations, etc. All have an interest and a role to play in making better, more sustainable places.

Chapter 2

Urban Change

Cities have changed significantly in recent years; so have ideas about how they should be designed, changed and improved. As means of physical and electronic communication between locations have evolved, traditional centralised city form has evolved into a less legible landscape of sprawling, polycentric 'cities'. As assumptions of centralised urban form and dominant central business districts become less tenable, the traditional vocabulary of 'city centre', 'suburb' and 'city edge' also becomes less meaningful. For Fishman (1987: 185), the new city's 'true centre' is no longer the downtown business district but each individual residential unit, whose members '... *create their own city from the multitude of destinations that are within suitable driving distance.*' Furthermore, their 'own city' may have little or no overlap with that of their neighbours. New advances in digital communication increasingly provide alternatives to physical travel between locations or render it unnecessary.

This chapter is split into five main sections. The first section discusses changing ideas of urban space design. The second section discusses early and mature industrial city form and post-industrial urban form. The third section discusses the impact of information and communication technology. The fourth section discusses the prospects of a return to urbanity. The fifth section reviews contemporary urbanisms.

CHANGING URBAN SPACE DESIGN

'Traditional' urban space can be regarded as the evolved state of urban form immediately prior to the onset of large-scale industrialisation and urbanisation. Until the Industrial Revolution, urban development was limited by transport methods, and speeds limited to those of the pedestrian and the horse and cart; the availability of construction materials was limited — each city was built of locally derived materials, giving it a relatively consistent appearance; and building methods were usually limited to load-bearing masonry and timber construction. Together with the absence of lifts to service high-rise buildings, these methods also limited the height that could be built and serviced to a maximum of six or seven stories — though taller buildings were occasionally built, usually for special purposes (e.g. church towers, cathedrals, watch towers, etc.).

Except when natural forces or war wreaked wholesale destruction, these limitations meant that change in the urban fabric was gradual, enabling successive generations to derive a sense of continuity and stability from their physical surroundings. With the growth of capitalism and rapid urbanisation, mainly during the nineteenth century, this older scale and pace of development was overtaken.

During the nineteenth century and early twentieth century, industrialisation, including new building materials and construction techniques — plate glass, steel, concrete, balloon frames, etc. — changed the scale of development. This coincided with other major developments in technology such as railways, the safety elevator and the internal combustion engine, and a host of related social and economic changes. Architects and engineers sought to meet the new demands and challenges of the period — ideas that came to be known as Modernism.

Emerging in the first half of the twentieth century, Modernism in architecture and planning was driven both by horror at the squalor and slums of nineteenth century industrial cities, and by perception of the start of a new age — the Machine Age — in which society would reap the benefits of new technology and industrialisation. The leading Modernist in city design was the Swiss architect and planner, Le Corbusier, and the period's most influential manifesto was the Charter of Athens — the report of the 1933 Congress of CIAM, the International Congress of Modern Architecture, established in the 1920s.

A number of contemporary problems and opportunities informed Modernist concepts of urban space design (see Box 2.1). Reacting to nineteenth century and early twentieth century industrial cities, Modernism is often seen as having an inherent anti-urban bias. More precisely, it was opposed to traditional urban form, with Modernists seeking to derive new principles of urban form: traditional, relatively low-rise streets, squares and urban blocks being eschewed in favour of rational, usually orthogonal, distributions of slab and point blocks, set in park land and other open space. Rather than being enclosed by buildings, space would flow freely around buildings to allow light in and air to circulate.

Opportunity and political will to develop Modernist ideas of urban space design came after 1945 with reconstruction in Europe, and later through slum clearance programmes and as a consequence of road-building schemes in all developed countries. Rather than incremental rehabilitation and infill development, comprehensive redevelopment was preferred, with the post-1945

Box 2.1 Characteristics of Modernist Urban Space Design

Healthier buildings

Early Modernist planning and urban design was a reaction to the physical conditions of industrial cities. Medical knowledge developed during the nineteenth century and early twentieth century provided criteria for designing healthier buildings and environments — the need for light, air, sun and ventilation, and access to open spaces. It was argued that the best way to achieve this was to detach buildings from each other, orientate them towards the sun (rather than, as previously, towards the street), spread them out to allow light and air to flow freely around them, and build upwards where light and air was plentiful.

Healthier environments

Modernists also sought to create healthier environments. At this larger scale, the solution was to provide light and air by decongestion, lower residential densities, and zoning housing away from industry — 'those dark satanic mills'. Functional zoning was a key element of the Charter of Athens, which proposed rigid functional zoning of city plans with green belts between areas reserved for different land uses. This was justified not only on environmental grounds but also because the resulting city would be more efficient and ordered, with new modes of transport tying the separated areas together.

City as machine

The car and the urban highway were potent symbols of the new age. Le Corbusier (1927) extolled the benefits and opportunities provided by cars:

'The cities will become part of the country; I shall live 30 miles from my office in one direction; my secretary will live thirty miles away

from it too, in the other direction, under another pine tree. We shall both own cars. We shall use up tyres, wear out road surfaces and gears, consume oil and gasoline.'

The Charter of Athens asserted that, because existing cities were ill-equipped to accommodate the car, 'great transformations' were necessary, with conflicts resolved by segregating vehicles and pedestrians, and by the rejection of 'streets' that slowed cars down. Cities were seen as machines for logically separating and ordering human movement and activities rather than places for people.

Architectural design philosophies

To express their function and functional requirements, buildings were designed from the inside out, responding only to their programme and functional requirements — for light, air, hygiene, aspect, prospect, recreation, movement and openness. Following their own internal logic without necessarily responding to the immediate urban context, they became sculptures or 'objects-in-space'. Such buildings would also express their modernity.

Architecture of time

Reacting to nineteenth century historicism, Modernism had an enthusiasm for the zeitgeist — the spirit of the age — and sought a radical break with the past. Differences, rather than continuities, with the past were emphasised, with the past seen as a hindrance to the future. Though largely 'rhetoric rather than reality', it was important in shaping attitudes and values (Middleton 1983: 730).

period seeing dramatic acceleration in the pace and physical scale of urban change. While the context for this was the ideas of CIAM, Le Corbusier and others, Harvey (1989a: 69) considers it less:

'... *a controlling force of ideas over production than a theoretical framework and justification for what practical-minded engineers, politicians, builders, and developers were in many cases engaged upon out of sheer social, economic, and political necessity.'*

Comprehensive redevelopment offered the prospect of higher quality environments and more efficient transport networks. At the same time, urban clearance, together with the design of new development, destroyed established street patterns (see Chapter 4). The process of redevelopment was highly disruptive to the economic and social infrastructure, while the resulting large blocks simplified the land-use pattern, removing the 'nooks and crannies' that housed economically marginal but socially desirable uses and activities giving variety and life to an area. Nevertheless, although often painful, through most of the 1945 to mid-1970s period, the destruction of the physical, social and cultural fabric of inner city areas, mixed-use functional neighbourhoods, and poorer, working-class residential areas

was accepted without serious question. But, with increasing force from the early 1960s onwards, there was increasing compliant, unrest and questioning of the conventional wisdom of urban renewal and redevelopment and a number of criticisms of, and reactions to, Modernist ideas of urban space design and prevailing practices of urban development can be identified (see Box 2.2). Contemporary urban space design has in large part drawn stimulus from these perceived shortcomings (see Chapter 4).

Critiques of Modernism often present it as more monolithic and all-embracing than it actually was. As Wells-Thorpe (1998: 105) observes, many of the benefits of Modernism are now taken for granted, while Harvey (1989a: 70) considers it '... *both erroneous and unjust to depict these "Modernist" solutions to the dilemmas of post-war urban development and redevelopment as unalloyed failures.'* In Europe, war-torn cities were rapidly reconstructed, and populations housed under much better conditions.

Indeed, Harvey (1989a: 71) regards it as 'completely wrong' to '... *lay all the blame for the urban ills of post-war development at the Modern Movement's door, without regard to the political-economic tune to which post-war urbanisation was dancing.'* Attributing the quality of late

Box 2.2 Critiques of Modernist Urban Space Design

Participation and involvement

Modernism was perceived to lack dialogue and interaction with the end user — Le Corbusier, for example, suggested '... *people would have to be re-educated to appreciate his visions.*' (in Knox 1987: 364); Walter Gropius considered it undesirable to talk to building users because '... *they were intellectually undeveloped.*' (in Knox 1987: 366). The shortcomings of built Modernist projects lead to arguments for consulting with users and local communities in order to understand — and perhaps respond to — their preferences and aspirations (see Chapter 12).

Conservation

By the late 1960s, the attributes of traditional environments, including how such environments seemed better able to accommodate and support urban life and activity, were increasingly recognised in contrast to, and as a reaction against, Modernist environments. During the 1960s and early 1970s, policies protecting historic areas were introduced, with conservation becoming an integral component of urban planning. With it came a related concern for context (in contrast to Modernism's internationalism), greater respect for the uniqueness of places and their history, and for continuity of local patterns and typologies (see Chapter 9).

Mixed uses

The logic of functional zoning, reinforced by transport developments and by high land values that excluded lower value uses and larger building complexes that internalised much of the traditional street life and activity, reduced the complexity and vitality of city centres. The sterility of such environments suggested the need for more mixed-use environments (see Chapter 8).

Urban form

With new awareness of the qualities and scale of the 'traditional' city, some theorists and practitioners advocated a morphological approach to urban design, based on existing 'tried-and-tested' spatial precedents and archetypes, and stressing continuity with, rather than a break from, the past. There was a growing influence from theorists unhappy with the

achievements of Modernist urban space design: while Modernism's 'best solo performances' may have been 'more virtuoso', they failed to produce 'good' streets or 'good' cities and there was recognition that '... *the typical fabric and its overall orchestration were better in previous eras.*' (Kelbaugh 1997: 95) (see Chapter 4).

Architecture of place

Disillusion with Modernist architecture — or, rather, its debasement through industrialised production and construction techniques — has been well documented in books (see Blake 1974; Wolfe 1981). In his 1966 book, *Complexity and Contradiction in Architecture*, Robert Venturi questioned the purist, minimalist and elitist dogma that, in his view, the International style and architectural Modernism had become. Influenced by this and his subsequent book, *Learning from Las Vegas* (Venturi *et al* 1972), new approaches emerged, recognising the built environment's decorative and contextual properties. This was not either/or, and could be an architecture of time and place (see Chapter 7).

Cities for people

Lacking the social qualities of streets, roads sliced up and fragmented urban areas, causing problems of severance. The centres of many American cities graphically illustrate the ultimate effect of the car on city form, becoming what Kostof termed 'automobile territory' with razed blocks given over to car parking adjacent to intensively developed blocks. Kostof (1992: 277) observes how — in Detroit, Houston, Los Angeles and elsewhere — there is 'Modernist urbanism', but not of the sort envisaged by Le Corbusier: '*His iconic ville verte — a vision of towers in a park — became in America a ville grise of towers in a parking lot.*' Although European cities were transformed in less dramatic ways, most cities saw major road building schemes (see Chapter 4). Reacting to the emphasis on cars, there has been a new concern for the pedestrian, and a desire to create pedestrian-dominant environments — environments accessible to cars, but designed to suit the scale, pace and comfort of pedestrians — and environments facilitating use by a range of modes of travel.

---

twentieth century urban environments solely to Modernism both gives too much credit to and heaps too much blame upon architects, planners and engineers, and understates the role of general development practices and the regulatory systems that permitted them.

Modernism is thus frequently misrepresented and caricatured. Rather than a visual style, it is properly a philosophy or approach to design, involving rational exploration of problems and challenges, and the development of responses exploiting new technologies. Marshall (2009: 33) describes it as '... *a belief in the possibility of progress through rational action*' — a definition that, in practice, encompasses most urban design. In different situations and different contexts, a Modernist approach *should* give rise to different forms — what is

manifest in one particular historical period should be different to that in another. The characteristics outlined in Box 2.1 are those of mid-twentieth century Modernism, when Modernists exploited the potential of steel and concrete frames and anticipated mass car ownership. Many contemporary designers retain the core sensibility of Modernism and respond to the problems and challenges of the present day by seeking to exploit the potential of new building materials and of computers to design and build shapes and forms not possible in earlier eras.

CHANGING CITY FORM

Cities and settlements have evolved through three historical eras. In the first era they were primarily market places; in the second era they were primarily centres of industrial production; and in the third era they were primarily centres of service provision, consumption and knowledge. The original basis for cities was the need to come together, for security and defence; for trade; for access to information, other people and resources that might only be available in particular places; to engage in activities requiring communal effort or organisation; and to use particular equipment or machines, etc. The essential factor was that activities required people to communicate, which, at least initially, meant being in the same place at the same time — that is, some form of concentration. The coming together of people in space and time facilities an important socio-cultural dimension, subsequently taken as the essence of 'the urban'. Oldenburg (1999: xxviii), for example, contends that, without public gathering places integral to people's lives, the 'promise of the city' is denied because the urban area '… *fails to nourish the kinds of relationships and the diversity of human contact that are the essence of the city.'* (see Chapter 6).

Since the first settlements the reasons for people coming together, and the interactions and transactions between them, have multiplied massively. So too have the

technologies of transportation and communication, the use and development of which has had significant effects on the form and nature of all settlements. The changing distribution of activities in space and the changing spatial form of cities and urban areas can be regarded as the product of successive waves of innovation and related technologies. Hargroves & Smith (2005) identify six waves of innovation that have shaped cities (Figure 2.1). The fifth wave was fuelled by relatively cheap, readily available oil. Moving into a post-cheap oil era, we are likely to face significant change, with Newman *et al* (2009: 13–4) suggesting the response to climate change and peak oil will be the impetus for the next burst of innovation — the sixth wave.

Rather than the technology itself, it is the pattern of infrastructure to support that technology — and subsequently social choice — that has been instrumental in directing spatial patterns of development. While defensive walls and fortifications initially constrained development, by compressing space-time (the distance that can be travelled in a unit of time), transport innovations — and subsequently information and communication technology (ICT) — were instrumental in allowing urban areas to spread out. Fifteen minutes' walking time in a medieval town might cover one

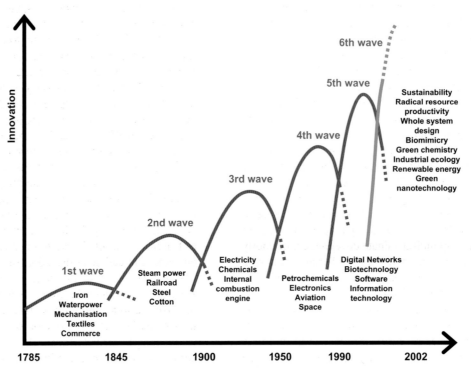

FIGURE 2.1   Six waves of innovation (*Image adapted from Hargroves & Smith 2005*). Hargroves & Smith (2005) identify six waves of innovation that have shaped cities, ultimately creating the polycentric urban regions of today. The first wave produced walking cities, with new industries developing along rivers and canals using water power. The second wave spread cities out along railway lines. The third wave saw linear development along electric tramways. Dominated by cheap oil and the automobile, the fourth wave enabled cities to spread and sprawl in all direction. The Internet and digital technologies of the fifth wave both minimised some of the negative consequences of sprawl and led to the regeneration of older industrial cities. Coinciding with the end of cheap oil, as Newman *et al* (2009: 52) explain, the sixth wave is '… *the beginning of a new era of resource productivity and investment in a new series of sustainability technologies related to renewables and distributed, small scale, water, energy, and waste systems … all of which are more local and require less fuel to distribute.'*

mile and take you from one side of the town to the other; 15 minutes' driving in a contemporary city might cover five or six miles, without ever leaving the city. Innovations in communications technology (e.g. telegraph, telephone, e-mail discussions, video-conferencing, etc.) now also provide alternatives to co-presence in communication. Urban design contributes to evolving trends in developing new urban form *and* reacts to the patterns of previous eras of growth.

(i) Early industrial city form

Before the full emergence of capitalist economies in the eighteenth century, and the Industrial Revolution in the nineteenth century, cities were essentially small-scale settlements. During the late eighteenth and nineteenth centuries, initially in England and subsequently elsewhere, major social and economic changes took place. As the population increased rapidly, changes in farming methods produced a labour surplus in agricultural districts. At the same time, the increasingly prosperous towns and cities of industrial and mining districts offered employment and a perceived higher standard of living, and there was a general migration of population into towns. Steam power necessitated a factory system, causing labour to be further concentrated in urban areas.

In the West, the urban population's growth was spectacular. In 1801, the urban population of England and Wales was three million — about one-third of the total population. By 1911, it was 36 million — almost 80% of the total population. The modern or industrial city was, thus, a product of the Industrial Revolution, a revolution that is today having similar impacts in cities across the global south.

Rapid growth of cities, however, led to severe overcrowding, squalor and poor public health. City authorities were inadequately organised for, and experienced in, coping with such rapid growth, and, with workers having to be within walking distance of factories due to the lack of mass public transport, there was a relatively indiscriminate development of poorly constructed workers' housing in and around factories, producing unsanitary and unhealthy conditions.

(ii) Mature Industrial City Form

Following the urbanisation precipitated by the Industrial Revolution, when the main means of transport had been by horse or by foot, mass transport systems broke the necessarily close spatial relation between workplace and residence. Industrial cities initially grew in density, but, after about 1870, with the development of suburban railway systems, they also grew in area. The early 1900s saw the development of horse-drawn, and then motorised, trams and buses, and, in the largest cities, underground railways. Such developments permitted decentralisation of — at

least initially — residential land uses. Suburbs were a new form of urbanisation that markedly differed from traditional urban form. Over time, these have evolved into two basic development patterns — higher density, more compact and walkable (traditional urbanism), and lower density, less compact drivable, poly-nucleated (sub)urbanism. These are development patterns rather than geographic locations: suburban locations may, for example, have more urban patterns of development. The defining characteristics are outlined in Table 2.1 — each characteristic is a spectrum ranging from 'more suburban' or 'more urban'.

The initial motivation for living in what became the suburbs was to escape the industrial city and its pollution, disease and crime. Additional attractions were better quality housing, a garden, healthier living conditions and the social status conferred. The growth of the Garden Cities movement in particular was highly influential in this period, providing an idealised suburban model that proved immediately attractive — though subsequently much abused — throughout the twentieth century (Box 2.3). Indeed, if one measured the influence of the Garden Cities movement by the extent of its direct descendent — suburban sprawl — its impact far outweighs that of Modernism.

In the 1930s, the movement towards decentralisation broadened its base as the steady-salaried employment of the burgeoning middle classes encouraged banks to lend money as mortgages. This fuelled speculative development, which, together with the expansion of transport systems — and, in most countries, ineffectual and nonexistent planning systems — led to more suburbanisation.

The post-1945 period saw further suburbanisation. Enabled by the individual mobility afforded by steadily increasing car ownership, spreading out the previously integrated activities of home, work, business and leisure, rapid urban decentralisation became a feature of most Western countries from 1945 onwards, and earlier in the USA (see Jackson 1985). The nature of decentralisation differed: in North America, Japan and Australia, it took the form of massive and sprawling suburbanisation, and in Europe it involved both suburbanisation of larger cities and towns and the growth of smaller towns and villages, partly as a result of green belts around larger cities (Breheny 1997: 21) (Figure 2.2).

A suburban population commuting to work in the city centre created problems of access and congestion, reducing the central business district (CBD)'s accessibility. In the 1950s and 1960s, road building schemes addressed the increasing need for access from the suburbs to city centres, and were

TABLE 2.1 Differences Between Suburban ('Sprawl') and Urban ('Compact City')

Low Density	High Density
Zoned development	Mixed-use development
Segregation of functions for living, working, recreation	Integration of functions for living, working, recreation
Segregation of demographic and economic groups	Mixed-income communicates
Car dependence	Predominance of pedestrians and cyclists
Disconnected public spaces	Interconnected walkable network of large- and small-scale public spaces
High-speed transport networks and increased road infrastructure	Minimised need for transport and planning for walking and cycling
Parking, buildings and freeways	Parks, landscape and cycle paths
Minimum parking spaces	Parking space capping requirements
Sense of anonymity	Sense of community
US urban model	European/Asian model
Developed from about 100 years ago	Developed from 9000 years ago
Large-scale developments	Neighbourhood-human-scale developments
Superstores and big shopping complexes	Corner shops, local shopping areas, farmers' markets
Mass housing and commercial/industrial districts	Capping of allowable space for commercial/industrial districts
Driven by market forces	Driven by vision and a masterplan
High energy	Low energy
High carbon dioxide emissions	Low carbon dioxide emissions

Source: Adapted from Dennis & Urry (2009: 113).

supplemented by other developments, such as ring roads, bypasses and connections to national motorway systems. At the time, it was confidently thought that suburbanites would continue to commute into the city for work, shopping and entertainment (Kunstler 2005: 41).

In time, however, the transport pattern was transformed from a hierarchical 'hub-and-spoke' pattern, where the hub was the most accessible point, to more integrated patterns where the most accessible locations are the junctions in the net. These developments materially changed the pattern of accessibility in the city region, removing the necessity to be close to the centre, which had kept city form compact and growth patterns concentric throughout the nineteenth century, and opening up the potential for scattered growth (Southworth & Owens 1993).

Furthermore, beyond the suburbs, which were still part of the morphological (built) city, were increasing extensive exurbs (a contraction of 'extra-urban') — a term coined by Spectorsky (1955) to describe the ring of prosperous communities beyond the suburbs that are, in effect, commuter towns and thus still part

of the functional city but no longer part of the morphological city.

Changes in the regional transportation network had two primary effects — central city decline and the emergence of 'perimeter cities' and edge cities. As the original CBD lost its primacy in the local transport network, central city decline and the emergence of new, less monocentric city forms were inevitable. In many cases this also precipitated the CBD's dissolution as a political economic, social and symbolic locus — a process termed the 'hollowing out' of cities and an outcome described as 'donut cities'. Fishman (1987: 17) observed the emergence of 'perimeter cities' functionally independent of the urban core — a phenomenon most prominent in the USA.

At a larger geographical scale, there has been inter-regional and international shift of population and investment. This is seen most clearly in the USA where there are no boundaries or linguistic constraints to tie people to place, and where the shift has been from the northern rustbelt to the southern sunbelt — that is, from the old manufacturing industrial cities of the north to the new service cities of the south.

BOX 2.3 Garden Cities

Originally envisaged by Ebenezer Howard and published in 1898 in *Tomorrow, A Peaceful Path to Real Reform*, the Garden Cities concept pursued a strong social agenda of creating socially mixed, working communities in healthy, green environments. In practice, built examples often failed to meet their social aims — Hampstead Garden Suburb, for example, was largely middle class and single use when built and remains so today — in part because they were being built as profit-making ventures.

Physically, as one of the movement's pioneers — Osborn (1918) — accepted in his own writings, a 'formula-based' approach quickly emerged, based on the visual image rather than the intended social and economic substance. In fact, the garden city formula developed, and was interpreted brilliantly by designers such as Raymond Unwin, Barry Parker and Louis de Soissons into a distinct and recognisable urbanism.

Suburban Idyll *(Image: Matthew Carmona)*

Hampstead Garden Suburb's distinguishing characteristics, for example, include:

Land uses
- Predominantly residential uses, with some civic buildings.
- Retail limited to the peripheral roads and no employment space.

Urban form
- The grouping of buildings to reinforce a sense of community around short lengths of narrow roads, greens, quadrangles and closes.
- Continuous building lines, punctuated by landscaped setbacks.
- Street junctions designed as urban spaces and entrances to the suburb marked architecturally.
- Picturesque layout of buildings — sometimes organised organically, sometimes as axial compositions.
- Low density — around 20 dwellings per hectare.

Landscape
- Urban form shaped by the underlying topography.
- Streets lined with grass verges and trees.
- Buildings separated from the street by generous front gardens.
- Plots separated by hedges, trees or fences, but not walls.
- Private rear gardens for most dwellings.

Architecture
- Landmark buildings to punctuate the urban composition.
- Houses designed to harmonise with each other.
- High quality building materials and traditional craftsmanship.
- Extensive use of pebbledash, generally unpainted, otherwise white or cream.
- Red, purple and brown stock brick, and handmade red plain tiles.
- Features such as chimneys, dormer windows and bays designed to add individuality.

Movement has thus been both from the central city to the suburban and exurban rings, and out of the region entirely. Those moving have been the ones with the capacity, skills and education to move, leaving a relatively more deprived, poorer and less educated population in the core cities and the economically distressed regions.

These shifts have given rise to the phenomenon of shrinking cities (see www.shrinkingcities.com) — those which have lost much of their original economic rationale and are losing population. The phenomenon is common in the USA's rustbelt, eastern Europe and much of northern Britain. In such cities, the existing infrastructure is now too large and too extensive for a much more dispersed population. The costs of maintaining this infrastructure with a diminished tax base, means that, rather than growth management, there are strategies for downsizing and planned shrinkage (Figure 2.3).

While the established centres were being eroded, on the urban periphery new concentrations of business, shopping and entertainment were being developed. To describe larger versions of these, Garreau (1991) coined the term 'edge city'.

For Garreau, edge cities were the result of a third wave of decentralisation — that of employment opportunities moving out to where people had lived and shopped for two decades. Garreau established five rules to identify an edge city:

- Having more than five million square feet (465 000 m²) of office space, housing between 20 000 and 50 000 office workers.

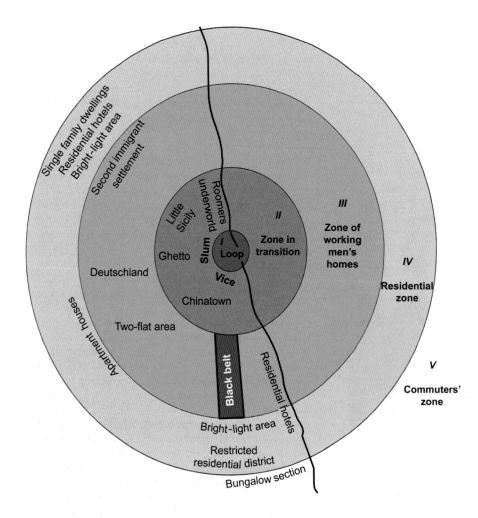

Single family dwellings
Residential hotels
Bright-light area
Second immigrant settlement
Apartment houses
Two-flat area
Deutschland
Ghetto
Little Sicily
Roomers underworld
I Loop
Slum
Vice
Chinatown
II Zone in transition
III Zone of working men's homes
IV Residential zone
V Commuters' zone
Black belt
Residential hotels
Bright-light area
Restricted residential district
Bungalow section

FIGURE 2.2 Burgess's concentric zone model (Image: Knox & Pinch 2000: 216). For much of the early twentieth century, the most influential ideas about, and explanations of, urban form and structure came from the University of Chicago's urban sociology department, subsequently known as the 'Chicago School'. Chicago was a new city, having grown rapidly and owing much of its growth to industrialisation. Models of urban structure — most famously Burgess's concentric zone model — were based on research on the city. The 'typical' mature industrial city had a dominant city centre or central business district (CBD), relatively homogeneous zones of land use and social groups, and a monocentric structure focused on the CBD — the most accessible point and focus of the transport network and system. Competition for sites and the ability of some land uses to outbid others meant land values were at their highest at the city centre. Around the centre would be concentric rings of different land uses. Land values and the intensity of development declined smoothly with distance from the centre of the city.

FIGURE 2.3 Detroit *(Image: Steve Tiesdell)*. The image captures a sense of the disinvestment and abandonment in central Detroit. For Fishman (2008: xv), Detroit encapsulates the fate that, as late as the end of the twentieth century, had been predicted for all American cities: '… *a downtown marginalised and semi-abandoned; once bustling factory zones turned into depopulated, deindustrialised and racially segregated "inner-cities"; suburbs in the "first-ring" just beyond the central city caught in a rolling wave of abandonment about to engulf them and — at the edges — the feverish, fragmented, low-density growth we know as sprawl.*'

- Having more than 600 000 square feet (56 000 m^2) of retail space, making it a centre of recreation and commerce as well as office work.
- Having more jobs than bedrooms.
- Being perceived as a single place.
- Being a new urbanisation (i.e. having had no urban characteristics 30 years previously).

Garreau's classic example of an edge city is Tysons Corner, Virginia, west of Washington DC. Typically having developed incrementally around a shopping mall or highway interchange, Garreau (1991: 111) termed this type 'boomers'. He identified two other types: 'uptowns' built over a pre-existing, pre-automobile settlement (Garreau 1991: 113) and 'greenfields' masterplanned as new towns, generally on the suburban fringe. For Garreau (1991: 116), these are 'most ambitious' and 'most awesome':

'A Greenfield occurs at the intersection between several thousand acres of farmland and one developer's monumental ego. It embraces an amazingly grand master-planned vision of human nature and rigid control of vast areas by private corporations.'

Edge city development was not unregulated and was typically permitted. For developers it was a path of least resistance (and highest profitability) through the regulations — that is, what the development industry found easiest to build. More precisely, though, the edge city is a product of the car, with most edge cities developing at or near existing or planned freeway intersections, or near major airports, and having hierarchical street arrangements centred on pedestrian-hostile arterial roads and winding parkways often without sidewalks/pavements. As well as in North America, the edge city is a common development form in China, India and parts of the Middle East.

(iii) Post-industrial urban form

Since the 1970s, new urban forms have been emerging that are significantly different from modern/industrial cities in their form, pattern of land values and social geographies. Processes of dispersal and decentralisation, enabled by mass car ownership and (relatively) cheap oil, combined with the changing transport network, resulted in a breaking down of the 'tent-like' density gradients stretching outwards from the central city to the suburbs: suburban densities of jobs and residents might appear next to the CBD, while new concentrations of residential, employment and retail development could sprout on the urban periphery (Hall 1998).

An extensive body of work by scholars based in California defines Los Angeles as the archetypal post-industrial city (Hall 1998: 10). The 'Los Angeles School' argues that post-industrial 'cities' are increasingly fragmentary in their form and chaotic in their structure, and generated by different processes of urbanisation than earlier cities (Box 2.4). A key theme is fragmentation, both in terms of the urban form and of the associated economic and social geographies (Figure 2.4). Graham & Marvin (2001: 115) describe how

'... complex patchworks of growth and decline, concentration and decentralisation, poverty and extreme wealth are juxtaposed. Whilst downtowns may maintain their dominance of some high level service functions, back offices, corporate plazas, research and development and university campuses, malls, airports and logistics zones, and retail, leisure and residential spaces spread further and further around the metropolitan core.'

Dear & Flusty (1999: 77) argue that in

'... the absence of conventional and transportation imperatives mandating propinquity, the once-standard Chicago School logic has given way to a seemingly haphazard juxtaposition of land uses scattered over the landscape.'

Box 2.4 The Los Angeles School

The value of the Los Angeles School lies in its early recognition of emergent processes shaping urban landscapes, economies and cultures. Soja (1995, 1996) identified six processes of restructuring:

(i) A combined process of deindustrialisation and reindustrialisation, resulting in the rise of new flexible forms of economic organisation and production, representing a shift *'... from the tight organisation of mass production and mass consumption around large industrial complexes to more flexible production systems,* [which are] *vertically disintegrated but geographically clustered in "new industrial spaces".'* (Soja 1995: 129).

(ii) The processes of internationalisation, the expansion of globalised capital, and the formation of a global system of 'world cities' in a combined process of 'globalising the local' and 'localising the global'.

(iii) The emergence of new post-industrial urban forms, involving a combination of decentralisation and recentralisation, the peripheralisation of the centre and the centralisation of the periphery, with the city simultaneously being turned inside-out and outside-in.

(iv) The development of new patterns of social fragmentation, segregation and polarisation, resulting in increasing inequality, new patterns of spatial segregation, a widening income gap and the multiplication of 'blatant contrasts' between wealth and poverty, revealing stark differences in income, culture and language, and lifestyles.

(v) The rise of 'carceral architecture' based on protection, surveillance and exclusion. With its 'kaleidoscope complexities', the postmodern city has both become 'increasingly ungovernable' and a 'carceral city' (see Chapter 6).

(vi) The increasing presence of simulation within urban landscapes is seen as a 'radical change' in *'... the ways we relate our images of what is real to empirical reality itself.'* (Soja 1995: 134).

The result is an urban landscape 'not unlike' that formed by a keno gamecard, in which

'Capital touches down as if by chance on a parcel of land, ignoring the opportunities on intervening lots. ... The relationship between development of one parcel and non-development of another is a disjointed, seemingly unrelated affair. ... Conventional city form, Chicago-style, is sacrificed in favour of a non-contiguous collage of parcelised, consumption-oriented landscapes devoid of conventional centres yet wired into electronic propinquity and nominally unified by the mythologies of the disinformation superhighway.' (1999: 81).

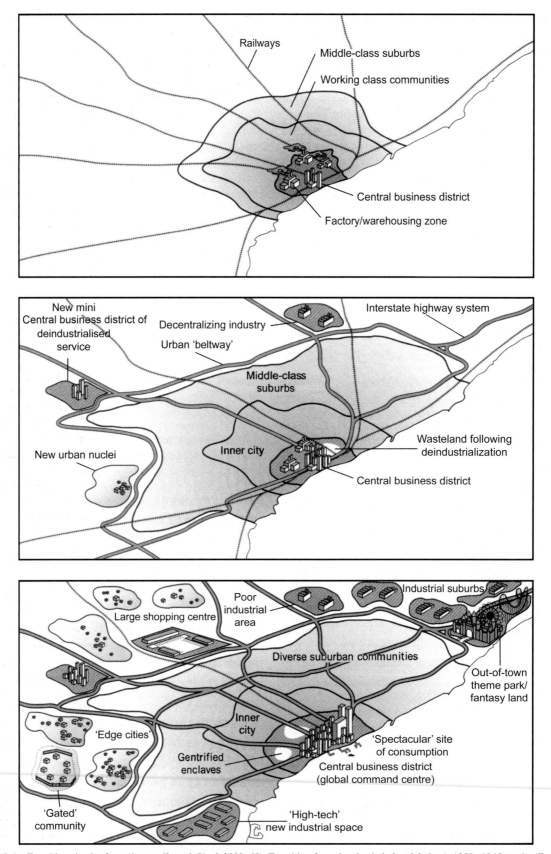

FIGURE 2.4   Transitions in city form (*Image: Knox & Pinch 2000: 69*). Transition from the classic industrial city (c.1850–1945) to the 'Fordist' city (c.1945–1973) and the 'post-Fordist' metropolis (c.1975 onwards).

Restructuring processes are nonetheless mediated by socio-cultural choice, by institutional structures and by pre-existing physical forms. The cities epitomising industrial (Chicago) and post-industrial (Los Angeles) urban form were relatively free from the constraints of earlier patterns. Most cities, particularly those in Europe, have extensive physical and socio-economic legacies of earlier urbanisations, but not (yet) the levels of disinvestment that have plagued many North American cities.

Thus, while Los Angeles-style — or perhaps Detroit-style — restructuring and urban form may be the future for some cities, it is not the future of all cities. Knox & Marston (1998: 449—53), for example, identify distinctive physical, social and economic features of European cities, distinguishing them from North American cities and providing resistance to large-scale restructuring:

- *Complex street patterns* — reflecting ancient patterns of settlement and long, slow growth.
- *The presence of plazas and squares* — many of pre-modern foundation, which remain important anchors and centres of activity.
- *High density and compact forms* — resulting from high levels of urbanisation, a long history of urban development, the constraints of defensive walls and, more recently, strong planning regulations limiting horizontal growth.
- *Low skylines* — limited by historic building materials and techniques, and by planning and building codes preserving the dominance of important buildings.
- *Lively downtowns* — due to the relatively late arrival of the suburbanising influence of the car and because of strong planning controls directed at urban containment.
- *Stable social and physical neighbourhoods* — Europeans move house much less frequently than Americans and, due to the past use of durable construction materials (e.g. brick and stone), the physical life cycle of neighbourhoods tends to be longer.
- *The scars of war* — defensive hill-top sites and city walls limiting and shaping the growth of modern cities.
- *Symbolism* — the legacy of a long and varied history, including a rich variety of valued symbols in the built environment.
- *A tradition of 'municipal socialism'* — European welfare states generally provide — or have provided — a broad range of municipal services and amenities, including public transit systems and public housing.

Thus, in much of Europe, there is a still vibrant — often revitalised (see below) — core surrounded by a 'shatter zone' — and then suburbia, with more prosperous residential developments and a mix of other developments — retail malls, leisure complexes, business parks and employment centres — surrounding it. The suburban and exurban rings, however, are not dissimilar to those of North America in either form or density (see Bruegmann 2005: 91—5).

Cedric Price wittily likened urban form to eggs. The early industrial city was very compact like a hard boiled egg. The mature industrial city was like a fried egg, with white suburbs centred on a yellow city centre. The post-industrial city was a scrambled egg, with white and yellow all mixed up. Interestingly, in *Suburban Nation*, Duany *et al* (2000: 10—1) compared the contemporary American city with '… *an unmade omelette: eggs, cheese, vegetables, a pinch of salt, but each consumed in turn, raw.*'

INFORMATION AND COMMUNICATION TECHNOLOGY

Contemporary restructuring of urban form is not only a consequence of the transition from an industrial to a post-industrial era, but also from an 'industrial' to an 'informational' era (Castells 1989). Precisely how cities and urban areas will develop in the informational age is, as yet, unknowable. What is new, and somewhat unexpected, for example, has been the popularity of virtual spaces — chat rooms, virtual worlds, Twitter, Facebook, etc. — that some argue will supplant our need to meet and interact in traditional public space, and will eventually lead to new forms of urbanism (see Aurigi 2005: 17—31).

Mitchell (1995), for example, asserts that digital telecommunications networks will transform urban form and function as radically as networks of water supply and sewers, electricity, and mechanised transportation, and telegraph and telephone networks have previously done. By supporting remote and asynchronous interaction, these networks will further loosen the spatial and temporal linkages that previously bound human activities together.

To illustrate the costs and benefits of local/remote and synchronous/asynchronous communication, Mitchell (1999: 136) uses the example of seeking information from a colleague and puts four modes of communication into a historical sequence that, *inter alia*, helps to explain the development of urban form (Figure 2.5). Face-to-face contact provides the most intense, high quality and potentially enjoyable interaction, but it is also the most expensive, requiring travel and consuming real estate. By contrast, despite separating participants in both space and time, remote asynchronous communication is far more convenient and often much less costly.

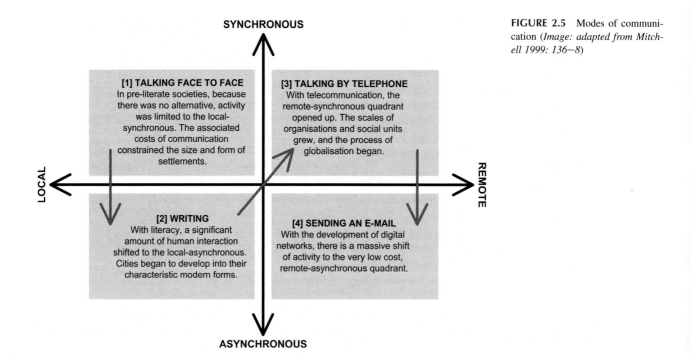

As urban history has shown, increased mobility — both physical and electronic — has reduced the need for spatial concentration. Electronic communication is perhaps the most powerful decentralising and dis-urbanising force ever experienced, with many experts seeing the 'information superhighway' further dispersing people and their jobs from cities. As Hall (1998: 957) observes,

'After all, that was the effect of previous technological breakthroughs, like the telephone and the car; the information superhighway will simply take the trend to its logical conclusion.'

For Mitchell (1995: 94), new technology is dissolving the 'glue' — the need for face-to-face contact with co-workers, for close proximity to expensive information-processing equipment, and for access to information only held and available at a central location — that held the old agglomerations together. Nonetheless, due to communication technology, while contemporary cities and urban areas might be more spatially diffuse and fluid, they are also more connected and integrated — albeit electronically rather than physically — than ever before.

Electronic communication *could* mean future 'cities' are aspatial and ageographic. Mitchell (1995: 8) argues that the Internet '... *negates geometry ... is fundamentally and profoundly aspatial ... The Net is ambient — nowhere in particular but everywhere at once.'* As it does not matter where computers are located, merely that they are connected, the Internet gets much closer to providing universal accessibility (where everywhere is equally accessible) than does the car.

The informational age thus advances the ideas of Webber (1963, 1964) who, extolling the freedom offered by freeways and the highly decentralised city, conceived of the 'non-place urban realm' (where 'place' refers to geographical location). Arguing that spread-out cities such as Los Angeles worked just as well as traditional high-density ones such as New York, Webber emphasised that the essential qualities of urbanness were cultural rather than territorial. In a celebrated passage, he concluded that

'... the values associated with the desired urban structure do not reside in the spatial structure per se. One pattern of settlement is superior to another only as it better serves to accommodate ongoing social processes and to further the non-spatial ends of the political community. I am flatly rejecting the contention that there is an overriding spatial or physical aesthetic of urban form.'

(Webber 1963: 52)

Recognising the instrumental impact of transport and communication technology does not equate to technological determinism — the application of technology is mediated by social trends. Decentralisation, the so-called 'death of distance' and the end of the city, are not foregone conclusions: technology creates opportunities, which people — at least those with choice — take advantage of. As Hall (1998: 943) argues,

'... new technology shapes new opportunities, to create new industries and transform old ones, to present new ways of organising firms or entire societies, to transform the potential for living; but it does not compel these changes.' (Figure 2.6).

FIGURE 2.6 Paris *(Image: Steve Tiesdell)*. Castells (1989: 1–2) noted *how 'intensely urban' Paris was '… the success story for the use of home-based telematic systems.'* Mitchell (1995: 169) asked whether Paris has '… *something that telepresence cannot match?'*

Universal mobility might result in an almost complete loss of significance associated with (geographic) centrality and traditional concepts of location. This argument is not wholly persuasive because place quality also matters. As location in space (geographical location) matters less in locational decisions, the quality of local 'place' starts to matter more. Kotkin (2001: 6), for example, argues that

'If people, companies, or industries can truly live anywhere, or at least chose from a multiplicity of places, the question of where to locate becomes increasingly contingent on the peculiar attributes of any given location.'

Predictions that new communication technologies would dissolve the city are challenged by evidence. Arguing that IT applications were largely metropolitan phenomena, Graham & Marvin (1999: 90) note how the value-added in IT industries has shifted to places able to sustain innovation in software and content — and crucially where the employees of such industries want to live and hang out. They cite a study of Manhattan's SoHo and TriBeCa, which found the raw material for such industries was:

'… the sort of informal networks, high levels of creativity and skills, tacit knowledge, and intense and continuous innovation processes that become possible in an intensely-localised culture, based on on-going, face-to-face contacts supported by rich, dense and interdependent combinations of meeting places and public spaces.'

(Graham & Marvin 1999: 97)

They also note how, despite the growth of some e-tailers, a wide range of consumer services both remain crucially embedded in urban locations — tourism, shopping, visiting museums and leisure attractions, eating and drinking, sport, theatre, cinema and so on — and seem likely to resist any simple, substantial substitution by 'online' equivalents (Graham & Marvin 1999: 95). Similarly, developing his thesis that cities need to attract talented workers, Florida (2002: xix) argues cities are the '… *key economic and social organising unit of our time',* providing '… *the "thick" and fluid labour markets that help match people to jobs'* and supporting '… *the "mating markets" that enable people to find life partners.'*

Rather than urbanity by economic necessity, it is presently a case of urbanity by cultural choice. Telecommuting — the ability to work from home, blurring distinctions between 'home' and 'workplace' — had been hailed as revolutionising living and working conditions, reversing the great historic divorce between home and workplace (Mitchell 1995) and completing the 'dissolution of cities which the automobile began' (Hall 1998: 959). But telecommuting does not necessarily mean a spatially remote electronic cottage and simply presents a greater choice of where one wants to live.

The actual choice, however, is more than an individual choice because it has collective outcomes and consequences. Leinberger (2008), for example, discusses the cardinal choice between walkable urbanism and drivable suburbanism (see Table 2.2), concluding that the latter has profound social, economic and environmental impacts on society at large. The costs, however, are often hidden from individuals who opt for a drivable lifestyle — hidden, that is, until it is too late, when the profound health costs and other costs become apparent.

TABLE 2.2 Costs and Benefits of Driveable Suburbanism

Benefits

- Terrestrial affiliation — having a piece of land to call one's own
- Lower costs, due to inherently cheaper construction and (hidden) infrastructure subsidies
- More land, particularly if one is willing to 'drive until you qualify'
- Lower community taxes
- Privacy
- Perceived safety
- Abundant free parking.

Costs

- Automobile dependence, leaving essentially only one means of transportation
- Social segregation
  - Concentration of poverty, resulting in major social problems
  - Lack of access to jobs for many lower income and minority households
  - Exclusion of non-drivers from society — those too old, too young, too poor, disabled, or not interested
  - Secession of the elites, propelling the growth of a two-class society
  - NIMBY (not in my back yard) development groups, trained to oppose driveable suburban development.

- Environmental effects
  - Land consumption at (probably) 10—20 times underlying population growth
  - Heat islands due to so much land being under asphalt
  - Water quality degradation due to the runoff from all that asphalt
  - Air quality degradation in spite of emission controls due to geometric growth in automobile use
  - Climate change due to the unproven but intuitive connection between low-density, car-based development and greenhouse gas emissions.

- Health implications
  - Respiratory diseases
  - Asthma
  - Obesity
  - Increased car accidents.

- Economic effects
  - Strained personal finance, as US households have shifted more of their spending to maintaining their fleet of depreciable cars
  - Declining infrastructure and economic competitiveness, due to building relatively lightly used, spread-out infrastructure that is too expensive to maintain and is massively subsidised
  - Oil dependency and the potential of global peak oil, with significant impacts on current trade deficits and foreign policy, and potentially serious implications when the peak oil is reached.

Source: Adapted from Leinberger (2008: 67, 84—5).

Telecommuting thus does not remove the need to create places where people want to live, work and play. In practice, it typically occurs on one or two days a week, allowing those who have choice more flexible and efficient lifestyles, but still necessitating face-to-face meetings on other days (Graham & Marvin 1999: 95—6).

Mitchell (1999: 7) thus suggests that, while future urban environments will retain much that is familiar, there will be a new layer consisting of

'... *a global construction of high-speed telecommunication links, smart places, and increasingly indispensable software, [which will] shift the functions and values of existing urban elements, and radically remake their relationships ... the new urban tissue will be characterised by live/work dwellings, twenty-four hour neighbourhoods, loose-knit, far-flung configurations of electronically mediated meeting places, flexible, decentralised production,* marketing and distribution systems, and electronically summoned and delivered services.'

A RETURN TO URBANITY?

Despite predictions of the end of cities and the notion of an urban crisis (Fishman 2008a), the period from the mid-1990s onwards saw remarkable resurgence of cities and a partial rediscovery — in policy and in practice — of the virtues and advantages of density and concentration, with urban renaissance policies becoming 'a defining feature of contemporary urban policy' globally from the early 1990s (Porter & Shaw 2009: 1). What was also witnessed was the economic recovery and cultural reinvention of cities — their CBDs and downtowns especially — as both vital points of concentration in their region and in the emerging global economy, and as key drivers of the regional and national economy, with population increases in the centres – the CBD/downtown and the inner city/first ring suburbs – of (some) cities. In the 1980s and early 1990s, economic development was pursued wherever it could be nurtured. In the late 1990s and early twenty-first century, it had a more urban focus, with cities and city regions seen as key sites and engines of economic development.

In the USA, for example, drawing on Lewis Mumford's prediction of a 'fourth migration', Fishman (2005, 2008a) describes a 'fifth migration' and a rebirth of the American city, due, in part, to the presence of relatively cheap housing close to the downtown regional employment cities and accessible to the suburbs:

'... reurbanism has been a major cultural force, challenging the suburban car culture with the classic urban values of density, walkability and diversity. Cities are now hip, especially for the growing cohort of the young for whom the city is the natural environment during college, and, increasingly, after college as well.' (2006: xvi).

In 1925, Mumford predicted that after a 'first migration' of pioneers settling the continent, and subsequent second (from farms to factory towns) and third migrations (to the great metropolitan centres), a 'fourth migration' would '... radically decentralise the functions of the great metropolis and spread population throughout whole regions.' (Fishman 2005: 358). Fishman (2005: 358) contends that we are witnessing the beginning of a 'fifth migration', where suburbanisation is '... now finally ebbing' and inner cities are being revitalised and in which a '... "virtuous cycle" replaces the vicious cycle of the fourth migration exodus from the city.'

Fishman sees four counter-trends to continued decentralisation: (i) downtown economic revitalisation as major US downtowns became crucial nodes in global finance and centres of knowledge production; (ii) immigrant reurbanism – the building of a new small-scale economy from the ground up; (iii) black reurbanism as a black middle class committed to the cities emerges; and (iv) white middle class reurbanism through a return to the city of the white middle class beyond isolated enclaves. Of these, the real fuel is immigrant reurbanism:

'... the global migration of immigrants from around the world as well as longer-term residents who are rediscovering the possibilities of inner cities located strategically between the downtown regional core and the suburbs.' (2005: 359).

The fifth migration nevertheless is '... likely to be a countermovement to the continuing power of decentralisation rather than the single dominant pattern within the region.' (2005: 360). In Western Europe, immigration from the EU's new member states to the east has driven a similar immigrant reurbanism, but steady economic growth (until late 2007), cheap credit and high demand for new housing, coupled with urban containment policies, has also been decisive in directing investment towards urban areas and away from the edge of city expansions.

Though the English urban renaissance was not formulated until 1999 and the publication of the Urban Task Force report, *Towards an Urban Renaissance*, the first decade of the twenty-first century saw a dramatic reversal – at least outwardly – in the fortunes of many city centres. Unpacking this urban renaissance, Colomb (2007: 6) identifies four key themes: the construction of a new urbanity, social mix as an engine for cohesion, strong local communities, and urban design as a precursor to civility and citizenship.

While acknowledging the unprecedented reinvestment and an increased role for conscious urban design, contributors to *Urban Design and the British Urban Renaissance* (Punter 2009) highlight various problems: the many design compromises necessary to accommodate an overheating housing market; the absence of local leadership; lack of adequate local planning to guide the renaissance; the poor quality of much new housing, in particular ubiquitous gentrification; the absence of community facilities and infrastructure; over-development in central areas; and an obsession with 'iconic' (meaning tall) buildings.

Part of this desire for greater urbanity is a cultural choice, deriving from dissatisfaction with suburbia – or perhaps more precisely the lack of choices other than suburbia, the lack of choice within suburbia and a general dissatisfaction with suburban life. More generally and positively, there has been a renewed desire for urban living; for time-thickened places; for places with high densities of social interaction; for cultural centrality – for being 'where the action is' rather than 'out in the sticks'; and for ready access to cultural and recreational amenities – theatres, museums, cafes, restaurants, bars, etc. – but also relatively ready access to natural landscapes.

But the desire for increased urbanity is neither universal, nor shared widely across lifestyle and social and age groups. In the US context, Fishman (2005: 363) argues the fifth migration's demographic potential

'... rests on such varied bases as aging baby boomers returning to the cities; their 20-something children rejecting the suburbs in favour of livelier inner city districts; the "natural increase" of unslumming households who choose to stay put; and of course the millions who seek to migrate to the United States.'

Recognising that these demographics are uneven and episodic, he argues that the planning challenge

'... is to implement policies that not only capitalise on and institutionalise present demographic trends but create diverse, livable, and vibrant cities that can sustain themselves long into the future.'(2005: 363).

The spatial dimension of cultural desires for increased urbanity encompasses concerns about sprawl; the decline of traditional city centres; brownfield rather than greenfield development; smart growth (see Box 2.5); environmental sustainability; transit-efficient and walkable urban forms; and more compact urban forms. As discussed below, it is likely that diminishing supplies of oil and climate change, rather than cultural preference, will result in a return to greater urbanity and greater concentration of population (though not necessarily in big cities).

Auto-dependency

A prime contributor to the pattern of contemporary urban form has been the car. Schwarzer's 'marketplace urbanists' (see below), for example, see the car as the 'elixir of city life', enabling dwelling, work and shopping to

---

BOX 2.5 Smart Growth

Growing concern about contemporary development patterns in the USA has led to the emergence of 'smart growth' (see www.smartgrowth.org). Smart growth advocates unify around the aim of changing what they regard as the undesirable impacts of (sub)urban sprawl, typically questioning the economic costs of abandoning infrastructure; the social costs of the mismatch between new employment located in the suburbs and the available workforce in the city; and the environmental costs of abandoning 'brownfield' sites, building on open space and prime agricultural lands at the suburban fringe, and increasing pollution by driving further (EPA 2001).

Acknowledging few would oppose 'smart growth' – the opposite being 'dumb growth' – Downs (2005) identifies four distinct groups supporting smart growth:

- *Anti- or slow-growth advocates,* aiming for slower outward expansion and reduced car dependence.
- *Pro-growth advocates,* aiming for outward expansion to fully accommodate future growth.
- *Inner-city advocates,* aiming to prevent the draining of resources from the inner city by outward growth processes.
- *Better-growth advocates,* aiming for reasonable growth but wanting, to reduce some of its negative impacts.

He also identifies 14 basic elements of smart growth:

Elements provoking widespread disagreement among groups supporting smart growth	• Placing limits on the outward extension of further growth. • Financing the additional infrastructure needed to deal with growth and maintain existing systems. • Reducing dependency on private automotive vehicles, especially one-person cars.
Elements with less-than-total agreement among groups supporting smart growth	• Promoting compact, mixed-use development. • Creating significant financial incentives for local governments to adopt 'smart growth' planning within ground rules laid out by the state government. • Adopting fiscal sharing among localities. • Deciding who should control land-use decisions. • Adopting faster project application approval processes, providing developers with greater certainty and lower project carrying costs. • Creating more affordable housing in outlying new-growth areas. • Developing a public–private consensus-building process.
Elements provoking agreement among groups supporting smart growth	• Preserving large amounts of open space and protecting the quality of the environment. • Redeveloping inner-core areas and developing infill sites. • Removing barriers to urban design innovation in both cities and new suburban areas. • Creating a greater sense of community within individual localities and neighbourhoods and a greater recognition of regional interdependence and solidarity throughout the entire metropolitan area.

Downs (2005) subsequently found that smart growth objectives are rarely supported by local residents, which, among other factors, forms a significant obstacle to its implementation. Indeed, Gosling (2003: 256) observes that community frustration with the impact of growth is increasingly driving a no-growth backlash. Opposing smart growth policies, a number of US communities have passed no-growth provisions, such as rigid urban growth boundaries, density limits and residential building permit limits, as well as mandatory voter approval for all new housing projects.

'... break free from their dependency on rail centres and corridors. Edge cities soar beyond inner-city constraints of land assembly, zoning regulation and high tax rates; they exploit fears of crime through privatised space, and desires for comfort and convenience via car-accessible and climatised space.'

(Schwarzer 2000: 131)

The car has allowed us to spread out but often only to do the things that we used to do by walking. Brog (1995, from Tolley 2008: 118), for example, shows how in Germany, in a single generation, increased car use and the extra speed conferred by the car led not to more trips, more activities or saved time for the average person, but, instead, resulted in longer trips, with people travelling further to access the same things accessed locally a generation previously.

Moreover, while cars have enabled cities and their activities to spread out and land-use patterns to evolve to privilege the car, to operate effectively cars become a necessity. The flexibility offered by the car is thus a 'coerced flexibility' (Sheller & Urry 2000: 745). By colonising public space networks, subordinating other forms of mobility and reorganising the distribution of activities in space, automobility — and the car system generally (see Dennis & Urry 2009: 47–61) — undermines other forms of mobility. Furthermore, by monopolising resources — leading to inadequate public transport and contributing to transformations of the city landscape such that important services become inaccessible to non-car users — the car system discriminates against non-car users (Lohan 2001: 43).

The major problem, and challenge, however, is that both society and environments are becoming increasingly auto-dependent (see Kunstler 1994; Kay 1997; Duany & Plater-Zyberk 2000; Leinberger 2008). Associated with a range of environmental, economic and social problems, automobile or car dependence exists where urban form and transport options are such that choices are limited to car use, with an associated range of environmental, economic and social problems (see Table 2.3).

Peak Oil

It is not merely car dependence that is a problem, but also the dependence of the global economy, contemporary society and the accustomed quality of life on the diminishing reserves of ready available and relatively cheap oil. An 'amazing substance' (Kunstler 2005: 31), oil enabled unprecedented technological growth and affluence for much of the world throughout the twentieth century. Its great advantages are '... *its cheapness, it high energy content, and, above all, its liquid nature, which makes it relatively easy to store, transport, and dispense.'* (Roberts 2004: 79). But the very advantages of oil also make it harder to find realistic and practicable alternatives:

'Nothing really matches oil for power, versatility, transportability, or ease of storage. It is all of these things, plus it has been cheap and plentiful ... the lack of these qualities is among the problems with the putative alternative fuels proposed for the post-cheap-energy area.'

(Kunstler 2005: 31)

By their very nature, all fossil fuels are limited in supply, and we are running out of the carbon-based fuels that have powered urban growth for the past 150 years. The situation is referred to as peak oil — the point when half the original supply has been pumped from the ground, after which the rate of production enters terminal decline.

A key issue is when peak oil will be reached. Optimistic predictions place such global decline beginning by 2020 or later, giving some scope — though not much — for major investments in alternatives, without requiring major changes in the lifestyle of affluent nations. Conversely, pessimistic predictions suggest it has already occurred, or will occur shortly. As Kunstler (2005: 25) observes, the peak may '... *only be seen in a "rearview mirror" once the terminal decline begins'* — at which point, it already may be too late for proactive mitigation.

TABLE 2.3 Problems of Car Dependency

Environmental	Economic	Social
• Oil vulnerability	• External costs from accidents and pollution	• Loss of street life
• Petro-chemical smog	• Congestion costs, despite road building	• Loss of community
• Toxic emissions such as lead and butane	• High infrastructure costs in new sprawling	• Loss of public safety
• High greenhouse gas contributions	suburbs	• Isolation in remote suburbs
• Urban sprawl	• Loss of productive rural land	• Access problems for those without
• Greater storm-water problems from extra hard surfaces	• Loss of urban land to bitumen	cars and those with disabilities
• Traffic problems such as noise and severance		

Source: Newman & Kenworthy (2000: 109).

As the supply of oil drops, prices will rise. The high dependence of contemporary industrial transport, and agricultural and industrial systems on low cost, readily available oil will hasten the post-peak production decline, with the probability of severe increases in oil prices having further negative implications for the global economy. Post-peak production will also deplete remaining reserves at a high rate, ensuring the eventual decline is far steeper and far more sudden. Roberts (2004: 46), for example, cites a US geologist as saying: '... *the edge of a plateau looks a lot like a cliff.'* For Kunstler (2005: 69), the prospects are bleak:

'At peak and just beyond, there is massive potential for system failures of all kinds, social, economic, and political. Peak is quite literally a tipping point. Beyond peak, things unravel, and the centre does not hold. Beyond peak, all bets are off about civilisation's future.'

Climate change will also bolster the impact of peak oil. As Kunstler (2005: 148) concludes:

'It may not matter anymore whether global warming is or is not a by-product of human activity, or if it just represents the dynamic disequilibrium of what we call "nature". But it happens to coincide with our imminent descent down the slippery slope of oil and gas depletion, so that all the potential discontinuities of that epochal circumstances will be amplified, ramified, reinforced, and torqued by climate change.'

The depletion of fossil fuel reserves and climate change and pollution will inexorably impact on urban form. The likely consequences are, as yet, unknown, and there are more pessimistic and more optimistic observers of the capacity to retrofit environments for a post-oil scenario. On the pessimistic side, Kunstler (2005: 275) highlights the prospects for many parts of the US's south-west, which has been made habitable through cheap energy:

'Practically all settlement in this region has occurred during the 150-year run of the oil age, with the most explosive growth phase only in the past fifty years ... Transportation, air conditioning, and water distribution will become critically problematic in the years ahead. As oil- and gas-based agriculture fails, and it becomes necessary to grow more food locally, places like Phoenix, Las Vegas, Albuquerque, and Los Angeles will painfully rediscover that they exist in deserts.' (see also www.lifeaftertheoilcrash.net and http://www.dieoff.com).

Others are more optimistic. Newman *et al* (2009), for example, argue that intelligent planning and visionary leadership can help cities meet the impending crises; they identify seven elements of the required paradigm shift to resilient cities:

- *The renewable energy city* — urban areas powered by renewable energy technologies from the region to the building level.

- *Carbon-neutral city* — every home, neighbourhood and business is carbon-neutral.
- *Distributed city* — cities will shift from large centralised power, water and waste systems to small-scale and neighbourhood-based systems.
- *Photosynthetic city* — the potential to harness renewable energy and provide food and fibre locally will become part of urban green infrastructure.
- *Eco-efficient city* — cities and regions will move from linear to circular (closed-loop) systems, where substantial amounts of their energy and material needs are provided from waste streams.
- *Place-based city* — cities and regions will understand renewable energy more generally as a way to build local economy, nurture a high quality of life, and create a strong commitment to place.
- *Sustainable transport city* — cities, neighbourhoods, and regions will be designed to use energy sparingly by offering walkable, transit-oriented options for all, supplemented by electric vehicles. (Newman *et al* 2009: 55—85).

Similarly, Dunham-Jones & Williamson (2009) catalogue ways of retrofitting suburbia to enable greater environmental sustainability, while the UN maintains a database of best practices in accommodating mobility within a dense environment and in reducing car dependence (see www.bestpractices.org).

Spatial Impacts

Some of the more spatial consequences of oil depletion will be an increased localism and perhaps also high density, more compact urban forms.

(i) **Localism**
The depletion of oil reserves and climate change may entail a return to localism and to greater concentration and density (i.e. urbanity). Discussing the post-peak oil period, Kunstler (2005: 255) asserts that our lives will become 'profoundly and intensely local':

'... the focus of society will have to return to the town or small city and its supporting agricultural hinterland. Those towns and small cities will have to be a lot denser.'

Accepting that a return to 'medieval villages and permaculture ruralised cities' is unlikely', Newman *et al* (2009: 136) argue: *'Localism is ... more likely to be the required modus operandi for the post-peak oil world, just as globalism was for the cheap oil era.'*

This will have impacts on personal travel — shorter journeys for employment/work and for food and other forms of shopping, perhaps, as discussed below, resulting in more compact cities and urban areas. Travel distances for leisure and vacation will also become shorter, with transatlantic and inter-continental holidays again becoming once-in-a-life-time experiences.

What will also be significant is shorter distances to supply and service cities and other urban areas. The highly integrated, global supply chains of companies such as Walmart, which ruthlessly exploit variations in labour costs, will not be sustainable in the face of steeply rising transport costs. Food supply and agriculture will also be affected — flying fresh fruit, vegetables, meats and fish thousands of miles will no longer be affordable, or even possible. To minimise travel for food, as Newman *et al* (2009: 136) suggest, '... *localities will need to explore more local production such as "fifty mile menus" and community-supported agriculture.*' Involving sourcing the menu entirely from within a 50-mile radius of the restaurant, 50-mile menus aim to allow customers to enjoy local produce, to reduce food miles and to support local farmers. At present, this is an artificial discipline but it also indicates what might be needed for a more sustainable way of life.

The increased localism of a post-peak oil future is perhaps prefigured by the 'slow movement' (see www.slowmovement.com), particularly its Slow Food and Slow City elements (see Knox 2005). The Slow Food movement was founded by Carlo Petrini in Italy in 1989 to combat fast food and fast life. Its forerunner organisation, Arcigola, had been founded in 1986 to resist the opening of a McDonald's near the Spanish Steps in Rome. Slow Food is a reaction to the disappearance of local food traditions and people's dwindling interest in the food they eat, where it comes from, how it tastes and how food choices affect the rest of the world. It seeks to preserve the cultural cuisine and the associated food plants and seeds, domestic animals, and farming within an eco-region.

Founded in Italy in 1999, the *Citta Lente* (literally Slow City) movement advocates a simpler, slower, more local and more sustainable lifestyle, celebrating and supporting diversity of culture and the specialties of a town and its hinterland, and seeking to improve the quality of life in towns by encouraging self determination while resisting the homogenisation and globalisation of towns and cities. As Knox (2005: 6) explains:

'The goal is to foster the development of places that enjoy a robust vitality based on good food, healthy environments, sustainable economies and the seasonality and traditional rhythms of community life.'

(ii) Compact cities

Another spatial consequence of oil depletion and rising oil prices may be that cities will be made more compact, with more dense centres being created within suburbia. Efforts to encourage this are already happening through more stringent land use and development regulation (e.g. through minimum densities, urban growth boundaries, green belts, etc.). What cannot be achieved by regulation may be achieved by market forces as post-peak oil fuel prices (and perhaps shortages) change the parameters of location choices.

Though some advocate more compact and centralised urban forms, there is considerable debate about whether these are practicable or even necessary. Breheny (1997: 20–1) identified the dominant motive for urban compaction and the compact city as reducing the need for travel by facilitating shorter journeys and public transport use (thereby reducing use of non-renewable fuels and vehicle emissions). Other motives are that it supports retention of open space and valued habitats; encourages and supports use of public transport, walking and cycling; and makes the provision of amenities and facilities economically viable and, thereby, encourages social interaction and enhances social sustainability.

Newman & Kenworthy's (1989) work relating petroleum consumption per capita to population density for a number of large cities has been central to the argument that more compact cities have lower levels of travel and thereby lower levels of fuel consumption and emission (Figure 2.7). Given the association of higher densities with lower fuel consumption, the conclusion was drawn that, to reduce fuel consumption and emissions, policies promoting urban compaction and public transport were needed.

Their ideas were criticised, however, for, *inter alia*, focusing too heavily on the single variable of density: Hall (1991) argued travel distances and modal splits also depend on urban structures. Cheshire (2006: 1237) argues the study did not include price data and that if economic variables and gasoline use were included then the relationship between density and fuel use '... *all but disappears; fuel use is largely explained by price and urban density is a function of city size and incomes.*'

More generally, Gordon *et al* (1989) have argued that market mechanisms would produce polycentric cities, with relatively low energy consumption and congestion. Gordon & Richardson (1991) also found that, despite continuing decentralisation, commuting distances in the USA had tended to remain stable or to fall, which they attributed to the co-relocation of people and jobs, with most work — and non-work — trips being from suburb to suburb, rather than suburb to city centre. Jobs and retail had generally moved closer to, rather than further

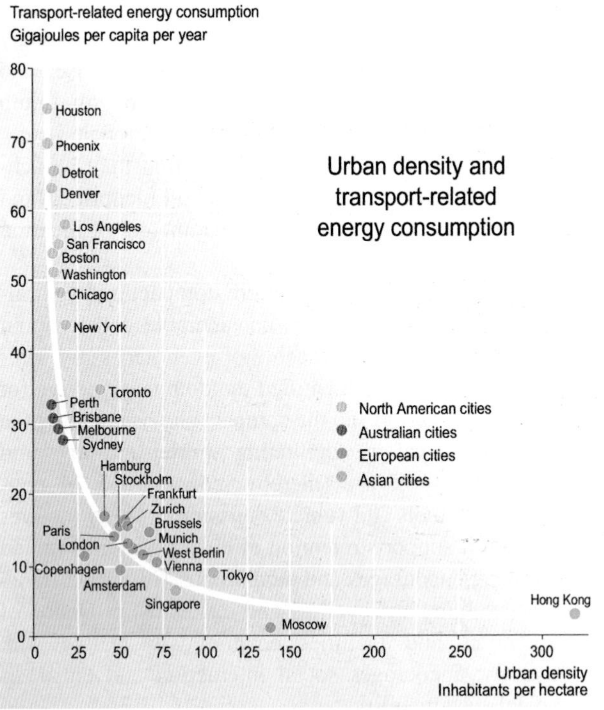

Transport-related energy consumption
Gigajoules per capita per year

FIGURE 2.7 Newman & Kenworthy's comparison of petroleum consumption per capita with population density (*Image: Newman & Kenworthy 1989; Atlas Environment duMonde Diplomatique 2007*). The cities with the lowest densities and highest consumption rates were all in the USA. European cities were relatively fuel-efficient, while, with its very high densities and a large mass transit system, Hong Kong was the most efficient.

from, where people lived, with commuting times falling rather than increasing (Pisarski 1987).

Various commentators suggest other future sustainable urban forms, such as decentralised but concentrated and compact settlements linked by public transport systems, and concentrated nodes and corridors of high-density development (see Frey 1999). Many such patterns are based on the aggregation of relatively small scale, walkable neighbourhoods (see Chapter 6), with the debates generally being concerned with how individual neighbourhoods are connected to form larger urban units (see Owens in Hall 1998: 972). A key factor is sufficient density to make mass transit and local services viable (see Chapter 8).

Future urban design could thus increasingly be about the design of mixed-use urban neighbourhoods/urban villages; business and employment parks; leisure and entertainment complexes; office complexes; shopping malls; home-work units — all cheek-by-jowl (or, equally, widely separated) with seemingly no overarching logic of land values providing an even transition of intensity and density of development. Terms such as 'city centre', 'suburb' and

'periphery' may become less meaningful, and social and spatial fragmentation may continue, with exclusive enclaves of wealth and privilege and areas of intense deprivation and disadvantage.

CONTEMPORARY URBANISMS

Some writers have conceptualised the trends and processes discussed above into a series of urbanisms. An outline of their characteristics provides a frame of reference for debates about the trajectory of contemporary urban design thought.

Schwarzer (2000: 128) presents four contemporary urbanisms neatly encapsulating the diversity of contemporary urban development processes and urban design paradigms:

- *Traditional urbanism* strives to renew the golden age of city building.
- *Conceptual urbanism* features those designs that, by going beyond customary frames, seek to accelerate the city's 'prodigious inventiveness'.
- *Marketplace urbanism* accepts the unplanned, vehicle-impelled (but immensely popular) growth on the edge of cities.
- *Social urbanism* seeks to heighten critical awareness of the injustices of capitalist urban development (see Table 2.4).

Though primarily based on US precedents and developments, Schwarzer's urbanisms have a more general applicability and can be seen as two pairs of opposites. Traditional urbanism and conceptual urbanism propose contrasting ideas about what should inform design and the creation of urban form. Marketplace urbanism accepts the forces shaping contemporary urban form, while social urbanism is a critique of the contemporary urban condition.

Also drawn primarily from an American context, Kelbaugh (2008a, 2008b) identified three 'self-conscious' urbanisms — New Urbanism, Post Urbanism and Everyday Urbanism — which '… *represent the cutting edge of theoretical and professional activity in Western architecture and urbanism.*' (2008a: 105 — see also Fishman 2005; Mehrotra 2005; Strickland 2005). These urbanisms are juxtaposed with what Kelbaugh (2008a: 105) refers to as 'market urbanism':

'… *current conventions and modes of land acquisition, professional planning and design services, government regulation, financing, and construction for the thousands of real estate development projects that spring up in places and at times determined by macro and micro market forces and by decisions of private developers.*'

As Kelbaugh (2008a: 112) notes, the differing clientele explains some of the contrasting tendencies, with New

TABLE 2.4 Four Urbanisms

Urbanism	Commentary
1. Traditional	Looking back '… *to an age of grids, public squares, moderately dense housing and pedestrian corridors*' (Schwarzer 2000: 129), traditional urbanism is a critique of the placelessness of the modern vehicular city and of urban sprawl. Depicted as 'pragmatic and populist' and a 'restoration of the ways and manners of city building', it seeks a more 'authentic' urban framework and asserts the value of the more meaningful places of nineteenth century and early twentieth century small towns and commuter suburbs.
2. Conceptual	Adopting a more radical attitude that attempts to '… *shake off assumptions of what the city was, is or should be*' (Schwarzer 2000: 136), conceptual urbanism demands appreciation of the 'fluid instabilities' of cities as well as their 'inertia of material residue'. Thus, rather than denouncing the 'chaos and congestion' of contemporary urban life, conceptual urbanists 'experiment out from disruption and disorder'.
3. Marketplace	Characterised by the '*immense financial, technological and political energies*' developing the edges of the contemporary city, Schwarzer (2000: 131) describes a '*mentality operating within the leading extremities of capital-driven urbanism*': '… *those nodes of dynamic intensity coalescing around the intersections of major freeways, atop tens of thousands of acres of farmland or waste land, on the borders of existing cities.*' For marketplace urbanists, the scale of suburban development and the economic power of edge cities are '… *proof of their harmony with popular values … Pragmatism is identified with what sells.*' (Schwarzer 2000: 131).
4. Social	Critiquing most aspects of contemporary US cities, particularly the 'uneven consequences' of commodity capitalism, social urbanism highlights areas of the city that 'capital ignores or flees from'. Schwarzer (2000: 135) describes it as an '… *indictment against the ongoing denigration of urban life at the hands of unequal capital concentration, relentless business and real-estate competition and ceaseless social movements.*'

Source: Adapted from Schwarzer (2000).

Urbanists typically working for land developers, especially on suburban greenfield projects, and also on less well-known urban redevelopment projects, sponsored by government agencies or public/private partnerships; Everyday Urbanists typically working for non-profit and community groups with limited resources and political power; and Post-Urbanist projects typically resulting from prestigious competitions, commissioned '… *by wealthy and powerful institutions, corporations and patrons who seek high profile, iconic buildings.*'

New Urbanism

New Urbanism characterises a set of ideas that appeared primarily in the USA during the second half of the 1980s and early 1990s. The movement was formalised by the creation of the Congress for New Urbanism (CNU) (see Chapter 1), publication of the Charter for New Urbanism (www.cnu.org) styled on CIAM's Charter of Athens (1933), subsequent annual conferences and a slew of publications.

According to their Charter (CNU 1998), New Urbanists are '…. *committed to re-establishing the relationship between the art of building and the making of community, through citizen based participatory planning and design.*' New Urbanism thus has a significant social agenda, but, as with Jane Jacobs, one linked to particular built forms: recognising that physical solutions would not solve social and economic problems, the Charter argues that '… *neither*

can economic vitality, community stability, and environmental health be sustained without a coherent and supportive physical framework.' (CNU 1998).

New Urbanism is a much — sometimes wilfully — misunderstood term and movement. Many, for example, confuse compromised practice with doctrinaire intent; others choose not to see the regional dimension — for Calthorpe (2005: 19) one of the 'greatest misnomers' is that: '… *it is only about a private little neighbourhood that's very pretty and isolated unto itself, as in the movie The Truman Show.*' Furthermore, though often taken as monolithic and doctrinaire, there are distinct East Coast ('historicist') and West Coast ('environmentalist') strands and, as Calthorpe (2005: 16) observes, debates regarding '… *whether the movement is guided by an open-ended set of principles or a design canon with specific forms and norms.*'

Providing a comprehensive and systematic discussion of New Urbanism, Ellis (2002) notes how, inter alia, much of the critical literature is characterised by use of caricature, premature judgements, unrealistic expectations and ideological bias (see also Brain 2005; Calthorpe 2005; Dunham-Jones 2008). It is particularly — and maybe harshly — criticised for its apparent nostalgia. For Post Urbanists (see below), New Urbanism's '… *desire for orderliness embodies nostalgia for a romanticised past that never existed.*' (Kelbaugh 2008a: 109). In terms of urban form, however, this criticism ignores the significance of embodied learning represented by tradition and the enduring, timeless qualities of spatial types (see Chapter 4).

The 'style' dimension is, nonetheless, problematic. Recognising that New Urbanism '... *is too often formulaic, realised in banal and cloyingly historicist architecture*', Kelbaugh (2008a: 112, 113) laments the use of historical styles lacking 'authenticity and tectonic integrity':

'Such skin-deep pastiche is more understandable for speculative housing which must sell in the marketplace or bankrupt the developer/builder. It is less excusable for non-residential buildings, especially public structures that are allowed to break the design code, but all too rarely rise to first-rate design.'

Despite many New Urbanists claiming the issue of architectural style is 'irrelevant or overblown', Kelbaugh (2008a: 112) observes that 'judging from the ferocity of the debates', '... *clearly it does matter to design professionals and academics.'*

Notably New Urbanism has sought to engage, to transform and to offer alternatives to contemporary regulatory systems — what Brain (2005: 230) refers to as 'the substantive irrationalities of technically rational regulatory structures' — and conventional (suburban) development practices in ways that support and promote, *inter alia*, better places. There is nonetheless a gap between theory and aspiration, and the outcomes on the ground. Projects may, for example, claim to be New Urbanist, but feature few of the Charter principles; they may adopt New Urbanist layouts but not be mixed-use, mixed-income, and mixed-tenure, nor be transit-oriented development (see Sohmer & Lang 2000) (Figure 2.8).

Walters (2007: 157) argues that, for all its flaws, no other activist-based approach to urban design in America matches New Urbanism in terms of projects built, nor in the impact on local government regulatory practice

(see Chapter 11). Its impact in the international field has also been significant. Talen (2005: 280–1) highlights what she sees as deeper routes by identifying four distinct urbanism 'cultures' informing New Urbanism — incrementalism, municipal planning, environmentalism and mixed-use development — and which New Urbanism seeks to integrate. Concluding that the ideas underpinning New Urbanism are nothing new, she suggests New Urbanists see all four cultures having value and needing to be incorporated in the promotion of US urbanism:

'The regulatory aspects of municipal planning are something to change, but their widespread acceptance and strength is also something to capitalise on ... [New Urbanists] value the broader objectives of environmental planning, and they are at the forefront of promoting mixed-use development within a regional context. All of these are valued at the same time that small-scale urban diversity, incrementalism, is the most revered approach of all.'

In the UK, where separate but allied traditional urbanism initiatives have proved influential, initially through the Urban Villages movement of the 1990s (Biddulph *et al* 2003) and subsequently through the work and influence of The Prince's Foundation (see www.princes-foundation. org), many similar debates have been heard (Figures 2.9–2.11). When the stylistic baggage is removed, much of

FIGURES 2.9–2.11   Poundbury, Dorset, UK; Kentlands, Maryland and Stapleton, Denver, Colorado *(Images: Matthew Carmona and Steve Tiesdell)*. Duany *et al* (2000: 208) complain that 'many architects' find it '... *impossible to see past the pitched roofs and wooden shutters of Seaside and Kentlands to the progressive town planning concepts underneath.'* Many have a similar difficulty with Poundbury's visual styling, which substantially derives from the particular tastes of its patron — HRH the Prince of Wales (Hardy 2005) — and which obscures the pioneering of a connected street pattern when most guidance was still recommending dendritic street patterns (see Chapter 4). Calthorpe (2005: 17) observes that, in his experience as a practitioner, '... *most of the neo-traditional style comes from the marketplace itself, not from the intentions of any designers or an intentional design ethos. And it is this marketplace force that must be understood and directed if the cartoons are to stop.'*

FIGURE 2.8   Seaside, Florida *(Image: Steve Tiesdell)*. Many projects (self-)described as 'New Urbanist', including some of the best known (e.g. Seaside, Florida and Kentlands, Maryland), do not conform with the core principles outlined in the CNU Charter. It is thus useful to distinguish 'deep' and 'shallow' variants, where deep New Urbanism conforms with a high proportion of the Charter principles (see also Sohmer & Lang 2000)

FIGURES 2.9–2.11 (*continued*).

what New Urbanism expounds is simply good place-making of the type advocated throughout this book, based on historic precedent and informed by critique of what works and what does not. Rather than the imposition of a design ideology, urban design should be about deploying design intelligence.

Post Urbanism

Acknowledging that the term Post Urbanism is not widely used and that no one formally labels themselves a Post Urbanist, Kelbaugh (2008a: 108) uses it '… *to refer to the avant-garde paradigm that has grown out of what has been called the post-structuralist or critical architectural project of the last several decades.*' Post Urbanism's origins lie in a radical 'New Modernist' approach, closely related to deconstructivism, which existed in the ideas and unbuilt projects – and more recently the built projects – of an architectural avant-

FIGURES 2.9–2.11 (*continued*).

garde. New Modernists aimed to create architecture – and perhaps also urbanism – reflecting the contemporary social condition. But, by reflecting, rather than attempting to shape, society, there was a turning away from Modernism's social ideals and a disavowal of the notion that architectural design could have a social programme. Kelbaugh (1997: 70) saw it as 'essentially nihilist', because it '… *accepts and even celebrates the fragmentation, dislocation, acuteness, and impermanence of contemporary life.*'

In their projects, Post Urbanists seek 'high art' architecture, with a focus on art rather than design. A product of a specific individual designer's artistic imagination, the notion of the 'author' is especially important: '*Celebrated in the media as solo artists or lone geniuses, they cultivate Howard Roarkish personas, despite the reality that large multidisciplinary teams are needed to realise their design.*' (Kelbaugh 2008a: 110). Their view of urban design thus tends to be one of 'big architecture' and of the 'grand project' rather than the wider (and less hubristic) sense intended in this book.

As individual buildings and small complexes, Post Urbanist projects represent significant urban events and extreme examples of contextual dissonance and juxtaposition but, equally, immensely rich visual and aesthetic experiences. For Kelbaugh (2008a: 111), Post Urbanist buildings can be 'spatial and formal tours-de-force': '*They can be sophisticated foreground architecture and icons of great formal skills and elegance, however convoluted, enigmatic, or haunting their shapes.*' Exploiting the ability of computers to draw, and then to construct, convoluted and twisted shapes and structures, Post Urbanist projects are 'bold and experimental', 'predictably unpredictable', relishing the chance to 'violate existing typologies' (Kelbaugh 2008a: 108, 110) (Figures 2.12 and 2.13) (see Chapter 7).

Yet Kelbaugh (2008a: 113) also laments how Post Urbanism is '… *too often an urbanism of trophy buildings, of which a city needs and can absorb only so many.*' He questions whether 'despite their theoretical and aesthetic sophistication', they '… *give back as much as they take from the city around them.*' (2008a: 109). Noting how they '… *often seem to be designed within an invisible envelope, with almost zero attention to offsite relationships*', he observes 'little direct reference to the physical context' with '… *avant-gardist shock tactics … deployed, no matter how modest the building programme or unimportant the site.*' (2008a: 108–9, 111). While Post Urbanism produces vibrant and potentially exciting buildings, environments and spaces, they seem to be for looking at or visiting occasionally rather than for living and working in. As Kelbaugh (2008a: 112) comments: '*Tourists in rental cars experiencing the city through their windshields may be better served than actual users.*'

FIGURE 2.12   Business School, Case Western University Campus, Cleveland (architect: Frank Gehry) *(Image: Steve Tiesdell)*

Everyday Urbanism

Post Urbanism's fetishising of the author contrasts with the humility of Everyday Urbanism. Crawford (2008a: 6) argues that Everyday Urbanism '… *emphasises the primacy of human experience as the fundamental aspect of any definition of urbanism.*' Kaliski (2008b: 216) explains its emergence as:

'… *a reaction against the determinism of any defined urban design practice. We were seeking means to observe and remain open to the diversity of cities. We were interested in the neglected places and experiences of cities that other urbanisms ignored. We thought these could be a starting point to construct a practice of inclusive non-dogmatic urbanism.*'

Its wider recognition was due to the 1999 publication (with a second edition in 2008) of an eponymous book, edited and substantially authored by John Leighton Chase, Margaret Crawford and John Kaliski. Rather than 'inventing a new idea', Crawford (2008b: 12) acknowledges that the book '… *encapsulated a widespread but not yet fully articulated attitude toward urban design.*'

Everyday Urbanism has three principal generators. First, an emphasis on the everyday experience of ordinary urban environments — based initially on the authors' daily experience of the 'endlessly fascinating urban landscape' of Los Angeles (Crawford 2008b: 12). Second, a critique of contemporary professional design discourses — as Crawford (2008b: 12) explains:

'… *urban designers often seemed unable to appreciate the city around them and displayed little interest in the people who lived in*

it. Instead, they approached the city in primarily abstract and normative terms.'

Third, the concepts of the everyday in the work of post-structuralist philosophers Henri Lefebvre, Michel de Certeau and Mikhail Bakhtin — again, as Crawford (2008b:12) explains:

'… *we proposed a new set of urban design values. These put urban residents and their daily experiences at the centre of the enterprise, encouraged a more ethnographic mode of urban research, and emphasised specificity and material reality.*'

Its proponents do not, however, disavow the importance of design and of design intelligence. Focusing on design rather than art, Everyday Urbanism's elemental formula can be summarised as 'present context' + 'democracy' + 'design intelligence'. As Kaliski (2008b: 220) explains:

'… *interest in present contexts as starting points; acceptance of democratic design discourses to reform these starting points; and application of design intelligence to addressing the concerns and needs of everyday design discourses.*'

Rather than an urbanism of risk-averse, conventional real estate development, traditional modes of development funding ('big projects' and the 'hard' city of buildings and spaces). Everyday Urbanism is an urbanism of unconventional real estate development; of innovative modes of development funding; of experimentation, innovation and creativity; of small, micro projects; and of the 'soft', more fluid and spontaneous city of people and activities. As such, it has resonance with other movements and initiatives, such

FIGURE 2.13 Guggenheim Museum, Bilbao (architect: Frank Gehry)
(Image: Matthew Carmona)

the initial premise is itself dubious). Waldheim (2006a: 11) argues that it involves a 'disciplinary realignment' in which

'… landscape replaces architecture as the building block of contemporary urbanism … landscape [is] both the lens through which the contemporary city is represented and the medium through which it is constructed.'

Some commentators justify its emergence due to the North American urban condition — the 'essentially horizontal character of contemporary automobile-based urbanisation' (Waldheim 2009: 227). Waldheim (2009: 235), for example, considers it 'no coincidence' that it has emerged at:

'… the moment when European models of urban density, centrality, and legibility of urban form appear increasingly remote and when most of us live and work in environments more suburban than urban, more vegetal than architectonic, more infrastructural than enclosed.'

Though one can credibly claim it as a 'New World' rather than a transplanted 'Old World' (European) urbanism, its relevance and applicability is not limited to North America.

The malleable conceptual elements of Landscape Urbanism are not 'buildings' and 'space', but 'ecology' and 'urban infrastructure'. The former is both deep ecology, represented by a concern for environmental sustainability, and ecology as metaphor — that is, integrated and mutually interactive systems. In terms of urban infrastructure, rather than *terra firma* — 'firm, not changing; fixed and definite' — Corner (2009: 30) suggests *terra fluxus* — the *'shifting processes through and across the urban field'*. Corner emphasises Rem Koolhaas' (1995: 969) proposition that urbanism is strategic and directed towards the '… *irrigation of territories with potentials.'*

Emerging over the last 10 years, Landscape Urbanism is perhaps best understood as a set of values. Its definitive projects have yet to be built, and so design competitions have been important for developing its core ideas. An influential and formative project has been Paris's Parc de la Villette — not just the built product designed by Bernard Tschumi but also the unbuilt design by the competition runner-up, Rem Koolhaas (Shane 2009) — while Fresh Kills Landfill in Staten Island, New York and Downsview Park in Toronto, both large-scale reclamation projects, are garnering critical attention.

as the Slow Cities movement (www.cittaslow.blog.com) and the various initiatives flourishing in the deindustrialised cities of the US rust belt and in central and eastern Europe, such as the 'shrinking cities' movement (see Oswalt 2006; www.skrinkingcities.com) and 'Pop-Up City' (Rugare & Schwarz 2008; Schwarz & Rugare 2009), with temporary uses for sites (Oswalt *et al* 2007).

Because so much of Everyday Urbanism is concerned with explanation of the urban condition rather than changing it through action, Walters (2007: 158) concludes its real challenge lies in moving beyond rhetoric to actual urban design intervention.

Landscape Urbanism

A further emergent urbanism is Landscape Urbanism — a self-consciously 'design-led' approach, where the object of design is landscape rather than buildings. The contention is that 'landscape', rather than 'architecture', is a better foundation for urban design (though one could argue that

Among the Urbanisms

What should urban designers take from these various urbanisms? The best response is to be critical, taking what is useful from each and seeking synergy rather than compromise. New Urbanism can become formulaic, producing the same answer to different problems and challenges, but it has much substantial common ground with principles of good place-making — many of which now exist in UK public guidance (see Tiesdell 2002) and in built form in contemporary Dutch urbanism — albeit in both cases without the style-prescription, branding and bandwagon that seem so essential in the US. From Post Urbanism, the excitement and exhilaration that good architecture can provoke, albeit probably through more respectful (and sustainable) urban buildings that add to, rather than subtract from, their context. From Everyday Urbanism, sympathy for and engagement with local place and with people, and the deployment of design intelligence. And from Landscape Urbanism, recognition of natural landscape and ecology as a starting point (rather than an afterthought).

Other self-conscious urbanisms, of course, exist, including:

- *Incremental organic (generative) urbanism*, reflecting the slow growth of the traditional city.
- *Garden Cities*, bringing together town and country in the 'suburban idyll'.
- *Modernism*, with its embrace of technology, the future and the potential of rational enquiry.
- *Sprawl*, representative of a market urbanism.
- *Sustainable place-making*, reflecting the conscious process of making better places for people, as advocated throughout this book.

In the future, the quest for sustainable place-making may transcend all these urbanisms. The aim should be to engage with ideas while avoiding being distracted by ideology and ideologues. Rather than high art, the 'design' in urban design is best understood as a problem-solving process (see Chapters 1 and 3). There are desirable (generic) principles of good urbanism and of place-making, but their application is tempered by, and contingent upon, the realities of the local situation.

CONCLUSION

This chapter has reviewed the context in which contemporary urban design operates: cities are changing and the future will be different from now, and different in ways that we do not yet know. Pollution, global warming and the depletion of fossil fuels are likely to provoke radical change. At present, there seems to be a cultural choice between urban form that is concentrated and urban form that is dispersed. But the latter's reliance on fossil fuels means it may well be unsustainable.

Urban design is not simply a passive reaction to change: it is — or should be — a positive attempt to shape change and to make better places. The structure of places matters and the need is to design well-functioning, people-friendly, sustainable places. The recent UK urban renaissance agenda and the smart growth movement in the USA reflect recognition that ignoring fundamental place-making considerations such as connectivity, accessibility and mixed uses results in less sustainable, less socially equitable and, in the long-term, less economically viable urban forms.

Chapter 3

Contexts for Urban Design

This chapter discusses a set of broad 'contexts' — local, global (sustainability), market (economic) and (governmental) regulatory (governmental) — that constrain and inform all areas of urban design action. Although these change over time, at any particular point in time they are relatively fixed and typically outside the scope of the urban design practitioner's influence. In relation to individual projects and interventions, they have to be accepted as given. They also underpin and inform discussions of the dimensions of urban design in the second part of this book — the dimensions represent the everyday material of urban design, which urban designers have scope to manipulate and change.

The boundaries between 'contexts' and 'dimensions' may, in practice, be blurred, but, in a general sense, while urban designers can make decisions about a development's form or visual appearance, they cannot change its situation in a particular local and global context, nor that it occurs within a market economy that, to a greater or lesser extent, is regulated by a governmental body.

Urban design's essential nature as a problem-solving process relates the four contexts and the six dimensions. Hence, after discussing each context, the final part of this chapter presents a discussion of the urban design process.

THE LOCAL CONTEXT

Where urban design action involves a public realm strategy or the design of street furniture, the 'site' is itself a part of a larger context. Where urban design action involves a development project, the local context includes both the site and the area outside its boundaries — that is, beyond the development parcel — upon which it impacts. The larger the development project or the project area, the greater the proportion of that development that creates its own context and the greater the scope to control or create the immediate context. Nevertheless, at all project scales, there is always a larger local context to which the project relates.

All urban design actions are, thus, contributions to a greater whole. Furthermore, all such acts are inextricably embedded within and contribute to a local context. Urban designers often operate within established, generally complex and frequently delicate contexts. Encapsulated in Francis Tibbalds' golden rule that 'places matter most' (see Chapter 1), respect for and informed appreciation of context is a prime component of successful urban design,

with the uniqueness of each place being a precious resource.

Disregard for local context, combined with an ideological imperative for constant innovation and novelty, was a contributory factor in the rejection of Modernist ideas of urban space design (see Chapter 2). Modernists visualised a new future in which cramped and unhealthy cities would be swept away and replaced by a new and radically different urban environment. Although such visions were never fully realised, the clean sweep mentality and the desire for a *tableau rasa* led to a preference for comprehensive redevelopment schemes rather than more incremental development that, *inter alia*, respected a place's existing character. This destruction of context hastened the growth of conservation movements, but, despite this experience, the lessons have not always been learnt (Figure 3.1).

Not all contexts or places require the same degree of contextual response: areas of highly unified character generally require more sensitive responses; those of low environmental quality offer greater opportunity to create new character. Most areas fall between these extremes. Furthermore, areas are often valued for a wide range of qualities and for many reasons. Many are not particularly historic, nor of high aesthetic quality, and are primarily

FIGURE 3.1 Isle of Dogs, London (*Image: Matthew Carmona*). New development in London's Isle of Dogs makes little reference to and is often not connected to its surrounding context. Despite significant investment in the area, the benefits have often been negligible in areas adjacent to the key developments

Public Places – Urban Spaces. DOI: 10.1016/B978-1-85617-827-3.10003-3

valued for social and cultural rather than physical qualities (see Hayden 1995).

Context must also be considered broadly. Buchanan (1988a: 33), for example, argued that context was not just the 'immediate surroundings', but the 'whole city and perhaps its surrounding region', and included:

'... *patterns of land use and land value, topography and micro-climate, history and symbolic significance and other socio-cultural realities and aspirations — and of course (and usually especially significant) the location in the larger nets of movement and capital web.*'

(Buchanan 1988a: 33).

Offering a useful point of departure for exploring the diversity of established urban contexts, a study of London's urban environmental quality (TCKWM 1993) identified eight key factors (Figure 3.2).

Similarly, Lang (1994: 19) suggests that all environments can be conceived of in terms of four interlocking components:

- *The terrestrial environment* — the nature of the earth, its structure and processes.
- *The animate environment* — the living organisms that occupy it.
- *The social environment* — the relationships among people.
- *The cultural environment* — the broader behavioural norms of a society and the artefacts created by it.

Factors contributing to context, therefore, include:

- *Terrestrial* and *animate* factors — the climate and associated local microclimates; the established natural environment; the underlying geology, land form and

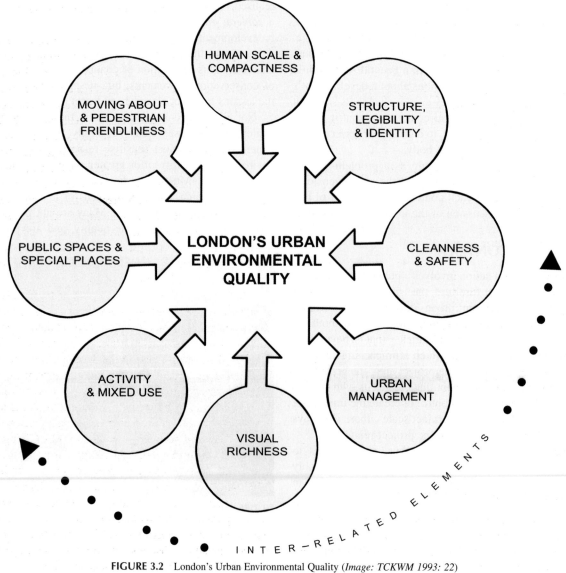

FIGURE 3.2 London's Urban Environmental Quality (*Image: TCKWM 1993: 22*)

topographical features; any environmental threats; and sources of food and water.

- *Social* and *cultural* factors — a settlement's original purpose; changes of purpose and subsequent human interventions over time; patterns of land ownership; the culture of the inhabitants; relations with neighbouring populations; and the ability to adapt to changing circumstances.

In any one place and at any one time, the 'urban environment' can be considered to be part of a particular terrestrial context, inhabited by a diverse animate community including multi-layered human social interactions and producing a distinctive local culture. The consequence is a proliferation of distinctive and complex urban contexts.

Although urban design and development has traditionally be concerned with the manmade elements, Yeang (2009) proposes eco-masterplanning, which seeks to retain the ecosystem's integrity, connectivity and functioning, by restoring and repairing stressed and disfigured ecosystems, while facilitating the human environment within ecologically acceptable bounds. His approach requires the bio-integration of four colour-coded infrastructural armatures:

- *Green* — the eco infrastructure provided by nature.
- *Blue* — the water infrastructure associated with systems of drainage, hydrological systems and water assets.
- *Grey* — the engineering infrastructure of roads, utilities and other support systems for human life.
- *Red* — the human infrastructure of buildings, spaces, activities and the complex social, economic and legislative systems they support.

Yeang (2009: 16) argues that these need to be understood and manipulated through the act of design as a '… *single dynamic living system that is both interactive and functional.*' The blue and green form the key organisational framework for the eco-masterplan, relating it both to the site and the wider context. He suggests that, in the past, we prioritised red and grey and neglected blue and green, and in the future, we will need to consider green and blue first, and then fit grey and red to them.

Yeang's analysis demonstrates how considerations of context involve not just 'place' in a physical sense, but also the people creating, occupying and using the built environment. Understanding local socio-cultural contexts and cultural differences allows urban places to be 'read' and understood, revealing, *inter alia*, the culture that created and maintains them.

Culture and the Environment

The relation between culture and environment is a two-way process: in aggregate and over time, people's choices create distinctive local cultures that both shape environments and are symbolised within that environment, with the environments created both reinforcing and representing that culture. People's choices are motivated by shifting criteria in terms of goals, values (both individual and societal) and preferences. While people — and the choices they make — collectively create socio-cultural contexts, they do not do so in a vacuum: their choices are limited by their ability and willingness to pay and are shaped by the constraints and opportunities offered by the local climate, and the availability and cost of technology and resources. The contemporary urban environment in the USA, for example, is a product of choices predicated on relatively low motoring costs; in much of Europe, it is a product of choices predicated on high motoring costs.

Technology, especially communication and transport technologies, provides new opportunities. The impact of such technologies on social and cultural life can be both dramatic and radical, but often occurs in incremental and subtle ways, such that we are less conscious of change as it happens, only becoming aware when looking back over a period of time.

The impact of new technology on social, cultural and economic life can be illustrated by comparing a traditional local bookshop with an e-tail bookseller (Table 3.1). Similarly, until recently banks were a ubiquitous presence on most high streets, offering face-to-face interaction and often occupying architecturally elaborate buildings (Mitchell 2002: 19). The high street bank's role has been affected by automatic cash points, which provide banking facilities 24 hours a day and anywhere the bank has cash points. As telephone and electronic banking further diminished the need for high street branches, bank branches closed, with many of the buildings finding other uses, becoming shops, café-bars, Internet cafes and so forth. These examples also illustrate how such changes come about through the aggregate effect of individual market choices facilitated by new technology.

While urban designers must respect and generally work with, rather than against, the grain of people's socio-cultural values and preferences, urban development both responds to cultural change and is itself a means towards such change. Through their involvement in the development process and in creating and managing the built environment, urban designers shape — but do not determine — patterns of social and cultural life and interaction. The last two decades, for example, have seen the emergence of 'café society', 'loft living' and, more generally, a culture of urban living in the centres of many English and North American cities — a cultural shift sometimes referred to as reurbanism (Fishman 2005, 2008a) or renaissance (Colomb 2007) (see Chapter 2). This is variously a result of people wanting these opportunities and seeking them out and the media and cultural industries presenting positive and attractive images of such lifestyles, but also a result of developers and designers making such opportunities available.

TABLE 3.1 Impacts of Communication Technology

Traditional Local Bookshop	E-Tail Bookseller
Provides a place where customers can browse and purchase books.	Book browsing and purchasing occurs at home or anywhere with an Internet connection (i.e. these activities are decentralised).
Book browsing and purchasing is undertaken in public and is thus a social activity.	Book purchasing becomes a private activity.
Book purchasing and browsing can only be undertaken during opening hours.	Book purchasing can be undertaken 24 hours a day.
Stores a stock of books on the premises.	Book storage and distribution is centralised where land is cheap and communications good.
Has to be located near to customers.	Retailer is both everywhere and nowhere.
The store has a 'real' presence and advertises/communicates itself as a bookshop within the local environment.	The retailer has a virtual presence.
The shop is managed and accounts are kept in an office within the building.	Administration can be undertaken anywhere where labour is available – the back office does not have to be near the customers or the books.

Source: Adapted from Mitchell (2002: 19).

Urban design also requires sensitivity to issues of cultural diversity. As processes of globalisation threaten to overwhelm and undermine cultural diversity, it is increasingly important to respect the cultural diversity that continues to exist, because this permits authentic local distinctiveness (see Chapter 5).

While discussion in this book draws primarily from a Western perspective, Shelton's *Learning from the Japanese City: West Meets East in Urban Design* (1999) offers an important reminder that ideas about urban space are culturally specific (Figure 3.3). He explains how Japan's urban forms are informed by ways of thinking and seeing that are both rooted deeply in the wider Japanese culture and quite different from those in the West. Japanese thinking about architectural and urban space, for example, has greater affinity with 'area' — as shown by the importance of the *tatami* mat and the floor in buildings — whereas Western thinking focuses on 'line'.

There are, of course, not only Eastern–Western differences but also differences both within these broad categories and elsewhere. Various debates, for example, exist about 'European' and 'American' traditions of urban design, often as attempts to identify a distinctively American tradition rather than a transplanted and remedial European tradition (see Dyckman 1962; Attoe & Logan 1989). Butina Watson & Bentley (2007: 13–4) highlight the complex and divergent range of local cultural landscapes found across the world, and the need for careful study of both historic precedent and of contemporary case study examples that have been able to capture important cultural references while avoiding pastiche. For these authors, there is a close association between the local built environment and the identity of individuals and local cultures. They argue that local landscapes should support a sense of identity and dispel any sense of rootlessness, since, in the process, this empowers those living there.

FIGURE 3.3 Streetscene, Shibuya, Tokyo *(Image: Steve Tiesdell).* For those steeped in Western traditions of urban design, exposure to Japanese cities can be a perplexing and baffling experience. Shelton (1999: 9) notes that, to most Western eyes, Japanese cities '… *lack civic spaces, sidewalks, squares, parks, vistas, etc; in other words, they lack those physical components that have come to be viewed as hallmarks of a civilised Western city.*'

Just as the economic, social, cultural and technological contexts for people's choices change, so does the urban environment, with local contexts continually in a process of change. Change is inevitable and often desirable. Prior to the Industrial Revolution, change in the built environment tended to be slow and incremental, owing much to local building materials and methods (see Chapter 2). Since then the pace and scale of change has quickened, with a corresponding increase in the intensity of the development pressures on particular places, many of which act to homogenise places and contexts (see Chapter 5). The pressures are diverse and include globalisation and internationalisation; the standardisation of building types, styles and construction methods; the loss of vernacular traditions; the use of mass-produced materials; decentralisation; the estrangement of people from the natural world; pressures for short-term financial returns both in the development industry and in the decisions people make about their living environments; the public sector's often unthinking and homogenising regulation of the built environment; and the increased personal mobility and dominance of cars. With both local and global dimensions, these pressures provide the link between the local and global contexts.

THE GLOBAL (SUSTAINABILITY) CONTEXT

Just as all acts of urban design are embedded in their local context, they are also inextricably embedded in the global context: local actions have global impacts and consequences, and global actions have local impacts and consequences. Given climate change, pollution of the natural environment and depletion of fossil fuels, a significant element of the global context relates to the need for environmental responsibility. Despite cities occupying just 1.5% of the earth's surface, the concentration of people and uses within them means they have a disproportionately large impact on the global climate. Research has nonetheless consistently shown that appropriately designed cities are the most efficient means of housing the existing global human population, and thus of addressing the environmental and human threats that might otherwise ensue. Globally, cities are growing at 2.3% per annum; this places a significant responsibility on those charged with their development to ensure the environmental impact is minimised (Newman 2006: 79).

Environmental responsibility impacts on urban design decisions at a number of levels, including:

- *Integration of new development with existing built form and infrastructure* — for example: choice of location/site, use of infrastructure and accessibility by various modes of travel.
- *Range of uses a development contains* — for example: mixed use, access to facilities/amenities and working from home.

- *Site layout and design* — for example: density, landscaping/greening, natural habitats and daylight/sunlight.
- *Design of individual buildings* — for example: built form, orientation, microclimate, robust buildings, building re-use and choice of materials.

Sustainable development entails not only environmental sustainability, but also economic and social sustainability. As well as considering environmental impacts, urban designers need to have regard to social impacts and long-term economic viability.

There is often tension between meeting (immediate) human needs, aspirations and desires and (longer-term) environmental responsibility (Figure 3.4). Human needs might be considered short-term and 'urgent' and those of the environment long-term and 'important', but these short-term and long-term interests must be balanced. The tendency is often to privilege short-term urgent needs at the expense of long-term important needs — but while the long-term necessarily includes the short-term, the short-term does not include the long-term. Commenting on the short-termism of market behaviour, John Manyard Keynes suggested that the market's view was short-term because '… *in the long term, we are all dead.*' A different sentiment is expressed in Chief Seattle's poetic statement: '*We do not inherit the world from our ancestors; we borrow it from our children.*' If future generations are to enjoy the environmental quality and quality of life enjoyed today, sustainable design is paramount.

The interpenetration of town and country was a key theme in the work of planning pioneers such as Ebenezer Howard, Patrick Geddes and Raymond Unwin, as were notions of local social and economic sustainability. As a consequence, some argue that planning, and to a lesser degree urban design, has always pursued notions of sustainability and that its public interest *raison d'être* necessitates balancing concerns for environment, economy and society.

Even if such notions have existed in theory, they have often been absent from practice, and have been compromised by the need to deliver outcomes largely through market processes, by public political agendas prioritising economic growth coupled to social (rather than environmental) well-being, and by private agendas seeing environmental impact as simply another cost category. The recent proliferation of writing on concepts of sustainable development has, however, helped to shift the urban design agenda towards broader environmental concerns. As with planning, the sustainable agenda gives urban design an additional legitimacy and importance — one highly compatible with a professional activity that emerged, at least in part, as a reaction to the unsustainable (anti-urban) development models of the mid- and late twentieth century.

Most recent conceptualisations of urban design demonstrate express concern for the impact of development on the

FIGURE 3.4   Supermarket, Greenwich Peninsula, London, UK *(Image: Matthew Carmona)*. This development epitomises the contradiction of an 'energy efficient' but car-dependent development

broader global environment. These have gradually worked their way into policy, both across the developed world (European Union 2004) and increasingly in the developing world (Romaya & Rakodi 2002). Little is straightforward in this fast-developing field, however, and arguments can be made for and against many of the new policy directions; not only from the perspective of whether sustainable principles are as laudable as much of the literature would suggest (Mantownhuman 2008), but also from that of those questioning whether the potential for intervention is sufficient to make a difference (Cuthbert 2006: 168—70).

Dismissing these critiques as misguided voices of the uninformed, economist Nicholas Stern (2009) asserts that there is 'no serious doubt' that emissions are growing as a result of human activity and that more greenhouse gases will inevitably lead to further climate change. There is no space to explore these arguments here, suffice to observe that an overwhelming consensus has emerged among researchers and writers on the subject, giving added legitimacy to developing policy in this area.

A key difficulty, however, is that environmental concerns are marginalised and seen as 'someone else's problem', such that concern for such issues in development is often limited to the extent to which it is either financially prudent or a requirement brought about by public regulation. The problem stems, in part, from the failure of the financial calculations within development processes — through inability, unwillingness or lack of compulsion — to recognise the full environmental costs (Rees & Wackernagle 1994). The developer is typically only concerned with the costs directly and immediately impacting on the project's viability

and rarely with wider environmental impacts bearing on, for example, the investor, the occupants and society at large, and impacting over the longer-term.

Yet, as Stern (2006) reported in his review of the economics of climate change, acting now to deliver more sustainable patterns of development will have costs, but these will be small compared with those of taking no action. As such, though an explicit sustainable goal is a relatively recent concern in urban design practice, it is arguably the most important and, as with the other contexts, one about which urban designers should be fully informed.

Developments have a much larger environmental impact than is immediately apparent. This can be visualised by considering a development's environmental footprint (Box 3.1). In essence, sustainable urban design involves reducing the total environmental footprint by, for example, reducing dependence on the wider environment for resources and reducing pollution of it by waste products. To achieve this, development — both in its initial construction and throughout its lifetime — should be as self-sufficient as possible (Figure 3.5). Although many urban design actions may be relatively small-scale, their aggregate effect has major effects on the overall natural systems of the neighbourhood, town, city, region and — eventually — the earth's biosphere.

Girardet (2008) discusses the metabolism of cities, defining metabolism as '… *the sum of all the biological, chemical and physical processes that occur within an organism or ecosystem to enable it to exist indefinitely.*' He argues that the metabolism of nature's ecosystems is circular, while the metabolism of rich, modern cities is

BOX 3.1. Environmental Footprints

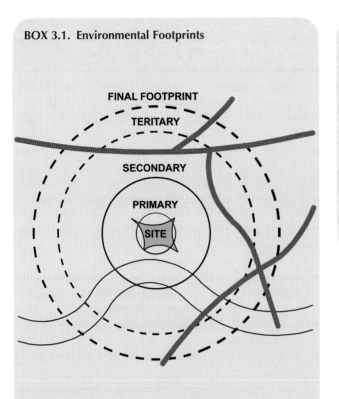

A development's environmental impact can be likened to a footprint. The footprint might initially appear to be small: the site area on which the development sits, together with the destruction of any natural environment that existed there. When the 'invisible' environmental capital inherent in constructing that development is considered, a second, larger footprint becomes apparent — the energy and resources expended in the manufacture and transport of materials, the energy required to prepare the site and construct the development, the energy required to extend the infrastructure needed to service the site, etc. When the development is occupied, there is a third, even larger footprint — the energy and resources expended to sustain the development: the maintenance requirements, the development's energy requirements, the waste disposal requirements, the occupants' travel to and from the development, etc. Finally, when the development reaches the end of its life, the energy required for altering or demolishing it and dealing with the resulting site and materials completes its lifetime environmental costs, thereby further enlarging the footprint. Typically concerned only with the environmental impact of construction (the first and second sets of costs), the developer is rarely concerned with the development's subsequent environmental impacts, which typically bear on the investor, the occupants and society at large.

This concept is reflected in the literature on environmental footprints, which argues that those in Western developed economies are unaware of the true environmental impact of their lifestyles (Wackernage & Yount 2000). This is certainly the case in most Western development processes where the initial developer is often only concerned with the direct development and construction costs — costs that directly impact on the project's economic viability — but rarely with the subsequent environmental impacts (or even management costs) over time. In the UK, for example, the footprint per person per year is 5.4 global hectares (gha). Research suggests that this needs to reduce by two-thirds, to 1.8 gha, to meet 'one planet living' objectives (BioRegional & CABE 2008: 8 & 11). Sustainable design approches can be utilised to allow residents to achieve this.

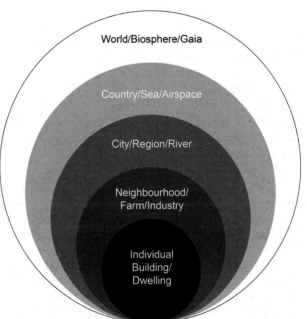

FIGURE 3.5 Nesting spheres of influence *(Image: Barton et al 1995: 12)*. Barton *et al* (1995) suggest viewing all development in terms of a series of spheres of influence. For more sustainable and self-sufficient development, the aim is to reduce the impact of the inner spheres on the outer spheres

essentially linear, taking resources and discarding wastes without much concern about environment impacts. Food provides an example of the linear metabolism. In *Hungry City*, for example, Steel (2009) traces food's journey from over far flung fields and oceans to the urban table, and thereafter to the sewer and landfill, exposing the inherent tension in the relationship between cities and their sources of, consumption of, and ultimately disposal of food products.

Girardet (2004: 124) argues that a linear model of urban production, consumption and disposal undermines the overall ecological viability of urban systems and that sustainable cities should mimic the circular metabolism of natural systems:

'To improve the urban metabolism, and to reduce the ecological footprint of cities, the application of ecological systems thinking needs to become prominent on the urban agenda. In future, cities need to adopt circular metabolic systems to assure their own long-term viability and that of the rural environments on whose viability they depend. Outputs will need to be inputs into the urban production system, with routine recycling of paper, metals, plastic and glass, returning plant nutrients back to farmland feeding cities to keep the soil in good health.'

Lang (1994) has argued that sustainable approaches to urban design should avoid the misconceptions that dealing with the environment is merely 'an engineering problem' to be overcome by technology and that designing to meet people's social needs at the expense of the natural environment is appropriate. Unfortunately, given (relatively) cheap and readily available energy throughout the twentieth century, the urban environment has been shaped by a technology the goals of which are economic rather than environmental or even social, resulting in an alienation of urban dwellers from the natural processes that in earlier times dictated the flux of life.

Some commentators propose seeing urban environments explicitly as natural ecosystems. In *Design with Nature* (1969), McHarg argued that towns and cities should be considered as part of a wider, functioning ecosystem. Hough (1984: 25) argued that, just as ecology has become the 'indispensable basis' for environmental planning of the larger landscape, '*... an understanding and application of the altered but nonetheless functioning natural processes within cities becomes central to urban design.*' (Figure 3.6). He identified five ecological design principles:

- Appreciation of process and change, on the basis that natural processes are unstoppable and that change is inevitable and not always for the worse.
- Economy of means, deriving the most from the least effort and energy.
- Diversity as the basis for environmental and social health.

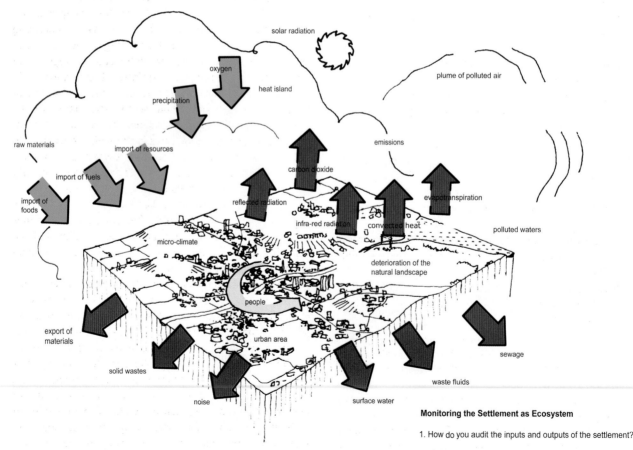

Monitoring the Settlement as Ecosystem

1. How do you audit the inputs and outputs of the settlement?

2. How do you reduce unsustainable inputs and outputs?

FIGURE 3.6 The settlement as ecosystem (*Image: Barton* et al *1995: 13*)

- Environmental literacy to form the basis for a wider understanding of ecological issues.
- Stressing enhancement of the environment as a consequence of change — and not just as damage limitation.

A number of commentators and organisations have proposed sets of principles for sustainable urban development and/or design (Table 3.2). Of these, Barton *et al*'s (1995) analysis of sustainable design principles is the most comprehensive (summarised in Barton 1996). More recently, through the auspices of its Working Group on Urban Design for Sustainability (EU 2004), the European Union has progressed its thinking, greatly expanding its agenda:

'Sustainable urban design is a process whereby all the actors involved work together through partnerships and effective participatory processes to integrate functional, environmental, and quality considerations to design, plan and manage [the] built environment'

Such places should:

- Be beautiful, distinctive, secure and healthy, and foster a strong sense of pride, social equity, cohesion and identity.
- Support a vibrant, balanced, inclusive and equitable economy.
- Treat land as a precious resource, reusing land, promoting compactness at a human scale and concentrated decentralisation regionally.
- Support city regions as functioning integrated networks and systems, with an integrated view of the urban and regional landscape.
- Strategically locate new development to address resource conservation, biodiversity, public health needs and public transport efficiency.
- Promote mixed-use development to maximise the benefits of proximity, vitality, security and adaptability of the built form.
- Have sufficient density to support public transport and services, whilst maintaining privacy and avoiding pollution.
- Have a green structure to optimise the ecological quality of urban areas, including their microclimate, and to give access to nature.
- Have high-quality public infrastructure, including public transport services, pedestrian and cycle networks, and an accessible network of streets and spaces.
- Make use of state-of-the-art resource saving and recycling technology.
- Respect the existing cultural heritage and social capital of places, whilst avoiding conservation for its own sake (EU 2004: 39).

A further overarching principle of sustainable urban design builds in, or leaves room for, future choice. Proposing a 'pragmatic principle' for urban design, Lang (1994: 348) argues that, rather than assuming technology will always find an answer, urban designers should take an environmentally benign position, designing flexible and robust environments that enable and facilitate choice and can accommodate change (see Chapter 9). Even though, in the short-term, people may continue to use their cars, a choice of means of travel should be available, including walking, cycling and public transit.

Table 3.3 summarises the 10 principles of sustainable urban design from Table 3.2 at a range of spatial scales — each principle is discussed further over the course of the following 10 chapters through a series of 'Sustainability Insets' (see also Carmona 2009a). In practice, however, these are cross-cutting concerns, with each relating in multiple, complex ways to all the 'dimensions' and 'processes' of urban design discussed in the second and third parts of this book.

THE MARKET CONTEXT

The third and fourth contexts represent different sides of a single state—market coin. With very few exceptions, we live in market economies. The necessity of operating within a market context and obtaining a reward (or, at least, a return that covers production costs) imposes, at minimum, budgetary constraints. Furthermore, in a market economy, many decisions with public consequences are made in the private sector. The context for the latter, however, is usually mediated by policy and regulatory frameworks and controls typically designed to offset or, at least, temper economic power and to produce better outcomes. Hence, as urban design actions typically occur in market economies that are regulated to a greater or lesser extent, to practice urban design, one must know political economy: Cuthbert (2006), for example, defines urban design as spatial political economy. This and the following parts of this chapter discuss the two main components of political economy.

To operate effectively, urban design practitioners need to understand the financial and economic processes by which developments come about. Market economies are driven by the search for profit (profit-seeking behaviour) and by the prospect of reward mediated by risk. In aggregate, the search for profit is often referred to as strategies or 'regimes' of capital accumulation. Development and redevelopment of the built environment is a means of making profits and accumulating capital. The production of the built environment and urban design more generally are often key components of such strategies (see Harvey 1989b).

TABLE 3.2 Matrix of Sustainable Design Principles (Carmona, 2009b)

	Hough (1984)	Bentley (1990)	Commission of the European Community (1990)	Blowers (1993)	Haughton & Hunter (1994)	Barton (1996)
1. Diversity and Choice	Diversity	Variety, permeability	Mixed development		Variety, permeability	
2. Distinctiveness			Regional identity	Heritage	Creative relationships, organic design	
3. Human Needs		Legibility		Aesthetics, human needs	Security, appropriate scale	Human needs
4. Biotic Support			Open space	Open space, biodiversity		Open space networks
5. Concentration		Vitality	Compact development		Concentration	Linear concentration
6. Resilience	Process and change	Resilience			Flexibility	
7. Resource Efficiency	Economy of means	Energy efficiency	Reducing travel/energy reduction, recycling	Land/minerals/energy resources, infrastructure and buildings	Economy of means	Energy-efficient movement, energy strategy
8. Self-sufficiency	Environmental literacy			Self-sufficiency	Democracy, consultation, participation	Self-sufficiency
9. Pollution Reduction		Cleanliness	Ameliorating pollution through planting	Climate/water/air quality		Water strategy
10. Stewardship	Enhancement through change		Integrated planning			

URBED (1997)	Rogers (1997)	Frey (1999)	Edwards (2000)	European Union Working Group on Urban Design for Sustainability (2004)	Jabareen (2006)	Clarke (2009)
Integration and permeability, a rich mix of uses	A city of easy contact, a diverse city	Mixed use, hierarchy of services and facilities	Mixed use, diversified tenure	Vibrant, mixed use, connected streets	Mixed uses, diversity in housing types and prices	Mixed use high streets, housing mix, permeable block structure, social streets
Sense-of-place		Sense of centrality, sense-of-place		Beautiful, distinctive, identity, sense of pride, respect for heritage	Diverse architecture	
Quality space, a framework of safe/legible space	A just city, a beautiful city	Low crime, social mix, imageability	Shelter and safety, open space for social interaction, healthy, secure, comfortable	Secure, healthy, equitable, cohesive, with privacy, supports social capital, human scale, balanced economy		Local community facilities, surveillance, privacy, mixed and inclusive communities
		Green space — public/private, symbiotic town/ country	Ecological well-being, natural habitat integration	Integrated landscape, biodiversity, green structure	Greening, biodiversity	
A critical mass of activity	A compact, polycentric city	Containment, densities to support services	High density	Compactness, density to support public transport	Compactness density to support transit	Polycentric urban structure, density gradients, reduce parking
Ability to adapt and change		Adaptability	Adaptable, extendable	Adaptable built form		Long-term maintenance
Minimal environmental harm	An ecological city	Public transport, reduce traffic volumes	Public transport, renewable energy, rainfall capture, low energy/water use	Land re-use, resource conservation, public transport efficiency resource and recycling technology	Sustainable transport, passive solar design	Orientation for solar energy, public transport
		Some local autonomy, some self-sufficiency		Integrated networks and systems, pedestrian and cycle networks	Walking and cycling	Walkable community, shared surfaces, participation
		Low pollution and noise	Pollution and waste strategies	Pollution avoidance, support microclimate	Green urban drainage	
A feeling of stewardship	A creative city		Integrated land use and transport planning			Urban management focused on sustainability

TABLE 3.3 Sustainable Design by Spatial Scale (Carmona, 2009b)

	Buildings	Spaces	Quarters	Settlements
1. Diversity and Choice (see Chapter 4)	Provide opportunity to mix uses within buildings Mix building types, ages and tenures Build accessible, lifetime homes and buildings	Mix uses along streets and in blocks Design for walking and cycling Combat privatisation of the public realm Remove barriers to local accessibility	Mix uses within quarters Design a fine-grained street and space network (micro scale) Support diversity in neighbourhood character Localise facilities and services	Integrate travel modes Connect route networks (macro scale) Centre hierarchy to boost choice Ensure variety in services and facilities between centres Remove barriers to accessibility
2. Distinctiveness (see Chapter 5)	Consider surrounding architectural character when designing Enhance locally distinctive building settings Retain important buildings and heritage	Reflect urban form, townscape and site character in design Retain distinctive site features Design for sense-of-place — local distinctiveness Retain important building groups and spaces	Reflect morphological patterns and history — incremental or planned Identify and reflect significant public associations Consider quarter uses and qualities	Protect any positive regional identity and landscape character Use topographical setting Preserve archaeological inheritance
3. Human Needs (see Chapter 6)	Support innovation and artistic expression in design Design to a human scale Design visually interesting buildings	Provide high quality, legible public spaces Combat crime through space design and management Enhance safety by reducing pedestrian/vehicle conflict Design for social contact and for safe children's play	Design visually interesting networks of space Enhance legibility through landmark and space disposition Mix communities socially Support social capital	Enhance legibility through quarter identity and disposition Promote equity through land use disposition Build settlement image foster sense of belonging
4. Biotic Support (see Chapter 7)	Provide opportunities for greening buildings Consider buildings as habitats	Design in robust soft landscaping Plant and renew street trees Encourage greening and display of private gardens	Provide minimum public open space standards Provide private open space Create new or enhance existing habitats Respect natural features	Link public (and private) open space into a network Green urban fringe locations Integrate town and country Support indigenous species
5. Concentration (see Chapter 8)	Design compact building forms to reduce heat loss, i.e. terraces Bring derelict buildings back into use Consider high buildings where appropriate	Reduce space given over to roads Reduce space given over to parking Increase vitality through activity concentration	Intensify around transport intersections Raise density standards and avoid low-density building Build at densities able to support a viable range of uses, transport and facilities Respect privacy and security needs	Enforce urban containment and reduce expansion Intensify along transport corridors Link centres of high activity
6. Robustness and Resilience (see Chapter 9)	Build extendible buildings Build adaptable buildings Build to last Use resilient materials	Design robust spaces, usable for many functions Design spaces able to accommodate above-and below-ground infrastructure requirements Design of serviceable space	Design to allow fine-grained changes of use across districts Ensure robust urban block layouts	Build a robust capital web — infrastructure to last and adapt Recognise changing patterns of living and work

TABLE 3.3 Sustainable Design by Spatial Scale (Carmona, 2009b)—cont'd

	Buildings	Spaces	Quarters	Settlements
7. Resource Efficiency (see Chapter 10)	Use passive (and active) solar gain technologies Design for energy retention Reduce embodied energy — local materials and low-energy materials Use recycled and renewable materials Design for natural light and ventilation	Design layouts to allow sun penetration Design spaces that reduce vehicle speeds and restrict vehicle circulation Design spaces that reduce wind speeds and enhance microclimate Use local, natural materials Capture and recycle water	Reduce parking standards Ensure urban block depths that allow sun and natural light penetration and that encourage natural ventilation Use combined heat and power systems Ensure local access to public transport	Invest in public transport infrastructure Use more efficiently before extending the established capital web (infrastructure)
8. Self-sufficiency (see Chapter 11)	Demonstrate a sense of public sector civic responsibility Encourage private sector civic responsibility Provide bicycle storage connecting to the Internet	Encourage self-policing through design Provide space for small-scale trading Provide bicycle parking facilities	Build a sense of community Involve communities in decision-making Encourage local food production — allotments, gardens, urban farms Pay locally for any harm Design to encourage cycling	Encourage environmental literacy through example and promotion Ensure consultation and participation in vision-making and design
9. Pollution Reduction (see Chapter 12)	Re-use and recycle waste water Insulate for reduced noise transmission — vertically and horizontally On-site foul water treatment using SUDs	Reduce hard surfaces and run-off Design in recycling facilities Design well-ventilated space to prevent pollution build-up Give public transport priority	Match projected CO_2 emissions with tree planting Plant trees to reduce pollution Tackle light pollution	Question 'end-of-pipe' solutions to water/sewerage disposal Control private motorised transport Clean and maintain the city
10. Stewardship (see Chapter 13)	Respond to and enhance context Design for easy maintenance	Respond to and enhance context Manage the public realm Allow personalisation of public space Introduce traffic calming	Design for revitalisation Develop a long-term vision Invest necessary resources	'Join up' governance regimes — design, planning, transport, urban management Ensure governance systems that support stakeholder involvement

Discussing architects but making a broader point, Knox (1984: 115) argues that, by helping to stimulate consumption and ensuring the circulation of capital, designers play an instrumental role in the development process. One aspect of this is a constant search for novelty and innovation:

'Without a steady supply of new fashions in domestic architecture, the filtering mechanism on which the whole owner-occupier housing market is based would slow down to a level unacceptable not only to builders and developers but also to the 'exchange' professionals' (surveyors, real estate agents, etc.) and the whole range of financial institutions involved, directly and indirectly, in the housing market.'

Although urban designers need to recognise and appreciate the processes driving development, two common misconceptions should be noted — that built environment professionals are the main agents in shaping urban space and that developers make the main decisions and, hence, designers merely provide 'packaging' for those decisions (Madanipour 1996: 119). The first overstates the role of designers, exposing them to criticism for developments (or aspects of development) outside their control. The second understates their role. Overstating the architect's role — and, indeed, other professionals in the development process generally — has been called a 'fetishising of design', which focuses on buildings and architects rather than on the broader social processes and relations surrounding the urban environment's production and meaning (Dickens 1980).

Subject to appropriate considerations of value, cost, risk/reward and uncertainty, market (as opposed to public)

development has to be economically viable before it is undertaken. In the private sector, viability is considered in terms of balancing risk and reward — with reward being seen primarily in terms of profits. A major barrier to achieving urban design quality, for example, is the perception that such development does not pay (and involves greater risk) — at least not on the timescale required by investors (see Chapter 10). In the public sector, viability is considered in terms of value for public (or taxpayer's) money, but also in terms of broader objectives such as achieving and maintaining a competitive economy and social cohesion.

The potential rewards and risks attached to any development opportunity reflect both the complexity of the process and the wider economic context within which development occurs. At all stages development projects are vulnerable to external and internal risks, not least market fluctuations and the need to maintain cash flow (Figure 3.7).

Urban development is substantially determined by those in control of, or in control of access to, resources, particularly those of land and capital. As buildings and urban developments are typically expensive to produce, those putting resources into developing them do so for their own purposes, which are usually concerned with obtaining some form of enhanced return. As Bentley (1998: 31) observes,

most major property developers are not interested in 'art for art's sake' and, even if they were, they have shareholders who, if acceptable profits are not achieved, will invest elsewhere. There is also, as Leinberger (2008: 49–51) highlights, a financial system that has commoditised the built environment into standard real estate products (see Chapter 10). Real estate is not just a product like oil or steel, however. It is the very stuff that constitutes place, and which marks out the context for real lives: the result of this commoditisation can be a perpetuation of standard, often unsustainable product types, and an absence of place-making as a factor in market-based decision-making.

The Operation of Markets

Before discussing markets, a distinction should be made between the market mechanism and capitalism. As Desai (2002: 176) argues, markets for economists are essentially mechanisms for allocating resources (perhaps efficiently and perhaps equitably); for capitalists, they are a means of making profits and of expanding their business (i.e. accumulating capital). For the economist, a market works when profits are eliminated; for capitalists this would be disastrous: '*Whether the market works or not the system has to be profitable, that is, to generate sufficient profits to keep*

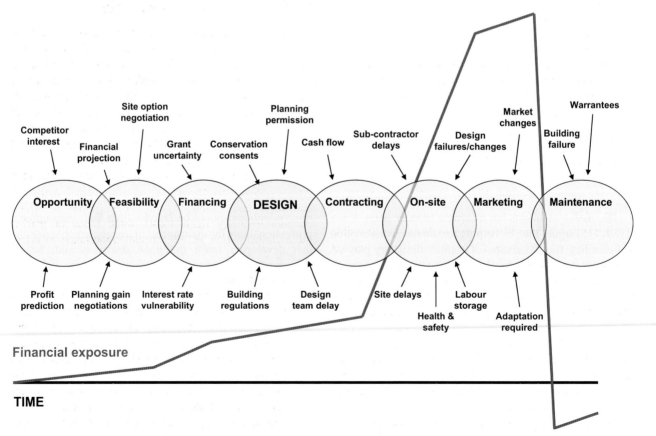

FIGURE 3.7 Risks in the procurement process

enough companies in business so that they can provide employment and generate output.' (Desai 2002: 176).

Regardless of their moral perspective on capitalism, to act in the world effectively, urban designers need to understand how markets work. A market exists when buyers wishing to exchange money for a good or service are in contact with sellers wishing to exchange goods or services for money. In simple terms it consists of supply (a stock of houses) interacting with demand (people seeking housing).

Advocates generally claim two main advantages to the market mechanism:

- First, competition between producers and suppliers of goods and services means markets are efficient allocators of goods and services. The prices of goods and services are determined (largely) by the interaction of the forces of supply and demand, with competition taking place on quality and/or price. This benefits consumers by providing goods and services at prices reduced by benign forces of competition, while ensuring all providers strive to offer goods or services as good as those available from other providers. Those that do not are forced to improve their product, reduce their price, move onto something else, or go out of business. Competition also provides incentives for entrepreneurs to innovate and exploit technology to gain an advantage over their competitors.
- Second, markets empower consumers by allowing them to choose between competing suppliers and to combine different packages of goods and services according to their own preferences rather than those of suppliers. In addition, people are able to maximise their individual welfare, constrained only by their willingness and ability to pay.

As Klosterman (1985: 6) explains, competitive markets

'... co-ordinate the actions of individuals, provide incentives to individual action, and supply those goods and services which society wants, in the quantities which it desires, at the prices it is willing to pay.'

Adam Smith famously referred to this as the 'invisible hand' — that is, the invisible hand of competitive market processes, or as Desai (2002) describes: *'... deep structures of interconnectedness beneath the seemingly chaotic and uncoordinated individual actions.'* Smith considered that, despite individuals pursuing their own advantage, the greatest benefit to society as a whole was achieved by their being free to do so, with each individual being *'lead by an invisible hand to promote an end which was no part of his intention'*. It is, as Varoufakis (1998: 20) suggests, *'... as if an invisible hand forces on those who act shamelessly a collective outcome fit for saints.'*

In market theory, the producer supplies precisely what the consumer wants. In practice, consumer sovereignty, and

situations approaching it, may not exist because the necessary competition does not occur. Critics argue that, as big business, corporate concerns and multi-national corporations dominate markets, consumers are inevitably manipulated into buying the products and services offered for sale rather than what they may really want or need. For Galbraith (1992: 134), the consumer

'... is very substantially in the service of the business firm. It is to this end that advertising and merchandising in all their cost and diversity are directed; consumer wants are shaped to the purposes and notably to the financial interest of the firm.'

A further difficulty is that big business and corporate interests typically represent economic interests, which are increasingly freed and estranged from allegiance to specific locations. Zukin (1991: 15), for example, highlighted a fundamental tension between mobile 'global capital' and immobile 'local community'. Harvey (1997: 20) argued that capital is no longer concerned about place: *'Capital needs fewer workers and much of it can move all over the world, deserting problematic places and populations at will.'* At the local level, the consequence is a loss of control and autonomy — the fate of local place being determined from afar by anonymous and impersonal economic forces.

Market Failure and Imperfection

To work efficiently, markets require 'perfect' competition, which, in turn, requires the following conditions: a large number of buyers and sellers; the quantity of any good bought by a buyer or sold by a seller being small relative to the total quantity traded; the goods or services sold by different sellers being identical; all buyers and sellers having perfect information; and perfect freedom of entry to the market. In practice, markets do not work perfectly and often 'fail' or are 'imperfect' in some way.

As well as problems of prisoners' dilemma conditions (individual actions that result in sub-optimal collective outcomes) and common pool goods (goods to which common property rights exist), three kinds of market failure/imperfection are of especial importance to urban designers:

(i) Externalities

Externalities are spill-over effects — that is, effects not taken into account in the process of the voluntary market exchange and thus external to the price paid. This can be illustrated by considering the social and environmental costs imposed by a car driver who pollutes the air and adds to road congestion (from Hodgson 1999: 64). The driver does not individually suffer most of these environmental costs; they are imposed on others. Furthermore, as the market does not (yet) impose a penalty on the driver commensurate with the social cost, the decision to drive is taken with regard to the driver's private costs and benefits rather than those for society as a whole. Negative externalities and spill-over effects are also shown by developers who ignore the congestion, noise and loss of privacy that their development imposes on neighbouring landowners.

Externalities can be positive as well as negative. Landowners, for example, gain positive externalities through new transportation links and other large-scale improvements to infrastructure that benefit their land. Although sometimes recouped by the state (e.g. through betterment taxes), for the most part private landowners benefit without incurring costs (see Chapter 10). Urban design is often about enhancing positive and minimising negative spill-over effects. The former is shown by the positive synergy deriving from a mix of uses within a limited geographical area. Similarly, many smaller stores benefit from the pedestrian flows generated by larger 'magnet' stores (see Chapter 8).

While real estate markets are well equipped to handle private costs and benefits, they are less able to take account of social costs and benefits imposed by externalities (Adams 1994: 70). Given the imperative of profit-maximising, or more simply profit-making, developers generally seek to minimise private development costs and to maximise private benefits. As social costs can often be ignored, markets are frequently characterised by highly individualistic behaviour, which prioritises individual (private) outcomes benefiting the individual over collective (social) outcomes benefiting society. The individual developer's profit maximisation, thus, tends to be achieved at the expense of the wider community. As a result, the process and product of development is often flawed because it is essentially concerned with, and concentrates on, individual developments rather than with the creation of places embedded in and forming part of the local context.

Adams (1994: 70–1) argues that externalities (and, indeed, other market failure in real estate markets) occur due to the intrinsic nature of land as a 'social' rather than a 'private' commodity, where 'private' refers to the costs and benefits to an individual and social refers to those to the community at large. Land is a social good because the potential use and value of any particular parcel of land is directly constrained by activity taking place on neighbouring land – that is, the activity inevitably spills over onto adjacent land parcels. Land is thus an interdependent asset, with a substantial proportion of its value (or lack of value) deriving from activities beyond its boundaries (see Chapter 10).

(ii) Public/collective consumption goods

A public good simultaneously benefits more than one individual because, ignoring congestion effects, one person's enjoyment does not inhibit the enjoyment of others. As a result, controlling access to these goods is difficult and sometimes impossible. By contrast, access to a private good can be restricted with a price charged for its enjoyment. For public goods, the benefit individuals receive is dependent on the total supply of the good rather than on their contribution towards its production. Thus, in making contributions to pay for a particular good, individuals have incentives to understate their real preferences in the hope others will pay for it. This enables them to free ride, enjoying the good at no personal expense. But, if everyone did this, the funds required to provide the good would not be available. Thus, as private actors cannot (exclusively) appropriate the benefits and rewards, the 'rational' developer contributes to the development of (say) the public realm only to the extent that she/he can accrue private benefits. The same argument applies to elements of infrastructure used collectively. For these reasons, the private sector is reluctant to supply such goods, and may need to be forced to do so, for example through development agreements tied to grants of planning/development consent. If, however, the private sector under-provides public goods, then either the State (which can raise funds through taxation) has to supply them or they are not supplied.

Urban development always has public and collective outcomes and impacts, and thus has some of the properties of a public/collective consumption good. Regardless of whether a development stands on private or public land or uses private or public resources, its exterior – at least – stands as a public object and – both aesthetically and functionally – forms part of the public realm.

(iii) Short-termism

Markets tend to focus on the short-term and the short run. The practice of discounting, for example, typically assumes that money now will be worth less in the future. Although once produced, the built environment is usually durable and lasts for many years, development funding normally depends on returns over the first few years of a building's life exceeding the costs of development by a sufficient margin to ensure the desired profit (Adams 1994: 71; Leinberger 2005, 2008). In conventional methods of development appraisal, costs and benefits occurring over longer periods are substantially discounted. A higher priority is, thus, accorded to short-term rather than long-term concerns, resulting in short-termism and a neglect of the long-term (see Chapter 10).

THE REGULATORY CONTEXT

The fourth context for urban design is the (governmental) regulatory context. The concern here is with the 'macro' context, which provides the overall context for the more detailed elaboration of public policy at lower governmental levels, which impacts more directly on development and place quality (see Chapter 11). While, in general, urban designers, developers and other development actors have to accept the macro regulatory context as a given, criticism is rife, and groups frequently lobby for change at the macro level, typically through professional societies and organisations.

Politics and Government

'Politics' and 'government' are related but different activities. Politics involves discussion and debate, and is a process by which individuals and groups input their opinions onto the agenda for government action — that is, an activity where alternative forms of action are debated as a prelude to choice. It is here, for example, that the balance between 'economic' and 'environmental' objectives is determined.

Government is where decisions are made on behalf of all and where legal and policy frameworks are established. The governmental context proper is, thus, informed by a political process and, before a policy can be enacted, the political arguments must be won. While a government's legitimacy to act in a particular area might be debated, the general assumption is that it represents '... *a democratically legitimised power factor, acting upon its power, and being held accountable for the way that power was wielded.*' (Bemelmans-Videc 2007: 4).

In representative democracies, decisions are made by elected politicians who, in principle, consider and reconcile the varied views and opinions held by the public prior to making those choices. Governments and individual politicians are elected for a limited period of office, after which they must seek re-election. Shorter periods of elected office and relatively frequent elections are positive for democratic accountability, but can militate against achieving more strategic long-term goals. This has significant implications for urban design and place-making.

Achieving significant improvements in urban areas is typically a long-term process and, thus, short periods of political office, coupled with various boom-to-bust economic cycles, do not provide a stable context for long-term investment, nor for implementing strategic visions. Indeed, the short-termism of elected politicians — either desiring instant effects or avoiding unpopular decisions — often inhibits the achievement of strategic urban design and place-making objectives, with long-term objectives being sacrificed for short-term electoral reasons.

Some politicians have, nevertheless, been both strong advocates of design quality and influential in raising the quality of development in their cities. A number of schemes from around the world have sought to convert once-hostile infrastructure into new and vibrant social spaces. These include New York's High Line Park, Boston's Big Dig, London's Mile End Park project, and, most dramatically, Seoul's Cheonggye waterfront scheme (see Figure 3.8).

As changes of administration can result in wavering commitment to particular policies, there is a need to take long-term views of a city's future and to propose strategic goals. Achieving long-term change requires the support of a broadly based coalition of interest groups and often requires the span of periods of different administrations and policy eras (Sabatier 1988). It is thus also essential to secure commitment to ideas and strategies. Studies of the planning histories of cities with track records in delivering design quality testify to the long-term commitment to, and struggle for, quality by a range of key local stakeholders (see Abbott 1997; Punter 1999, 2002, 2003a, 2003b).

FIGURE 3.8 Reclaiming space through political commitment *(Image: Matthew Carmona)*. Seoul's Cheonggye waterfront scheme is often attributed to the city's former Mayor — Myung-Bak Lee. In 2002, acting on his campaign promise to remove the Cheonggye Expressway and reveal the ancient river below, Lee announced the scheme. Where once there was a highway, a river now flows again. Lee subsequently became South Korea's president. The scheme brought 5.6 km of buried historic stream back to the surface, removing in the process the 1960s concrete elevated highway that previously stretched along the line of this once natural feature of the city. Today Cheonggye offers a new linear space through the heart of Seoul, softened by flowing water and careful landscaping that together cool the air. In a city with little public open space and dominated by its roads, the scheme provides a means to escape from the harsh urban surroundings. It reconnects the city physically along its length and through numerous transverse crossings, as well as perceptually to its heritage, as a former political and social boundary in the city. Described as Seoul's Las Rambas, it continues to prove popular among residents and tourists alike

The Structure of Government

A key element of the regulatory (governmental) context is the relation between the different tiers of government and the relative autonomy of each tier. A focus for much political science enquiry and debate, centre–local relations are especially relevant in the urban design field due to the ability and capacity of local governments to develop local responses to local problems, opportunities and contexts.

In unitary systems of government — such as Spain, France, the UK and Japan — sovereignty is located at the centre and all subsidiary forms of government (local government or municipalities) only exist and have powers at the discretion of the centre. In the UK, where the role of central government is strong and local authorities are less able to determine their own agendas, the result gives potential for a more consistent design emphasis, but — until the mid-1990s — a general undermining of initiative at the local level. In France, the strong mayoral system facilitates innovation at the local level as and when the individual mayors value urban design, while, at the national level, prestige projects act as design exemplars.

In federal systems — such as the USA, Canada, Australia and Germany — sovereignty is shared between a national or federal government and the governments of a number of states or provinces. A formal constitution sets out the areas in which the federal government has competence and those where the states/provinces have competence. Within the state or province, all subsidiary forms of government (e.g. local government or municipalities) only exist and have powers at the discretion of the state or provincial government. In the USA, where the Federal Government has little or no role in planning or urban design, individual states and cities have greater autonomy and freedom to develop their own responses. This allows a greater variety of approaches and outcomes, and also fertile ground for policy innovation and development.

Network Governance

Rather than hierarchical and tiered systems of government, more complex systems of 'governance' have emerged over the past 30–40 years in most developed countries, with various central government bodies and other arm's length governmental organisations (e.g. quangos and non-governmental organisations — NGOs), complemented by an expanding array of public–private partnerships, being established at various levels and across different functional sectors and geographical areas. This more distributed — some argue fragmented — structure of government adds to the complexity and challenge of place-making and especially to the delivery and maintenance of good places (Figure 3.9).

Governments do not have a monopoly on power, nor control over all resources, and are thus dependent on the power and resources of other actors. Rhodes (1994, 1996, 1997), for example, argues that governments must manage and steer policy networks to achieve their policy objectives.

When governments are seen as hierarchies, power flows downwards and outwards from the top or centre — the mode of operation of such systems is one of 'command and control'; seen as interacting networks of public and private actors, power is diffuse, with all actors having some power and some resources to exchange. Thus, rather than through command and control, contemporary governments increasingly operate through bargaining and negotiation and through exchanging resources. In this changed era of governance, public/state actors must operate differently. As Salamon (2002: 15) neatly puts it, they must '... *learn how to create incentives for the outcomes they desire from actors over whom they have only imperfect control.*'

Arguing that network governance shifts the emphasis from management to enablement, Salamon (2002: 16–7) identifies three specific enablement skills:

- *Activation skills* — those required to activate the networks of state and non-state actors required to address public problems.
- *Orchestration skills* — analogous to those required of a conductor getting a group of skilled musicians to perform a given work in sync and on cue so that the result is music rather than a cacophony.
- *Modulation skills* — those required to manipulate rewards and penalties to elicit cooperative behaviour from interdependent actors.

Governments' need to create incentives for the desired outcomes from actors over whom they have only imperfect control resembles the task facing urban designers working in or for the public sector. The delivery skills required by urban designers are thus similar to those of other public managers.

Governmental Actions

Decisions made by governmental bodies may be implemented through direct action by government agencies or through the various ways and means of influencing and shaping the decisions of private actors by creating policy and legal frameworks and through fiscal measures (by imposition of taxes and provision of tax breaks and subsidies).

The public sector sometimes acts directly on private sector actors (e.g. developers, landowners, etc.). More typically, it establishes the policy framework, which, in turn, provides the context for private sector decision-making (i.e. with respect to private sector investment decisions). It, thereby, influences the set of incentives and sanctions available, making some actions more likely than

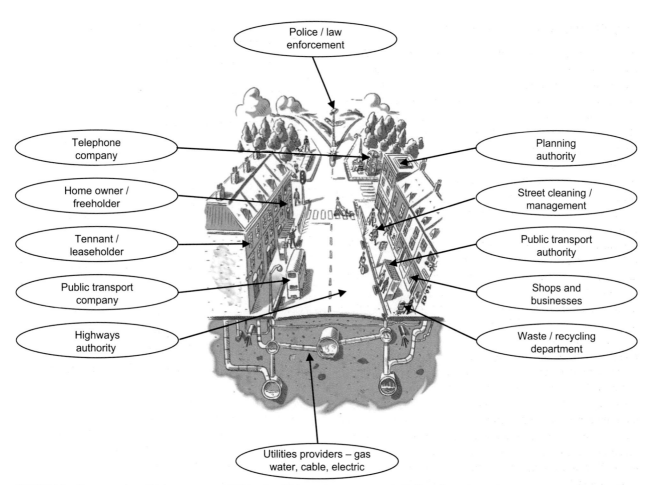

FIGURE 3.9 Fragmentation of high street responsibilities. In addition to the estrangement of built environment professions, there is a more widespread and pervasive institutional fragmentation which, *inter alia*, results in the neglect of the totality and suggests a need for joining-up. This diagram highlights the fragmentation of responsibilities in a typical UK high street. Quality often falls between the gaps in these responsibilities

others. Tiesdell & Allmendinger (2005) and Adams *et al* (2003) classified policy actions (instruments) by how they affect the decision environments — and hence the behaviour — of key development actors:

- Those intended to *shape* behaviours — that is, setting the context for market decisions and transactions, by shaping the decision environment.
- Those intended to *regulate* behaviours — that is, controlling and regulating market actions, by defining the parameters of the decision environment.
- Those intended to *stimulate* behaviours — that is, lubricating market actions and transactions, by restructuring the contours of the decision environment.
- Those intended to develop the *capacity* of development actors/organisations — that is, enhancing the ability of actors to operate more effectively within a particular opportunity space (see Table 3.4).

These policy actions/instruments operate neither in isolation nor in a vacuum, and may also be new initiatives in already crowded policy contexts. In addition, they may often operate as bundles or packages of policy instruments — masterplans, for example, are typically bundles of shaping, regulating and stimulus instruments.

State–Market Relations

An important part of the governmental context is the balance between state and market, and between public and private sectors. Virtually no development project now occurs entirely within the private sector unmediated by any form of public regulation and intervention, and urban development is increasingly a process of co-production between public and private sectors. As shown by the proliferation of public–private partnerships, each sector depends on the other to achieve its goals and their roles are often complimentary rather than antagonistic. Nonetheless, development will often be perceived differently when viewed by the public and private sectors. Table 3.5 identifies some basic differences.

Many urban design actions, particularly those by the public sector, involve (public) interventions into real estate markets. In urban design terms, the main argument for state

TABLE 3.4 State Actions/Urban Design Policy Instruments

Instrument Types	Common Sub-types
Shaping Instruments	
Shape behaviour by providing the general rules of the game – that is, shaping the general context for decision-making	• *Market-structuring instruments* – actions establishing the overarching context within which market actions and transactions occur. Examples include legal frameworks, property rights, national taxation systems, etc. • *Investment instruments* – actions involving macro level (non-site-specific) public investment in the provision of public and collective goods, through either direct (e.g. by a public agency) or indirect (e.g. by providing funding to third parties) provision. • *Information-provision and coordination instruments* – actions providing information to inform decision-making (e.g. listed building registers) and/or to increase the coordination of otherwise independent actions. Examples include plans, policy statements, guidance, advice, etc., produced by governmental agencies/authorities (and others).
Regulatory Instruments	
Affect decisions by restricting the set of choices available	• *Regulatory instruments* – actions compelling, eradicating and/or managing aspects of an activity. Examples include the more general controls over development (planning systems and development controls, highways, historic preservation, etc.) and more specific controls over development design (design policies/design review procedures). • *Enforcement instruments* – actions ensuring regulatory action is undertaken. • *Regulatory procedures* – actions relating to the fact of, and procedures for, regulation, which add time, uncertainty and other costs. Examples include deregulation/streamlining, such as fast-tracking applications from registered architects, simplified planning zones/enterprise zones, etc.
Stimulus Instruments	
Make some actions more – or less –attractive to actors, and rewarding them for particular development	• *Direct state actions* – actions at the site- or area-specific level, usually intended to overcome particular obstacles to development. Examples include providing public infrastructure (e.g. access roads, public spaces, etc.), environmental improvements, land assembly/sub-division, etc. • *Price-adjusting instruments* – actions adjusting the price to the actor of an activity. Examples include imposing activity- or site-specific taxes, tax credits/incentives/breaks, subsidies/grants, etc., which offer scope for quid-pro-quo stipulations, including design requirements. • *Risk-adjusting instruments* – actions adjusting the risk to the actor associated with an activity. Examples include creating a more predictable investment environment through demonstration projects, policy stability, investment actions, active place management, etc. • *Capital-raising instruments* – actions facilitating the availability of development finance or, alternatively, enabling selected developers to access sources of finance previously or otherwise inaccessible to them or on more favourable terms.
Capacity-building Instruments	
Facilitate the operation of the other policy instruments	• *Developing human capital* – actions involving developing the skills and abilities of development actors, both as individuals and as organisations, to deploy the other instruments more effectively. Examples include on-the-job training, CPD, expert seminars, exposure to good or innovative practices, field visits, etc. • *Enhancing institutional and organisational networks and capacity* – actions involving establishing formal and informal arenas or organisations for exchanging information and knowledge and for building or extending actor networks and relationship webs. Examples include job swaps and secondments, architecture/design centres, etc. • *Reframing cultural mindsets* – actions seeking to challenge mindsets and encourage 'mindshifts'. Examples include instruments facilitating and encouraging blue-sky thinking, thinking outside the box, and creativity (e.g. through ideas competitions). They may also enhance the receptivity of decision-makers to new ideas, by challenging and perhaps changing their worldview.

Source: Adapted from Adams *et al* (2003); Tiesdell & Allmendinger (2005).

intervention is that it produces better quality development and/or better places than would be created by otherwise unfettered markets. But, because perfect government does not exist, state intervention cannot guarantee delivery of these objectives. Thus, while the case for state intervention is to 'correct' market failures, this view risks the fallacy of supposing that the alternative to imperfect markets is 'perfect government'. Van Doren (2005: 45, 64), for

TABLE 3.5 Differences between Public and Private Sectors

The Public Sector	The Private Sector
• Is concerned that development creates a tax base to raise revenues.	• Looks for a good (and preferably immediate) return on investment mediated by considerations of risk and liquidity (the profit margin).
• Aims to enhance long-term investment opportunities in its area of responsibility.	• Pursues investment opportunities wherever and whenever they arise.
• Aims to enhance the existing or create a new high-quality environment.	• Is more concerned that the surrounding context both supports the particular development and does not undermine its asset value for as long as the investment is held.
• Is concerned that development creates jobs and has a social benefit.	• Bases its investment decisions on local purchasing power and the availability of a ready market.
• Will look for opportunities to support public services.	• Looks to the cost and availability of financing for development.

example, cites the work of regulatory economists, who have generally come out against regulation, arguing that in most cases no market failure existed in the first place and the regulation acts as a barrier to change and innovation. Ultimately, however, it is a political question of which imperfect form of organisation will lead to a better outcome (see Wolf 1994). Governmental agencies must, nonetheless, be market-aware, which, in urban design terms, requires urban designers to appreciate the market-driven and market-led nature of the development process (see Chapter 10).

In considering market–state relations, a broad distinction can be made between 'mixed' and 'market-led' economies. More properly, the distinction is between instances where the state plays a more significant and more direct role in the management of the economy and intervenes more in private sector decision-making, and those where it plays a less significant direct role:

- In *mixed economies* the State generally has a more executive role — a more 'hands-on' approach, with direct action through public agencies. Urban design policies and decisions here have, in principle, the potential to more fully reflect the public interest, address context, and incorporate design, place-making and local concerns.
- In *market-led economies* the state has a more facilitative role — a more 'hands-off' role, with direct action being undertaken by the private and voluntary sectors. In such economies, for reasons of economic and construction efficiency, design decisions are based on market analysis and the contribution to the wider public interest is rarely a major consideration unless public regulation requires it. Similarly, context is not a major concern unless seen as a financial asset, with the qualities and attributes of buildings as individual objects (as commodities) prioritised over their contribution to the wider place.

The key question, however, is the degree to which the activities of the private sector are or should be regulated, which — in turn — raises issues regarding the purpose of urban design and whose interests it serves: the interests of capital accumulation or the interests of the public at large?

Direct state intervention often involves public spending, and the degree of such intervention is often a function of politicians' — and political parties' — perceptions of the willingness of the taxpayer to fund (for example) public infrastructure. Lang (1994: 459–62) distinguishes between paying and non-paying clients of urban design. Whether in the public or private sector, the paying clients include developers/entrepreneurs and their financial backers. In the public sector, the entrepreneurs are government agencies and politicians. Their financial backers are taxpayers (though increasingly it might also be the private sector).

Traditionally, the public sector has acted in the public or collective interest in the public realm promoting, and often substantially funding, the development of the 'capital web' (in essence, public or collective infrastructure — see Chapter 4) and those elements of the urban environment regarded as beneficial to society as a whole, but which would not pay for themselves directly through user fees or for which it is administratively impossible to collect fees, and which are therefore funded through general taxation (i. e. public goods).

People often expect the state to provide infrastructure and services, but do not always connect this with tax collection. Alternatively, taxpayers may connect it directly with tax collection and be unwilling to fund or subsidise any activity that does not directly (and manifestly) benefit them: weighed down by self-interest, they are only concerned with public infrastructure and the design of the built environment when it directly affects them (Lang 1994: 459). As Galbraith (1992: 21) suggests, expenditure and new investment in public infrastructure is 'powerfully and effectively resisted' because '... *present cost and taxation are specific, future advantage is dispersed. Later and different individuals will benefit; why pay for persons unknown?*' Alternatively, they are concerned that the state will not make good use of their money. As a consequence, there are pressures for tax limitation, which, in turn, imposes budgetary constrains on state action.

Though sometimes presented as a binary choice between permitting unfettered play of market forces or state intervention, there is no such thing as a 'free market'. Thus, rather than a matter of state intervention or non-intervention, the question is actually why and how the state intervenes. Furthermore, while there are debates about whether the State should have a greater or lesser direct role, and whether it should intervene to a greater or lesser degree in the operation of markets, these debates may only be of academic interest since projects have to be designed and implemented in accordance with prevailing and (anticipated) future market conditions and the regulatory context that exists at that point in time. The latter is thus substantially a given, though it is not immutable and changes over time.

Neo-Liberalism

It is useful to consider the contemporary governmental context within which urban design operates. Over the past 40 years, there has been increased discussion and debate about the appropriate roles of the private and public sectors and the relationship between state and market. The 1970s saw increasingly critical views on big government and assumptions that 'more government' was the solution. Arguments were advanced that government was part of the problem and that the solution involved freeing market forces through deregulation and by rolling back the frontiers of the state.

Influenced by the work of key public choice economists, the 1970s and 1980s saw neo-liberal arguments come to prominence and subsequently to political power. In general, as Dennis & Urry (2009: 141) observe, neo-liberalism asserts:

'... *the power and importance of private entrepreneurship, private property rights, the freeing of markets and the freeing of trade. It involves deregulating private activities and companies, the privatisation of previously 'state' or 'collective' services, the undermining of the collective powers of workers and providing the conditions for the private sector to find ever new sources of profitable activity.*'

Elevating market exchanges over and above all other sets of connections between people, neo-liberalism seeks to minimise the role of the State and to allow Adam Smith's invisible hand to do its work. Based on public choice critiques of government, the reduced role for the State was both because

'... *it is presumed that states will always be inferior to markets in "guessing" what is necessary to do and because states are thought to be easily corruptible by private interest groups.*' (Dennis & Urry 2009: 141).

Much effort was thus directed at reducing the State's powers, resulting in a shift towards (more) market-led economies (Brenner & Theodore 2002).

Initially occurring during the Thatcher era in the UK (1979–1990) and the Reagan era in the USA (1980–1988), the neo-liberal hegemony continued under subsequent administrations and governments, whether notionally of the political left or the political right (see Peck 2001). Harvey (2005: 3) argues that neo-liberalism has become '... *incorporated into the common-sense way many of us interpret, live in and understand the world.*'

Though presented as a political choice, when implemented these changes went hand in hand with national governments losing the power to shape their economies and societies as a result of increasing globalisation and the increasing power of multi-national corporations. The consequence, according to many commentators, was a 'hollowing-out of the nation state', as national governments lost powers upwards to supranational government bodies and organisations; downwards to local governments and other local governmental bodies; and outwards to arm's-length government agencies and to the private and voluntary sectors.

Competing Cities

Globalisation, the increasing power of multi-national corporations and the hollowing-out of the nation state, shifted the emphasis from nation states to individual cities, which would then compete with neighbouring cities and cities elsewhere for the most lucrative modern industries. Castells & Hall (1994: 7), for example, observed a change of territorial scale in competition from competing nation states to competing city regions:

'... *the most fascinating paradox is the fact that in a world economy whose productive infrastructure is made up of information flows, cities and regions are increasingly becoming critical agents of economic development ... Precisely because the economy is global, national governments suffer from failing powers to act upon the functional processes that shape their economies and societies. But regions and cities are more flexible in adapting to changing conditions of markets, technology, and culture. True, they have less power than national governments, but they have a greater capacity to generate targeted development projects, negotiate with multinational firms, foster the growth of small and medium endogenous firms, and create conditions that will attract the new sources of wealth, power, and prestige. In this process of generating new growth, they compete with each other; but, more often than not, such competition becomes a source of innovation, of efficiency, of a collective effort to create a better place to live and a more effective place to do business.'*

The focus of city (municipal) government/governance thus shifted from a primary concern with welfare provision towards promoting the physical and economic conditions that facilitated inward investment and economic growth. Harvey (1989a) characterised this as a change from a 'welfare state' to an 'entrepreneurial state'. Economic competition, often at the region or city level rather than that of the nation state — and sometimes, but not always, balanced by calls for social cohesion and environmental sustainability — still provides the prevailing context within which contemporary activities of planning and designing cities are situated (see Gordon & Buck 2005).

A prominent neo-liberal policy theme has been that of 'reinventing government', where government should 'steer' rather than 'row' (e.g. Osbourne & Gaebler 1992) and, more generally, operate like the private sector. Rather than as a direct provider, the state's role increasing became one of regulator and strategic enabler, with a distinct shift towards private provision and privatisation as new political ideologies, combined with fiscal constraints on municipal governments, dictating the public sector's dependence on private sector investors and developers and, more generally, the voluntary sector for the achievement of public objectives, including place quality.

But while there was much less rowing, there also seemed to be less steering. In many countries, the 1980s and 1990s witnessed a retreat from direct state action and intervention in the built environment (with the notable exception of road building) and a retreat from directive planning and proactive urban design. In this respect, Harvey (1990) identified two design/planning approaches responding to the volatility of capitalism. The more common approach was essentially reactive and involved being highly adaptable and fast-moving in responding to markets. A second, much less common, approach was proactive and involved shaping market shifts through, *inter alia*, longer-term city planning.

But, as cities and city governments became increasingly entrepreneurial, Harvey argued that 'planning' was increasingly downgraded in favour of 'designing', with city planning and urban design reduced to merely facilitating and managing (mostly) private sector real estate development 'projects' — flagship office projects, spectacular spaces of consumption, iconic architectural projects, upscale residential developments and cultural activities, typically for the most affluent. Thus, rather than (social and economic) urban planning, the focus was on the planning of real estate (physical) development projects — an approach labelled 'property-led' regeneration. What also became apparent was that rolling back the state required significant state expenditure.

Another core neo-liberal policy theme was privatisation and private provision of what had previously been public services and public provision. Graham (2001: 365), for example, observes how elements of the public realm and public infrastructure of urban areas were privatised and sold off, either to private, profit-seeking companies or to various types of public—private partnership. Similarly, Loukaitou-Sideris (1991, from Loukaitou-Sideris & Banerjee 1998: 87) attributes the privatisation of public space in US downtowns to three interrelated factors:

- The public sector's desire to attract private investment and to relieve its financial burdens by using private resources.
- The private sector's responsiveness to development initiatives and its willingness to participate in public—private partnerships and provide (quasi-)public spaces within private development projects.
- The existence of a market demand for the facilities and services offered by privately built open spaces.

She notes how the desire of office workers, tourists and conventioneers to be separated from 'threatening' groups provided the market opportunity for spaces produced, maintained and controlled by the private sector (see Chapter 6).

The top-down imposition of private sector property development projects and the creation of semi-privatised environments divorced from effective public engagement, scrutiny and accountability was seen by some as accompanied by a turning away from a concern for democracy (see Chapter 6) (Figure 3.10).

Against this background, Loukaitou-Sideris & Banerjee (1998: 280) examined the outcomes of market-led urban design in West Coast American cities, observing the following themes:

- Urban design was losing any larger public purpose or vision.
- Urban design was being privatised and increasingly dependent on private initiatives.
- To maximise returns on investment, urban design interventions were designed exclusively for tenants rather than the wider public.
- Design initiatives were opportunistic and public policy responses reactive — as a result, developments were ad hoc, episodic and disjointed.
- Privatisation was exacerbating the polarisation of rundown, public downtowns of the indigents and the glamorous, private downtowns of corporate America.

Similar observations can be made in the UK's major cities, where, with a few notable exceptions, throughout much of the late twentieth century and early twenty-first century, public agencies were characterised by short-termism, lack of strategic vision, and an absence of

FIGURE 3.10 Melbourne Riverfront *(Image: Steve Tiesdell)*. Discussing the revitalisation of Melbourne's riverfront, Sandercock & Dovey (2002) show how concern for image and identity overpowered core issues of democratic control and accountability

public sector interest in design quality. The result, *inter alia*, was a lack of commitment to place quality. Commenting on early developments in the Docklands area, for example, and, as he saw it, the folly of not providing a framework to guide development, Wilford (1984: 13) had warned that:

'Dependence on the capacities of non-regulated capitalism as fairy god-mother has been demonstrated time and again to be a deluding myth and cowardly evasion on the part of those charged with the task of designing our cities.'

In the midst of the public sector's apparent neglect of design and place-making in the UK during the 1980s, the Canary Wharf development in London Docklands marked a turning point. To protect their development's long-term viability, the developers — who intended to own and manage the development in the long-term — insisted on higher design and infrastructure standards, which — at least within its own terms — produced a high-quality development, albeit one that remains introspective, commercial and private. To achieve this, the developers created and imposed a design framework that acted to overcome the absence of any such framework from the public sector. In doing so they not only guaranteed the design coherence of their own development, but effectively launched a new model of design-led development that both demonstrated the folly of the public sector withdrawal from leadership in design and quickly became the norm for prestige commercial development in the UK (see Carmona 2009a, 2009b, 2009c). Since then, a growing number of other projects and developments demonstrate how the public sector can work in partnership with the private sector to produce high-quality places (Figures 3.11 and 3.12).

Beyond Neo-liberalism?

Global economic recession, which may, in time, provoke wider changes in economic and political thinking rather than merely a return to business as usual; climate change; peak oil; and other major events suggest challenges and sources of resistance to the prevailing neo-liberal orthodoxy. Dennis & Urry (2009: 144), for example, point to an 'emergent contradiction at the heart of contemporary capitalism and unfolding catastrophes', which might '... *just tip economic and political discourse and practice away from neo-liberal orthodoxy.'* They cite Stern's *The Economics of Climate Change* (2007: 644), which concludes with a post-neo-liberal rallying cry about

'... reducing the risk of climate change [requiring] collective action ... It requires a partnership between public and private sectors, working with civil society and with individuals.'

FIGURE 3.11 Broadgate, London *(Image: Steve Tiesdell)*. At the same time as the relatively deregulated development of the London Docklands, the Broadgate development was completed within a frenzied development context in the City of London. The Broadgate development provides a coherent addition to the City of London, is integrated into its context and creates successful and coherent privately owned 'public' space. It also illustrates the potential of the private sector to innovate and its ability to deliver quality outcomes

FIGURE 3.12 Millennium Village, Greenwich, London (*Image: Matthew Carmona*). A high-quality development project produced by public and private sectors working together

The roots and antecedents of change exist in mainstream governance and in urban design practices. During the 1990s and into the twenty-first century, attempts to go beyond simplistic notions of 'government good, market bad' and 'government bad, market good' coalesced around the notion of a 'third way' — or, more precisely, third ways (see Giddens 2001). Third way advocates sought to go beyond conventional political categories of 'left' and 'right', typically defined in terms of attitudes to the role of the market. In contrast to the 'first way' (social democracy), the third way recognised important limits to state action. In contrast to the 'second way' (neo-liberalism), it accepted the need for intervention by government to moderate the impact of market forces.

Though the term 'third way' became associated with particular politicians and governments/administrations and lost credibility along with them (and indeed has been labelled 'neo-liberal lite' — see Peck 2001), the general concept of focusing on the strengths of markets and the strengths of the state, without ideological prejudice for one or the other, remains valid. This requires a nuanced understanding of state–market relations, in which they are complimentary rather than antagonistic and in which, for example, local governments and municipalities use their powers to provide leadership, enable a coordinated local approach and, more generally, harness the creativity, energy and resources of the private and voluntary sectors — in short, exercise leadership, and be proactive and enabling.

During the 1990s, and continuing into the twenty-first century, in the UK — and in other countries, for example New Zealand (see http://www.mfe.govt.nz) — positive changes in the regulatory context and culture were made that recognised the importance and value of urban design (see Carmona 2001). Punter (2007a: 169), for example

observed several new agendas driving a new urban design policy agenda:

- Greater public concern with the protection of a sense-of-place and local distinctiveness in a globalising world.
- Greater environmental concern with the sustainability of development at macro and micro scales.
- A more strategic view of urban design as a shaper of urban form city-wide.
- Greater concern with urban regeneration (particularly reversing the loss of population from major cities).

These desires underpinned the UK government's 'Quality in Town and Country Initiative' from 1994 to 1997 and were epitomised by the Urban Task Force report, *Towards an Urban Renaissance* (UTF 1999), giving rise to the influential Commission for Architecture and the Built Environment (CABE — see www.cabe.org.uk).

The UK was, however, merely catching up with those countries and cities where approaches recognising the value of proactive design in ensuring place quality had already become well established. Express, proactive urban design was seen as a means of ensuring and adding quality in the development of, for example, the Berlin IBA, Barcelona and Copenhagen — projects and cities regularly cited as exemplars.

THE DESIGN PROCESS

Urban design as a process is a reoccurring theme in this book — design process relates the four contexts discussed here with the six dimensions discussed in Part II. 'Design' in urban design is not merely an 'art'-type design process, it is also a research and decision-making process; a creative, exploratory and problem-solving activity through which objectives and constraints are weighed and balanced, the problems and possible solutions explored and optimal resolutions derived.

Design is holistic: what matters is the totality — the whole — being created. It thus involves making design investigations and addressing several aspects of a design problem simultaneously rather than sequentially. Consequently, all design responses must satisfy multiple criteria *simultaneously*. Vitruvius' 'firmness, commodity and delight' can be taken as criteria of good design in a product design sense — firmness is where a design achieves the necessary technical criteria; commodity where it achieves the necessary functional criteria; and delight where it has aesthetic appeal. A fourth criteria of 'economy' should also be added, not merely in a narrow financial sense of respecting budget constraints, but also in the wider sense of minimising environmental costs. These (and other desirable) criteria cannot be put into a hierarchy of importance: good design must achieve them all simultaneously.

Designers are often accused of concentrating too much on visual appearance. In some cases this may be true — though Richard Buckminster Fuller gave a much better explanation of the role of beauty in the design process:

'When I am working on a problem, I never think about beauty. I think only how to solve the problem. But when I have finished, if the solution is not beautiful, I know it is wrong.'

Design involves more than just aesthetics and superficial styling: what matters in the design of a car, for example, is not just the styling of the external shell, but also the power, performance, reliability and fuel economy of its engine; its internal comfort and the ergonomic design of the driver's seating position; its weather resistance and longevity; its security system; etc. A similarly 'deep' understanding of design applies to the design of the built environment. Aesthetic appeal should not be dismissed too lightly though — if something appeals to us aesthetically, we *care* more about it.

As argued in Chapter 1, urban design processes take two distinct forms:

- *Unknowing or Un-self-conscious urban design* — an ongoing incremental process involving relatively small-scale decisions and interventions without any overall vision of where they might lead, or knowledge that they are necessarily part of a process that shapes places. In part, this is a process of 'trial and error' and incremental improvement. Many towns developed in this fashion in which the resultant environment was unintended — or, at least, never designed or planned as a whole. In the past, this appeared to work — at least, in

terms of the environments that have survived and are highly valued today. It also worked because the pace of change was relatively slow and the increments of change relatively small and relatively easily undone (see Chapter 9). For better or worse, much of the design of contemporary environments also happens in this ad hoc and piecemeal fashion without express (knowing) planning or design.

- *Knowing or Self-conscious urban design* — a process by which different concerns are intentionally shaped, balanced and controlled by producing and implementing development and design proposals, plans and policies.

All self-conscious 'design' activity follows an essentially similar process. A self-conscious design process might be considered to follow four key development phases: brief setting, the design phase, the implementation phase, and the post-implementation review. In each development phase, particularly the design phase, the urban designer's thought processes can be disaggregated into a series of stages:

- *Setting goals* — in conjunction with other actors (particularly clients and stakeholders) and having regard to economic and political realities, proposed timescale, and client and stakeholder requirements.
- *Analysis* — gathering and analysing information and ideas that might inform the design solution.
- *Visioning* — generating and developing possible solutions through an iterative process of imaging and presenting — usually informed by personal experience and design philosophies.

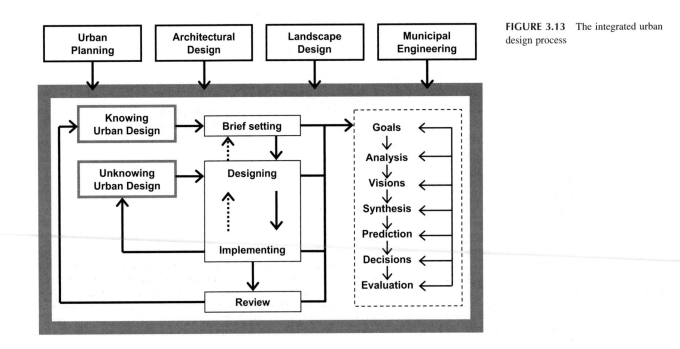

FIGURE 3.13 The integrated urban design process

- *Synthesis and prediction* − testing the generated solutions as a means to identify workable alternatives.
- *Decision-making* − identifying alternatives to be discarded and those worthy of further refinement or promoting as the preferred design solution.
- *Evaluation (appraisal)* − reviewing the finished product against the identified goals.

Each stage represents a complex set of activities, which, while generally portrayed as a linear process, is iterative and cyclical, and less mechanistic and more intuitive than diagrams of the design process suggest. Furthermore, in each phase, the nature of the problem changes and evolves as new information and influences come to bear, resulting in an iterative process with designs − including design policies and other guidance − reconsidered in the light of new objectives, or implemented in part and later changed and adapted as new influences come to bear. At this level, urban design parallels similar design processes in urban planning at the city-wide scale, architectural design of individual buildings and landscape design across the range of scales (Figure 3.13).

Two further aspects of the design process must also be highlighted − its exploratory nature and its essential uncertainty.

First, design is exploratory and unfolds over time. Schon (1991) described it as a 'conversation' or dialogue between definitions and understandings of the 'problem' and possible responses or 'solutions', which takes place over time, during which understanding of the problem and potential responses change, develop and evolve. As Popper (1972: 260) stresses, design is exploratory:

'We start ... with a problem, a difficulty. ... Whatever it may be when we first encounter the problem we cannot, obviously, know much about it. At best, we have only a vague idea what our problem really consists of. How, then, can we produce an adequate solution? Obviously, we cannot. We must first get better acquainted with the problem. But how?

'My answer is very simple: by producing an inadequate solution and by criticising it. ... And if we have worked on a problem long enough, and intensively enough, we begin to know it, to

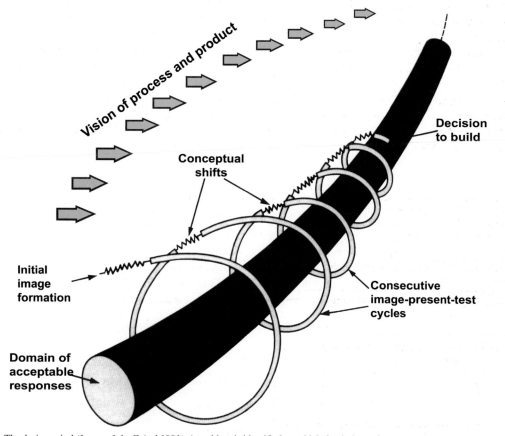

FIGURE 3.14   The design spiral *(Image: John Zeisel 1981)*. A problem is identified, to which the designer forms a tentative solution, a range of solutions or, more generally, approaches to a solution. These are evaluated in terms of the original problem or a set of objectives, and then refined; developed and improved through testing, discovering and purging of 'errors' or inappropriate ideas; or abandoned. The problem itself is also reconsidered. Design is thus a continuous and repeated process of image-test-evaluate, involving imaging (thinking in terms of a solution), presenting, testing and then re-imaging (reconsidering or developing alternative solutions). The process moves towards a better solution, until a decision is taken to proceed and implement the proposal. The proposal will also be further modified and (hopefully) improved through the implementation process

understand it, in the sense that we know what kind of guess or conjecture or hypothesis will not do at all, because it simply misses the point of the problem, and what kind of requirements would have to be met by any serious attempt to solve it. In other words, we begin to see ramifications of the problem, its sub-problems, and its connection with other problems.'

Zeisel (1981, 2006) conceived of a 'design spiral', in which design interconnects three basic activities — imaging, presenting and testing — relying on two types of information — heuristic and catalytic for imaging, and a body of knowledge for testing. He conceived of design as a cyclical and iterative process through which solutions are gradually refined through a series of creative leaps or 'conceptual shifts' as designers continuously modify their results in the light of new information (Figure 3.14).

Second, because it unfolds over time, and is contingent and opportunistic, there is an essential uncertainty within the design process: one never quite knows what one is going to end up with. Those outside the design process — the public, politicians, clients, etc. — often have difficulty in appreciating this and the skills involved in handling it (Meiss 1990: 202). Kelbaugh (2002: 16), for example, explains how designers are:

'... used to making intuitive trade-offs and weighing costs against benefits often without all the data. In fact, the mark of a good designer, unlike a scientist, is the very ability to make good decisions without all the requisite information, because it is rarely all available at the proper time. (Nor are all necessary, because good design is about getting most of the answers mostly right ...). Holding a great number of design variables up in the air as long as possible and bringing them together synergistically at the last possible moment is an essential skill and talent for design.'

CONCLUSION

Presenting four fundamental contexts for urban design action, this chapter has argued that effective urban design action requires respect for the local and global contexts and understanding of the market and regulatory contexts, and has emphasised the nature of urban design — like all forms of design — as a cyclical, iterative and creative process.

The four contexts are subsumed within the definition of urban design given at the start of Chapter 1 — urban design is *the process* of making *better* places for people *than would otherwise be produced*. This definition asserts the importance of four themes that occur throughout this book:

- That urban design is for and about people, involving considerations of equity, gender, income group, etc., and generally prioritising broader, collective outcomes over narrower, individual outcomes.
- The value of place and the need for an explicit concern for issues of place-making, encompassing a response to the local context and to the global imperatives for greater sustainability.
- That urban design operates in the real world and that the field of opportunity for urban designers is typically constrained and bounded by forces (market and regulatory) beyond its control or influence. Urban designers can, nonetheless, challenge and push the boundaries of their field of opportunity.
- The importance of design as a process.

The six chapters in Part II each discuss a different dimension of urban design — 'morphological', 'perceptual', 'social', 'visual', 'functional' and 'temporal'. Overlapping and interrelated, these dimensions are the 'everyday matter' of urban design. As urban design must be understood holistically as a joined-up activity, this separation is for the purpose of clarity in exposition and analysis only. The cross-cutting contexts outlined here relate to and inform all the dimensions. The dimensions and contexts are linked and related by the conception of design as a design process — a process grounded in an appreciation of and respect for local and global contexts and an understanding of prevailing economic (market) and political (regulatory) realities. Without this, urban design is just 'development', naive aspiration or wishful thinking with little potential for successful implementation.

The Dimensions of Urban Design

Chapter 4

The Morphological Dimension

This chapter focuses on urban design's morphological dimension — the configuration of urban form and space, and the spatial patterns of infrastructure that support it. There are essentially two types of urban space system — one is where buildings define space; the other where buildings are objects-in-space (Box 4.1). The former typically consists of buildings as constituent parts of urban blocks, with urban blocks defining and enclosing external urban space — as shorthand, we refer to this as traditional urban space. The latter typically consists of freestanding buildings in landscape settings — we refer to this as Modernist urban space.

During the second half of the twentieth century, the morphological structure of the public space network changed in two highly significant ways:

- From buildings embedded in urban blocks defining streets and squares to buildings as separate freestanding 'object-buildings' standing in an amorphous 'space'.
- From interconnected, small-scale, finely meshed street grids to larger-scale road networks surrounding super-blocks with discontinuous road layouts within (see Pope 1996; Bentley 1999).

This chapter is in four main parts. The morphological transformations are discussed in the second part. The third and fourth parts each discuss aspects of the contemporary reaction. First, however, discussion of urban morphology is necessary.

URBAN MORPHOLOGY

Urban morphology — the study of change in the physical form and shape of settlements over time — focuses on patterns and processes of growth and change. Moudon (1994) identifies three distinct schools of thought in typomorphology, but concludes that:

- Each studies the volumetric characteristics of built structures with their related open spaces to define a built landscape type.
- Each includes land and its sub-divisions as a constituent element of type, making land the link between building scale and city scale.
- Each considers the built landscape type as a morphogenetic unit because it is defined by time — the time of its production, use and mutation.

Morphologists showed settlements could be broken down into several key elements. Conzen (1960), for example, distinguished the street (cadastral) pattern, the plot pattern, building structures and land uses (see below). He also emphasised the difference in stability of these elements. Buildings and, in particular, the land uses they accommodate are the least resilient elements. Although more enduring, the plot pattern changes over time as individual plots are subdivided or amalgamated. The street plan tends to be the most enduring element. Its stability is variously a consequence of being a capital asset, of ownership structures and, in particular, of the difficulties in organising and implementing large-scale change. Such changes do happen, however, through the destruction caused by war and natural disaster and, in the twentieth century, through programmes of comprehensive redevelopment.

Differences in street and block patterns, plot patterns, the arrangement of buildings within plots and the shapes of buildings create very different environments — the different patterns are commonly referred to as 'urban tissue' (Caniggia & Maffel 1979, 1984). Usually taking the form of figure-ground studies (see Chapter 7), tissue studies demonstrate the profoundly different morphological patterns characterising, for example, a medieval town, Georgian London, or an American grid-iron plan — each of which can be compared with a Modernist landscape (Figure 4.1a–c). An invaluable resource for tissue studies is Jenkins' *To Scale* (2008), which contains 100 fragments of cities from around the world drawn to the same scale. Jenkins (2008) argues that only by comparing tissue can we establish a sense of scale when designing, or when coming to terms with, the size of a site or a particular precedent. He further argues that urban precedent helps establish a conversation between the past and the future, linking the known to the unknown.

The notion of tissue refers to more than just (static) form and is better understood as a (dynamic) system. As Panerai *et al* (2004: 158) explain:

'The concept of tissue … with the double textile and biological connections, evokes ideas of interweaving and of connections between parts, together with a capacity for adaptation. It is in contrast to the completed or fixed work and, instead, implies a process of transformations.'

Public Places – Urban Spaces. DOI: 10.1016/B978-1-85617-827-3.10004-5

BOX 4.1 Types of Urban Space

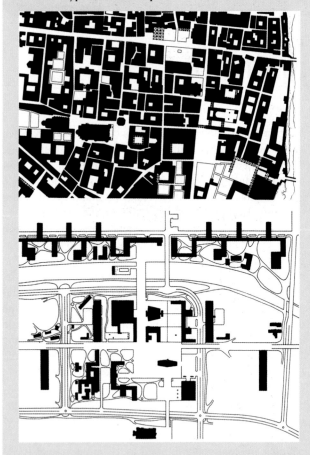

Figure-ground diagrams of Parma and Saint-Die—Adapted from Rowe & Koetter 1978.

These figure-ground diagrams show different patterns of urban space. In the plan for Parma (top), buildings are constituent elements in a generalised, highly connected mass (urban blocks), which defines streets and squares and a small-scale, finely meshed street grid. Buildings are generally low-rise and of similar height. Taller buildings are generally exceptions and usually have some civic significance (i.e. religious or major public buildings). The street pattern consists of a grid, the cells of which are relatively small.

In the plan of Saint-Die (bottom), buildings are separate freestanding pavilions/objects standing in a more generalised type of 'space' and a coarsely meshed 'road' grid. The buildings are set within a 'superblock' system, the cells of which are relatively large (perhaps two to three square kilometres in area). The superblocks are typically surrounded by major roads carrying all non-local traffic. This type of urban space generally only appears in its pure form when built on greenfield sites.

Each space system consists of two component parts: a two-dimensional pattern (either small blocks or superblocks) and a three-dimensional form (either buildings-enclosing-space or buildings-in-space). In what can be considered the ideal systems they are paired in a particular way: small blocks and buildings-enclosing-space (Parma — Type A) and superblocks and buildings-in-space (Saint-Die — Type D). These are rarely seen in their ideal form.

	Small Blocks	Super blocks
Building defining and enclosing space	Type A	Type B
Buildings as objects-in-space	Type C	Type D

Other combinations are also possible. These are hybrid or compromised versions of the ideal systems (Type B or C). Type C, for example, represents situations where freestanding buildings are located in small block street patterns; tall buildings may also be developed within small block patterns (e.g. the City of London and central Hong Kong).

Morphological Elements

Returning to Conzen's four main morphological elements, it is possible to see how morphological structures are composed of interrelated layers:

(i) Land uses

Compared to buildings, plot divisions and the street pattern, land uses are relatively temporary. Changes to land uses include both new uses coming in and existing uses moving to other areas. Incoming uses often lead, through redevelopment, to new buildings, plot amalgamations or subdivisions and, in some instances, changes to the street pattern. By contrast, displaced land uses generally re-locate to buildings in older areas and, rather than redeveloping them, adapt and convert them.

(ii) Building structures

There has often been a recognisable cycle of building development on each plot. In England, this process has been described and explained in terms of the transformation of burgage plots, which started out as long narrow fields laid out perpendicular to a street or circulation route (Conzen 1960) (see Figure 4.2). Although Conzen's work focused on English medieval towns, Loyer (1988) describes similar processes in eighteenth century and nineteenth century Paris. The cycle has also been shown in nineteenth century industrial towns and twentieth century suburbs (e.g. Whitehead 1992).

With no indigenous tradition of burgage plots, many countries — especially those in the New World — witnessed

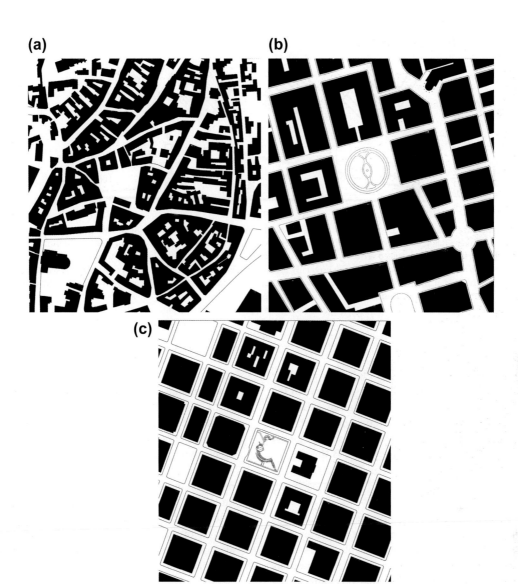

FIGURE 4.1   Morphological tissues of (a) Raehoja Plats, Tallinn; (b) Cavendish and Hanover Square, London; and (c) Pioneer Courthouse Square, Portland *(Images: Jenkins 2008)*

an early focus on grids. Moudon's (1986) comprehensive study of San Francisco's Alamo Square neighbourhood, for example, details the evolution of block, lot and buildings patterns. As plot owners exploited frontage onto the surrounding streets, many grid developments began with outward-facing perimeter block development, with subsequent organic/incremental development extending into the heart of the block.

Some buildings — churches, cathedrals and public buildings — will last longer than others for a variety of reasons, including the greater investment — both financial and symbolic — in their design, construction and ornamentation, and may become particularly meaningful to residents, symbolically representing the city. With the exception of major buildings and in the absence of conservation controls, other buildings will only tend to survive if able to adapt to new uses or the contemporary demands of existing uses — a quality known as robustness (see Chapter 9). Buildings that endure over time will often accommodate different land uses or different intensities of use during their lifetime. The same building, for example, may successively be an upmarket single-family house, then offices, then student bedsits.

(iii) Plot pattern
Cadastral units (urban blocks) are typically subdivided or 'platted' into plots or lots (Figure 4.3). These may be 'back-to-back' plots, each having a frontage onto a main street or circulation route and a shared or

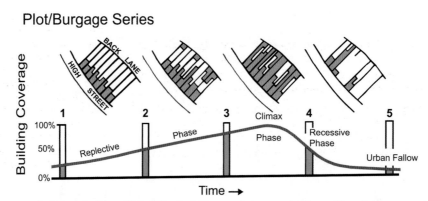

FIGURE 4.2   The burgage cycle (Image: Larkham 1996: 175). Exploiting proximity to pedestrian traffic and the opportunities for access, trade and commerce, the first building — the 'plot dominant' — is built on the street frontage or head of the plot. As the land uses on the plot and within the building change over time, the initial building is extended vertically and/or horizontally towards the rear of the plot. Exploiting access at the back of the plot, the tail of the plot may become built up. The intermediate space — originally fields or gardens — may also be built upon in the form of freestanding buildings or, more typically, through horizontal additions. There might also be vertical growth in terms of building height. New and larger buildings may replace the initial buildings. Over time and with continuing development, the open spaces within the plot are reduced to small courts. As greater densities are achieved by creating rooms without direct access to the street and without adequate light and air, development reaches its choke point. After this there may be a partial or complete clearance before total redevelopment. There might also be changes in the plot pattern as plots are amalgamated to create development sites for larger buildings or truncated by a new mid-block alley, thereby creating independent plots (Larkham 1996: 175)

common plot boundary at the rear. Plots may also face onto main streets at the front with service alleys at the rear. These arrangements form an alternating A-B-A-B-A-B street pattern, where A is the main street with a high degree of spatial definition, pedestrian interest and active frontages (see Chapter 8) and B the service alley (Figure 4.4) (see Duany *et al* 2000: 161). Less common are 'through' plots with frontage at each end onto a main street.

As a defined unit of ownership, the initial pattern is instrumental in the block's subsequent evolution (see Panerai *et al* 2004: 162—4). Over time, plots are bought and sold, and plot boundaries may change. Large plots may be subdivided, with the original owner retaining one part and selling or leasing the other. Alternatively, to provide a larger development site and enable

construction of larger buildings, several plots may be amalgamated and plot sizes become larger. In extreme cases — such as the construction of shopping centres in central areas — not just plots but whole urban blocks can be amalgamated, the public street between the two blocks being privatised and built over.

Although plot and block amalgamation of this nature removes most of the evidence of earlier plots and buildings, in many cities — especially in Europe — evidence of plot patterns persists from earlier periods. As few of those plots have a building of that period, it also demonstrates how buildings change more rapidly than plot patterns.

(iv) Cadastral (street) pattern

The cadastral pattern is the layout of urban blocks and public space/movement channels between those blocks. The spaces between the blocks can be considered to be the public space network (see below). Patterns of streets and spaces have often developed over many hundreds of years, changing and evolving in the process. The ground plan of most settlements can, therefore, be seen as a series of overlays and additions from different ages, with fragments and 'ghosts' of patterns from different eras evident. In Florence, for example, the original Roman street pattern is still evident in the plan of the city's central core (Figure 4.5). In Rome, the Piazza Navona's form derives from development on the site of an ancient Roman stadium. In the twentieth century, new roads have often been cut through the street patterns of older areas, frequently leaving fragmented townscapes in their wake.

The term 'palimpsest' is used to describe such processes of landscape change, where current uses

FIGURE 4.3   Central Prague, Czech Republic *(Image: Steve Tiesdell).* These buildings show evidence of long narrow plots fronting onto a public space

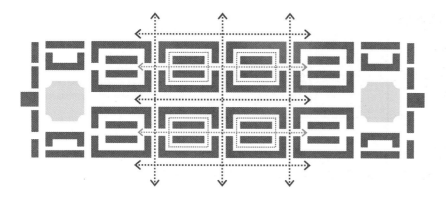

FIGURE 4.4 Edinburgh New Town. This stylised plan shows three circulation meshes in James Craig's plan for Edinburgh New Town. The primary mesh (shown in red) is the principal movement mesh. The secondary mesh (green) consists of service lanes or alleys through the centre of the street blocks. These meshes are the equivalent of an A-B street grid. The tertiary mesh (blue) is for circulation within the street block. In Edinburgh, the secondary mesh has become an important pedestrian thoroughfare and the site of small shops, bars and restaurants

over-write, but do not completely erase, the marks of prior use. Tissue studies of different historical periods enable identification and exploration of changes in the urban pattern.

An important place quality established by the cadastral pattern is permeability — the extent to which an environment allows people a choice of routes through and within it. In general terms, it is a measure of the opportunity for movement (a structural facet of the system) (see Chapter 8). A related quality — accessibility — is what is achieved in practice. As visual permeability refers to the ability to see the routes through an environment, while physical permeability refers to the ability to move through an environment, there may be visual permeability but not physical permeability (and vice-a-versa).

Cadastral patterns composed of many small-sized street blocks are considered to have a *fine* urban grain, while patterns with fewer, larger blocks have a *coarse* urban grain. Although urban blocks can vary dramatically in size, an area with smaller blocks offers a greater choice of routes and generally creates a more permeable environment than one with larger blocks (Figure 4.6a–d). Smaller blocks also increase *visual* permeability, thereby improving people's *awareness* of the choice available — the smaller the block, the easier it is to see from one junction to the next in all directions.

FIGURE 4.5 Central Florence, Italy *(Image: adapted from Braunfels 1988)*. The contemporary core retains the layout of the original Roman settlement

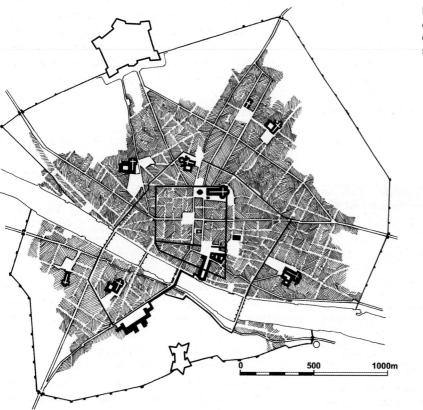

0   500   1000m

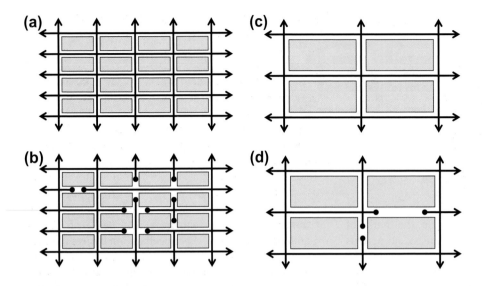

FIGURE 4.6 (a–d) Permeability. Finely meshed grids (networks) offer many different ways to get from place to place. Coarser grids offer fewer ways. If the grid becomes discontinuous through the severing of routes and the creation of dead ends, permeability is reduced

Regular and Deformed Grids

A basic distinction in cadastral patterns can be made between regular or 'ideal' grids characterised by geometric regularity and organic or 'deformed' grids characterised by apparent irregularity. The cores of pre-industrial cities tend to have 'deformed' grids (Figure 4.7). Having developed incrementally, deformed grids are often described as 'organic' – their layouts having been generated naturally – or, at least, having the appearance of having been generated naturally – rather than being consciously man-made. Generally based on pedestrian movement and strongly influenced by topography, they were integral parts of the immediate area, rather than through-routes, and evolved and developed through use.

Regular and ideal grids are typically planned – or, at least, were planned at some point – and have some degree of geometric discipline. Most grids have had ad hoc alterations in the period after they were first laid out and have thus developed organically. Due to the ease of laying out streets, the most basic planned layouts have generally been rectilinear and many settlements with regular or semi-regular grids exist. Many European cities have their foundation as Greek or Roman planned settlements. In Europe, regular grid patterns have frequently been overlaid on or added alongside more organic patterns (e.g. Cerda in Barcelona; Edinburgh New Town). Many New World cities – in USA, Australia, much of South America – have regular, orthogonal grids in their central areas.

The grids used to lay out cities in the USA became simpler over time. The public squares and diagonal streets, which constituted important features of earlier street patterns – Savannah, Philadelphia, Washington – were omitted in later street patterns in favour of simpler, unadorned systems of straight streets and rectangular blocks, by which large, relatively plain tracts of land could

easily be divided into manageable plots and sold off (Reps 1965). Noting that few American cities used the grid-iron as 'more than an equitable expedient', Morris (1994: 347) regards Savannah as an important exception and suggests the urban mid-west's geometry might have been 'less monotonously debasing' under its influence (Figure 4.8).

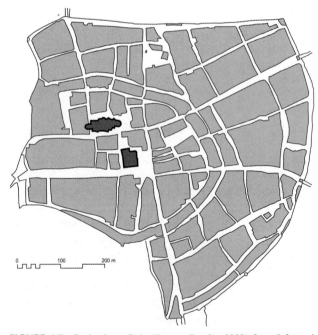

FIGURE 4.7 Rothenburg, Italy *(Image: Bentley 1998)*. In a deformed grid, the public space network is deformed in two ways. First, the shaping and alignment of urban blocks mean that sight-lines do not continue right through the grid from one side to the other but continually strike the surfaces of the building blocks. Second, as one passes along lines, the spaces vary in width. Hillier (1996a, 1996b) argues that deformities in the grid affect visual permeability and are thus an important influence on movement (see Chapter 8)

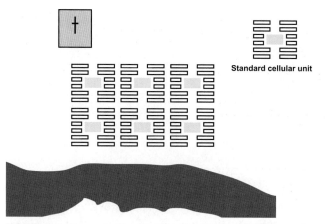

Standard cellular unit

FIGURE 4.8 Savannah, Georgia, USA. Savannah was laid out on the basis of cellular units with growth intended to be by repetition of those units. Each unit had an identical layout consisting of four groups of ten house lots and four 'trust lots' (reserved for public or more important buildings) surrounding a public square. Through-traffic was on the streets between cellular units, leaving the public squares to quieter traffic. At intervals, tree-lined boulevards replaced ordinary streets

Some planned street patterns have an important symbolic function with certain meanings written into the overall plan. Traditional Chinese capital cities, for example, were planned as perfect squares, with twelve city gates, three on each side, representing the twelve months of the year; Roman new towns had two intersecting main streets representing the solar axis and the line of the equinox. Such layouts are not always religious or ancient. In Washington DC, for example, the locations of the White House and the Capitol symbolise the separation of executive and legislative powers.

While deformed grids usually have a picturesque character as a result of the changing spatial enclosure, regular grids have been criticised for their supposed monotony. Sitte (1889: 93), for example, condemned Mannheim's 'unrelenting thoroughness', where there were no exceptions to '... *the arid rule that all streets intersect perpendicularly and that each one runs straight in both directions until it reaches the countryside beyond the town.*'

Rybczynski (1995: 44−5), however, contends that apparently mechanical grids do not necessarily lack poetic character, with more picturesque elements occurring where, for example, grids meet the natural landscape, such as the fracturing of the grid by ravines in Los Angeles. Equally, grids do not have to be homogeneous and entirely regular. The 1811 plan of midtown Manhattan had broad, short-block avenues for large buildings and narrow, long-block streets for smaller row houses, while open squares (e.g. Washington Square), wider avenues (e.g. Park Avenue) and the meander of Broadway introduce differentiation and interest.

During the late nineteenth century and early decades of the twentieth century, the dominance of rectilinear patterns provoked reaction in the form of continuous curvilinear

layouts, where wide, shallow plots (in contrast to deep, narrow plots) gave an impression of spaciousness. Curvilinear layouts derived from English picturesque design of the early nineteenth century, such as John Nash's 1823 design for Park Village, near Regent's Park. Another early example was Olmsted and Vaux's 1868 plan for Riverside, near Chicago. Later examples were by Unwin and Parker at New Earswick (1898), Letchworth Garden City (1905) and Hampstead Garden Suburb (1908). While the curves contain views and add visual interest to newly developing neighbourhoods and suburbs, they also reduced visual permeability, discouraging non-residents from entering.

Most of the earlier curvilinear patterns developed from the late nineteenth century through to the 1920s and 1930s were variations of grids. A refinement (introduced by Unwin and Parker at New Earswick) that become increasingly commonplace during the late 1950s involved cul-de-sacs, which sought to retain the aesthetics of curvilinear layouts while mitigating the nuisances and dangers of cars and other traffic. As discussed later in this chapter, cul-de-sac road forms changed the nature of the public space network: rather than a grid, the street pattern became a hierarchical and discontinuous tree-like pattern.

The Public Space Network

The cadastral pattern establishes the main elements of the public space network, and is also a key element in the broader concept of the capital web (see below). As well as providing access to and displaying the 'public face' of private property, the public space network facilitates and accommodates the overlapping realms of 'movement space' and 'social space' (i.e. space for people to engage in various forms of exchange − economic, social and cultural) (see Chapter 6).

Pedestrian movement is compatible with the notion of streets as social space, and there is a symbiotic relationship between pedestrian movement and economic, social and cultural exchange and transactions. By contrast, car-based movement is pure circulation, with private cars also facilitating an essentially private control over public space. Opportunities for most forms of social interaction and exchange only occur once the car has been parked. Over time, (vehicular) movement space has overwhelmed social space.

When the principal modes of transport were by foot or horse, the realms of movement and social space had considerable overlap. With the development of new modes of land-based travel, the realms became more separated and increasingly compartmentalised into vehicular movement space and pedestrian movement/social space (Figure 4.9). At the same time, public space was colonised by the car and the street's social aspects were suppressed in favour of movement and circulation − urban 'streets' thus become

FIGURE 4.9   Movement and social space — Seoul, South Korea *(Image: Matthew Carmona)*. Public space can be considered in terms of movement space and social space. A crucial difference is that movement space for pedestrians is also social space, but movement space for vehicles often annihilates its potential as social space

FIGURE 4.10   Highway severance — Chicago, USA *(Image: Matthew Carmona)*. Major roads act as barriers to movement, creating severance and fragmenting urban areas. Lefebvre (1991: 359), for example, observes how urban space is '… *sliced up, degraded, and eventually destroyed by … the proliferation of fast roads*'

'roads'. Containing only movement space, *roads* divide and separate areas; containing social space and movement space, *walkable* streets connect buildings and activities across space. Provision for the car thus frequently fragments the city, with movement between fragments becoming a purely movement experience (Figure 4.10).

The pattern of urban blocks and the public space network, plus the basic infrastructure and any other relatively permanent elements of an urban area, constitute the above-ground elements of David Crane's 'capital web'. For Buchanan (1988a: 33), the capital web:

'… *structures a city, its land uses and land values, the density of developments and the intensity of their use, and the way the citizens move through, see and remember the city as well as encounter their fellow citizens.*'

In designing or working within the capital web, urban designers need to be aware of patterns of stability within change — that is, to differentiate elements that either do not change or change over longer periods of time (which, in turn, may give a measure of consistency of character and identity), from those that change over shorter periods of time (see Chapter 9). Buchanan (1988a: 32) argued that it is the movement network, together with the services buried beneath it and monuments and civic buildings within and adjacent to it — plus the images these structured in the mind — that are the relatively permanent parts of the city. Within this more permanent framework, individual buildings, land uses and activities come and go.

The capital web and the public space network can be seen as a generative framework or structure, and thus instrumental in determining patterns of development and urbanisation. Many designers refer to this as an 'armature', meaning a generator or framework — as in the framework

used by a sculptor to support a figure being modelled in a plastic material. As Calthorpe (2005: 34—6) observes:

'*The armature of urbanism has and always will be its streets, from medieval donkey trails through the surveyor's grid, Haussmann's boulevards, the superblock, or the unholy alliance of Arterial and Collector Street. The structure of circulation is a fundamental postulate of community form. For example when the assumption was avenues with a mix of streetcars and autos the result was a form of low-rise mixed-use urbanism unique to America, the streetcar suburb. Likewise our historic fine-grained grid became the fixed framework for the evolution of almost all our cities.*'

As the urban armature often consists of movement channels, both for circulation and distribution, transport infrastructure can be a powerful generator of new urbanisation and arguably also of re-urbanisation. Sites with direct access to, or connections to, movement channels and interchanges are privileged (and thus more likely to be developed) over those with less access to or that are more remote from them. The movement channels might be important new boulevards or a new transit route, but, equally, might simply be new roads that increase accessibility – though, as discussed later in this chapter, these armatures may have significantly different outcomes.

MORPHOLOGICAL TRANSFORMATIONS

This part discusses the transformation in the public space network's morphological structure in the twentieth century from buildings as constituent elements of urban blocks defining streets and squares towards buildings as separate freestanding object-buildings standing in amorphous 'space'.

Substantially a product of the need to accommodate fast-moving vehicular traffic in urban areas, the other major morphological transformation of the twentieth century was from relatively small-scale, integrated and connected, finely meshed grids, usually originating when pedestrian traffic was dominant, to hierarchical road systems surrounding superblocks and segregated and introverted enclaves.

Buildings Defining Space and Buildings in Space

In traditional urban space, the urban fabric is relatively dense, and buildings are normally built adjacent to one another and flush with the street. Building facades thus provide the 'walls' of open space. As the only part exposed to view, the facade also conveys – and is designed to convey – the building's identity and character. Embedded in a dense urban fabric, the building's backs and sides can be more mundane without detriment to the public realm. The facade also contributes to larger systems of 'street' and 'urban block'.

By contrast, freestanding buildings were, characteristic of Modernist design. According to 'functionalist' ideas of design, the convenience of a building's internal spaces was the principal determinant of its external form. Le Corbusier (1927: 167), for example, likened a building to a soap bubble: *'This bubble is perfect and harmonious if the breath has been evenly distributed and regulated from the inside. The exterior is the result of interior.'* Designed from the inside out, responding to their functional requirements and considerations of light, air, hygiene, aspect, prospect, 'movement', 'openness', etc., buildings became objects-in-space, whereby the exterior form – and, hence, its relationship to public space – was merely a by-product of its internal planning. The approach also, *inter alia*, enabled expression of the potential of new building technology and materials.

At the larger scale, the notion of freestanding buildings was further supported by the imperatives of providing healthier living conditions, accommodating cars in urban areas and aesthetic preferences. Modernist urban space was also intended to flow freely around buildings rather than being enclosed and contained by them: Le Corbusier

(in Broadbent 1990: 129), for example, saw the traditional street as: *'… no more than a trench, a deep cleft, a narrow passage. And although we have been accustomed to it for more than a thousand years, our hearts are always oppressed by the constriction of the enclosing walls.'* (see Chapter 2). Desires for the physical separation of buildings were reinforced and exacerbated by public health and planning rules and standards, such as density zoning, road widths, sight-lines, the space required for underground services, and day-lighting angles.

The shift towards freestanding buildings was often a path of least resistance for building developers and, in addition, was fuelled by the desire for buildings to stand out or otherwise be distinctive as a consequence of real estate interests. Buildings can stand out in a number of ways: by being physically separated from adjoining buildings; by being taller; and/or by being architecturally distinctive. Not insignificant though was that, as a development form, freestanding buildings were easier and cheaper. Through separation and physical distance, freestanding buildings can insulate and protect themselves from negative spill-over effects – noise, smells, disturbance, etc. – though they might also be isolated from positive spill-over effects such as busy pedestrian flows.

Prior to the modern period only a few building types used separation as a means of gaining distinction. These were typically public rather than private buildings – churches, town halls, palaces, etc. – where the exterior had significance for the city and its people. The typical traditional city thus had a few 'special' buildings that were separated from the general mass of buildings either through their architectural ornament and/or by being freestanding (i.e. object-buildings) and a much greater number of 'ordinary', anonymous and mundane buildings that were embedded within the general built matrix (i.e. fabric or texture) (Figure 4.11). In the twentieth century, many more buildings were designed and built as freestanding buildings.

For Meiss (1990: 77), the fundamental problem of twentieth century urbanisation was the multiplication of 'objects' and the neglect of 'fabrics'. He argues that, as the number of object-buildings multiplied, their value as exceptions was lost, complaining that contemporary production methods confer object-status on buildings whose *'… content and significance are ordinary.'* (1990: 77).

When applied across a wider range of building types and within traditional urban space systems, freestanding buildings gradually broke down the urban block system. As a direct consequence, the public space network changed from definite spatial types (streets and squares) towards a more amorphous type of space that – unless expressly designed and thereafter maintained – was residual, accidental and merely occupied by objects standing within that space (Figure 4.12).

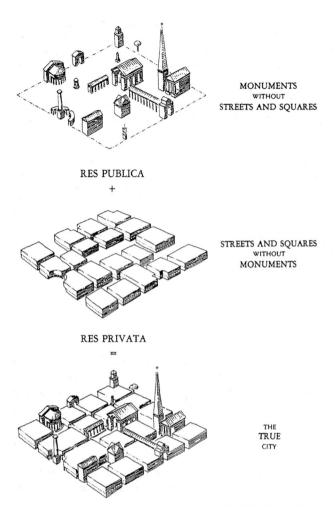

RES PUBLICA
+

STREETS AND SQUARES
WITHOUT
MONUMENTS

RES PRIVATA
=

THE
TRUE
CITY

MONUMENTS
WITHOUT
STREETS AND SQUARES

FIGURE 4.11 Leon Krier's true city *(Image: Krier 1990)*. Leon Krier's model of the traditional city combines a *res publica*, monumental buildings, often in Classical style and sometimes as object-buildings, and a *res privata*, consisting of urban blocks forming streets and squares, made up of vernacular buildings

FIGURE 4.12 Building as object-in-space — Littlejohn Street, Aberdeen *(Image: Steve Tiesdell)*. The police station — the slab block building in the centre of the image — was designed as an object-in-space, set back from the street behind a car park and failing to define the street space. The space around the building is SLOAP — space left over after planning

As such developments became more common during the second half of the twentieth century, cities lost their spatial coherence, becoming a series of unrelated and competing or isolated monuments and small complexes of buildings surrounded by roads, parking and a rather disparate landscaping (see Hebbert 2008). Lefebvre (1991: 303) argues the outcome was a 'fracturing of space': '... *a disordering of elements wrenched from each other in such a way that the urban fabric itself — the street, the city — is also torn apart.*' A new kind of city emerged — made up of amorphous spaces, 'punctuated with monumental buildings' and 'arbitrary and disconnected individual features' (Brand 1994: 10).

Explaining how Modernist ideas of urban space design, combined with modern development practices, created a phenomena he aptly describes as 'lost' space, Trancik (1986: 21) observes how '... *without any conscious intention on anyone's part — the ideals of free flowing space and pure architecture have evolved into our present urban*

situation of individual buildings isolated in parking lots and highways.'

Without explicit concern for the spaces between buildings, many environments became mere accretions of individual buildings rather than synergistic combinations of buildings and spaces. The spaces between object-buildings need to be, but often are not, expressly designed. Furthermore, rather than the free-flowing, manicured Arcadian landscapes envisaged, they were more often SLOAP (space left over after planning) (Hebbert 2008). Curiously, the spaces between buildings-defining-spaces seem to have less need to be expressly designed — while the spaces around object-buildings frequently fail, street spaces more rarely failed.

The Road Hierarchy

Accommodating different forms of travel has been a historical evolution. When the dominant modes of land-based travel were walking and by horse, there were relatively few conflicts between the needs of movement and social space. While canals and railways were, for the most part, always separate systems, horse-drawn carriages and then cars shared the same space as pedestrian movement, exacerbating the tension between the competing demands of movement and social space. Provision for vehicular traffic, thus, initially evolved by usurping pedestrians from (large) parts of the public space network.

The separation of pedestrian movement from vehicular movement in conventional streets occurred in many cities at various points during the eighteenth century and nineteenth century through the introduction of sidewalks

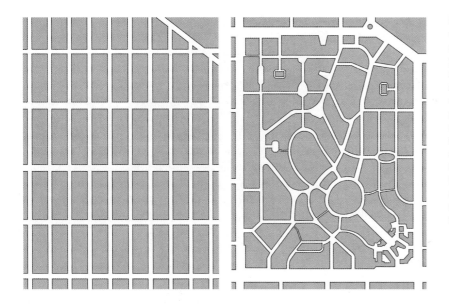

FIGURE 4.13 Clarence Perry's neighbourhood unit and standard gridded street system. Perry aimed to organise space in a way that was more pedestrian-friendly and which provided space for residents to socialise. Seeing through-traffic as an obstacle to community formation and busy traffic routes as obvious boundaries for residential areas, rather than places, as was the case in traditional settlements (e.g. the traditional high street), he proposed that arterial roads bypass rather than penetrate his neighbourhood unit, thereby protecting it from through-traffic. Within the unit was a hierarchy of roads, each sized according to the intended traffic load and deliberately less well-integrated than in a grid layout to minimise opportunities for rat runs

(footways or, in the UK, pavements), which also served to separate pedestrians from the new side channels and cambered roads, designed to improve health through the more efficient disposal of sewage and run-off (Taylor 2002: 28). Sidewalks/pavements were for pedestrians, while the centre of the street was for vehicles — pedestrians entered this zone at their peril.

The twentieth century saw more radical ideas. The best way to accommodate growing numbers of cars seemed to involve giving them their own dedicated movement network. Noting Le Corbusier's well-known dislike of the 'hurly-burly' of streets, Boddy (1992: 132) regards formulating a 'more rationalised alternative' as the generative idea of his urbanism. Le Corbusier's city plans featured radical separation of the various modes of travel — and then their equally radical re-integration in vast transport interchanges.

With increasing levels of car ownership and increased speed and size, there was a shift in the design of urban road transportation systems. Rather than combining movement and access, the shift was towards separation through the introduction of a hierarchical system. The intention was to distribute traffic through a hierarchy of routes closely matched to traffic volume and purpose, with free-flow movement at one end (e.g. a dedicated expressway) and local access at the other, and with each level linked dendritically to the next.

The street hierarchy concept was first elaborated by the German architect and urban planner Ludwig Hilberseimer (1885–1967). Hilberseimer's chief concerns were increasing the speed of traffic circulation and making it safe for primary school-age children to walk to school. Similar ideas informed Perry's Neighborhood

Unit concept (1929) (Figure 4.13) (see Chapter 6). Ideas for separating different modes of traffic were further developed during the late 1920s — by, for example, Benton MacKaye, who conceived of the 'highwayless town' and the 'townless highway' — and in the 1930s and 1940s through Tripp's *Road Traffic and Its Control* (1938) and *Town Planning and Road Traffic* (1942).

An exceptionally clear statement of the principles of hierarchy came in the 1963 Buchanan Report, *Traffic in Towns*:

'The function of the distributory network is to canalise the longer movements from locality to locality. The links of the network should therefore be designed for swift, efficient movement. This means that they cannot also be used for giving direct access to buildings, nor even to minor roads serving the buildings, because the consequent frequency of the junctions would give rise to traffic dangers and disturb the efficiency of the road. It is therefore necessary to introduce the idea of a 'hierarchy' of distributors, whereby important distributors feed down through distributors of lesser category to the minor roads which give access to the buildings. This system may be likened to the trunk, limbs, branches, and finally the twigs (corresponding to the access roads) of a tree. Basically, however, there are only two kinds of road — distributors designed for movement, and access roads to serve the buildings.'

(Buchanan 1963: 43–4).

The idea remains through to today — though, as discussed below, it is being increasingly challenged. In England, for example, until 2007 and the publication of the *Manual for Streets* (DfT 2007), *Design Bulletin 32: Residential Roads and Footpaths* (DoE/DoT 1992: 15) advocated a four-level hierarchy: primary distributor roads; district distributor roads; local distributor roads; and residential access roads. Streets directly serving buildings were only allowed for groups of less than 300 houses.

Hierarchical systems are seen in their purest forms on previously undeveloped (greenfield) land, where a pure hierarchical system could be laid out with few constraints. As access to the major road network would be at widely spaced intervals, each cell within the network would be quite large (i.e. a superblock system). The major road network would thus have a relatively coarse grain and would carry the non-local traffic, allowing the streets/ roads within each cell of the major road network to carry local traffic only. This pattern of road infrastructure becomes an important armature determining the form of development, which is frequently known as pod development (see below).

In established urban areas, hierarchical systems are seen in a hybrid form as quasi-hierarchical systems. Where comprehensive redevelopment and urban renewal schemes occurred, new development was often based on hierarchical road patterns and the creation of superblocks — larger than a traditional city block, a superblock is typically bounded by widely spaced, high-speed, arterial or circulating routes rather than by local streets. Superblocks, rather than traditional urban grids, for example, were frequently used in public housing projects during the second half of the twentieth century.

Where comprehensive redevelopment was not possible or did not happen, traffic engineers and planners began to create quasi-road hierarchical patterns and to modify existing street networks into quasi-cellular or superblock patterns through incremental redevelopment. Road planning thus involved both the cutting of limited-access roads through established urban areas and the creation of enclaves/precincts. As Hebbert (2005: 40) notes, in a frequently used organic analogy, these were arteries and cells.

The Arteries

Municipalities and highway engineers sought direct and cost-efficient routes for new limited-access urban highways (Figure 4.14). In terms of routes, a chief criterion was land acquisition costs, with highways directed through public parks, declining industrial and dock areas, and open space. Many cities lost access to their waterfronts. Some historic areas, such as New York's SoHo and New Orleans' Vieux Carre, were saved by successful anti-highway campaigns, but many others were less fortunate.

In additional to limited-access highways, the goal of a quasi-road hierarchical pattern was also achieved by designating certain streets as major roads with selective widening, waiting restrictions, turning prohibitions, one-way routings and access limited to allow traffic to move

FIGURE 4.14　Urban highway — Glasgow *(Image: Steve Tiesdell)*. Inner ring-roads (the downtown loop) were built close to the business core, often devastating its fringes and cutting it off from surrounding neighbourhoods

more freely and quickly. Hierarchical road systems meant expressly designing and, in existing urban areas designating, some roads to handle higher traffic loads. The smooth flow of traffic on such roads would be assisted by reducing their connectivity (i.e. by limiting the number of other roads connecting into them and by prohibiting private driveways from opening onto them). The number of pedestrian crossings was limited by creating dedicated crossing points — subways, bridges or light-controlled crossings. At permitted crossing points, traffic flow took priority, and pedestrian movement was limited by barriers and railings.

To attain the design speed, urban roads were designed or modified to provide long forward vision and wide visibility splays at corners. Building frontages onto the road were controlled to avoid distractions to drivers, while railings and other barriers sought to prevent intrusion of 'traffic interruptions' (i.e. people). In his 1964 book *Planning for Man and Motor*, Ritter (1964: 34) argued that safety had to be assured by keeping pedestrians away from cars and motorists away from 'kerbside distractions' such as shops, advertisements and 'pretty girls on the pavement' — ' ... *the more attractive the girl, the greater the menace.*' (cited in Hebbert 2005: 43).

A key consequence, as Hebbert (2005: 42) observes, was that, while traditional urbanism measured a street's importance by the height and adornment of its building frontages, hierarchical road systems '... *turned that upside down, putting traffic capacity in an inverse relation to building capacity, so the most important arteries would carry no building at all.*' Typically, the major road network was seen as a negative living environment onto which other land uses should turn their backs, resulting in anonymous movement space (Figure 4.15).

FIGURE 4.15 Anonymous movement space *(Image: Matthew Carmona)*. As social space provides opportunities for interaction and exchange, development facing onto it is socially active. By contrast, movement space has few opportunities for interaction and exchange — and, because there is no incentive to be anything else, abutting development tends to be socially passive

The Cells

In existing urban areas where comprehensive redevelopment was not possible or did not happen, quasi-cellular pattern was achieved by closing off intersections and side streets and consolidating blocks to create larger superblocks, with the new perimeters of the enlarged street/super blocks becoming large-scale gyratory systems. Through planning control, new buildings were oriented away from thoroughfares. In accordance with planning principles first proposed in Clarence Perry's neighbourhood unit, high traffic generators such as shops and apartments were also banished to the arterial roads forming the boundaries of the superblock, while schools, churches and parks were concentrated at the centre. Within the block, culs-de-sac prevented through-traffic. The local road network within the superblock was intended to carry lighter traffic loads. To prevent or deter traffic from taking short cuts ('rat running'), the local road network was designed (or redesigned in existing environments) to be relatively discontinuous (e.g. through the use of cul-de-sacs) or at least poorly interconnected.

The traffic-calmed, even traffic-free, superblock was a common design idea. Clarence Perry's neighbourhood unit of 1929, for example, was a superblock surrounded by major arterial roads. Similarly, Tripp (1942) advocated a 'precinct principle' from which extraneous traffic would be excluded. Given the ideas of his day, Tripp saw the precincts as specialised, single-land-use areas. A similar idea appears in the Buchanan Report (1964) — though rather than specialised single land use precincts,

Before

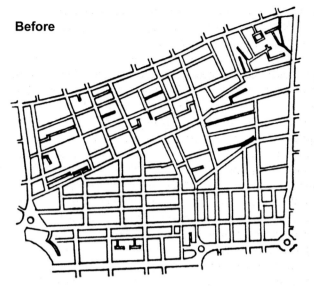

After

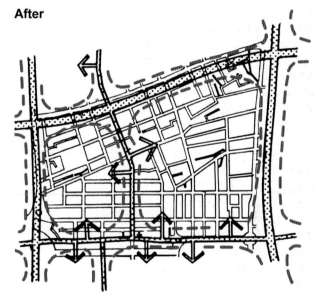

FIGURE 4.16 Buchanan's environmental areas *(Image: adapted from Scoffham 1984)*. Buchanan proposed dividing the city into 'environmental areas' each bounded by major roads and kept free from through-traffic

Buchanan's environmental areas were intended to be mixed-use (Figure 4.16).

Pope (1996: 189) describes these processes as 'grid erosion', whereby open grid street systems become 'ladder' street systems — a grid allows movement in a variety of directions and through a variety of paths; a 'ladder' permits movement from A to B and vice versa (Figure 4.17a–c). In the most car-dependent US cities, as Graham & Marvin (2001: 229) note, the publicly developed infrastructure 'grid' is 'splintering' into infrastructure 'ladders' where '*... the terminal point of each link is geared towards exclusively servicing a single secessionary space.*'

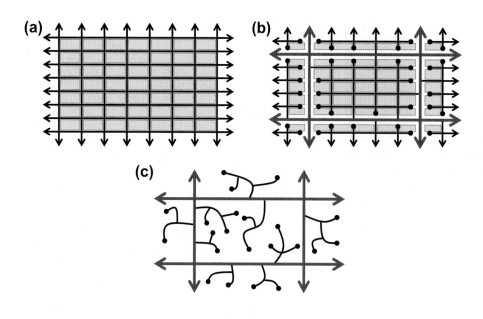

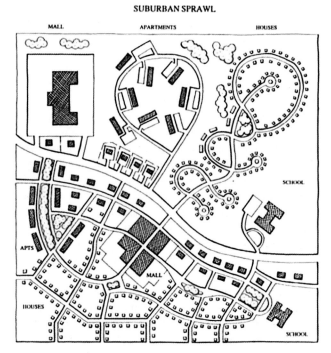

FIGURE 4.17 (a) Phase I: Grid street system. (b) Phase II: Grid erosion. (c) Phase III: Ladder street system. *(Images: redrawn and adapted from Pope 1996).* As illustrated in these diagrams, Pope (1996: 189) describes the phenomenon of grid erosion — the process by which traditional grids are transformed into superblocks and, in particular, into 'pod' systems. Many contemporary developments, especially those on greenfield sites, start out with laddered rather than grid layouts

Hierarchical road networks thus segregate and fragment urban areas into enclaves. Such enclaves may be justified by arguments that defining discrete territories helps generate sense of identity, sense of community and a sense of safety and security for those living in the area, but it is also a short step to the gated community, where the public space of the street is closed to public access by a gate (see Chapter 6). Pope (1996), for example, argues that ladders support broader desires for exclusivity, isolation and separation — resulting in what he terms 'xenophobic enclaves'. Interestingly, contemporary practice is to reintegrate public housing estates into the local street/movement system, thereby breaking their social and physical isolation. In France, such programmes are known as 'desenclavement'.

Pod Developments

A further transformation in the morphological structure of urban areas is that from outward-facing urban blocks to inward-focused complexes of buildings served by an exclusive road connection — often referred to as 'pods' (see Ford 2000). In pod development, each use — shopping mall, fast-food outlet, strip mall, office park, apartment complex, medical centre, hotel and convention facility, etc. — is conceived as a separate element, surrounded by its associated parking and usually with its own individual and exclusive access onto a collector or main distributor road (Figure 4.18).

While individual pods may be better (or less well) designed, they are almost always introverted and unconnected to — if not positively separated from — adjacent developments; geographically proximate, they have very little other relation. Separation is not just by roads but also by expanses of car parking. Indeed, apart from a road

FIGURE 4.18 Grid and tree-like street patterns *(Image: Duany et al 2000).* In the upper part of this diagram, each development is a self-contained pod, unrelated to other pods and having its own exclusive connection to the collector road. This type of road pattern is dendritic or tree-like. In the lower part of the diagram, there is a traditional grid with a more synergistic arrangement of buildings and spaces. Furthermore, rather than concentrating traffic onto arterial roads, the grid disperses it through a network: a single accident on the local distributor or on any of the access roads in the upper network will block traffic flows; if a similar accident occurs in the lower network, traffic can find alternative routes

link, there is little need to link them up because almost everyone drives between them. As Ford (2000: 21) comments: *'The idea is to separate — often to the point of walling off — land uses into distinctive social and functional worlds.'*

With no pedestrian flow — only vehicular flow — pod developments do not generally front onto the main traffic distribution roads. Development becomes introverted, focused inwards either onto the internal road/street network within the superblock and at the points where people can park and leave their cars. Alternatively, there might be 'large lump' developments — shopping centres, office complexes, multi-screen cinemas, hotel complexes — which offer some form of pedestrian realm within the centre of the block, surrounded by car parking, but not connecting to any wider area. Such pedestrian-oriented spaces are usually private spaces where access and behaviour are closely controlled and regulated (see Chapter 6). Bentley (1999: 88) observes how the city becomes *'... transformed into a series of islands, with spectacular interiors, set in a "left over" sea.'*

Driven by a narrow real estate and regulatory logic, pod development is also the characteristic form of new suburban development and indeed much other contemporary development. But pods fragment the city: instead of urban areas being conceived in terms of connected urban space defined by urban blocks, they are conceived in terms of roads and transport routes creating cells within which individual buildings (and/or inward-focused complexes of buildings) stand in space, sometimes in landscaped settings but more often amid car parking. There is no synergy though the spatial concentration of different uses and the whole is only the sum of the parts. Because the road structure, in effect, determines everything else, it is a default urbanism: it is not how we intended it, nor what we want it to be; it is what happens when we do not take positive action to stop it and to do something better or simply different (Figure 4.19).

Residential Pods

Residential cul-de-sacs are a particular kind of pod. In its typical suburban manifestation, it is a relatively short, dead-end street with a turning hammerhead or circle, serving perhaps 20 or 30 dwellings. As its name suggests, it is a place *'... where one does not enter by chance because it does not lead anywhere other than to private houses.'* (Panerai *et al* 2004: 43).

Unwin & Parker pioneered cul-de-sac street patterns at New Earswick at the end of the nineteenth century. At the time the reasons for their use included savings in road costs: with a lighter traffic load, they could be built with a lower specification. As traffic engineers began to address the safety problems associated with through-traffic in residential streets, the use of culs-de-sacs became much more frequent from the mid-1950s onwards (Southworth & Ben-Joseph 1995: 77). Many contemporary residential areas are now laid out in 'dendritic' (tree-like) street patterns, in which a curvilinear collector road loops off a major highway, with a number of cul-de-sacs branching off it. In its ideal form, all houses are situated on cul-de-sacs with none placed on the busier and noisy loop road. Due to their shape on plan, the system is sometimes referred to as 'loops and lollipops'.

For many, the term cul-de-sac is pejorative and represents:

'... the essence of suburbia today: the isolated, insular, private enclave, set in a formless sprawl of similar enclaves, separated socially and physically from the larger world, and dependent upon the automobile for its survival.'

(Southworth & Ben-Joseph 1997: 120–1).

Nonetheless, the cul-de-sac seems much loved by suburban residents and developers (see Table 4.1). The competing needs suggest potential for a better-designed solution: Southworth & Ben-Joseph (1997: 126), for example, contend it is possible to design new residential districts — and, perhaps less easily, to retrofit old ones — to achieve both interconnected pedestrian networks and limited-access vehicular systems (see also Marshall 2005; Dunham-Jones & Williamson 2009).

FIGURE 4.19 Pod development — Braehead Retail Park, Paisley, Scotland *(Image: Steve Tiesdell)*. Many pod developments are entirely standardised and repetitive developments — Duany *et al* (2000) refer to them as 'cookie cutter' developments — substantially determined by real estate funding requirements (Leinberger 2005, 2008) (see Chapter 10) and imposed on a location with little regard for the local context, topography or landscape. Typical characteristics of pod development include free-standing single-use developments with very 'functional' layouts; abundant on-site parking; target-hardened, defensible space; detachment from the public realm; general pedestrian unfriendliness; architecture lacking any stylistic consistency but with gratuitous local place references; and minimal landscaping (Punter 2007b: 394)

TABLE 4.1 Cul-de-sac Street Systems

Arguments for

- *Provides quieter and safer streets:* From the point of view of residents, the pattern offers quiet and safe streets, where children can play with minimal fear of the hazards of fast-moving traffic.
- *Promotes resident interaction:* A discontinuous short street system, unlike the grid, may promote neighbouring, familiarity and interaction.
- *Provides a local sense of identity:* The scale of the cul-de-sac provides a local sense of identity.
- *Reduces opportunities for crime:* Compared with traditional street layouts, hierarchical discontinuous layout systems deter burglaries because criminals avoid street patterns where they might get trapped (Mayo 1979; Newman 1995) (see Chapter 6).

Arguments against

- *Lack of interconnectedness:* Isolation from through-traffic may result in isolation from nearly everything else. To go somewhere/ anywhere, one must always leave the cul-de-sac and travel on a collector road. Furthermore, designed for car access, such layouts often have poorly developed networks of pedestrian routes — required to follow the vehicular routes, pedestrian walks are often long and inconvenient.
- *Creates car-dependency:* Going almost anywhere beyond the cul-de-sac means going out to a major road, virtually necessitating a car journey, and, thereby, isolating and excluding those too young, old or poor to drive and sentencing the rest to a life ferrying themselves and their dependants around.
- *Generates traffic congestion:* As every trip from one component to another necessitates entering the collector road, the area's traffic relies on a single road. As a result, it is generally congested during much of the day, while any major accident on the collector road will block the entire system.
- *Enhances opportunities for crime:* Cul-de-sac patterns interrupt the through-movement of people and, thereby, reduce the policing effect of people presence (see Chapter 6).
- *Lack of identity and character:* The sense of being part of a neighbourhood or town, with a clear structure and identity, is often lost because through streets connecting places are missing. There is a sense of identity within the cul-de-sac, but not with anything beyond the cul-de-sac.

Source: Adapted from Southworth & Ben-Joseph (1997: 121–5).

The reaction to the impact of road hierarchies and pod developments has three interrelated elements: a return to interconnected street patterns; a return to the urban block; and the design of streets as places (i.e. reconciling their roles as movement and as social space). In combination these reactions represent a shift towards a more self-conscious and normative urbanism, rather than the default urbanism of a roads-first approach. They are discussed in the next three parts of this chapter.

CONNECTED STREET PATTERNS

The desire to return to connected street networks has come from various sources. In the USA, New Urbanists have been prominent critics of cul-de-sacs and committed advocates of connected street networks (Duany *et al* 2000). In the UK, while the 1973 edition of the *Essex Design Guide* had reluctantly accepted 'the road engineers' concept of a tree-like street network', the second edition (1997) was '… *radically different … in its concern to achieve connected street networks and acceptance of the urban block.*' (Panerai *et al* 2004: 175). By 2001, government guidance also commended the connected street pattern, recognising that:

'… *the block structure defined by a network of interconnected roads has been the predominant form of housing layout for centuries. Only recently have structures created primarily for the*

car resulted in formless residential environments characterised by a dead-end system of "loops and lollipops"'

(DETR/CABE 2000: 40–1).

Connected street patterns do not necessarily mean a rigid grid-iron. Marshall (2005), for example, distinguished qualities of connectivity and complexity in street patterns. Dendritic patterns have low connectivity, while grids have high connectivity. But complexity involves other qualities — even with equal connectivity; for example, deformed grids have greater complexity than regular grids. Marshall analysed 60 street network patterns in terms of their relative connectivity and their relative complexity (see Figure 4.20).

On the spectrum of connectivity, he identified four broad types:

- *Tributary* — deep branching with systematic use of cul-de-sac and/or layered loop roads, and often associated with hierarchically based suburban expansions of the second half of the twentieth century (see below).
- *Semi-tributary* — with some degree of layering and use of cul-de-sacs, but with less division between minor and major access roads and use of T junctions, found in older suburban neighbourhoods.
- *Semi-gridded* — referring to typical distorted grid systems with a variety of T and X junctions, often found in inner areas or traditional settlements.

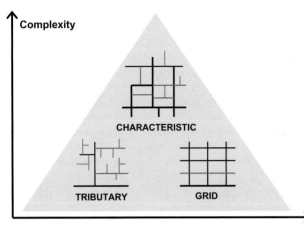

FIGURE 4.20   Street structure *(Image: adapted from Marshall 2005: 154)* . Analysing street network patterns in terms of their relative connectivity and their relative complexity, Marshall found a triangular distribution. Tributary patterns were less connected and less complex; grid patterns were most connected but similarly less complex. Most streets patterns, however, had a 'characteristic' structure: a medium level of connectivity and a high degree of complexity

- *Gridded* — featuring a high proportion of X junctions and reflecting the type of planned, regular layouts of grid-iron urban extensions or new cities.

Marshall found most existing street structures were neither pure grids nor pure tributary forms, and instead combined features of both, exhibiting a combination of connectivity but also of complexity. The intermediate positions between grid and tributary were not inferior, however, and had their own positive qualities (e.g. complexity) and it might be that these are the more desired street patterns.

Connected street patterns can also be justified on sustainability grounds — if a high level of permeability is provided initially, segregation can usually be achieved later — if necessary — through design or management: the layout is robust and capable of adaptation. Conversely, it is difficult, even impossible, to adapt an environment designed for segregation into one for integration. To ensure permeability, all streets should connect to other streets and should terminate in other streets. Such a principle creates connected and permeable street patterns.

Urban Blocks

Reaction to object-buildings and pod developments saw new interest in the conscious design of the space between buildings and in the creation of well-defined, positive space. This has led to explicit attempts to compose and organise the parts so that the whole — the place — is greater than the sum of the parts (individual buildings and developments).

Connected street patterns and block structures generally go together and many contemporary development projects are conceived using connected street patterns and urban blocks (Figure 4.21). As Kropf (2006: 12) observes: *'The block is the result of connecting streets. The block only comes into being when streets are connected. The perimeter block only arises when streets are connected and well defined by buildings.'* Similarly, Panerai *et al* (2004: 162) argues *'… the block is not an architectural form, but a group of independent building plots. It has a proper meaning only when it is in a dialectical relationship with the road network.'*

While Modernist urban space design and development practices had largely undermined the urban block, a prominent block-based development occurred at Battery Park City, New York from the early 1980s onwards. The masterplan by Cooper-Eckstut for the 37-hectare (92-acre) site set out a regular arrangement of streets and blocks, respecting and extending the city's long-established street grid and requiring most buildings to line up in a uniform distance from the kerb to form consistent street walls. Enormously successful as a real estate venture, Fishman (2008b: xvii) considers the model's strengths are *'still compelling compared to the Modernist model it replaced'*, though *'… so too is the need to get beyond it.'* (see Box 4.2).

Demonstrating new interest in and concern for the continuity of places, such approaches have often also shown a willingness to examine and learn from precedent, and have often taken reference from traditional urban

FIGURE 4.21   Granton, Edinburgh *(Image: Llewelyn-Davies 2000).* Many contemporary urban development schemes use urban block structures. It is also a means of 'designing cities without designing buildings' (Barnett 1974), allowing some design decisions to be 'down-streamed' to later in the development process. While street block structures are a useful default, in any particular context or situation, other typologies and configurations may perform better — though the performance benefits should be persuasively demonstrated

BOX 4.2 The Battery Park City Method

Masterplanned by Cooper & Eckstut (adopted in 1979), Battery Park City has become established as a 'durable paradigm for larger-scale urban real estate development in North America (Love 2009: 210). Based on extending the streets of the Manhattan grid, as Panerai *et al* (2004: 181) explain:

'Instead of the superblocks and megastructure that implied one designer and a single investor for a few very large and expensive projects, these streets defined moderately sized urban blocks that were capable of accommodating buildings designed by a variety of architects using different developers'

Love (2009: 212) suggests it has endured because of its real estate development logic, whereby dividing large development parcels into independent 'blocks' has two main benefits: first, it is divided into flexible phases, readily adaptable to suit the changing real estate market and, second, by dimensioning blocks to correspond to the optimum parcel size for a typical residential or commercial development project, the resulting building is guaranteed open exposures and free access on all sides (i.e. no party walls). The development is thus both capable of incremental build-out and can attract funding on an on-going basis.

The apparent exigencies of initial (short term) real estate development (and financing), however, often coarsen the model, removing much of the architectural/visual and social vitality and variety. As Love (2009) argues, Battery Park City's sterility derives not only from the architectural design but also the urban framework. In essence, the approach becomes formulaic, with life-giving nuance and quality stripped out for efficient profit-making and risk-reduction. Typical shortcomings are:

- *Uniform and standardised street block sizes.* Furthermore, as Love (2009: 212) observes, '... *the flexible phasing logic of a long range commercial masterplan ... all but codifies a block size that persists from plan to plan.'* A solution is to mandate a variety of block sizes (Love 2009: 223), and which, *inter alia*, would also permit a wider range of development companies to contribute to the development.

- *The blocks being single buildings,* often with a single entrance. A possible solution is internal block subdivision and perhaps plot-based development and thus several developers on each block.

- *The increment of repetition being too large,* whereby only developments above a certain threshold size are possible. As Love (2009: 213) comments: *'... more than the style of the architecture, it is the monopoly of a single scale of building that is the problem. ... the serial repetition of a single building type – successful in Boston's Back Bay or in Bath, England – does not work for buildings with 35,000 square-foot floor plates.'*

- *Retail units being too large.* Love (2009: 214) suggests the building footprint is often the problem, with only 'urban versions of American big-box retailers' being able to fill 'the big leasable voids'. A solution is to develop a range of retail unit sizes and combine this with a retail letting policy that reserves space for micro-retail.

Battery Park City (*Image: Matthew Carmona*)

---

space. A significant strand in this approach can be labelled typo-morphological.

Typo-Morphological Approaches

A key figure in re-evaluating urban space design was Colin Rowe. Under Rowe's influence an approach explicitly relating new development to a city's historical structure and to traditional typologies of urban space was explored at Cornell University from the early 1960s (Figure 4.22). In *Collage City*, Rowe subsequently described the Modernist city's 'spatial predicament' as one of 'objects' and 'texture': objects are sculptural buildings standing freely in space, while texture is the background, continuous matrix

of built form defining space (Rowe & Koetter 1978: 50–85).

Using figure-ground diagrams of traditional and Modernist cities, Rowe & Koetter showed how the former was the inverse of the latter: one diagram was an accumulation of solids in largely unmanipulated void; the other an accumulation of voids in largely unmanipulated solid. Nevertheless, rather than privileging the positive space (space-fixation) or the positive building (object-fixation), they recognised situations where one or the other would be appropriate, but also a 'desired situation' being *'... one in which both buildings and spaces exist in an equality of sustained debate. A debate in which victory consists in each component emerging undefeated.'*

FIGURE 4.22   Extract of the Nolli plan of Rome. Colin Rowe was instrumental in reviving the use of figure-ground diagrams — famously the Giambattista Nolli map of Rome — and in encouraging tissue studies. Figure-ground diagrams were to teach students not to consider buildings only as objects but also as backgrounds

(Rowe & Koetter 1978: 83) — in other words, a state of figure-ground reversal (see Chapter 7).

Another morphological approach developed in the mid-1960s, initially by Aldo Rossi and the Italian Rationalist School and subsequently by others, including brothers Rob and Leon Krier. Rossi's book *The Architecture of the City* (1966, 1982) was instrumental in resurrecting ideas of architectural types and typology. In contrast to building type, which generally refers to function, architectural type is morphological and refers to form. Abstractions of basic principles, ideas or forms, architectural types are, in a sense, three-dimensional templates that can be repeatedly copied with endless variation (Kelbaugh 1997: 97).

Discussing limits and constraints in design — and how, for example, site and programmatic constraints often make the design process easier — Kelbaugh (2002) argues that interest in architectural and morphological types formalised and systematised processes of learning from experience and precedent. Typologists asserted that, when designing a building or urban space, architectural types that had evolved over time offered a superior point of departure to Modernist functionalism, which sought to discover new forms latent in 'programme' or 'technology'.

The historic city is a source of durable types: as Gosling & Maitland (1984: 134) note:

'Until the point at which it was destroyed by the disastrous innovations of the twentieth century, the city is seen as having developed certain "type" elements ... universal solutions of great simplicity and integrity, arrived at over a period of time by the operation of anonymous forces of selection.'

The key urban type is the 'urban block', together with a variety of more specific types such as 'streets', 'avenues', 'arcades', 'colonnades', etc.

In *Urban Space* (1979), Rob Krier developed a typology of urban squares (Figure 4.23). In contrast to Sitte (1889) and Zucker (1959) (see Chapter 7), who focused on the aesthetic effect, Krier focused on elementary geometry. Krier's brother, Leon, also developed a critique of Modernist urban space design rooted in a preference for traditional urban spatial forms and types (Krier 1978a, 1978b, 1979) (Figure 4.24). Architectural types were also the basis of DPZ's form-based code at Seaside (Figure 4.25).

Use of types and typology has been more readily accepted in urban design than in the architectural community. This relates both to much urban design being readily

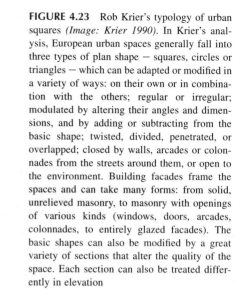

FIGURE 4.23 Rob Krier's typology of urban squares *(Image: Krier 1990)*. In Krier's analysis, European urban spaces generally fall into three types of plan shape — squares, circles or triangles — which can be adapted or modified in a variety of ways: on their own or in combination with the others; regular or irregular; modulated by altering their angles and dimensions, and by adding or subtracting from the basic shape; twisted, divided, penetrated, or overlapped; closed by walls, arcades or colonnades from the streets around them, or open to the environment. Building facades frame the spaces and can take many forms: from solid, unrelieved masonry, to masonry with openings of various kinds (windows, doors, arcades, colonnades, to entirely glazed facades). The basic shapes can also be modified by a great variety of sections that alter the quality of the space. Each section can also be treated differently in elevation

understood as an indirect or 'second-order' design activity (see Chapter 1) and to the value placed on originality and novelty within the architectural community (see Lawson 1980: 110; Bentley 1999). While Modernists' belief in the zeitgeist made an ideological virtue of innovation and novelty, an important distinction must be drawn: novelty means something is new; innovation involves it being better than existing alternatives. The ideological imperative for originality, creativity and endless novelty is thus often misplaced; rather than being valued as ends in themselves, they are means to create better buildings and better places.

Although much contemporary urban space design has been informed by a reaction to Modernism's stance on history and tradition and has a strong historicist dimension, many are sceptical of such approaches. Read (1982), for

example, warned that the industrial city's problems were real problems and that:

'... *while it may be reasonable now to reject the forms which [Modernists] evolved in their response to the problems of the industrial city, those problems will not be removed simply by looking further back to the pre-industrial city.*'

Urban Block Sizes

Conceived as a public space network, urban block structures open up possibilities and — in conjunction with basic typologies/codes/rules about physical parameters — can provide coherence and 'good' urban form without necessarily being overly deterministic about architectural form

(a)

(b)

(c)

(d)

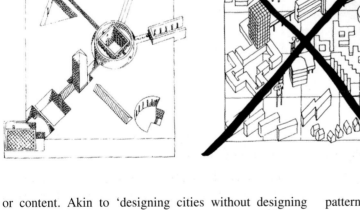

FIGURE 4.24 (a–d) Leon Krier's four types of urban space *(Image: Krier L 1990)*. Krier identified four models or systems of urban space — in the first three buildings-define-space, while, in the fourth, buildings are objects-in-space: (a) the urban blocks are the result of the patterns of streets and squares: the pattern is typologically classifiable; (b) the pattern of streets and squares is the result of the position of blocks: the blocks are typologically classifiable; (c) the streets and squares are precise formal types: the public 'rooms' are typologically classifiable; and (d) the buildings are precise formal types: there is a random distribution of buildings standing in space

or content. Akin to 'designing cities without designing buildings' (Barnett 1974), it also allows detailed building design to occur later in the development process.

The street pattern/block structure is important in determining the pattern of movement, setting the parameters for subsequent development and in contributing to an area's character. As a key element of the capital web, the street pattern is generally the most resilient part of the infrastructure and should have dimensions allowing it to accommodate, rather than inhibit, change. The size and shape of urban blocks is also important. In designing new patterns of urban development — or in 'healing' established patterns — a balance needs to be struck between providing sufficient area for development (i.e. to make it commercially viable), for efficient and convenient circulation and for social space.

Microclimate and issues of wind and sun penetration also need to be considered: tall, narrow streets in northerly or southerly climes, for example, will have limited sunlight penetration for much of the year (see Chapter 8) and thus a balance must be struck within the design process between environmental performance and urban

(a)

(b)

(c)

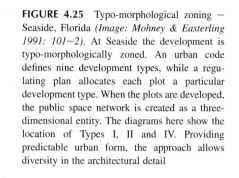

FIGURE 4.25 Typo-morphological zoning — Seaside, Florida *(Image: Mohney & Easterling 1991: 101−2).* At Seaside the development is typo-morphologically zoned. An urban code defines nine development types, while a regulating plan allocates each plot a particular development type. When the plots are developed, the public space network is created as a three-dimensional entity. The diagrams here show the location of Types I, II and IV. Providing predictable urban form, the approach allows diversity in the architectural detail

form. Street blocks typically feature buildings of between 2−7 storeys and natural limits of about 10−12 stories (although this depends on the size and width of surrounding streets). Beyond these limits other building configurations may produce better outcomes. An insistence on urban block and perimeter block configurations can, however, be seen as frustrating other development typologies that, for example, place greater emphasis on orienting towards the sun and limiting overshadowing. A common hybrid urban form, for example, is the podium-and-tower configuration (Figure 4.26).

A balance also needs to be struck between arguments for smaller blocks — based on considerations of pedestrian permeability, walkability and the social use of space — and those for larger blocks based on the optimum distribution of built form and open space (see below). Rather than a single, repeated block size, a range of block sizes (including small blocks) may encourage and facilitate greater diversity of building types and land uses (see Love 2009).

Block size can be determined by the local context. In established urban contexts or on brownfield sites the block size may be inferred by working with the existing and remnant patterns of previous urbanisations, reintegrating isolated fragments of those urbanisations and re-establishing — and/or creating new — linkages with the wider context to facilitate movement and to connect and integrate the new development with the surrounding context (Figure 4.27).

Greenfield sites usually have fewer contextual cues to suggest appropriate block sizes. In such cases, they could

FIGURE 4.26 Podium development — Chicago *(Image: Steve Tiesdell).* Common in many North American cities, especially Vancouver and Toronto — and as shown here in Chicago — podium-and-tower configurations are a hybrid urban form offering a number of advantages. The podium element forms a perimeter edging the street block and is relatively low-rise — usually between three and eight storeys. In Vancouver, the podium element is often up to eight storeys; in Toronto the podiums are lower as the city authorities like them no taller than the street is wide. The podium element typically has street-oriented housing and some commercial uses providing a continuous street wall of a domestic scale and character, and activities overlooking and animating the street. Beneath the podium is underground car parking. Private, highly landscaped courtyards are usually located within or on top of the podium element. With a smaller footprint, the tower element rises either directly from the ground or from the podium

be determined by analysing the requirements of particular land uses — offices, housing, shops, industry, etc. Alternatively they may be based on an analysis of historical precedents and tissue studies — patterns that have endured by being able to accommodate growth and change over time.

Noting that the size of an ideal block cannot be established any more precisely than the ideal height of a human body, Krier (1990: 197) argues that through 'comparison and experience' block sizes 'more apt' to form a 'complex urban pattern' can be deduced. He also observes that, in cities that have evolved organically, the smallest and typologically most complex urban blocks are found at the centre, with blocks growing larger and typologically simpler towards the periphery before finally dissolving into single freestanding objects.

Small Blocks

Small blocks are nevertheless often advocated for a variety of reasons including vitality, permeability, visual interest and legibility — Jacobs (1961: 191–9), for example, devoted a chapter of *The Death and Life of Great American Cities*, to 'The Need for Small Blocks' because of the

increased vitality and choice such layouts offer. Krier (1990: 198) also prefers small blocks for reasons of increased urbanity:

'If the main cause for small blocks and a dense pattern is primarily economic, it is this very same reason which has created the intimate character of a highly urban environment. Such an environment is the basis of urban culture, of intense social, cultural and economic exchange.'

Small blocks may often be either a single building or entirely built over with perhaps a light well or atrium space in the centre of the block. Panerai *et al* (2004: 162) term these 'monumental blocks' and, despite the building generally taking the form of a traditional urban block, they liken their effect to that of object-buildings with a single point of entry and raising front-back problems (see Box 4.3). They also identify another special case — that of facilities blocks — where a group of street blocks form a single functional complex (and that may, in practice, be a superblock).

Panerai *et al* (2004) also lament how the urban block's return to the foreground has some perverse effects. Noting how new developments are 'filled with pseudo-blocks' — an 'urbanistic rendering of a valueless postmodern formalism' — they argue that urban blocks should be understood as a system rather than as an a priori form. Emphasising the importance of internal sub-divisions, they caution against '… *showing the outward appearance of urbanity without ensuring the conditions to allow it to happen.'* (2004: 164) (see Chapter 9).

Large Blocks

Larger blocks are likely to be perimeter blocks where the ribbon of buildings around the edge of the block provides the public front to the development, with private or semi-private space in the block's interior. As the cross-sectional depth of building able to be naturally lit and ventilated is limited, so is the effective depth of the perimeter ribbon of building. Hence, as the dimensions of the block get larger, the size of the central space increases. Depending on its size, the central space can be used for various purposes — residents' car parking, private gardens, a communal garden for residents, a location for community or sports facilities, etc.

With a larger space within the block, larger perimeter blocks provide greater opportunities for biodiversity. Llewelyn Davies (2000: 58), for example, recommends that blocks of external dimensions of about 90 m × 90 m, containing private or communal gardens, provide a good trade-off between biodiversity and other considerations. Krier (1990), however, criticises larger perimeter blocks because they compete with the street and internalise (privatise) 'public' life (Figure 4.28).

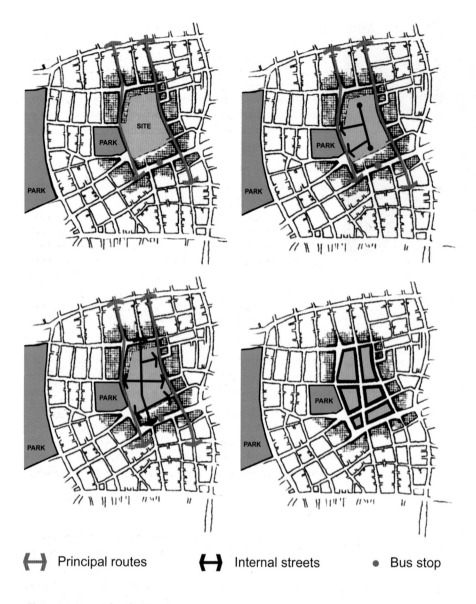

FIGURE 4.27   Block size *(Image: Lle-welyn-Davis 2000: 36)*. Block sizes can be established by considering existing linkages and connections, and by working within the grain of the local context. The diagrams start by showing how the site can be connected with nearby main routes and public transport facilities. The second diagram shows how cul-de-sac layouts create an introverted layout that fails to integrate with the surroundings. The third diagram suggests a more pedestrian-friendly approach that integrates with the surrounding context, linking existing and proposed streets. The street pattern then forms the basis for urban blocks — shown in the fourth diagram

⊢⊣ Principal routes   ⊢⊣ Internal streets   • Bus stop

Comparing Block Sizes

Compared to small block patterns, larger block structures may be more efficient in terms of the distribution of built form and open space because there is less circulation space. Research by Martin & March (1972) examined the densities and land use intensities of different development patterns, providing mathematical arguments both for larger block sizes and for perimeter rather than pavilion development. Looking at housing layouts in particular, they showed that, subject to certain environmental criteria, perimeter blocks had higher land use intensity than other built forms, such as pavilion or tower block forms.

Taking central Manhattan between Park and Eighth Avenue, and 42nd and 57th Streets as an example, Martin (1972: 21–2) showed how the same volume of development could be organised in radically different ways.

Imagining the whole area developed in the form of thirty-six-storey 'Seagram'-type buildings, he calculated the amount of floor space achieved. Replacing the Seagram buildings with perimeter blocks and enlarging the street block by omitting some of the cross streets, he showed the same amount of floor space could be accommodated in buildings eight storeys high. Furthermore, the spaces within the perimeter blocks would each be equivalent in area to Washington Square and there would be twenty-eight such spaces.

For Martin (1972: 22) this raised 'far-reaching questions' about the relationship between built form and open spaces. The open space provided in the Seagram building layout, for example, was in the form of a series of traffic corridors; in the perimeter block form, it was a series of traffic-free courts. Although this example provides support for larger, coarser and less permeable block

BOX 4.3 The Front-Back Distinction

Perimeter blocks, Paris (*Image: Matthew Carmona*)

The apparent choice between buildings-defining-space and freestanding object-buildings is more than one of aesthetic preference because the resultant space has different social characteristics. As Bentley (1999: 125) argues, the latter ignores 'socially-constructed' notions of front and back, which are vital in the relationship between public and private and in establishing conditions of privacy (see Chapter 8).

Development generally benefits from having a front onto public space (e.g. for entrances, social display, and the most public activities) and a back where the most private activities can go. In terms of layout, public fronts should face onto public space and other fronts, while private backs should face onto private space and other backs. As freestanding object-buildings are surrounded by public space, at least some public space has to be faced by backs:

'The privacy barriers, which are necessary in these situations, create increasing proportions of inactive, blank edges to public space — edges without windows or doors — as the transition from perimeter blocks to pavilions proceeds.'

(Bentley 1999: 184).

Though other development configurations are possible, recognition of the front-back distinction tends to lead to perimeter block development, which also has a number of other advantageous characteristics/features: explicit public and private sides; the capacity to accommodate different densities of development; and a public facade that both physically defines and addresses an urban space 'socially'. Most importantly, however, it produces (or results from) a connected street pattern.

structures (i.e. superblocks), it also demonstrates the need to consider the layout of the urban framework in three rather than two dimensions (i.e. possible configurations of urban form).

To examine the development and sustainability of urban patterns, particularly block sizes and circulation meshes, Siksna (1998) studied the CBDs of four American and four Australian cities (Figures 4.29 and 4.30). Laid out in the first half of the nineteenth century and before the onset of the automobile age, each city plan had had more than 150 years of growth and evolution.

Two interrelated aspects of the evolution of the block and street patterns are of particular interest — their persistence and the size of the circulation meshes.

- *Persistence of block and street pattern* — Demonstrating their durability in changing circumstances, the original block and street patterns of the small block cities (Portland and Seattle) were substantially intact. Although the original block and street patterns of the medium block cities (Chicago, Indianapolis, Melbourne and Brisbane) were largely intact, changes had occurred through the insertion/deletion of alleys and arcades — more so in

Melbourne and Brisbane. The original street patterns of the large block cities (Perth and Adelaide) were also largely intact, but the block and street pattern had changed considerably, with the original blocks having been broken down into smaller blocks with the street patterns altered significantly by insertion of alleys and arcades. In Adelaide all the blocks had been divided and typically contained four or five smaller blocks or subblocks. In Perth, they had been subdivided into two or three blocks. In both cities, the blocks now approached the dimensions of the blocks in the other cities.

- *Circulation mesh* — Regarding the area available for circulation, Siksna concluded a good proportion was one where circulation occupied 30–40% of the total area. All the American cities attained or exceeded this range in their initial layouts and needed few additional streets or alleyways. Those layouts where streets and alleys initially occupied less than 30% of the area needed additional routes, thereby demonstrating a lack of sufficient initial circulation space. By the same argument, layouts with small and medium blocks (i.e. where streets and alleys initially occupied more than

FIGURE 4.28   The Poundbury Block. Through his practice, Leon Krier has been credited with the design of a new urban block structure described by Biddulph (2007: 105) as the 'Poundbury Block' after the Poundbury development in Dorchester, where it can be found. Resembling earlier historic block structures containing mews courts, the model consists of medium-sized blocks with buildings lining the perimeter and facing on to a picturesque street environment. Behind these can be found parking courts linked to the street network to provide a series of secondary pedestrian routes. The courts have houses located within them and living spaces above garages facing onto the interiors to ensure they are well overlooked. The result is a highly permeable pedestrian network − though Biddulph (2007) questions the necessity to provide supplementary routes through areas that already have relatively small perimeter blocks, and the layout confuses the front-back principle

40% of the area) could be regarded as too generous. By inserting additional streets, alleys, arcades and other routes, most CBDs had developed fine-meshed pedestrian networks in their retail cores. Siksna concluded that circulation meshes of between 80 and 110 m was an optimal provision, though, in some cases, finer pedestrian meshes (from 50 to 70 m spacing) had emerged in intensively used retail blocks. Although the vehicular mesh of most cities had coarsened, cities with small blocks (Portland and Seattle) had retained a convenient mesh size (below 200 m), while in medium and large block cities the mesh size generally exceeded 300 m, which was considered inconvenient for local traffic movement.

As well as evolution towards optimum block sizes, Siksna concluded that incremental change generally overcame or, at least, reduced the deficiencies of the initial layout. Such changes also generally emerged through the initiative of individual or adjacent owners rather than through direct public intervention. The initial pattern had, nevertheless, played an instrumental role, with certain block forms and sizes proving either more robust or more amenable to adaptation over time.

STREETS AS PLACES

The final part of this chapter discusses the increasing desire to design streets as places. The terms streets, boulevards, avenues, etc., imply design elements lacking in the term 'road': rather than separation, they suggest accommodating and reconciling the demands of movement and social space within substantially the same physical space.

While some 'roads' will always be needed, many commentators advocate re-discovering 'streets' as both social space and as connecting − rather than dividing − elements within cities, emphasising the association of streets with quality of public life (Appleyard 1981; Moudon 1987; Hass-Klau 1990; Jacobs 1995; Loukaitou-Sideris & Banerjee 1998; Hass-Klau *et al* 1999; Banerjee 2001; Jacobs *et al* 2002). Similarly, a number of organisations have lobbied for road/street design to consider all users. Campaigning against streets designed only for speeding cars, for example, the US-based Complete Streets movement (see www.completestreets.org) advocates transportation planners and engineers designing and operating the entire roadway with all users in mind − including cyclists, public transportation vehicles and riders, and pedestrians of all ages and abilities (see also www.livingstreets.org.uk).

Noting how the downtowns of many Californian cities had been fragmented into a series of unrelated and spatially limited realms, Loukaitou-Sideris & Banerjee (1998: 304) argue that, rather than treating the street as a 'channel for efficient movement' (as in the Modernist era) or as an 'aesthetic visual element' (as in the City Beautiful era), contemporary urban design '... *should rediscover the social role of the street as a connector that stitches together and sometimes penetrates the disparate downtown realms.*' The diversity and choice that comes with this reflects the complexity of the traditional city, and is the opposite of tree-like simplicity. It is also a key tenet of sustainable urban design (see Sustainability Insert 1).

Sustainable urban design requires patterns of development able to accommodate and integrate the demands and needs of the various movement systems, while supporting social interaction and exchange. Despite tensions and conflicts between the public space network's role as movement space and its role as social space, there is also a need for a multi-purpose public space network, where social space and movement space are separated if absolutely necessary, but otherwise have considerable overlap (see Chapter 8).

Alexander (1965) uses the separation of pedestrians from moving vehicles as an exa!mple of what he terms a 'tree'-like organisational structure inherent in over-ordering of the built environment. He argues that, while this can be a good idea, it is not always a good idea and there are times when the 'ecology of a situation' demands the opposite. To illustrate his point, he uses the example of taxis, which can only function when pedestrians and

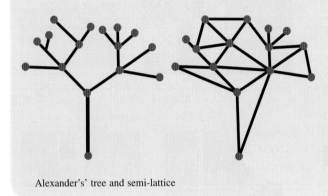
vehicles are not strictly separated: the 'prowling taxi' needs a fast stream of traffic so that it can cover a large area to be sure of finding a passenger; the pedestrian needs both to be able to hail the taxi from any point and, thereafter, be taken to any other point in the 'pedestrian world'. Thus, the taxi system must overlap with the vehicular traffic and the pedestrian circulation systems.

Designing for Cars or People

Writing about residential areas, Engwicht (1999) argues that:

'... *the more space a city devotes to movement, the more the exchange space becomes diluted and scattered. The more diluted and scattered the exchange opportunities, the more the city begins to lose the very thing that makes a city: a concentration of exchange opportunities.*'

(Engwicht, 1999: 19).

He suggests comparing streets with houses: the latter are designed to reduce movement space (corridors), while maximising exchange spaces (rooms). However, the combination of vehicular movement space and social space in the same physical space tends to cause a variety of problems. The first is simply that major urban roads provide obstructions to pedestrian movement, creating problems of severance and reducing connectivity. Though subways and

pedestrian bridges are often used to re-connect the areas either side, such measures often cause significant inconvenience to pedestrians. Many cities have now removed subways, replacing them with surface-level crossings. More dramatically, in Boston, severance was removed by burying an eight-lane highway in The Big Dig.

Another problem is that heavy traffic frustrates the social use of streets. In well-known research, Appleyard & Lintell (1972) compared three San Francisco streets, which, while similar in many ways, varied in the amounts of vehicular traffic and social use (Figure 4.31).

Related to this is how privileging vehicular movement often results in cars monopolising space: Sheller & Urry (2000: 745) contend that car travel 'rudely interrupts' the use of urban space by others '... *whose daily routines are merely obstacles to the high-speed traffic that cuts mercilessly through slower-moving pathways and dwellings.*' (Figure 4.32a and b). Similarly, Buchanan (1988: 32) complained that, often considered solely in terms of (vehicular) circulation, public space had lost its social function:

'*Even when formalised as streets, these are little more than voids ... They merely provide access and form boundaries between neat parcels of development in which all functions, even shopping, are located at some remove from the street, each as a distinct and separate destination.*'

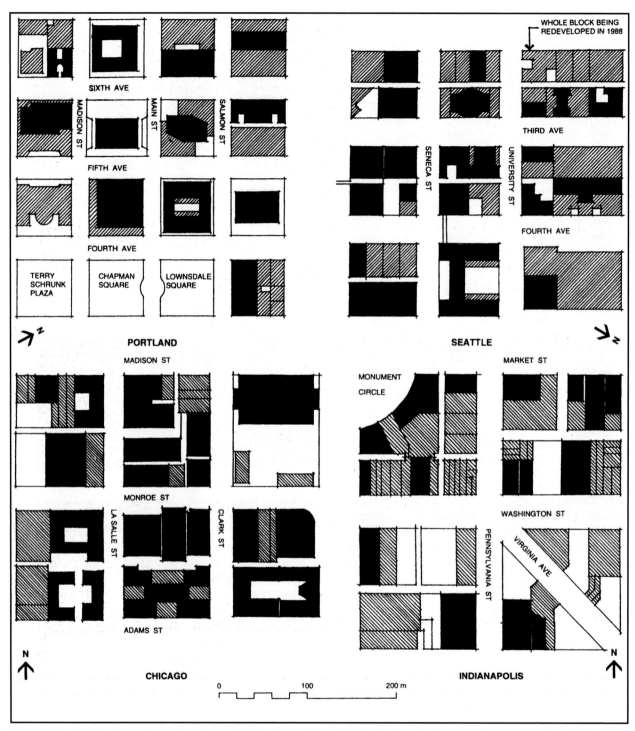

FIGURE 4.29   CBD block structures and sizes in four US cities *(Image: Siksna 1998)*. Portland and Seattle are small square and rectangular block cities. Chicago and Indianapolis are medium square block cities

But these 'problems' are not inevitable, and different design approaches and priorities can achieve different outcomes. Before those different design approaches can be employed, however, a change of attitudes and approaches is required among key actors and decision-makers, especially highway engineers and politicians. Road engineers have sometimes been likened to religious fundamentalists: if it isn't in the manual, then it can't be done because children will die. The safety claims of road designers are, however, increasingly questioned (Noland 2000; Jones 2003).

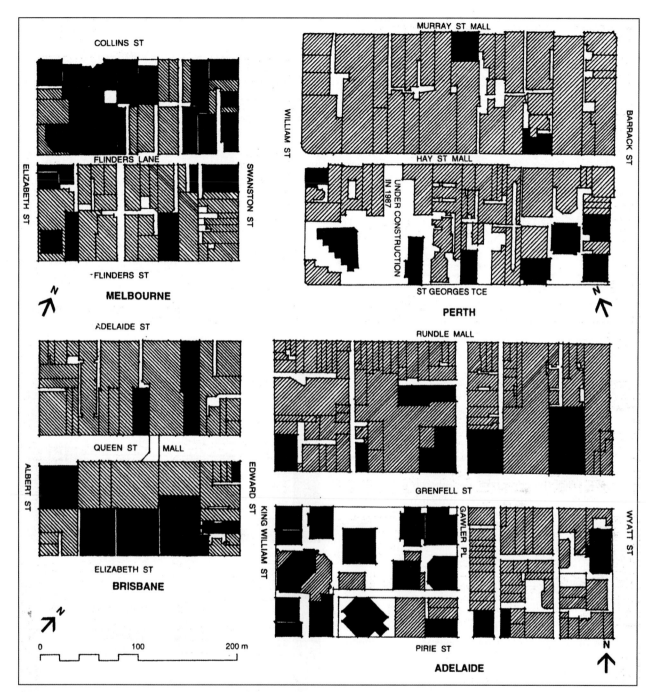

FIGURE 4.30   CBD block structures and sizes in four Australian cities *(Image: Siksna 1998).* Melbourne and Brisbane are medium rectangular block cities. Perth and Adelaide are large rectangular block cities

In part the challenge is one of changing entrenched, institutional practices (see Hess 2009) and encouraging highway engineers to break free from the rule books, to exercise discretion and to design in-the-round, relating generally desirable principles to particular contexts and by focusing on the whole rather than the part. The drive for more enlightened road/street design and thus better places

is ongoing. For Hebbert (2005), it is a 'struggle for street design', while Jacobs *et al* (2002: 92) sound a note of pessimism:

'*... many design and planning professionals and social theorists have argued that it is time to rethink the concept of vehicle and pedestrian separation ... Yet overwhelmingly the voices of separateness continue to rule in regard to roadway location, size and*

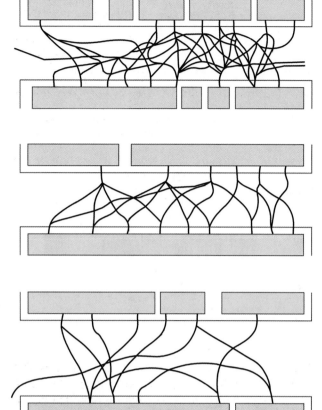

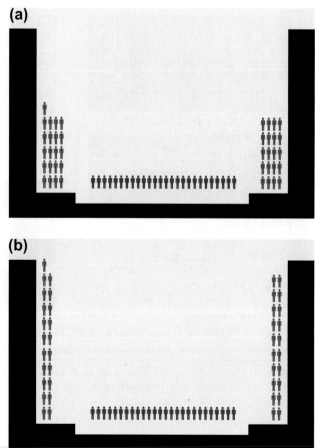

the CNU's assistance — encourages engineers to make fuller use of the discretion available to them.

In the UK, *Places, Streets and Movement* (DETR 1998), based on Alan Baxter's pioneering work with innovative street layouts at Poundbury, sought to modify the standard hierarchical model through professional discretion based on contextual evidence and public consultation. As Hebbert (2005: 54–5) explains, it '... *asks the engineer to be an urban design participant and fit roads to the space formed by building fronts, instead of requiring development to fit a pre-ordained, rule-based road pattern.*' In England, a new generation of guidance is exemplified by the publication of a new *Manual for Streets* (DfT 2007). Recognising that streets encompass more than their movement function and also have a place function, the manual encourages highway engineers to design-in-the-round and to '... *break away from previous approaches to hierarchy, whereby street*

FIGURE 4.31   Social life and traffic loads. Comparing three San Francisco streets that varied in the amount of traffic travelling along them, Appleyard & Lintell (1972) found that, on the heavily trafficked street, people tended to use the sidewalk only as a pathway between home and final destination. On the lightly trafficked street, there was an active social life: people used the sidewalks and the corner stores as places to meet and initiate interaction. The high-volume street was also seen as a less friendly place to live than the lightly trafficked street

design in favour of separate uses, separate lanes, separate functions, separateness.'

It is only relatively recently that calls for place-making and design-in-the-round have gained leverage on orthodox engineering priorities. In Germany, for example, Hebbert (2005: 51) describes how, under permissive federal guidelines introduced in 1985:

'... *engineers could abandon some or all of their conventional requirements in terms of visibility splays, corner geometry and signage, opening the way to forms of interaction in which the environment "speaks" to the driver through surface materials, building enclosure, on-street parking, trees and shrubs, art and decoration. ... the aim of such approaches is to achieve speed reduction and attentive driving through an enhanced sense-of-place and locality.*'

Similarly, in the USA, the Federal Highways Administration's Context Sensitive Design initiative — developed with

FIGURE 4.32   (a and b) William H. Whyte's studies of pedestrian and vehicle flow rates and movement space in central New York. In diagram (a), 26 000 people travel in cars on a road 50 feet wide and 41 000 people travel on sidewalks that are 13 feet wide on each side of the street. Because the sidewalk is cluttered the effective space for pedestrian movement is six feet each side of the street. Thus, as shown in diagram (b) 41 000 people travel on sidewalks only six feet wide

FIGURE 4.33 Social and movement emphasis of streets *(Image: DfT 2007).* *Manual for Streets* (DfT 2007) promotes a place and movement matrix, which defines, for different situations, the relative importance of these functions: a motorway (freeway) has a high movement function and a low place function; a residential street has the opposite, and is primarily a place where movement should be subservient. A high street (main street) lies somewhere in between, with a medium movement function and a high place function

designs were only based on traffic considerations.' (DfT 2007: 19) (Figure 4.33).

From Arterial Roads to Streets and Boulevards

Cities around the world have sought to change the character of urban roads — and to re-discover them as 'streets', 'avenues' and 'boulevards', and to re-conceive them as connectors rather than dividers. As noted previously, transport infrastructure can be a powerful generator of urban form. There is, however, a highly significant difference between a road-based armature and a street- or boulevard-based armature: roads promote a discontinuous urbanisation with points of concentration where cars can stop and park; pedestrian-friendly streets promote a more continuous urbanisation.

Bonamoni (1990: 63–6, in Hebbert 2005: 50) advocates a shift in engineering practice, with main roads again becoming boulevards and avenues:

'In the town a road is not a route, it's a polyvalent space. The town has to run alongside the highway. Every object speaks to the motorist. Bitumen, white markings, standard signs say car and indicate that it's the motorist in charge. But trees, pavements, row parking, non-bituminous paving material and such-like elements of urban vocabulary say town, pedestrians. The motorist no longer feels that he's on conquered territory, he slows down and becomes attentive to urban life.'

A key source of precedents and examples for this is a pair of books authored by Allen Jacobs. In *Great Streets*

(1995), the key observation and demonstration is that many of most loved urban streets manage to safely accommodate both high traffic volumes and high pedestrian flows, without need for undue separation, while still maintaining strong place character. Rome's Via del Guibbonari, London's Regent Street, the Champs Élysées in Paris and New York's Fifth Avenue are all cases in point where the highway design rule books would make building such places impossible today.

In *The Boulevard Book* (Jacobs *et al* 2002: 206), the authors challenge the hierarchical paradigm and propose an alternative, '... *one that maintains access and multi-functionality at all street scales.'* They focus on a particular type of a great street — the multi-way thoroughfare. With parallel roadways serving distinctly different traffic functions, the multi-way thoroughfare addresses the functional problems posed by the co-existence of through-movement and access to land uses abutting major urban streets. The central lanes carry non-local through-traffic, while, separated by medians, the side lanes carry local traffic. Tree-lined median strips serve both to modulate the scale of the street and narrow its apparent width, while also providing additional pedestrian areas. Most of the road surface might be equivalent to a typical American commercial strip, but what is different are the layers at the edge of the road — the local lanes, the sidewalks and trees — which make it a multi-lane boulevard. The building frontages, medians and trees enable it to function not only as a through-traffic route but also a space for sitting, driving, parking and delivering, cycling, and public transport, adding tremendous value to local real estate.

Around the world cities are seeking to change the character of urban roads. Toronto, for example, has an 'arterial road to boulevards' programme (Hess 2009). In New York, the Westway and West Side Highway have been replaced with a ground-level urban boulevard. In San Francisco, the elevated Hayes Valley section of the earthquake-damaged Central Freeway has been replaced by the ground-level multi-lane Octavia Boulevard. Once simply fenced-off land beneath the elevated US Route 101, the new boulevard has four central lanes, two in each direction, separated by a median strip with elm trees and low shrubs. On either side of these — buffered by a median strip with poplar trees and more shrubs — are local lanes for neighbourhood traffic, with homes and businesses fronting directly onto them. Another freeway-removal project in the city involved rebuilding earthquake-damaged Embarcadero Freeway as a much more accessible tree-lined boulevard involving light rail and pedestrian and cycle space, with a new public space in front of the Ferry Building at the foot of Market Street. Peter Calthorpe has also explored the use of multi-lane thoroughfares in new developments (see Dunham-Jones & Williamson 2009).

In the UK, Birmingham, the first city to complete a 50-mile per hour ring and radial motorway system, was also among the first to dismantle its flyovers and underpasses, to replace free-flow intersections with light-controlled crossroads and to reinstate pedestrian flows at street level (Hebbert 2005: 49) (Figure 4.34a and b). Similar actions are happening in many European cities (Figure 4.35).

Shared Spaces

At the more local level, careful design is required to reconcile and integrate the needs and demands of different forms of movement: protecting social space from the impacts of cars and creating areas that, while accessible by cars, are pedestrian-dominant (see Moudon 1987; Hass-Klau 1990; Southworth & Ben-Joseph 1997). Such ideas are epitomised by the concepts of 'shared space'. Based on consultation with users, shared space aims to accommodate pedestrian activity and vehicular movement on a single shared surface. The concept is also based on Hans Monderman's argument that behaviour in traffic is more positively affected by the design of the built environment than by conventional traffic control devices and regulations. Thus, by its design, shared space encourages negotiation of shared areas at appropriate speeds and with due consideration for the other users.

Shared space typically involves replacing conventional road priority management systems and devices (kerbs, lines, signs, signals, etc.) and the segregation of vehicles,

FIGURE 4.34 Birmingham, UK *(Images: Steve Tiesdell)*. As an explicit strategy of 'breaking the concrete collar' of the inner ring-road and making a more pedestrian-friendly environment, a section of Birmingham's inner ring-road was lowered and a wide pedestrian bridge created to link the existing city centre with a new public space at Centenary Square

FIGURE 4.35 Champs Élysée, Paris *(Image: Matthew Carmona)*. The footway of the Champs Élysées has been widened from 12 to 24 m, kiosks and clutter have been removed to ensure the pedestrian a clear line of vision, and the public realm has been refurbished

pedestrians, cyclists and other road users, with an integrated, people-oriented understanding of public space, such that walking, cycling, and driving cars become integrated activities. Examples include '*woonerfs*' and Home Zones (Biddulph 2001). In the late 1960s, Niek De Boer, a professor at Delft University of Technology, designed streets so that '… *motorists would feel as if they were driving in a "garden" setting, forcing drivers to consider other road users.*' (Southworth & Ben-Joseph 1997: 112). De Boer named his innovation *woonerfs* ('living street').

The keys to shared space are lower design speeds for cars and more attentive drivers: as Duany *et al* (2000: 160) argue: '… *the solution is not the removal of cars from the city — far from it. The most vital American public spaces are full of cars. But those cars move slowly, due to the appropriate design of the thoroughfares.*' Well-engineered, modern roads designed according to the rule book seem, somewhat paradoxically, to encourage higher speeds and less attentive drivers: as Hebbert (2005: 53) argues:

'*Linear safety devices such as white lines, crash barriers and pedestrian guard rails combine in the driver's visual field into a race-track. … The standardised carriageway with its consistent geometrical configuration increases motorists' sense of comfort and reduces their level of caution.*'

The shared street concept thus establishes a pedestrian orientation by giving pedestrians primary rights, having lower design speeds (which, *inter alia*, widen the driver's lateral vision and shorten the braking response distance) and a design character that makes the driver feel like an intruder — sensing they are intruding into a pedestrian zone, motorists are more attentive and drive more cautiously (Figure 4.36).

Shared space schemes have developed considerably in recent years. At the most elementary level, as Pharoah (2008) observes, perhaps 90% of urban streets have a recognisable carriageway flanked by footways either side. Sometimes pedestrian and road users are separated by kerbs and barriers — 'hard separation' — though increasingly by designs demarking pavements (perhaps through colour) without changes in level — 'soft separation'. At a more sophisticated level of design, shared space is where vehicles and pedestrians share the same surface without demarking boundaries.

No longer limited to low-traffic residential streets, shared space concepts are being applied to high-traffic commercial areas. In Friesland (Netherlands) and Chambery (France), for example, the concept has been applied to junctions carrying in excess of 20 000 vehicles a day and where '… *all indications of priority including traffic lights, white lines and signs are removed, and instead both pedestrians and drivers use eye contact to negotiate who goes first.*' (Pharoah 2008: 17). In all such cases the key is

FIGURE 4.36 Shared space — London *(Image: Matthew Carmona)*. Rather than assuming the driver needs a behavioural environment of complete predictability, degrees of uncertainty are used to stimulate driver alertness: the absence of priority signs and kerbs, and the surface patterning signal crawling speeds to drivers, while building fronts are grouped to form 'places' with restricted visibility where drivers will reduce speed without need for overt controls. As Stemmet (2002) advocates, the engineer becomes a 'key enabler' in this process of holistic urban design

reducing vehicle speed by designing roads so that drivers sense that caution is required and the need to drive with greater care and consideration. The needs of users with impaired sight need careful consideration, however, and increasingly, some form of protected footway is being integrated into shared surface schemes. Other conflicts arise because, for example, older people do not hear cyclists.

It is also notable that shared space schemes have developed more rapidly in some countries than in others, which may, in part, be due to the system of legal liability. In most English-speaking countries, for example, a fault liability system operates, whereby the one who is at fault pays compensation for losses due to road traffic collisions. By contrast, other countries use a risk liability system. Where a conflict occurs between a motor vehicle and a vulnerable road user, there is a legal assumption that motorists are liable, regardless of fault, for injuries and property damage suffered by cyclists or pedestrians.

CONCLUSION

This chapter has discussed urban design's morphological dimension, focusing on urban form and urban layout and highlighting contemporary preferences for urban block and interconnected street patterns. In essence, it has focused on the public space network and the physical public realm — the physical setting or stage for public life. Underpinning this discussion is one of the critical tensions at the heart of contemporary urban design: the conflicts, complexity and, of course, synergies between the need for movement and space required for social and economic exchange and everyday life. As Jan Gehl has long argued, urban design priorities should be 'life' first, then 'space', then 'building'. The physical structure will be determined by the types of activity envisaged for the space when it is designed; from then on, it will limit them. Getting the shape and structure of the urban morphology right in the first place is thus crucial if the spaces created are to be robust and adaptable, and able to cope with both movement and activity.

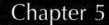
The Perceptual Dimension

Awareness and appreciation of environmental perception and, in particular, the perception and experience of 'place' is an essential dimension of urban design. Since the 1960s, an interdisciplinary field of environmental perception has gratually developed. While the initial work examined environmental images, this work has been supplemented by work on symbolism and meaning in the built environment. More generally, the interest in environmental perception has been reinforced by a body of work focusing on the experiential 'sense of place' — which, in turn, is associated with place image and synonymous with place identity.

This chapter is in three main parts. The first part discusses environmental perception. The second part discusses the construction of place in terms of place identity, sense of place and placelessness. The third part discusses place differentiation and place-theming.

ENVIRONMENTAL PERCEPTION

We affect the environment and are affected by it. For this interaction to occur, we must *perceive* — that is, be stimulated by sight, sound, smell or tactile information, which offer clues about the world around us (Bell *et al* 1990: 27). Perception involves gathering, organising and making sense of information about the environment. A distinction is generally made between two processes that gather and interpret environmental stimuli — 'sensation' and 'perception'. These are not discrete processes and, in practice, it is not clear where sensation ends and perception begins.

Sensation refers to the simple biological experiences elicited by environmental stimuli (i.e. human sensory systems reacting to individual sounds or a flash of light). The four most valuable senses in interpreting and sensing the environments are vision; hearing; smell; and touch. These are not the only senses, however. We also have senses of heat, balance and pain, for example.

- *Vision* — The dominant sense, vision provides more information than the other senses combined. Orientation in space is achieved visually. As Porteous (1996: 3) observes, vision is active and searching: '*We look; smells and sounds come to us.*' Visual perception is also a highly complex phenomenon and relies on space, distance, colour, shape, textural and contrast gradients, etc.

- *Hearing* — While visual space is sectoral — our arc of vision involves only what lies before us — 'acoustic' space is all-surrounding, has no obvious boundaries, and, in contrast to vision, emphasises space rather than objects in space (Porteous 1996: 33). While vision is information-rich, hearing is information-poor. Hearing is, nevertheless, emotionally rich — screams, music, thunder arouse us; the flow of water or the wind in the leaves soothes us (Porteous 1996: 35).
- *Smell* — As with hearing, the human sense of smell is not well developed. Nevertheless, while even more information-poor than sound, smell is emotionally richer than sound.
- *Touch* — Much of our experience of texture comes through our feet and through our buttocks when we sit down rather than through our hands (Porteous 1996: 36).

These sensory stimuli are usually perceived and appreciated as an interconnected whole. The individual dimensions can only be separated by deliberate action (i.e. closing one's eyes, blocking one's nose or ears) or by employing selective attention. Vision is the dominant sense, but the urban environment is not only perceived visually — sounds, smells, touch and movement are also essential dimensions of our perception of the environment. Bacon (1992: 20), for example, argued that the 'changing visual picture' was:

'*... only the beginning of the sensory experience; the changes from light to shade, from hot to cold, from noise to silence, the flow of smells associated with open spaces, and the tactile quality of the surface under foot, are all important in the cumulative effect.*'

Although contributing to the richness of the experience, these non-visual dimensions of the sensation and perception are often underdeveloped and underexploited, and an emerging literature focuses on the design of multi-sensory environments.

Lang (1994: 226–7) argues that, rather than focusing on removing the negative, concern for the 'sonic environment' should — in specific settings — also focus on increasing the positive, such as birdsong, children's voices and the crunching of autumn leaves. He argues that an environment's 'soundscape' '*... can be orchestrated in much the same way as its visual qualities by the choice of materials* *used for the surfaces of the environment and the nature of objects within it.'* (Lang 1994: 227). In particular, positive sounds − waterfalls, fountains, etc. − can mask negative sounds like traffic noise.

Perception (sometimes confusingly referred to as 'cognition') concerns more than just seeing or sensing the urban environment, however, and refers to the more complex processing or understanding of stimuli. Ittelson (1978, from Bell *et al* 1994: 29) identifies four types or dimensions of perception, each operating simultaneously:

- *Cognitive* − involves the thinking about, organising and keeping of information about the environment. In essence, it enables us to *make sense* of the environment.
- *Affective* − involves our feelings, which − in turn − influence our perception of the environment; equally, our perception of the environment influences our feelings.
- *Interpretative* − encompasses the meaning or associations derived from the environment. In actively processing information, we rely on memory of past stimulation for comparison with newly experienced stimuli.
- *Evaluative* − incorporates values and preferences and the determination of 'good' or 'bad' elements in the environment.

Rather than simply a biological process, perception is socially and culturally learnt. While sensations may be similar for everyone, individuals filter, react to, organise and value those sensations differently. Differences in environmental perception can be attributed to a number of factors − age, gender, ethnicity, lifestyle, length of residence in an area, usual travel mode − but also to the physical, social and cultural environments in which we live and were raised. Thus, despite everyone effectively living in their 'own world', because of similarities in their socialisation, past experience and the present urban environment, certain aspects of imagery will be held in common by large groups of people (Knox & Pinch 2000: 295). Mental 'maps' and images of places and environments, particularly shared or common images, are therefore a central part of studies of environmental perception in urban design.

Place Images

The 'environment' can be considered as a mental construct − an environmental image, created and valued differently by each individual. Images are the result of processes through which personal experiences and values filter the barrage of environmental stimuli. For Lynch (1960: 6), for example, environmental images were the result of a two-way process between the observer and the environment: the environment suggested distinctions and

relations, from which observers selected, organised and endowed with meaning what they saw. Similarly, Montgomery (1998: 100) distinguishes between 'identity' and 'image'. *Place identity* could be understood as what a place is actually like, but, more precisely, it relates to the common elements of beholders' individual place images. While it resides substantially (but not entirely) in the place itself, it cannot be taken as a 'given' nor simply 'read off' because place identities are socially constructed; they are produced and reproduced as a communication process, evolving and adapting over time. Place images and identities are often contested, with a power struggle regarding whose images are dominant: places thus rarely have a single place identity and, instead, there are multiple, possibly divergent place identities.

To make sense of their surroundings, people reduce 'reality' to a few selective impressions − that is, they produce *place images*. Such images are *partial* (not covering the whole place); *simplified* (omitting much information); *idiosyncratic* (each individual's place image is unique); and *distorted* (based on subjective, rather than real, distance and direction) (Pocock & Hudson 1978: 33). Image is thus a combination of place identity and how the place is perceived by the individual (i.e. it includes that individual's set of feelings about and impressions of the place).

Physical and visual distinctiveness aid the creation of place images and identities. Kevin Lynch, for example, discussed 'imageability' − the likelihood of a place creating a strong image in the mind of the beholder. Although place images form in the mind of the beholder, they are not created in a vacuum and, instead, draw upon and filter external stimuli. In short, they are based on real places, albeit in a partial and simplified manner. The place itself is not the only source of stimuli, however − place images are informed by received information about the place (e.g. its reputation, its media coverage, stories and anecdotes heard). Furthermore, as Relph (1976: 106) observes, place images are '*... not just selective abstractions of an objective reality but are intentional interpretations of what is or what is not believed to be.*' As is discussed below, this is the basis of intentionality and phenomenology.

Based on cognitive (mental) mapping techniques and interviews with residents of Boston, Jersey City and Los Angeles, Lynch's *The Image of the City* (1960) was a key initial work in the field of urban imagery. Rather than image, Lynch had initially been interested in legibility − that is, how people orientated themselves and navigated within cities. Lynch argued that the ease with which we could mentally organise the environment into a coherent pattern or 'image' was related to our ability to navigate through it − a quality he referred to as 'legibility'. A clear image enables one to 'move about easily and quickly', while an 'ordered environment' can '*... serve as a broad* *frame of reference, an organiser of activity or belief or knowledge.'* (Lynch 1960: 4).

Through his research, Lynch found the minor theme of orientation through legibility grew into the major theme of the city's mental image. Observing that cities had districts, landmarks and paths that were easily identifiable and easily grouped into an overall pattern lead to what he called 'imageability': *'... that quality in a physical object which gives it a high probability of evoking a strong image in any given observer.'* (Lynch 1960: 9). Accepting that images could vary significantly between different observers, in his research Lynch sought to identify a public or city image.

Lynch (1960: 8) argued that 'workable' environmental images required three attributes:

- *Identity* — an object's distinction from other things and its recognition as a separable entity (e.g. a door).
- *Structure* — the object's spatial relation to the observer and to other objects (the door's position).
- *Meaning* — the object must have some meaning for the observer, whether practical or emotional (recognition of a 'door' as a hole for getting out).

Recognising that meaning was less likely to be consistent at the city level and across disparate groups of people than were perceptions of identity and structure, Lynch's study separated meaning from form, with imageability being explored in terms of the physical qualities relating to identity and structure.

Through mental mapping — cognitive geography — exercises, Lynch aimed to identify those aspects of the environment that left a strong image in the observer's mind. Aggregating individual images would discern a public or city image. From his research, Lynch derived five key physical elements — paths, edges, districts, nodes and landmarks (see Table 5.1). None of Lynch's element types exists in isolation; they combine to provide the overall image: *'... districts are structured with nodes, defined by edges, penetrated by paths, and sprinkled with landmarks ... elements regularly overlap and pierce one another.'* (Lynch 1960: 48–9).

Lynch's study also indicated that there may not be a single comprehensive image for the entire environment, and that sets of images often overlap and interrelate. Images, for example, are often arranged in a series of levels reflecting the scale of the area. Observers move as necessary from an image at street level to those of the neighbourhood, the city and beyond.

Beyond *the Image of the City*

Lynch's original study and its method have been replicated in various contexts. Lynch (1984: 249) contended that in 'every case' the basic ideas had held, *'... with the important proviso that images are much modified by culture and familiarity.'* He noted that the existence of the basic elements of the city image *'... seem astonishingly similar in some very diverse cultures and places. We were lucky.'* (Lynch 1984: 249).

From various studies in the Lynch tradition, there is a wealth of information about the way different groups in different places structure their city images. De Jonge (1962), for example, found Amsterdam was more legible to its inhabitants than were Rotterdam and The Hague to theirs. Comparing Milan and Rome, Francescato & Mebane (1973) found that, while both cities were highly legible, they were legible in different ways. The mental maps of the Milanese were structured by a clearly connected set of paths relating to their city's radial street pattern, whereas Romans' mental maps exhibited a greater diversity of content and were structured around landmarks and edges associated with the city's historic buildings, its hills and the River Tiber.

Nevertheless, some of the work following on from Lynch was highly critical of his findings and his methods — though, to some extent, this is unfair because Lynch had explicitly offered it as a 'first initial sketch'. Three areas of criticism are of note:

(i) Observer variation

The validity of aggregating the environmental images of people with different backgrounds and experience has been questioned. While finding that common city images could be identified, arising from common human strategies of cognition, culture, experience and city form, Lynch (1984: 251) acknowledged his 'deliberate and explicit' neglect of observer variation in his original study. Francescato & Mebane's study of Milan and Rome (1973) and Appleyard's study of Ciudad Guyana (1976), for example, each showed how factors such as social class and habitual use caused people's city images to differ.

(ii) Legibility and imageability

In *Good City Form*, Lynch (1981: 139–41) reduced the emphasis on legibility, seeing it as one kind of 'sense' that was just one dimension of city experience. Further downplaying its significance in a 1984 article, 'Reconsidering *The Image of the City*', he accepted that way-finding was a 'secondary problem for most people' — *'If lost in a city, one can always ask the way or consult a map'* — and questioned the value of legible environments: *'What do people care if they have a vivid image of their locality? And aren't they delighted by surprise and mystery.'* (Lynch 1984: 250). This raised an important distinction between imageable environments — that is, memorable and legible — and liked environments. De Jonge's study in Holland suggested people liked 'illegible' environments, while Kaplan & Kaplan

TABLE 5.1 Lynch's Five Elements

Paths

Champs Élysées, Paris (*Image: Steve Tiesdell*). Certain paths are significant in supporting clear mental maps of cities or parts of cities.

These are channels along which observers move — streets, walkways, transit lines, canals, etc. Lynch noted that paths were often the predominant elements in people's image with the other elements being arranged and related along paths. Where major paths lacked identity or were easily confused with each other, the whole image would be less clear. Paths could be important features in city images for several reasons including regular use, concentration of special uses, characteristic spatial qualities, facade characteristics, proximity to special features in the city, visual prominence and dominance, or by virtue of their position in the overall path structure.

Edges

Weymouth, England (*Image: Matthew Carmona*). The sea edge is a powerful organising element for coastal towns and cities.

These are linear elements either not used or considered by observers as paths, and often forming boundaries between areas or linear breaks in continuity (e.g. shores, railroad cuts, edges of development, walls, etc.). As Lynch (1960: 47) notes: '… *edges may be barriers, more or less penetrable, which close one region off from another; or they may be seams, lines along which two regions are related and joined together.*' The strongest edges are visually prominent, but also continuous in form and often impenetrable to cross-movement. Nonetheless, while continuity and visibility are important, strong edges need not be impenetrable. Edges are important organising features, particularly when they perform the role of holding together generalised areas, as in the outline of a city by water or a wall. Many cities have clearly identified edges. Istanbul's image, for example, is structured by the River Bosphorus, which forms an edge for both the European and Asian sides of the city. Water gives a distinctive edge to cities located on coasts — Istanbul, Hong Kong, Stockholm, etc. — and along rivers — Paris, London, Budapest, Vienna, Prague, etc.

(Continued)

TABLE 5.1 Lynch's Five Elements—cont'd

Districts	 Manchester's Gay Village (*Image: Mathew Carmona*) has developed a clear identity distinct from surrounding districts.	These are the medium-to-large areas, which observers mentally enter 'inside of', and/or have some common identifying character. Distinctive physical characteristics might include 'thematic continuities', such as texture, space, form, detail, symbol, building type, uses, activities, inhabitants, degree of maintenance, and/or topography. Given some distinctive elements, there may not be enough for a 'full thematic unit' — the district only being recognisable to someone already familiar with the city — and reinforcement of clues may be needed to produce a stronger image. Some districts may have hard and precise boundaries, while others might have soft or uncertain boundaries. A district might, for example, possess no clear edges, with its distinct qualities gradually fading away into surrounding areas.
Nodes	 New York's Times Square (*Image: Matthew Carmona*). The crossing of routes through the centre and the concentration of activity make this a key node in the city.	These are point references: '... *the strategic spots in a city into which an observer can enter, and which are the intensive foci to and from which [s/he] is travelling.*' (Lynch, 1960: 47). Nodes may be primarily junctions, or simply 'thematic concentrations' of a particular use or physical character. As decisions are made and attention heightened, junctions can be significant. The most dominant nodes are often 'concentrations' and 'junctions', with both functional and physical significance. While not essential, distinctive physical form is likely to make the node more memorable (Lynch 1960: 72–6).

(Continued)

TABLE 5.1 Lynch's Five Elements—cont'd

Landmarks

Grand Arch, La Defense, Paris (*Image: Steve Tiesdell*).
A powerful local and city-wide landmark.

These are other types of point references, which, in contrast to nodes, are external to the observer. Some landmarks — towers, spires, hills — are distant and are typically seen from many angles and from distances, over the tops of smaller elements. Other landmarks — sculpture, signs, trees — are primarily local, being visible only in restricted localities and from certain approaches. As landmarks with a clear form contrasting with their background and a prominent spatial location are more easily identifiable, they are more likely to be chosen as significant by the observer. Lynch (1960: 78–9) argued that a landmark's key physical characteristic was 'singularity': '... *some aspect that is unique or memorable in the context.*' He also noted that 'spatial prominence' could establish some elements as landmarks by, for example, making the element visible from many locations and/or by creating a local contrast with nearby elements. How an environment is used may also strengthen a landmark's significance through, for example, its location at a junction involving path decisions or because of a particular activity associated with it.

(1982) highlighted the need and value of 'surprise' and 'mystery' in environments. Based on an environmental preference framework relating issues of 'making sense' (order) and 'involvement' or engagement (complexity) with a time dimension (Figure 5.1), they argue that making sense of environments is not sufficient and that, over time, we also seek opportunities to expand our horizons — that is, we seek and cherish the potential for involvement and engagement.

(iii) Meaning and symbolism

While Lynch focused on the structure of people's mental images, others argued more attention needed to be paid to the 'meaning' and 'affective' dimensions of environmental perception — what the urban environment meant to people and how they felt about it. Cognitive mapping techniques tend to neglect these issues. Appleyard (1980) extended Lynch's work by identifying four ways in which buildings and other urban elements were known:

- By their imageability or distinctiveness of form;
- By their visibility as people move around the city;
- By their role as a setting for activity; and
- By the significance of their role in society.

Gottdiener & Langopoulos (1986: 7) argued that, in the Lynchian tradition, 'signification' — the process by which places, people and things are given representational meaning — is reduced to a perceptual knowledge of physical form, with other aspects of the environment, such as the 'meaning' of an environment and whether people liked it, being neglected. Environments could be memorable or forgettable, liked or disliked, meaningful or not, but Lynch's method tended only to record the first options.

Although he had sought to set aside meaning, Lynch (1984: 252) considered it had 'always' crept in because '... *people could not help connecting their surroundings with the rest of their lives.*' The conclusion drawn was that the social and emotional meanings attached to, or evoked by, the elements of the urban environment were at least as

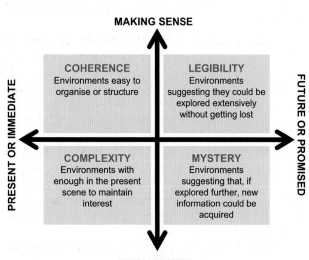

FIGURE 5.1 Environmental preference framework (*Image: adapted from Kaplan & Kaplan 1982: 81*). Kaplan & Kaplan (1982: 82–7) suggest 'coherence', 'legibility', 'complexity' and 'mystery' as informational qualities of environments that contribute to people's preferences for particular physical environments. For immediate appreciation of environments, understanding is supported by environmental coherence (to make sense) and complexity (to encourage involvement). In the longer term, legibility and mystery encourage further exploration

important — and often more so — than the structural and physical aspects of people's imagery — that is, not only what people perceive as being *where* but also how they *feel* about those different elements (Knox & Pinch 2000: 302).

Environmental Meaning and Symbolism

All urban environments — or 'landscapes' — are repositories of symbols, meanings and values. The study of 'signs' and their meanings is known as 'semiology' or 'semiotics'. As Eco (1968: 56–7) explains, semiotics studies '… *all cultural phenomena as if they were systems of signs.*' The argument is that the world is replete with 'signs', which can be interpreted and understood as a function of society, culture and ideology. Following Ferdinand de Saussure, the process of creating meaning is called 'signification': 'signifieds' are what are referred to; 'signifiers' are the things that refer to them; the 'sign' is the association or relationship established between them. A sign stands in for or represents something else — thus, in a language a word stands for a concept. Different types of sign are usually identified:

- *Iconic signs* — have a direct similarity with the object (e.g. a painting).
- *Indexical signs* — have a material relationship with the object (e.g. smoke signifying fire).
- *Symbolic signs* — have a more arbitrary relationship with the object and are essentially constructed through social and cultural systems (e.g. classical columns representing grandeur) (from Lane 2000: 111).

Just as the words of a formally codified language have agreed-upon meanings, the meanings of non-verbal signs arise from social and cultural conventions. There is greater flexibility, however, to interpret the latter. As society changes, so does signification: meanings attached or attributed to the built environment are modified as social values change in response to changing patterns of socio-economic organisation and lifestyles (Knox 1984: 112).

A key idea in semiotics is layering of meaning. The first layer or 'first-order' sign is that of *denotation*, meaning the object's 'primary function' or the function it makes possible (Eco 1968). The 'second-order' sign — or 'secondary function' — is that of *connotation* and is of a symbolic nature. Layering allows distinctions to be made between the use of objects for immediate function and their second-order, connotative (symbolic) meaning. If made of Italian marble with Doric columns, for example, a porch — primary function: providing shelter from the weather — connotes a different 'symbolic function' or meaning from one made of roughly sawn timber and a wood slat roof (Figure 5.2).

Eco (1968: 64) shows how the secondary function can be more important than the primary function: a chair typically denotes the function of being able to sit down,

FIGURE 5.2 Lakelands, Maryland, USA (*Image: Steve Tiesdell*). In addition to their primary function of providing shelter, porches can connote 'community' or 'sociability'. Contending that New Urbanist developments are based on a 'past ideal of community', Huxtable (1997: 42) argues that by reducing '… *the definition of community to a romantic social aesthetic emphasising front porches … they have avoided the questions of urbanisation to become part of the problem.*' Nevertheless, while the porches may symbolise or connote 'community', they also have a practical function (use value) that may assist the creation of contacts between neighbours (see Chapter 6)

but, when it is a throne, it should be sat on with a certain dignity. The connotation can become so functionally important as to distort the basic function — in connoting 'regalness', a throne '… *often demands that the person sitting on it sit rigidly and uncomfortably … and therefore seats one "poorly" with respect to the primary utilitas.*' (Eco 1968: 64).

The second-order meaning also provides the means to differentiate between objects. As Gottdiener (2001: 41) notes: '*Producers of consumer goods that are very similar or identical use signs and symbolic appeals to differentiate their products.*' Commodities consist of more than their material qualities; we also consume the 'idea' of them and what they will allow us to become. The idea of the commodity can become more important than the commodity itself — rather than selling houses, for example, developers sell images of desirable lifestyles (see Dovey, 1999). Economic and commercial forces are, therefore, highly influential in creating the symbolism of the built environment.

Because meanings in environments and landscapes are both interpreted and produced, meaning resides both in the object and in the mind of the beholder — though certain elements in the built environment have relatively stable (i.e. socially accepted) meanings. Knox & Pinch (2000: 273) note the difference between 'intended' messages sent by owners/producers, via architects, planners, etc., and messages 'received' by users. The gap between the intended and the perceived meaning of architecture and architectural symbolism can be related to Barthes' (1968) discussion of the 'death of the author' — that is, the figurative death of those authors who proposed a system of meaning based upon 'mimesis' — the belief that an image, word or object (or work of architecture) carries a fixed message determined by the author (architect or sponsor). For Barthes, the reader inexorably constructs a new text in the act of reading. Reading an environment thus involves understanding how it comes to mean different things to different people and how meanings change. Accordingly, much of the built environment's social meaning depends on the *audience* and on the concepts of audience held by architects, other creators, designers and managers of the built environment (Knox 1984: 112) (see Figure 5.3).

The symbolic role of buildings and environments is a key part of the relationships between society and environment. Power (and control) is often a key theme, with all manmade environments effectively symbolising the power to make or change the environment, and much critical attention focuses on how environments represent, communicate and embody patterns of power and dominance. The symbolic content of the contemporary built environment is, however, multi-layered, open to interpretation and often ambiguous. Lasswell (1979, from Knox 1987: 367) suggests the 'signature-of-power' is manifest in two ways — through strategies of awe that 'intimidate' the

audience with 'majestic displays of power' and strategies of admiration that 'divert' the audience with 'spectacular' design effects. While, as Knox (1984: 110) argues, the source of this symbolisation of power has changed over time — from royalty and aristocracy, through industrial capital to present-day big government and big business — the purpose has always been the same: '... *to legitimise a particular ideology or power system by providing a physical focus to which sentiments could be attached.'*

There may, however, be competing associations and interpretations: for some, large office blocks symbolise financial strength and influence; for others, corporate greed (Knox & Pinch 2000: 55). Political and economic power is not the only message conveyed, as elements of counter-ideology also generate their own symbolic structures and environments.

Knox (1984: 107) argues that the built environment is not simply an expression of the power exerted at different times by various individuals, social groups and governments, but is also a means by which the prevailing system of power is maintained. The expression of power is often overt: many totalitarian and imperial/colonial regimes, for example, have used the built environment to symbolise political power (see Saoud 1995).

As it may not always be desirable to display power, symbolism may '... *involve "modest" or "low profile"*

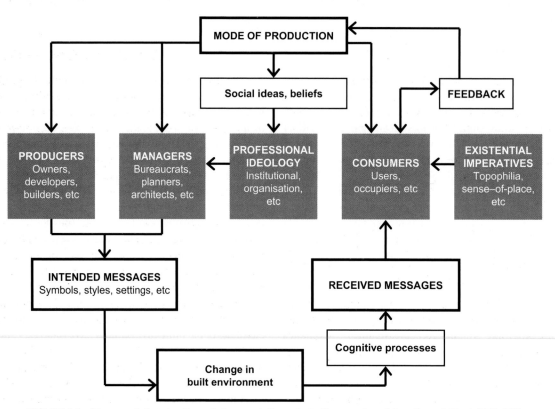

FIGURE 5.3   Signs, symbols and settings: A framework for analysis (*Image: adapted from Knox & Pinch 2000: 273*)

architectural motifs; or carry deliberately misleading messages for the purposes of maintaining social harmony.' (Knox 1987: 367). Dovey (1999: 2) observes how: *'The more that the structures and the presentations of power can be embedded in the framework of everyday life, the less questionable they become and the more effectively they can work.'* He argues that: *'... the exercise of power is slippery and ever-changing. Power naturalises and camouflages itself, chameleon-like within its context. The choice of the mask is a dimension of power.'* (1999: 13).

The danger of this approach, however, is that it can lead to a one-dimensional view of design, which is reduced merely to the production of signs, whereby the sign value outweighs the use value and design is seen as concerned primarily with surface meanings rather than deeper functions (see Evans 2003).

Symbolism and Architectural Modernism

Acknowledging the impact of explicit symbolism in the built environment, architectural Modernists rejected its display in the form of applied ornament. As Ward (1997: 21) observed, Modernist buildings were to carry no associations beyond their own 'magnificent declaration of modernity'. Intended to be capable of reproduction anywhere, their universally applicable 'modern style' transcended national and local cultures — Hitchcock & Johnson (1922) introduced it to America as 'the International style'.

Despite rejecting traditional forms of symbolism, Modernists were unable to reject all symbolism because all elements of the built environment are inescapably symbols. In *Complexity and Contradiction in Architecture* (1966), Venturi challenged both the minimalism and elitism of the International style, and the role of symbolism and meaning in Modernist architecture. In a subsequent book, *Learning from Las Vegas*, Venturi *et al* (1972) identified three ways of expressing a building's function or meaning:

- The 'Las Vegas way' — placing a 'big sign' in front of a 'little building'.
- The 'decorated shed' — designing a simple building form and then covering the facade with signs.
- The 'duck' — making the building's overall form visually express or symbolise its function (a deliberate strategy in attempts at iconic sign).

Venturi *et al* argued that most pre-twentieth century buildings were decorated sheds, while many Modernist buildings, designed to express their internal functions, were ducks. Influenced by Venturi's arguments, new 'post-modern' — both 'post-modern' meaning 'after modernism' and postmodernism as a set of ideas — ideas about architecture emerged, emphasising stylistic pluralism and scenographic, decorative and contextual properties, with building designers embracing and exploring the variety of ways in which people gained meanings from the environment.

In contrast to Modernism's univalent style, Jencks (1977) argued that postmodernism was 'multivalent', open to many different meanings and interpretations, with many postmodern buildings being collages of different visual styles, languages or codes, making allusions variously to popular culture, technology, local traditions and place. This shift has elicited much debate in the architectural literature.

Because it uses pre-existing forms of explicit symbolism, much postmodern architecture is characterised as 'historicist'. Jameson (1984) suggested a two-part categorisation — 'parody', the mimicry of old styles, which, as Ward (1997: 24) suggests, has a critical edge and '... *mocks rather than merely plunders from tradition'*, and 'pastiche' — a 'neutral practice', possessing none of 'parody's ulterior motives' and, instead, being 'speech in a dead language' (Jameson 1984: 65). Jencks (1977) distinguished between 'straight revivalism' — problematic because it simply repeated rather than challenged tradition — and 'radical eclecticism', the ironic mixing of styles and references, expressing a more critical attitude to tradition and architecture (Ward 1997: 23–4). While the historicist influence can be ironic or earnest, Davis (1987: 21, from Ellin 1999: 160) argues that, in ignoring the specific ideological or religious implications of the periods quoted, historicist architects and urbanists are, in fact, anti-historicist, preferring history-as-arcadian-symbol, rather than history-as-reality.

THE SOCIAL CONSTRUCTION OF PLACE

Having discussed environmental perception/cognition and the generation of meaning in the urban environment in the first part of this chapter, this part discusses one kind of meaning — that of 'sense of place'. Sense of place is often discussed in terms of the Latin concept of 'genius loci' — a notion suggesting people experience something beyond the physical or sensory properties of places and feel an attachment to a spirit of place (Jackson 1994: 157). As places change over time, there is a 'continuing narrative' involving past, present and future sense of place (see Chapter 9). Many places have retained their identities through significant social, cultural and technological changes (Dubos 1972: 7, from Relph 1976: 98) — and, hence, though subject to constant change, some essence of their place identity is maintained. How places are managed and controlled over time also impacts on sense of place (see Chapter 11).

For Relph (1976: 99), the spirit of place retained through such changes is 'subtle and nebulous', and not easily analysed in 'formal and conceptual terms', but is, nonetheless, 'extremely obvious'. From a more commercial perspective, Sircus (2001: 31) likens the sense or spirit of place to a brand that connotes certain expectations of quality, consistency and reliability:

'Every place is potentially a brand. In every way as much as Disneyland and Las Vegas, cities like Paris, Edinburgh and New York are their own brands, because a consistent, clear image has emerged of what each place looks, feels like, and the story or history it conveys.'

Typically there is significant physical continuity — in terms of street patterns and property boundaries if not necessarily of buildings. Identifying and recognising patterns of stability within change involves differentiating the more stable and the less stable elements — the former giving a measure of consistency of character and identity (see Chapter 9). Although space and particularly patterns of urban space are generally more enduring than individual buildings, some buildings — often the most important — have lasted for hundreds of years, helping to further sustain and contribute to the sense of time within the place (see Chapter 4).

By embodying and representing 'social' and 'public' memory, the materiality and physicality of places provide both a tangible record of the passage of time and a major contribution to place images and identities. The physical permanence concretises a meaningful place — its simple endurance over time giving it time-thickened qualities enhancing place identity. As Brand (1994: 2) suggests: *'Old buildings embody history … we glimpse the worlds of previous generations.'* Nonetheless, while the built environment contributes significantly to place images and identities, these are essentially intangible. For Tuan (1975: 164), the 'communal past' is not 'vividly present' *'… unless objectified in things that can be seen and touched, that is, directly experienced.'*

Sense of Place

As Montgomery (1998: 94) observes, it is a relatively straightforward task to think of a successful place, to be able go there and know that this is a good place; it is much more difficult to discern why it is successful, and whether similar success can be generated elsewhere. This section discusses sense of place. Providing a wider frame of reference, the following sections discuss placelessness and the phenomenon of 'invented' places.

The past 40 years have seen increasing interest in people's ties to, and conceptions of, places. This has often drawn on 'phenomenology', which, based on Edmund Husserl's notion of intentionality, aims to describe and understand phenomena as experiences through human consciousness, which takes in 'information' and makes it into 'the world' (Pepper 1984: 120). While place meanings are rooted in the physical setting and in activities, they are not a property of them but a 'property of human intentions and experiences' of those

places (Relph 1976: 47). Phenomenology argues there is no objective world external to and separate from ourselves. Hence, what 'the environment' represents is a function of our own subjective construction of it — in other words, what matters is how we 'come-to' a place.

Dovey (1999: 44) sees phenomenology as a 'necessary but limited' approach to the understanding of place, since focusing on the everyday, lived-in experience involves a 'certain blindness' to the effects of social structure and ideology on everyday experience. As the basis for his communications theory of society, Jurgen Habermas makes a useful distinction between the 'life-world' — the everyday world of place experience, social integration and 'communicative action' — and the 'system' — the social and economic structures of the state and the market (Dovey 1999: 51–2). Phenomenology tends to focus on the former to the exclusion of the latter.

Focusing on the psychological and experiential sense of place, Relph's *Place and Placelessness* (1976) drew on phenomenology. Relph (1976: 8) argued that, however, 'amorphous' and 'intangible', whenever we feel or know space, there is typically an associated concept of 'place'. For Relph, places were essentially centres of meaning constructed out of lived experience. By imbruing them with meaning, people — as individuals or as groups — change 'spaces' into 'places'. Some places are meaningful to people in groups or as a society or a nation as a whole. Wenceslas Square as the Velvet Revolution's epicentre, for example, is particularly meaningful to the citizens of Prague. Other places may be especially meaningful for individuals, for example, a place where a couple agreed to get married.

Concepts of place often emphasise the importance of a sense of 'belonging' and of emotional attachment (see Chapter 6). Place can be considered in terms of an unconscious 'rootedness' or a conscious sense of association or identity with a particular place. Rootedness tends to refer to a generally unconscious sense of place. Arefi (1999: 184) suggests it is *'… the most natural, pristine, unmediated kind of people-place tie.'* For Relph (1976: 38), it meant having *'… a secure point from which to look out on the world, a firm grasp of one's own position in the order of things, and a significant spiritual and psychological attachment to somewhere in particular.'*

It is often argued that people need a 'sense of belonging' to a specific territory or with a group of people, who, in turn, may or may not occupy a specific territory. Crang (1998: 103) suggested that *'… places provide an anchor of shared experiences between people and continuity over time.'* Individuals need to create and express a sense of both belonging to some collective entity or place and of personal or individual identity, which may often be gained by a degree of physical separation, by physical distinctiveness and/or a sense of entering into a particular area. Design strategies may purposefully emphasise these themes (see Chapter 6). For Norberg-Schulz (1971: 25), 'to be inside' was '... *the primary intention behind the place concept.*' Similarly, for Relph (1976: 111–2), the 'essence of place' lay in the – perhaps unconscious but frequently conscious – experience of an 'inside' that is distinct from an 'outside'. He distinguished types of identity of place based on notions of 'insiders' and 'outsiders' (see Table 5.2).

Territoriality and Personalisation

The concept of inside–outside relations is most easily understood in terms of territoriality: people's definition and defence of themselves – physically and psychologically – by the creation of a bounded, and often exclusive, domain (Ardrey 1967). Suggesting that people structure groups and define each other by distinguishing between 'insiders' and 'outsiders', territoriality is frequently the basis for distinctive social milieus that '... *mould the attitudes and shape the behaviour of their inhabitants.*' (Knox & Pinch 2000: 8–9).

Individual identity is associated with 'personalisation' – the putting of a distinctive stamp on one's environment. Typically this occurs at, and makes explicit, the threshold or transition between public and private domains, where small-scale design details contribute to symbolising or delimiting of space. Personalising private space expresses tastes and values and has little impact on the wider community. Personalising elements visible from the public realm communicates these tastes to the wider community. Although generally designed and built by someone else, individuals adapt and modify the given environment – re-arranging furniture or changing decoration, external planting in a garden, or front door colour.

Meiss (1990: 162) identified three design strategies to assist sense of identity when designing for people and groups:

- Environments responsive to, and based on, designers' deep understanding of the values and behaviour of the people and groups concerned, and the environmental features crucial to their identity. This requires recognition of difficulties posed by the designer–user gap (see Chapter 12).
- Participation of future users in the design of their environment. This also requires recognition of difficulties posed by the designer–user gap (see Chapter 12).
- Environments that users can modify and adapt. Herman Hertzberger (from Meiss 1990: 162) advocated an 'architecture of hospitality' reconciling mass production and individual identity. This involves issues of robustness and of the differing time frames of change of the different elements of the urban environment (see Chapter 9). It also demands that opportunities for group and individual personalisation be considered within the design process (see Bentley *et al* 1985: 99–105).

The Dimensions of Place

Personal or group engagement with space gives it meaning as a 'place', at least to the extent of being different from other places. Sense of place is, however, more than this. Lynch (1960: 6) defines 'identity of place' as that which provides '... *individuality or distinction from other places ... the basis for its recognition as a separable entity.*' For Relph, this acknowledges that each place has a 'unique address', without explaining *how* it becomes identifiable. He argued 'physical setting', 'activities' and 'meanings' constitute the three basic elements of place identity. But, rather than sensing place through simply residing in these elements, this feeling comes instead from human interaction with the elements (i.e. it was phenomenological).

The Dutch architect Aldo Van Eyck emphasised this succinctly in his famous description of place: '*Whatever*

TABLE 5.2 Types of Identity of Place

Existential insideness	Place is lived and dynamic, full with known meanings and experienced without reflection.
Empathetic insideness	Place records and expresses the cultural values and experiences of those who create and live in it.
Behavioural insideness	Place is ambient environment, possessing qualities of landscape or townscape that constitute a primary basis for public or consensus knowledge of that place.
Incidental outsideness	The selected functions of a place are what is important, and its identity is little more than the background for those functions.
Objective outsider	Place is reduced either to the single dimension of location, or to a space of located objects and activities.
Mass identity of place	An identity is provided more or less ready-made by the mass media, and remote from direct experience. It is a superficial and manipulated identity, which undermines both individual experiences and the symbolic properties of the identities of places.
Existential outsideness	Where identity of place represents a lost and now unattainable involvement; places are all and always incidental, for existence itself is incidental.

Source: Adapted from Relph (1976: 111–2).

space and time mean, place and occasion mean more. For space in the image of man is place, and time in the image of man is occasion.' The impact of occasion is dramatically demonstrated by contrasting a sports stadium full of people with the same stadium empty.

Drawing on Relph's work, Canter (1977) saw places as a function of 'activities' plus 'physical attributes' plus 'conceptions'. Building on Relph and Canter's ideas, Punter (1991) and Montgomery (1998) located the components of sense of place within urban design thought (Figure 5.4). These diagrams illustrate how design can contribute to and enhance the potential sense of place. While useful in simplifying and organising our notion of place and sense of place, we must also be careful not to simplify or reduce the concept of place — real places are complex and messy.

The contribution of each of Relph's three components to sense of place identity varies. In particular and, challenging what has been said previously, the significance of the materiality and physicality of places may often be overstated — activities and meanings associated with places may be as or more important in creating sense of place. Any individual's conception of place will have its own variation of Relph's three components of place.

Suggesting that identity is intimately tied to *memory*, Hayden (1995: 9) sees urban landscapes as 'storehouses'

for social memories. In Edward S. Casey's formulation, 'place memory' is:

'... the stabilising persistence of place as a container of experiences that contributes so powerfully to its intrinsic memorability. ... We might even say that memory is naturally place-oriented or at least place-supported.'
(from Hayden 1995: 46).

For Hayden (1995: 46) place memory

'... encapsulates the human ability to connect with both the built and natural environments that are entwined in the cultural landscape. It is the key to the power of historic places to help citizens define their public pasts; places trigger memories for insiders, who have shared a common past, and at the same time places can represent shared pasts to outsiders who might be interested in knowing about them in the present.'

Seen from a temporal perspective, the physical dimensions of places are most salient in the short term, being displaced in the longer term by the activities and events that happen there and how these change over time (i.e. the socio-cultural dimensions of place). As Tuan (1975: 164) argues, place experience involves time:

'To know a place well requires long residence and deep involvement. It is possible to appreciate the visual qualities of a place with one short visit, but not how it smells on a frosty morning, how

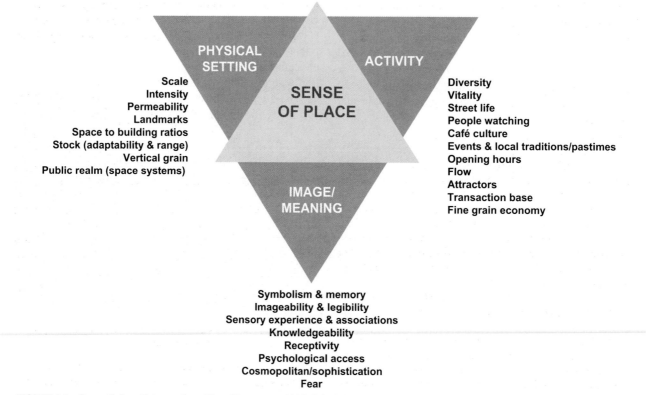

FIGURE 5.4   Sense of place (*Image: adapted from Montgomery 1998*). John Montgomery's diagram illustrates how urban design actions can contribute to, and enhance, the potential sense of place

city sounds reverberate across narrow streets to expire over the broad square, or how the pavement burns through gym shoe soles and melts bicycle tyres in August.'

Though particular parts or elements may be highly influential, place identities (sense of place) are a creation of the area as a whole rather than any specific part or element. The sense of place does not exist in any particular part but in the combination of those parts into a greater whole. A building, for example, is part — but only one part — of the place experience. Dovey (2010: 16—7) thus describes places as 'assemblages', arguing that:

'The senses or meanings of a place are neither found within the material urban form nor are they simply added to it, rather they are integral to the assemblage. ... To see places as assemblages is to avoid the reduction of place to text, to materiality or to subjective experience. What we call 'sense of place' is a phenomenon that connects or spans this materiality/expression dimension.'

For him, the whole experience of place is constituted from the interaction between the parts — the activity, form and meaning.

Similarly, place identities exist across property ownership lines. Indeed, property lines are often entirely irrelevant to experiential sense of place — we experience urban places as wholes, with place identity deriving from multiple properties (and the spaces between them) developed, owned and managed by separate owners with differing interests. The buildings themselves were commissioned from disparately motivated architects, and designed and developed at widely varying times. Sense of place can thus

be considered as a common or collective property resource and, as with all such resources, is vulnerable to a tragedy-of-the-commons (see Chapter 6).

While urban designers cannot make places in any simplistic or deterministic manner, they can increase the 'place potential' — the likelihood that people will consider the space a significant and meaningful place. The social and functional dimensions of place are discussed in Chapters 6 and 8.

Placelessness

The quality of being a distinctive and meaningful place — which, in the absence of a more elegant term, could be called 'placefulness' — is a continuous quality, with real places existing on a continuum from placeful (i.e. a strong sense of place) to placeless (i.e. a lack of place distinctiveness). Whereas constituting a sense of place tends to be associated with something of intrinsic value, placelessness is generally viewed negatively. Gertrude Stein's dismissal of Oakland — 'There's no there there' — aptly captures this. Nonetheless, appreciation of 'placelessness', for example, provides a frame of reference for urban design and place-making. Relph (1976: ii) considered it unrealistic to investigate place without considering the parallel phenomenon of 'placelessness' — which he defined as the 'casual eradication of distinctive places' and the 'making of standardised landscapes', a concern regularly addressed in the sustainability literature (see Sustainability Insert 2).

Placelessness tends to signify absence or loss of meaning. Embedded within a narrative of loss (e.g. Arefi

---

Sustainability Insert 2 — Distinctiveness

Supporting local distinctiveness firmly ties the global sustainability agenda to urban design's local place-making context (see Chapter 3). It is also intimately related to achieving other sustainable goals: to careful stewardship, in that conservation of the built fabric is a process of management and maintenance through time; to the delivery of human needs, because perceptions of place are intimately tied to the familiar and cherished local scene; and to resilience, because distinctiveness inevitably requires that built and natural assets are valued over the long term (see Chapter 9). It also represents a key objective of progressive planning systems through legislation covering the protection and enhancement of valued buildings, townscapes and natural landscapes.

Distinctiveness is concerned fundamentally with preserving and enhancing what is special about places (Clifford & King 1993), in that (as described by Philips 2003: 42—5) places can be viewed as constructs of often unique geographic, physical and environmental characteristics, combined with unique cultural circumstances manifest in a settlement's original form and purpose and subsequent human interventions over time — the interconnected parts.

Taipei, Taiwan (*Image: Matthew Carmona*). Social and cultural practices as part of the distinctive local scene.

The result is environments of distinctive character in building design, space composition, mix of uses and spatial layouts, which, like eco-systems, once damaged are difficult to

(Continued)

Sustainability Insert 2 — Distinctiveness—cont'd

repair. This does not imply that change is inappropriate and should be resisted — an environment may be distinctive in a negative as well as a positive sense — merely that, to be sustainable, the precautionary principle should be applied (Biddulph 2007: 70) with careful consideration given to identifying what is special, to resisting pressures for homogenisation, and to ensuring new development across all scales respects and enhances the best of what already exists and what works, rather than continuously reinventing the wheel.

1999; Banerjee 2001), there has been growing concern about its consequences. Various factors contribute to the contemporary sense of placelessness, including the contemporary market and regulatory approaches (see Chapters 3, 10 and 11). Three interrelated processes will be discussed here: globalisation; the emergence of mass culture; and the loss of the social and cultural relations embedded in specific places/territories.

(i) Globalisation

Many of the trends homogenising place meaning relate the creation of a global space through improved communications (both physical and electronic). Globalisation is a multi-faceted process in which the world is increasingly interconnected, with centralised decision-making exploiting efficiencies and economies of scale and standardisation. The changing, and problematising, of the relationship between local and global has significant implications for place meaning. Castells (1989: 6) described the emergence of a 'space of flows', which '... *dominates the historically constructed space of places.*' For Zukin (1991: 15), there is a fundamental tension between 'global capital' that can move and 'local community' that cannot, while Harvey (1997: 20) observes capital is no longer concerned about place: '*Capital needs fewer workers and much of it can move all over the world, deserting problematic places and populations at will.*' At the local level, there is loss of control and autonomy as the fate of local place is increasingly determined from afar by anonymous and impersonal economic forces. For Knox (2005: 3), globalisation has been complicit in creating a 'fast world': '...*a world of restless landscapes in which the more places change the more they seem to look alike, the less they are able to retain a distinctive sense of place, and the less they are able to sustain a public social life.*'

A globalised economy does not, *ipso facto*, mean globalised culture. As Entrikin (1991) notes, in some locations forces of convergence create sameness through standardisation, but elsewhere forces of divergence maintain cultural and spatial differentiation and distinctiveness. Local cultures provide 'one-of-a-kind' places, whose unique qualities are an important place asset: '*If places are becoming increasingly alike, the rewards for standing out are increasing.*' (Crang 1998: 117).

The situation is more complex, however. King (2000: 23) argues that, being embedded in a local context, urban design is '... *torn between the representation, and even celebration, of the global and the enhancement and often rescue of the local.*' He further notes how global trade is dependent on '... *the riches of local culture that it threatens to commercialise, degrade, swamp, and eventually destroy.*' Madanipour (2003: 224) suggests that, as cities increasingly compete for inward investment, they need to create environments seen as safe, attractive and offering the range of amenities and facilities expected by their (increasingly white collar) workers, and the tourists they hope to attract. So, while globalisation may lead to an erosion of place meaning, in other ways it may also bring benefits. Dovey (1999: 158—9) argues that, because local differences of urban culture are attractive to global marketing strategies, globalisation '... *does not simply iron out differences between cities, it also stimulates them.*' This is discussed later as 'place differentiation'.

(ii) Mass culture

With globalisation has come 'mass' culture, emerging from processes of mass production, mass marketing and mass consumption, which homogenise and standardise cultures and places, transcending, crowding-out, even destroying local cultures. For Crang (1998: 115), worry over placelessness can be interpreted as fear that local, supposedly 'authentic' forms of culture are being displaced by mass-produced commercial forms imposed on the locality. In Relph's (1976: 92) view, these:

'... *are formulated by manufacturers, governments, and professional designers, and are guided and communicated through mass media. They are not developed and formulated by the people. Uniform products and places are created for people of supposedly uniform needs and tastes, or perhaps vice versa.*'

Sometimes the process involves a deliberate creation of sameness, copying a formula that has worked elsewhere — for example, the emergence of formulaic China Towns in many cities across the world, or the cloning of high streets with the same national and international brands (New Economics Foundation 2004).

(iii) Loss of (attachment to) territory

Placelessness is also a reaction to the loss, or absence, of environments that, in Heidegger's terms, we 'care' about. Such environments promote what Relph termed 'existential outsideness': because people do not feel that they belong, they no longer care for their environment (Crang 1998: 112). In *Non-places*, Auge (1995: 94) contrasts 'places' where there is an 'organic sociality' — that is, where people have long-term relationships and interactions serving more than immediate functional purposes — with 'non-places' dominated by 'contractual solitariness' — where individual or small groups relate to wider society only through limited and specific interactions.

Discussing the emergence of a 'placeless' society, Meyrowitz (1985) highlighted the shift from cultures inhabiting specific areas, to a more mobile society. Mobility and communication technology have unprecedented implications for existing concepts of 'place' and 'community', as communities of interest supplant place-based communities (see Chapter 6). Crang (1998: 114) suggests few cultures remain 'place-bound', and that past geographic links may have been due more to the limitations of communications and transport than to any more fundamental connection. If so, he suggests, 'loss of place' does not really matter.

PLACE DIFFERENTIATION

A response to the standardisation of place and placelessness is the deliberate creation (or invention) of place distinctiveness and differentiation through design. This relates to, but differs subtly from, enhancing local distinctiveness: local distinctiveness should come from within; place differentiation generally comes from without. Conservation should enable place differentiation and local distinctiveness — and yet the paradox, as commentators such as Tunbridge (1998) and Ashworth (1998) argue, is that contemporary conservation practices tend to homogenise historic places (see Gospodini 2002, 2004).

That the physical landscape is often both more responsive and more immediately amendable to change than a city's economic structure and activity explains, in part, the willingness of city authorities and stakeholders to invest in image-building campaigns and physical change as means of place differentiation, creating competitive advantage and perhaps also of stimulating more fundamental economic change (Figure 5.5). Place marketing and city branding have thus been seen as important dimensions of city development.

Urban design is often complicit in this, with iconic buildings and the serial repetition of exemplar urban design projects — a classic example being Baltimore's Inner

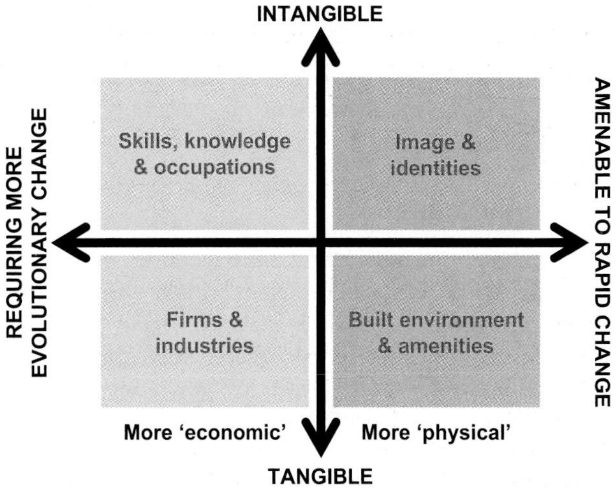

FIGURE 5.5 Economic and physical means of place differentiation (*Image: adapted from Turok 2009*)

Harbour — becoming key elements of place-marketing strategies (Harvey 1989a) (Figure 5.6). A typical 'formula' for physical regeneration and renewal involves derelict industrial sites becoming heritage parks; old canals and waterfronts becoming upscale residential or restaurant quarters; obsolete warehouses becoming chic lofts, plus an iconic/signature building or two (or more) preferably designed by one of a limited number of 'starchitects' (see below).

The spread of this formula raises doubts about the competitive edge that can be attained. If the result is that all cities ultimately look similar, then a consequence is loss of identity and that pursuing distinctiveness as a competitive strategy becomes a zero-sum game (see Sklair 2006b). In the specific case of iconic buildings, Sklair (2006a: 37) refers to the problems of oversupply (and hence diminishing returns) and of undersupply:

FIGURE 5.6 Inner Harbor, Baltimore (*Image: Doshik Yang*). Since its regeneration in the 1970s and 1980s, Baltimore's Inner Harbor has spawned copycat leisure spaces around the world (Yang 2006: 102–7)

'... *a delicate balancing act to perform in its efforts to feed the stream of iconic buildings, spaces and architects, in the knowledge that too few means the loss of profits but too many means the devaluation of the currency of iconic architecture.*'

Place Marketing

Imagineering — manufacturing place identities — involves deliberate use of symbols/themes (often drawn from existing places) to enhance place distinctiveness. At a larger scale this is termed place marketing, which attempts to change place identity by presenting carefully selected place images to identified local and non-local audiences. Since the 1980s, places (especially cities) have attempted to challenge negative perceptions and/or to construct new images for investors, visitors and residents (Kearns & Philo 1993). Place images thus become a tool to shape perceptions of a place in a particular way.

While place images form autonomously, place marketing involves developing such images for an ulterior purpose — revitalisation, tourism, economic development, etc. Because the supply (place) is capable of being tailored to better suit demand, place marketing raises questions regarding manipulation of place associations and meanings for commercial purposes and the commodification of place (see below).

Use of images in place marketing has a number of recognised problems, including mismatches between image and reality; being elitist by appealing only to youthful talent, higher income households and high value-added businesses; and being simplistic and sanitised (Turok 2009).

Place marketing involves attempts to, first, change the perceptual place image in the minds of target audiences through advertising and place promotion campaigns and, second, as a means to achieve this, to carry out physical changes to the place through public realm improvements; real estate development; external rehabilitation; and the establishment of new attractions, activities and events. These changes are related — the place is changed to substantiate the place-marketing image, while the changed place provides additional material from which to construct and reinforce place-marketing images. Though it serves much wider purposes, the physical re-imaging of cities — Evans (2003) describes it as 'hard branding' — shows how urban design supports place marketing (see also Hannigan 1998; Gospodini 2002, 2004) (Figure 5.7).

Icons and Iconicity

Iconic buildings have raised much debate in recent years (Sklair 2006a, 2006b; Silber 2007; Jencks 2005). An architectural icon is a building or a space — and sometimes an architect — that is not only different and unique but also famous, not just among the architectural

FIGURE 5.7   Milwaukee Art Museum, Milwaukee (architect: Santiago Calatrava) *(Image: Steve Tiesdell)*

cognoscenti but also among the general public. Most architectural icons are landmarks in the sense of being physically distinctive and identifiable within an urban landscape, but they are not just landmarks, because they have a '... *special meaning that is symbolic for a culture and/or a time,* [which] *has an aesthetic component.*' (Sklair 2006a: 25).

Distinctive buildings symbolise their city — the Eiffel Tower and Sydney Opera House are obvious examples (Figure 5.8) — and thus the lure of new iconic buildings is to create similar distinctiveness *quickly*. Moreover, over and above the building's core function, its physical distinctiveness is seen as an economic asset (Figure 5.9).

In the past, the status of building and other structures as icons was acquired over time through physical distinctiveness *and* time-thickened social significance. In a more

FIGURE 5.8   Sydney Opera House *(Image: Steve Tiesdell)*. Sydney Opera House symbolises the city, and is also a powerful visual magnet within Circular Quay and Port Jackson

FIGURE 5.9 CCTV Building, Beijing (architect: Rem Koolhaas) (*Image: Matthew Carmona*)

global age with cities competing globally, certain buildings are increasingly designed to be *immediately* iconic. International architectural competitions are routinely expected to generate iconic buildings.

This poses two related questions about the precise nature of iconicity (Sklair 2006a). First, whether it resides primarily in the building/space *or* is socially created and thus primarily exists in images of that building/space. If the latter, then one must look at the institutions that create iconicity. Second, whether it exists in the building/space *or* in the designer (architect) of that building/space (i.e. it is the designer that bestows iconicity on the building or space rather than vice versa). Thus, in addition to how certain buildings become iconic, one must also consider how certain architects become iconic (and thus their every building become *ipso facto* iconic).

Much of the fad for iconicity is attributable to the architectural and popular media, where discussion and knowledge of buildings and design are based on highly selective images and accounts of building design and development, which, *inter alia*, fetish buildings and are propelled by an incessant search for novelty and sensation. In such discourses, buildings and spaces are consumed as

images rather than experienced as places. There is thus a phenomenon of iconicity being attached to designers on the basis of a completed project or two, or alternatively through winning — even being highly placed in — a competition and often without that project being built. Contemporary architects can thus come to be iconic on the basis of 'paper architecture', which is typically unbuilt (even unbuildable), yet well-known through frequent reproduction in the architectural and popular media.

This is also associated with 'signature architects' and 'starchitects'. Signature architects are those who place unique signatures, in the sense of recognisable features, on their buildings (Sklair 2006a: 31). Despite differing sites and contexts, the signature architect's designs are recognisably similar and identifiable — indeed, designing a highly contextually responsive building may jeopardise their signature, which, in part, was the reason for their appointment. A contraction of 'star' and 'architect', starchitects are those architects whose celebrity and critical acclaim goes beyond the architectural world and who have some degree of fame among the general public. As celebrity status is generally associated with delivering the 'wow factor', the starchitect's designs are almost always intended to be iconic.

Iconic Buildings and Civic Boosterism

The principal rationale for deliberately created iconic architecture is civic boosterism, with iconicity valued as a resource for, and contributor to, place identity but also, and more importantly, as a contributor to a *particular* place identity. As Sklair (2006a: 36) explains: '*Analytically, iconicity in architecture may be seen not simply as a judgment of excellence or uniqueness but like celebrity in popular culture, as a resource in struggles for meaning and, by implication, for power.*' Iconic buildings are thus typically intended to signify a city's cultural significance, its economic dynamism, the quality of life possible there and other desirable attributes.

This has been labelled the 'Bilbao Effect' — the notion that a single building can transform the fortunes of an entire region. Rather than merely symbolising it, the suggestion is that the Frank Gehry designed Guggenheim museum was of itself instrumental in the regeneration of Bilbao's regional economy by bringing the city to the attention of the world, who, in turn, rushed to visit it. The regeneration formula was thus reduced to the need to procure an iconic building — though more considered accounts give the full story (see Del Cerro Santamaria 2007).

Sklair (2006a: 36) distinguishes professional (architectural) icons and public (popular) icons. Put simply, this is a distinction between buildings famous within the architectural community and buildings famous beyond that community. To be effective as economic icons — that is,

FIGURE 5.10   Pompidou Centre, Paris (*Image: Steve Tiesdell*). Iconic buildings are frequently place-signifying, but less frequently place-making. A key indicator is the (often poor) quality of the spaces surrounding the iconic building. Designed by Renzo Piano and Richard Rogers, the Pompidou Centre is an exception — an architectural and a popular icon, it works at many levels and, in particular, defines and engages with a series of well-used public spaces around it

enhancing and transforming the city's external image — aspiring iconic buildings must first have sufficient status and acclaim as an architectural icon. But this is a necessary, not a sufficient, condition: they must also become public icons, which is the real reason for their commission.

A key problem with many supposedly iconic buildings is that, while seductive and alluring in images, they do not make good places — producing the desired image seems, somewhat curiously, inimical with creating a good place (Figure 5.10). Designed to modify the image and impression of the host city and to incite people to visit them (or merely to think more positively of the city), fulfilling the promise implied in the image is less important.

Place-Theming

Place-theming involves a deliberate shaping and packaging of place and place images around a particular theme. Crang (1998: 116–7), for example, notes an industry '... *that sets out to "imagineer" places, to create "uniqueness" in order to attract attention, visitors and — in the end — money.*' For Hayden (2004: 102), theming describes '... *designing and decorating restaurants, hotels, shopping malls, casinos, and even small towns to exaggerate stereotypes and recreate lost places.*'

Intended to further the purposes of consumption, place-theming occurs in a variety of settings, including shopping malls, historic districts, urban entertainment districts, central city redevelopments and tourist destinations (see Relph 1976; Zukin 1991; Hannigan 1998; Gottdiener 2001). Depending on the extent of existing source material, place-theming can involve reinventing or inventing places.

'Re-invented places' start from a basis in reality, but involve significant change, distortion and loss of authenticity. Invented places spring from the creative minds of authors, artists, architects, designers and imaginers. *Invention* as an attempt to deceive is problematic, but the real issue is when *seduction* (and perhaps misapprehension) becomes manipulation (and possibly deception) — though, it may be the *extent* rather than the mere *fact* of invention that is important (Figure 5.11).

Invented Places

Prior to widespread industrialisation, the physical distinctiveness of places arose substantially through the use of local building materials and a limited range of construction methods. Industrialisation, and subsequently globalisation, enabled the emergence of a universal or 'International' style, which made virtues of industrialised production methods and new building materials (and, not insignificantly, greatly reduced their cost), enabling, *inter alia*, all places to be similar. More generally, as Gottdiener (2001: 4) notes, before the 1960s, buildings '... *reflected their functions with a minimum of symbolic trappings ... Symbolic marking was muted.*'

As further advances in construction methods and building materials yielded yet more choice and enabled buildings and thus places to be made (at least outwardly) distinctive, Modernism's limited palette and aesthetic broadened into postmodernism, which legitimised a wider range of styles and aesthetics and the use of historical motifs. Sternberg (2000: 274) notes how, reacting to Modernism, a new generation of thinkers stressed '... *another integral facet of the city: its capacity to exhibit history, tradition, nature, nationality, or other themes that heighten meaning and solidify identity.*'

The turn to postmodernism coincided with a transition to overtly symbolised and commercialised urban environments: '*The use of symbols and motifs more and more frequently characterises the space of everyday life in both the city and the suburb.*' (Gottdiener 2001: 4). Similarly, Sternberg (2000: 274) observes how, in professional design practice, '... *purposeful thematisation is now widespread, extending from shopping malls to festival markets to urban waterfronts*' (see below).

Although it did not invent the practice — Robert Venturi, for example, observed how throughout history most buildings were 'decorated sheds' (see Venturi *et al* 1972) — postmodernism showed how standard boxes could be packaged or 'wallpapered' to give meaning in a variety of ways. The basic premise — separation of content and image, enabling symbolisation to be applied, and thereby superficial, rather than deep and innate — involves artificiality but simultaneously offers choice.

Applied symbolisation can reflect the local or the global. The preferred choice is often to emphasise the local,

FIGURE 5.11   The Palace in the 'new' Old Town development, Dubai *(Image: Matthew Carmona)*

with many commentators favouring the local and indigenous as the only legitimate form of symbolisation — the endogenous is acclaimed as authentic; the exogenous dismissed as alien. But the 'local' is merely one choice — and rather than an autonomous creation, it can also be an applied theme (and every bit as artificial as any other applied theme). Noting how '... *most writers on this topic disdain mere thematisation and assert that design for meaning should be rooted in indigenous character*', Sternberg (2000: 274—5) argues that choices other than indigenous correctness exist:

'In one place, the local identity we wish to articulate may well derive from strands of local history, but in another that identity might best evolve from today's living culture. Things made new or brought in from afar may better express the aspirations of the place than trivial legends dressed up as history.'

Whatever its merits and demerits, theming at least acknowledges the significance of place and place values. Acknowledging criticism of historic preservation for 'inventing histories', for example, Ellin (2000: 104) also suggests it represents '... *a welcome corrective to Modernism's obsession with forgetting the past and starting over on a clean slate.'*

Theme parks are perhaps the epitome of invented places. For Sircus (2001: 30), Disneyland is the quintessential invented place:

'It creates reality out of fantasy in ways that are often symbolic and subliminal; digging deep into the user's psyche, connecting with cross-cultural images and multi-generational, hard-wired memories. It is successful because it adheres to certain principles of sequential experience and storytelling, creating an appropriate and meaningful sense of place in which both activities and memories are individual and shared.'

In their purest forms, invented places depend on a high degree of control — particularly of context but often also of behaviour (see Chapter 6) — and a certain scale of operation. Graham & Marvin (2001: 264) refer to the phenomenon of 'bundled' urban environments — invented street systems within shopping malls, themes parks and urban resorts, often with strong tie-ins to leading sports, media and entertainment multi-nationals (Disney, Time-Warner, Sony, Nike, etc.), thereby exploiting merchandising spin-offs. Such developments cover increasingly large footprints as developers attempt to bundle together the maximum number of 'synergistic' uses within a single complex — retailing, cinemas, IMAX screens, sports facilities, restaurants, hotels, entertainment facilities, casinos, simulated historic scenes, virtual reality complexes, museums, zoos, bowling alleys, artificial ski slopes, etc.

Hannigan (1998) discusses a particular kind of invented place — the urban entertainment destination (UED) or 'fantasy city'. According to Hannigan (1998: 3—4), the typical UED is:

- Theme-o-centre: '... *everything from individual entertainment venues to the image of the city itself conforms to a scripted theme, normally drawn from sports, history or popular entertainment.'*
- Not only themed, but also 'aggressively branded': *'Urban entrainment destinations are not financed and marketed exclusively on the basis of their ability to*

deliver a high degree of consumer satisfaction and fun but also on their potential for selling licensed merchandise on site.'

- Open day and night, reflecting *'... its intended market of "baby boomer" and "generation X" adults in search of leisure, sociability and entertainment.'*
- Modular: *'... mixing and matching an increasingly standard array of components in various configurations.'*
- Solipsistic: *'... isolated from surrounding neighbourhoods, physically, economically and socially.'*
- postmodern: *'... insomuch as it is constructed around technologies of simulation, virtual reality and the thrill of the spectacle.'*

Criticisms of Place-Theming and Invented Places

Invented places and place-theming provide opportunities for urban design and place-making, but the practices raise a number of place-making issues and there has been much critical comment:

(i) Superficiality

Despite much contemporary urban development paying greater attention to place, critics lament the 'depthlessness' of overtly themed places, suggesting it is a superficial attention that undermines and even destroys, rather than reinforces, the real place identity. Dovey (1999: 44), for example, observes how sense of place's intangibility has been 'widely exploited' to legitimise design projects and, in so doing, *'... is reduced to scenographic and rhetorical effect as a cover for place destruction.'* Similarly, Huxtable (1997: 3) complains that *'... themed parodies pass for places ... even as real places with their full freight of art and memories are devalued and destroyed.'*

Some see this 'superficiality' as a defining characteristic of postmodernism (see Jameson 1984). A form of architectural 'fetishism', Harvey (1990: 77) suggests it involves *'... direct concern with surface appearances that conceal underlying meanings.'* In *Variations on a Theme Park*, Sorkin (1992: xiv) asserts that the profession of urban design was 'almost wholly preoccupied' with the 'creation of urbane disguises':

'Whether in its master incarnation at the ersatz Main Street of Disneyland, in the phoney history of a Rouse market place, or the gentrified architecture of the "reborn" Lower East Side, this elaborate apparatus is at pains to assert its ties to the kind of city life it is in the process of obliterating. ... The architecture of this city is almost purely semiotic, playing the game of grafted signification, theme-park building.'

Gottdiener (2001) identifies positive and negative sides to the proliferation of themed environments. They offer a 'qualitatively new source of entertainment in the history of human civilisation', but their:

'... essential purpose of merchandising and profit-making, their control by private commercial interests rather than public ones, and their reduction of all meanings to superficial images, raises serious questions about the quality of our daily life.'

(Gottdiener 2001: 75).

Such highbrow critiques often contain elements of elitism. Fainstein (1994: 232) observes how the popularity of many out-of-centre shopping complexes and revitalised areas drives *'... cultural critics into paroxysms of annoyance as they attempt to show that people ought to be continually exposed to the realities of life at the lower depths.'* Gottdiener (2001) suggests critics of themed environments adopt *'... a critical, elite perspective that finds only consumer manipulation behind themed facades and only corporate greed behind the proliferation of themed environments.'* Despite seeing some truth in this, he notes a reductionist critique, which is only partially true because many elements *'... converge to create an emphasis on a meaningful environment in daily life. These factors create multi-leveled experiences and symbolic milieus.'*

Similarly, Ellin (2000: 103) argues that, despite being criticised for being contrived and 'artificial', people may like these qualities:

'Accused of distracting people from the injustices and ugliness of their lives, of placating them, and of being places of "spectacle and surveillance", themed environments might also be applauded for the diversion they offer, for simply providing places in which people can relax and have fun in the company of family and friends.'

(ii) The commodification of place

As their symbolism tends to come 'from without' rather than 'from within', invented places are, in Relph's terms, 'other-directed' — that is, 'outside inventions' rather than expressions of the local culture. Here, 'economic space' invades 'lived space' and the life-world becomes less an end in itself and increasingly a means to the system's ends. As Dovey (1999: 51–2) explains, *'... places of everyday life become increasingly subject to the system imperatives of the market and its distorted communications, advertising and constructions of meaning.'*

By seeking to sell or market the place, place-theming actions, and place-marketing images, necessarily commodify, and distort, the place, by making its exchange value its primary quality. Such actions are often geared towards a place's commercial exploitation (usually for outsiders) rather than its 'authentic' development for the benefit of local people and businesses. In the context of tourism, Cohen (1988: 372) explains the consequence of commodification: '... *"colourful" local costumes and customs, rituals and feasts, and folk and ethnic arts become touristic services or commodities, as they come to be performed or produced for touristic consumption.*'

Sometimes termed theme park-isation or heritage-isation, commodification is perhaps best known, and disparaged, as Disney-fication. Disney-fication involves presenting an existing, perhaps historic, place in ways that encourage tourism, but do not encourage exposure to, and may trivialise, the actual history. More generally, Rojek (2001 cited in Hedges 2009: 37) refers to a 'cult-of-distraction' that '... *valorises the superficial, the gaudy, the domination of commodity culture.*' The overarching question though is whether commodification of place matters and, if so, how much.

(iii) Simulacrum and the real

Reviewing Huxtable's *The Unreal America* (1997), Rybczynski (1997: 13) suggests her analysis presumes the public's inability to distinguish between what is real and what is not. But, he contends, people watching the erupting lava outside *The Mirage* in Las Vegas do not mistake it for a real volcano; commuters using the neo-classical concourse of the old Pennsylvania Station know they were not in ancient Rome. He concludes that '... *the relationship between reality and illusion has always been blurred; Pennsylvania Station was simultaneously a surrogate Baths of Caracalla and a real place.*' (1997: 13)

As the sophistication of simulation develops, however, it becomes increasingly difficult to tell reality from simulation. Discussing the 'real' and the 'simulation' − or, more precisely, simulacrum, because simulation can connote a copy made for the purpose of deceit − Baudrillard (1983, from Lane 2000: 86−7) identified three levels of simulation: first-order simulations are obvious copies of reality; second-order simulations are copies that blur the boundaries between reality and representation; while third-order simulations − 'simulacra' − are imitations of things that never actually existed.

In first- and second-order simulation the real still exists and the simulation can be distinguished from it. With third-order simulation, the real does not exist. For example, if the real is a territory or landscape, a first-order simulation might be a portrait of the territory or landscape, second-order simulation is a map of that territory, and third-order simulation − which

Baudrillard calls 'hyper-reality' − is a map of a territory that does not exist.

Nonetheless, while Disney's Main Street, USA may be mistaken for a 'real' main street, the real danger is that people do not have a real main street − or, indeed, real places − to compare it against, especially if, over time, the ability to distinguish the real from the simulated atrophies. In *Empire of Illusion: The End of Literacy and the Triumph of Spectacle* Hedges (2009: 44, 51) argues that a public no longer able to 'distinguish between truth and fiction' must interpret 'reality through illusion', and laments how contemporary America has become '... *a culture that has been denied, or has passively given up, the linguistic and intellectual tools to cope with complexity, to separate illusion from reality.*' He, thus, reflects Jean Baudrillard's contention that we live in a Disney-esque world in which our understanding is shaped by media-driven signs, and that the tools of historical intelligibility − without which we can no longer tell what is real, if indeed anything is real.

(iv) Authenticity

Relph (1976: 113) recognised sense of place may be 'authentic' and 'genuine' or, equally, 'inauthentic', 'contrived' or 'artificial'. Many critics regard development that copies or draws explicit reference from historical precedent as 'false' and lacking authenticity. For Boyer (1992: 188), development at New York's Union Square, Times Square and Battery Park City involving '... *the reiteration and recycling of already-known symbolic codes and historic forms to the point of cliché...*' were literal representations of the past − 'retro urban designs' − designed for 'inattentive viewers'. This is not a new phenomenon: writing 50 years ago, Boorstein, in *The Image: A Guide to Pseudo-events in America* (1961), argued that, in contemporary culture, the 'fabricated, inauthentic and theatrical' had already displaced the 'natural, genuine and spontaneous', such that reality had been converted into stagecraft.

Use of the terms 'authentic' and 'inauthentic' is often contingent − authentic being what particular critics like. Commenting on the 'exaltation of authenticity', Fainstein (1994: 230) notes difficulties with the 'implied definition' of authenticity: '... *the critical literature is replete with accusations of fakery,* [but] *the nature of the authentic, late twentieth-century design is rarely specified.*'

Arguing that a 'deeper critique' ought to demonstrate precisely how such landscapes fail to satisfy important human needs, Fainstein (1994: 232) notes how critics seem reluctant to do this because it puts them on the '... *thorny ground of explicating exactly what activities afford genuine as opposed to false satisfaction.'* For Fainstein (1994: 231), Disney World *'… is an authentic reflection of underlying economic and social processes … It is the genuine thing.'* She thus questions whether authenticity is the appropriate value to apply because *'… deconstruction of the urban environment reveals a reasonably accurate portrayal of the social forces underlying it.'* (1994: 232).

Debates are thus raised about precisely what is meant by authenticity in an urban design context. Boyle (2004: 16–22), for example, identifies 10 elements of authenticity or realness, which convey something of its character – 'ethical'; 'natural'; 'honest'; 'simple'; 'unspun'; 'sustainable'; 'beautiful'; 'rooted'; 'deep'; and 'human'. Analogy is instructive. In a guide to malt whisky, Jackson (2004: 37) contrasts drinks that *'… come from nowhere, taste of nothing much, and have a logo for a name …'* with those that *'… come from somewhere, have complex aromas and flavours, and may have a name that is hard to pronounce.'* He continues:

'Such drinks reflect their place of origin. They have evolved. They have a story to tell. They are good company, and they require something of the drinker in return: that he or she experiences the pleasure of learning to drink. Real, evolved drinks … arise from their own terroir: geology, soil vegetation, topography, weather, water, and air. To what extent they are influenced by each of these elements is a matter for debate, often passionate. People care about real drinks.'

(2004: 37).

Florida (2002: 228) offers an understanding of authentic as the opposite of generic – that is, distinctive or one-of-a-kind. His interviewees equated:

'… authentic with being "real", as in a place that has real buildings, real people, real history. An authentic place offers unique and original experiences. Thus a place full of chain stores, chain restaurants and nightclubs is not authentic. Not only do these venues look pretty much the same everywhere, they offer the same experience you could have anywhere.'

(2002: 228)

In contrast to purpose-built, packaged experiences aimed at maximising consumption and tourist/visitor spend, Florida (2002: 232) emphasises how real places permit, facilitate and reward participation: *'You can do more than be a spectator; you can be part of the scene.'* The experience can also be modulated: *'… to choose the mix, to turn the intensity level up or down as desired, and to have a hand in creating the experience rather than merely consuming it.'* (2002: 232).

Thus, in these readings, real, authentic places permit and enable two-way interaction, inviting and rewarding intellectual and emotional engagement. Arguably, what is found in authentic places equates to 'truth'; 'depth' and 'art', rather than (relatively effortless) 'entertainment' and shallow or superficial 'beauty'. Focusing on the latter may, however, crowd-out, distort and distract from the former, which ultimately diminishes and undermines the real experience. This is generally what critics mean when they refer to a lack of authenticity.

People may be less concerned about authenticity than experts. They may be fooled or misled, but it may not matter (much) to them and what may be more important is whether they like a place – in this sense, their concern is for 'experience' authenticity rather than 'document' authenticity (see Jiven & Larkham 2003: 78). People's perceptions are important: Nasar (1998: 69), for example, asserts that: *'Historical content may be authentic or not. If observers consider a place historical, it has historical content to them.'* As Sircus (2001: 31) argues:

'Place is not good or bad simply because it is real versus surrogate, authentic versus pastiche. People enjoy both, whether it is a place created over centuries, or created instantly. A successful place, like a novel or a movie, engages us actively in an emotional experience orchestrated and organised to communicate purpose and story.'

But it is precisely the scripting, orchestration and organisation – manipulation and seduction are alternative terms – that worry critics: we can choose whether and how to read a book; we have less control over our everyday place experiences (see Chapter 6).

CONCLUSION

The value of the perceptual dimension of urban design is the emphasis placed on people and how they perceive, value and both draw meaning from and add meaning to the urban environment. Places that are 'real' to people invite, require and reward involvement – both intellectual and emotional – and provide a sense of psychological connectedness. Although urban design inexorably creates/invents and reinvents places and does so with a greater or lesser degree of finesse, contrivance and authenticity, people make places and give them with meaning; messages are 'sent', but also 'received' and interpreted – individuals and society determines whether a place is authentic or not, and the quality and meaning of their experience there. Most places are discretionary environments and their success can be measured in terms of the number of people freely choosing to use them. Urban designers thus need to learn how to make better people places by observing existing places (see Chapter 8) and through dialogue with their users and stakeholders (see Chapter 12).

Chapter 6

The Social Dimension

This chapter discusses urban design's social dimension and the relationship between space and society. Space and society are clearly related: it is difficult to conceive of 'space' as being without social content and, equally, of society without a spatial component. This chapter focuses on six key aspects of the social dimension of urban design: the relationship between people and space; the concept of the public realm; neighbourhoods; safety and security; the control of public space; and equitable environments.

PEOPLE AND SPACE

Understanding the relationship between people ('society') and their environment ('space') is an essential component of urban design. Consideration of the relationship between people and their environment starts with architectural or environmental determinism, where the physical environment has a determining influence on human behaviour. But, by negating the role of human agency and social influences, it assumes environment–people interaction is a one-way process. Similarly, Kashef (2008: 416) describes an attitude within social science that sees space '... *as a backdrop or a neutral container for economic and social activities (i.e. urban space may be configured and reconfigured by societal and cultural changes but not vice versa).*'

People are not passive, however, and influence and change the environment as it influences and changes them. It is, thus, a continuous two-way process in which people create and modify spaces while at the same time being influenced in various ways by those spaces. Social process happens neither in a vacuum, nor against a 'neutral backdrop', and the built environment is thus both the medium for and the outcome of social process and change.

By shaping the built environment, urban designers influence patterns of human activity and, thus, of social life. Dear & Wolch (1989), for example, argue that social relations can be:

- *Constituted through space* – where site characteristics influence settlement form.
- *Constrained by space* – where the physical environment facilitates or obstructs human activity.
- *Mediated by space* – where the friction-of-distance facilitates, or inhibits, the development of various social practices.

Physical factors are thus neither the exclusive nor necessarily the dominant influence on behaviour, though what people are able to do is constrained by environmental opportunities available to them. A room's physical form clearly affects what its users can and cannot do: a window in an otherwise solid wall allows a person to see out; a solid wall without a window does not afford that opportunity. Human behaviour is thus inherently situational, embedded in physical – but also 'social', 'cultural' and 'perceptual' – contexts and settings.

There are different perspectives on the degree to which the environment influences people's actions. Physical determinism haunts all discussions of urban design. Franck (1984) identified four major weaknesses and limitations of determinist views of physical design: exaggerating the influence of the physical environment by understating the influence of other factors; assuming the physical environment has only direct effects on behaviour; ignoring the active role of human choice and goals; and neglecting active processes of creating and modifying environments. The relationship is thus not deterministic: the creation or modification of environments merely creates potentials; what actually happens depends on the choices made by people. Lang (1987) discusses this in terms of the opportunities or 'affordances' for action that an environment affords.

Variants on 'hard' determinism are 'environmental possibilism' and 'environmental probabilism' (see Porteous 1977; Bell *et al* 1990). In the first, people choose among the environmental opportunities available to them. The second suggests that in a given physical setting some choices are more likely than others, and can be illustrated by a simple example (from Bell *et al* 1994: 365). A seminar involving a small number of people is held in a large room with a formal layout of chairs and tables. There is minimal discussion. When the chairs and tables are arranged differently, there is more discussion. Thus, when the environment is changed, behaviour also changes. The latter outcome is not inevitable: had the seminar been scheduled late in the day or had the convenor failed to motivate participants, the rearrangement may not have been any more successful than the original layout. The example shows *design matters* but not absolutely. What happens in any particular environment depends on those using that environment (see Chapter 8).

Gans (1968: 5) drew a valuable distinction between 'potential' and 'effective' environments, whereby a physical

Public Places – Urban Spaces. DOI: 10.1016/B978-1-85617-827-3.10006-9

FIGURE 6.1   Pyramid of human needs

setting is a potential environment, providing a range of environmental opportunities regarding what people are able to do. At any moment in time, what people actually do is the 'resultant' or effective environment. Thus, while designers create potential environments, people create effective environments. The relationship between people and their environment is, thus, best conceived as a continuous two-way process in which people create and modify spaces while at the same time being influenced by those spaces. Rather than determining human actions or behaviour, urban design can be seen as a means of manipulating the probabilities of certain actions or behaviours occurring. It can thus be argued credibly that environments with, for example, a high concentration of street-level doors are more conducive to social interaction than environments characterised by fortress-like structures with blank walls; similarly, residential neighbourhoods where houses have front porches present a more gregarious setting than neighbourhoods where three-car garage doors face onto public space (Ford 2000: 13).

The choices that individuals make in any particular environment are responsive to the individual's ego, personality, character, goals and values, available resources, past experiences, life stage, etc. Nevertheless, despite the individualistic and complex nature of human values, goals and aspirations, a number of authors have proposed an overarching hierarchy of human needs. Such hierarchies often derive from Maslow's original work on human motivations, which identified a five-stage hierarchy of basic human needs:

- Physiological needs (for warmth and comfort);
- Safety and security needs (to feel safe from harm);
- Affiliation needs (to belong — to a community, for example);
- Esteem needs (to feel valued by others); and
- Self-actualisation (for artistic expression and fulfilment) (Maslow 1968) (Figure 6.1).

The most basic human physiological needs have to be satisfied before progress can be made to the higher order needs. Although there is a hierarchy, the different needs are related in a complex series of inter-linked relationships (Figure 6.2). Thus, if the most basic human needs of individuals are not met, it will be difficult for them, or society at large, to focus on higher order collective needs such as sustainability (see Sustainability Insert 3).

'Society' and 'culture' also influence the choices people make in any given setting. Society can be understood as any self-perpetuating human grouping occupying a relatively bounded territory, that interacts in a systematic way and possesses its own culture and institutions. Culture is probably best understood in an anthropological sense as a '... *particular way of life, which expresses certain meanings and values not only in art and learning, but also in institutions and ordinary behaviour.'* (Williams 1961: 41).

Lawson (2001: 2–3) argues that whenever we find people gathered together collectively inhabiting some part of our world we also tend to find rules governing their use of space. The queue, for example, is a form of conventionalised behaviour triggered by environmental signals:

'When someone pushes in front of you in a queue, you feel offended not just because you are one place further back but also because they failed to respect the rules. In most situations where we queue there are also token signals from the physical environment that we should behave in this highly artificial way. The rope barriers sometimes used to form queues in public places are hardly able to contain a crowd physically, and yet without them the crowd would probably push and shove in a chaotic and possibly aggressive manner. Our civilisation and our culture enables us to be remarkably co-operative, even when we are actually competing for limited tickets at the theatre or sale bargains in the shop.'

(2001: 7–8).

Behaviour in public spaces is often discussed in terms of civility and incivility (see below). Civility involves awareness of and respect for other people's use of public space. As Brain (2005: 223) explains:

'Civility is a matter of respect expressed in the form of social distance and discretion, a recognition of the distinction between those things that it is appropriate to share (or impose on one's fellows) and those that are best kept private. It is not simply a tolerance of difference but recognition and allowance for occupation of a shared world without demand that differences be either erased or ignored.'

In recent years, there seems to have been a decline in the apparent civility of the public in space. Though suggestive of a 'golden age' when public behaviour was of a higher order, it is also an extremely common observation (see

Sustainability Insert 3 — Human Needs

Recognising that environmental needs are unlikely to be met if human needs are ignored, conceptualisations of sustainability have increasingly been underpinned by notions of social and economic sustainability. Relating such broad concerns to that of sustainable urban design, human needs encompass many of the perceptual and social needs discussed in this and the previous chapter, including local access to varied economic opportunities, and also the creation of comfortable environments that are at a human-scale and visually attractive; that allow safe and crime-free human contact, and ease of movement and navigation (legibility); that are socially mixed; and that through their design and the disposition of uses are available to all.

The work of the Coin Street Community Builders on London's South Bank represents a successful attempt to build a sustainable community in all senses, from tangible environmental objectives, such as the sourcing of building materials from sustainable sources, to the more intangible and challenging provision of a socially mixed and engaged community with associated local job opportunities; the latter achieved by a combination of careful fine-gained masterplanning over time (as opposed to a single 'big-bang' vision), the provision of affordable housing through a cooperative structure, and cross-subsiding housing, light industrial space, public spaces and community programmes through commercial elements such as shops and restaurants (Haworth 2009).

At the larger scale of settlement and quarter design, human needs can be met through positive image building to foster identification with place to build commitment to, and sense of ownership of, the environment (Chaplin 2007). At this scale, one increasingly prevalent effect illustrates how environment also directly impacts on human well-being, health and comfort. With global warming, inhabitants of urban areas increasingly suffer from the tendency of hard, built-up areas to store and retain heat longer than surrounding green areas. These urban heat island effects (a form of environmental pollution) can leave city centres 10% warmer than surrounding suburban areas, and were blamed for 35 000 deaths across Europe in August 2003. Yet simple design measures can help to rectify the situation: increasing tree cover by 10%, for example, can reduce the surface temperature of a city by between 3 and 4 °C (CABE 2009:19). At the same time, street trees improve biodiversity, provide daily shade and shelter, filter dust and pollution, are psychologically restful and attractive and, critically, reduce carbon dioxide.

Gabriels Wharf, South Bank, London (*Image: Matthew Carmona*), built and managed by Coin Street Community Builders.

Lofland 1973; Milgram 1977; Davis 1990; Carter 1998; Fyfe 1998).

While designers can manipulate functional and cognitive cues to increase the probability of (more) respectful behaviour in public spaces, what can be achieved through design is inevitably limited. Many urban design practitioners, nonetheless, remain optimistic about the probability of particular behaviours in certain environments and advocate good design as a means to achieve certain desirable outcomes. As Ford (2000: 199) argues, writers such as Jane Jacobs and William H Whyte (supposedly) believed that: *'Good streets, sidewalks, parks, and other public spaces bring out the best in human nature and provide the settings for a civil and courteous society. Everything will be fine if we can just get the design right.'*

Those holding a more pessimistic view argue that parks will inevitably attract undesirables; front porches will attract nosy neighbours; grid street patterns will invite strangers into the neighbourhood; benches in public spaces will encourage vagrants; and so forth. These attitudes often translate into highly risk-averse approaches, whereby, rather than risking the possibility of anti-social behaviour, spaces discouraging all and any behaviour are preferred. Such attitudes frequently lead to hostile and anti-social environments, which, rather perversely, seem to foster anti-social behaviour.

While needing to find arguments countering pessimistic views and attitudes, over-optimism and exaggerated claims by urban designers invite charges of environmental determinism. The claim might be that, if houses have front porches, then residents will be more neighbourly and, in time, will form communities. The reality is that they may do but, equally, may not. If benches are provided, vagrants might sleep on them, but if benches were not provided, vagrants could not sleep on them but neither could people sit on them. Urban design should provide rather than denying choice. It is thus preferable to provide the opportunity and, thereafter and as appropriate, to manage or regulate its use.

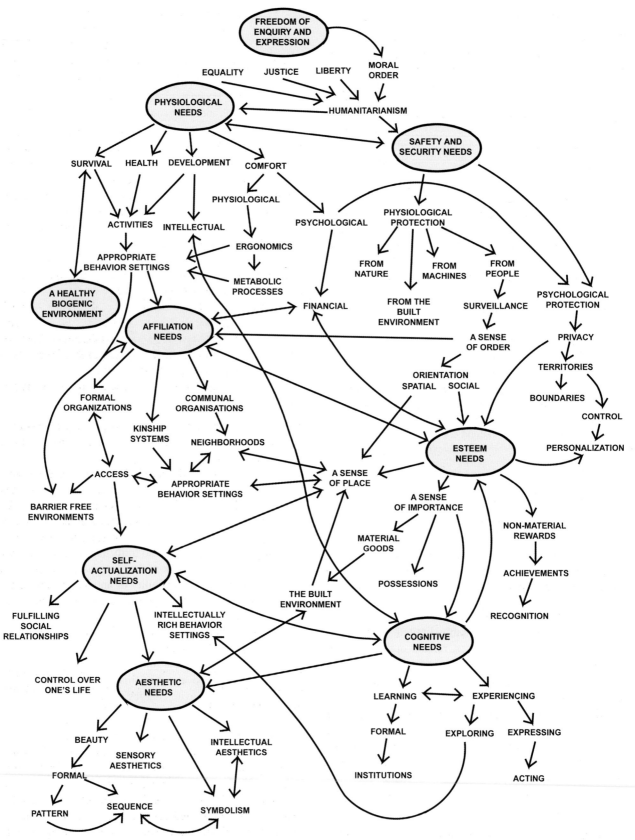

FIGURE 6.2   Hierarchy of human needs *(Image: Lang 1987: 10)*

THE PUBLIC REALM

In Chapter 1, urban design was defined as a process of making better places for people than would otherwise be created. Implicitly we meant public places and in this section we explore the meaning of 'the public'. Commonly evoked in discussions of urban design and place-making, 'public realm' is an often taken-for-granted term and it is important to review what the concept of the public realm — and the related concept of 'public life' — might mean. Frequently reduced to merely the physical public space, it is more than just a physical setting — it is also the activity happening within the container.

The public realm has 'physical' (i.e. space) and 'social' (i.e. activity) dimensions. For the purpose of this book, the *physical* public realm means the series of spaces and settings — which may be publicly or privately owned — that support or facilitate public life and social interaction. The activities and events occurring there can be termed the *socio-cultural* public realm.

The concept of the public must also be understood vis-à-vis private. In broad terms, as Loukaitou-Sideris & Banerjee (1998: 175) observe: *'Public life involves relatively open and universal social contexts, in contrast to private life, which is intimate, familiar, shielded, controlled by the individual, and shared only with family and friends.'* Nonetheless, while private is often the opposite of public, there is also a sense in which public means collective, the opposite of which would be individual. Thus, we must be mindful of a collective/individual axis as well as a public/private axis.

Defining Public Space

Public space is an integral part of the public realm, and is receiving increased attention across the range of social science and humanities disciplines. Each academic discipline views through a different lens and with particular interests and concerns to the fore. Political scientists, for example, generally focus on democratisation and on rights (Arendt 1963; Mitchell 1995; Mensch 2007); geographers on sense-of-place and 'placelessness' (Massey 2005; Amin & Graham 1997); anthropologists and sociologists on the historical construction and subjective value of place (Sorkin 1992; Zukin 1995); legal scholars on access and control in public places (Biffault 1999).

Although an often taken-for-granted term, public space is actually a complex concept for which a definitive definition may be elusive. This section will discuss what is understood by public space and the related concept of public life, before returning to the public realm.

The UK government has adopted the following definition of public space:

'Public space relates to all those parts of the built and natural environment where the public have free access. It encompasses: all the streets, squares and other rights of way, whether predominantly in residential, commercial or community/civic uses; the open spaces and parks; and the "public/private" spaces where public access is unrestricted (at least during daylight hours). It includes the interfaces with key internal and private spaces to which the public normally has free access.'

(Carmona *et al* 2004: 10).

Another way of defining public space is to consider it as all the spaces shown as 'white' in a figure-ground diagram. In Nolli's map of Rome (see Figure 4.22), this definition includes the interiors of key public buildings, such as churches. These are simple and straightforward definitions that are easily understood, the first focusing on whether space is free and unrestricted to enter, and the second on the physical (open) nature of that space.

For many, however, this presents, as Sommer (2009: 145) observes, a *'... false and too easy conflation of the architectural figure with the private and the urban ground with the public.'* Debates thus surround the extent to which public space also includes the wider range of 'pseudo-public' spaces that make up the full public realm, some of which will be 'indoors' spaces, or for which a fee needs to be paid on entering (e.g. a sports stadium).

The relative 'publicness' of space can be considered in terms of three qualities:

- *Ownership* — whether the space is publicly or privately owned, and whether — and in what sense — it constitutes 'neutral' ground.
- *Access* — whether the public has access to the space. This poses the question of whether a place becomes private when an admission fee is charged: consider, for example, the difference between museums for which an entry fee is charged and for which no entry fee is charged: is one public and the other not, or are neither public? While, in urban design terms, 'accessibility' is the capacity to enter and use a space, as discussed later in this chapter, not all public spaces are 'open' and accessible to everyone.
- *Use* — whether the space is actively used and shared by different individuals and groups.

If the distinction between public and private is clear-cut and obvious, then public and private are clearly defined realms and cannot be confused. If it is indistinct and difficult to define, then public/private would be a continuous quality and there are degrees of publicness (Figure 6.3).

So far we have adopted an *objectivist* view, in which public space is something that is 'out-there' and external to people. An alternative perspective is an *interpretivist* or *constructivist* view where 'reality' is socially constructed — that is, it is constructed and constantly reconstructed in minds. From this perspective there is no such thing as a real public space that can, for example, be captured like

FIGURE 6.3 Political activity in public space, Seoul *(Image: Matthew Carmona)*. Public space should offer the opportunity for political display. Rarely allowed in quasi-public space, the presence of such activities is an indicator of publicness — here, in Seoul, solitary political protests are permitted. Another indicator of publicness is whether photographs can be taken. As urban designers, architects and others are aware, property owners are increasingly sensitive to having pictures taken

FIGURE 6.4 Street cafes as informal public life, Barcelona *(Image: Matthew Carmona)*

a butterfly in a net and pinned to a board as an ideal specimen. Instead, there are varying and competing perspectives in terms of both what things are and what they mean. Thus, if people *think* it is a public space, then it is a public space. We thus always need to ask 'to whom' a space might be more (or less) public.

The difficulty with an interpretivist approach is that it prevents us from generalising across spaces. From this perspective, perhaps the best one can hope to find is a temporary, partial consensus on what constitutes public space. But as public space will mean different things to different people, the consensus may often be weak or non-existent. For this reason the broader concepts of public realm and public life are particularly useful.

Public Life

Banerjee (2001: 19) recommends urban designers focus on the broader concept of public life, rather than public spaces (Figures 6.4–6.6). Public life is traditionally associated with public spaces. But, as Banerjee (2001: 19–20) observes, it is increasingly '… *flourishing in private places … in small businesses such as coffee shops, bookstores and other such third places.*' Public life occurs in what might be referred to as social space. This is space used for social interaction, regardless of whether it is publicly owned or privately owned space, provided it is accessible to the public. Oldenburg's 'third place' concept provides a useful way of understanding informal public life and its relation to the public realm (see Box 6.1).

Public life can be broadly grouped into two interrelated types — 'formal' and 'informal'. Of most interest in urban design is informal public life, which, occurring

FIGURE 6.5 Informal public life: browsing on the Left Bank, Paris *(Image: Matthew Carmona)*

FIGURE 6.6 Informal public life: Michigan Avenue, Chicago *(Image: Steve Tiesdell)*

BOX 6.1 Oldenburg's Third Place

Hair-braiding Salon, The Bahamas (*Image: Matthew Carmona*)

Oldenburg's (1999) central thesis is that, to be 'relaxed and fulfilling', daily life must find its balance in three realms of experience — 'domestic', 'work' and 'social'. Drawing on contemporary US society, where domestic life might consist of isolated nuclear families or single people living alone and the work environment essentially solitary, Oldenburg argues that people need the release and stimulation that more sociable realms can provide.

Oldenburg argues that, while seemingly 'amorphous and scattered', informal public life is actually highly focused and emerges in 'core settings'. His term 'third place', therefore, signifies the '... *great variety of public places that host the*

regular, voluntary, informal, and happily anticipated gatherings of individuals beyond the realms of home and work.' (Oldenburg 1999: 16).

Third places are often specific to cultures and to historical eras: Paris has its sidewalk cafes; Florence its piazzas; Vienna its coffee houses; and Germany its beer gardens. Such places emerge and decline; are sustained or neglected; and are replaced or usurped by new 'third' places. As Banerjee (2001: 14) suggests, in many American cities, Starbuck's coffee shops, Borders bookstores and health clubs have become 'major icons' of the third place.

Core qualities of third places, also core qualities of the public realm, include:

- Their existence as neutral ground, where individuals can come and go as they please;
- Being highly inclusive, accessible and not having formal criteria of membership, thereby serving to expand possibilities;
- Their taken-for-granted-ness and low profile;
- Being open during but also outside office hours;
- Their character being marked by a 'playful mood';
- Providing psychological comfort and support; and
- Their 'cardinal and sustaining' activity being conversation and, hence, their being 'political fora of great importance'.

The last quality highlights the overlap between third places and the democratic public realm, with Oldenburg (1999: xxiv) observing that it is not difficult to understand why, at various points in history, coffee houses '... *came under attack by government leaders'*.

---

beyond the realm of formal institutions, entails choice and voluntarism. Many parts of the public realm are discretionary environments — people do not have to use them and can choose whether or not to use them: there may be various ways of getting from A to B, for example, and the choice of which route to follow is made on a number of interrelated grounds — convenience, interest, delight, safety, and, of course, rights of access.

The Public Realm

The public realm can be considered to be the sites and settings of formal and informal public life. This definition includes some notion of public space, whether material or virtual. It includes the media, the Internet, etc., though the particular interest here is with physical and material settings rather than virtual settings.

The concept of physical public realm extends to all the spaces accessible to and used by the public, including:

- *External public space* — those pieces of land lying between private landholdings (e.g. public squares, streets, highways, parks, parking lots, stretches of

coastline, forests, lakes and rivers). These are all spaces that, in principle, are accessible and available to all. This is public space in its purest form.

- *Internal 'public' space* — various public institutions (libraries, museums, town halls, etc.) plus most public transport facilities (train stations, bus stations, airports, etc.).

- *External and internal quasi-'public' space* — although legally private, some public spaces — university campuses, sports grounds, restaurants, cinemas, theatres, nightclubs, shopping malls — also form part of the public realm. This category also includes privatised external public spaces. As the owners and operators of all these public spaces retain rights to regulate access and behaviour within these spaces, they are only nominally public.

The public realm has a number of key functions. Drawing on a range of literature, Loukaitou-Sideris & Banerjee (1998) identified three key functions: (i) a political stage/forum — for political representation, display and action; (ii) neutral or common ground — for social interaction, intermingling, and communication; and (iii) a stage for information exchange, personal development and social learning — that is, for the development of tolerance.

Similarly, Tiesdell & Oc (1998) identified four generally desirable qualities of the public realm: (i) universal access (open to all); (ii) neutral territory (free from coercive forces); (iii) inclusive and pluralist (accepting and accommodating difference); and (iv) symbolic and representative of the collective and of sociability (rather than individuality and privacy). Rarely, if ever, wholly attained in practice, they argued these qualities should be regarded as an analytic ideal providing a measure of the degree to which 'real' public realms fall short. In this sense, they are similar to the qualities of a perfect market (see Chapter 3). A related discussion is whether the analytic ideal is also a normative ideal and thus something to be sought after.

Accessible Public Realm

The criterion of universal access (open to all) suggests a single or unitary public realm. A constructivist interpretation, however, suggests there is no single or *unitary* public realm since a space that is public for citizen A may not be public for citizen B. Many commentators thus argue that there can be no unitary public realm, only a series of overlapping public realms, and instead emphasise the notion of 'multiple publics' (Young 1989; Iveson 1998) — a notion that resonates with a key theme in many critiques of contemporary city development, the 'privatisation' of public space.

Thus, in contemporary society, rather than a 'unitary' polis or public sphere, it may be better to conceive of a series of separate yet overlapping public spheres involving, for example, different socio-economic, gender and ethnic groups (see Calhoun 1992; Boyer 1993; Sandercock 1997; Featherstone 1998). Boyer (1993: 118), for example, argues that:

'Any contemporary references to the "public" is by nature a universalising construct that assumes a collective whole, while in reality the public is fragmented into marginalised groups, many of whom have no voice, position or representation in the public sphere.'

Similarly, according to other commentators, what we are presently witnessing is an *'... increasing diversity of lifestyles and cultures [that] is splintering public space into a patchwork of specialised monocultural enclaves.'* (Mean & Tims 2005). More pertinent, and difficult, questions are whether, and how much, this matters.

The Democratic Public Realm

The key functions and qualities of the public realm relate to a notion of a 'democratic' (and political) public realm — one that has a physical or material basis, but which variously facilitates and symbolises socio-political

activities regarded as important to democratic citizenship.

The democratic nature of public space has pedigree in the urban design literature. Frederick J Olmstead, for example, regarded public parks as a means of allowing different social classes to mix, while, in an early essay, Lynch (1965) argued that 'open' spaces (note *open* rather than *public*) were open to the '... *freely chosen and spontaneous actions of people.'* He later argued that free use of open space may '... *offend us, endanger us, or even threaten the seat of power'*, but is also one of our 'essential values' (Lynch 1972a).

As a political stage, the public realm can be considered to involve or symbolise socio-political activities regarded as important to 'citizenship' and to the existence of a civil society — that is, wider social relations and public participation as against the narrower operations of state or of market. Though not predicated on the existence of material public space, the concept of a 'political' public realm has interested many writers (e.g. Arendt 1958; Habermas 1962, 1979). Arendt (1958), for example, conceived the city as a 'polis' — a self-governing political community whose citizens deliberate, debate and resolve issues. She saw the public realm as satisfying three criteria: by outlasting mortal lives, it memorialised and, thereby, conveyed a sense of history and society to individuals; it was an arena for diverse groups of people to engage in dialogue, debate and oppositional struggles; and it was accessible to and used by all (from Ellin 1996: 126).

Existing between the domain of the state and the private domain of the individual and the family, Jurgen Habermas' 'public sphere' relates to the sphere where public affairs are discussed and debated (Habermas 1962). His ideas are based on the development of various spaces — coffee houses, salons, etc., together with newspapers, journals, periodicals and reviews — in eighteenth century Europe, that encouraged new forms of reasoned argumentation.

Rather than public realm, Habermas used the term 'public sphere' and it could be argued that the concept of the public realm (by contrast) bridges — perhaps too easily and too unproblematically — public space and public sphere. It is perhaps more accurate to say that the public realm includes some elements of public sphere and of public space. Low & Smith (2006: 5) discuss the relationship between public sphere, seen as an essentially political concept — the 'politics-of-the-public' — and public space, seen as an essentially physical concept. They note the considerable literature — developed by philosophers and political theorists and literary and legal scholars — concerning the *public sphere*, which

'..... emphasises the ideas, media, institutions, and practices that all contribute to the generation of something that we can call the public, publics or public opinions, and the work is generally

nested both in a larger historical framework concerning the state and the transformation of bourgeois social relations and in a normative search for political and moral effectiveness. ... So viewed, the public sphere is rarely if ever spatalised.'

They then note that, at the same time, architects, geographers, planners, anthropologists, urbanists and others have discussed *public space*:

'This work is explicitly spatial, seeking to comprehend the ways in which social and political, and economic and cultural processes and relations make specific public places and landscapes, and the ways in which, in turn, these geographies reaffirm, contradict, or alter their constituent social and political relations.'

(Low & Smith 2006: 5).

They conclude that, while these public spaces and public sphere literatures overlap, they typically occupy separate domains: *'The public sphere remains essentially ungrounded while public space discussions insufficiently connect to mediations on the public sphere.'* Low & Smith (2006: 6) subsequently assert that the *'... spatiality of the public sphere potentially transforms our understanding of the politics of the public. An understanding of public space is an imperative for understanding the public sphere.'*

The Decline of the Public Realm

Many commentators observe the declining significance of public space and the public realm. In part, this is attributed to the reduced availability of, and significance attached to, public space – and a related diminution of public life. Use of the public realm has also been challenged by various developments, such as increased personal mobility – initially through the car and subsequently through the Internet (see Chapter 2). Contemporary social interaction is also affected by the conflict within public space between social space and movement space, with private cars facilitating an essentially private control over public space (see Chapter 4).

More generally, there has also been a retreat from, and disengagement with, public space and public facilities – both as causes and as consequences of the trend towards privatisation (see Chapter 3). In *The Fall of Public Man*, for example, Sennett (1977) documented the social, political and economic factors leading to a privatisation of people's lives and the 'end of public culture'. Similarly Ellin (1996: 149) observes how many of the social and civic functions that traditionally occurred in public spaces have been abandoned or usurped by more private realms as activities such as leisure, entertainment, gaining information and consumption can increasingly be satisfied at home through the television or the Internet. Activities once only available

in collective and public forms have become available in individualised and private forms. The domestication of leisure – through, for example, mass ownership of radios, televisions, hi-fis, video recorders and computers – has also meant that public space and other areas of public assembly are less significant as a focus of people's lives.

Ellin (1999: 167) also observes how, as the public realm has grown increasingly impoverished, *'... there has been a corresponding decline in meaningful space and a desire to control one's space, or to privatise.'* She suggests that the appropriation of public space by private agencies epitomises this 'privatisation impulse': *'... the inward-turning shopping mall which has abandoned the central city for the suburbs and which turns its back entirely on its surroundings with its fortress-like exterior surrounded by a moat-like car park.'* (Ellin 1999: 168).

Observing the process of privatising and selling off standardised infrastructure systems, Graham (2001: 365) suggests it is most familiar and widespread in the domain of public streets: *'The municipally-controlled street systems, that once acted as effective monopolies of the public realm in many cities, are being paralleled by the growth of a set of shadow, privatised street spaces.'*

Loukaitou-Sideris (1991, from Loukaitou-Sideris & Banerjee 1998: 87) notes how the desire of office workers, tourists and conventioneers to be separated from 'threatening' groups provides the market opportunity for spaces produced, maintained and controlled by the private sector.

Nevertheless, some commentators (e.g. Brill 1989; Krieger 1995) argue that perceptions of the public realm's apparent decline are based on a false notion and that, in reality, the public realm has never been *'... as diverse, dense, classless, or democratic as is now imagined.'* (Loukaitou-Sideris & Banerjee 1998: 182). Other commentators note resurgence in the use of public space, seeing it as a process of socio-cultural transformation. For Carr *et al* (1992: 343), the relationship of public space to public life is dynamic and reciprocal, with new forms of public life requiring new spaces (Figures 6.7 and 6.8).

But there is the possibility of a vicious spiral: if people use public space less, then there is less incentive to provide new spaces and to maintain existing spaces. With a decline in their maintenance and quality, public spaces are likely to be used less, thereby exacerbating the spiral of decline. As is discussed in Chapter 8, use of the public space is also a function of its quality and the extent to which it provides a supportive and conducive environment.

NEIGHBOURHOODS

A well-developed tradition of neighbourhood design exists. Perhaps the most influential has been Clarence Perry's neighbourhood unit developed in the USA during the 1920s

FIGURE 6.7 Promenade Plantee, Paris *(Image: Matthew Carmona)*. Discussed railway viaducts in Paris have been reclaimed as green pathways, elevated above the city streets and providing often surprisingly direct connections between places

FIGURE 6.8 Madison Square Park, New York *(Image: Matthew Carmona)*. In this park, dogs are only permitted off the lead in the Designated Dog Pound. The regulation creates a new form of meeting space for those with dogs

(Box 6.2). Perry's ideas were developed as a means of organising and developing parts of cities in a systematic and logical fashion. In the USA, New Urbanism brought together neo-traditional neighbourhoods (NTDs) and traditional neighbourhood development (TNDs), which exhibit a clear lineage from Perry's ideas (see Box 6.3). In Europe, stimulated by Leon Krier among others, there has been interest in the idea and concept of urban quarters. This found resonance in the Urban Villages movement in the UK in the 1990s, with the Urban Villages Forum (later incorporated into the Prince's Foundation) established to advocate and promote such developments (Aldous 1992; Biddulph 2000).

Overlaid on the physical and spatial design of a neighbourhood were more social ideas and objectives, such as social balance (mixed communities), neighbour interaction and the creation of identity and sense-of-community. Three interrelated strands of thinking thus informed neighbourhood design:

First, neighbourhoods have been proposed and/or designed as a planning device – that is, as a relatively pragmatic and useful way of structuring and organising urban areas (with or without associated social objectives). Rather than a highly atomistic development, these are attempts to contribute to something larger, so that the 'whole' is greater than the sum of the parts: for example, an attempt to create mixed-use or 'balanced' neighbourhoods rather than monofunctional housing estates. Increasingly the pursuit of more sustainable modes of development has acted as justification for such approaches. Neighbourhoods, for example, can be designed to be more self-sufficient in terms of reducing the need to travel by encouraging walking – that is, walkable neighbourhoods – and by providing opportunities for work and recreation closer to home.

Second, neighbourhoods have also been proposed and/or designed as areas of identity and character to create or enhance a sense-of-place. While this may be a relatively superficial sense of identity with the area's physical character, it may also be a deeper and perhaps more meaningful sense of identity with the place's socio-cultural character (i.e. through time-thickened experience).

Third, neighbourhoods have been proposed and/or designed as a means of creating areas of greater social/resident interaction and enhancing neighbourliness. A frequent theme in neighbourhood design has been that of 'community' and, as such, neighbourhood design has often been associated with the idea that certain layouts, and the configuration of particular forms and land uses, assist the formation of 'communities'. The conflation of 'physical' neighbourhoods – defined by such physical properties as territory or boundaries – and 'social' communities – defined by such social properties as character, reputation and associations – has, nonetheless, increasingly been challenged.

Blowers (1973) identified five types of neighbourhood. While each is recognisable as a neighbourhood, only the final one has the attributes of a community:

- *Arbitrary neighbourhoods* based on a common territory, where the only common feature is spatial proximity.
- *Ecological* and *ethnological neighbourhoods* with a common environment and identity.
- *Homogeneous neighbourhoods* inhabited by particular socio-economic or ethnic groups.
- *Functional neighbourhoods*, derived from the geographical mapping of service provision.

Perry proposed each neighbourhood unit should contain four basic elements: (i) an elementary school; (ii) small parks and playgrounds; (iii) small stores; and (iv) a configuration of buildings and streets that allowed all public facilities to be within safe pedestrian access. Six physical attributes were also specified:

- *Size* – the population required to support one elementary school.
- *Boundaries* – arterial roads to bypass rather than penetrate the unit.
- *Open spaces*.
- *Institutional sites* – at the central point so that the sphere of influence coincided with the unit.
- *Local shops* – located on the edge of the unit so that larger units would be formed at junctions.
- *An internal street system* – proportional to the expected traffic load.

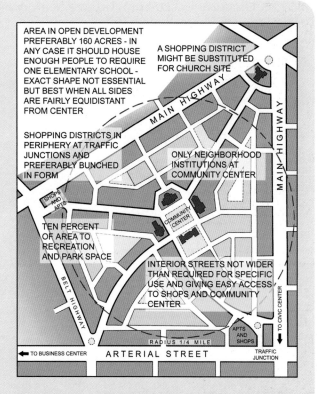

Clarence Perry's neighbourhood unit (*Image: Duany et al 2000*)

- *Community neighbourhood*, in which a close-knit, socially homogeneous group engages in primary contacts.

While some critics presume all attempts to design better neighbourhoods are, *ipso facto,* also attempts to create communities, advocates of neighbourhood planning expose themselves to criticism by claiming certain design strategies will (inexorably) create a stronger sense-of-community. In making claims about creating communities, for example, some New Urbanists have overreached themselves (see Brain 2005).

Advising 'steering away' from the term community in connection with physical design, Talen (2000: 179) suggests using more specific elements of community – such as resident interaction – that make better sense in the context of urban design. Resident interaction can be influenced by design strategies providing opportunities to increase the frequency of visual contacts, such that, through repetitive visual contact, more meaningful contact may be provoked. Visual contacts stimulate a relatively superficial form of social interaction. For more in-depth, meaningful and sustained or enduring interaction, those interacting must have something in common. As Gans (1961) noted in his studies of residential environments, propinquity may initiate many

social relationships and maintain less intensive ones, but (physical) friendships require social homogeneity.

The central issues regarding neighbourhood design concepts can be reviewed under four headings – size; boundaries; social relevance; and mixed communities.

(i) Size

Considerable debate has occurred regarding optimal neighbourhood size, which has usually been expressed in terms of area or population, sometimes both. The preferred area is often limited to what is considered to be a comfortable walking distance – this is either 5 minutes or 10 minutes or 300–800 m (1000–2000 feet) (see Chapter 8). The preferred size is sometimes derived from the catchment's population for a primary or elementary school or, in the case of transit-oriented development (TOD), the population required to make public transit viable.

The population size has also been derived from that of smaller – supposedly more social – communities in small towns and villages. Jacobs (1961), however, highlighted the fallacy of trying to establish a rigid threshold population, arguing that a population of 10 000 in a large city would not have the innate cross-connections that would occur among the same

BOX 6.3 Characteristics of Urban Villages and New Urbanist Neighbourhoods

Urban Villages

Poundbury Farm, Dorchester (*Image: Matthew Carmona*)

- *Size* – small enough for all places to be within walking distance of each other and for people to know each other.
- *Size* – large enough to support a wide range of activities and facilities and to be able to stand up for itself when its interests come under threat.
- *A range of uses* – mixed within street blocks as well as within the village as a whole.
- *A balance of houses and flats and workspaces* – such that there is a theoretical one-to-one ratio between jobs and residents able and willing to work.
- *A pedestrian-friendly environment* – catering for the car without encouraging its use.
- *A mixture of different building types and sizes*, including some degree of mixed use with buildings.
- *Robust building types.*
- *Mixed tenure* – both for residential and employment uses.
- Compact, pedestrian-friendly, mixed-use and identifiable areas that encourage citizens to take responsibility for their maintenance and evolution.
- Daily living activities within walking distance, allowing independence to those who do not drive.
- Appropriate building densities and land uses within walking distance of transit stops, thereby permitting public transit to become a viable alternative to the automobile.

New Urbanist Neighbourhoods

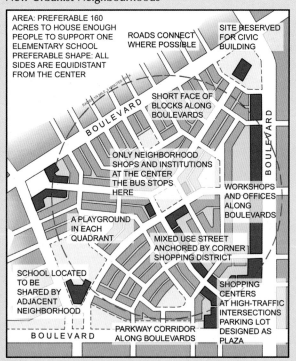

Duany & Plater-Zyberk's neighbourhood concept (*Image: Duany et al 2000*)

- Interconnected networks of streets, thereby encouraging walking, reducing the number and length of automobile trips, and conserving energy.
- Broad range of housing types and price levels, thereby bringing people of diverse ages, races and incomes into daily interaction.
- Concentrations of civic, institutional and commercial activity.
- Schools sized and located to enable children to walk or cycle to them.
- A range of parks/open space.

---

population in a small town. She argued only three kinds of neighbourhood were useful: the city as whole; the street-neighbourhood; and districts of large, sub-city size composed of 100 000 people or more (i.e. those large enough to be politically significant).

Research has shown how the size of physically identifiable neighbourhoods does not necessarily correspond with people's social relations and, furthermore, that residents do not perceive the neighbourhood unit as a neighbourhood. Such conceptions of neighbourhood and community are often top-down constructions with little meaning when viewed from the

bottom up. Gans (1962: 11), for example, found patterns of activity within his Boston West End neighbourhood were so diverse that only outsiders ever considered it a single neighbourhood. Lee (1965) identified three neighbourhoods that residents themselves perceive: the 'social acquaintance' neighbourhood; the 'homogeneous' neighbourhood (i.e. people in homes like ours); and the 'social provision' or unit neighbourhood. The most congruent with people's social relations was the social acquaintance neighbourhood:

'The schema includes a small physical area, perhaps half-a-dozen streets containing only houses, apart from the few

corner shops and pubs that invariably go with them. Sheer propinquity produces a state of affairs in which the family knows everyone else.'

(Lee, 1965).

(ii)   Boundaries

A prevalent idea has been that clear boundaries to neighbourhoods (i.e. a distinct territory) will enhance functional and social interaction, sense-of-community and identity within those boundaries. Different opinions have, however, been expressed about the value of such boundaries. Jacobs (1961) argued against identifying the boundaries because, where neighbourhoods worked best, they had no beginnings or ends, and their success depended on overlapping and interweaving.

In his seminal essay '*A City is Not a Tree*', Alexander (1965) criticised the use of the neighbourhood as a discrete unit within the city. Alexander's argument concerns the properties of 'tree' and 'semi-lattice' structures as ways of combining a number of small systems into larger and more complex systems (see Sustainability Insert 1, Chapter 4). Tree structures consist of separate and discrete systems organised into hierarchies, but in semi-lattice structures the systems are variously and complexly related and overlapped. Accordingly, Alexander argued that cities should not be designed as neatly branching tree-like structures and, *inter alia,* condemned city plans establishing discretely bounded neighbourhoods and/or functionally zoned areas. Similarly, Lynch (1981: 401) argued that planning a city as a series of neighbourhoods was either 'futile' or, alternatively, would support social segregation, because '*... any good city has a continuous fabric, rather than a cellular one.*'

(iii)   Social relevance and meaning

The idea of discrete and self-sufficient neighbourhoods has also been criticised for being anachronistic — that is, being outmoded and having limited relevance to contemporary society, particularly in consideration of increased mobility, especially car-based mobility, and more recently by mobility enabled by electronic communications. While communities-of-place still exist, they have been supplemented and often supplanted by communities-of-interest detached from any specific locale. Common territory is, thus, no longer a prerequisite of community and social interaction.

Furthermore, in a highly mobile age, it is argued that people no longer want, or need, the same sense-of-community and neighbourliness. They are not geographically limited to the neighbourhood or local area and can pick and choose from the entire city (and beyond) for jobs, recreation, friends, shops, entertainment, their children's schools, etc. — and in the process form communities of choice. Nevertheless, it is not an issue of an either/or choice between mobility and spatially diffuse contacts and acquaintances or spatially proximate networks of friendships; it is — more correctly — one of providing opportunities for both and allowing people to find their own balance. Whether they have certain social characteristics or not, neighbourhoods are also places with distinct characters that residents can identify with and that offer, where sought or desired, a sense-of-belonging.

(iv)   Mixed communities

Advocates of neighbourhood design consistently emphasise mixed use. Mixed-use neighbourhood design concepts, for example, are considered to be valuable for environmental and social sustainability purposes (i.e. mixing tenures and providing facilities and activities close to homes) (Figure 6.9). Arguing that zoning resulted in a mechanical segregation of urban functions rather than their organic integration (see Chapter 8), Krier (1990) based his proposals for reconstructing the European city as mixed-use urban quarters rather than monofunctional zones. For Krier, a city should be conceived of as a 'family' of quarters, with each quarter being a 'City within a City' integrating all the daily functions of urban life (dwelling, working, leisure) within a territory not exceeding 35 ha and 15 000 inhabitants.

While a general criticism of all attempts at creating neighbourhoods/communities, the charge of social engineering has commonly been levelled at attempts to create socially balanced neighbourhoods and communities (see Banerjee & Baer 1984). Some element of social mix is, nevertheless, desirable and there are various benefits from mixed and (better) balanced neighbourhoods. Both the Urban Villages Forum and the Congress of the New Urbanism, for example, emphasised the need for a variety of house prices and tenures. DTLR/CABE (2001: 34) lists the following advantages:

- Providing a better balance of demand for community services and facilities (e.g. schools, recreation facilities and care for elderly people).
- Providing opportunities for 'life-time' communities (e.g. where people can either age-in-place or move home without leaving the neighbourhood).
- Making the neighbourhoods more robust by avoiding concentrations of housing of the same type.
- Enabling community self-help (e.g. assistance with childcare, help with shopping, the garden or during the winter freeze).
- Assisting surveillance through people coming and going throughout the day and evening.

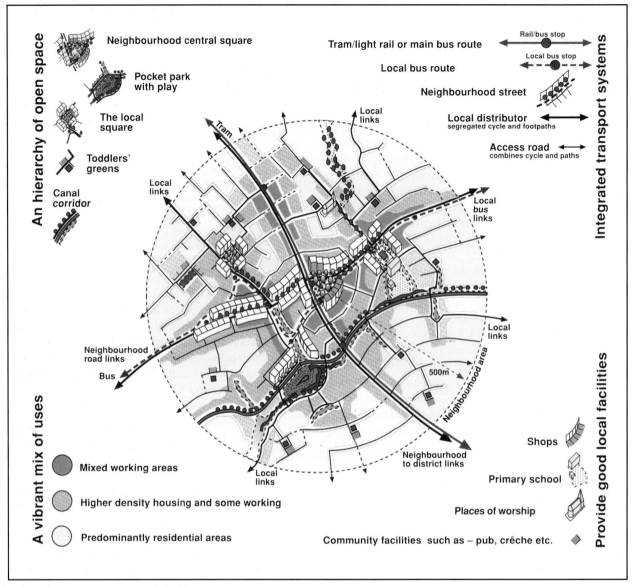

FIGURE 6.9   Mixed-use neighbourhood *(Image: Urban Task Force 1999: 66)*

Mixed neighbourhoods also provide a greater diversity of building form and scales, which (potentially) makes the neighbourhood more visually interesting and provides greater scope for local distinctiveness and character (Figure 6.10).

Achieving social mix is often problematic (Kintrea & Atkinson 2000). Moreover, in the contemporary period, there is an increasing trend towards segregation. In the USA, the desire for social homogeneity is often a function of race, while in Europe, especially the UK, it is a function of socio-economic class. In all cases, however, it is driven by a desire to protect property values.

Segregation, however, compromises the public realm's role as an important stage for social learning, personal development and information exchange. Within the urban design literature, the social segregation of urban space and the damaging effects of exclusion are receiving increasing attention. Segregation allows a certain ignorance regarding social difference and thus a fear of 'the other' (Ellin 1996: 145–6). Social segregation, for example, has been central to Richard Sennett's work (e.g. Sennett 1970, 1977, 1990). Sennett (1990: 20) argues that people living in 'sealed communities' are 'diminished in their development':

'The wounds of past experience, the stereotypes which have become rooted in memory, are not confronted. Recognition scenes that might occur at borders are the only chance people have to confront fixed, sociological pictures routinised in time.'

FIGURE 6.10 Stapleton, Denver, Colorado *(Image: Steve Tiesdell)*. Accessory units allow a more diverse range of house types within a neighbourhood

Echoing Sennett's arguments, Duany *et al* (2000: 45−6) argue that the segregationist pattern is self-perpetuating because children growing up in such homogeneous environments are

'... less likely to develop a sense of empathy for people from other walks of life and [are] *ill-prepared to live in a diverse society. The other becomes alien to the child's experience, witnessed only through the sensationalising eye of the television.'*

Given a relatively free property market and contemporary desires for social homogeneity (to live with people 'like us'), it is difficult for a diverse social mix to be achieved or sustained: neighbourhoods that start out diverse often evolve through market processes towards greater social homogeneity (see Cheshire 2006). This social tendency can, nevertheless, be reinforced and exacerbated by certain development patterns and design strategies. In residential development, a high degree of market segmentation is obtained by dividing developments into separate pods − each pod being designated for a different type of dwelling, occupant and price bracket (see Chapter 4). Observing a suburban landscape composed of housing pods each composed entirely of one type and price of housing unit, Duany *et al* (2000: 43) highlight the 'ruthless segregation by minute graduations of income': *'There have always been better or worse neighbourhoods, and the rich have often taken refuge from the poor, but never with such precision.'*

Conversely, however, certain patterns of development provide an element of exclusivity without strict separation. In traditional neighbourhoods, house prices and types may vary considerably from street to street, with the transition typically occurring at mid-block where backyards and gardens meet. Discussing how design can support neighbourhood diversity, Talen (2009a: 184−5; see also Talen 2008b) lists some of the ways in which design can help make diversity viable:

- By showing how multi-family units can be accommodated in single-family blocks.
- By designing links between diverse land uses and housing types.
- By creating paths through edges that disrupt connectivity.
- By increasing density near public transit.
- By demonstrating the value of non-standard unit types like courtyard housing, closes and residential mews.
- By fitting small businesses and live/work units in residential neighbourhoods.
- By developing codes that successfully accommodate land-use diversity.
- By softening the impact of big box retail development in under-invested commercial strips.
- By designing streets that function as collective spaces.
- By connecting institutions to their surrounding residential fabric.

She explains that:

'... these are some of the "mundane" ways that urban design addresses, the basic requirements of human integration, the fears that arise from uncomfortable proximities, and often contentious fitting together of wide-ranging uses. ... Design is needed not to smooth out every wrong but to help make diversity liveable and even preferable.'

(Talen 2009a: 185).

Research on mixed tenure development in the UK (see Jupp 1999), however, has shown that only by mixing tenures within streets (rather than street-by-street or block-by-block) do the benefits of building cross-tenure social networks occur − indicating, *inter alia*, that the street is the strongest social unit. The research, thus, recommended mixing tenures along streets.

The criticisms and comments made above do not negate the value of neighbourhood design patterns and merely qualify their use. Most of the principles of neighbourhood design advocated by the Urban Villages Forum and the CNU, for example, are also principles of sustainable urban design. Problems often stem, however, from an over-rigid application of the principles of better neighbourhood design. Lynch (1981: 250), for example, concluded it was *'... the concept of the large, autonomous, sharply defined, and rigid neighbourhood unit of a standard size, to which all physical and social relations are keyed, that seems to be inappropriate for our society.'* Rather than dogma, they are generally desirable design principles to be adapted in the light of the local context and prevailing social, economic and political realities.

SAFETY AND SECURITY

People face a variety of threats in the urban environment − crime; 'street barbarism'; acts of terrorism; fast-moving vehicles; natural disasters/phenomena; and unseen problems such as air pollution and water contamination. In some parts of the world, the threats of natural disasters — earthquakes, floods, volcanic eruptions — are everyday concerns to be addressed in the design of buildings and settlements. To some degree, building techniques and technology allow such problems to be managed and the resultant threats reduced. Other threats — real or imagined — seemingly continue to increase. This section deals principally with crime, safety and security and particularly their relationship to the public realm. Road/pedestrian safety is discussed in Chapter 8.

Security relates to the 'protection' of oneself, one's family and friends, and individual and communal property. Lack of security, perceptions of lack of safety and fear-of-victimisation are threats both to the use of the public realm and to the creation of better places. Creating a sense of security and safety is, thus, an essential prerequisite of successful urban design.

Fear of Victimisation

A distinction should be made between 'fear' and 'risk' — the difference between 'feeling safe' and actually 'being safe'. In general, women are more fearful of victimisation than men. Although the gender-fear gap narrows with increasing age, men do not ever become as fearful as women. Fear-of-victimisation may also be out of proportion with the risk-of-victimisation: those most at risk statistically in the UK, for example, are young males, while those exhibiting most fear are women, the elderly and ethnic minorities. There is, however, an explanation: being more risk-averse, vulnerable people take precautionary measures. Hence, as a direct result of fewer women and older people putting themselves at risk, they are less likely to be victimised.

In terms of its impact, the perception of crime can be as instrumental as its actuality (i.e. the statistical risk). Perceptions come from many sources, such as reporting of crime in the media. In response to fear-of-victimisation many people take precautionary actions either to avoid the risk or, where risk avoidance is not possible or desirable, to reduce their exposure through risk management. Hence, fear-of-victimisation is a cause of exclusion not just from particular places but from much of the public realm (see Ellin 1997; Oc & Tiesdell 1997).

If people choose not to use a particular place or environment because, at best, they feel uncomfortable there and, at worst, they are afraid and feel unsafe, the public realm is impoverished. Such avoidance is a consequence of fear of certain environments as well as fears of particular incidents. Many people, for example, are apprehensive about or fearful of certain parts of urban areas, such as pedestrian subways, dark alleys and areas that are deserted or crowded with the 'wrong kind of people'. Many are disturbed by situations restricting choice or offering no alternatives — for example, subways as the only means of crossing busy roads or narrow pavements and constricted entrances, particularly when obstructed by 'people who create anxiety' — winos, beggars, rowdy or drunken youths, etc. Similarly, signs of physical and social disorder, such as graffiti, litter, broken windows, vandalised public property, vomit and urine in shop doorways, suggest an out-of-control, and thus unpredictable, environment.

Fear-of-victimisation (rather than actual levels of crime) is often the driver of moves to privatise parts of the public realm, segregating communities in the process (Minton 2006: 24). This privatisation usually translates into express control of certain territories or spaces — through the use of different means of segregation and isolation, such as physical distance, walls, gates and fences or other, less visible barriers to shut out and exclude the outside world and its perceived threats and challenges — and also by means of active policing strategies and surveillance cameras.

Privatisation is akin to the phenomenon of 'voluntary exclusion', whereby some — usually more affluent groups — choose to live separately. Described as the 'succession of the successful' from the civic life of the broader society by former US Labour Secretary Robert Reich (see also Lasch 1995), it is manifested in a variety of ways, including opting out of public education and public health systems and opting out of privatising public space. In the urban design field, the most visible manifestation is the gated community (see Box 6.4).

Crime, Disorder and Incivility

Considerations of safety are related to — but distinct from — concerns about crime. Crime is about offenders and offences; safety about victims and fear-of-victimisation. In public space, it is often disorderly rather than necessarily criminal behaviour that is problematic. Hence, it is important to distinguish between criminal and disorderly behaviour. While the general definition of a crime is a transgression of a formally constituted law (and, thus, prosecutable as an offence), much of the disorderly conduct and anti-social behaviour associated with public space is an incivility rather than a crime (though there have been attempts to criminalise some incivilities).

Common problems in public space are disorderly conduct and incivilities:

- *Disorderly conduct:* Kelling (1987: 95) defines 'disorder' as a '... *condition resulting from behaviour that, depending on location, time and local traditions, is offensive in its violation of expectancy for normalcy and peace in a community.*' Hence, disorder generally refers also to disorderly conduct.
- *Incivilities:* Provoking anxiety and apprehension, La Grange *et al* (1992: 312) define incivilities as '... *low level breaches of community standards that signal an*

BOX 6.4 Gated Communities

Security settlement — Pretoria, South Africa (*Image: Steve Tiesdell*)

Gated communities can be seen as a dramatic manifestation of fragmentation, polarisation and divisions within society. In their book, *Fortress America* (1997), Blakely & Snyder chronicle how, attempting to find like-minded neighbours, secure property values, and/or reduce or escape from the impact of crime, communities erect walls and gates, controlling who can — and, more importantly, who cannot — enter. Gated communities differ from apartment blocks — which may have entry control systems or door personnel to prevent public access to lobbies, hallways, and parking lots — because the geographical scale of enclosure is much greater: the gated community's walls and fences prevent public access to streets, pavements, parks, beaches, rivers, trails, playgrounds, etc., which would otherwise be open and shared by all the citizens of a locality.

Rather than public institutions, amenities and space being public or 'quasi-public' goods (see Chapter 3), such facilities become private 'club' goods, with explicit criteria of membership determining who benefits (i.e. those that can only be consumed if one is a member of the club) (see Webster 2001, 2002). The chief criterion for membership is usually ability to pay.

Gating, however, does little to address the cause of the problems it is a response to: the neighbourhood remains embedded within a wider society, which it cannot wholly escape nor wholly insulate itself from. The supposed safety advantages of gating are gained at the expense of those left outside : '... *the relatively influential and law-abiding citizens on the inside are no longer motivated or, probably, even able to make any contribution to the safety, or the sense of safety of conditions outside.*' (Bentley 1999: 163). The gates are, in essence, a private solution imposing significant public and social costs, and Blakely & Snyder (1997: 173) argue the entire public realm should be considered when gating.

The impact of gated communities can be militated, though not removed, by limiting the size of the gated enclosures; by softening the design of the boundary (e.g. through landscaping measures); and by requiring facilities and amenities to be located outside the enclosure and made accessible to non-residents (see Miao 2003; Xu & Yang 2009). Gated communities are an increasingly common form of development in many parts of the world. In China, for example, more than 80% of new housing development takes this form. Arguably gating is a traditional form in China where courtyard housing was often located in compounds and in workers' compounds during the communist era — though, today, they have security guards and non-residents are excluded whereas in the past they were not.

---

erosion of conventionally accepted norms and values.' Sometimes referred to as 'quality of life' crimes, Jacobs (1961: 39) aptly referred to them as 'street barbarism'. There are *social* incivilities and *physical* incivilities: the presence of vagrants and down-and-outs, for example, is a physical incivility; 'aggressive begging' is a social incivility (and may also be a crime). Women are often disproportional victims of incivilities and suffer greater distress as a result of them (see Fyfe *et al* 2006; Boyd 2006; Philips & Smith 2006; Banister *et al* 2006).

Whatever the causation, today's society is generally seen as less law-abiding and more prone to disorder than in the past (see Field 2003). The decline in civility also involves disregard for — or ignorance of — conventions of good or respectful behaviour necessary for life in a well-functioning society. Wherever people collectively inhabit and share a space or territory, rules — sometimes formal, but often informal — govern the use of that space (Lawson 2001: 2–3).

Levels of tolerance relating to anti-social street activity also contribute to the problem. Realist criminologists see crime rates as a product of two forces — changes in behaviour *and* changes in definitions. Young (1992: 44) argues these are not necessarily covariant: vandalism may increase but people become more tolerant about graffiti; acts of violence may decrease, yet people become more sensitive to it.

Younger people often seem to accept a certain amount of rowdiness as an inevitable part of a night out and may often tolerate actions older people would find offensive and a deterrent to their use of certain places, particularly in the evening or at night. Those more familiar with the evening/night-time scene, for example, are better able to decode signals, and can assess whether they are threatening and decide what action needs to be taken. Having lost or never having developed those skills, those less familiar may often interpret general rowdiness as an immediate personal threat.

Approaches to Crime Prevention

'Dispositional' and 'situational' represent two main approaches to crime prevention. The dispositional approach involves removing or lessening an individual's motivation to commit criminal acts, through education and moral guidance; sanctions and penalties as deterrents; and/or community, social and economic development. The main thrust of the situational approach is that *once* an offender has made the *initial decision* to offend (i.e. has become motivated), then the techniques make the commission of *that* crime in that *particular place* more difficult.

Principally developed and codified by Clarke (1992, 1997), the situational approach focuses attention on the opportunity for crime:

'Proceeding from an analysis of the circumstances giving rise to specific kinds of crime, [situational crime prevention] *introduces discrete managerial and environmental change to reduce the opportunity for those crimes to occur. Thus, it is focused on the settings for crime, rather than upon those committing criminal acts.'*

(Clarke 1997: 4).

Situational measures manipulate not just the physical but also the social and psychological settings for crime. There are four overarching opportunity reduction strategies:

- Increasing the perceived effort of the offence.
- Increasing the perceived risk of the offence.
- Reducing the reward from the offence.
- Removing excuses for the offence. (Clarke 1997) (see also Wortley 1998, 2001; Cornish & Clarke 2003).

There is a continuing debate regarding which approach is most effective. In theory, reducing the offender's motivation to offend is innately superior, but, because it is often difficult to effect, the situational approach and opportunity reduction measures are often justified on practical grounds. Nevertheless, while design may affect crime and/or perceptions of safety, it can only create the preconditions for a safer environment: it is not a substitute for changing the conduct or reducing the underlying motivation of offending individuals.

Dispositional and situational approaches may also produce radically different environments. To illustrate the difference Bottoms (1990: 7) provides an analogy with child-raising:

'... some parents might lock cupboards or drawers to prevent their children from helping themselves to loose cash, chocolates and so forth (opportunity reduction); others will prefer ... not to lock up anything in the house but so to socialise their children that they will not steal even if the opportunities are available.'

Dispositional approaches are, however, generally outside the scope of urban design action and, thus, outside the remit of this book.

Opportunity Reduction Methods

Opportunity reduction methods have been developed within the mainstream urban design literature, with key themes of activity, surveillance, territorial definition and control occurring throughout these discussions (see Table 6.1). Originating with Jacobs (1961), these ideas were developed through Oscar Newman's ideas of 'defensible space' and the Crime Prevention Through Environment Design (CPTED) approach. More recently, Bill Hillier's perspective on crime and safety re-engages with Jane Jacobs.

Jacobs stressed the need for activity to provide surveillance and for sufficient territorial definition to distinguish between 'private' and 'public' spaces. Jacobs' (1961: 40) prerequisite of a successful neighbourhood was that '... *a person must feel personally safe and secure on the street among all these strangers.'* She argued that, rather than by the police, the 'public peace' was kept by an intricate network of voluntary controls and standards and that sidewalks, adjacent uses and their users were 'active participants' in the 'drama of civilisation versus barbarism':

'... the streets of a city must do most of the job of handling strangers, for this is where strangers come and go. The streets must not only defend the city against predatory strangers, they must protect the many, many peaceable and well-meaning strangers who use them ensuring their safety too as they pass through.'

(Jacobs 1961: 45).

Oscar Newman developed some of Jacobs' ideas further, emphasising surveillance and territorial definition. To explore the relationship between physical design and crime, Newman studied the locations of crimes in housing projects in New York. The resulting book, *Defensible Space: People and Design in the Violent City* (1973), proposed restructuring urban environments based on his interpretation of territoriality: '... *so that they can again become liveable and controlled not by police but by a community of people sharing a common terrain.'*

Newman identified three factors associated with increases in the crime rate in residential blocks: *anonymity* — people did not know their neighbours; *lack of surveillance* — making it easier for crimes to be committed unseen; and the *availability of escape routes* — making it easier for criminals to disappear from the scene. From these he developed his concept of 'defensible space':

'... the range of mechanisms — real and symbolic barriers, strongly defined areas of influence, and improved opportunities for surveillance — that combine to bring an environment under the control of its residents.'

(Newman 1973).

TABLE 6.1 Situational Approaches

	Jane Jacobs	Oscar Newman	CPTED	Space Syntax
Control of space/ territoriality	*Clear demarcation* between public and private spaces.	*Territoriality* — capacity of the physical environment to create perceived zones of territorial influence (including mechanisms symbolising boundaries and defining a hierarchy of increasingly private zones).	*Natural access* control aimed at reducing opportunities by denying access to the crime target. *Territorial reinforcement* — physical design. Creating or extending a sphere of influence so that users of a property develop a sense of proprietorship.	Spaces integrated with other spaces, so that pedestrians are encouraged to see into and move through them.
Surveillance	Need for eyes-on-the-street' belonging to street's 'natural proprietors' (street users and residents). Enhanced by a diversity of activities and various functions that naturally create peopled places.	*Surveillance* — capacity of physical design to provide surveillance opportunities for residents and their agents.	*Natural surveillance* as a result of the routine use of property.	Surveillance provided by people moving through spaces.
Activity	Sidewalks need '... *users on it fairly continuously, both to add to the number of effective eyes on the street and to induce people in buildings along the street to watch the sidewalks in sufficient number.'*	Rejects the argument that more activity on the street and the presence of commercial uses necessarily reduces street crime.	Argues for reduced through-movement and hence reduced levels of activity.	As feeling safe depends on areas being in continuous occupation and use, areas should be designed to enable this (e.g. by making them better integrated with regard to the movement system).

The CPTED approach has many elements in common with Newman's concept of defensible space. The main idea is that the physical environment can be manipulated to produce behavioural effects that would reduce the incidence and fear of crime by reducing the propensity of the physical environment to support criminal behaviour, thereby improving quality of life (Crowe 1991: 28–9). 'Secured by Design' approaches, widely adopted by police agencies around the world, are similar to CPTED approaches. In the UK, for example, most police authorities have police architectural liaison officers who ensure such principles are adopted in new developments. Analysis of these approaches both in the UK (BRE 1999) and in the USA (Sherwin *et al* 2001) provides a basis for modifying crime prevention strategies according to the particular characteristics of each place, rather than adopting a one-size-fits-all policy.

The emphasis on territorial definition in Newman's defensible space and the CPTED approaches has tended to support hierarchical (segregated) and discontinuous streets and road layouts, such as cul-de-sacs. Such layouts have been found to deter burglary rates compared with more easily travelled street layouts since, it is argued, criminals avoid street patterns where they might easily be trapped (Mayo 1979). Segregated residential areas can be distinguished into two broad groups — those where the means of segregation is relatively implicit and those where the means of segregation is explicit, active and physical. Both involve some definition of territory — in the former, 'strangers' are passively deterred from entering the territory; in the latter, they are actively prevented from entering the territory.

Hillier (1988, 1996a) has criticised defensible enclaves that exclude the natural movement of people, thereby excluding all strangers without distinguishing between Jacobs' predatory and peaceable, well-meaning strangers. He argued that, while the creation of enclaves of defensible space effectively assumes all strangers are dangerous, the feeling of safety in public space is enhanced by the presence of people — the latter is the primary means by which a space is naturally policed: Jacobs referred to this as 'eyes on the street'. The more this is eliminated, the greater the danger once — as was always possible — a potential criminal appeared on the scene. Hillier (1996a, 1996b) argued that certain spatial characteristics increased the likely presence of people and, thereby, enhanced the feelings of safety (see Chapter 8). Research has also shown that burglary rates for locations that are 'less integrated' are higher than for dwellings in 'more integrated' locations (Chih-Feng Shu 2000).

Within these sets of ideas, a basic contradiction exists between design strategies advocating people presence and eyes on the street to ensure the safety of people and property ('open solutions'), and those restricting access and permeability and providing territorial spheres of interest to prevent people from using particular areas ('closed solutions'), thereby ensuring the safety of people and property within those areas (Town & O'Toole 2005). While both ideas have their merits and applications, the crucial issue concerns the *density* of pedestrian movement.

To provide a sense of security and sufficient surveillance to act as deterrents, integrated layouts need a threshold density of pedestrian movement. High-density, mixed-use urban areas may provide the required density. If achieving the necessary density of pedestrian movement is unlikely (e.g. in low-density, mainly residential areas that may, in practice, be dormitory communities), then defensible space-type design strategies may be more appropriate.

These sets of ideas are not necessarily mutually exclusive — indeed, examining patterns of crime in an area of London covering in excess of 100 000 dwellings, Hillier revised his earlier position, acknowledging both sides were 'right about some things and wrong about others':

'The advocates of the closed solution seem to have been too conservative in overstating and oversimplifying the case for cul-de-sac and closed areas, in insisting on small rather than larger groupings of residents, and in underestimating the potential for, and the importance of, life outside the cul-de-sac and the closed-off-area. The advocates of the open solution have been too optimistic about exposing the dwelling to the public realm, in not linking permeability to a realistic understanding of movement patterns, and perhaps, in not appreciating the interdependence between residential numbers and the safety of mixed-use areas.'

(Hillier & Sahbaz 2009: 185).

He concludes:

- The relative safety of different dwelling types is affected by the number of sides on which the dwelling is exposed to the public realm (flats are most safe; detached dwellings least safe).
- Living in higher density areas reduces risk, with ambient ground-level density (as opposed to off-the-ground density) correlating particularly strongly with safer living.
- Good local movement is beneficial, but larger-scale through-movement across areas is not.
- Where larger-scale movement exists, the greater movement potential provided by more integrated street systems lowers risk.
- Relative affluence and the number of neighbours has a greater effect than layout type, whether grid or cul-de-sac.

- Larger number of dwellings per street segment reduces risk in grid, cul-de-sac and mixed-use areas.
- Higher wealth increases safety in flats but decreases it in houses, particularly in low-density cul-de-sacs.
- Dwellings should be arranged linearly on two sides of the street in larger residential blocks that allow good local movement but that are not over-permeable.

There are also related conflicts between enabling surveillance and restricting access. Although, in many residential areas, high, impermeable fences are considered unneighbourly, such fences prevent 'criminals' from accessing — or, at least, make it more difficult for them to access — the private space surrounding the dwelling. Fences around such private spaces are more common in Europe. Typically the fence at the front of the dwelling — where there is a fence — is of modest height, allowing interaction between dwelling and street, with the dwelling providing eyes on the street. The fence to the rear is usually taller. Nevertheless, because police officers or security personnel cannot easily spot suspicious activity, fences can make it more difficult to police residential areas. Where private spaces are open and unfenced — an approach common in parts of the USA — those attempting to break into the house, or merely loitering suspiciously, are open to view and surveillance. This approach, however, reduces the privacy of the backyard and exposes all facades of the dwelling to view. As well as security issues, there may also be aesthetic preferences for one type of arrangement or the other.

Criticisms of Opportunity Reduction Approaches

Opportunity reduction approaches are criticised on two main grounds — their image and the possibility of displacement.

(i) Image

Use of opportunity reduction techniques has often raised concerns about the image presented and the ambience of the resulting environment. Express concerns for security, protection from crime and increased feelings of safety, for example, have resulted in the emergence of highly defensive urbanisms. Sorkin (1992: xiii–xiv) noted an '... *obsession with "security", with rising levels of manipulation and surveillance over its citizenry and with a proliferation of new modes of segregation.*'

The features of what Soja termed the 'carceral city' (see Chapter 2) are explored in Davis' *City of Quartz* (1990) and include panopticon-like shopping centres with advanced forms of spatial surveillance; 'smart' office buildings impenetrable to outsiders; 'bunker' and 'paranoid' architecture; neighbourhood watches backed by armed home owners; a police force armed with advanced military technology; 'sadistic' street environments with razor-protected trash bins; and cunningly designed park benches to prevent indigents sleeping on them. Nevertheless, urban areas and public spaces made safe but no longer appealing, or generating fear and intimidating potential users, defeat their *raison d'être*. Reassuring to some, expressly policed environments are oppressive to others.

Opportunity reduction methods can be subtler in their application. In this respect, it is instructive to consider the controls operating in theme parks. Disney, for example, handles large crowds of visitors — 100 000 per day — in an orderly fashion. Opportunities for disorder are minimised in a variety of ways: by constant instruction and direction; by physical barriers limiting the choice of available actions; and by surveillance from '... *omnipresent employees who detect and rectify the slightest deviation.'* (Shearing & Stenning 1985: 419). The control strategies are embedded in both the environmental design and its management, with other functions typically overshadowing the control function; thus, every Disney Productions employee '... *while visibly and primarily engaged in other functions, is also engaged in the maintenance of order.'* (Shearing & Stenning 1987: 419) — the overall effect being to embed the control functions into the 'woodwork'. Shearing & Stenning argue that Disney Productions' power rests both in the physical coercion it can bring to bear — if and when needed to — and in its capacity to induce co-operation by depriving visitors of a resource they value. Control thus becomes consensual.

(ii) Displacement

The second criticism of opportunity reduction techniques is that of displacement, whereby restricting opportunities for crime in one location simply redistributes it. Displacement takes different forms:

- *Geographical displacement* — the crime is moved from one location to another.
- *Temporal displacement* — the crime is moved from one time to another.
- *Target displacement* — the crime is moved from one target to another.
- *Tactical displacement* — one method of crime is substituted for another.
- *Crime type displacement* — one kind of crime is substituted for another (Felson & Clarke 1998: 25).

Conclusive demonstrations of the absence of displacement are elusive: inability to detect it does not mean it is not present, and its possibility can never be precluded by research. Equally, it is probable that the frictional effect of displacement or deflection dissipates at least some

'criminal' energies and motivation. The degree of displacement is likely to correlate with the availability of alternative targets and with the offender's strength of motivation.

Displacement is not, however, a compelling argument against opportunity reduction measures. Barr & Pease (1992), for example, distinguish between 'benign' displacement, involving a less serious offence being committed, and 'malign' displacement, involving a shift to a more serious offence or to offences that have worse consequences. The aim is crime reduction, but benign displacement is generally better than malign displacement. Research indicates that integrated approaches to crime prevention through design can reduce displacement to neighbouring areas, as well as improve residents' perceptions of their areas (Ekblom *et al* 1996).

The approach adopted in any specific place has an impact on the character and appeal of the resulting environment. Synthesising opportunity reduction approaches with more general design ideas, Oc & Tiesdell (1999, 2000) identified four approaches to creating safer environments:

- *The fortress approach* — walls; barriers; gates; physical segregation; privatisation and control of territory; and deliberate strategies of exclusion.
- *The panoptic approach* (the 'police state') — the explicit control of public space; the privatisation of public space; an explicit police presence; the presence of security guards; closed circuit television (CCTV) systems as tools of control; covert surveillance systems; and exclusion.
- *The management or regulatory approach* (the 'policed' state) — the management of public space; explicit rules and regulations; temporal and spatial regulations; CCTV as a management tool; and ambassadors/city centre representatives in public space.
- *The animation or 'peopling' approach* — people presence; people generators; activities; a welcoming ambience; accessibility; and inclusion.

These are not exclusive approaches. The approach to be adopted depends on the local context and may combine different elements of these approaches. Fortress and panoptic approaches are positive actions — something is being seen to be done — but are also essentially private-minded behaviours. The consequence of such individual actions is that, while it becomes safer for some, it may become increasingly unsafe for others. In effect, individual solutions of this nature both inhibit collective solutions and result in situations less good for everyone. Thus, while elements of fortress and panoptic strategies may have their place, there are other more positive ways of making urban places feel safer. Management and animation approaches, for example, offer inherently more expansive and positive notions of urban areas and public spaces.

CONTROLLING SPACE: ACCESS AND EXCLUSION

As noted above, a key element in any discussion of the public realm is access. While, by definition, the public realm should be accessible to all, some environments — intentionally or unintentionally — are exclusionary and are less accessible to certain sections of society. Exclusion is often used to reinforce or establish connotations of social status or, as discussed in the previous section, 'security' and, in essence, is a manifestation of power through the control of space and access to that space. Various forces in society purposefully reduce accessibility. For the most part, these are a function of desires to control particular environments and settings (and, *inter alia*, to protect investments). Nevertheless, if access control and exclusion are practised explicitly and widely, the public realm's publicness is compromised. Although design strategies can be used both to enable and further the aim of exclusion or — at least in part — to promote and enable inclusion, that environments should increase choice and be inclusive is a central tenet of much urban design thinking.

Public space is a collective asset or resource. Such assets are prone to a problem commonly referred to as the tragedy-of-the-commons. Writing about public space, Kohn (2004) refers to a tragedy-of-the-agora. This tragedy arises for two reasons. First, there is no incentive for self-restraint in one's own use of the resource because others will not limit themselves in the same way. Second, there is no incentive to invest in improving the resource because the investor cannot appropriate the benefits of that investment. The solution is usually a call for some form of management of the resource in the interest of the community and/or to assign (individual) property rights (i.e. to privatise the resource, which, *inter alia*, means it is no longer a common property resource).

Managing public space necessarily involves balancing collective and individual interests and also balancing freedom and control. In turn, this often requires 'rules' regulating what is acceptable and unacceptable within that space — 'acceptable' should relate to the 'community' constituting the public, but, as discussed below, this is frequently not the case.

Lynch and Carr (1979) identified four key public space management tasks:

- Distinguishing between 'harmful' and 'harmless' activities — controlling the former without constraining the latter.
- Increasing the general tolerance towards free use, while stabilising a broad consensus of what is permissible.
- Separating — in time and space — the activities of groups with a low tolerance for each other.
- Providing 'marginal places' where extremely free behaviour can go on with little damage.

They support the principle of freedom in public space, arguing that:

'We prize the right to speak and act as we wish. When others act more freely, we learn about them, and thus about ourselves. The pleasure of an urban space freely used is the spectacle of those peculiar ways, and the chance of an interesting encounter.'

(Lynch & Carr 1979: 415).

Freedom of action in public space is, nevertheless, necessarily a 'responsible freedom'. According to Carr *et al* (1992: 152), it involves '… *the ability to carry out the activities that one desires, to use a place as one wishes but with the recognition that a public space is a shared space.'*

Management of public space may involve some forms of exclusion. Minton (2006: 2), for example, describes the potential for social exclusion in terms of 'hot spots' of affluence and 'cold spots' of exclusion. 'Hot spots' — such as urban regeneration areas or business improvement districts (BIDS) (see Chapter 11) — are characterised by having 'clean-and-safe' policies that often displace social problems. On the other hand, 'cold spots' are characterised by the socially excluded, who are unwelcome in the hot spots. By this analysis, public space management is actively creating socially polarised urban public spaces.

Exclusion can be considered in terms of (i) excluding behaviour or conduct; (ii) exclusion through design; and (iii) the exclusion of people.

(i) Excluding conducts

Managing public space can be discussed in terms of preventing or excluding certain undesirable social behaviours. Managers and owners of quasi-public space have various motivations for seeking to control activity, due, for example, to their responsibility for maintenance, their liability for what may happen within the space, and their concern for marketability. The exclusion of certain behaviours or activities from urban spaces can be a function — even an objective — of the prevailing management or control regime. Murphy (2001: 24) highlights the proliferation of 'exclusion' zones (i.e. zones designed to be free of some undesirable social characteristics). This is a broad phenomenon. There are, for example: smoke-free zones; campaign and politics-free zones; skateboard-free zones; mobile or cell-phone-free zones; alcohol-free zones; and car-free zones (Figure 6.11).

Although public spaces may be regulated through a series of bylaws and other regulations, the existence of explicit controls on behaviour and activity is more pronounced and evident in quasi-public space. In such space, the tendency is towards control. While public- and privately owned public spaces facilitate and encourage uses and users, Nemeth & Schmidt (2007)

FIGURE 6.11 Love Square, Philadelphia *(Image: Steve Tiesdell)*. Skateboarders had colonised an underused space; when the city authorities wanted to upgrade the space, the skateboarders were moved out

found that, in general, privately owned spaces do more to 'control' uses and behaviours. Different management regimes also operate, with publicly owned spaces focusing more on laws/rules and design/image, and privately owned spaces focusing on these but also on surveillance/policing and access/territorial control (Nemeth & Schmidt 2007).

Ellin (1999: 168–9) illustrated the intensity of regulation and control by reference to a sign that used to hang at the entry to Universal Studio's CityWalk, Los Angeles, warning visitors against:

'... *obscene language or gestures, noisy or boisterous behaviour, singing, playing of musical instruments, unnecessary staring, running, skating, roller-blading, bringing pets, "non-commercial expressive activity", distributing commercial advertising, "failing to be fully clothed", or "sitting on the ground more than five minutes".'* (Figure 6.12).

Loukaitou-Sideris & Banerjee (1998: 183–5) note two types of control:

- *Hard (active) control* uses vigilant private security officers, surveillance cameras and express regulations either prohibiting certain activities from happening or allowing them subject to the issue of permits, programming, scheduling, or leasing. Over the past 10 years surveillance cameras have become an increasingly common feature of the urban scene. With more than two million cameras in operation, for example – and a total currently increasing by 20% per year – the UK is the most surveyed country in the world and, on average, each person is observed by 30 cameras per day.

- *Soft (passive) control* focuses on 'symbolic restrictions' that passively discourage undesirable activities and on *not* providing certain facilities (e.g.public toilets).

Whatever the control strategy, if public spaces are to be successful as people places, they must still be attractive – though, equally, the sense of 'control' might be part of the appeal (Figure 6.13). While many favour greater regulation of the public realm in the interest of the greater good of public order and public safety, there is a danger of a progression from rules enacted in the wider public interest becoming rules enacted to prohibit certain behaviours objectionable to certain (dominant) groups for much narrower reasons (profitability or marketability). The latter provides much of the rationale for exclusion and reduced accessibility within public space.

(ii) Exclusion through design

Carr *et al* (1992: 138) identify visual, physical and symbolic as different forms of access. Visual access – visibility – is important for people to feel free to enter a space. If people are able to see into a space before

FIGURE 6.12   Rules in 'public' space *(Image: Matthew Carmona)*

FIGURE 6.13 Peace Gardens, Sheffield, UK *(Image: Sheffield City Council)*. The recently redeveloped Peace Gardens in Sheffield, UK provides a lively and vibrant place for people. On the first sunny weekend after its opening local people used it more like a beach than a traditional European square. Management staff considered how to regulate its uses but quickly appreciated that, provided the square was not being damaged, such free behaviour suggested a feeling of ownership and affinity with the space

they enter it, they can judge whether they would feel comfortable, welcome and safe there.

Physical access concerns whether the space is physically available to the public, with physical exclusion being the inability to access or use the environment, regardless of whether or not it can be seen into. Exclusion can thus be directly facilitated through physical design strategies. Observing Los Angeles, Flusty (1997: 48–9) characterised five types of space designed to exclude:

- Stealthy space cannot be found; it is camouflaged or obscured by intervening objects or level changes.
- Slippery space cannot be reached due to contorted, protracted or missing paths of approach.
- Crusty space cannot be accessed due to obstructions such as walls, gates and checkpoints.
- Prickly space cannot be comfortably occupied (e.g. ledges sloped to inhibit sitting).
- Jittery space cannot be used unobserved due to active monitoring by roving patrols and/or surveillance technologies.

Similarly, evaluating 'public' plazas in central Los Angeles, Loukaitou-Sideris & Banerjee (1998: 96–7) found 'introversion' and a 'deliberate fragmentation' of the public realm, with plazas designed to inhibit visual access and, thus, to be exclusive. Spaces were hidden, with exteriors giving few clues to the space within, while certain design strategies – isolation from the

street, de-emphasis of street-level access, major entrances through parking structures, etc. – were used to achieve an inward orientation of the spaces, insulating them from the outside environment and thus disconnecting them from the surrounding city (Loukaitou-Sideris & Banerjee 1998: 97).

Symbolic access involves visual cues or symbols suggesting who is and who is not welcome in the space. Individuals and groups perceived either as threatening, or comforting or inviting, for example, may affect entry into a public space. Similarly, certain design elements may act as symbolic cues regarding the type of people who are desired: particular kinds of shops, for example, signal the type of people welcome there. Noting that '... *one could be forgiven for thinking that power is largely about guards or gates or that it is present through surveillance techniques ....'*, Allen (2006: 441) highlights the role of 'ambient power' in public spaces. Using Berlin's Potsdamer Platz as an example, he describes a 'logic of seduction' in which

'... the layout and design ... represent a seductive presence that effectively closes down options, enticing visitors to circulate and interact in ways that they might not otherwise have chosen ... Power in this instance works through the ambient qualities of the space, where the experience of it is itself the expression of power.'

(2006: 441).

Another form of access is economic access. A form of direct exclusion, for example, is practised by charging an entry fee, whereby the entrance ticket contains an undertaking to obey the rules at the sanction of being ejected from the place. While common in some parts of quasi-public space (e.g. cinemas, theatres, etc.), this is less common in other parts, such as public parks and civic space. A subtler form of exclusion is practised through visual cues symbolising and communicating the *ability* to pay – or, perhaps more precisely, the ability to consume – which in turn ensures access to the space. Those not communicating the appropriate visual cues are treated with suspicion, made to feel uncomfortable or unwelcome, refused entry or asked to leave. Thus, although a fee is not charged, a sufficiently prosperous appearance is needed to ensure access.

(iii) Excluding people

Exclusion through design is typically a passive means of exclusion; other means of exclusion are more active. Thus, rather than excluding particular behaviours, some exclusion strategies seek to actively exclude – or, better, prevent the entry of – certain individuals or social groups. One of the principal rights of private ownership is the ability to exclude and/or to prevent access. Most legal systems permit exclusion on the grounds of *conduct* (that is, behaviour over which people have, in principle, a choice) but, rarely, on the grounds of *status* (that is, factors over which people have no choice — skin colour, gender, age, etc.).

A device that has caused controversy in the UK is the Mosquito, which emits an irritating and uncomfortable high frequency noise that, because hearing deteriorates with age, can only be heard by younger people. Over 3000 of the devices had been installed outside shops and in other public spaces as a means of deterring teenagers from gathering there. The device does not discriminate: all young people (including babies) are discomforted by the noise regardless of their conduct or behaviour: they are discriminated against simply because of their status as young people.

Unless special exclusion orders have been created, one cannot — in principle — be legally excluded from true public space. The public realm nevertheless includes spaces that are accessible to the public but private in terms of ownership. Such spaces have often been provided with some form of public contribution or subsidy (e.g. through density bonuses or through direct financial subsidies), a condition of which is that they should be publicly accessible. Commenting on the design of such spaces, Banerjee (2001: 12) observes that the public is welcome as patrons of shops and restaurants, office workers, or clients of businesses located on the premises, but access to and use of the space remains a privilege rather than a right. The attraction of such spaces may be enhanced by — or contingent upon — the removal, control or displacement of certain groups and activities deemed to have no commercial value. Thus, certain 'undesirable' individuals or groups, such as those whose mere presence creates anxiety in others, may be excluded both for the well-being and security of others and to further profit-making.

Access control of this nature is usually risk-averse: it is better — at least, from the perspective of those doing the excluding — to exclude too many rather than too few. Seen positively, such strategies are based on 'profiling' (i.e. identifying the characteristics of groups or individuals deemed likely to contravene the desired behaviours, so that attention can be concentrated on such groups); seen negatively, this is stereotyping and discrimination.

The 'Policing' of Public Space

Greater management and regulation of the public realm may be favoured for reasons of the greater good of public order and public safety, but, as noted above, the danger is a progression from rules enacted in the wider public interest to rules enacted to prohibit certain behaviours objectionable to dominant groups.

Rather than the legality of power, the key question is the legitimacy of the rule-makers — the former is judged in the court of public opinion; the latter in a court of law (Hague & Harrop 2004: 15). Legality is a technical matter — it denotes whether the rule was made correctly. Legitimacy is a political question: '*A legitimate system of government is one based on authority: that is, those subject to its rule recognise its right to make decisions.*' (Hague & Harrop 2004: 15). A further consideration here is the distinction between a police state that protects the interests of the powerful or a private interest — Big Brother — and a policed state that protects the freedoms of its citizens — Big Father.

Managing and 'policing' public space commonly involve more than just the public police. Nearly 50 years ago, Jacobs (1961: 41) argued that, 'necessary as the police were', the public peace was not kept primarily by them and, instead, was

'*… kept by an intricate, almost unconscious, network of voluntary controls and standards among the people themselves … No amount of police can enforce civilisation where the normal, casual enforcement of it has broken down.*'

Policing thus has to be considered in terms of 'social control' and in terms of public and private police.

Jones & Newburn (2002: 139) distinguished different types or levels of social control:

- *Primary (formal) social controls* — these are direct and are exerted by those for whom crime prevention, peacekeeping, and investigatory and related policing activities are a primary and defining part of their role. Typical examples are the public police, other policing (regulatory) bodies and the commercial security sector.
- *Secondary (informal) social controls* — these are more indirect and are those exerted by those for whom social control activities are an important secondary aspect of their role. Typical examples include teachers, park-keepers, caretakers, railways guards, bus conductors, etc.
- *Tertiary (informal) social controls* — these are also indirect and are those exerted by 'intermediate' groups within local communities. Typical examples include workgroups, churches, trade unions, clubs and societies, and community groups.

Jones & Newburn (2002: 140–1) argue that current trends in policing relate to the decline of indirect sources of social control, evinced by the marked decrease in the numbers employed in the range of occupations providing indirect social control, through, for example, natural surveillance and other low-level controls as a corollary to their primary functions. In part, this has been a consequence of labour-saving technologies (e.g. self-purchasing ticket machines and automatic barriers, CCTV and automated access control).

Noting how the rise of private security is often attributed to reductions in — or, at least, restrictions on the growth of — public policing, Jones & Newburn argue that the decline of secondary social control occupations — bus conductors, railway station masters, train guards, ticket inspectors, park-keepers, etc. — is more significant. More particularly, they argue that the declining visibility of such occupations contributes to the growth of primary forms of social control.

'Private police' are an increasing presence in public space, with the commonest form being security guards and the door stewards of bars, pubs and nightclubs. There is much criticism of this situation. Concluding that, in the absence of adequate state control mechanisms, door stewards and bouncers are the *de facto* '... *custodians of a liminal zone, using violence and intimidation as a commercial resource'*, Hobbs *et al* (2000) advocate the state (in the form of the public police) regaining the policing and regulatory imperative from commercial forces: '... *while the police face the routine frantic mustering of skeleton shifts of officers, the good, the bad, and the tattooed of an unaccountable security industry will continue to prosper.'*

In addition to public accountability, another problem is that private security's only function is security (Figure 6.14). By contrast, the indirect social control occupations discussed above offer a primary service or hospitality function with 'order maintenance' being secondary. To supplement the public police, many cities now employ public safety representatives or ambassadors to work in public space — part of their role is hospitality, but another part includes safety and security.

'Human' policing and surveillance is also being supplemented and sometimes replaced by 'electronic' policing through CCTV systems. Closed circuit television (CCTV) cameras and systems have become a pervasive and common feature of British and many other city centres. Systematic research on the impact of such measures reveals, however, that while the popularity of such systems grows at a seemingly exponential rate, their impact on reducing crime is minimal (Welsh & Farrington 2002).

EQUITABLE ENVIRONMENTS

If urban design is about *making better places for people*, then the 'people' referred to are *all* the potential users of the built environment — old/young, rich/poor, male/female,

FIGURE 6.14 Security in 'public' space *(Image: Matthew Carmona).* An increasing presence in 'public' space, private security's only function is security. By contrast, indirect social control occupations offer a primary service or hospitality function with order maintenance and security being secondary functions. Here at Canary Wharf in London, the private security guards have uniforms that emulate Police officers

those able-bodied and those with disabilities, the ethnic majority and ethnic minorities. Just as good urban design is sustainable, so is it equitable and thereby inclusive. For large sections of society, however, the day-to-day reality is often very different.

Disability, Ageing and Exclusion

For many — the disabled, the elderly, those with young children in pushchairs, pregnant women, etc. — various physical barriers prevent them from using the public realm. Hall & Imrie (1999: 409), for example, observe how people with disabilities experience the built environment as a series of obstacle courses

'Most buildings are not wheelchair accessible and few contain sufficient tactile colouring or colour contrasts to enable vision-impaired people to navigate with ease. The design of specific items, such as doors, handles, and toilets, are also standardised to the point whereby many people with a range of physiological and/or mental impairments, find them impossible to use.'

In the developed world, as populations live longer, disability is no longer the exception and is increasingly the expectation as ageing takes its toll on the physical and mental faculties of even the healthiest individuals. For most, at some point in their lives, ageing will leave them less able to cope with the physical demands of using the built environment, typically as a result of a combination of minor impairments to hearing, eyesight, dexterity, mobility, bladder control and memory problems. By 2020 close to half the UK adult population will be over 50 years old, while 20% of the US population and 25% of the

Japanese population will be over 65 (Burton & Mitchell 2006: 5—7).

There are two main models of disability. The 'medical model' defines disability in terms of a medical condition (the person is described as 'arthritic' or 'epileptic') and places the disabling factors on the individual rather than taking account of the disabling factors in society. The 'social model' focuses on the limitations of society. Barriers imposed by society are the disabling factor, not personal impairments — hence, the impairment is not the barrier, it is the inability of society to make adjustments that is the barrier. In the social model the emphasis is placed on a society and/or environment that is *disabling* rather than on the individual who has a *disability*.

Arguing that design and development process are both disabling and disablist, Imrie & Hall (2001: 10) contend that inclusive design is about attitudes and processes as much as it is about products. They found that most built environment professionals have little awareness of the needs of disabled people and only react to such needs when forced to do so by legislation. In such a context, the provision of features for the less able-bodied in society is regarded as an 'add-on' extra and as an extra cost to be resisted. Unsurprisingly, they found that people with disabilities were often alienated from the built environment as well as from the broader social and development processes that give rise to it. Significantly, however, where local policy frameworks supported provision of higher access standards, they found developers rarely resisted (Imrie & Hall 2001: 69—82).

In an urban design context, addressing environmental disability involves understanding social disability and the ways in which the environment is disabling; designing for inclusion rather than exclusion or segregation; and ensuring proactive and integrated consideration rather than reactive 'tacked-on' provision. Attention to disability, however, detracts from the fact that universal access and design features make it easier for all to use the built environment. The overarching argument, therefore, is that the needs of those with disabilities should be considered an integral part of the design process and that, by meeting these needs, buildings and environments will perform better for all users.

Thus, for urban designers, the delivery of barrier-free environments should be the aim, preferably following principles of universal design (see Nasar & Evans-Cowley 2007). The US-based Centre for Universal Design (in Sawyer & Bright 2007: 3) defined these as follows:

- *Equitable* — the design should be usable by people with diverse abilities and should appeal to all users.
- *Flexible* — the design should cater for a wide range of individual preferences and abilities.

- *Simple and intuitive* — use of the design should be easy to understand, regardless of experience, knowledge, language skills or current concentration level.
- *Perceptible* — the design communicates necessary information effectively to the user, regardless of ambient condition or the user's sensory abilities.
- *Tolerance for error* — the design minimises hazards and the adverse consequences of accidental or unintended actions.
- *Low physical effort* — the design can be used efficiently and comfortably with a minimum of fatigue.
- *Size and space for approach use* — appropriate size and space is provided for approach, reach, manipulation and use, regardless of the user's body size, posture or mobility.

In practice, narrow perceptions of disability and the needs of people with disabilities often mean that 'disabled provision' is geared only to the needs of wheelchair users and rarely considers other forms of disability. In the UK, the 1995 *Disability Discrimination Act* contains a much broader definition: '… *a physical or mental impairment which has a substantial and long-term adverse effect on a person's ability to carry out day-to-day activities.*' To be regarded as disabled for the purpose of the Act, a person must be affected in at least one of the following respects: mobility; manual dexterity; physical co-ordination; continence; ability to lift, carry or otherwise move everyday objects; speech, hearing or eyesight; memory or ability to concentrate, learn or understand; and/or perception of risk of physical danger. Recognition of the range of disabilities and impairments expands our appreciation of the way in which the built environment is disabling: for example, just 4% of the population with disabilities in the UK are wheelchair users (Imrie & Hall 2001: 43).

Disabilities are often unseen. Among the ageing population, for example, dementia is an increasing problem, affecting one in twenty between the ages of 70 and 80 and one in five thereafter (Burton & Mitchell 2006: 27). Among this group, particular problems are apparent with how to read and interpret the cues that signal the use of buildings, the location of entrances, the behaviour that is expected in different places, and the intentions of people around them. For such users of the built environment, clarity of function and distinctive features in the built environment help them to navigate (Burton & Mitchell 2006: 37). Design can thus play a part in helping to overcome the problems experienced by many elderly people of effectively being trapped and isolated indoors.

Burton & Mitchell (2006: 7) argue that the cause of disability is gaining a large number of new and influential advocates as the baby boom generation begins to experience difficulties with mobility. As a generation with considerable wealth and influence, combined with expectations for living full, active and independent lives, this generation will have a profound impact by demanding better provision. Burton & Mitchell (2006) argue that this will require the creation of 'streets for life', demonstrating a range of design features (see Table 6.2) and helping to deliver six design attributes:

- *Familiarity* — streets that are recognisable, with long-established forms and features and designs that are familiar to older people.
- *Legibility* — streets that help older people to understand where they are and to identify which way they need to go.
- *Distinctiveness* — streets that reflect local character in their built form and uses and thereby give a clear image of place.
- *Accessibility* — streets that enable older people to reach, enter, use and walk around places they need or wish to visit, regardless of any physical, sensory or mental impairment.
- *Comfort* — streets that enable people to visit places of their choice without physical or mental discomposure and to enjoy being out of the house.

TABLE 6.2 Seventeen 'Streets-for-Life' Design Features

Ranked from Most to Least Important

1	A mix of uses, including plenty of services and facilities and open space
2	Wide, smooth, non-slip footways (without cycle lanes)
3	Frequent road crossings with audible and visual cues suitable for older people
4	Clear signs throughout
5	Frequent wooden seating, with arm and back rests
6	Small blocks laid out on an irregular grid (with minimal crossroads)
7	Clearly marked level changes, with handrails
8	Grade-level toilets
9	Enclosed bus shelters, with seating
10	Varied urban form and architecture
11	Buffer zones between busy roads and footways (e.g. trees and grass verge)
12	Landmark, distinctive structures and places of activity
13	A hierarchy of streets from main to side
14	Special/distinctive features at junctions
15	Buildings with evident (i.e. prominent) entrances
16	Buildings designed to reflect uses
17	Gently winding streets

Source: Burton & Mitchell (2006: 145).

- *Safety* — streets that enable people to use, enjoy and move around the outside environment without fear of tripping or falling, being run-over or being attacked.

These have been specifically constructed with the needs of the older population in mind, but relate equally well to the range of users that find the built environment disabling.

Mobility, Wealth and Exclusion

Mobility can also be considered in terms of car-based and non-car-based accessibility. Environments are inaccessible if they rely on users reaching them by private modes of travel. Car-dependant developments reduce the ability of many people to reach such places (see Chapter 2). Inclusive urban design relies to some degree on the spatial concentration of different land uses to make places and facilities accessible and to make public transport viable. Groups with low mobility also tend to have low accessibility.

In the contemporary period, 'automobility' — a term meaning car-based mobility but referring more generally to the various economic and political systems that support and further the interests of a car-based society — has been especially privileged and frequently has resulted in a prevalence of car-dependant environments. On the positive side, as Sheller & Urry (2000: 743) argue, automobility is a 'source of freedom', whose flexibility enables car drivers to travel at speed, at any time, in any direction. Cars also provide a means of security. Sheller & Urry (2000: 749) observe how, in some respects, women's 'emancipation' has been predicated on the automobile: *'Cars afford many women a sense of personal freedom and a relatively secure form of travel in which families and objects can be safely transported, and fragmented time-schedules successfully intermeshed.'*

This flexibility and freedom is, nevertheless, itself necessitated by automobility: many people's working, social and home lives could not be undertaken without the flexibilities of the car and its 24-hour availability (Sheller & Urry 2000: 744). Urry (1999: 13–4) contends that the flexibility of the car is a 'coerced flexibility' in the sense that automobility supports an ever-increasing spatial separation of uses, which, in turn, necessitates greater and greater use of the car to recombine the separated and fragmented facilities. Thus, despite — as Urry (1999: 14) observes — the 'widespread depiction in advertising and the media of cars as 'harbingers of unproblematic liberation', mass mobility does not generate mass accessibility.

While the particular advantage of cars is the ability to make (virtually) 'seamless' journeys, with, in principle, a high degree of personal safety, provision for the car often simultaneously interrupts or severs the linkages that make other forms of transport possible. Seamless car journeys also make other modes of travel seem more fragmented and inconvenient. Various 'gaps' occur in the use of, for example, public transport: the walk to the bus stop; the wait at the bus stop; the walk through the bus station to the train station; the wait on the station platform; etc. (Sheller & Urry 2000: 745). Each gap is a source of uncertainty, inconvenience and perhaps danger. Gaps exist for car drivers (e.g. in using a multi-storey car park), but they are 'much less endemic' than for other modes of travel.

These gaps unduly impact on lower income groups (and women – see below) because of their greater reliance on public transport. But this is just the first of a range of disadvantages that economically disadvantaged groups face from the built environment. CABE (2008) identified some of these, including the poorest people tending to live in the least safe and healthy environments (see Chapter 8), with the greatest likelihood of environmental hazards such as flooding and pollution. Exclusion for such groups is a product of inaccessible facilities, poorly managed parks and public spaces (if they exist at all), dilapidated housing, living in locations with high traffic volumes, and the disturbance, pollution, noise and potential injury this causes. Moreover, with climate change becoming an increasing concern, such groups will be less able to adapt their homes to be resilient to extreme weather conditions such as heatwaves.

For CABE (2008: 6) the challenge is '… *to find ways in which design and management of the built environment alleviates and does not exacerbate income inequality* …' – not least by being aware of the equity impact of public and private investment decisions. This awareness may extend beyond the short-term impacts of particular development decisions to the long-term social impacts of attempts to improve the physical fabric, such as the gentrification that such process often gives rise to (see Chapter 9).

Exclusion of the Young

Some heavy users of public space have been actively denied access to it, or parts of it, prominent among which are the poor, homeless and teenagers. Exclusion because of fear or an inability to consume has been discussed above – teenagers are excluded for both these reasons. They are also at risk of exclusion because of the way public spaces are increasingly privately owned and subject to corporate rather than public-interest ideologies. Investigating the exclusion of teenagers in Brisbane's shopping centres, Crane (2000: 5) found teenagers are routinely split up if in groups larger than three, excluded on the basis of appearance (e.g. hairstyle), recorded in photographic and written dossiers, and moved on from the entrances of premises or when congregating in common areas. They are also excluded because of their pastimes, the most written about being skateboarding, regarded, by some, as 'anti-social' because of the conflict it creates with other groups and due to the damage to street furniture (Johns 2001).

Rather than positively designing for and managing such activities, the more common strategy is to banish such uses to dedicated spaces, and to design or police them out of shared spaces. However, as Malone (2002: 165) observes: '*It has become obvious from research that skate ramps and other youth-specific spaces on the margins of city centres are less than appealing places for young people (especially for young women).*' In such places teenagers experience problems of safety and security and feelings of exclusion, while what they seek in a public space is '… *social integration, safety and freedom of movement*'. These all represent failures to appropriately manage shared public spaces in a manner allowing equitable use by all groups without diminishing the welfare of others. For Malone (2002: 167), there needs to be recognition and acceptance of difference, and of streets as appropriate venues for expressing the collective culture of all components of a community.

Beunderman *et al* (2007: 3) argue that the health of the public realm can be judged by the extent of access it provides as a shared resource. For them

'… *children and young people suffer from a mix of invisibility, segregation and exclusion. They are, for example, invisible in economically dominated town centre regeneration strategies which prioritise commercial interests and uses; they are segregated spatially, temporally and by age into designated play areas and supervised activities; and finally, they face exclusion from public spaces and places through a combination of adult fears and complaints, legal controls and dispersal orders.*'

Younger children – also traditionally heavy users of public space – have increasingly been excluded from this territory. In England, despite three-quarters of adults having, as children, played outside in the street or in areas close to their homes, only a fifth of their children have similar opportunities (Beunderman *et al* 2007: 1). Despite dedicated play spaces being an important part of the built environment for younger children (see Chapter 8), some argue that the resources lavished on such spaces owe more to the lobbying of the industry now built up around manufacturing playground equipment and to the angst among adults no longer willing to allow their children to play freely within the wider built environment. As Cunningham & Jones (1999: 12) ask:

'*Are we forgetting, in our desire to improve the environment of the playground and make it an appropriate, exciting, beautiful and even challenging children's place, that the play environment extends well beyond the confines of the playground and properly embraces the whole city and countryside? Can enrichment of the small, local and generally confined spaces that are the playground, essential as that enrichment is, ever compensate for impoverishment of the broader environment that constitutes the child's more general universe and playscape?*'

The play ranges of children are increasingly restricted and constrained, with girls in particular suffering from greater restriction in their local neighbourhoods. As well as anxieties born from sensationalist news reporting of violence against children and from fear of liability on the part of the professional carers of the children of working parents (see Box 6.5), the restrictions also stem from steady increase in vehicular traffic on the roads and the reduced ability of children to use streets safely − the latter despite a continuing real reduction in child mortality from traffic incidents (Cunningham & Jones, 1999: 15). In England, for example, Department of Health data suggest only 52% of children walked to school in 2002/2003, compared with 61% 10 years previously (Beunderman *et al* 2007: 45). Growth of the 'school run' further increases the number of vehicles on the streets, increasing perceptions of danger while reducing opportunities for exercise and for children to learn how to interact with others in the socio-cultural public realm.

The trends lead to a greater pressure on designated 'safe' play spaces, and even to the spread of privatised play spaces − indoor adventure soft playgrounds, and play zones in retail outlets and in family pubs/restaurants. Although evidence suggests this new market in play has not reduced the use of public playgrounds, there is concern that the trend towards the commercialisation of play space could exclude children of families with mobility or financial constraints (McKendrick *et al* 1999: 56). As a consequence, such children could suffer a double exclusion: first, as those most likely to live in unfavourable and potentially dangerous local neighbourhoods (e.g. in the vicinity of major roads) and, second, through exclusion from the new private spaces.

At the other end of the youthful spectrum, the activities of young adults have been seen as part of the problem, and criticised for excluding others through their colonisation of town centre locations. Roberts & Turner (2005) argue that increasing emphasis on the evening economy and support for 24-hour city policies, for example, has brought with it forms of behaviour that even the perpetrators would feel is unacceptable in their own neighbourhoods. In such places the conflicts often revolve around the needs of local residents versus those of the revellers and local businesses serving the evening economy. Leisure and entertainment destinations such as London's Soho are of this type.

In the UK, the 24-hour city and concepts of the evening economy became a major component in the regeneration of towns and cities throughout the 1990s. Subsequent government-led deregulation of liquor-licensing and of the drinks industry fuelled this heady mix, turning many urban centres into what have come to be termed 'youthful

---

BOX 6.5 The Constraints of Risk and Liability

Risk and the attendant fear of litigation increasingly dictate how public space is designed and managed. Health and safety regulations and safety audits are now regarded as indispensable for public authorities to protect themselves from being sued by parties injured while in public space. Such tools are inevitably blunt instruments and are frequently implemented in a technocratic manner by unknowing urban designers (see Chapter 1). The result is potential for restrictions on innovation leading to standardised designs and less interesting places.

There has also been a reaction to the perceived 'compensation culture', as a result of which public authorities have sought to design out any risks in public space as a means to manage their liabilities in case of accidents and other dangers (Beck 1992). Research in the UK (CABE 2007) suggests the compensation culture is over-stated and, in fact, personal injury claims are declining. Moreover, when made, such claims largely focus on maintenance deficiencies rather than design faults. The research revealed that, despite perceptions among some professionals, the public are far more concerned about risks associated with personal security (e.g. mugging) than trip-and-fall type hazards that can never be fully designed out − not least because it is almost impossible to predict how individuals will actually behave in space.

It is thus more important to view risks as opportunities that can be creatively managed (rather than eliminated). This involves distinguishing between minor hazards and substantial risks; challenging weak evidence that might otherwise lead to dumbing-down design; avoiding playing safe; and rejecting 'tick box' solutions that may simply encourage perverse behaviours. Risk is an inexorable element of the built environment and people, even children, are quite capable of understanding and negotiating it, particularly when the benefits are clear, such as in the enjoyment of well-designed, liveable public space.

Beyond the railings (*Image: Matthew Carmona*)

playscapes' (Chatterton & Hollands 2002). These spaces are not neglected, but have nevertheless been given over to market forces and to a clientele of the young with disposable income to burn (Worpole 1999), in the process deterring other users from these previously shared spaces and perpetuating a form of exclusion. For Roberts & Turner (2005: 190), more active management and more sophisticated planning controls are required. Without suitable controls, they argue, the ideal of a European 'continental ambience', so admired by the original proponents of the 24-hour city, will not be achieved. It is clear that youthful users of the built environment can easily be failed as children, teenagers and young adults – this also occurs at what is a critical stage in their life cycles, when healthy and appropriately social behaviours are being learnt.

Cultural Difference and Public Space

Concluding her examination of youth culture and street life, Malone (2002: 167) proposes replacing multiculturalism, which links difference within the terrain of false equality, with a radical view of cultural difference that recognises the contested character of youth culture within the community – cultural difference should also be celebrated rather than alleviated. As communities have become more ethnically diverse, these notions of different cultures colliding in the melting pot of public space can also be extended to how different ethnic groups use space, and to concerns that these different patterns of use are inadequately recognised in urban design processes.

Ethnic minorities, like the rest of the population in a society, consist of diverses groups of individuals with varying aspirations, social standing, and engagement with their localities. Moreover, in many cosmopolitan cities, many (often very different) minority groups constitute the non-indigenous population. It is thus difficult to generalise about a particular minority perspective on urban design, particularly as research has shown these perspectives are shaped more by where a person is raised than by their ethnic make-up, with people typically showing a preference for the types of environment that they knew as children; second-generation immigrants have similar preferences to the indigenous population (Rishbeth 2001: 354).

Analysing public space in East London, for example, Dines & Cattell (2006) found certain spaces played an important role in supporting ethnic networks among first-generation Asians, while second-or third-generation Asians did not consider the same spaces to be important social arenas. So, if urban design is to be appropriately responsive to the needs of local populations, it is critical to understand the diversity of views and perspectives among minority groups (see Chapter 12), as well as among the majority population – though, for a range of religious and cultural

reasons, some minority groups are particularly hard to engage in participatory processes.

Analysis shows different groups use urban space in different ways. Focusing on the use of public parks in Los Angeles, Loukaitou-Sideris (1995) found Hispanics primarily viewed parks as places for social gatherings, typically involving a shared meal, while Afro-Americans more often used parks for sporting purposes. Chinese groups used parks far less often, with the exception of elderly men who practiced Tai Chi. Whites typically used parks for solitary purposes, for walking or jogging, and highly valued their aesthetic qualities. Despite this, Dines & Cattell (2006) conclude that the urban public realm provides a valuable role as the venue for inter-ethnic interaction and social encounter, and thus for encouraging tolerance. Certain spaces provided opportunities for dissimilar people to mix:

- *Neighbourhood and semi-domestic spaces*, such as shared forecourts, the school lobby and residential streets, were a first point of contact between neighbours of different ethnic groups.
- *Neighbourhood parks* were where young people in particular interacted.
- *Local markets* encouraged casual encounters between groups who would otherwise not come into contact.

Asking whether existing environments can be made more inclusive to the multi-cultural societies common in many cities, Rishbeth (2001: 356–2) usefully distinguishes between design responses based on 'symbolic reference', 'experiential reference' and 'facility provision'.

- *Symbolic reference* involves inserting elements into the public realm that symbolise (often in a simplistic manner) another culture. Most Chinatowns, for example, use stereotypical visual cues imported in an exaggerated or idealised manner to give users a sense of Chinese culture (Figure 6.15). Typically, however, because little thought is given to developing relation-ships between the indigenous environment and the imported elements, the latter often amount to a carica-ture of 'otherness'.
- *Experiential reference* does not rely on visual cues, and instead attempts to shape the whole environment so that it reflects users' experience of other cultures. This is most easily and convincingly achieved in natural land-scapes such as public parks where exotic planting can provide evocative reminders of overseas landscapes – though it can also be found in the scale, texture and density of an urban street (Rishbeth 2001: 359). There is always the danger, however, with both these approaches that the visual manifestations of one culture serve to exclude as well as include – such as when, for example, long-established residents feel such interventions represent the cultures of newcomers but not their own (Rishbeth 2001: 357). This raises questions about who

decides what is acceptable and what is alien in different built environments; how different tastes and sensibilities are catered for; and how democratic those decisions should be.

- *Facility provision* does not rely on visual cues either, and instead attempts to understand how different cultures use the environment, and to provide facilities appropriate to that use. Rishbeth (2001: 361), for example, identifies how some cultures have long traditions of growing their own food, and that the provision of allotments can allow them to continue these culturally important behaviours in a manner respective of local visual sensibilities. Alternatively the provision of appropriate social, sporting, housing and other leisure facilities may meet particular minority needs without impacting on the perceived welfare of others. Such provision is inclusive because it neither differentiates between different users nor defines specific spaces for minority groups.

Such design responses are compatible with management responses that actively encourage the sharing of spaces — for example through events and festivals celebrating the cultural diversity of places, or policing that is sensitive to cultural norms and practices, and which is aware of any ethnic tensions that exist. Lownsbrough & Beunderman (2007) argue that public spaces can play a key role as venues for practical solutions that increase the sense of society and mutuality between ethnic groups, which might otherwise be divided through ignorance of the 'other'. For them '... *it is about coming together and, more specifically, doing things together.*' (Lownsbrough & Beunderman 2007: 3). They argue the number of spaces that might be described as 'public yet not civil' is higher for minorities than for other groups, because there are likely to be additional deterrents created by unfamiliarity and fear of hostile or discriminatory behaviour (Lownsbrough & Beunderman 2007: 14). Indeed, they cite evidence that poor physical

surroundings can represent a causal factor in violent racial attacks. Rather than seeking answers in tightening security measures, their case study research suggests solutions require:

- Understanding the grain of people's everyday lives and taking small steps that encourage interaction, for example improving the physical conditions at a school gate or bus stop, or adjusting the opening times at a local market.
- Creating 'trusted' spaces where people feel secure and able to take part in unfamiliar interactions, for example places that are well managed and maintained with no signs of crime or vandalism.
- Fostering positive interactions while not explicitly promoting them, using the built environment and activities within it as a means to break down barriers while not focusing on the barriers themselves.
- Embracing innovative new uses for spaces that will transform interactions between people, bearing in mind that the spaces occupied by communities extend far beyond the formal hard public spaces of the city.

Gender Perspectives

Perhaps the largest body of literature addresses how environmental design — intentionally or otherwise — excludes women (Day 1999). This literature begins by challenging the essentially exclusionary notion that a woman's proper place is in the home, culminating in a city of separate spheres, the masculine city and feminine suburb (Saegert 1980). For Sandercock & Forsyth (1992: 53), this sums up the dominant twentieth century metropolitan spatial form, and underpins the feminist political struggle, which emerged slowly across the fields of the built environment and which campaigns for women to become full actors in the public domain of the city.

Women make up over half the population and just like men constitute an almost infinitely diverse group about which it is difficult to generalise. Nevertheless, as Cavanagh (1998: 169−71) has argued, women often have very different lifestyles and patterns of movement to men, related to the traditional divisions of labour and the fact that women continue to carry greater responsibility for caring for children and the elderly and for household tasks. As a consequence, compared with men, many women spend a greater proportion of their time in and around the home environment, they take shorter cross-town rather than into-centre trips (for example taking children to school), and generally have less access to cars. They are also under-represented in many of the built environment professions, ensuring women's needs are less often heard in discussions about design. As a result,

'... *women frequently experience inconvenience and obstruction in the designed environment, inadequate solutions are imposed on*

FIGURE 6.15   Chinatown, Washington DC *(Image: Steve Tiesdell)*

them and they encounter a widespread lack of knowledge and understanding among professionals about how they use space.'

(Cavanagh 1998: 169-1).

Greed (2003) illustrates this gender blindness through her study of public toilet provision in the UK. She argues there is a general under-provision of public toilets, which makes public environments less comfortable and healthy places to be. Often exacerbated by local authority cost-cutting, the lack and poor standards of provision inequitably impacts on the elderly and on women, who for biological reasons need to use toilets more often and for longer, while women are, on average, faced with only half the provision of men. She suggests that:

'While the majority of user groups are female, the majority of providers and policy-making groups are male, and according to women toilet campaigners, it simply does not occur to them, it's not important to them, they don't find it a problem.'

(Greed 2003: 6).

Cuthbert (2006: 137—8) has argued that:

'Entire city structures have been generated on the basis of patriarchal capitalism: land-use zoning patterns, including the form, location and type of residential areas, transport networks, public open space, and the relationship between work and home result from male-dominated expectations and values …'

Although today people may not occupy the spaces created according to the same conventions and constraints, for Cuthbert the location of housing as well as how space is arranged and occupied within residential units are all expressions of a gendered society, one in which men and women's perceptions of space differ markedly. This, he suggests, relates primarily to the removal of economic production activities from the domestic sphere within western capitalist societies, and the consequential generation of separate environments for production and for consumption/reproduction. This, in turn, led to feminist critiques of the resulting space (particularly low-density suburban space), which disadvantages women by, *inter alia*, detaching them from social networks and the facilities of central areas.

Empirical evidence supports these critiques. Whitzman (2007), for example, has shown how fear-of-victimisation, particularly at night, unduly impacts on women; McGuckin & Murakami (1999) demonstrated that women take more complex trips than men, between childcare, school, work and shops in a series of complex trip-chains; while, in the UK, Greed (2007) showed that only 35% of women have access to a car during the day and that 75% of daytime bus journeys are taken by women.

Of course, not all women live in the suburbs, and such critiques have been criticised for disproportionately focusing on the lives of white middle class, heterosexual women and neglecting the distinct problems and needs of other groups. With this in mind, Cavanagh (1998: 172—7) suggests a range of generic prescriptions for designing more women-centred environments. For her, good residential environments provide appropriate spatial arrangements within homes (e.g. decent internal space standards to accommodate family activities such as sitting down together for a meal, and being flexible enough to accommodate changes in family size and circumstances), and externally are well-served with local amenities such as public transport, schools, health and leisure facilities, shops and local employment opportunities — the latter allowing women to manage their complex overlapping lives as carers and earners. In town centres, women again seek a good and convenient mix of public services, not least for socialising; areas free from the fumes and danger of traffic congestion; and places that are well-lit with good natural surveillance and thus not perceived as dangerous. In essence, they seek the sorts of good urban design outcomes discussed elsewhere in this book.

For others, however, more radical action is required to address the conventional division between private and public spaces that, they argue, physically imprints sexual inequality into the built fabric. Hayden (1980: 266), for example, argues that no less than 'a new paradigm of home, the neighbourhood and the city' is required if a non-sexist city is to be built that will '… *support rather than restrict the activities of employed women and their families.'* For her this necessitates breaking down the spatial separation of home and workplaces that has become the norm in Western cities — by, for example, families pooling resources to share domestic burdens, including childcare, in a manner that emancipates women. The physical manifestation of this is the cooperative unit with private homes sited around communal spaces and facilities such as day-care centres, laundrettes, communal kitchens, shared vehicles, etc. For different reasons — namely those of social interaction and latterly environmental sustainability — this model reflects the structures of co-housing that have grown in popularity since the 1960s, and which, some argue, provide a more equitable model of housing (Williams 2005).

For Cuthbert (2006: 139), the best course of action for professionals seeking to promote a more equitable environment for women is to ensure they are fully aware of how decisions in the past have (by commission or omission) created gendered environments. In this way future design decisions can be better informed as to their gender consequences, bearing in mind that '… *there may be some aspects of gender difference that are wholly constructive, that individuals of whatever gender might agree should be maintained.'* (Cuthbert 2006: 139). Nevertheless, what is good for women will also be good for men, particularly as gender roles (in the West at least) are far less prescribed than in the immediate past. Equally, by contributing to a more contented and harmonious society, urban design that is responsive to the needs of different groups, the young, those with disabilities and the elderly will also be good for the rest of society — this is the object of inclusive design.

Inclusive Design

The move from exclusionary modes of design to inclusive ones requires a change in mindset among those responsible for designing and managing the built environment. Keates & Clarkson (2004: 1) argue that, whatever the product, inclusive design is not a niche activity, nor one addressing 'special needs' and, instead, it is about ensuring design outcomes are of greatest value to the widest possible range of users: '... *it cannot be split out from the main design thrust and addressed at the end of the design process ... it needs to be a core activity, as tightly integrated into the design process as quality is.*'

They then set out a number of arguments to support inclusive design (Keates & Clarkson 2004: 19—32). Adapted to the built environment, these are:

- *The societal argument* — reflecting the need to cater for the changing nature of many societies, for example in Western Europe, where populations are ageing, where those with disabilities are now fully integrated into society and encouraged to lead full and active lives, and where the technology needed to live such lives is becoming ever more complex (e.g. the replacement of local banks with 'hole-in-the-wall' ATMs and phone boxes with mobile phones).
- *The sociological argument* — born from a population that is more demanding and less willing to accept sub-standard conditions as the norm: for example, under-investment in local parks or a poorly managed public realm.
- *The self-interest argument* — most people (including designers) at some point in their lifetime will experience a reduction in their functional capacity.
- *The legal argument* — governments around the world are responding to these ethical arguments by putting in place regulatory regimes that strive to combat exclusion. Legislation of this nature is most often developed as regards building design (for example Part M of the British Building Regulations), but less so in public space.
- *The financial argument* — the way the built environment is designed has a major impact on the available pool of customers and employees to which companies have access, and the degree to which they can retain them across their lifespan. For the public sector, an inclusive built environment will reduce expenditure on the need to make special provision for otherwise excluded groups.
- *The good design argument* — inclusive design is by its very nature user-centred and this responsiveness to user needs is a hallmark of good urban design.

In pursuit of inclusive design, urban design and place-making generally should be considered in terms of how it increases or reduces the choices available to different social groups. Yet the gap between the intentions of designers and the outcomes achieved can often be wide, simply because the likely users of space and their needs have not been thought through — for example the provision of attractive new public spaces that are sterile and lifeless because they fail to provide adequate attractions, amenities or connections to existing economic and social networks (Worpole & Knox 2007: 13).

For CABE (2006: 1) inclusive design is simply about making places everyone can use; it should also aim '... *to remove the barriers that create undue effort and separation. It enables everyone to participate equally, confidently and independently in everyday activities ...*' ensuring that places can be used safely, with dignity, comfort and convenience. It argues that, by its very nature, good design is inclusive and is the responsibility of all built environment professionals, as well as land and property owners. Inclusive design thus aims to:

- Place people at the heart of the design process;
- Acknowledge diversity and difference;
- Offer choice where a single design solution cannot accommodate all users;
- Provide for flexibility in use; and
- Create environments that are enjoyable to use for everyone.

CONCLUSION

More than any other dimension, urban design's social dimension raises a host of issues concerning values and difficult choices regarding the effects of urban design decisions on different individuals and groups in society. In a 1995 article, Don Mitchell asked whether we were witnessing the end of public space: '*Have we created a society that expects and desires only private interactions, private communications, and private politics, that reserves public spaces, solely for commodified recreation and spectacle?*' Similarly, Graham & Marvin (2001: 232) observed how the public space network of many cities was giving way to:

'... *instrumental quasi-public spaces geared overwhelmingly to consumption and paid recreation by those who can afford it and who are deemed to warrant unfettered access ... In many cases "public space" is now under the direct or indirect control, of corporate, real estate or retailer groups, which carefully work with private and public police and security forces to manage and desire out any groups or behaviour seen as threatening.*'

What is evident here is both express desires for exclusiveness and segregation and the ability of urban design — and urban designers — to respond to those needs. In practice desires for a more inclusive public realm can be thwarted in various ways — not least, by demand for spaces predicated on some degree of exclusion. Discussing public space in southern California, Loukaitou-Sideris & Banerjee (1998: 299) argued the character of such spaces reflected a 'collective apathy and reluctance' to create a more inclusive public realm.

The social dimension thus involves challenging questions for urban designers. While the aim should be to create an accessible, safe and secure, equitable public realm for all, economic and social trends can make this increasingly difficult to deliver. This is the contemporary context in which urban designers necessarily work, but, equally, the question arises whether to acquiesce with or to confront illegitimate uses of power, thereby raising important ethical issues and requiring urban designers to consider their values and their actions in designing and creating public spaces.

Chapter 7

The Visual Dimension

This chapter discusses the visual–aesthetic dimension of urban design and place-making. Movements such as 'City Beautiful' and 'Townscape' established a predominantly visual perspective on the design of development, which was dominant until Lynch, Jacobs and others broadened the discipline's scope, shifting its focus from civic to urban design.

The urban environment's visual–aesthetic character derives from the combination of its spatial (volumetric) and its visual qualities, the artefacts in those spaces and the relationships between them all. Accordingly this chapter is in three main parts. The first part discusses aesthetic preferences. The second part discusses the visual–aesthetic qualities of urban spaces and townscape. The third part discusses the design of elements defining and occupying urban space – the architectural walls, the floorscape, street furniture and landscaping.

AESTHETIC APPRECIATION AND PREFERENCES

Architecture and urban design are among the very few inescapable – and thus public – art forms. As Nasar (1998: 28) notes, while observers can choose whether to experience art, literature and music, urban design and urban architecture do not afford such a choice: *'In their daily activities, people must pass through and experience the public parts of the city environment.'* Thus, while we may *'… accept the idea of "high" visual arts that appeal to a narrow audience who choose to visit a museum, city form and appearance must satisfy the broader public who regularly experiences it.'* (1998: 2). Similarly, Childs (2009: 138) comments:

'In many arts, an audience member may choose without significant consequence to engage and disengage with the work. We can buy and then put down a book, or go to a movie and walk out. These arts have voluntary audiences. Similarly, the owners of built places are voluntary audiences. However, buildings, landscapes and public works also have significant involuntary audiences.'

Aesthetic appreciation of the urban environment is primarily visual and kinaesthetic (through movement). Experiencing urban environments is, nonetheless, multi-sensory – hearing, smelling and tactility can be more important than vision. Meiss (1990: 15), for example, urges designers: *'… to imagine the echo in the spaces that we are designing, the smells that will be given off by the materials or the activities that will take place there, the tactile experience that they will arouse.'*

Visual–aesthetic appreciation of urban environments is a product of perception and cognition – that is, what stimuli we perceive and how we process, interpret, judge and feel about the information gathered (see Chapter 5). It is inseparable from, and significantly influenced by, how we feel about a particular environment – whether we *care* about it – and what that environment means to us – whether we *value* it.

Aesthetic appreciation also has a significant personal component and raises issues of individual taste, but, because it also has socially and culturally learnt components, it goes beyond simple expressions of personal preferences. Accepting that notions of 'beauty' are socially and culturally constructed means that beauty resides – at least in part – in the object rather than purely in the mind of the beholder. But recognising that beauty is socially constructed also raises issues of power and whether accepted notions of beauty within a society have been imposed in the form of elite canons of good taste and/or whether they have emerged authentically and uncoerced from within that society.

Although this chapter focuses on urban design's visual–aesthetic dimension, the general public's liking for particular environments is much broader than aesthetic criteria. Rather than narrower aesthetic qualities, Nasar (1998) found people evaluated their environments in terms of much broader criteria. He identified five attributes of 'liked' environments, with disliked environments having opposing attributes. In each case, it was the observer's perception of the attribute that was important. The attributes translate into a series of generalised preferences:

- *Naturalness* – environments that are natural or where there is a predominance of natural over built elements.
- *Upkeep/civilities* – environments that appear to be looked after and cared for.
- *Openness and defined space* – the blending of defined open space with panoramas and vistas of pleasant elements.
- *Historical significance/content* – environments that provoke favourable associations.
- *Order* – organisation, coherence, congruity, legibility, clarity (Nasar 1998: 62–73).

Patterns and Aesthetic Order

We always experience the 'whole' rather than any single part in isolation — moreover, as Walter Benjamin observed, architecture is always '... *perceived unconsciously and in passing ... distractedly and through the collective.*' Because of this, all interventions into urban settings are inexorably contributions to an ensemble. We may, however, emphasise parts of an environment to make the environment more ordered, visually coherent and harmonious. Gestalt psychologists, for example, argued that aesthetic order and coherence comes from the grouping and recognition of patterns, and that people use principles of organisation or grouping to make environments more coherent visually (see Arnheim 1977; Meiss 1990). Based on Gestalt theory, Meiss (1990: 32) argues that: '*Part of the pleasures and difficulties we experience with the built environment can be explained by our ease or difficulty in mentally grouping different elements from the visual field into synoptic units.*'

Fundamental 'factors of coherence' or principles of grouping have been identified (see Table 7.1). Pure situations are rare, and in most environments several principles come into play simultaneously, though one principle may often be dominant. More generally, Smith (1980: 74) argues our intuitive capacity for aesthetic appreciation has four distinct components that transcend time and culture (see Table 7.2).

An overarching issue in Gestalt theory and in Smith's four components is the apparent need for balance between order and complexity in environments, which changes over time and with familiarity. A fine line exists between the richness of diversity and the bewilderment of visual chaos: as Cold (2000: 207) observes, we desire '... *an environment with a richness of detail that is larger than our immediate ability to process it.*' Nasar (1998: 75) observes that *interest* increases with the complexity of an environment, while our *preference* also increases with complexity up to a point, after which it decreases.

Reflecting on his concept of legibility and noting that we are 'pattern makers' not 'pattern worshippers', Lynch (1984: 252) argued the 'valuable' city was not an ordered one, but one that could be ordered — that is, with a 'complexity that unfolds as one experiences it'. Acknowledging that 'some overarching, patent order' was necessary for the 'bewildered newcomer', he argued that cities should have an 'unfolding order':

'... *a pattern that one progressively grasps, making deeper and richer connections. Hence our delight ... in ambiguity, mystery and surprise, as long as they are contained within a basic order, and as long as we can be confident of weaving the puzzle into some new, more intricate pattern.*'

(Lynch 1984: 252).

The Kinaesthetic Experience

The urban environment is not experienced as a static composition and the kinaesthetic experience of moving through space over time is an important part of urban design's visual—aesthetic dimension. Urban environments are thus experienced in some form of dynamic, emerging, unfolding and temporal sequence.

To describe the visual experience of townscape, Cullen (1961) conceived of the concept of 'serial vision' (Figure 7.1). Cullen argued that the environment is typically experienced on the move in a series of jerks or revelations. In addition to the view that is immediately present (the 'existing view'), there are also hints of a different view (the 'emerging view'). While there is an awareness of the sense of being in a particular place (of being 'here'), there might also be an equally strong sense that around and outside it are other places that are 'there' (Figure 7.2). Similarly, Frederick (2007) observes how our experience of a space is strongly influenced by how we arrive at it — wide, bright urban squares will feel wider and brighter when counterpointed by arriving through narrow, tall, darker streets.

For Cullen, delight and interest are stimulated by contrasts (the 'drama of juxtaposition'), and by concealment and revelation: a city view is first glimpsed, then hidden and later revealed again from a new angle or highlighting an interesting detail. This process of 'denial-and-reward' is a means of enriching the passage through the built environment. He, therefore, argued the urban environment should be considered and designed from the point of view of the moving person, where '... *the whole city becomes a plastic experience, a journey through pressures and vacuums, a sequence of exposures and enclosures, of constraint and relief.*' (Cullen 1961: 12).

New modes of travel have provided additional ways of seeing, engaging with and forming new mental images of urban environments. Drivers see the urban environment at speed and through a windscreen, while concentrating on the road, other traffic and any signs or directions. Although they still see it at speed and generally through glass, passengers have greater scope to observe the environment than the driver but are equally unable to fully engage with it. By contrast, pedestrians (and cyclists) both see the urban environment differently and have more freedom to stop and engage with it (see Chapters 4 and 8).

By recording the experience on film in slow motion, Appleyard *et al* explored the motorist's visual experience in their book *The View from the Road* (1964). Played back at regular projection speed, the film condensed the experience in time, making some passages stand out and showing a rhythmic spacing of bridges and overpasses. Similarly, based on the experience of driving the Las Vegas Strip of the mid-1960s with its billboards and neon signs, Venturi

TABLE 7.1 Gestalt Principles of Organisation and Coherence

(i) *Similarity* — enables recognition of similar or identical elements amid others through repetition of forms or of common characteristics (e.g. window shapes).

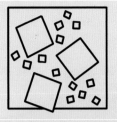

(ii) *Proximity* — enables elements that are spatially closer together to be read as a group and to be distinguished from those that are further apart.

(iii) *Common ground/common enclosure,* whereby an enclosure or a ground defines a field or group. Those elements within the field or ground are distinguished from what lies outside.

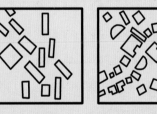

(iv) *Orientation,* whereby elements are grouped through a common orientation, either through parallelism or convergence towards a void or solid.

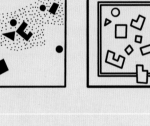

(v) *Closure* — enables recognition of incomplete or partial elements as wholes.

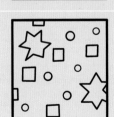

(vi) *Continuity* — enables recognition of patterns that may not have been intended.

Source: Adapted and extended from Meiss (1990: 36–8).

TABLE 7.2 Components of Intuitive Capacity for Aesthetic Appreciation

Sense of rhyme and pattern	Rhyme involves (some) similarity in the elements and presupposes the simultaneous existence of both complexity — a mass of visual detail and information — and patterns. Over time, as the mind 'organises' and makes sense of the information, the latter becomes more dominant, but not in an obvious way.

Central Bologna *(Image: Tim Heath)*. Colonnades provide rhyme and pattern, contributing to character and identity.

Appreciation of rhythm	Rhythm is the product of the grouping of elements to create, for example, emphasis, interval, accent and/or direction. Differing from rhyme, its impact relies on a stricter repetition with visual pleasure being derived from rhythmic elements varying from a simple binary kind to more complex repeated sub-systems (Smith 1980: 78).

Facade rhythms in Edinburgh and Chicago *(Images: Steve Tiesdell and Mathew Carmona)*. Strict rhythms can be monotonous, and contrast and variety are essential in providing interest.

Recognition of balance	Visual 'balance' can be readily conceived but is difficult to define precisely. Balance is a form of order and generally relates to harmony among the parts of a visual scene or environment. It can also be recognised in scenes that are complex and seemingly chaotic. In such cases, it is rarely immediately obvious and may only become apparent over time. Smith (1980: 79) suggests one of the major attractions of historic towns is the discovery of views where everything suddenly — and perhaps surprisingly — seems to cohere to produce perfect balance. Leon Krier suggests a test of visual balance involving rotating a building relative to the ground line — the building should *only* visually balance where in its normal position relative to the ground. Although symmetry can be a powerful tool in achieving balance, symmetrical compositions can appear mechanical, contrived and leaden. Asymmetrical compositions often use elements of symmetry to achieve visual balance but in more complex and potentially interesting ways than straightforward 'mirror' symmetry. Balance can also be perceived in situations that are not obviously symmetrical (e.g. in highly complex organisations of colours, textures and shapes, which cohere into a state of balance). Appreciation of asymmetrical balance is considered by many to demonstrate a capacity for higher-order thinking. Balance is inherent in a symmetrical composition, but asymmetrical compositions can be balanced or unbalanced (Frederick 2007).

TABLE 7.2 Components of Intuitive Capacity for Aesthetic Appreciation—cont'd

There are also different types of balance: Georgian, neo-classical townscapes, for example, usually have a 'static' form of balance whereby all the elements contribute and are subservient to the greater whole, while in Victorian, neo-Gothic townscapes, the elements often compete and there is a 'dynamic' balance.

Gravesend, UK (*Image: Matthew Carmona*), an asymmetrical facade with symmetrical elements to balance the composition

Sensitivity to harmonic relationships	Harmony is concerned with the relationships between different parts and how they fit together to form a connected whole. Certain relationships, such as those related to the golden section, also contribute to the quality of harmony. Gifted designers often manipulate proportions to achieve more harmonious effects. Perspective effects, for example, may be used to suggest building elements and features are taller or more slender or more elegant than they actually are. Equally, deliberate distraction might be employed to concentrate attention on some design aspects rather than on others.

Founding Hospital, Florence (*Image: Matthew Carmona*), design based on simple harmonic properties

Source: Adapted from Smith (1980: 78).

FIGURE 7.1   Gordon Cullen's serial vision (*Image: Cullen 1961: 17*)

FIGURE 7.2   Rhodes — Cullen saw particular significance in the tension between 'hereness' and 'thereness' *(Image: Matthew Carmona)*

FIGURES 7.3—7.5   Three contrasting walks: (i) Rome, Italy; (ii) Copenhagen, Denmark; and (iii) Kyoto, Japan (Images: Bosselmann 1998: 70, 79, 81). The walks illustrated are the same length in terms of distance but the experience and perception of time taken varies. Drawn at a consistent scale and read as a set, these diagrams are also tissue studies illustrating different textures, block sizes and urban grains (see Chapter 4)

et al (1972) highlighted how it had been designed to suit car-based observers (e.g. quickly read signs). The overarching lesson, however, is that, while environments seen only from cars can — and perhaps should — be designed to suit motorists and their passengers, environments seen by both motorists and pedestrians should be designed for the pedestrian's more discerning and prolonged attention.

Noting how Cullen and Ed Bacon's work (Bacon 1992) showed how movement can be read and understood as a pictorial sequence, Bosselmann (1998: 49—60) describes the rich and varied experience of a walk — measuring 350 m and taking about four minutes — from the Calle Lunga de Barnaba to the Rio de la Frescada in Venice. He uses this to show how our perception of time passing and distance travelled differs from reality, and is, in part, a function of the visual and experiential qualities of the environment we are moving through. Noting that the Venice walk seems both to be longer and to take more time than it actually does, he assesses the aesthetic experience of the same length of walk in 14 other cities (Figures 7.3—7.5). In most cities, the same length of walk appears to take less time; in a few cities, it appears to take almost the same time.

Bosselmann (1998: 90) argues that people tell the length of their walks in terms of the 'rhythmic spacing', which relates to different types of visual and spatial experiences along the walk — Gordon Cullen referred to these as (spatial) 'episodes'. The Venice walk had many different types of rhythmic spacing. The other environments had fewer types and the visible information engaged walkers less frequently. While Bosselmann's four-minute walk in Venice needed 39 drawings of unequal spacing to explain it, the other walks required far fewer drawings.

Nonetheless, the paradox remains that a short walk in Venice seems longer in terms of both distance and time than

FIGURES 7.3—7.5   *(continued).*

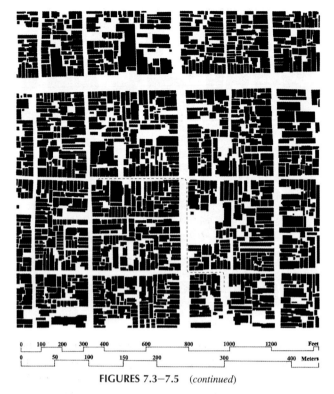

0   100   200   300   400   600   800   1000   1200   Feet
0   50   100   150   200   300   400   Meters

FIGURES 7.3–7.5 (continued)

the walks in the other cities. James (1892: 150, from Isaacs, 2001: 110) identifies a similar paradox: '… *a time filled with varied and interesting experiences seems short in passing, but long as we look back. [Equally] … a tract of time empty of experiences seems long in passing, but in retrospect short.*' Isaacs (2001: 110) explains this paradox: when walking through an environment that engages the mind, one is less aware of the passing of time, but when one reflects on that experience and the variety of sensations contained within it, one assumes more time must have passed. Conversely, when walking through an environment that does not engage the mind, one is more aware of the passing of time, but, in retrospect, the absence of sensations leads one to believe that less time has passed.

VISUAL QUALITIES OF SPACE

Urban spaces can be analysed in terms of their types (streets or squares), relationships (townscape) and volumetric qualities. Taking the latter first, external (outdoor) space can be considered in terms of 'negative' and 'positive' spaces (Figure 7.6) (Alexander *et al* 1977: 518):

- Positive space has a distinct and definite shape. In Paterson's terms, it is 'conceivable', can be measured and has definite and perceivable boundaries suggesting a sense-of-boundary or threshold between 'inside' and 'outside' (Paterson 1984, from Trancik 1986: 60). Defined by buildings, trees, columns, walls, level

changes, etc., the boundary need not be continuous and might be substantially implied. The shape of the space is as important as those of the buildings that surround it.
- Negative space is shapeless. In Paterson's terms, it is 'inconceivable' — it lacks perceivable edges (i.e. it is difficult to imagine the space being filled with a liquid because, quite simply, it is difficult to conceive of the space) (Figure 7.7).

The difference between 'positive' and 'negative' outdoor spaces can also be considered in terms of 'convexity' (Figure 7.8).

Creating Positive Space

Three major space-defining or -enclosing elements exist — the surrounding structures (the walls to the space); the floor; and the imaginary sphere of the sky overhead, which, Zucker (1959) argued, was perceived as three to four times the height of the tallest building. Enclosure and spatial containment must be considered in both plan and vertical section, with the amount of enclosure and the resulting degree of spatial containment depending on the ratio of the width of the space to the height of the enclosing walls. Not all buildings are — or should be — designed to be seen in a single view and greater variety in visual experience is created by spaces that, in different ways, restrict views of the surrounding structures. As demonstrated in Box 7.1, the plan arrangement is an important determining factor in creating a sense of spatial containment. The ideas set out in Box 7.1 are schematic and real squares have a high degree of both complexity and subtlety — see Baker (1996) for a thorough analysis of the spatial qualities of Venice's Piazza San Marco and Sienna's Campo.

Questioning why people feel comfortable in a space at least partly enclosed, Alexander *et al* (1977: 520) note that it is not always true. For example, people feel comfortable on an open beach. Nevertheless, they concede that in

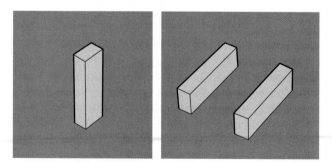

FIGURE 7.6   The sense-of-space. It is much easier to conceive of space that has clear limits. Consider the diagrams above. Asked what they see in the left-hand diagram, many people might say a tower block. For the right-hand diagram, they might say two blocks — though a few people might say two blocks *with a space between them*. Few people would readily describe the left-hand diagram as a tower *surrounded by space*

FIGURE 7.7 Figure—ground reversal. Depending on which is the 'figure' and which the 'ground', the image is either a vase or two faces. Positive and negative spaces can be distinguished through figure-ground *reversal*. Where outdoor spaces are negative, the buildings are the figure and outdoor space is the ground, but it is rarely possible to reverse this and to see the outdoor space as figure and the buildings as ground. Where outdoor spaces are positive, figure-ground reversal is possible and the buildings can be considered as figure or ground

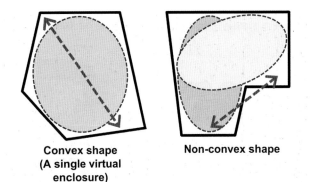

Convex shape
(A single virtual enclosure)

Non-convex shape

FIGURE 7.8 Convexity. A space is 'convex' when a line joining any two points inside the space lies totally within the space. The left-hand space is convex and, therefore, positive. The right-hand space is non-convex because a line joining two points cuts across the corner and goes outside the space. According to Alexander *et al* (1977: 518), 'positive' spaces are enclosed — at least to the extent that their areas *seem* bounded (i.e. the 'virtual' area is convex). The L-shaped space thus contains (at least) two large virtual spaces (thereby adding to its interest). The oval shapes represent the virtual area. 'Negative' spaces are often so poorly defined that it may not be possible to identify their boundaries

smaller outdoor spaces — gardens, parks, walks, plazas — enclosure seems to create a feeling of security:

'*... when a person looks for a place to sit down outdoors, he rarely chooses to sit exposed in the middle of an open space — he usually looks for a tree to put his back against; a hollow in the ground, a natural cleft which will partly enclose and shelter him.*'

(Alexander *et al* 1977: 520—1).

While noting people's apparent environmental preference for openness, Nasar (1998: 68), for example, cites research indicating preferences for 'defined openness' or, in other terms, 'open *but* bounded spaces'.

Sitte (1889; Collins & Collins 1965: 61) argued that: '*The ideal street must form a completely enclosed unit! The more one's impressions are confined within it, the more perfect will be its tableau: one feels at ease in a space where the gaze cannot be lost in infinity.*' Based on his analysis of a large number of European squares, Sitte showed that those that were well used tended to be partly enclosed but also open to one another so that each led into the next. Bentley (1998: 14), however contends that Sitte made a 'highly selective reading of the pre-capitalist city', arguing that —

although Sitte considered a sense-of-enclosure to be the most important quality of public space and stressed the medieval street system's spatial enclosure — its more valuable quality was actually its 'integrated continuity'.

In this respect, Cullen (1961: 106) made a valuable distinction between 'enclosure' and 'closure'. Enclosure, he argued, provided a complete 'private world' that is inward-looking, static and self-sufficient. Closure, by contrast, involved the division of the urban environment into a series of visually digestible and coherent 'episodes' while retaining a sense of progression. Each episode is effectively linked — sometimes surprisingly — to the others so that progress on foot is made more interesting by reason of these episodes.

A conclusion, therefore, is that rather than full or complete enclosure, a degree of enclosure is required. Furthermore, a balance must also be struck between achieving enclosure and other considerations, such as connectivity and permeability, which are important influences on how well the space is used (see Chapter 8).

Putting some empirical rigour on such observations, Ewing *et al* (2006) correlate a range of largely visual qualities of public space with the walkability of that space as perceived by an expert panel. They found that five key qualities explained more than 95% of the variation in walkability for a range of spaces. 'Human scale' ranked first in significance as a determinant of overall walkability, followed by 'imageability' (see Chapter 5), 'enclosure', 'transparency' (the degree to which activity is perceived beyond the building edge, through windows, doors and other openings — see Chapter 8) and 'tidiness'. This suggests spaces that are visually of a human scale, that have a strong image, that exhibit a sense-of-enclosure, and that

BOX 7.1 Principles of Spatial Containment and Enclosure

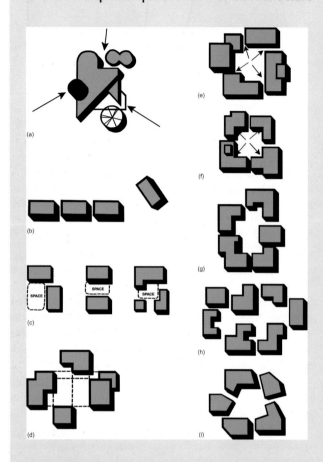

buildings with them (d). As with wholly rectilinear layouts, this method also sometimes appears contrived. An alternative to the rigidity of a rectilinear layout is where some of buildings are at varying angles to each other, introducing a degree of variety into the layout. When several buildings (or urban blocks) are clustered together in a more organised manner, 'positive' spaces can be created.

The most straightforward means of creating a sense of spatial containment is to group buildings around a central space (i.e. to enclose the space with an encircling wall of building facades) – the space becomes the primary focus and the buildings are subservient to it. Where the corners of the central space are open (i.e. where they form street intersections or where there is a gap between two separate buildings), the space is defined only by the facades of the enclosing buildings, with space leaking out through the corner openings. To better contain the space, building facades can be overlapped to prevent or limit views into or out of the space (e). When the building walls themselves fill and turn the corner of the central space, the corners keep views within the central space and create a much stronger sensation of enclosure (f).

If the whole space can be easily observed, it is not intriguing and may not invite further involvement. It may also lack sub-spaces and implied movement. When the perimeter becomes more varied and complex, with indentations and projections in the building facades, the resulting space has a number of implied sub-spaces and offers a richer experience. For a person standing within it, other points and sub-spaces are hidden or partially disguised, thereby creating a sense of mystery or intrigue (g). Nevertheless, as a simple urban space becomes more complex, there is a danger that it seems to break into a disjointed series of separate spaces (h). A dominant spatial volume helps establish a focus for the composition, the smaller sub-spaces being unable to compete with the major space. Alternatively the spaces might be organised by means of an axis or by a single dominant building.

A further key factor in creating a strong sense-of-enclosure is the design of openings into the space. Booth (1983: 142) refers to this as a 'windmill' or 'whirling' square; Sitte (1889) referred to it to a 'turbine' plan, describing it as the 'most favourable condition' (see Figure 7.12). As the streets do not pass directly through the space, the space has a strong sense-of-containment. Not only does this plan organisation contribute to strengthening the sense-of-enclosure, it also forces pedestrians entering to experience the space: they walk through – rather than pass by – the space (i).

The organisational and relational principles described here can be emphasised and reinforced – or indeed ignored – in the design of the floorscape.

Booth (1983) has usefully discussed the quality of enclosure through a series of simple diagrams. A single building of relatively simple form does not define or create space and, instead, is simply an object-in-space (a).

The weakest definition of space typically occurs when buildings are organised in a long row or are sited indiscriminately with no effort to co-ordinate relationships between them (b). In both these situations, there is no containment – the buildings are individual, unrelated elements surrounded by 'negative' space (i.e. space without containment or focus).

A simple most commonly used means to achieve compositional order is to site buildings at right angles to one another (c). However, this easily becomes monotonous when overused. The building-to-building association can be further strengthened by relating the forms and lines of one building to those of nearby buildings – by, for example, extending imaginary lines from the edges of a given building and aligning nearby

Images Adapted from Booth 1983.

are tidy and appear to be the venue for a range of active uses, will be perceived as more walkable.

Although urban spaces come in a variety of different sizes and shapes, there are two main types of positive space – 'streets' (roads, paths, avenues, lanes, boulevards, alleys, malls, etc.) and 'squares' (plazas, circuses, piazzas, places, courts, etc.). Streets are 'dynamic' spaces (there is a sense-of-movement), while squares are static spaces (there

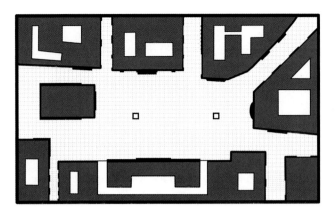

Ratio approx. 1:3

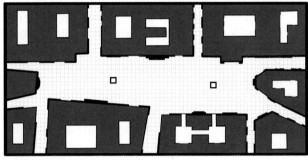

Ratio approx. 1:5

FIGURE 7.9 Width-to-length ratios. Width-to-length ratios help distinguish between 'streets' and 'squares'. If the ratio of width to length is 2:3 neither axis dominates and the space can be considered a square. Ratios of about 1:3 form the transition between street and square, as one axis begins to dominate. Where the ratio is 1:5, one axis clearly dominates and movement is suggested along that axis. Proportions of more than 1:5 suggest a street — a dynamic space

is less sense-of-movement). As one axis of potential movement begins to dominate, width-to-length ratios on plan greater than 3:1 begin to suggest dynamic movement — a ratio defining the upper limit for the proportions of a square and, by inference, the lower limit for a street (Figure 7.9). Streets and squares can also be characterised as either 'formal' or 'informal' (Figure 7.10).

The Square

A 'square' usually refers to an area framed by buildings. A distinction should, however, be made between squares designed for civic prestige, 'grandeur' or simply to exhibit a particular building, and those designed as 'people places' — that is, as settings for informal public life (see Chapter 8). This distinction is not absolute, and many public spaces function as both. Nonetheless, if we judge one type in terms of the other, difficulties arise: spaces designed to show off a particular building or for certain civic functions, for example, may be judged unsuccessful as people places.

The ideas of Camillo Sitte and Paul Zucker are of particular value for the visual–aesthetic appreciation of squares. Rob Krier's typology of urban spaces is also useful, but, whereas both Sitte and Zucker focused on the visual–aesthetic effect, his was a morphological structuring based on geometric patterns (see Chapter 4).

Camillo Sitte's Principles

Sitte (1889) advocated what is seen as a 'picturesque' approach to urban space design. Collins & Collins (1965: xii) contend Sitte meant picturesque in a pictorial rather

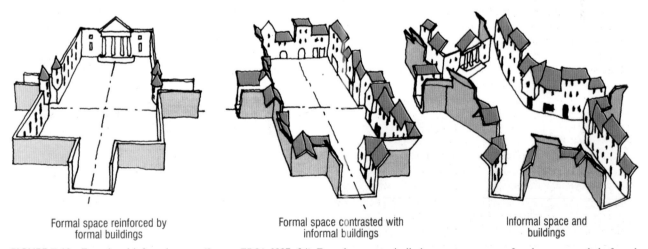

Formal space reinforced by
formal buildings

Formal space contrasted with
informal buildings

Informal space and
buildings

FIGURE 7.10 Formal and informal spaces *(Image: EPOA 1997: 24)*. Formal spaces typically have a strong sense-of-enclosure; an orderly formal floorscape and arrangement of street furniture; surrounding buildings that enhance the formality; and often a symmetrical layout. Informal squares typically have a more relaxed character; a wide variety of architectural treatments in the surrounding buildings; and an asymmetric layout. In any given context, neither is necessarily more appropriate than the other. Krier (2009: 163) comments that modest architecture is not appropriate for highly formal public spaces: *'Regular and parallel public spaces require a high degree of architectural order and design quality. Streets and squares with non-parallel configurations can accept more modest architecture with freer, less imposing compositions.'* Geometrical regularity is, however, less ambiguous and, when new development is proposed, it is more likely that it will respect that boundary or, alternatively, that the developer can be persuaded or required to respect the boundary

than romantic sense — that is, '*... structured like a picture and possessing the formal values of an organised canvas.*' Based on an analysis of the visual and aesthetic character of the squares of a range of European towns, particularly — although not exclusively — those resulting from incremental, organic growth, Sitte derived a series of artistic principles:

(i) **Enclosure**

For Sitte, enclosure was the primary feeling of urbanity and his overarching principle was that '*... public squares should be enclosed entities.*' (Figure 7.11). The design of the intersection between side streets and the square was one of the most important elements in enclosing the square, and Sitte argued that it should not be possible to see out of the square along more than one street at a time. One means for achieving this was the 'turbine' plan (Figure 7.12).

(ii) **Positive space**

Sitte rejected the concept of buildings as freestanding, sculptural objects. To create a better sense of enclosure, Sitte also argued that buildings, rather than being freestanding, should be joined to one another. For Sitte, a building's principal aesthetic was the manner in which its facades defined space and how the facade was seen from within that space. In most squares, observers can stand sufficiently far back to appreciate a facade as a whole and to appreciate its relation — or lack of relation — with its neighbours.

(iii) **Shape**

Arguing that squares should be in proportion to their major building, Sitte identified 'deep' and 'wide' types, depending on whether the main building was long and low or tall and narrow (Figure 7.13). The depth of a square was best related to the need to appreciate the main building (i.e. the depth should be between one and two times the main building's height), while the corresponding width depended on the perspective effect. In terms of plan shape, Sitte recommended that no relationship should be more than 3:1 and favoured irregular layouts.

Sitte's observations here relate to Von Meiss's notion of radiance, which refers to how some building facades command the space in front of them, creating a sense-of-space: '*A freestanding sculpture or building exerts a radiance which defines a more or less precise field around it. To enter the field of influence of an object is the beginning of a spatial experience.*' (Meiss 1990: 93). Radiance can be understood by reference to the human head: faces command the space immediately in front in a way that the backs and sides of our heads do not. In general, more formal architecture (i.e. symmetrical and regular) will have a greater sense of command.

(iv) **Monuments**

Sitte's general principle was that the centre of the square should be kept free. He also recommended putting something into it to provide a focus, but preferably along the edge of the square or off-centre — indeed, Collins & Collins (1965: ix) note Sitte book's *raison d'être* was the proper placement of public statues and monuments. In terms of detailed placement, he made an analogy with where children built snowmen — on the islands left by the paths through the snow. Likening the paths through the snow to routes crossing the square, he recommended that, when placing monuments within a space, one should avoid the natural routes through the space. While the positioning of such monuments had a functional logic, he argued that it was also aesthetically pleasing.

FIGURE 7.11 Piazza Navona, Rome, Italy *(Image: Matthew Carmona).* A well-enclosed space usually provides enough symmetry within the cone of vision to suggest an 'outdoor room'

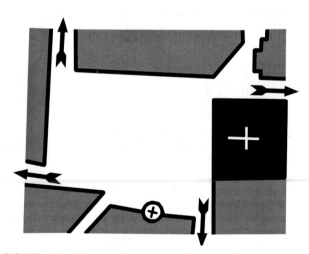

FIGURE 7.12 Sitte's turbine plan — Piazza del Duomo, Ravenna *(Image: Collins & Collins 1965: 34)*

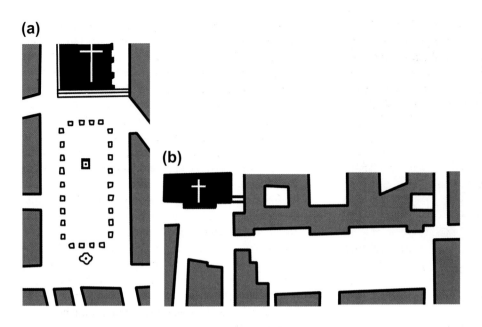

(a)

(b)

FIGURES 7.13 (a and b) Sitte's 'deep' (Piazza Santa Croce, Florence) and 'broad' piazza types (Piazza Reale, Modena) *(Image: Collins & Collins 1965: 39, 40)*

Paul Zucker's Typology of Urban Squares

In *Town and Square* (1959), Zucker discussed 'artistically-relevant' squares, which represented 'organised' and contained space. He argued that squares such as Rome's Piazza San Pietro and Venice's Piazza San Marco were 'undoubtedly art' because the '… *unique relationship between the open area of the square, the surrounding buildings, and the sky above creates a genuine emotional experience comparable to the impact of any other work of art.*' (Zucker 1959: 1). Zucker outlined five basic types of 'artistically relevant' urban square (Figure 7.14). Squares rarely represent only one pure type and frequently bear the characteristics of two or more. Venice's Piazza San Marco, for example, could be regarded as a closed square or, equally, as a set of grouped squares. He also noted that the specific function of a square did not automatically produce a definite spatial form and that each particular function could be expressed in many different shapes.

(i) The closed square: space self-contained

A closed square is a complete enclosure interrupted only by the streets leading into it, often exhibiting a regular geometric form and sometimes a repetition of architectural elements (e.g. Place des Vosges, Paris). For Zucker (1959), the closed square represents '… *the purest and most immediate expression of man's fight against being lost in a gelatinous world, in a disorderly mass of urban dwellings.*' Important elements in the appearance of closed squares include the layout on plan and the repetition of similar buildings or building facade types (Figure 7.15). Often a rhythmical alternation of two or more types is employed, with richer treatments concentrated on the corners or on the central parts of each side (Place Vendome, Paris), or framing the streets running into the square (Place des Victoires, Paris).

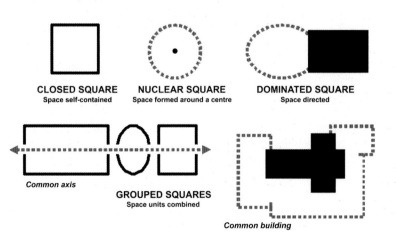

CLOSED SQUARE
Space self-contained

NUCLEAR SQUARE
Space formed around a centre

DOMINATED SQUARE
Space directed

Common axis

GROUPED SQUARES
Space units combined

Common building

FIGURE 7.14 Zucker's typology of urban squares. Note both that it is not possible to convey the key attributes of Zucker's amorphous square through a simple sketch and that the surrounding enclosure for the nuclear and dominated types is shown as a broken line. Though the material continuity of the enclosing elements may be weak, Zucker (1959: 2–3) argues that, when considered as a work of art and provided there is a virtual space, it is not important whether the boundaries of the 'space' are tangible or have to be partially imagined

FIGURE 7.15 Zucker's closed square — Place des Vosges, Paris, France (*Image: Steve Tiesdell*)

(ii) **The dominated square: space directed**

Recognising some buildings create a sense-of-space (Von Meiss's radiance) in front of them, Zucker's dominated square is characterised by a building or group of buildings towards which the space is directed and to which all other surrounding structures are related. Although typically the dominant feature is a building, this need not be the case and the square's dominant feature could, for example, be a view — provided a sufficiently strong sense-of-space is created (Piazza del Campidoglio, Rome).

(iii) **The nuclear square: space formed around a centre**

The nuclear square has a central feature — a vertical nucleus — sufficiently powerful to create a sense-of-space around itself and to charge the space with a tension that keeps the whole together. The force exerted by the nucleus governs the effective size of such spaces.

(iv) **Grouped squares: space units combined**

Zucker compared the visual impact of a group of aesthetically related squares with the effect of successive rooms inside a Baroque palace, where the first room prepares for the second, the second for the third, etc., with each being both a meaningful link in the chain and having additional significance because of it. Hence, provided the successive mental images can be integrated into a greater whole, individual squares can be fused organically or aesthetically. The squares may also be linked by means of an axis or axial relationships (the Place Royale, Place de la Carriere and the Hemicycle in Nancy) or have non-axial relations being, for example, grouped around a dominant building (Piazza San Marco, Venice).

(v) **The amorphous square: space unlimited**

Amorphous squares are those that do not fall into one of the above categories. For Zucker, an amorphous square shared at least some of the necessary qualities with other types, even if — on further analysis — it appeared to be unorganised or formless. For example, in London's Trafalgar Square the nuclear character suggested by Nelson's column is not sufficient to create a sense-of-space that relates to the size of the square. Similarly, the apparently dominating effect of the National Gallery is not sufficient to create a sense-of-space that relates to the size of the square, while there is a general lack of closure formed by the facades of the buildings surrounding the space.

The Street

Streets are linear three-dimensional spaces, enclosed on opposite sides by buildings. As discussed in Chapter 4, a 'street' is distinct from a 'road' — the primary purpose of the latter being a thoroughfare for vehicular traffic. Street form can be analysed in terms of a number of polar qualities, the combination of which gives scope for great diversity: visually dynamic or visually static; enclosed or open; long or short; wide or narrow; straight or curved; and formality or informality of the architectural treatment. To these might be added other considerations, such as the scale, proportion and rhythm of a street's architecture and its connections to other streets and squares. Furthermore, the presence of another opposite or counter-posing quality — rough/smooth; horizontal/vertical; large/small; etc. — usually enhances the initial quality.

Unlike urban squares — where, in most cases, the degree and nature of the enclosure gives a visually static character — most streets are visually dynamic and there is a sense-of-movement. As horizontal lines are visually faster than vertical lines, the character of streets — and the visual character of squares — can be modified to make them more (or less) visually dynamic, by, for example, vertical emphasis in the street wall checking the horizontal flow of space (horizontal emphasis would tend to increase that flow); irregular skylines slowing the eye; and incidents and setbacks reducing the impact of otherwise converging perspectives. The space can also be modulated into a number of discrete sections (Cullen's episodes and Bosselmann's rhythmic spacings) or through elements punctuating the flow of space (e.g. street termination features).

In streets with strong physical character, the street volume generally takes a positive form and possesses a strong sense-of-enclosure. The continuity of the street wall and the height-to-width ratio determine the sense of spatial enclosure within the street, while its width determines how the surrounding architecture is seen (Table 7.3). In narrow streets, vertical features become more prominent;

TABLE 7.3 Height-to-Width Ratios for Street Enclosure

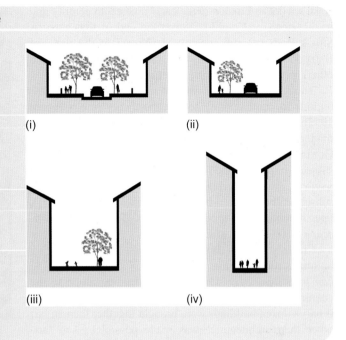

(i) Unlike a square, a street has only two walls to define space. If the walls are low in relation to the street width, outward views are not sufficiently contained to provide a sense of enclosed space. Streets with 1:4 ratios have three times as much sky as wall within the cone of vision, giving a weak sense-of-enclosure.

(ii) If the ratio is 1:2 the peripheral glimpses of sky equal the amount of visual field devoted to the street wall. The view of the sky is in the less dominant peripheral vision, thereby increasing the sense-of-enclosure. Ratios between 1:2 and 1:2.5 provide a good sense-of-enclosure in a street.

(iii) A street wall height that equals the street width severely limits the sky view and gives a strong sense-of-enclosure. Ratios of 1:1 are often considered the minimum for comfortable urban streets.

(iv) If the surrounding building height exceeds the width of the space then the tops of buildings will no longer be visible without looking up. Such ratios reduce light penetration into the space and may be claustrophobic. Combined with other street profiles, however, they create dramatic contrast and counterpoint.

projections are exaggerated; and eye-level details more important. The observer sees facades at acute angles and, when facing in the direction of the street, only sees parts of facades. Wide symmetrical facades may be inappropriate because the viewer is unable to stand far enough back to appreciate the symmetry. The most comfortable viewing distance for a building is from a distance of about twice its height. In broad streets, the observer is sufficiently removed to see the surrounding facades as wholes and their relationship — or lack of it — becomes evident. The floorscape and the skyline become more important elements in the street's character.

Winding, twisting streets and those with irregular street frontages enhance the sense-of-enclosure and provide a constantly changing prospect for the moving observer. Many commentators (e.g. Sitte 1889; Cullen 1961) prefer such streets, arguing that, while straight roads have their place, their selection is often made without sufficient consideration of terrain, local circumstances, townscape effect and potential for visual delight and interest (i.e. without an artistic sensibility).

For Le Corbusier (1929: 5), straight roads were the 'way of man' because man had a purpose and took the shortest route. The winding way, by contrast, was the 'way of the pack-donkey' who '... *zigzags to avoid the larger stones, or to ease the climb, or to gain a little shade; he takes the line of least resistance.*' Le Corbusier (1929: 13), thus, dismissed Camillo Sitte's *City Planning According to Artistic Principles* as a 'most wilful piece of work', a 'glorification of the curved line' and a 'specious demonstration of its unrivalled beauty' — though, as Broadbent (1990: 130)

wryly comments, Corbusean man would clearly '... *hack away the stones, scrambling upwards in a straight line, whatever the gradient whilst eschewing any shade to lighten his physical labours!*'

Successful design of straight streets — in visual terms, at least — generally depends on such factors as good proportions between length and width; the quality and unity of facades along the length of the street; and on their visual termination on a focus or other feature that brings the eye to rest. The design of streets as a coherent whole is a skill that has atrophied through the twentieth century and is only now being rediscovered.

Townscape

As well as the spatial properties and qualities of streets and squares, urban designers are concerned with how they are connected up to form streets, social space and, most importantly, movement systems. The public space network (see Chapter 4) creates a series of townscape effects, involving, for example, changing views and vistas, the interplay and varying relation of landmarks, and visual incidents and design features, together with changes and contrasts of enclosure. In broad terms, townscape results from the weaving together of buildings and all the other elements of the urban fabric and street scene (trees, nature, water, traffic, advertisements, etc.) such that — in Gordon Cullen's phrase — visual drama is released.

Although the term was first used in Thomas Sharpe's 1948 study of Oxford, a self-consciously 'picturesque' approach to townscape had already been evident in John

Nash's work in London in the early nineteenth century and in the views of Camillo Sitte at the end of that century. Sitte's lead was subsequently developed in the work of Barry Parker and Ray Unwin, Clough Williams-Ellis and others in the early twentieth century.

Though a number of writers made significant contributions to contemporary townscape theory (e.g. Gibberd 1953b; Worskett 1969; Tugnutt & Robertson 1987), the modern 'townscape' philosophy is closely associated with Gordon Cullen, whose beautifully illustrated essays on the subject initially formed a series of articles in the *Architectural Review* during the mid- and late 1950s and subsequently appeared in book form as *Townscape* (1961), later republished in amended form as *The Concise Townscape* (1971) (see also Gosling 1996).

Cullen's (1961: 10) main contention was that bringing buildings together gave a '… *visual pleasure which none can give separately.*' One building standing alone in the countryside was experienced as a work of architecture, but if half a dozen buildings were brought together then an 'art other than architecture' was made possible – an 'art-of-relationship'. Cullen's argument was essentially a contextualist one in which the whole was greater than the sum of the individual parts and where each building should be seen as a contribution to a larger whole. Cullen also suggested a vocabulary of terms to describe particular aspects of townscape (Figures 7.16–7.19 and 7.2).

Cullen argued that townscape could not be appreciated in a technical manner and had to be appreciated with an aesthetic sensibility. Although primarily visual, for Cullen townscape was not only visual, because vision evoked memories, experiences and emotional response.

While Cullen's concept of townscape is a useful means of analysis and appraisal, it is more difficult to translate into a design method. Indeed, it might be better not to attempt that translation. Townscape was primarily criticised for its tendency to isolate – and, to some extent, overemphasise – urban design's visual–aesthetic dimension. In his 'Introduction' to *The Concise Townscape*, Cullen (1971) himself lamented that townscape had resulted in '… *a superficial civic style of bollards and cobblestones.*' The essence of Cullen's argument, however, was that, as well as appreciating established townscapes, his ideas could be used to inform the design of new townscapes and interventions into existing townscapes. Unfortunately, when Cullen tried to do so, although the resulting proposals were often beautifully presented, they were rarely credible as serious pieces of functional, developable urban fabric (see, for example, Carmona 2009c: 96–8).

VISUAL ELEMENTS OF SPACE

The visual–aesthetic character of urban places derives from more than their spatial qualities. The colour, texture

FIGURE 7.16 Closed vista – Vienna *(Image: Matthew Carmona).* Cullen's 'closed vista': '… *which puts a building down and then invites you to stand back and admire it*'

and detailing of the surfaces defining urban space make significant contributions to its character. As warm colours seem to advance into a space while cool colours retreat, a space surrounded by facades in warm colours will tend to feel smaller, while a similar space surrounded by facades in cool colours will tend to feel larger. Similarly, a space can feel harsh and inhuman if its surfaces lack fine detail and visual interest, while, if finely detailed, it might feel delicate, airy and inviting. The activities occurring within and around the space also contribute to its character and sense-of-place (see Chapter 6).

Urban Architecture

For the purpose of this discussion, 'urban' architecture can be considered to be that which responds to and contributes positively to its context and to the physical definition of the public realm. The notion of object-buildings and 'textures/ fabrics' (building mass) was introduced in Chapter 4.

FIGURE 7.17 Deflection — Oxford *(Image: Matthew Carmona)*. Cullen's 'deflection': '*… in which the object building is deflected away from the right angle, thus arousing the expectation that it is doing this to some purpose*'

FIGURE 7.18 Projection and recession — Savora, Italy *(Image: Matthew Carmona)*. Cullen's 'projection and recession': '*Instead of the eye taking in the street in a single glance, as it would in a street with perfectly straight facades, it is caught up in the intricacy of the meander*'

FIGURE 7.19 Narrows — Shad Thames, London *(Image: Steve Tiesdell)*. Cullen's 'narrows': '*The crowding together of buildings forms a pressure, an unavoidable nearness of detail, which is in direct contrast to the wide piazza.*'

A visually coherent townscape might be considered to combine a limited number of 'special' or iconic object-buildings — which might typically be religious buildings, government buildings, prominent residences, civic monuments — usually, though not always, standing either slightly or dramatically apart from their context, balanced by a greater number of 'ordinary' or quotidian ('texture') buildings. Kelbaugh (2002: 99) refers to the latter as 'background' or 'collateral' buildings, which '*… gain their strength from the public space they define.*' The iconic/quotidian distinction is not one of design quality — both should be well designed. Many cities, however, suffer from both a surfeit of poorly designed iconic/special buildings and too many poorly designed quotidian/ordinary buildings, both transgressing basic principles of good urban architectural design.

As noted previously, Meiss (1990: 93) uses the notion of radiance to describe the spatial impact of facades. He suggests that, while the built fabric gives an '*image of continuity, of expansiveness, stretching to infinity*', the object is '*… a closed element, finite, comprehensible as an entity.*' (1990: 75). Standing out against a background, it concentrates visual attention. He also notes that, even where buildings are embedded within urban blocks, the front facade may take on an object role, forming an object-facade with radiance and commanding the space in front of that facade. While the object-facade has radiance onto public space, the building's other (three) sides are embedded in the general fabric. The extent of radiance depends on the nature and size of the object or facade and on the context — although it may also be suggested or reinforced by the design of the surrounding space. It is also unlikely that object-buildings will have the same degree of radiance in all directions and, moreover, as the aesthetic effect works by contrast with the fabric (the object needs a 'ground' to stand out against), the design of buildings as freestanding objects-in-space should be occasional exceptions.

Concern merely for a building's facade might be seen as relegating the design of buildings to a process akin to two-dimensional stage set design. As Meiss (1990) observes, stage sets are a kind of architecture, but architecture is more than a stage set. Freestanding buildings are more difficult to design successfully than those embedded within an urban block, which present only their main facade to public space. Freestanding buildings are seen, and thus subject to aesthetic critique, from many points — a more demanding task, it is also one that their designers are more likely to fail at. Furthermore, the cost of ornamenting and elaborating four (or more) exterior walls is inevitably higher than elaborating a single front facade.

Writing at the end of the nineteenth century, Camillo Sitte considered that freestanding buildings would inevitably be over-exposed like a 'cake on a serving-platter'. Moreover, he argued that, because it involved the additional 'expense of finishing lengthy facades', it was greatly to the client's disadvantage and that, if the building was embedded within an urban block, its main facade '... *could then be carried out in marble from top to bottom.*' (Sitte, 1889 from Collins & Collins 1965: 28).

Facade Design

This section concentrates on facade design and the integration of new buildings into established urban settings. In essence, facades are designed for private interests, whose actual interests may differ from the public interest of good place-making. Successful facade design is a contemporary design problem. Going beyond the visual–aesthetic role of facades, Buchanan (1988b) argues that facades should:

- Create a sense of place.
- Mediate between inside and out, and private and public space, and provide gradations between the two.
- Have windows suggesting the potential presence of people and that reveal and 'frame' internal life.
- Have character and coherence that both acknowledge conventions and enter into a dialogue with adjacent buildings.
- Have compositions that create rhythm and repose and hold the eye.
- Have a sense of mass and materials, which should be combined with an expression of the form of construction.
- Have substantial, tactile and decorative materials, which are natural and which weather gracefully.
- Have decoration that distracts, delights and intrigues.

Defining what made a 'good building' the Royal Fine Art Commission (RFAC) (Cantacuzino 1994) identified six criteria:

- *Order and unity* — 'satisfying and indivisible unity' created through the 'search for order' (1994: 70). In terms of building elements and facade design, order is manifest through such means as symmetry, balance, repetition, the grid, the bay, the structural frame, etc.
- *Expression* — '... *the apt expression of the function of a building which enables us to recognise a building for what it is.*' (1994: 70). While subject to debate, symbolic appropriateness is often considered a key requisite of good architecture. A house, for example, should communicate its function as a house, a church its function as a church, etc. The symbolic differentiation of building types also produces a hierarchy of building types, which increases the legibility of urban areas.
- *Integrity* — '... *a strict adherence to principles of design, not in the sense of rules which may determine the design of a classical facade, but in the sense that Gothic architecture embodies principles of construction which are quite different to the principles of Classical architecture.*' (1994: 71). In other words, buildings should express through their form and construction the functions they and their individual parts fulfil.
- *Plan and section* — to ensure its integrity as a three-dimensional construction, there should be a positive relationship between a building's facade and its plan and section (i.e. between its interior and the exterior) (see Chapter 9).
- *Detail* — detail is what holds the eye, thus a lack of detail '... *deprives us of a layer of experience that brings us into close contact with a building where we can admire the beauty of the materials and the skill of the craftsman or engineer.*' (1994: 76).
- *Integration* — the first five qualities are those of individual buildings, but what matters in urban design is how that building relates to the larger whole. The sixth criterion thus involves whether a building harmonises with its surroundings and the qualities it needs to integrate with those surroundings. As Frederick (2007) observes, integration is primarily about relationships and, furthermore, 'beauty' is usually due more to harmonious relationships among elements of a composition than to the elements themselves — thus it is the ensemble that matters, both within the individual building and in terms of the building with its neighbours.

In this area, perhaps above all others, there is a need to avoid turning generally desirable principles into dogmatic imperatives: strict adherence to 'the rules' often leads to mediocrity and uniformity. The RFAC, for example, stressed that a building could embody every criterion and not be a 'good' building and, conversely, could be a 'good' building without complying with any of the criteria. Moreover, 'good' designers successfully break the rules, and generally know what the criteria are — or, at least, have an intuitive understanding of them. For these reasons, rather than as a design prescription, the RFAC's criteria are best understood as means of structuring and informing an appreciation of urban architecture. It may also be important that they are considered, either explicitly or intuitively, in the design process.

Integration

The sixth RFAC criterion — integration — is a problematic area of urban architectural design. During the late 1980s, for example, HRH the Prince of Wales (1989: 84) famously described the design of an extension of the National Gallery in London's Trafalgar Square as a 'monstrous carbuncle' on the face of a 'much-loved friend'. More generally and stressing his basic principle that 'places matter most', Tibbalds (1992: 16) argued that, in most instances, individual buildings should be subservient to the needs and character of the place as a whole: *'If every building screams for attention, the result is likely to be discordant chaos. A few buildings can, quite legitimately, be soloists, but the majority need simply to be sound, reliable members of the chorus.'* He further argued that, while there are occasional needs for the unusual 'prima donna' set piece, *'... the greater need is for a better vocabulary of well-designed, interesting 'back cloth' buildings.'* (Tibbalds 1992: 16).

Integration — or, as it is sometimes disparagingly (and incorrectly) called, 'fitting-in' — does not require slavish adherence to a certain architectural style. The 'stylistic' dimension is only one aspect of 'fitting-in'; other visual criteria — scale, rhythm, etc. — will often be more important — and setting too much store by it denies the opportunity for innovation and excitement. Many successful groups of buildings are of dramatically different materials and styles (Figure 7.20). Accordingly, the RFAC suggested six criteria for the harmonious integration of new buildings into existing contexts: siting; massing; scale; proportion; rhythm; and materials (Cantacuzino, 1994: 76–9). These are discussed further below.

Different approaches to creating harmony with the existing context can be identified, each representing and reflecting particular design philosophies. Rather than discrete approaches, they exist along a continuum. At one extreme, (stylistic) *uniformity* or *matching* involves imitating or copying the local spatial and visual character. Such an approach can, however, dilute and weaken the qualities it seeks to retain.

At the other extreme, *juxtaposition* or *contrast* involves designing a new building with few apparent concessions to

FIGURE 7.20 Piazza San Marco, Venice *(Image: Matthew Carmona)*. Dramatically different materials and styles, but few would dispute the aesthetic harmony of the composition. Note, however, that each building defines space

the existing spatial and visual character (Figures 7.21–7.24). While there can be vibrant contrast, the approach is eminently capable of producing '... *a disastrous result in the form of arrogant exhibitionism.'* (Wells-Thorpe 1998: 113).

Between matching and juxtaposition lies *continuity*. Involving interpretation — rather than mere imitation — of the local spatial and visual character, the approach reflects a desire for new development to reflect *and* develop the existing sense of place. Spatial and visual character can be separated such that a design may match the area's spatial character but juxtapose with its visual character.

One approach to discussing the integration of new development is by analogy with both human characters and a dialogue or debate among them. Moreover, much of

FIGURE 7.21 Contextual juxtaposition — The Glass Pyramid, Le Lourvre, Paris *(Image: Steve Tiesdell)*

FIGURE 7.22 Contextual juxtaposition — 'Ginger Rogers and Fred Astaire building', Prague *(Image: Matthew Carmona)*

FIGURE 7.23 Contextual juxtaposition — Delft *(Image: Matthew Carmona)*

the same language and conventions (including references to manners, which are, in essence, about respect for others and for the collective) can be employed. Buildings can be bold, confident, brash, self-effacing, reserved, shy, witty, cheeky, etc. Appreciation of character is also in the mind of the beholder — for one beholder a person may simply be self-confident; to another they may be rude or presumptuous — and also situational and contextual: conduct appropriate at a sports match, for example, may not be appropriate at a formal dinner party. Linguistic analogies are frequently made in this context — dialogue, grammar/syntax, language — arguably because it is about communication. These analogies might nevertheless be rendered trite by the context in which they are used.

Whether a building harmonises with its context, however, is ultimately a matter of personal judgement. Pearce (1989: 166) succinctly encapsulates the challenge: *'All that is required for the rewarding addition of a new building in an old setting is the genius of the place to be complemented by the genius of the architect.'* But genius is rare, and what is often needed is well-mannered urban buildings. What is noticeable, however, is that, though most traditional buildings are well-mannered, such qualities are much rarer in buildings built after 1945.

Areas of homogeneous architectural character are relatively rare, and the variety inherent in most contexts permits opportunities for contrasting design. Wells-Thorpe (1998: 113) suggests that in assessing whether a *more* contextualist approach is appropriate the following qualities of the 'old surroundings' should be considered: (i) their extent; (ii) their worth (i.e. their quality); (iii) their consistency and homogeneity; (iv) their uniqueness; and (v) their proximity (whether they can be seen in the same sweep of the eye).

While variety is of particular value in creating visually interesting street scenes, certain principles of well-mannered urban architectural design enable new buildings to better harmonise with the existing context. Rather than absolute or hard-and-fast rules, these are generally desirable principles

and occasional transgressions may be desirable. What is important, however, is the win/loss ratio, as per Andres Duany's comment:

'I would have no problem with modernist architecture were it not for its appalling win-to-loss ratio. I am not prepared to tolerate the thirty million modernist buildings that have destroyed the cities of the world in exchange for the three thousand (or is it three hundred?) undeniable masterpieces of modernism'

(cited in Kelbaugh 2002: 94).

These principles can be considered in terms of volumetric (spatial), visual, social and functional characters.

Integration — Volumetric (Spatial) Character

Volumetric/spatial integration relates to the new building's overall three-dimensional form and disposition relative to its setting or context.

FIGURE 7.24 Contextual juxtaposition — Delft *(Image: Matthew Carmona)*

(i) Street patterns and block and plot sizes

Respect for existing street patterns and block/plots sizes aids harmonious integration. Plot amalgamation, for example, alters the scale of city buildings and breaks down the traditional grain of urban areas.

(ii) Siting

Siting concerns how a building sits on its site and how it relates to other buildings and to the street or other urban spaces. Respect for the established building line and street frontage is important in ensuring the continuity and definition of external space: breaks in the street line should be deliberate — rather than arbitrary or accidental — and should create positive space or incident. Highly sculptural buildings — objects-in-space — should generally be exceptions and major incidents in the townscape, their impact being more significant for their relative scarcity. An urban rule-of-thumb when designing an infill building, suggested by Frederick (2007), is, unless there is a compelling reason to do otherwise, that its front should be placed at the prevailing building line of the street. Setting buildings back from the street makes them less accessible to passers-by, reduces the economic viability of ground floor businesses and weakens the street's spatial definition.

(iii) Size/massing

Massing is the three-dimensional disposition of the building volume. A useful urban rule, derived from observing traditional urban environments, suggests symmetry of building height (and, indeed, uses) across spaces, and asymmetry across blocks (see Chapter 8) — as noted previously, sufficient symmetry within the cone of vision gives a sense-of-enclosure and suggests an outdoor room. The impact of new development also needs to be considered from a range of viewing points and angles. Although sometimes used to control the volume of development acceptable on a particular site, plot ratios (gross floor area divided by site area) and floor area ratios (FARs) are a rather crude tool as the same volume of development can be organised in a variety of different ways (see Chapter 8). Plot ratios should always be accompanied (or replaced) by some form of indicative massing.

(iv) Building scale

Scale is different from size: size represents the literal dimensions of an object; scale is the perception of that object relative to other objects around it and to our perception of those objects. Scale concerns, first, the building's dimensions and all its parts relative to the dimensions of a human being (i.e. human scale) and, second, its dimensions relative to those of its setting (i.e. generic scale) (Figure 7.25). Hence, a building can be understood to be in or out of scale with its surroundings and, separately, to be of human

FIGURE 7.25 Visual scale — Mansion House, London, UK (*Image: Matthew Carmona*). It is difficult to read the scale of this building. It initially reads as a three-storey building, until the clues given by the traffic signs and the cars are noted — it is realised that it is a much larger building than initially supposed, but also seems to be a small building trying to be large

scale or not. Building scale relates to the size of adjacent buildings — that is, whether one dwarfs another or whether there are design elements that form a (visual) bridge or transition in terms of size.

Integration — Visual Character

Visual integration relates primarily to the design of a building's facade(s).

(i) Proportions and relationships

Proportion is the relation between the different parts of a building, and also between any individual parts and the whole. It may relate to the ratio of solid to void in a building's facade or to the way in which window openings are arranged in relation to solid wall elements. Traditional street scenes built in load-bearing masonry and consisting of a series of different buildings tend to have relatively consistent ratios of window-to-wall area. Figure-ground studies of the street elevation in which each facade is reduced to solid (white) and void (black) are a means of investigating fenestration proportions and rhythms (see below). By removing extraneous detail, this technique permits a clearer focus on the proportions (and rhythms) of solid-to-void along the street.

(ii) Relative visual scale

New buildings in established contexts may be more harmoniously integrated if they have complimentary proportions with — that is, a similar visual scale as — neighbouring buildings.

(iii) Articulation and richness

Low relief, 'surface' texture detail is what holds the eye and provides interest. Facades can be appreciated in terms of their visual 'richness' and 'elegance'. Richness relates to the visual interest and complexity that holds the eye. Elegance is a function of the proportions that the eye finds pleasing and harmonious. Some facades will have both elegance and richness; where facades are elegant, detail is normally used sparingly. An elegant facade, however, does not necessarily hold the eye and could be construed to be lacking visual interest and even to be boring. Detail and visual interest help to humanise environments. As buildings are seen in different ways — near and far (and at all stages in between), straight on, or obliquely — detail is typically required at varying scales on facades depending on their position in the townscape. Small-scale detail, for example, is especially important at ground floor level to provide visual interest for the pedestrian, while larger-scale detail is important for viewing over longer distances (Figure 7.26a–c). There is also typically an increase in the intensity of detail about windows and especially about doorways and at building corners. Appropriate emphasis of entrance points also allows users to 'read' the facade and facilitates movement from the public to private realm (Figure 7.27).

(iv) Pattern and rhyme

Rhyme involves (some) similarity in the elements of the building and its neighbours, and presupposes the simultaneous existence of both complexity (i.e. a mass of visual detail and information) and patterns. Smith (1980: 74) argues that rhyme patterns do not comprise simple repetition, as in fabrics and wallpaper, and are better considered as a system in which, while there may not be 'point-to-point correspondence', there is nevertheless 'substantial affinity'. At the level of the street, some streets are unified through repetition of a particular architectural 'style', while others exhibit great variety and yet are unified by common underlying design patterns or motifs. Unifying elements may be present in the form of, for example, the building silhouette; consistent plot widths; fenestration patterns; proportions; massing; the treatment of entrances; materials; details; scale; style; etc.

(v) Rhythm

Differing from rhyme, rhythm relies for its impact on a stricter repetition. Rhythm is the arrangement and size of the constituent parts of a building's facade (i.e. its windows or bays), which are normally repeated. Of particular significance for rhythm is the facade's wall-to-window ratio (i.e. solid-to-void); the horizontal or vertical emphasis of the fenestration; and the expression of structure. Dividing a facade into a series of bays is one means of integrating a large building into a street scene.

(vi) Horizontality and verticality

Although most facades have both vertical and horizontal elements, one or the other tends to dominate such that it has a vertical or horizontal emphasis (Figure 7.28). As the constituent parts of a building's facade traditionally had a vertical emphasis, buildings with a strong horizontal emphasis tend to disrupt the visual rhythm of traditional streets. Furthermore, as the combination of buildings with horizontal emphasis and the horizontality of streets can result in excess horizontality, a general principle is that urban buildings have a vertical emphasis to which the street provides a balancing horizontality. An additional argument for verticality is that horizontal lines are visually faster than vertical lines (the eye runs more quickly along them). As the eye is detained for a shorter period of time, strong horizontal lines are less interesting.

(vii) Materials

Providing a building with colour and texture, the choice of materials also affects weathering, detailing, visual interest at various distances and facade patterning. Judicious use of materials can sharpen or soften differences between the various parts of the building, and the relation between it and its neighbours. With appropriate modelling, incidents of shade and shadow on a facade give a sense of visual depth and solidity and can dramatically alter the perception of materials. Materials also help establish local distinctiveness. The UK's exceptional geological diversity, for example, has led to a diverse range of

FIGURES 7.26 (a−c) Visual detail on facades − Barcelona *(Images: Matthew Carmona)*. This building is richly detailed at a series of different levels. At distance only the main elements of the facade are apparent. Coming closer, other major elements become apparent. Closer still, materials and constructional detailing are apparent, with additional detail at ground level

FIGURE 7.27   Tripartite division of facade — Gdansk *(Image: Matthew Carmona)*. Many traditional urban facades are organised into three elements — typically 'base', 'middle' and 'top'. The base is usually designed to express its structural support, relates to the street and is often more richly decorated as this is the part that pedestrians are better able to see and appreciate; the middle is often more visually restrained, while the top and skyline are again more visually complex to detain the eye. The relative proportions of elements can also be important — traditionally the base is substantial and can visually take the weight of the building's upper storeys. Although this practice is less commonly followed in contemporary development, these buildings have been designed in the traditional manner

vernacular building traditions, and thus to significant local distinctiveness. Consistent use of local building materials, or a limited palette of colours, can give a town or city a strong sense of place, while their use in new development helps it to integrate visually (see Porter 1982; Lange 1997; Moughtin *et al* 1995: 133–44).

Integration — Social and Functional Character

As much, and perhaps more, significant in successful integration are 'functional' and 'social' considerations — that is, how a building integrates with the social context and how it is designed to achieve its functional programme. It relates, for example, to how taxis arrive, queue and load at the entrance to a hotel.

(i) Human scale

Although the height of buildings is not necessarily of significance in achieving human scale, the articulation of facades and the visual interest at pedestrian level is. As noted previously, a building can be understood to be of a human scale or not and, separately, to be in or out of scale with its surroundings (Figure 7.29). Certain scale-giving elements, such as windows, doors and construction materials, are particularly important because we have a clear perception of their size relative to that of our own bodies. Scale derives not just from the elements of the building or the facade but

also the intrinsic size of building materials. In the past, the limitations of the human body dictated the size of materials used in construction and, where the individual unit can be seen, such elements gave the building scale. With mechanised building techniques, the need for construction units that could be easily handled became less important and many buildings and urban spaces do not have the benefit of such scale-giving elements (Figure 7.30).

(ii) Active frontages

Frontage — how buildings address the street — is a key determinant of the quality of streets and of public space. Active frontages have a strong sense of 'human presence'. In essence, this relates to whether there is

FIGURES 7.28   Verticality and horizontality — South Beach, Miami (Image: Matthew Carmona). Although most facades have both vertical and horizontal elements, one tends to dominate. The emphasis is shown by the tendency to look *up and down* or *along* the facade. This pair of buildings illustrate this principle. Individual windows or the fenestration pattern as a whole are often a key element in determining the emphasis. Buildings in load-bearing masonry tend to have a vertical emphasis. In framed buildings, the facade is simply a cladding or skin. Openings in that skin can be made in any shape or form, and, to emphasise the potential of new construction methods, many early nineteenth century architects designed buildings with a horizontal emphasis

FIGURE 7.29 Public art playing games with scale — Rome *(Image: Matthew Carmona)*

a sense of activity at the ground floor (e.g. interaction with the street) and/or a sense of activity on the upper floors within a building animating the street space (e.g. eyes-on-the-street), and, more generally, to the notion of active frontages (see Chapter 8).

(iii) **Iconography and visual cues to functionality**
Social integration requires visual clues to aid the building's functionality (e.g. in locating its main entrance). In many established locations, there is a well-developed iconography and symbolism relating to entrances as transitions between, for example, public and private spaces, with gradations and distinctions defining different degrees of publicness.

FIGURE 7.30 Scale-giving elements — Boston *(Image: Matthew Carmona)*. Here the contrast in scale between buildings is dramatic, not just in absolute size, but also between the highly modulated Old State House in the foreground and the facade behind, which lacks similar scale-giving elements

(iv) **Transition from public to private realm**
The design of the transition from public to private should respect and protect both the public and the private realms (Figure 7.31). The key design elements are often the organisation of entrances, changes of level through steps and ramps, and the treatment of views into and out from the building's lower levels. To maintain a degree of privacy and control, those in the building ought to be at a slightly higher level than those on the street outside. There may also be design features (e.g. railings or heavily textured pavements) that keep pedestrians away from the building wall and windows, discouraging them from peering into the more private parts of a building (Figures 7.32 and 7.33).

Floorscape

Floorscape is an important part of making a harmonious and integrated whole. In general terms, there are two main types of flooring within urban areas — 'hard' pavement and 'soft' landscaped areas. The focus here is on hard pavements. The materials used — brick, stone slabs, cobbles, concrete, macadam, etc. — determine a floorscape's basic character but what also matters is how they are used; how they are arranged; and how they interrelate with other

FIGURES 7.31 Transition from public to private — Blythswood Hill, Glasgow *(Image: Steve Tiesdell)*. To cope with the functional, and in turn aesthetic, problems/challenges of building on a hill, the Georgians set buildings back from the street line and introduced a well with access to a basement. The well was functional, giving a number of ways: the main rooms of the building were raised above the street level and were separated from the street, thus providing privacy; the lower level was for servicing and could accommodate coal deliveries, and screen refuse and waste. Continued by the Victorians, the well device is one of the design patterns (together with street pattern and plot sizes) that is instrumental in giving the area its genius loci. The basement wells now accommodate a range of small businesses, bars and restaurants. More modern buildings, which are larger due to plot amalgamation, have dispensed with the well but have struggled to resolve the problems of designing on a hill

FIGURES 7.32 and 7.33   The Gherkin, London *(Images: Steve Tiesdell and Matthew Carmona)*. Successful buildings work at many levels. Though a distinctive contribution to London's skyline, the 'Gherkin' does little to aid successful integration at ground level

materials and landscape features (Figure 7.34). The edging detail is also important in visually linking and, thereby, aiding the transition from the horizontal to the vertical plane — a transition that often indicates the quality of a paving design.

Floorscape patterns result from functional considerations, which may *inter alia* have an aesthetic effect, and/or from attempts to organise the space aesthetically. Considering the former first, the primary function of any paved area is to provide a hard, dry, non-slip surface that will carry the traffic load. Different traffic loads can be reflected in different flooring materials and construction methods, which may also indicate where different types of traffic should go. Junctions between materials are often articulated. The most common edge between vehicular and pedestrian traffic is the ubiquitous granite or concrete kerb with a shallow step from pavement to road. Using materials to add further parallel lines both gives greater definition to the change of function and has a decorative effect.

Change of flooring materials can indicate a change of ownership (e.g. between public and private spaces),

potential hazards or provide a warning. Textured pavements at road crossing points, for example, assist those with impaired sight. Paving might also be designed to guide pedestrians or vehicles through an area where there are few other indications of the route to be taken: lines across otherwise monolithic surfaces, for example, give strong directional qualities. Equally, directional paving may have a purely aesthetic function and may simply be used within a space to reinforce a linear form and so enhance the sense-of-movement.

Floorscape can also be consciously designed to enhance the character of the space, by introducing scale (both human and generic); modulating the space (organising it into a series of hierarchical elements); reinforcing spatial and visual character; and aesthetically organising and unifying the space. A sense of scale in the floorscape of an urban space can derive from the intrinsic scale of the materials, from the patterning of different materials, or from a combination of both. Sized to permit easy handling, stone paving slabs generally give a human scale to urban spaces. Smaller spaces often require no additional patterning to provide a sense of scale; larger spaces generally require some form of additional patterning.

Floorscape patterns often modulate large, hard surfaces, breaking them down into more visually manageable and/or human proportions. The floorscape can be enriched in a fashion similar to the design of a building facade by repeating and echoing particular motifs or themes, by emphasising changes of materials and/or by dramatising the edge of a paved area. In the Piazza San Marco, Venice, for example, the scale of the space is modulated and humanised by a simple grid of white travertine and black basalt. Floorscape patterns can also be used to manipulate the apparent size of the space: the addition of detail and

FIGURE 7.34   Unity of materials — Castlegate, Aberdeen *(Image: Steve Tiesdell)*. Unity of materials and design between the floorscape and the surrounding architecture creates a visually harmonious townscape

modulation tends to make a big space seem smaller, while a simple and relatively unadorned treatment makes a small space seem larger.

In streets, floorscape patterns can reinforce the linear character of space, by emphasising its character as a 'path', by providing a sense of direction, by checking the flow of space or by suggesting a feeling of repose (Figure 7.35). Parallel lines following the length of the street reinforce the sense-of-movement. Conversely, paving that does not follow the linearity of the street tends to slow the visual pace and reinforce its qualities as a place at which to stop or linger. Interplay between floor patterns alternating between movement and rest brings qualities of rhythm and scale to the urban scene.

Floorscapes designed to provide a sense of repose are usually associated with areas where people stop and rest (i.e. with urban squares). The floorscape pattern of squares can perform a number of functions: providing a sense of scale; unifying the space by linking and relating the centre and edges; and/or bringing order to a space that would otherwise be a disparate group of buildings. In the latter case, a strong and simple geometric figure (a rectangle, circle or oval) can organise the central part of the space, providing focus and discipline, and allowing the more irregular line of the surrounding buildings to form more localised relations with the edge of the geometric figure (Figure 7.36). By relating the floor and the walls to the space and by focusing the space, the geometric figure organises the square into a single aesthetic whole. Michelangelo's design for the floorscape of Campidoglio in Rome achieves all of these functions (Figure 7.37). Key buildings may be emphasised by having their geometry continued or their features reflected in the floorscape — a device that unifies the composition.

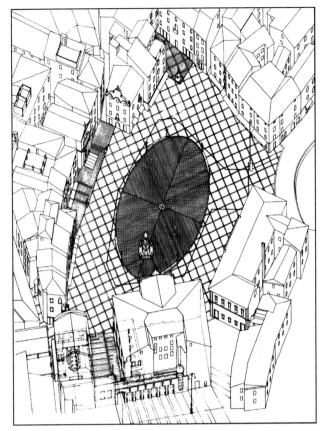

FIGURE 7.36 Floorscape — Piazza Giuseppe Tartini, Pirano, Slovenia *(Image: Favole 1997)*. A simple geometric floorscape unifies and organises the irregular trapezoidal space

FIGURE 7.35 Vibrant street floor pattern — Izmir, Turkey *(Image: Matthew Carmona)*

FIGURE 7.37 Floorscape — Campidoglio, Rome *(Image: Matthew Carmona)*. The Campidoglio's floor pattern expands out from the base of the equestrian statue. The sunken oval containing the pattern reinforces the centrality of the space while the expanding ripples of the central pattern emphasise movement to the edge. Constantly and repeatedly linking the centre and the edge, the design unifies the space and its enclosing elements

Street Furniture

Street furniture includes all the hard landscape elements other than the floorscape: telegraph poles, lighting standards, telephone boxes, benches, planters, traffic signs, direction signs, CCTV cameras, police boxes, bollards, boundary walls, railings, fountains, bus shelters, statues, plinths, etc., and myriad other items. Public art in all its forms is also a type of street furniture (Figures 7.38 and 7.39).

In addition to contributing to identity and character, the quality, organisation and distribution of street furniture is a prime indicator of the quality of an urban space and can also establish quality standards and expectations for subsequent development. Furthermore, rather than buildings, the clutter of street furniture and other paraphernalia often diminishes the quality of the visual scene. In some cases, however, 'clutter' provides the street's essential character (Figure 7.40).

Street furniture can be procured in various ways. The most basic are 'off-the-peg' systems, where items are simply selected from manufacturers' catalogues. Alternatively, standard items can be customised to give a degree of local identity, which could be further developed by the design of a suite of items to be used only in that particular place or locality. In locations where a particularly strong

FIGURE 7.39   Public art, Delft *(Image: Matthew Carmona)*

design character is desired, artists might be invited to design furniture for that space or area (Gillespies 1995: 67).

Although an integral, and necessary, part of the public realm, myriad items of street furniture are often distributed with little concern for their overall effect, resulting in a visually and functionally cluttered urban scene. In 2004, recognising that the towns and villages of England were blighted by superfluous signs, haphazard paving and obstructed footways, English Heritage launched a campaign to 'save our streets', intended to rid them of excessive furniture, make them more friendly to pedestrians and cyclists, and generally to return them to '... *places where people want to be, where all street users are accommodated and where communities thrive as a result.'* Working with the Department of Transport, it published *Streets for All*, setting out principles of good practice in street management (see www.english-heritage.org.uk/).

FIGURE 7.38   Public art, Pittsburgh *(Image: Steve Tiesdell)*

FIGURE 7.40   Signage in Japanese streets forms a more significant component of the townscape than in European cities — Tokyo *(Image: Steve Tiesdell)*

Extraneous and unnecessary street signs were a *bête noir* for Dutch traffic engineer and urbanist, Hans Monderman. Arguing that increasing control and regulation by the state reduced individual and collective responsibility, Monderman pioneered an approach that, rather than relying on traffic signals and physical barriers, respected drivers' common sense and intelligence (Figures 7.41–7.43; see also Chapters 4 and 8). Following Monderman's lead, many European cities are removing traffic lights, sidewalks, kerbs, signage, painted markings and other extraneous street furniture (Figure 7.44). Backing up these professional and political preferences, analysis by Nasar (1999) of street signage has demonstrated a profound public preference for reducing sign obtrusiveness and the complexity of street signs.

Accepting that some items of street furniture are necessary, Gillespies (1995: 65) offers six basic design principles:

- Design to require and to incorporate the minimum of street furniture.
- Wherever possible, integrate and combine elements into a single unit.
- Remove all superfluous pieces of street furniture.

FIGURES 7.41–7.43   *(continued)*

- Consider street furniture as a family of items, in keeping with the quality of the environment and assisting in the unification of the urban area to provide a coherent sense of identity.
- Position street furniture to help create and delineate space.
- Locate street furniture so as not to impede pedestrian or vehicular traffic or 'desire lines' (Figure 7.45).

FIGURES 7.41–7.43 Bollards – Leith, Edinburgh; Sheffield; and Chelsea, London *(Images: Steve Tiesdell and Matthew Carmona)*. Rather risk-averse, UK environments seem to need a vast range of bollards, railings, etc., to prevent people from disrupting the smooth – and speedy – flow of vehicular traffic. Practice in many countries trusts people to learn, the principle being to allow people to experience risk and thereby to learn from it; shielding people from all risk renders them helpless and vulnerable when confronted by risk. Illustrated here are three solutions to separating cars and pedestrians

FIGURES 7.41–7.43   *(continued)*

FIGURE 7.44 Street furniture — Kensington High Street, London *(Image: Steve Tiesdell)*. Informed by Hans Monderman's minimalist approach, large areas of pedestrian guard-railing were removed in London's Kensington High Street, traffic signals were combined with lamp columns and signage was rationalised. On first encountering the decluttered street the viewer senses that something is missing but cannot initially identify what it is. One comes to realise that what is missing is the 'usual' high street clutter. As important as the actual changes was the process of making them: to achieve this required a local politician prepared to challenge standard highway engineering practices and the risk-averse culture of the engineers. The changes have yielded significant and sustained reductions in injuries to pedestrians

Landscape and Landscaping

With a narrower meaning than landscape, 'landscaping' is the main focus in this section because of its more limited visual–aesthetic connotations. Landscaping is frequently an afterthought in urban design — something to be added (provided funds allow) once the major decisions have been taken, to hide/conceal poor-quality architecture/buildings or as a way of filling left-over space. If a completed

building needs (remedial) landscaping — an act known as putting-paisley-round-the-pig (see Hayden 2004: 86) — it has already failed as a design. While well-designed landscaping adds quality, visual interest and colour to development, poorly designed landscaping detracts from otherwise well-designed developments.

As Neal & Hopkins (2005: 152) argue, landscape design has four critical drivers:

- Working *on* the land — art.
- Working *with* the land — ecology.
- Working *through* the land — society.
- Working *for* the land — sustainability.

The broader landscape — and, by inference, landscape design — thus relates not just to visual–aesthetic concerns, but also to the full range of design dimensions discussed in this book. As part of the pursuit of sustainable design, urban designers should be concerned with the underlying natural processes and with the potential of new development to support the local ecology, hydrology and geology, as much as with the problems and opportunities offered by particular

FIGURE 7.46 Soft landscape can be used simply to bring colour and joy to otherwise hard urban landscapes — Soeul *(Image: Matthew Carmona)*

FIGURE 7.45 Zoning of street furniture — Edinburgh *(Image: Steve Tiesdell)*. The pavement here has been 'zoned' into a smoother area for walking and a 'textured' area for signage, bus shelter, cycle stands, etc. — though seemingly not for the local authority's waste bins!

Sustainability Insert 4 — Biotic Support

Across the different design scales, green landscape is fundamental to meeting the challenge of maintaining environmental diversity. Landscape design is often the forgotten dimension of the urban environment, too often being treated as an afterthought or as a purely visual concern, for example, to reduce the impact of poorly designed buildings or expanses of parking; or alternatively forced and overly conceptual, in the process losing its human connection (Denton-Thompson 2005: 126). More fundamental approaches to landscape have long been advocated, in which urban areas form just one part of a wider functioning ecosystem, and in which the biotic environment (fauna and flora and space for them to flourish) exist side by side, and even dictate the form of the human-made environment (McHarg 1969). Thus, like the associated need to reduce pollution and the use of natural resources, the need for biotic support equates to support for the ongoing natural processes in and around human settlements. CABE (2009: 21), for example, argues that, in a context where urban gardens often feature greater biodiversity than surrounding intensively farmed countryside, space needs to be consciously provided for flora and fauna within urban areas to supplement the role these areas already play in supporting wildlife.

At the level of buildings and spaces, this might include the integration of soft landscaping and trees and the nurturing of habitats in new and established developments. The *Urban Design Compendium*, for example, argues that urban blocks of about 90 by 90 m allow for permeability while providing adequate space for biodiversity and wildlife support (Llewelyn-Davies 2007: 58).

At the scale of the urban quarter or district, the concern extends to respect for existing, and provision of new, open spaces and corridors within settlements and to their nurturing as natural habitats (Woolley 2003: 36–44).

At the settlement-wide scale, the concern relates to integrating town and country through the design of open space networks and a careful transition between town and country at the urban fringe (Von Borcke 2003).

Greening buildings, Paris (*Image: Matthew Carmona*)

sites. The 'greening' of towns and cities thus represents a key sustainability objective (see Sustainability Insert 4).

Trees and other vegetation can be particularly effective in reducing carbon dioxide build-up and restoring oxygen; reducing wind speeds in urban spaces; acting as shelterbelts; and filtering dust and pollution (see Chapter 8). A positive approach to landscaping is therefore necessary, in which its contribution to the totality of the urban environment is considered. Landscape design strategies should be developed before — or, at least, in parallel with — the building design process, and should be an integral part of any overarching development framework.

Soft Landscaping

Soft landscaping can be a decisive element in adding to place character, personality and identity — Oak Street, for example, differs from Pine Street. Trees and other vegetation also add a sense of human scale, providing a contrast with, and a foil to, hard urban landscapes (Figure 7.46). They also express the changing seasons, enhancing temporal legibility. Landscaping often plays an important aesthetic role in adding coherence and structure to otherwise disparate environments. In some streets, trees reinforce — or where the buildings themselves lack it, provide — a sense-of-enclosure and continuity. Much of the appeal of older, more mature (garden) suburbs, for example, derives from the continuity of the landscape structure, which enables a diversity of architectural treatments to cohere harmoniously.

Much of the floorscape pattern — and, indeed, the three-dimensional effect of urban space — can be reinforced and enhanced by tree planting. Trees in the urban environment need to be sited positively. Where there is a formal setting,

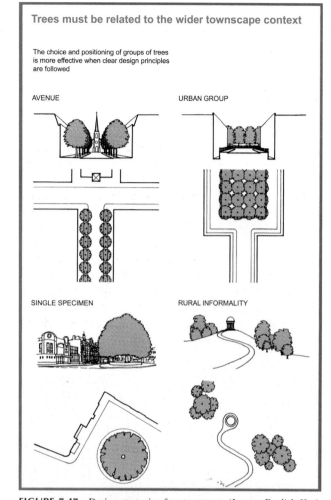

Trees must be related to the wider townscape context

The choice and positioning of groups of trees is more effective when clear design principles are followed

AVENUE

URBAN GROUP

SINGLE SPECIMEN

RURAL INFORMALITY

FIGURE 7.47 Design strategies for street trees *(Image: English Heritage 2000a: 49)*. Trees are not always appropriate in urban areas and, where used, they should be chosen and located in relation to the overall townscape effect

this may involve a degree of regimentation (e.g. the use of trees planted in straight lines or in formal geometric patterns) rather than picturesque groupings (see Robinson 1992: 41–81). Trees can also be used to reinforce or complete the sense of spatial containment within an urban space or to create a 'space-within-a-space'. When deciduous trees are used, the sense-of-containment and character changes with the seasons.

The theme of street trees can be overdone, however. To give greater emphasis to landscaped garden squares, for example, Georgian streets rarely contained street trees. Similarly, Camillo Sitte (Collins & Collins 1965) calculated that the boulevards of nineteenth century Vienna contained enough trees to form an entire forest, and would, he argued, be better deployed as two or three parks. In *Streets for All,* aimed at guiding the management of

London's streets, English Heritage (2000: 48) argue that soft landscaping (including trees) in urban areas is not always appropriate and, where used, should be chosen and located in relation to the overall townscape effect (Figure 7.47). For all landscape schemes — hard or soft — it suggests eight considerations:

- *Appearance* — regard for historic context and local distinctiveness.
- *Suitability of materials* and their combination for the tasks they perform.
- *Robustness* — in terms of long-term maintenance.
- *Cleansing* — refuse collection, sweeping and washing, specialist cleansing of graffiti and gum.
- *Avoiding clutter* — keeping signage to a minimum and using existing posts or wall mountings.
- *Concern for pedestrians* — a welcoming atmosphere and clear directional signage.
- *Concern for people with disabilities* — safety, convenience and removal of obstacles.
- *Traffic and related matters* — such as public transport, cyclists and concern for the comfort and safety of pedestrians crossing the carriageways (English Heritage 2000).

CONCLUSION

This chapter has emphasised the necessity of considering the visual–aesthetic effect of additions to the urban environment while also underlining the need to consider the whole. Buildings, streets and spaces, hard and soft landscaping and street furniture should, therefore, be considered together to reinforce or enhance the sense of place, and to create drama and visual interest. The key question when considering any new intervention (and, more generally, any new increment of development) is what kind of place will be created. This also emphasises the need to avoid overstating the importance of building (architectural) design in creating successful urban places. Urban designers must, for example, avoid conflating the visual dimension of urban design with architectural (building) design: good places do not need to be 'special' architecturally and will often be architecturally 'ordinary'; architecturally acclaimed buildings do not *ipso facto* make good places. Nonetheless, as Montgomery (1998: 112–3) notes, issues of architectural style are 'not unimportant' for they also convey meaning, shape identity and create image. The aesthetic dimension of architecture matters to the extent that we care more about environments that we find attractive and visually appealing — attractive environments are thus more likely to be robust and sustainable (see Chapter 9).

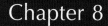

The Functional Dimension

Urban design's functional dimension relates to how places work and how urban designers can make 'better' places or, more precisely, increase the potential for them to develop. Though the visual–aesthetic and the social usage traditions each had a functionalist perspective, they were interpreted differently. In the visual–aesthetic tradition, drawing on the physical sciences, the human dimension was often abstracted out and reduced to technical or aesthetic criteria, with function considered in terms of daylighting, overshadowing, traffic flow, access and circulation, etc. In the social usage tradition, drawing on the social sciences, the concern was for how the design of the environment supported its use by people.

This chapter is in five parts. The first part discusses movement. The second part discusses the design of 'people places'. The third part discusses environmental design. The fourth part discusses designing for healthier environments, while the fifth part discusses aspects of the infrastructure necessary to support contemporary life.

MOVEMENT

Movement is fundamental to understanding how places function. Pedestrian flows through public space are both at the heart of the urban experience and important in generating life and activity (Figure 8.1). Where people choose to sit or linger in public space is often based on opportunities for people-watching, which, in turn, are related to the life and activity within the space and how people move through it. Similarly, the prime retail locations in urban areas (as opposed to out-of-town locations) are based on pedestrian footfall, which, in turn, is a by-product of pedestrian movement between places. The convention for valuing retail space, for example, is based on Zone A rents – the rent for the first (usually) 6 m of floor area back from the street edge. Zone A rents are a function of pedestrian flow rates.

Vehicular and Pedestrian Movement

A basic distinction can be made between vehicular and pedestrian movement. As discussed in Chapter 4, car-based movement is pure circulation; pedestrian movement is circulation but also permits economic, social and cultural exchange.

The great advantage of cars is that they provide seamless travel from origin to destination – though, as noted in Chapter 6, designing for vehicular traffic often creates gaps in the pedestrian movement experience. In urban terms, however, the experience of car travel is essentially discontinuous and primarily involves the arrival at – rather than the experience of travel between – particular destinations. Opportunities for most forms of social interaction and exchange only occur once the car has been parked. Vehicular movement is thus about spatially isolated and fragmented origins and destinations – and the quality and continuity of urban space are less important for car drivers,

FIGURE 8.1 Harajuka, Tokyo (*Image: Steve Tiesdell*). Generating life and activity, pedestrian movement through public space lies at the heart of the urban experience. Rather than merely movement-to and movement-through, however, the key to a successful people place lies in encouraging people to stop and spend time within the space

Public Places – Urban Spaces. DOI: 10.1016/B978-1-85617-827-3.10008-2

201

while breaking a journey is both inconvenient and time-consuming, and direct journeys to a single destination are preferred (i.e. 'park once' strategies). As Lefebvre (1991: 312–3) contends, while in motion, the driver is concerned only with steering himself to his destination and

'… in looking about sees only what he needs to see for that purpose; he thus perceives only his route, which has been materialised, mechanised, and technicised, and he sees it from one angle only — that of its functionality: speed, readability, facility.'

The car trip itself may consist of boarding the car in the garage at home and getting out in the secure car park of the final destination. From the refuge and sanctuary of their personal private realms, people tend to make car trips to private and self-contained attractions — shopping malls, theme parks, cinema multiplexes, sports stadia, etc. By comparison, for pedestrians, the continuity of urban space — the connections between destinations — is important and successful people places must be (and are) integrated with and embedded in local movement systems.

Pedestrian travel is rarely single-purpose: in going from one place to another, we stop to buy a newspaper or a bottle of milk; talk to a neighbour, colleague or friend; window shop; have a drink at a pavement café; or, more simply, enjoy a view or watch the 'world go by' Jane Jacobs (1961) famously highlighted walking as the mechanism that turns roads into streets where social interaction and economic exchange flourish. Pedestrian travel is thus both circulation and exchange: as Gehl (2000) argues, *'… there is much more to walking than walking.'*

Thus, while often useful for tracing vehicular movement, when used to study pedestrian movement, origin-destination studies ignore a key component of the movement experience. Hillier (1996a, 1996b) terms this the 'by-product' of movement — the potential for other (optional) activities in addition to the basic activity of travelling from origin to destination. By ensuring origin-destination trips take people past outward-facing building blocks *en route*, he argues that the traditional urban grid represents a 'mechanism for generating contact' allowing maximisation of the by-product effect (Hillier 1996b: 59). The impact and value of the by-product of movement can be illustrated by its exploitation in shopping centre design (Figure 8.2).

Successful people places may be destinations (go-to places) in their own right but, more likely, they are also places on the way to many other places (i.e. go-through places). The reality is that very few successful people places work solely as destinations in their own right. Almost all are places with favourable locations within the wider strategic movement network and, as discussed later, they have the benefit of centrality within those networks. This point is neatly illustrated by considering two points in a grid — one on the edge and one more central (Figure 8.3) and also

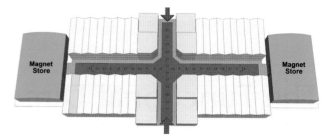

FIGURE 8.2   Shopping centre design. Industry guidance on the design of retail environments argues that: *'Retail-led developments are only successful in retailing and financial terms if they generate profit. Therefore, urban design cannot be seen as a static imposition of an idealised physical blueprint. It must embrace the dynamics of the way in which people move around town or city centres — understanding pedestrian flows (the key to retail value), walking distances, retail circuits and trips for different types of shopping (the modal shopper). These behavioural considerations are at the core of the way in which shopping works and therefore need to be at the core of the urban design process'* (Building Design Partnership 2002: 53). Retail developers and designers are skilled in exploiting shopper psychology and manipulating shopper movements within retail environments. In the simplest form of shopping centre, the 'magnet' stores are located at either end of a central mall lined with smaller stores. The magnet stores attract shoppers to the mall. As shoppers enter the mall, they are drawn towards the magnet stores and in the process pass the smaller stores, generating footfall and potential trade for those smaller stores. If shoppers enter through one of the magnet stores, the other magnet stores provide the stimulus for movement along the mall. This is admittedly a simplified account of movement — the magnet stores attract people in the aggregate, but may not attract any particular individual. Equally, it may be the ambience and character of the mall's 'public' spaces that are the real attraction

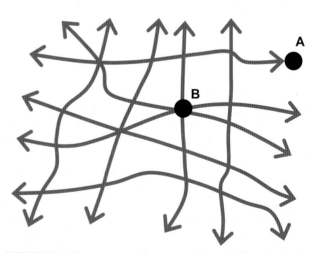

FIGURE 8.3   Movement-to and movement-through. Point A only has movement directly to it (i.e. it is only a destination). Point B is a destination, but it also benefits from movement through it to other points (i.e. it is on the way to many other places). As all successful shopkeepers know, getting people to enter your shop if they are already outside is much easier than getting them to travel to your shop in the first place. Similarly, getting people who are already moving through the space to stop is much easier than getting them to come to the space in the first place

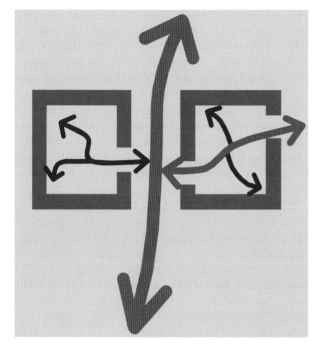

FIGURE 8.4 Courtyards-that-live. In Christopher Alexander's *Pattern Language*, 'courtyards-that-live' are those with paths running through them (i.e. they are not cul-de-sacs or dead ends). Thus, as well as being destinations, they are also on the way to other places

by Christopher Alexander's pattern of 'courtyards-that-live' (Figure 8.4).

As explained further below, this also explains why we tend to over-estimate the power of 'magnets' (or destinations) to attract people. Most shops, for example, are not a sufficient magnet and have to be well-located with respect to the existing movement patterns. The land-use activity merely reinforces/multiplies the basic movement.

Space Syntax

With colleagues at University College London's Space Syntax Laboratory (www.spacesyntax.com), Bill Hillier (Hillier & Hanson, 1984; Hillier, 1988, 1996a, 1996b; Hillier *et al* 1993) has extensively explored and theorised the relationship between − primarily, but not exclusively, pedestrian − movement and the configuration of urban space, and thereafter the relationship with pedestrian densities and land uses. Hillier's empirical research supports his idea that movement densities can be accurately predicted by analysing spatial configuration and the structure of the urban grid. The analytic process involves what Hillier terms 'natural movement' − the proportion of movement determined by the structure of the urban grid rather than by the presence of specific attractors or magnet land uses. He argues that the configuration of space, particularly its effect on visual permeability, is most important in determining movement densities.

Known as Space Syntax, his theory measures quantitatively the relational properties of urban space (see Hillier & Hanson 1984; Hillier 1996):

'Such relational properties rest on assumptions that longer lines of sight, fewer turns, higher connectivity and a high ability to reach points from every other point in space are desirable. The evidence … has shown a positive relationship between the occurrence of activity and spaces that exhibit these desirable properties.'

(Baran *et al* 2008: 8).

Using complex mapping and mathematical techniques, Hillier's analysis is based on certain key geometric properties of the spatial configuration of urban areas. Spatial configuration is represented by an axial plan consisting of a series of 'convex' spaces linked by 'axial' lines − the longest and fewest set of lines of sight passing through all the convex (open) spaces in the area (Figure 8.5). The lines can be thought of as streets, though they do not need to be streets.

From the network of lines, two syntactical properties are calculated for each line:

- Its *connectivity* − the number of lines that are directly connected to it. 'Control' is a modification of connectivity, which measures the degree to which a line controls access to its immediate neighbours, taking account of the number of alternative connections each

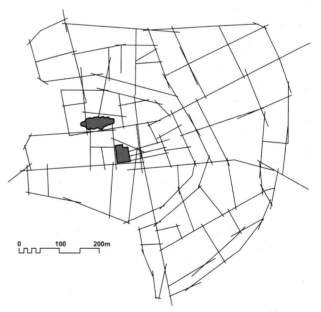

FIGURE 8.5 Axial map of Rothenburg. In an axial map, the plan view of the study area is drawn with axial lines ensuring all convex spaces are linked. Straight or axial lines are important because, for Hillier, people move along lines and, furthermore, need to be able to see along lines in order to know where they can go. Hillier notes that longer lines tend to strike facades at an open angle (i.e. suggesting further movement), while shorter lines tend to strike them at angles closer to a right angle, thereby, reducing the potential for movement in that direction. He also notes that patterns of land uses generally change slowly along lines of movement and more sharply with the increasing angle of turn onto different lines

of these neighbours has. A high control value indicates that the line is important for accessing neighbouring lines (Baran *et al* 2008: 9).

- Its *integration* — the number of lines that must be traversed if one were to move from every line (street) to every other line (street) in the axial map. In other words, it indicates how easily one can reach a specific line. The higher a line's integration value, the lower the number of axial lines needed to reach it. Integration is often considered in terms of 'global integration' (i.e. access from all other lines) and 'local integration' (i.e. those lines that are accessible up to a given number of lines away) (Baran *et al* 2008: 9).

The integration value is regarded as a good predictor of natural movement — the more integrated the line, the more movement along it; the less integrated the line, the less movement along it (Figure 8.6a and b).

Research to date has focused mainly on the presence of activity on a street, finding that high-integration streets have higher numbers of pedestrians and car movements (Hillier & Hanson 1984; Peponis *et al* 1989; Hillier *et al* 1993; Hillier 1996b; Penn *et al* 1998; Read 1999). As Baran *et al* (2008: 10–1) note, the syntactical properties of space have also been used in explaining the location of crime occurrence, pedestrian safety and spatial cognition.

Hillier argues his analysis gives a 'true-to-life functional picture' of movement densities due to the influence natural movement has had on the urban pattern's evolution and on the distribution of land uses. The by-product concept also enables Hillier to explain how the pattern of

land uses derives from the pattern of natural movement rather than, as might intuitively be expected, the other way around. Hillier argues that every trip in an urban system has three elements: an origin, a destination and a series of spaces passed through on the way from one to the other (the 'by-product'). Regardless of the specific locations of all the origins and destination, some locations have more potential to generate contact than others because they have more by-products. Hence, those spaces prioritised by the spatial configuration for through-movement are, and have been, selected as locations for 'passing trade' land uses.

Hillier acknowledges potential confusion between the effects of spatial configuration and that of particular land uses on movement. Acknowledging that particular land uses can attract people, he contends this is a multiplier effect — uses cannot change the line's integration value. In other words, as the patterns of (natural) movement and of space come before the land uses, land uses merely reinforce the basic movement pattern or system. Hillier (1996a: 169) argues that:

'It is this positive feedback loop built on a foundation of the relation between the grid structure and movement which gives rise to the urban buzz, which we prefer to be romantic or mystical about — but which arises from the co-incidence in certain locations of large numbers of different activities involving people going about their business in different ways.'

Hillier (1996a: 169) illustrates this by a negative example — London's South Bank, an area built in the 1970s of Modernist megastructures and separated pedestrian

(a)   **(b)**

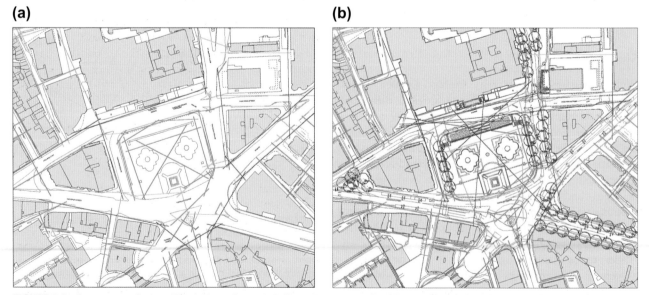

FIGURE 8.6 Space syntax diagram *(Image: Space Syntax Ltd)*. Space Syntax maps show degree of integration in terms of colour, with red being the most integrated lines and green the least. Accordingly, red lines have the most potential movement and activity along them; green lines have the least. The figures here show the Space Syntax analysis before and after proposed improvements to London's Trafalgar Square. The analysis suggested that, following the improvements, there would be more movement through the centre of the space

walkways. Despite (at the time) the co-existence in a small area of many major functions, there was little 'urban buzz'. Hillier attributed this to the configuration of space, which failed to bring the different groups of space users — concert attendees, gallery visitors, residents, office workers, etc. — into patterns of movement prioritising the same spaces — groups moved through the area like 'ships in the night', depriving the area of the multiplier effects of different space users 'sparking off' each other. Since that time many of the high-level walkways have been demolished, fundamentally changing the local integration value of the remaining grade level pedestrian routes. This, alongside new cross-river connections along the Thames, improving the area's integration into the wider movement pattern, has helped to bring it back to life.

Criticisms of Hillier's work tend to take two main forms. The first set is the more technical criticisms of Space Syntax as a method (see, for example, Ratti 2004a, 2004b; Steadman 2004; Hillier & Penn 2004). Some argue, for example, that Space Syntax measures one form of 'centrality' but that several other forms exist and, thus, the approach is partial (see Porta & Latora 2008); others question the link between axial lines and visual permeability.

The second set of criticisms of Space Syntax theory relates to it seeming not to consider human agency. Cuthbert (2007: 202), for example, argues that:

'… Hillier & Hanson's approach is unavowedly structuralist, making it in principle, singularly indifferent to any human qualities at all … It is an exercise in abstraction based on a model of human relations that is so far removed from the social that its usefulness in any sphere of human development must be seriously questioned. Despite the extensive content of much of the work, people are reduced to atoms moving about in urban space, and with about as much character.'

Although, in essence, movement comes first in Hillier's system, the movement is unrelated to specific purpose. In practice, the purpose of that movement is usually related to land use, with movement between certain points being more likely for certain land uses (e.g. a public building) than for others (e.g. a private house). Hillier's argument, however, is that — both initially and over time — the by-product of movement is more important than any particular origin or destination. Nevertheless, as land uses and the purpose of movement are entwined, the instrumental — deterministic — role ascribed to configuration and natural movement remains problematic. Changing the location of land uses changes the pattern of movement, while changing the pattern of movement will — over time — change the pattern of land uses. It is, thus, a two-way interactive process.

Returning to the London South Bank example (above), although local integration was undoubtedly improved by re-modelling the complex, the area's greater liveliness might also be attributed to the programming of events in its public spaces and the insertion of a wide range of new active and cultural uses along the southern bank of the Thames. As the changes to land uses and routes emerged over time, it is perhaps a case of 'chicken and egg'.

Space Syntax challenges urban designers to think critically about the relationship between the configuration of space, movement and land uses. It is widely used as an analytic and design tool, and the theories behind its use continue to be developed by Hillier and others. Although Hillier's theory may be based on a rather mechanistic view of people and their behaviour, its predictions have a high correlation with observed patterns of movement. In particular, it reminds urban designers both of the importance of connectivity and of the overarching need to consider movement in the design of urban areas (especially pedestrian movement). The key message is that well-connected places are more likely to encourage pedestrian movement and to support a vital and viable range of uses.

DESIGNING (BETTER) 'PEOPLE PLACES'

As discussed in Chapter 6, 'public space' is a highly nuanced term and, rather than public spaces, the term 'people place' is used here. People places are those intended to be used by people, usually through spontaneous, everyday and informal use. Not all formal public spaces achieve, or are intended to achieve, this. Some, for example, are designed to provide a foil to buildings or to act as grand performance or display spaces, perhaps as an expression of state or other power and the ability to control space.

Successful People Places

Successful public spaces are characterised by the presence of people, in an often self-reinforcing process. They typically have animation and vitality, an 'urban buzz'. Jacobs (1961) argued that bringing people onto the street created animation and vitality, and likened street life to an intricate street ballet:

'… we may fancifully call it the art form of the city and liken it to a dance — not to a simple-minded precision dance with everyone kicking up at the same time, twirling in unison and bowing off en masse, but to an intricate ballet in which individual dancers and ensembles all have distinctive parts which miraculously reinforce one another and compose an orderly whole.'

Stevens (2007: 213) uses the same quote to conclude his discussion of play in the city. For Stevens, playful behaviour implies the range of spontaneous and creative behaviours that people of all ages will engage in if the conditions are right: 'To understand and optimise the richness of the place ballet requires attention to the stage: to props, to entries and exits, and to the immense variety of acts which discover and engage these spatial opportunities.'

In this regard public spaces are essentially discretionary environments: people have to choose to go to and use them and conceivably could go elsewhere. If they are to become peopled and animated, they must offer what people want and desire, and do so in an attractive and safe environment. In other words people need to feel psychologically comfortable or engaged enough to want to stay and play.

The Project for Public Space (2000) identifies four key attributes of successful places: comfort and image; access and linkage; uses and activity; and sociability (see Table 8.1).

For Montgomery (1998: 99), the key to successful places are their transaction base, which should be 'as complex as possible': '... *without a transaction base of economic activity at many different levels and layers, it will not be possible to create a good urban place.*' As not all transactions are economic, urban areas and cities must also provide space for social and cultural transactions. Montgomery lists a number of key indicators of vitality:

- Extent of variety in primary land uses, including residential.
- Proportion of locally owned or independent businesses, particularly shops.
- Patterns of opening hours, and the existence of evening and night-time activity.
- Presence, size and specialisms of street markets.

- Availability of cinemas, theatres, wine bars, cafes, pubs, restaurants, and other cultural and meeting places offering service of different kinds, prices and quality.
- Availability of spaces, including gardens, squares and corners, enabling people-watching and activities such as cultural animation programmes.
- Patterns of mixed land use enabling self-improvement and small-scale investment in property.
- Availability of differing unit sizes and costs of property.
- Degree of innovation and confidence in new architecture, providing a variety of building types, styles and design.
- Presence of an active street life and active street frontages (see also Montgomery 2008).

Different places are, nonetheless, animated in different ways. Some are louder, busier and more vibrant, animated by people and traffic; others are quieter, perhaps animated by nature — the wind in the trees, changing cloud formations and so forth.

Movement and Activity

According to Space Syntax theory, the basic movement patterns suggest potential movement and activity within a location. The potential may be unrealised however, because the space is unattractive or lacks active frontages. Therefore how the space is designed makes a difference

TABLE 8.1 Attributes of Successful Places

Key Attributes	Inner Ring Intangibles		Outer Ring Measurables
Comfort and image	• Safety • Charm • History • Attractiveness • Spirituality	• Sittability • Walkability • Greenness • Cleanliness	• Crime statistics • Sanitation rating • Building conditions • Environmental data
Access and linkage	• Readability • Walkability • Reliability • Continuity	• Proximity • Connectedness • Convenience • Accessibility	• Traffic data • Mode split • Transit usage • Pedestrian activity • Parking usage patterns
Uses and activity	• Realness • Sustainability • Specialness • Uniqueness • Affordability • Fun	• Activity • Usefulness • Celebration • Vitality • Indigenousness • 'Homegrown' quality	• Property values • Rent levels • Land-use patterns • Retail sales • Local business ownership
Sociability	• Co-operation • Neighbourliness • Stewardship • Pride • Welcoming	• Gossip • Diversity • Story telling • Friendliness • Interactivity	• Street life • Social networks • Evening use • Volunteerism • Number of women, children and the elderly

Source: Adapted from Project for Public Space (2000).

to the density of use as a multiplier of the basic movement pattern.

If a space is poorly located within the local movement pattern (i.e. 'off the beaten track'), it matters little how well it is designed as it is unlikely to ever be well-used unless there are changes in the wider area — either greater density of uses or changes to the movement network that increase connectivity and/or reduce severance (i.e. through better quality connections or by new connections, such as new bridges across rivers, or the removal of obstacles to movement to a site).

Conversely, if the space is well-located within the local movement system, then upgrading the space and environmental improvements is likely to have a major impact on the density of its use. In many cities, for example, vehicular traffic interferes with and reduces the freedom of pedestrian movement. But there are now numerous instances where the spatial configuration is not changed but streets are closed to car traffic and left open only for pedestrians: the new space is subsequently used more intensively by a greater number of pedestrians (see Hass-Klau *et al* 1999; Gehl & Gemzoe 2000).

Thus, if a space is well-located, then good design can enable it to realise its previously untapped potential — in effect, the act of designing involves metaphorically pushing against an open door (exploiting the place's latent potential). Quality thus affects density of use. This point is also made in Jan Gehl's discussion of necessary, optional and social activities and their relationship with the design quality of the public environment (see Box 8.1). Gehl's essential point is that design makes a difference (Figure 8.7).

Connectivity and Visual Permeability

While there are various aesthetic ideas about the desirable shape and configuration of public spaces (see Chapter 7), various functional considerations relating to how design features support use and activity are particularly important. In particular, and as discussed above, we can usefully distinguish between the *macro-design* of a space — its relationship with its hinterland, including the routes into and connections with its surroundings — and its *micro-design* — the design of the space itself.

In terms of the macro-design, Hillier (1996a, 1996b) contends that various functional considerations related to movement need to be taken into account. He argues that attempts to account for the pattern of well- and poorly used informal public space in the City of London that, *inter alia*, fail to emphasise the role of movement have been 'singularly unsuccessful':

'... *some spaces hemmed in by traffic are several times better used than adjacent spaces without traffic, exposed spaces often perform better than spaces with good enclosure, some of the most successful spaces are in the shadow of tall buildings, and so on.*'
(Hillier 1996b: 52).

BOX 8.1 Activities and Design Quality

In *Life Between Buildings,* Gehl (1996) adopts a probabilistic approach to the relationship between design and activity. He argues that, through design and within certain limits — regional, climatic and societal — it is possible to influence *how many* people use public spaces, *how long* individual activities last and *which* activity types can develop.

He argues that 'greatly simplified' outdoor activities in public spaces can be divided into three categories:

- *Necessary activities* are more or less compulsory (e.g. going to school or to work, shopping, or waiting for a bus) and, as the participants have no choice, their incidence is only slightly influenced by the physical setting.
- *Optional activities* are participated in if there is a wish to do so and if time and place make it possible — for example, taking a walk to get a breath of fresh air, stopping for a coffee in a street café, people-watching, etc. Such activities only take place when exterior conditions are optimal — that is, when weather and setting invite them.
- *Social activities* depend on the presence of others in public space, such as greetings and conversations, communal activities of various kinds and passive contacts (i.e. simply seeing and hearing other people). These activities occur spontaneously as a direct consequence of people moving about and being in the same spaces, and are, therefore,

indirectly supported whenever necessary and optional activities are given better environmental conditions.

The crux of Gehl's argument is that, when public spaces are of poor quality, only strictly necessary activities occur. When public spaces are of higher quality, necessary activities take place with approximately the same frequency — although people choose to spend longer doing them — but, more importantly, a wide range of optional (social) activities also occur.

	Quality of the physical environment	
	Poor	**Good**
Necessary activities	●	●
Optional activities	•	●
'Resultant' activities (Social activities)	•	●

Jan Gehl's diagram of relation between quality and use

FIGURE 8.7 Design matters *(Image: Matthew Carmona)*. Given injunctions against smoking in the workplace, groups of smokers outside office buildings are common. If the space is not designed for this, there is often an unsightly straggle of people smoking and perhaps also obstructing the pavement/sidewalk. Sometimes, the smokers are herded behind screens, but if a space is better designed for the activity, what might be seen is a group of people using a public space who also happen to be smoking. Design means that what in one setting was the primary activity, in another becomes an incidental activity

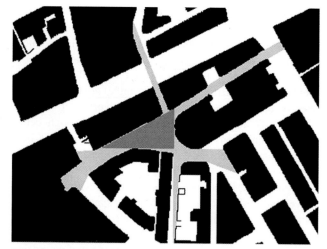

FIGURE 8.8 Visual permeability. A shape is convex if all points within it can be seen from all other points within that shape. The *convex isovist* is the shape defined by all the points that can be seen from any point within the convex space. A *strategic isovist* is similar but for a point source. Hillier argues that sight lines are important in terms of influencing movement. The convex isovist thus represents the opportunity space – the space that a pedestrian within a convex space can see and could move into. The diagram shows the convex element (darker shading) and the strategic isovist (lighter shading) for The Green – an historic but underused space in the centre of Aberdeen. Located close to the main pedestrian thoroughfare of Union Street, it is not visually linked to it and has a low pedestrian density

Hillier argues that the only variable that correlates consistently with the degree of use is what he calls the 'strategic value' of the isovist – in effect, a measure of the visual permeability of the space – which, in Space Syntax theory, is the sum of the integration values of all the lines passing through the body of the space. He argues this makes intuitive sense because, if the primary activity of those who stop to sit in public spaces is people-watching, then '... *strategic spaces with areas close to – but not actually lying on – the main lines of movement are optimal.*' (Hillier 1996b: 52) (Figure 8.8).

For Hillier, the main fault in many contemporary public spaces is that designers prioritise sense-of-enclosure within the space over visual permeability into the space. His key principle is that urban spaces should not be too enclosed. Moreover, rather than enclosure, the key quality in terms of the pedestrian use of public spaces is their 'connectedness' or, in Hillier's terms, integration. Hillier (1996a: 161) argues that, if design is over-localised, the natural movement pattern is disrupted and the space will be underused.

Activities in Public Space

As successful places support and facilitate the activities of people, their design should be informed by an awareness of how people use them. For Bacon (1992: 20), it was only through 'endless walking' that designers could 'absorb into their being' the true experience of urban space, while, as the Project for Public Space (PPS 2000: 51) advises: '*When you observe a space you learn about how it is actually used, rather than how you think it is used.*' Successful designers generally develop a detailed knowledge of, and sensitivity to, people places based on first-hand experience.

Many of the best commentaries on the design and use of public space are based on first-hand observation: Jacobs' *Death and Life of Great American Cities* (1961) was based on observations in North American cities; Gehl's *Space Between Buildings: Using Public Space* (1971) on observations in Scandinavia (see Table 8.2); and Whyte's *The Social Life of Small Urban Spaces* (1980) on observations in New York (see Box 8.2). More recent contributions to the genre include Marcus & Sarkissian's *Housing As If People Mattered* (1986), the Project for Public Space's *How to Turn a Place Around: A Handbook for Creating Successful Public Places* (1999), and Stevens' *The Ludic City* (2007).

Synthesising research and ideas on the use and design of public space, Carr *et al* (1992) argue that, as well as being *meaningful* – allowing people to make strong connections between the place, their personal lives, and the larger world (see Chapter 5) – and *democratic* – protecting the rights of user groups, being accessible to all groups and providing for freedom of action (see Chapter 6) – public spaces

TABLE 8.2 What Public Space Should Provide

Protection		Protection Against Crime and Violence (Feelings of Safety)	Protection Against Unpleasant Sense-Experiences
	Protection Against Traffic and Accidents		
	Traffic accidents *Fear* of accidents Other accidents	Lived in/used Street life Street watching Overlapping functions in space and time	Winds/draughts Rain/snow Cold/heat Pollution Dust, glare, noise
Comfort	**Possibilities for walking**	**Possibilities for standing/staying**	**Possibilities for sitting**
	Room for walking Untiring layout of streets Interesting facades No obstacles Good surfaces	Attractive edges – 'edge effects' Defined spots for staying Supports for staying	Zones for sitting Maximising advantages – primary and secondary sitting possibilities Benches for resting
	Possibilities to see	**Possibilities for hearing/talking**	**Possibilities for play/unfolding activities**
	Seeing distances Unhindered views Interesting views Lighting (when dark)	Low noise levels Bench arrangements – 'talkscapes'	Invitation to physical activity, play, unfolding and entertainment – day and night, summer and winter
Enjoyment	**Scale**	**Possibilities for enjoying positive aspects of climate**	**Aesthetic quality/positive sense-experiences**
	Dimensions of buildings and spaces in observance of important human dimensions related to senses, movements, sizes and behaviours	Sun/shade Warmth/cool Breeze/ventilation	Good design and detailing Views/vistas Trees, plants, water

Source: Adapted from Gehl (2008: 108).

should be *responsive* – that is, designed and managed to serve the needs of their users.

They identify five primary needs people seek to satisfy in public space:

(i) Comfort

Comfort is a prerequisite of successful public spaces. The length of time people stay in a public space is a function and an indicator of its comfort. Sense of comfort includes environmental factors (relief from sun and wind, etc. – see below); physical comfort (comfortable and sufficient seating, etc.) and social and psychological comfort (the space's character and ambience) (Figure 8.9). Carr *et al* (1992: 97) argued this is '... *a deep and pervasive need that extends to people's experiences in public places. It is a sense of security, a feeling that one's person and possessions are not vulnerable.*' The inability to see into or out of a space also raises concerns about safety, which undermine comfort. Comfort may also be enhanced by physical design and/or management strategies (see Chapter 6).

(ii) Relaxation

A sense of psychological comfort is a prerequisite of relaxation, but relaxation is a more developed state with the 'body and mind at ease' (Carr *et al* 1992: 98). Relaxation often involves respite from, or contrast with, the immediate environment. In urban settings, natural elements – trees, greenery and water features – and separation from vehicular traffic help accentuate contrast, making it easier to be relaxed. Features that help make a space a sanctuary may, however, also obstruct visual permeability, creating safety problems and discouraging people from using it. Similarly, during low-occupancy times, separation from traffic flows may increase concerns about safety and security. But, as in all aspects of design, it is necessary to achieve a balanced whole.

(iii) Passive engagement

While passive engagement with the environment can lead to a sense of relaxation, it also involves '... *the need for an encounter with the setting, albeit without becoming actively involved.*' (Carr *et al* 1992: 103).

BOX 8.2 The Social Life of Small Urban Spaces

William 'Holly' Whyte's work (Whyte 1980, 1988) is of particular interest in terms of how people use public spaces. Using photographic studies of New York's open spaces created as a result of the city's incentive zoning regulations, Whyte noted many were little used and did not justify the extra floor-space given to developers. Initially published as *The Social Life of Small Urban Spaces* (1980), Whyte's work was reissued as a more substantial book, *City: Rediscovering the Centre* (1988). The Project for Public Space, established in 1975, has continued his work (see www.pps.org), pioneering the use of video to analyse patterns of space usage over time.

Whyte considered that off-peak use provided the best clues to people's preferences. When a place was crowded, people sat where they could rather than where they most wanted to. Later, some parts of a public space became empty while others continued to be used. He also found most spaces tended to have well-defined sub-places – often around the edge – where people preferred to be and arranged to meet. Whyte noted that, in general, women were more discriminating in their choice of Jan Gehl's diagram of relation between quality and use space and that a low proportion of women generally indicated something was wrong. Women also sought a greater degree of privacy than men, who tended to prefer more prominent seating.

The most sociable spaces often possessed the following features:

- A good location, preferably on a busy route and both physically and visually accessible.

- Streets being part of the 'social' space – cutting a space off from the street with railings or walls isolated it and reduced its use.
- Being level or almost level with the pavement – spaces significantly above or below this were less used.
- Places to sit – both explicit (benches, seats, etc.) and integral (steps, low walls, etc.).
- Moveable seats, enabling choice and the communication of character and personality.

Less important factors included sun penetration, aesthetics (what mattered was how people used the space), and the shapes and sizes of spaces.

Bryant park, New York (*Image: Matthew Carmona*) well-defined sub-places and moveable seats

The primary form of passive engagement is people-watching. Whyte (1980: 13), for example, found that what attracts people is other people, and the life and activity they bring. The most-used sitting places are generally adjacent to the pedestrian flow (Figures 8.10 and 8.11). Street cafes, for example, provide opportunities, and excuses, for people-watching and other forms of passive engagement, as do fountains, public art, commanding views, and activities occurring in public spaces, ranging from formal lunch-time *al fresco* concerts to informal street entertainment (Figures 8.12 and 8.13).

FIGURE 8.9 Gadynia, Poland *(Image: Matthew Carmona)*. Rather than sitting with their backs to the pedestrian flow, people often choose to sit facing it

FIGURES 8.10 and 8.11 Passive engagement *(Images: Steve Tiesdell and Matthew Carmona)*. Raised vantage points (e.g. steps, balconies, upper levels, etc.) allow observers to watch people while avoiding eye contact

FIGURES 8.10 and 8.11   (*continued*)

FIGURES 8.12 and 8.13   (*continued*)

(iv) Active engagement

Active engagement represents a more direct experience with a place and the people in it. Carr *et al* (1992: 119) note that, while some find sufficient satisfaction in people-watching, others desire more direct contact, whether with friends, family or strangers. The simple proximity of people in space and time does not *ipso facto* mean they will spontaneously interact — Whyte (1980: 19) found public spaces were 'not ideal places' for 'striking up acquaintances', and that, even in the most sociable, there was 'not much mingling'. The coincidence of people in time and space does, nevertheless, provide opportunities (affordances) for contact and social interaction.

Discussing how design supports interaction, Gehl (1996: 19) refers to 'varied transitional forms' between

FIGURES 8.12 and 8.13   Active engagement *(image: Matthew Carmona).* Street entertainment enhances the animation and vitality of public spaces

being alone and being together and suggests a scale of 'intensity of contact' ranging from 'close friendships' to 'friends', 'acquaintances', 'chance contacts' and 'passive contacts'. If activity in the spaces between buildings is missing, then the lower end of this contact scale also disappears: *'The boundaries between isolation and contact become sharper — people are either alone or else with others on a relatively demanding and exacting level.'*

Successful people places provide opportunities for varying degrees of engagement, and also the potential to disengage or withdraw from contact. Design can create, or inhibit, such opportunities for contact. Unusual features or occurrences in a public space, such as an entertainer or the configuration of design features, can result in what Whyte (1980: 94) calls 'triangulation': *'… the process by which some external stimulus provides a linkage between people and prompts strangers to talk to other strangers as if they knew each other.'*

The arrangement of different elements — benches, telephones, fountains, sculptures, coffee carts — can be configured in ways that are more — and less — conducive to social interaction (Figure 8.14). The Project for Public Space (2000: 63) observes how triangulation occurs spontaneously where there is something of interest, such as life-size fibreglass cows (Chicago 1999) or pigs (Seattle 2001) painted by artists and set up on streets as public art: *'The cows created an excuse for people who didn't know each other to talk to one another.'* (Figure 8.15).

'Play', in all its myriad forms, is an important part of active engagement. Arguing that the presence of playful behaviour is a good indication of place quality, Stevens (2007: 214) suggests play may require environments that *'… are more arresting to the senses, more disorderly and more risky.'* For Stevens, higher

FIGURE 8.14 Government Square, Boston, USA *(Image: Steve Tiesdell)*. The design of some public spaces can inhibit their function as people places

FIGURES 8.16 and 8.17 Play in public space *(Image: Matthew Carmona)*.

density and greater diversity, complexity and even disorder in the urban environment allow more play possibilities, helping to stimulate such behaviours by challenging space users emotionally.

In this respect Stevens (2007: 208–9) provides a useful counterpart to Lynch's five elements (see Chapter 5). For him, three of Lynch's elements have a dual role in both practical cognition for way-finding and in the diverse, unplanned activities of play — paths, nodes (intersections) and edges (boundaries). He suggests these elements are critical in physical, perceptual and psychological terms while Lynch's other elements — districts and landmarks — have only a very limited role in spatial experience beyond way-finding. Instead, two further elements important for play are identified:

FIGURES 8.16 and 8.17 *(continued)*

FIGURE 8.15 Crown Fountain, Millennium Park, Chicago (artist: Jaume Plesna) *(Image: Matthew Carmona)*. Public art helps the process of triangulation — providing a linkage between people, and prompting strangers to talk to other strangers

- *Props* encompass the range of small-scale physical components — such as public artworks, play equipment and street furniture — placed in public space to meet aesthetic and functional needs, but which also provide a catalyst to stimulate playful behaviours: posing with or climbing on a sculpture; dodging a water-jet from a fountain; or 'leapfrogging' bollards (Figures 8.16 and 8.17).
- *Thresholds* represent the points of transition between inside and outside, a place to focus attention and channel movement: doorways, colonnades, porches, stairways, etc. They are places of meeting and interaction that stimulate a wide range of playful behaviour: '*Observation of playful behaviour involving props and thresholds reveals a rich scope of interrelations between perception, memory, intention, symbolism, human bodies, actions and spatial form.*' (Stevens 2007: 210).

(v) Discovery

Representing the desire for new experiences, 'discovery' depends on both variety and change. Change may occur as a result of the 'march of time' and the cycles of the seasons (see Chapter 9). It may also involve a more deliberate action by those responsible for managing and animating public space — by, for example, cultural animation programmes involving lunch-time concerts, art exhibitions, street theatre, live music and festivals, parades, markets, fairs, society events, trade promotions, etc. — across a range of times and venues. Such programmes may be annual events, such as the Edinburgh Festival, London's Notting Hill Carnival or New Orleans' Mardi-Gras, or special one-off events and celebrations. Similarly, involving a break from the routine and the expected, desires for discovery may be satisfied by tourism and travel to new locations.

Given the potential sterility of over-programming events in public space, discovery may require some sense of unpredictability and even danger, whether real or imagined. As Hajer & Reijndorp (2001: 128) suggest:

'The new public domain does not only appear at the usual places in the city, but often develops in and around the in-between spaces. … These places often have the character of "liminal spaces": they are border crossings, places where the different worlds of the inhabitants of the urban field touch each other.'

They cite a broad group of supporters (Sennett 1990; Shields 1991; Zukin 1991, 1995; Lovatt & O'Connor 1995) for the idea of 'liminality' — spaces formed in the interstices of everyday life and outside 'normal' rules, where different cultures meet and interact — supporters who, in different ways, argue that such spaces bring together disparate activities, occupiers and characters, creating valuable exchanges and connections. Worpole & Knox (2007: 14) term such spaces 'slack' spaces, arguing that they should be regulated with a light touch. For them, urban areas need places where certain behaviours are allowed that in other circumstances might be regarded as anti-social.

Franck & Stevens (2007: 23) develop a typology around the idea of 'looseness' and 'tightness' of space, which they argue are '… *related conditions, emerging from a nexus of the physical and the social features of a space.'* Loose space is adaptable, un-restricted and used for a variety of functions, ad hoc as well as planned. Tight space, by contrast, is fixed, physically constrained or controlled in terms of the types of activities that can occur there. For them, while these qualities are adjustable and relative, existing along a continuum from tight to loose, new types of public space (see Chapter 6) are often more restrictive in nature than they have been in the past, and actively discourage the kinds of unplanned activities that lead to looseness, and, by implication, discovery and re-discovery.

(vi) Display

Public space also satisfies a sixth need, that of display. By definition, in any public space, we are on display: how we appear, dress and behave in public space not only represents a display but may also be important to our sense of identity and belonging. We may purposefully dress to remain inconspicuous and relatively unnoticed or, alternatively, to stand out as different or to define our sense of association with a particular group (and so perhaps engender a sense of belonging to that group). Teenagers and other young people dress in an expressly alternative fashion in order to signal belonging to particular social groups or, more simply, their difference from the mainstream. Other social groups send their signals of difference in other, perhaps more subtle, ways — for example, through the trappings of conspicuous consumption (e.g. through particular clothing labels or through shopping bags). These activities and behaviours form a display for other users of the public space.

The design and management of public spaces often needs to accommodate these needs, while also handling any conflict between them. Rather than spaces that are comfortable, ordered and controlled, to better support active engagement, play and discovery, spaces may need to allow for spontaneity and unscripted, unprogrammed activities. Although Stevens (2007) acknowledges behaviours cannot always be predicted and designed for, he argues that it is through urban design as place-making in-the-round that the possibility of chance, discovery, diversity, risk and thus play can best be enabled.

Franck & Stevens (2006) argue such spaces should be regulated with a light touch and should allow for a variety of unplanned, unprogrammed, unmediated and improvised uses. For them, urban areas need places where certain behaviours are allowed, which, in other circumstances, would be regarded as anti-social. Because of their 'edgy' nature, such activities are often relegated to locations and spaces that more mainstream activities eschew, in turn helping to justify the existence of such places and the physical environments in which they are found.

The poor physical state of these types of public space seems to be a consequence of a lack of clarity regarding who should be managing them. As a consequence, they are often neglected, with Hajer & Reijndorp (2001: 129) arguing that greater attention needs to be given to them. In Europe, the opportunity provided by such spaces has spawned a movement dedicated to re-populating such places with temporary and alternative uses. As pioneers Urban Catalyst observe many examples across Europe

FIGURE 8.18 Public life in liminal space — Paddington, London (*Image: Matthew Carmona*)

FIGURE 8.19 Post Office Square, Chicago (*Image: Matthew Carmona*). The sculpture provides a focus and sense of visual completeness for the space — try imagining the space without it — but it is difficult for people to engage with it

'*... demonstrate that the phenomena of derelict sites caused by de-industrialisation, abundance of infra-structure or political faults ... represent a common part of the urban fabric in nearly all European cities.*' (Oswalt *et al* 2007: 273). They argue temporary uses can thrive in such localities, where conventional planning and design processes have typically failed. The experience emphasises a key argument — that the physical environment is only one element in place-making and that different types of social places can form and be nurtured in even the most physically unpromising spaces (Figure 8.18).

The Design of The Edge

The micro-design and use of successful people places can be considered in terms of the 'centre' and the 'edge'. Alexander *et al* (1977: 606) assert that a public space '*... without a middle is quite likely to stay empty.*' They recommend that between

'*... the natural paths which cross a public square ... choose something to stand roughly in the middle: a fountain, a tree, a statue, a clock-tower with seats, a windmill, a bandstand ... Leave it exactly where it falls, between the paths; resist the impulse to put it exactly in the middle.*'

(Alexander *et al* 1977: 606—8).

As well as providing a sense of identity and character, such features can also provide prompts for triangulation (see above).

While something in the middle provides a focus and a sense of visual completeness (Figures 8.19 and 8.20), this is secondary and what really matters for a successful people place is the design of the edge. Alexander *et al* (1977: 600) argue that the life of a public square forms naturally around its edge, to which people gravitate rather than lingering out

in the open: '*If the edge fails, then the space never becomes lively ... the space becomes a place to walk through, not a place to stop.*' Rather than treating the edge of the space as a 'line or interface with no thickness', they recommend conceiving it '*... as a "thing", a "place", a zone with volume to it.*' (Alexander *et al* 1977: 753).

As a support for people-watching, the edge of a space can be enhanced by providing formal (seating, benches, etc.) and informal (stringcourses, column bases, low walls, steps, etc.) places to sit (Figure 8.21). If the edge is set at a slightly higher level than the space itself, and partly protected from the weather (e.g. by an arcade), then both the prospect and the potential for people-watching are enhanced. For Alexander *et al* (1977: 604—5), the most

FIGURE 8.20 Cloud Gate, Millennium Park, Chicago (artist: Anish Kapoor) (*Image: Tim Heath*). The public art installations in Millennium Park invite active engagement. Nicknamed 'The Bean', this art project provides an activity focus for the space. Nearby is the Crown Fountain. Both are immensely popular

FIGURE 8.21 Primary and secondary seating opportunities *(Image: Matthew Carmona)*. Formal seating opportunities are those primarily designed for seating. Secondary seating is where seating is possible but seating is not the primary function. Informal seating opportunities do not look forlorn when unused

inviting spots are high enough to provide a vantage point, but low enough to be used.

Active Frontages

Frontage is how a building addresses the street. Facades can be designed so that buildings metaphorically 'reach out' to the street, offering 'active' frontage onto public space, adding interest, life and vitality. As windows and doorways suggest human presence, the more doors and windows onto public space, the more active the frontage. Conceptualising the boundary between public and private realms, Madanipour (2003: 59–67) suggests it faces two directions: on the one hand it protects the public sphere from private encroachment; on the other it protects the private sphere from the public gaze. Yet as well as separating private and public spheres and protecting them from each other, the boundary also acts as a site of interface and communication between the two. Sometimes there will be a desire to facilitate interaction (e.g. a row of shops onto a street) and, at other times, to limit interaction (e.g. a police station). For Madanipour (2003: 64):

'… the more ambiguous and articulate the boundary, the more civilised a place appears to be. When the two realms are separated by rigid walls, the line of interaction becomes arid, communication limited and the social life poorer for that.'

The interface also needs to be designed to enable a range of indoor and 'private' activities to co-exist in close physical proximity with a range of outdoor and 'public' activities. Views into buildings, for example, provide interest to passers-by, while views out put 'eyes on the street', contributing to its safety. The number of doors/entrances, with activity directly visible from public space, is a good indicator of potential street life and activity: the greater the intensity, the greater the potential (see Table 8.3).

TABLE 8.3 Scale of Active Frontages

Grade A	• More than 15 premises every 100 m • More than 25 doors and windows every 100 m • A large range of functions/land uses • No blind/blank facades and few passive ones • Much depth and relief in the building surface • High-quality materials and refined details
Grade B	• 10–15 premises every 100 m • More than 15 doors and windows every 100 m • A moderate range of functions/land uses • A blind/blank or few passive facades • Some depth and modelling in the building surface • Good-quality materials and refined details
Grade C	• 6–10 premises every 100 m • Some range of functions/land uses • Less than half blind/blank or passive facades • Very little depth and modelling in the building surface • Standard materials and few details
Grade D	• 3–5 premises every 100 m • Little or no range of functions/land uses • Predominantly blind/blank or passive facades • Flat building surfaces • Few or no details
Grade E	• 1 or 2 premises every 100 m • No range of functions/land uses • Predominantly blind/blank or passive facades • Flat building surfaces • No details and nothing to look at

Source: Adapted from Llewelyn-Davies (2000: 89).

Blank frontage is the antithesis of active frontage. Whyte (1988) railed against the blank walls, designed as such, which he felt were becoming the dominant townscape feature of US cities: *'They are a declaration of distrust of the city and its streets and the undesirables who might be on them.'* While a 'technical explanation' (e.g. the need for consistent light levels) might be offered, this was rarely the real reason — blank walls were an end in themselves: *'They proclaim the power of the institution, the inconsequence of the individual, whom they are clearly meant to put down, if not intimidate.'* Blank frontages not only deaden that part of the street, they also break the continuity of experience vital for the rest of the street (Figures 8.22 and 8.23).

Issues of active and blank facades also feature in residential design. Analysing residential design in the USA, Southworth & Owens (1993: 282–3) note how, in role and position, the garage has usurped the porch — a transformation highlighting social change and symbolising the primacy of the car in the design of residential environments. Contributing formally and functionally to a human-scale

FIGURE 8.22 Sixteenth Street, Denver, USA *(Image: Steve Tiesdell)*. Although residential uses bring life and activity to city centres, the configuration and integration of such developments affect vitality in adjacent public spaces. In this instance, the ground level consists of a parking structure providing the street edge and frontage with a residential tower above. Presenting a blank frontage to the street, the parking structure has a deadening effect on the city centre. Spatial concentration of such developments would further undermine activity and vitality, and safety and security

street, the porch traditionally enables and symbolises 'entry'. The garage, by contrast, was traditionally a small structure towards the back of the plot, but gradually it came forward to a position of prominence next to the house. In the process, it expanded from a single bay to two or even three bays. As lots narrowed, the garage moved in front of the house, becoming the primary place of access and a primary element of the streetscape, and displacing the front porch, which completely disappeared, with pedestrian access to the house via a narrow alley alongside the garage to a side door. Intriguingly, Southworth & Owens (1993: 282–3) note how some residents had begun to use their garages as

FIGURE 8.23 East London, UK *(Image: Matthew Carmona)*. With no windows facing onto the street, this house is a regular target for graffiti

FIGURE 8.24 (a and b) The garage in the street scene *(Image: Steve Tiesdell)*. The garage door has become the dominant feature of the street scene of many residential developments, and also the main entry point for residents who arrive and depart by car. New Urbanists have both re-asserted the importance of the front porch and have returned the garage to the rear of the plot. Unless the porch reclaims its functional role as the point of entry and of the transition between public and private realms, however, this may simply be a symbolic gesture

social spaces, equipping them with lawn chairs, radios and televisions, and treating them in a manner analogous to the old front porch. Unlike the old front porch, however, these 'human' qualities are only conveyed when the garage door is open; when closed, it becomes a blank facade (Figure 8.24a and b).

For more lively people places, the public edge of buildings surrounding the space should accommodate activities both benefiting from interaction with the public realm and contributing to the vitality there. MacCormac (1983) discussed the 'osmotic' properties of streets – the way in which activities within buildings percolate through and infuse the street with life and activity. Some land uses have very little relation to people in the street; others involve and engage people.

FIGURE 8.25 Street markets provide an intense series of local transactions — Den Bosch, Netherlands *(Image: Willie Miller)*

MacCormac characterised the activity generated by different land uses as their 'transactional' quality, distinguishing 'local' and 'foreign' transactions. Local transactions are those peculiar to place and sensitive to change, with a significant impact on street life and active frontages, and generating many comings and goings. Foreign transactions are those that could be located anywhere because they are carried out on a regional or national scale, and have very little impact on street life because the activity is essentially internalised.

From this, MacCormac (1983) established a spectrum of uses supportive of an animated public realm. At the greater interaction end were street markets; restaurants, cafes, bars and pubs; housing; small-scale offices and shops; and small-scale industry. At the other end were car parking; warehouses; large-scale industry; large-scale offices; blocks of flats; and supermarkets (Figure 8.25). This is not to imply some uses are unnecessary or have no place within an urban area — merely that they have lesser claims to key street and public space frontages. To ensure busier, livelier spaces, the more interactive uses must be adjacent to them (Figure 8.26a and b).

Large buildings with a single entrance can have a deadening impact on streets. In many urban environments, larger firms, with less necessity for contact with the immediate locality, have sought prestigious locations on the street frontage (or other prime spaces such as waterfronts), where they offer little sense of activity relevant to the public outside. In traditional urban environments, large buildings with little to contribute to street life — such as law courts, churches, theatres, etc. — were often embedded in the urban fabric with a limited presence on the street

FIGURE 8.26 The impact of local and foreign transactions *(Images: Matthew Carmona)*. Two sides of the same street illustrating the impact of foreign transactions on one side, and local transactions on the other

FIGURE 8.27 Coliseum Theatre, London *(Image: Steve Tiesdell)*. Although a foreign transaction, this theatre avoids causing a deadening effect on local street life by being embedded in the core of the street block, and (partially) surrounded by a perimeter of local transactions. While the theatre is a foreign transaction, the front of house, box office and its bar are all potentially local transactions that will benefit the street edge. As a foreign transaction, it attains civic presence through symbolism and iconography, and by appearing emblematically on the skyline.

frontage, freeing it for uses that interacted better with the street (MacCormac 1987) (Figure 8.27).

This traditional development pattern suggests a way of incorporating foreign transactions — such as 'big box' retail developments, which often stand alone with exposed 'dead' frontages — into urban settings without causing a deadening effect on local street life: the core of the development contains the foreign transactions, while the perimeter houses the local ones (Figure 8.28). For office buildings, locating active uses at the ground floor level can overcome their deadening effect on the street.

In the USA, practices have developed whereby larger single-use buildings — big box retail, department stores, movie theatres, etc. — are completely or partially wrapped in what are termed 'liner' buildings (see Mouzon, in Steuteville *et al* 2009: 90−106, 291−2) − '… *a relatively shallow building that conceals a larger, outwardly uninteresting structure such as a parking garage, cinema complex, or big box store.'* Containing retail and small businesses at ground level and offices or residential above, liner buildings have a shallow footprint in terms of depth (6−12 m; 20−40 ft) and are often single-loaded, though sometimes they are detached from the big box and have

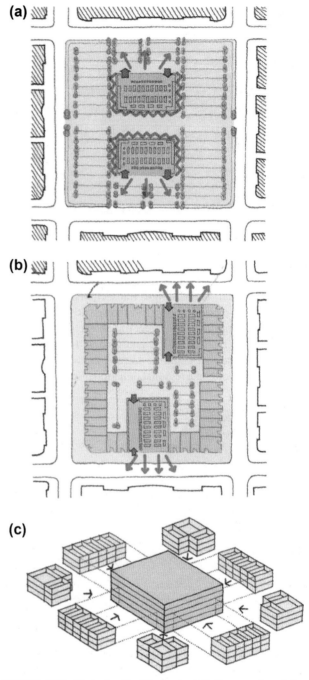

FIGURE 8.28 Designing for 'big box' retail *(Image: adapted from Llewelyn-Davies 2001)*. These illustrations show design strategies for incorporating big box retail units. (a) Where big box sheds are surrounded by parking, the potential active frontage is projected into the car park, rear elevations are exposed and the streetscape is undermined. (b) By turning the sales floor through 90 degrees and inserting the building into a perimeter block, access is provided from both sides, while creating active street frontage. (c) To create active frontage, big box sheds can be surrounded by smaller units (Source: Adapted from Llewelyn-Davies, 2000: 43). A difficulty arises, however, where there is mismatch between the number of big box retailers and a much smaller number of smaller retailers. It may also be considered an 'urbane disguise' because there is still the economic impact (both positive and negative) of big box retail

FIGURE 8.29 Integrating big box development – Philadelphia *(Image: Matthew Carmona)*. Here, a big box car park is surrounded by single aspect housing, which animates the street scene

a service-way between them and the big box unit allowing rear servicing. The shallow footprint generally means that retail units are occupied by independent rather than chain retailers and thus add to the diversity of the retail offer (Figure 8.29).

Sociability and Privacy

Providing the interface between public and private realms, the edge of the public space network needs to both enable interaction and protect privacy. For Madanipour (2003: 240) this role is essentially ambiguous because the boundary is simultaneously part of the public and private spheres, both shaped by and shaping these two spheres, and helping to define the power relations between the two:

'The wall that separates two neighbours, home from street, and city from countryside, lies at the heart of the notion of law and society. City building therefore is partly a boundary setting exercise, sub-dividing space and creating new functions and meanings, establishing new relationships between the two sides.'
(Madanipour 2003: 240).

He observes how a host of mechanisms – colonnades, porches, semi-public gateways, foyers, elaborate facades and courtyards – has been developed to facilitate communication between public and private while maintaining their distinctive roles (see Chapter 7). A central challenge of good urbanism is finding a balance between the two.

As discussed in Chapter 4 and based on an understanding of the public/private interface, public 'fronts' should face onto other fronts or onto public space, while private 'backs' should face onto private space and other backs. Used consistently, such a strategy generally reduces the need for blank walls (i.e. instances where private uses front onto public space) – perimeter block systems generally provide this distinction.

In urban design terms, privacy is usually defined in terms of selective control of access (to individual or group) and of interaction (especially that which is unwanted). Need for privacy and interaction varies among individuals, with respect to personality, life stage, etc., and across different cultures and societies. In many eastern cultures, concern for privacy has often been a major structuring element of urban areas.

Privacy is nonetheless a complex and multi-facetted concept. Westin (1967, from Mazumdar 2000: 161), for example, distinguished four types: 'solitude' (being alone); 'intimacy' (the ability of a small number of people to be by themselves undisturbed); 'anonymity' (the ability to interact with others without being identifiable or account-able; and 'reserve' (the ability to limit communication about oneself). Mazumdar (2000: 161) added three further types: 'seclusion' (being out of the way and difficult to find); 'not neighbouring' (i.e. avoiding contact with neighbours); and 'isolation' (being away from others). Some of these types of privacy are based on physical distance, others on the control of interaction, but can require a different design response.

Privacy can be attained in a number of ways, which may include behavioural/management mechanisms or, alternatively, strategies involving physical distance or sonic or visual 'screens'. Built-form determinants of privacy take two forms – 'barriers', which physically establish the general privacy state and cannot be easily changed, and 'filters', which allow the individual to modify or control that general state. In functional terms, privacy can usefully be discussed in terms of 'aural' and 'visual' privacy.

Visual Privacy

Issues of visual privacy typically relate to the interface between public and private realms and, in particular, the physical and visual permeability between these realms. Rather than a simple duality of privacy/no privacy, there is a spectrum of privacy needs. Chermayeff & Alexander (1963: 37), for example, argued that '... *to develop both privacy and the true advantages of living in a community, an entirely new anatomy of urbanism is needed, built of many hierarchies of clearly anticipated domains.'*

Designers must enable the requirements of each privacy domain, while balancing these with opportunities for interaction. In domestic space, privacy levels typically structure the position of rooms, grading from the most accessible, public spaces such as the entrance hall, to the least accessible and most private spaces (e.g. bedrooms and bathrooms) – an ordering that also relates to the position of outdoor public space and access to the dwelling (Figure 8.30). Indeed, Madanipour (2003) sees the whole experience of the city as a transition from the personal space of the body, to the exclusive and intimate space of the

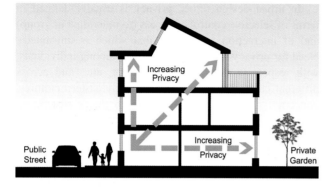

FIGURE 8.30 Privacy gradient *(Image: Adapted from Bentley 1999).* Positive privacy gradients maintain and respect the public/private distinction

home and private property, to the interpersonal and communal spaces of sociability and the neighbourhood and to the institutional and impersonal space of the common world.

Rather than a hard and impermeable interface between public and private realms, a softer and more permeable one is often desirable. Activities in private space are not all equally private, and softer permeable interfaces may create important interstitial or transitional spaces (e.g. pavement cafes or dwellings with verandas where internal activities can be seen from outside). Visual permeability can enrich the public realm, but can also confuse the vital public/private distinction. The permeability of the public/private interface should thus be controlled by private users. In practice, the necessary degree of control is often absent. Instead of enabling users to choose how much privacy they want through adjustable filters, designers often decide for them by making permanent physical and visual barriers.

At a development-wide scale, inflexible use of 'space-between-dwellings' standards to ensure privacy can result in regimented and monotonous layouts and low densities with associated high land-take (Carmona 2001: 225–7). Designers should, therefore, balance distance with designed-in strategies.

Aural Privacy

Undesired sounds — usually termed 'noise' — can disturb and invade one's privacy and activities. Noise is 'unwanted' sound, but it also raises issues of by whom it is unwanted: one person's unwanted sound is another's music. 'Sonic comfort' depends not only on the decibel level of sound, but also on its pitch, its source and perceptions of the degree to which hearers have control over it (Lang 1994: 226). Noise disturbance also has a temporal dimension: the same type and level of noise is more acceptable at some times of the day or week and less acceptable at others. While people adapt to extraordinarily noisy environments, sonic pollution is an increasing concern.

Rather than the physical characteristics of noise, Glass & Singer (1972, from Krupat 1985: 114) found it was the social and cognitive contexts in which it occurred that determined whether it was intrusive. Furthermore, rather than the inability of people to adapt, psychic after-effects were the major source of noise-induced problems. Research, for example, has indicated that continual exposure to background noise, such as that found in a relatively noisy neighbourhood, can lead to raised blood pressure, heart rates and stress in children, reducing their maturation and leading to 'learned helplessness syndrome' (Evans *et al* 2001).

Design strategies can combat noise nuisance. A broad distinction can often be made between noise-generating activities — cafes, bars, night-clubs, traffic, street entertainment, amplified music, etc. — and noise-sensitive uses, primarily housing and other residential uses (see Tiesdell & Slater 2006). Measures can be taken to prevent or reduce the 'break out' of noise, and/or to separate it from noise-sensitive uses, by physical distance, sound insulation and/or through screens and barriers. Within buildings, noise-sensitive uses and activities can be located away from noise sources. As change may be unpredictable and impossible to control, a necessary precautionary principle should be to ensure appropriate insulation is provided for noise-sensitive uses from the outset. As physical distance from the noise source is often impractical, the other main means to obstruct the sound path is by solid screening (i.e. solid fencing) or earthbund. The insulation effect of trees and tree belts, however, is primarily psychological.

Vitality, Mixed and Continuous Use

A key aspect of creating a lively and well-used public realm is the spatial and temporal concentration of different land uses and activities. Although a fundamental part of Modernist planning (see Chapter 2), functional zoning approaches had, over time, led to cities dominated by a coarsely gained collage of single-function areas rather than the more fine-grained mixed-use areas of previous eras and have been much criticised.

Jacobs (1961: 155), for example, argued that the vitality of city neighbourhoods depends on the overlapping and interweaving of activities, and that understanding cities requires dealing with mixtures of uses as the 'essential phenomena'. She also outlined four conditions indispensable to generating 'exuberant diversity' in a city's streets and districts:

- The district must serve more than one primary function, and preferably more than two.
- Most blocks must be short — streets and opportunities to turn corners must be frequent.

- The district must mingle buildings varying in age and condition.
- There must be a sufficiently dense concentration of people, for whatever purposes they may be there (Jacobs 1961: 162–3).

The response to the sterility produced by the functional zoning policies and practices of much post-war planning and urban development was a concern for a mix of land uses, which has become a widely accepted, multi-benefit urban design objective. Llewelyn-Davies (2000: 39) identifies the following benefits of mixed-use development:

- More convenient access to facilities;
- Minimising travel-to-work congestion;
- Greater opportunities for social interaction;
- Socially diverse communities;
- A greater feeling of safety through more eyes on the street;
- Greater energy efficiency and more efficient use of space and buildings;
- More consumer choice of lifestyle, location and building type;
- Greater urban vitality and street life; and
- Increased viability of urban facilities and support for small business.

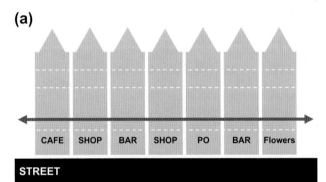

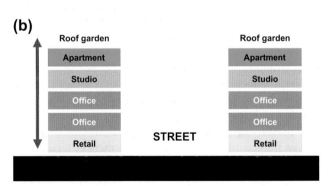

FIGURE 8.31   (a) Horizontal and (b) vertical mixed uses *(Source: Adapted from Montgomery 1998)*

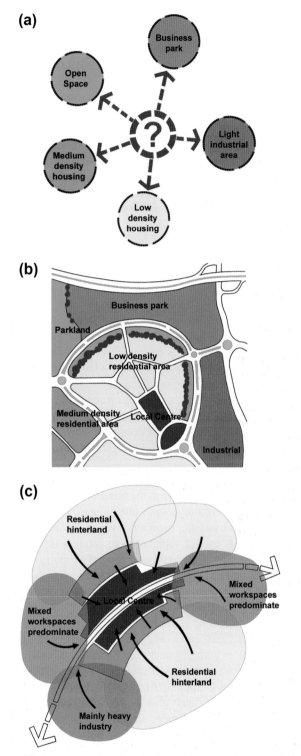

FIGURE 8.32   Designing for mixed uses *(Source: Adapted from Llewelyn-Davies 2000: 39)*. (a) If all the potential 'mixed-use elements' are located at the edge of the development, it undermines the role of the centre. (b) Geographically proximate, the uses remain zoned with roads forming the boundaries between uses. (c) More vibrant and sustainable neighbourhoods and areas result from the complex interweaving of uses and by blurring the distinctions between uses

Areas may have mixed uses in either or both of two ways: by having a mix of single-use buildings or by having buildings each containing a mix of uses (e.g. 'living over the shop) (Figures 8.31a and b and 8.32). The latter is generally preferable.

Rather than zoning per se, it is the type of zoning and how it is applied that may be problematic. Contrasting 'exclusive' with 'inclusive' zoning, Krier (1990: 208–9) illustrates different attitudes to zoning. In exclusive zoning, 'all that is not specifically obligatory is strictly forbidden'. Zoning of this type is a routine and largely unquestioned activity, resulting in mechanical separation of different land uses and functions for no real purpose other than a misguided sense of order. By contrast, in inclusive zoning, 'all is permitted and promoted that is not strictly forbidden', with exclusion based on environmental 'nuisance' or incompatibility ('bad neighbour' uses) and — in principle — different uses can occupy the same area.

Criticisms of functional zoning do not, however, invalidate the mechanism of zoning, which, in practice, can be used in different ways. Kropf (1996: 723) argues that, rather than the general principle of defining areas controlled by particular regulations, what is important is the specific content of zoning ordinance. Some commentators suggest shifting the emphasis from use to form (e.g. from functional to 'typo-morphological' zoning) (e.g. Moudon 1994). Over the past decade, a more explicit use of form-based zoning codes has been adopted (see Chapters 4 and 11).

In many countries, although post-war functional zoning policies have been abandoned, the mindset has proved more enduring. Furthermore, social, institutional, financial and political conservatism, together with interests such as discrimination, market segmentation, product differentiation and desires to maintain and protect property prices, perpetuate *de facto* functional zoning. In many parts of the USA, strict segregation — once applied only to incompatible uses — is now applied to every use, with typical contemporary zoning codes having several dozen land-use designations, and producing an extremely segregated environment — both physically and socially. This derives from, and appeals to, the self-interest of many local property owners, but is often detrimental to place quality.

Market factors may also result in mono-functional areas, because, for example, all developers and property owners seek the 'highest-and-best' possible use. This tendency is reduced where secondary uses have a symbiotic relation with the area's dominant one — for example local shops serving a community. Where it has sufficient powers, the public sector can intervene to limit the area that can be developed for the primary use, and/or to protect certain sites for other uses. It might also specify maximum and minimum amounts of floorspace that can be occupied by given uses (see Chapter 11).

While functional zoning strategies and mono-functional developments often create or exacerbate car-dependency and reduce choice, mixed-use developments generally enable walking or, at least, choice in travel mode, and are thus more sustainable. They also offer more lifestyle choices. Duany *et al* (2000: 25), for example, argue that traditional neighbourhoods provide for an array of lifestyles — one can live above the store; next to the store; five minutes from the store; or nowhere near the store. By contrast, contemporary suburbia frequently offers only one lifestyle — to own a car and to need it for everything.

Despite general support for the principle of mixed-use buildings, developments and areas, the property industry in general, developers and some occupiers, have — until quite recently — been averse to mixed uses within the same building. Several interrelated factors account for this:

- *Development reasons* — the additional costs of developing mixed-use buildings (for different fire escape requirements, etc.) and the institutional structure of the development industry, with developers tending to specialise in a particular development type (residential or commercial, etc.).
- *Management reasons* — occupiers not wanting other users within the same building for reasons of incompatibility or security; and additional costs involved in having different users in the same building, due to different leasing requirements, or safety or environmental health requirements.
- *Investment reasons* — different leasing periods reduce the development's liquidity and value.

However, market volatility provides a rationale for mixed-use developments. Primary office locations are likely always to be fully let, but in secondary locations office property markets are more volatile and the effects of downturns more keenly felt. All or part of a building in these locations may be periodically vacant, and it may produce a better overall return to have a mix of office and residential uses, because the building may be let more readily for residential use (albeit at a lower return). A mixed-use building with flexibility between land uses thus spreads the risk of vacancy.

There may also be physical, legal or financial obstacles that prohibit or increase the cost of accommodating different land uses within one building. The need, therefore, is to find ways of providing or enabling mixed uses within buildings, through persuasion, regulation, or financial incentives. Planning policies, masterplans or urban design frameworks could require an element of mixed uses in developments or even within buildings.

Although a mix of uses may occur spontaneously through market action, appropriate physical provision of robust buildings or development patterns increases the possibility of a mix of uses emerging over time. If no provision is made, this is unlikely to occur. The need, therefore, is for enabling design that facilitates (rather than inhibits) mixed uses (see Chapter 9).

Creating a mix of uses in existing areas often involves introducing residential uses into non-residential areas (e.g. the downtown or city centre) or non-residential uses into residential areas (e.g. suburbs). The design challenge is to gain the synergy and benefits of mixed uses while avoiding bad neighbour situations. Examining the land-use pattern of traditional urban neighbourhoods, MacCormac (1987) noted the tendency for symmetry of land uses across spaces and asymmetry across blocks. This suggests ways of incorporating different uses into an area while reducing the potential for negative or bad neighbour effects. There might, for example, be a grading of uses across a series of blocks with intermediary uses between those that would be incompatible as direct neighbours.

Another useful development pattern is that of perimeter blocks, which can accommodate a mix of uses in a number of different ways. Mixing uses within perimeter blocks can occur through, for example, inserting managed workspaces or compatible employment uses into the back land or block interior or introducing a mews line through the block lined with single-aspect offices, workshops or studios, or a residential mews within a commercial block (see Urban Task Force 1999; Llewelyn-Davies 2000: 96; Komossa *et al* 2005).

Density

A sufficient density of activity and people has often been regarded as a prerequisite of animation and vitality, and for creating and sustaining viable mixed use. Jacobs (1961: 163) considered that density was essential to urban life. For her, New York's Greenwich Village, with densities ranging from 310 to 500 dwellings per net hectare of residential land, was the optimum environment (1961: 216). The UK's Urban Task Force (1999: 59) noted that Barcelona — described as

the 'most compact and vibrant European city' — has an average density of about 400 dwellings per hectare.

Recent debates about creating more sustainable and compact towns and cities have led to a renewed focus on issues of density, especially residential densities. The argument is that compact cities can offer a high quality of life while minimising resource and energy consumption. Achieving higher densities than have been the norm during the latter part of the twentieth century in the UK and the USA, for example, is regarded as a prerequisite of more sustainable environments (see Chapter 2). Llewelyn-Davies (2000: 46) suggests a range of benefits from higher development densities:

- *Social* — by encouraging positive interaction and diversity; improving viability of and access to community services; and enabling more and better integrated social housing.
- *Economic* — by enhancing the economic viability of development and providing economies of infrastructure (e.g. basement car parking).
- *Transport* — by supporting public transport and reducing car travel and parking demand.
- *Environmental* — by increasing energy efficiency; decreasing resource consumption; creating less pollution; preserving and helping to fund the maintenance of public open space; and reducing overall demand for development land.

Although more compact and higher-density development is currently encouraged, it often conflicts with socio-cultural preferences for lower density environments and for car-based mobility (see Breheny 1995, 1997). Whether to seek more concentrated forms of development thus remains one of the most challenging of the sustainable urban design principles outlined in Chapter 3 (see Sustainability Insert 5).

Sustainability Insert 5 — Concentration

Concentration (increasing densities) across spatial scales is widely held to be a sustainable strategy. Nevertheless, in a challenge to those advocating higher-density living, it has been argued that a renewed emphasis on higher-density development could mean more congestion and pollution and probably the demolition of at least part of the historic fabric (Hall 1995). Furthermore, that higher-density living, although technically sustainable in the short term, may be individually unacceptable and perhaps unsustainable in the long term as working from home becomes more the norm, as non-polluting motorised transport is developed and as the reduced supply of greenfield land drives up densities at the expense of open space in established urban areas (Davison 1995). Research sponsored by the retail industry has even shown that in some circumstances new out-of-town shopping development can

result in fewer car journeys over town centre alternatives on the basis that customers will travel to such developments come what may, and therefore that the more such developments there are, and the closer they are to each other, the less individuals will need to travel to reach them (JMP Consultants 1995).

Despite the debates, Breheny (1992a, 1992b) reflected a broad consensus by arguing that urban containment policies should continue to be adopted and decentralisation slowed down, and that this should go together with rejuvenating existing urban areas, with intensification prioritised around transport nodes, but with extreme 'compact city' proposals rejected as unreasonable. Reviewing the case for compact cities Jenks *et al* (1996: 342) supported this view, arguing that, while intensification can support urban living and reduce land-take,

(Continued)

Sustainability Insert 5 — Concentration—cont'd

the case for widespread compaction of many existing urban areas was not persuasive. For Clarke (2009: 17) a critical issue is not density per se, but how efficiently and for what purpose land is used. For example, reducing the space given over to cars from two to one off-street space per unit can increase site capacity by 50%, and reduce the site area required for roads and parking from 40 to 20%. Such arguments have been influential in London where minimum density thresholds across the city from 35 to 45 dwellings per hectare (dph) have been determined by maps of Public Transport Accessibility Levels (PTALs) and related car parking standards.

At the building scale, compact building forms such as terraces are clearly more energy-efficient than, for example, detached ones (the higher the ratio of floor area to external skin area, the lower the loss of energy — Chalifoux in Farr 2008: 189—92), while factoring in all consumption patterns has shown that denser patterns of housing design reduce the environmental footprint of housing due to differences in household size, private lawns and parking (Moos *et al* 2006).

The variation in impact resulting from concentrating urban form is illustrated by Newman (2006: 285), who concludes that, with population densities of around 100 persons per hectare, most Chinese cities consume around 2 gigajoules (GJ) of transport energy per person. By contrast, with a density of six persons per hectare, Atlanta (USA) consumes 103 GJ per person. The 200 million Chinese who moved into cities between 1996 and 2006 are thus equivalent to just over one Atlanta with its four million people.

Richmond-upon-Thames, London, PTAL map

While preferences and arguments for low and lower densities were initially a response to conditions within nineteenth century industrial cities, during the twentieth century it became an objective in its own right, backed by various regulations that, by effectively prohibiting higher-density development, virtually mandated suburban sprawl. Reviewing twentieth century British housing, Scoffham (1984: 23) notes how density zoning, road widths, sight lines, the space required for underground services, street by-laws and daylighting angles were all blamed for pushing buildings further and further apart.

While higher densities are sometimes equated with poor-quality environments, high-quality urban design is — in principle — achievable at all densities. At higher-density levels, however, it becomes essential to protect amenity (particularly privacy standards) and to provide liveable environments. Although preconceptions of high-density development can elicit concerns, studies by Denby (1956) and others showed that the densities of highly desirable Georgian and early Victorian terraces were often much higher than those achieved by high-rise, supposedly high-density housing developments. Studies by Martin & March (1972, March 1967) also dispelled some of the preconceptions (see Chapter 4). These studies showed density must be considered in terms of the configuration of urban form —

that is, as a product or outcome rather than as a determinant of design (see Box 8.3). Used in isolation, for example, plot ratios or floor area ratios (FARs) are a particularly blunt tool to prescribe desirable urban form: the same plot ratio could enable a ten-storey block in the centre of the site or a three-storey perimeter block. When plot ratios are used, they must be integrated with other controls.

Despite her overarching preference for higher densities, Jacobs (1961: 221) concluded that 'proper' city densities were a 'matter of performance' and could not be based on abstractions about the quantity of land needed for X number of people. Similarly, Llewelyn-Davies (2000: 46) suggests the aim should be to generate a critical mass of people able to support urban services such as local shops, schools and public transport. Research by Owens (from Hall 1998: 972) also suggests there is no need for very high densities: 25 dwellings per hectare, for example, allow facilities with

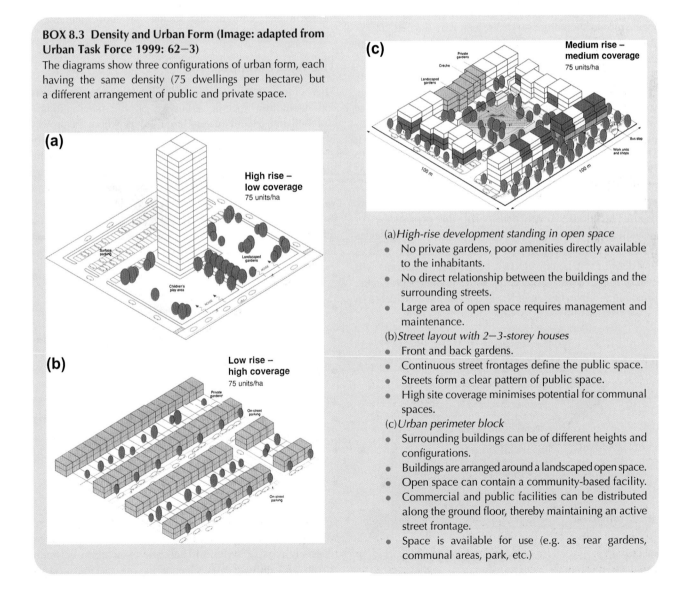

BOX 8.3 Density and Urban Form (Image: adapted from Urban Task Force 1999: 62–3)
The diagrams show three configurations of urban form, each having the same density (75 dwellings per hectare) but a different arrangement of public and private space.

(a) *High-rise development standing in open space*
- No private gardens, poor amenities directly available to the inhabitants.
- No direct relationship between the buildings and the surrounding streets.
- Large area of open space requires management and maintenance.

(b) *Street layout with 2—3-storey houses*
- Front and back gardens.
- Continuous street frontages define the public space.
- Streets form a clear pattern of public space.
- High site coverage minimises potential for communal spaces.

(c) *Urban perimeter block*
- Surrounding buildings can be of different heights and configurations.
- Buildings are arranged around a landscaped open space.
- Open space can contain a community-based facility.
- Commercial and public facilities can be distributed along the ground floor, thereby maintaining an active street frontage.
- Space is available for use (e.g. as rear gardens, communal areas, park, etc.)

a catchment area of 8000 people to be within 600 m of all homes, while a pedestrian-scale cluster of 20 000–30 000 people would provide a sufficient threshold for many facilities without resort to high densities. Similarly, the UK's Urban Task Force (1999: 61) calculated that a population of 7500 would support a viable local hub of facilities. Assuming 5 ha of communal area per 400 dwellings and 2.2 persons per dwelling (42 ha of communal space for 7500 persons), then at a gross development density of 100 people per hectare (the population density necessary to support good bus service, given a socially mixed population), the population could be contained within an area with a radius of 610 m. It also calculated, however, that under these circumstances, 31% of the population would be more than 500 m from the centre and may tend to drive for local trips. Increasing gross development density to 150 people per hectare would mean the population could be contained within 540 m with 13% being over 500 m from the centre. Many, however, doubt the economic viability of local walk-to shopping districts: research by Bartlett (2003), for example, indicates little chance of neighbourhood retail districts surviving on local walk-to shoppers alone.

Considerations of density – particularly the density required to make public transit schemes viable – have often formed the basis of transit-oriented development (TOD) (see www.transitorienteddevelopment.org) and of neighbourhoods designed for sustainability (see Calthorpe 1993; Dittmar & Ohland 2004; Loukaitou-Sideris 2010) (Figure 8.33). Research in the UK suggests that net densities of 100 persons per hectare (approximately 45 units/ha) are necessary to sustain a good bus service, while, in more central locations, a net density of 240 persons/ha (or 60 units/ha) will sustain a tram service (Llewelyn-Davies 2000: 47). Conversely, if new neighbourhoods are built at low densities, it is unlikely that public transit systems will ever become viable. This accords with Jon Lang's pragmatic principle of urban design: if travel options are considered in terms of providing choice, then flexibility is built-in when relative travel costs change in the future.

ENVIRONMENTAL DESIGN

An essential part of urban design is the need to provide comfortable conditions within public spaces – comfort being a prerequisite of successful people places (see above). Levels of sunlight, shade, temperature, humidity, rain, snow, wind and noise have an impact upon our experience and use of urban environments. A number of design actions can help to make conditions more acceptable, including the configuration of space and the use of buildings, walls, trees, canopies and arcades for shade and shelter. Desirable conditions will vary by season and by the activities that take place.

The following sections consider environmental conditions in public spaces and around buildings in terms of microclimate; sunlight and shelter; air movement about buildings; and lighting.

The Microclimate

Microclimate is often neglected in urban design. Designers can have little specific influence on the macroclimatic situation and, except on very large sites or where the project is the design of a new settlement, they often have only a limited effect on features affecting the climate at the meso-scale. Such features include the nature of the surroundings and topographical features such as hills and valleys, which affect exposure to wind. Design decisions, however, have an important influence in modifying the microclimate to make spaces more comfortable. Relevant factors at this scale include:

- Building configuration and its effect on and relationship to buildings and other influences at the site boundary.
- Positioning of access roads and pedestrian paths, trees and other vegetation, walls, fences, and other obstructions.
- Orientation of internal and external spaces and facades with respect to the direction of sunlight and shade.
- Massing and grouping of buildings, including the space between buildings.
- Wind environment.
- Positioning of main entrances and other openings acting as transitions between inside and outside conditions.
- Landscape, planting and water pools/fountains to enhance natural cooling.
- Environmental noise and pollution (Pitts 1999).

Responding to both the local and global contexts, the need is for 'climate-sensitive design'. Traditional designs were well-suited to the local climate and, moreover, were often relatively passive systems. The close association between design and climate was severed by the use of modern

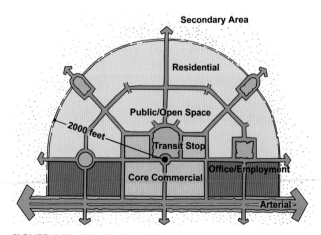

FIGURE 8.33 Transit-oriented development (TOD) *(Image: Adapted from Calthorpe 1993)*

construction techniques, by the availability of cheap fuels and by active building services systems able to overcome any detrimental effects. The architectural vogue for an International style also resulted in the inappropriate translation of building designs from one climate region to another and/or the design of buildings without regard to the local climate. As Kunstler (2005: 121–2) explains:

'Pre-modernist architecture was developed to take advantage of sunlight heating and lighting buildings and breezes for cooling, which are also produced by solar action on air. The development of these traditional techniques was a slow and painful accretion of experience over scores of centuries. It has only been the anomalous abundance of cheap oil and gas in our time that permitted builders, and especially architects preoccupied with style issues, to depart from traditional practices that took advantage of passive solar energy.'

The contemporary need is to use technology to design *with* rather than *against* climate.

Designing for Sun and Shade

Sunlight penetration into urban places and into buildings helps make them more pleasant places. It also encourages outdoor activities; reduces mould growth; improves health by providing the body with vitamin E; encourages plant growth; and provides a cheap, readily available source of energy for passive and active collection. The value of sunlight penetration varies over the cycle of the seasons and, while places in the sun are desirable at some times of the year, at other times shade is preferred.

Two major issues are of concern: orientation – in northern latitudes, for example, south-facing elevations receive the maximum sunlight and north-facing elevations the least – and overshadowing and shading. In terms of the latter, the following should be considered:

- The sun's position (altitude and azimuth) relative to public spaces and to the principal facades of buildings.
- Site orientation and slope.
- Existing obstructions on the site.
- The potential for overshadowing from obstructions beyond the site boundary.
- The potential to overshadow nearby buildings and spaces (Pitts 1999).

Solar access can be evaluated using sun charts such as a stereographic sun chart and bespoke computer programmes. As well as graphical and computer prediction techniques, physical models can be tested using a heliodon. If overshadowing is to be avoided during winter months (when solar gain is most advantageous), the spacing of buildings is very significant. Trees will also provide obstructions to solar access, but, when deciduous, will perform the dual function of permitting solar penetration

during the winter and a degree of shading in the summer. The spacing between tree and building is again critical.

Design must strike a balance between physical definition of space for visual and social reasons and for egress of light and air for functional and environmental reasons. As discussed in Chapter 3, good design achieves all criteria simultaneously.

Air Movement – The Wind Environment

Wind flow has a substantial effect on the comfort of pedestrians, the environmental conditions within public spaces and around building entrances and the activities that might occur there (Table 8.4). Wind tunnel tests during the design development process are often critical – particularly where proposed buildings are significantly taller than their neighbours.

TABLE 8.4 Windspeed and Effects

Situation	Windspeed (m/s)	Effect
Calm, light air	0–1.5	• Calm • No noticeable wind effect
Light breeze	1.6–3.3	• Wind felt on face
Gentle breeze	3.4–5.4	• Wind extends light flag • Hair is disturbed • Clothing flaps
Moderate breeze	5.5–7.9	• Raises dust, dry soil, loose paper • Hair disarranged
Fresh breeze	8.0–10.7	• Force of wind felt on body • Drifting snow becomes airborne • Limits of agreeable wind on land
Strong breeze	10.8–13.8	• Umbrella used with difficulty • Hair blown straight • Difficult to walk • Wind noise on ears unpleasant • Wind-borne snow above head height (blizzard)
Near gale	13.9–17.1	• Inconvenience felt when walking
Gale	17.2–20.7	• Generally impedes progress • Great difficulty with balance in gusts
Strong gale	20.8–24.4	• People blown over by gusts

Source: Bentley *et al* (1985: 75, after Penwarden & Wise 1975).

If, as is usually the case, the wind effect is to be minimised, the following factors should be considered:

- Building dimensions should be kept to a minimum to reduce wind pressures.
- The larger building dimension should not face into the predominating wind (i.e. the long axis should be parallel to the prevailing wind).
- Building layouts should avoid creating tunnel effects (e.g. long parallel rows of relatively smooth-faced buildings should be avoided).
- As sheer vertical faces to tall buildings can generate substantial down draughts, which can obstruct pedestrian access and create uncomfortable conditions at ground level, the facades of tall buildings should be staggered and stepped back with increasing height away from the prevailing wind (i.e. tending towards a ziggurat form).
- Protection of pedestrians by the use of canopies and podiums, which reduce down draught at ground level.
- Buildings should be grouped in irregular arrays, but within each group the heights should be similar and the spacing between them kept to a minimum.
- Shelter belts (trees, hedges, walls, fences, etc.) can provide a degree of protection for buildings and pedestrians. They are most effective when correctly oriented with airflow permeability of about 40%, which allows wind to be diffused rather than forced over an obstruction, thereby causing increased turbulence (Pitts 1999; BRE 1990).

In very humid climates external spaces may need to be designed to encourage a greater through flow of cooling air. In more arid climates positioning fountains and water features in public spaces help cooling through the evaporation of water vapour.

Air quality is an increasingly important consideration in urban areas. Trees and other vegetation will tend to filter air, while rainfall will scrub it, although, in high concentrations, pollution will kill natural vegetation. The London Plane Tree — a hybrid of American and European types — for example, is tolerant of atmospheric pollution and root compaction. The pores on the trunk may get blocked, but the bark flakes off (exfoliates). Its glossy leaves are washed by the rain, and new leaves have small hairs, which fall off, cleaning the leaves. To dissipate air pollution, good air circulation flow about buildings and within urban spaces is required — which may conflict with desires for a greater sense of enclosure in urban spaces (see Chapter 7) (Figure 8.34).

Airflow inside buildings can be created by natural ventilation, or by mechanical ventilation or air conditioning. In general, designers should seek to minimise the need for artificial systems. If airflow is to provide natural ventilation and cooling, the plan form needs to be relatively shallow. For successful cross-ventilation, the cross-

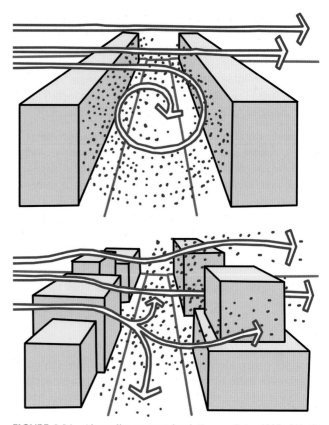

FIGURE 8.34   Air quality at street level *(Image: Spirn 1987: 311–2, from Vernez-Moudon 1987: 311)*. Street canyons lined with buildings of similar height, oriented perpendicular to the wind direction (upper diagram), tend to have poorer air circulation than street canyons lined with buildings of different heights and interspersed with open areas (lower diagram)

sectional depth should be a maximum of five times the floor-to-window head height.

Lighting

Natural lighting makes an important contribution to the character and utility of public space. The play of light in urban spaces also has aesthetic dimensions. As Louis Kahn wrote: *'The sunlight did not know what it was before it hit a wall.'* (in Meiss 1990: 121). Frederick (2007: 49) observes how the altitude, angle and colour of daylighting vary with orientation and time of day. In the northern hemisphere, daylight:

- From north-facing windows is shadowless, diffuse and neutral or slightly greyish most of the day and year.
- From the east is strongest in the morning, is of low altitude, with soft, long shadows, and is grey-yellow in colour.
- From the south is dominant from late morning to mid-afternoon, renders colours accurately, and casts strong, crisp shadows.

- From the west is strongest in the late afternoon and early evening, has a rich gold-orange cast, and can penetrate deeply into buildings, but occasionally is overbearing.

The amount of visible sky — particularly the sky overhead, which is brighter than that at the horizon — is crucial to the quality of daylighting. Except where particularly tall or large buildings surround the space, adequate daylighting — as distinct from direct sunlight — of an urban space is rarely a problem. In general, buildings should make as much beneficial use of naturally available light as possible. A basic rule-of-thumb used in the UK is that obstructions subtending an angle of less than 25 degrees to the horizontal will not usually interfere with good daylighting, while obstructions greater than 25 degrees need not interfere provided they are relatively narrow (Littlefair 1991). The quality of the daylighting in a room depends on the design and position of fenestration relative to the depth and shape of the room, and on whether surrounding buildings obstruct the light penetration into a building. Shallower plans will be better lit than deeper plans.

Although artificial lighting can make a positive contribution to the character and utility of urban spaces, it is often designed only with vehicular traffic in mind and tends to be inefficient in energy use, resulting in light pollution. It has two key functions:

- *Statutory lighting* — which provides basic lighting levels, to aid pedestrian way-finding and the secure use of the public realm at night, and the safe passage of vehicles.
- *Amenity lighting* — which enhances the street scene through flood, feature and low-level lighting; and gives colour and vitality through signs, shop-lighting and seasonal lighting.

In practice, the lighting of streets at night derives from a wide range of sources — street lamps, borrowed light from buildings, shop signs, etc. — and the ensemble needs careful consideration to meet both statutory and amenity needs. To achieve this and to enhance the night-time economy, a number of towns and cities, such as Washington DC, Melbourne and Edinburgh, have adopted comprehensive lighting strategies. The subdued lighting at Washington DC, for example, allows floodlit buildings to stand out and a view of starry skies, making the city one of the world's great night-time walking cities. Well-lit streets and spaces are also particularly important in making users feel safe and secure (see Chapter 6).

DESIGNING HEALTHIER ENVIRONMENTS

Although a developing research and policy literature relates public health to the design of the built environment, the act of building has long been regulated in order to reduce the threat posed to human health by poor-quality development. An early example was the rebuilding of London after the Great Fire of 1666. As Hebbert (1998: 26) recounts, there was to be no Baroque master plan, but, to reduce fire risk, Charles II's Act for the Rebuilding of the City of London (1667):

'*... left a legacy for town planning just as decisive. The Act established a typology of streets and matching buildings, prohibited buildings with jutting projections, dispensed with timber famed construction, and prescribed materials, ceiling heights, wall thicknesses, and structural requirements such as the placing of joists*'

(Hebbert 1998: 28).

Today, building regulations of much greater complexity and sophistication exist all over the world, addressing such issues of fire spread, structural stability, and materials safety (see Chapter 11). Ultimately, such regulations protect the health and well-being of building inhabitants and the wider community.

The emergence of planning at the end of the nineteenth century owed much to a concern for health — in particular to a desire to address issues of over-crowding and sanitation in industrial cities. These factors, and in particular a concern to create environments with better sunlight penetration, ventilation and open space provision, were the driving force behind Modernism's growth and spread in the first half of the twentieth century, while, in the second half, the built environment was increasingly shaped by concerns for health and safety. The highways standards used by traffic engineers to design the road network (see below), for example, are typically predicated on separating pedestrians from vehicles in the — some would argue — misguided (see DfT 2007) belief that this will reduce the likelihood of accidents (see Chapter 4). In different ways and for different reasons, questions of health have always been at the forefront of urban design.

Health as a Strategic Design Concern

Today, the impact of the built environment on a range of new health-related concerns has again come to the fore, meshing with a wider agenda for healthy cities (Hancock & Duhl, in Barton & Tsourou 2000: 31) encompassing:

- A clean, safe physical environment of high quality (including housing quality).
- An ecosystem that is stable now and sustainable in the long term.
- A strong, mutually supportive, non-exploitative community.
- A high degree of participation and control by the public over decisions affecting their lives.
- The meeting of basic needs for food, water, shelter, income, safety and work.

- Access to a wide variety of experiences, resources, contact and interaction.
- A diverse, vital and innovative city economy.
- The encouragement of connectedness with the past.
- An urban form that is compatible with and enhances the above.
- An optimum level of public health services available to all.
- High levels of positive health and low levels of disease.

Playing a critical role in achieving many of these aims, urban design — and the processes that give rise to it — is of central importance to delivering an agenda enshrined in the constitution of the World Health Organisation in 1946, where health was seen as encompassing complete physical, mental and social well-being rather than merely the absence of disease or infirmity.

In some parts of the world, however, the problems faced by the early planners in Europe and the USA and associated with a poor-quality physical built environment continue to cause endemic health and social problems. In China, for example, the State Environment Protection Administration reported in 2007 that 585 cities faced major air and water pollution problems (see http://www.china.org.cn). In additional to technological solutions to clean up industry and investment in new infrastructure (e.g. for water purification), the response to these problems will require separating local populations from heavy and noxious industry, the source of much local pollution. In much of the global south the pursuit of further development poses various hazardous challenges, with, for example, the spread of car ownership posing significant health problems as dense urban areas with poor public transport infrastructures are increasingly choked with traffic fumes.

In the developed world, the contemporary challenge increasingly focuses on encouraging a diverse mix of uses rather on separating them and on creating liveable environments that support a sense of mental well-being through being safe and secure, legible, comfortable, stimulating, inclusive, etc. Nevertheless, some physical health issues remain a concern, and have risen up the agenda in recent years, including those associated with traffic congestion. These concerns are linked to a wide range of health problems: respiratory diseases such as asthma and bronchitis; increased allergies among children; DNA damage; increased risk to those with heart disease; and mental health problems in children. In Boston, for example, studies of 200 children found that, even after controlling for socio-economic factors, scores on verbal reasoning, visual learning and other tests were significantly lower among those exposed to more traffic fumes (Suglia *et al* 2008). At the same time, the Royal Society (2008) published findings highlighting the dangers of ground-level ozone, caused in large part by traffic fumes, and thought to be the cause of more than 1500 deaths a year in the UK alone.

A further major impact at this scale has been the increasing prevalence of urban heat islands brought on by the geographical spread of hard urban surfaces (roads and rooftops) and the allied reduction in vegetation and shade in urban areas (Figure 8.35). Data also shows an increasing trend towards extreme weather events in urban areas. While natural climate change may be responsible for some of this, Gallo *et al* (1999) argue that the rate of increase far exceeds the rate of global warming, suggesting urban growth patterns may be primarily responsible. The health impacts of these effects range from uncomfortable but minor complaints (fainting, swelling, cramps, hyperventilation, etc.), to heat exhaustion and heat stroke — the latter featuring high fatality rates, particularly among elderly and economically disadvantaged groups.

The macro-location of land uses, green space and the provision and management of transport infrastructure all raise questions about the planning of urban areas at a strategic scale. As decisions taken at this scale have a profound impact on the way settlements function at a local level, they necessitate a creative design process that, when translated to localities, will have a profound impact on the ability to create sustainable, healthy places (see Box 8.4).

The Local Environment

At the local level, a wide range of detailed technical factors impact on the healthiness of the local built environment. Protection against communicable diseases requires a safe water supply, sanitary sewerage and waste disposal, good drainage of surface water, and provision of facilities for

FIGURE 8.35   Dubai *(Image: Matthew Carmona).* Large areas of hard surfaces on buildings and landscape can quickly raise external street temperatures, leading to heat island effects

BOX 8.4 Strategic Urban Design, Dongtan Eco Village

Dongtan East Village and East Lake *(Image: Arup)*

Designed by Arup for the financier/developer Shanghai Industrial Investment Corporation (SIIC), Dongtan is planned to occupy 86 km^2 at the eastern tip of Chongming Island, close to Shanghai, for an eventual target population of 500 000. Although it is planned to build the project out over a period of 20–30 years, the project has been designed in its entirety from the start to deliver what has been heavily trailed as the world's first eco-city.

At the mouth of the Yangtze River, the island is a migratory stop for birds, including the rare black-faced spoonbill. As such only 40% of the land area will be built upon and the project will feature large areas of 'managed' and 'natural' wetlands. Other features are planned to include:

- A continuous network of cycle and footpaths.
- An integrated public transit system of fuel-celled buses and solar-powered water taxis.

- An energy plant to burn waste rice husks near the city centre.
- A hundred percent of energy generated from renewable sources by its completion.

The concept for the first phase of Dongtan is three villages, each with their own character, that together will form a town. Each town will have two economic centres, one at the core and one at the periphery. As more towns are added, the peripheral economic zones will overlap to form the economic core of the emerging city of Dongtan. Connecting the towns will be several modes of sustainable transit, with residents connected to a centre in 7 minutes or less.

Although, as yet, Dongtan remains unrealised, it illustrates the potential benefits of strategic design as a means to deliver a healthy, sustainable and functional city.

Source: *adapted from http://agemtsofurbanism.com*

personal hygiene and safe food preparation. Protection against injuries, poisonings and chronic diseases requires adequate structural and fire safety safeguards, low air pollution, safety from harmful materials and from injury on the roads, and through ready access to appropriate emergency services. Reduction of psychological and social stress requires adequate living space, privacy and comfort, personal and family security, protection from noise, and access to recreation, community and cultural facilities (adapted from Barton & Tsourou 2000: 102–3).

In the West, many of the preconditions for healthy living are now in place, forming part of the everyday infrastructure of contemporary cities, and have helped give rise to dramatic extensions in life expectancy. Particularly in the USA and UK, however, new health concerns, including increases in obesity, cardiovascular disease, diabetes, asthma, depression, violence and a range of other mental disorders, are now linked to contemporary lifestyles influenced by the way the local built environment is designed, for example the spread of 'obsesogenic' environments: places that — by encouraging the over-consumption of energy-dense foods (foods high in fat and sugar) and reducing the opportunities for exercise; for example, walking — promote weight gain and are not conducive to weight loss (Booth *et al* 2005).

As Jackson (2003) observes, the link between health and the design of the built environment comes as no surprise:

'Hippocrates, the Romans, and Jung knew our physical environment affects our physical and mental health. We physicians focus well on our patients as individuals with health problems, but when so many of our patients have the same problems, such as cardiovascular disease, diabetes, and depression, we must realise that their poor health is not caused only by a lack of discipline but may be the result of the built environments in which we live.'

Much of the urban design literature advocates mixing uses, connected street networks and higher residential densities to support social contact and to promote physical exercise through walking and cycling — see, for example, the Centre for Livable Communities' (1999) guidelines for healthy streets. Although Jackson (2003: 194) notes that the full health benefits of many of these claims have yet to be proven, she cites a growing body of evidence supporting the claims. Survey evidence in the USA, for example, suggests that the presence of sidewalks, animated streets and enjoyable scenery all promote walking and exercise, and that, while pedestrian paths separated from the street and human activity are hardly used, those winding through mixed land uses with small lot sizes are well used. She cites Balfour & Kaplan (2002), who show that poor lighting, excessive noise and traffic, and lack of public transport are all associated with loss of physical condition in adults aged over 55. For her, detrimental environmental conditions discourage neighbourhood excursions and undermine health.

Reviewing the literature on urban design and human health, Jackson (2003: 192—3) notes how the majority of urban design-related medical and social science research focuses on visual and physical access to the outdoors. Supporting the intuitive (if often crudely implemented) assertions of the Modernists, she argues that the most healthful architecture exposes inhabitants to natural light and ventilation, views of greenery and close proximity to outdoor green space. In doing so, she cites evidence showing that the presence of trees near public housing reduces domestic violence; views of greenery rather than pavements increase cognitive function in low-income children; and window views of greenery aid speed of recovery in hospital. Conversely, inadequate exposure to ultraviolet radiation impairs the body's use of calcium, while radiation from televisions and fluorescent lights is associated with nerve dysfunction and even, in the case of fluorescent lighting, with melanoma.

In a further systematic review of over 500 articles on physical activity and urban design practices (Heath *et al* 2006), interventions at both community and street scale were proven to be effective in promoting physical activity. At the community scale, policies encouraging transit-oriented development, attractive and connected pathways, raised densities, and the mixing of uses were all effective. At the street scale, policies and practices for creating/renovating playgrounds, forming squares, traffic calming, bicycle lanes, improved lighting and enhanced aesthetics through landscaping all support physical activity.

Evidence gathered in the UK has also revealed a range of health benefits from local environments that include high-quality green space, and that give good opportunities for an active lifestyle (Woolley *et al* 2004). Only 7% of urban park users in England, for example, are there for sporting activities. Sports such as football (soccer) are part of the weekly routine for many people and require good-quality open space, while, as people get older, the types of sports they enjoy may change, with golf, bowls and cycling becoming more popular with the over-sixties. These activities help people to keep fit by protecting the cardiovascular system and preventing the onset of other health problems. If appropriately designed, many hard urban public spaces also offer opportunities for less formal but equally beneficial sports — such as skate-boarding, which mostly attracts younger males.

Evidence suggests patterns of activity and exercise are established early in life, and an absence of exercise when young can create problems in adulthood (Kuh & Cooper 1992). For children, well-designed spaces with trees and grass offer better play opportunities than places without such landscape elements. In inner-city Chicago, for example, children were observed playing in areas surrounding apartment blocks; the areas were similar but not all of them had trees and grass. Significantly higher levels of creative play were found in the green spaces than in the barren areas, improving social and interpersonal skills, as well as developing motor fitness and cognitive development (Taylor *et al* 1998). In this regard, the provision of adequate space for creative play is considered vital for child development and future health — preferably the 10 principles for designing play set out by CABE Space (2008) (Box 8.5).

As discussed in Chapter 6, the design of the built environment can be critical in supporting social relationships. A key contribution in this area has been Putnam's *Bowling Alone* (2000), which explores how the design of many contemporary American suburbs results in isolation and loss of social capital, undermining family, religious and other social ties that seem to support healthy, happy lifestyles. For Putnam, this is as detrimental to human health as smoking, obesity, and high blood pressure. Part of the problem is due to the stress of commuting long distances on

BOX 8.5 10 Principles for Designing Play

Well-designed play spaces positively impact on children's lives, encouraging exercise, physical development, socialisation and learning through play. They are also spaces for adults, serving as meeting places and places of relaxation (McKendrick 1999 p76). CABE Space (2008) advocates a fresh design-led approach to play, based on 10 principles and encapsulated in one golden rule: a successful play space is a place in its own right, specially designed for its location, in such a way as to provide as much play value as possible. A play space should be:

1. Designed to enhance its setting
2. Located in the best possible place where children would naturally play
3. Close to nature
4. Designed so that children can play in different ways
5. Geared towards encouraging disabled and able-bodie children to play together
6. Based on a successful community engagement process and thereby loved by the community
7. Where children of all ages play together
8. Designed to enable children to stretch and challenge themselves
9. Constructed from sustainable materials
10. Designed to be flexible with the potential for development and change

Image: A creative play environment, Norfolk, England (*Image Matthew Carmona*)

ever more crowded roads, leading, in turn, to stress that reveals itself both in incidents of road rage and in negative impacts on work and family relations (Frumkin 2001: 207–8). Putnam (2000) argues that every 10 minutes added to commuters' driving time equates to a 10% decline in civic involvement and consequential loss in social capital.

Evidence in the USA has shown that the isolating nature of such environments is particularly profound on children, the elderly and the disabled, who are also particularly affected by vehicular hazards. Laura Jackson, for example, cites evidence that pedestrian fatalities are most common in those parts of the USA where urban sprawl is the dominant form – despite walking being less prevalent in such locations, with consequential increases in obesity and hypertension (Ewing *et al* 2008). More profoundly, while a higher quality and quantity of social relationships are associated with health benefits, social stratification and income inequality is associated with increased mortality. Because urban sprawl is strongly associated with an absence of social capital, and with higher stratification in society, it is also increasingly seen as a main contributing factor to a range of negative health impacts culminating in the potential for higher mortality (Frumkin 2001: 209).

Health-Promoting Environments

The public health literature is unequivocal that significant improvements in public health can be obtained through increased levels of moderate physical activity. In one study, each additional hour spent in a car per day was associated with a 6% increase in obesity, while each additional kilometre walked was associated with a 4.8% fall (Frank *et al* 2004: 87).

Frank & Engelke (2001: 214–5) argue that health benefits can be most efficiently achieved through creating 'health-promotive' environments in which physical activity is encouraged as a by-product of urban form. They argue that all modes of travel are not equal in this respect – non-motorised modes have clear health consequences, while motorised modes have negative associations. For them, despite the associations being well-known, a fundamental disconnect exists between public health professionals and those responsible for shaping the built form, often exacerbated by a separation of responsibilities and institutional barriers. Thus, for example, planning continues to support car-dependent, rather than pedestrian- or cycle-friendly, development because the public health costs of such development are not fully considered.

Their findings suggest it is much easier to encourage physical activity that will be sustained over time if it is of a moderate type, such as walking, rather than a vigorous or competitive form. This is particularly the case among middle-aged and older persons (Frank & Engelke 2001: 207). Walking is the favoured form of exercise of most adults and can be incorporated into daily living routines. Thus, for them, the public health benefits of designing environments that encourage walking are clear. Walking has become a central element of health promotion activity in the UK — not least because, as Tolley (2008: 120) observes, by '... *being easy to incorporate into daily lives and split into "bite-sized chunks", it is actually more likely to be taken up by people and maintained, especially since this means it "doesn't feel like exercise".*'

Fundamental to this is the provision of a connected route network and a wide range of facilities and amenities locally (Frank *et al* 2004). Urban design cannot force those who do not wish to take exercise to do so, but it can provide choice, and make exercise of some choices more likely (Figure 8.36a and b).

THE CAPITAL WEB

As discussed previously in Chapter 4, the capital web is made up of the above and below ground elements of the city's infrastructure. This infrastructure is mainly horizontal — though Duany *et al.* (2000) also refer to a 'vertical infrastructure' of community centres, churches, mosques, libraries, sports pitches, etc. The major capital web considerations in urban design are the provision of public open space; road and footpath design; parking and servicing; and other infrastructure.

External Public Open Space

External public open space offers recreational opportunities; wildlife habitats; venues for special events; and the opportunity for the city to breathe. At the larger scale, areas of public open space should link into a network, with opportunities for movement of people and wildlife between areas. At a smaller scale, standards are often set by public authorities to ensure a minimum provision: in the UK, the most common is the National Playing Fields Association's 2.4 hectares (6 acres) per thousand population (1.6—1.8 hectares for outdoor sport plus 0.6—0.8 hectares for children's playing space). Such provision should be locally accessible and within easy walking distance of all homes, and the NPFA (1992) suggest dividing it between local areas of play (LAPs) within 100 m of all homes and larger locally equipped areas for play (LEAPS) within

FIGURE 8.36   Walkable environments — Barcelona *(Images: Matthew Carmona and Steve Tiesdell)*

every 400 m. In some places, provision may be adequate in terms of size, but the facilities are unused for other reasons, such as fear-of-victimisation (see Chapter 6).

The provision of open space is particularly important in higher-density environments. Appropriate standards should be established in all new developments, with aspirational targets in areas with low levels of existing provision. Rather than being treated as an afterthought — as a use for space left over after planning (SLOAP) — open space should be an integrated and important part of the urban design vision for a place, often as a key focus for public life. A number of towns and cities have developed sophisticated open space frameworks and green space networks to link open spaces and create 'green' corridors through urban areas for recreational purposes and for wildlife. Integration of natural and built environments is a key objective of sustainable development (see Insert 4 sustainability Biotic Support chapter, 7).

Road and Footpath Design

The requirements of cars rather than people often undermine the design of urban environments. If vehicular speeds can be lowered — by speed bumps or other obstacles or, more subtly, by manipulating and configuring sight lines — then car-oriented street standards can be relaxed as well. As discussed in Chapter 4, in the post-war period concern for the segregation of pedestrian and vehicular traffic, initially on the grounds of personal safety, often meant pedestrians could only cross busy roads by underground subways or overground foot bridges. Car-free pedestrian precincts have also been used, with mixed success: some are deserted outside office hours, while others are very successful. Detailed analysis is necessary to determine why some are successful and others not, but the mix of uses and the opportunity they provide for activity at different times of the day play a major part.

In general, the contemporary ethos is to design pedestrian-dominant rather than car-dominant environments: such approaches give priority to pedestrians without banishing the car. This has seen extensive pedestrianisation of city centres; pavement widening/road-narrowing schemes; the closing and blocking up of underground pedestrian ways; and the re-introduction of surface-level crossings. Many residential streets have been traffic-calmed — the Dutch, for example, have employed the concept of the car-free *woonerf* (see Chapter 4), while, at a larger scale, there are road pricing schemes (e.g. in London where traffic has reduced by 16% on average since its introduction in 2003) and in some cities — typically historic European cities — the banning of all cars from the core city centres.

As discussed in Chapter 4, there will inevitably be parts of environments where cars dominate and parts where pedestrians dominate. In resolving competing claims for space, the aim must also be to avoid car-dependant environments, because this reduces their potential to be sustainable, and to increase the potential for walking. Cars can be reconciled to systems designed to give pedestrians, cycling and public transport priority, but it is difficult for these other modes of travel to fit into systems designed for cars. Thus, the priorities for movement should be: first by foot and bicycle, then public transport and, finally, the car. This may require routes for pedestrians or cyclists being designed in from the outset because fitting them in later will be difficult, if not impossible.

Road and footpath design thus needs to achieve a set of basic requirements:

- Maintaining safety and personal security through reducing vehicle speeds, discouraging road and footpath separation and increasing passive surveillance.
- Increasing permeability and access by all modes of travel but particularly by foot.
- Encouraging directness by acknowledging and emphasising 'desire lines' in development (the most convenient route to where people wish to go).

- Designing in sympathy with the local context to ensure an attractive development in which clearly defined spaces, landscaping and buildings dominate rather than roads or cars.
- Increasing legibility through the design of layouts in which the overall structure and local visual references are clear.

While these requirements must be reconciled with the needs and efficiency of the road network, the concerns of highways (traffic) engineers to attain road safety and efficiency may often conflict with the broader aim of overall environmental quality.

Local municipalities have often adopted hierarchical highway standards with specifications for alignments, widths, corner radii, etc., given according to the design speed and volume of the traffic, which have led to the over-engineering of many (particularly residential) environments, and over-reliance on simple standards to design new road systems (see Chapter 4). Traffic-calming methods are increasingly being used to slow vehicles and increase pedestrian safety at the lower ends of these hierarchies. In addition, more sophisticated design guidance has seen authorities abandoning hierarchical approaches to designing road layouts.

New design guidance proposes highway considerations should move beyond matters of safety and vehicle flow efficiency to encompass a concern for environmental quality, pedestrian permeability and three-dimensional space design (Carmona 2001: 283). In the UK, *Manual for Streets* (DfT 2007) is representative of a new generation of policy and design guidance (see Chapter 4), taking forward earlier guidance (DETR 1998), which suggested:

- Spaces should come first, with buildings arranged to fit the context, and roads 'plumbed' in later (see Figures 8.37–8.39).
- Designating 20 mph zones in residential areas.
- Adopting a network of spaces rather than a hierarchy of roads.
- Adopting a sustainable movement framework well related to public transport and an integrated mix of uses.
- Using 'connected' rather than cul-de-sac road layouts.

Designing For Walking

Walking and walkability have attracted much recent urban design scholarship and research (see Forsyth & Southworth 2008; Baraa *et al* 2008; Alfonzo *et al* 2008; Lindsey *et al* 2008; Tahrani & Moreau 2008; Wunderlich 2008; Johnston 2008; Ewing & Handy 2009). Distinctions are often made between 'necessary' or utilitarian walking and 'optional' or recreational and leisure walking. Wunderlich (2008: 131) labels these 'purposive' and 'discursive' and adds a third type — conceptual walking (e.g. walking in

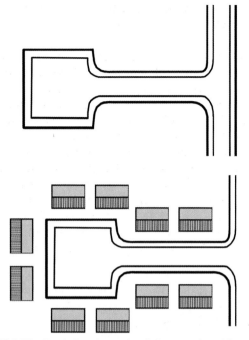

FIGURE 8.39 Innovative street design — Poundbury, Dorchester *(Image: Matthew Carmona)*. One of the most significant features of Poundbury was the spaces first approach to street design

FIGURE 8.37 'Roads first, houses later' *(Image: Adapted from DETR 1998: 23)*. Many housing developments are laid out around roads without considering the spaces created between individual (usually standard) housing units. A 'roads first, houses later' approach produces a form of road-dominated design that neglects other important elements of the residential environment. It is, in effect, a default urbanism (see Chapter 4)

a deliberately reflective mode, for example planning a walk to experience and/or become familiar with a place). At one level, the relationship between necessary and optional walking and the quality of the physical environment is similar to Gehl's discussion of the incidence of necessary and optional activities in public space. At another level, the issue relates those design actions encouraging and supporting a modal shift towards more walking. Rather than focusing on walking *per se*, the

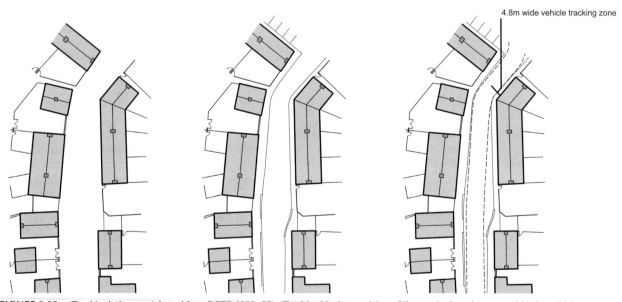

FIGURE 8.38 'Tracking' *(Image: Adapted from DETR 1998: 55)*. 'Tracking' is the provision of the required carriageway width for vehicle movement within the overall width of the street. The idea is an attempt to suggest alternatives to the 'roads first, houses later' approach to residential design. Instead of taking highway engineering requirements as the starting point for design (i.e. a 'roads first' approach), the arrangement of buildings and enclosure is considered first and the roads are plumbed in later (i.e. a 'spaces first' approach). In the first diagram, buildings are arranged to form street enclosure. In the second, footways are laid out in front of buildings to reinforce the space and enclosure. In the third, the carriageway width is checked by plotting vehicle-tracking paths

approach endorsed by, for example, the English *Manual for Streets* (DfT 2007) is to create high-quality, pedestrian-friendly environments in which walking becomes a natural and pleasurable activity (Tolley 2008: 132).

Many traffic-calming measures enhance walkability, including widening the sidewalks/pavements, thereby reducing the street width — as a general rule-of-thumb, Dan Burden (in Steuteville *et al* 2009: 151) recommends dividing the width of the right-of-way of any street equally between walking and driving. Adding parking to the street and/or adding a median strip will also serve to calm traffic — median strips also reduce the visual width of the street. Another method is 'bulb-outs' — the widening of the side-walks or planter strips at the end or in the middle of a street block (Steuteville *et al* 2009: 146). These both narrow a portion of the street and reduce the crossing distance for

pedestrians. Narrow-radius kerbs at the street corners also reduce both the crossing distance for pedestrians and car speeds.

Walkability also requires destinations within walking distance that are worth walking to. A design device for assessing this is the concept of a 'pedestrian shed' (or ped shed) — the area within (typically) a five-minute walk/quarter-mile radius of a key destination, which is used both to locate key destinations and to maximise homes within the catchment area. Another analytical device is the 'amenities distance wheel' (Barton *et al* 1995), which pictorially represents the distance of key amenities from a point source — the more compact the wheel, the more destinations within a walkable distance (Figure 8.40). A web-based instrument (www.walkscore.com) uses a similar method to evaluate the walkability of locations.

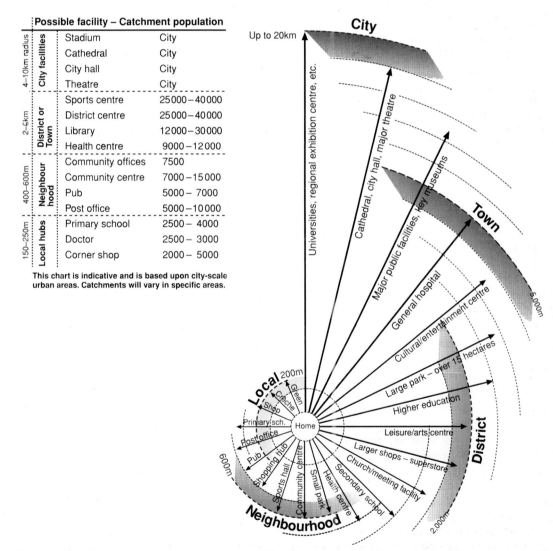

Possible facility – Catchment population		
City facilities (4–10km radius)	Stadium	City
	Cathedral	City
	City hall	City
	Theatre	City
District or Town (2–6km)	Sports centre	25000–40000
	District centre	25000–40000
	Library	12000–30000
	Health centre	9000–12000
Neighbourhood (400–600m)	Community offices	7500
	Community centre	7000–15000
	Pub	5000–7000
	Post office	5000–10000
Local hubs (150–250m)	Primary school	2500–4000
	Doctor	2500–3000
	Corner shop	2000–5000

This chart is indicative and is based upon city-scale urban areas. Catchments will vary in specific areas.

FIGURE 8.40   Amenities distance wheel *(Image: Urban Task Force 1999 originally adapted from Barton et al 1995)*. The more compact the wheel, the more destinations within a walkable distance. The viability at different amenities will, however, depend on the presence of a large enough population to support them

Inserting an address or postcode gives a walk score rating for that location on a scale from 0 to 100, where:

- 0–24 is *car-dependent (driving only)* with virtually no destinations within walking range.
- 25–49 is *car-dependent* where only a few destinations are within easy walking range and where driving or public transportation is a must.
- 50–69 is *somewhat walkable*.
- 70–89 is *very walkable*.
- 90–100 represents a *walker's paradise* where most errands can be accomplished on foot and many people get by without owning a car.

The algorithm, however, appears to measure distance as-the-crow-flies rather than how one would walk to them, and thus does not take account of connectivity and obstructions to pedestrian movement (see Steuteville *et al* 2009: 380).

Designing For Cycling

The personal health benefits of cycling are greater than those of walking. Cycling is an aerobic activity, uses major muscle groups, expends significant amounts of energy and has the potential to raise the heart rate to an extent that benefits cardiovascular health (Tolley 2008: 122).

A contemporary design challenge is to create environments that encourage more cycling. As Tolley (2008: 122) argues, making the cycling environment less intimidating – by, for example, reducing traffic speeds and constructing more cycle paths and lanes – would mean that existing cyclists would be less likely to come into fatal contact with cars, but, more importantly, would help to release the known latent demand for cycling. Jones (2001), however, reports practitioners repeatedly noting how levels of cycling were being depressed by the poor quality of cycling provision in the UK, including conflict with pedestrians on shared-use paths, lack of continuity of routes, dangerous road junction design and poor cycle facilities at destinations.

As with urban design generally, designing for cycling must be considered in-the-round. As Tolley (2008: 125–6) observes, safety is often pursued at the expense of the four other standard cycle route design criteria – coherence, directness, attractiveness and comfort. Installing barriers, staggered crossings and routes through subways, for example, may make routes safer, but it also makes them less coherent and direct, and more uncomfortable and unattractive, and risks destroying the quality of the urban environment, particularly for pedestrians (Badland & Schofield 2005; Tolley 2008: 125–6).

A significant constraint to cycling is the lack of storage for bicycles within private homes and flats – not least because cycles take up valuable space when parked in the hallway of a typical house or flat. To facilitate more cycling, sufficient space must be provided for parking bicycles in or near homes. Communal indoor or under-cover cycle storage can make owning and using a cycle much easier and more attractive, especially in high-density areas (Llewelyn-Davies 2000: 73).

Parking and Servicing

Despite well-aired arguments for reducing reliance on private cars, parking requirements are a necessity of contemporary living likely to remain for the foreseeable future. Indeed, space for parking is required within all environments – whether urban, suburban or rural. A particular problem, however, involves integrating parking successfully into the street scene and near developments. Parking needs to be:

- Sufficient to cater for contemporary needs.
- Convenient (i.e. located close to destinations) for all users, including those with disabilities.
- Attractive (e.g. by limiting its visual intrusion – use of landscaping and quality materials can successfully integrate on- and off-street parking).
- Safe and secure.

Where locations are well-served by public transport, required parking standards can be reduced. Charging for parking is one approach to managing demand for parking space – Shoup (2005), for example, documented the high and 'hidden' costs of free parking (see Box 8.6). Everyday Urbanists (see Chapter 2) have also demonstrated some of the opportunity costs of giving over precious real estate to parking spaces (see Chase 2008). Beginning in 2005, Rebar – a San Francisco-based interdisciplinary studio, operating at the intersection of art, design and activism (see www.rebargroup.org/) – instituted a series of PARK(ing) Days – an annual, one-day event where volunteers feed the meters and appropriate a parking space, turning it into a temporary public park. Installed, occupied and removed within a single day, each PARK highlights the opportunity cost of a small unit of urban space. As Chase (2008: 195) explains: *'This unsanctioned appropriation of the virtually inviolate public parking space is a way of questioning the domination of urban public space by the automobile.'* (see Figure 8.41).

Car-free housing, where residents contract not to own cars, has been developed in a few locations well-served by public transport, while, in some developments, dwellings are sold without parking spaces, with purchasers making extra payments for parking spaces. Some cities and developments have car club and car pool schemes, where a range of cars – from people carriers and four-wheel drive vehicles to small city 'run-arounds' – are owned and used collectively by members. Car clubs are well established in several northern European countries. In Germany, for example, a club called *StattAuto* has 20 000 members and serves 18 cities with 1000 cars of varying sizes (see Richards 2001: 122–3). In some countries, location-specific mortgages are available. Where a property is bought in a location well-served by public transit, the ratio between the mortgage loan and the applicant's salary is higher than normal because the buyer does not have the expense of owning and running a car, and thus has more disposable income.

Contemporary developments also require space for servicing, including business deliveries; waste disposal, storage and collection; recycling points; emergency access; removals; cleaning and maintenance; and utilities access. However, due to their scale, many of these elements can be very disruptive in the street scene. Service vehicles, for example, require wider streets, larger setbacks, open service yards and gaping service bays. In residential areas, intimacy and variety in the street scene can be disrupted by

the requirements of service vehicles, including the statutory requirement for adequate access provision to be made for emergency vehicles. Servicing arrangements should be integrated with care and should not dictate the overall layout or character of an area.

Infrastructure

An area's infrastructure — both that above and that under ground — has often been built up over several centuries. With each urban intervention, it is either adapted or extended. Above ground, the capital web incorporates the public space network and landscaping framework; any public transport network and infrastructure; and public facilities (e.g. shops) and services (e.g. schools). Below ground, it incorporates water supply networks; sewage disposal systems; electric grids; gas supply network; telephone networks; cable networks; combined heat and light systems; and underground transit systems.

These infrastructure networks are becoming increasingly important, and a key generative element, in the development of urban areas (see Mitchell 1994, 1999; Horan, 2000; Graham & Marvin 2001; Allen no date). Unless there is ubiquitous provision, the network inevitably advantages some locations relative to others and the pattern of infrastructure is a significant factor in determining where development occurs (see Chapter 4).

Until relatively recently, traditional street systems adapted well to the requirements for below ground infrastructure. Incremental and ad hoc provision, however, has overloaded many streets causing conflicts — as shown by the poor and dying state of many street trees with damaged root systems. In general, there is a need to consider the seen and unseen capital web in the design process; to plan for flexibility and future changes/additions; and to integrate development in a sustainable manner, thereby minimising

FIGURE 8.41 Parking space reclaimed as a cafe terrace — Birmingham, Michigan (*Image: Robin Boyle*)

FIGURE 8.42 Increase in development intensity around transit stops — Salford Quays, Manchester *(Image: Matthew Carmona)*

the need for new infrastructure and reducing disruption to that which exists (see Graham & Marvin 1996, 2001). New elements of infrastructure, especially public transport, are also a means to improve the public realm (see Richards 2001) more generally; rather than just engineering projects, they are a crucial place-shaping infrastructure (Figure 8.42). Intensification around railway and transit stations, for example, can introduce new residential and commercial uses on previously underused sites, thereby increasing an area's vitality and allowing residents on the surrounding (unchanged) suburban streets to meet more of their everyday needs locally.

CONCLUSION

Discussing the functional dimension of urban design, this chapter reiterates the importance of understanding urban design as a design process. As discussed in Chapter 3, the criteria of good design — 'firmness', 'commodity', 'delight' and 'economy' — must be satisfied simultaneously. In any design process, there is a danger of narrowly prioritising a particular dimension — aesthetic, functional, technical or economic — and of isolating it from its context and from its contribution to the greater whole. Design must be considered as a totality and in-the-round.

Discussing the design of speed humps from the perspective of engineers and urban designers, Appleyard (1991: 7—8) argued that:

'The engineer will tend to design a speed hump solely for the purpose of slowing the traffic in a safe and cheap way. These humps can be quite ugly — lumps of asphalt that convey a negative controlling impression to the drivers. The urban designer favours more pleasant humps, perhaps made of bricks, that can also serve as raised crosswalks for pedestrians.'

The latter is a holistic solution. Appleyard (1991: 8), thus, argues that while the economist sees resolution of differences in terms of 'compromise' and 'trade-offs', the urban designer offers creative ingenuity and adds value in resolving the differences — in the example, combining functionality with visual and social objectives.

Chapter 9

The Temporal Dimension

This chapter discusses urban design's 'time' dimension. Sometimes considered to be a matter of working in three dimensions, urban design is actually four-dimensional – the fourth dimension being time. As time passes, spaces become lived-in, places made more meaningful by their time-thickened qualities. In *What Time is This Place?* Lynch was concerned how the 'evidence of time' is made manifest in the physical form of the city. He argued that we experience the passage of time in the urban environment in two ways (Lynch 1972: 65). The first is through 'rhythmic repetition': '... *the heartbeat, breathing, sleeping and waking, hunger, the cycles of sun and moon, the seasons, waves, tides, clocks.*' The second is through 'progressive and irreversible change': '... *growth and decay, not recurrence but alteration.*'

Time and space are intimately related. In his overview of the relationship between time and the built environment, *What Time is This Place?* Lynch (1972: 241) argued that space and time '... *are the great framework within which we order our experience. We live in time-places.*' For Patrick Geddes, one of the fathers of city planning, a city '... *is more than a place in space, it is a drama in time.*' (from Cowan 1995: 1).

This chapter discusses three aspects of urban design's temporal dimension. First, as activities are dynamic in space and time, environments are used differently at different times. Urban designers, thus, need to understand and appreciate time cycles and the time management of activities in space. Second, although environments relentlessly change over time, a high value is often placed on some degree of continuity and stability. Urban designers, thus, need to understand how environments change, what stays the same and what changes over time. They also need to be able to design and manage environments that accept the inevitability of time's passage. Third, environments will change over time, while, equally, urban design projects, policies, etc., will be implemented over time.

TIME CYCLES

The first way in which we know that time has passed is through rhythmic repetition. The main time cycles are based on natural cycles, with the dominant cycle being the circadian – or 24-hour – cycle that results from the Earth's rotation. This is the continuous cycle of day and night, involving sleeping and waking and various bodily cycles.

Other cycles – those of working and leisure time, the cycle of meals, etc., – are overlain on this basic cycle. The cycle of the year and the changing seasons is also rooted in natural processes: the period of the Earth's rotation around the sun. The tilt in the Earth's axis changes the angle of the sun relative to the Earth's surface, thereby varying the length of sunlit daytime through the year and creating the cycle of the seasons. Moving away from the equator, the effect of the different seasons and the changing period of sunlight hours become increasingly pronounced: in higher latitudes, winter days are much shorter and summer days much longer.

Facilitation and encouragement of the use of urban spaces require understanding the effects of the cycle of light and dark, day and night and of the seasons, which promote related cycles of activity. At different times of the day and night, the urban environment is both perceived and used differently. Various factors, such as perceptions of safety, also change during the course of the day, which – in turn – affect how the space is perceived and used. A rewarding and enlightening experience for urban designers is to observe a 'life in a day' of a public space or the same space over the course of the seasons: that is, to study its social anthropology and to witness its changing rhythms and pulses – now busy, now quiet – and the different people using the space – more women at some times, more men at others.

Lefebvre (1991) observed how places are often characterised by particular rhythmic identities, composed of multiple everyday and overlapping time–space rhythms, of people walking, of social encounter, of rest, of particular users (e.g. shoppers, tourists, theatre-goers, etc.). These social rhythms are influenced by the types of rhythms engrained in the physical environment (see Chapter 7) that may in turn suggest a fast or slow place. Wunderlich (2008: 134–5) describes these as 'place-rhythms', arguing that:

'They include functional routines of our lifeworld overlaid by patterns of sound and smell, light and dark, heat and cold, movement and stillness that synchronize within the same time-space framework and define a place temporal milieu.'

Thus, she argues, cities and places are commonly perceived as fast or slow:

'Fast cities are represented as complex, busy and agitated, and their everyday social life portrayed as repetitive, accelerated and

homogenized. In contrast, slow cities are conceived as somewhat easy to understand, quiet and ordered, and their everyday social life as patterned, and rather slow and distinct.'

(Wunderlich 2010: 135).

Moreover, within all cities, certain places will be perceived as fast, frenetic hubs of activity, while other places will be perceived as slow, relaxed, perhaps, more social places.

Cycles of activity are also grounded in the changing seasons. During the winter in northern temperate climes, for example, the hours of sunlight are few, snow may lie on the ground, there are no leaves on the trees, and, even at noon, the sun is low in the sky. Winter days are typically grey, wet, windy and cold. People wrap up warm when venturing out and may use external spaces only when necessary. In the spring, leaves start to appear on trees and people begin to linger in urban spaces, enjoying the warmth of the sun. In the summer, the trees are in full leaf, the sun is high in the sky, the days are long and light, and people stay longer in urban spaces. In the autumn, the leaves turn a rich variety of reds and browns and eventually fall from the trees. People may linger in urban spaces to enjoy the last warmth of the sun before the onset of winter.

Urban designers may deliberately exploit the changing seasons to bring greater variety and interest to urban spaces. Environments designed to reflect and enhance the changing times of the day and the changing seasons add to the richness of the urban experience. Windows in buildings, for example, not only provide light and ventilation, but also allow occupants to remain in contact with the world outside and to be aware of weather and of the time of the day through the movements of the sun. Features exploiting the passing of the seasons add to the temporal legibility of urban spaces. In the course of a year, for example, deciduous trees develop new sprigs, grow new leaves, and develop blossoms and then fruits, and then their leaves change colour and eventually fall from the tree.

Discussing 'winter Copenhagen' and 'summer Copenhagen', Gehl & Gemzoe (1996: 48) observe how, in winter, people may walk but their stride is generally brisk and purposeful; their stops few, brief and of necessity. During the summer, people still walk but in greater numbers; strides are slower and more leisurely. More strikingly, though, people stop more frequently, start to sit down and generally spend time in the city. Although only twice as many people walk in the city centre in the summer as in the winter, each person spends — on average — four times as much time there. The summer people density is thus eight times that of the winter, explaining quiet winter streets and squares swarming with people during the summer (Gehl & Gemzoe 1996: 48). Elsewhere, temperature swings can be far more severe, making external life in all but the shortest doses very difficult, although not impossible (Figure 9.1). In such

FIGURE 9.1   Harbin Ice Festival (*Image: Matthew Carmona*). In Harbin, Northern China, temperatures swing from an average of +25 °C in the height of summer to −25 in the depths of winter. Yet, even here, the city continues to celebrate its external environment with its annual ice fair, during which the whole city is transformed by ice sculptures

places exploiting the period where external life is more comfortable becomes very important.

Some of the time cycles by which we structure and organise our lives have less relation to natural cycles. Zeubavel (1981 in Jackson 1994), for example, argues that much of our daily lives are structured by 'mechanical time'. We no longer, for example, rise with the dawn and retire at sunset. Despite its historical — but increasingly less relevant religious and economic — basis, the rhythm of the week is also artificial. Zeubavel (1981, from Jackson 1994: 160) suggests we are '... *increasingly detaching ourselves from "organic and functional periodicity" which is dictated by nature and replacing it by "mechanical periodicity" which is dictated by the schedule, the calendar and the clock.'*

More generally, as Kreitzman (1999: 2) argues, the 'old time-makers' — night and day, morning, noon and night, weekday and weekend — are less dominant and the grip of the old discipline of time and time constraints is weakening. While this has been a historical process — candles, gas lamps and then electric light, for example, all extended the useful hours of the day — the pace of this change is accelerating. Kreitzman (1999: 2) argues the term '24-hour society' is useful shorthand for the changes underway, serving as a metaphor for a 'different type of world'. While more pronounced in certain cities, Kreitzman (1999: 10) shows how the UK is becoming a 24-hour society. Since the late 1980s, for example, the National Grid has recorded an increase in electricity usage between 6 pm and 10 pm, which it attributes to shops staying open later and staying lit, while telephone companies have noted an increase in night-time telephone traffic.

The 24-hour society is emerging from the weakening and breakdown of time structures — in particular, the traditional structure of the working day beginning at eight or nine o'clock in the morning and ending at five o'clock or so in the afternoon, which, in the recent past, constrained and regimented our lives. As a consequence, the use of time and the pattern of activities is being variously stretched and squeezed. Kreitzman (1999: 2) argues that '… *we cannot create time but we can provide the means to use the available time more effectively so that we can free ourselves from the coiled grip of the time squeeze.'*

In the same way that the Internet and electronic communications have given freedom from the constraints of space, there is greater freedom from the constraints of time. If the distinctions between night/day and weekend/weekday are increasingly being eroded, what does this mean for the ways in which people use their time? In the short-term, at least, it results in greater freedom and diversity and, at least initially, results in greater uncertainty. In a 24-hour society, patterns of use and activity are less regimented, potentially more responsive to individual needs and preferences and, thereby, less predictable. Among other issues, it provides the opportunity for individuals to avoid peak times, thereby reducing congestion. But while the breakdown of such time structures offers new freedoms and opportunities, the costs and benefits fall on different social groups: those at the top have more freedom and flexibility; those at the bottom increasingly work longer shifts, often at unsocial hours.

The Time Management of Public Space

Those advocating mixed uses have generally done so on the basis that it creates more life and activity in a location. While a key aspect of creating lively and well-used public places is the spatial concentration of different land uses (see Chapters 6 and 8), activity must also be considered in temporal terms. Monofunctional areas — whether a consequence of functional zoning or market processes — tend to be narrowly time-specialised. While housing is often thought of as a land use providing 24-hour life and activity, this is — more precisely — a function of occupancy. Where there is a high proportion of retired people and families, it

may have good day-time levels of activity, while occupancy mainly by working people results in low levels of activity during the working day, but more in the evening and at night.

A downside of the 24-hour society is that it reduces the likelihood of the coincidence of people in time and space. This raises the spectre of increasing atomisation of society and the loss of the social bounding that occurs through events happening at a specific time, serving both to bring people together and to give them something in common. Jackson (1994: 161), for example, highlights the 'periodicity' provided by the arrival of trains in the towns of the great plains of North America. Similarly, Zerubavel (1981, from Jackson, 1994: 161–2) describes the social consequences of the sharing of schedules and calendars and routines: '*A temporal order … shared by a social group and … unique to it* [as, for example, in a religious calendar] … *contributes to the establishment of inter-group boundaries and constitutes a powerful basis of solidarity within a group.'* Nevertheless, because shops, cafes, etc., can open 24 hours per day, it does not follow that they will: efficiencies and economies in the supply of services qualify these new freedoms.

Urban designers need to understand activity patterns, how to encourage greater levels of use throughout all time periods, and how to achieve synergies from activities happening in the same space and at the same time. For Lynch (1981: 452), although 'activity timing' is as important as 'activity spacing', it is less often 'consciously manipulated':

'We have tended towards a greater precision of activity timing, and greater time specialisation: weekends, office hours, peak travel, and the like. Many spaces are used intensively for certain periods, and then stand empty for longer times.'

Timing has not been wholly neglected. One of Jacobs' four conditions for generating 'exuberant diversity' was to ensure the presence of people who go outdoors on different schedules (Jacobs, 1961: 162). However, the timing of activities may need to be managed. Lynch (1981: 452), for example, recognised that activities may be prohibited at certain times to prevent conflicts; separated in time to alleviate congestion; or brought together in time to allow connections and a sufficient density of use (e.g. the establishment of market days). Well-peopled places enable complementary activities to overlap in space and complexly interrelate, resisting the narrow time specialisation that fragments and compartmentalises activity.

Describing single-use buildings and single-purpose spaces, which are occupied between certain hours and empty the rest of the time, as 'mono-chronic', Kreitzman (1999: 146) argues that in a 24-hour society buildings and spaces need to be poly-chronic. While public space is often naturally animated by the everyday ebb and flow of people moving through spaces going about their everyday business, Montgomery (1995b: 104) argues it can also be stimulated through planned programmes of 'cultural animation', which involve programming events across a range of times and venues to encourage people to visit, use and linger in urban places. Programmes usually involve a varied diet of events and activities, such as lunch-time concerts, art exhibitions, street theatre, live music and festivals, across a range of times and venues. Thus, as people visit an area to see what is going on, urban vitality is further stimulated and the public realm becomes animated by having more people on the streets and in the cafes, etc. Montgomery stresses how the 'soft', infrastructure of events, programmes and activities is as important for successful urban revitalisation as the 'hard' infrastructure — buildings, spaces, street design, etc.

For people to choose to use public spaces, they must not only offer what they want but also do so in an attractive and safe fashion. As discussed in Chapter 6, safety is a prerequisite of a successful urban place. Peopled places are often safer places, while the areas people are most concerned about are those that are deserted or crowded with the 'wrong kind' of people.

Although the public spaces of many cities and urban areas are well-used during the day and during working hours, a widespread problem is the lack of activity during the evening and at night, with few uses and activities to attract a broad range of social groups. A particular issue is the so-called 'dead' period in city centres between the end of the typical working day and the start of the night-time economy when people come back into the centre in search of recreation and entertainment. The '24-hour city' concept and explicit promotion and development of the 'evening economy' are approaches to revitalising city centres that attempt to address these issues (see Bianchini 1994; Montgomery 1994). They also form responses to the functional zoning policies and the 'hollowing out' of the central area of cities.

The evening economy and the 24-hour city concepts (see Chapter 6) are influenced both by cities in continental Europe that are inherently 24-hour in their nature and those that have developed policies to revitalise their urban nightlife, and more generally to regenerate and create safer city centres (see Heath & Stickland 1997: 170). Unless evening economy and 24-hour city strategies are broadly based, they are susceptible to being male-oriented and alcohol-fixated with

'... nothing to offer those workers with "carer" responsibilities who have no time to stay on in the town centre drinking the night away, as they have to get back home and start on the "second-shift" of cooking, housework and childcare.'

(Greed 1999: 203).

The need is for evening economies based on encouraging 'entertainment', rather than alcohol, and activities for a wide range of social and age groups. There are also a series of micro-management issues relating to conflicts between, for example, noise-generating activities (cafes, bars and music venues) and noise-sensitive activities (city centre residential uses) (see Chatterton & Hollands 2002; Tiesdell & Slater 2006; Roberts & Eldridge 2009).

THE MARCH OF TIME

As well as the repetitive rhythms of time, a second way in which we know that time has passed is through evidence of progressive and irreversible change. In a very real sense, the past is fixed and the future open. While we may yearn to turn back the clock, to return to the city we knew as a child, or to relive a wonderful moment, we are unable to do so. This is the relentless 'march of time' or — in the astrophysicist Arthur Eddington's (1927, from Coveney & Highfield 1990) evocative term — the 'arrow of time'. The immediate kinaesthetic experience of urban space was discussed in Chapter 7. The long-term experience and passage of time within places will be discussed here.

Urban environments are continuously and inexorably changing. From the first drawing through to the final demolition, environments and buildings are shaped and reshaped by technological, economic, social and cultural change. Brand (1994: 7) argues that commercial buildings have to adapt particularly quickly: *'Most businesses either grow or fail. If they grow, they move; if they fail, they're gone. … Commercial buildings are forever metamorphic.'*

Furthermore, any intervention into the physical fabric of a place irreversibly changes its history for all time, becoming part of that history. All urban design actions are, thus, contributions to broader, open and evolving systems and contributions to a greater whole. Although never static, the built environment stands as testament to processes of continuity, change and the passage of time within a particular place. Knox & Ozolins (2000: 3), for example, argue that:

'... a building or other element of the built environment of a given period and type tends to be a carrier of the zeitgeist, or "spirit" of its time. Every city can therefore be "read" as a multi-layered "text", a narrative of signs and symbols. … the built environment becomes a biography of urban change.'

Similarly, for Mumford (1938), it is by the 'diversity of its time structures' that *'... the city in part escapes the tyranny of a single present and the monotony of a future that consists in repeating only a single beat heard in the past.'* (Figure 9.2)

Until the Industrial Revolution, and except when natural forces or war wracked wholesale destruction, change in the urban fabric was both gradual and relatively small-scale. Cities evolved over time through seemingly 'natural' processes: that is, they grew — or at least appeared to

FIGURE 9.2 Sacramento Old Town, Sacramento, California, USA (*Image: Steve Tiesdell*). Except as museums — and increasingly as simulacra — of themselves, what is the future of such places?

grow — organically. Successive generations were able to derive a sense of continuity and stability from their physical surroundings. Since the Industrial Revolution both the pace and scale of change have increased, as both the processes of change and the impact of those processes radically altered. Modernists argued that the means of controlling and directing these processes of change also needed to be radically rethought: societies needed large-scale, social and economic organisation and to harness the benefits of science, technology and rationalism.

One consequence of Modernism's enthusiasm for the zeitgeist was to emphasise differences, rather than to acknowledge continuities, with the past. The legacy from the past was seen as a hindrance to the future. The pioneer Modernists, for example, visualised sweeping away the cramped and unhealthy cities of their time, replacing them with a new and radically different environment consisting of high-rise buildings standing among trees and vegetation. The clean-sweep mentality and the desire for a *tableau rasa* lead to a preference for comprehensive redevelopment schemes, rather than more incremental — and arguably sensitive — development. It was also confidently and persuasively argued that comprehensive redevelopment would provide significant physical improvements, and further justified by claims and desires for progress and modernity.

The opportunity to develop such ideas came after 1945 in the reconstruction of war-damaged cities in Europe, and subsequently through slum clearance programmes and road-building schemes. Accordingly, the post-war period saw dramatic acceleration in the pace and physical scale of the cycle of demolition and renewal in most cities in the developed world. Ashworth & Tunbridge (1990: 1), for example, note how this period

'… led to an abrupt break in the centuries-long evolution of the physical fabric of cities. The past and its values [were] rejected in favour of a "brave new world" whose creation threatened to destroy all trace of preceding architectural achievement.'

For most of the initial post-war period, the destruction of much of the physical, social and cultural fabric of central and inner city areas was accepted without serious question. But, by the mid-1960s, the social effects of this destruction were becoming evident. Frequent and increasingly widespread public protest ushered in a period of increased concern for — and subsequently a widespread public consensus in favour of — conservation, which involved a desire to retain existing and familiar environments. The consensus was initially reactionary: the public had had enough of the brutal and insensitive change and desired familiar environments to be improved but kept substantially intact. Policies protecting historic areas were introduced all over the developed world during the 1960s and early 1970s. At the same time, conservation became an integral, rather than a peripheral, part of urban planning and development. The emergence of conservation also provoked a fundamental questioning and re-evaluation of ideas in architecture, planning and urban development, and was critical to the emergence of express concerns for urban design and place-making.

Conservation

Lynch (1972: 35–6) outlined a series of questions encapsulating various debates about the purpose and practice of conservation:

'*Are we looking for evidence of climatic moments or for any manifestation of tradition we can find, or are we judging and evaluating the past, choosing the more significant over the less, retaining what we think of as best?*

'*Should things be saved because they were associated with important persons or events? Because they are unique or nearly so or quite the contrary, because they were most typical of their time? Because of their importance as a group symbol? Because of their intrinsic qualities in the present? Because of their special usefulness as sources of intellectual information about the past?*

'*Or should we simply (as we most often do) let chance select for us and preserve for a second century everything that has happened to survive the first?*'

Accepting that the reasons for conserving historic building and environments are many, and often culture-, context- and building-specific, Tiesdell *et al* (1995: 11–7) list the more common justifications:

- *Aesthetic value* — historic buildings and environments are valued because they are intrinsically beautiful or because they have a scarcity value.
- *Value for architectural diversity and contrast* — existing environments are valued for the architectural diversity

that results from the proximity of buildings of many different ages.

- *Value for environmental diversity and contrast* – within many cities, there is often a stimulating contrast between the human-scale environment of their historic areas and the monumental scale of their Central Business Districts.
- *Value for functional diversity* – a diverse range of different types of space in buildings of varying ages, enabling a mix of uses. Older buildings and areas may offer lower rents allowing economically marginal but socially important activities to have a place in the city.
- *Resource value* – as buildings are committed expenditure, their re-use constitutes conservation of scarce resources, a reduction in the consumption of energy and materials in construction and good resource management.
- *Value for continuity of cultural memory and heritage* – visible evidence of the past can contribute educationally to the cultural identity and memory of a particular people or place, giving meaning to the present by interpreting the past.
- *Economic and commercial value* – older environments provide a distinctive sense-of-place, offering opportunities for economic development and tourism.

In most countries, preservation and conservation as a widespread and coherent practice are relatively recent. Lefebvre (1991: 360) describes how attitudes to conservation have typically changed over time:

'... countries in the throes of rapid development blithely destroy historic spaces – houses, palaces, military or civil structures. If advantage or profit is to be found in it, then the old is swept away. Later, however... these same countries are liable to discover how such spaces may be pressed into the service of cultural consumption, of "culture itself", and of the tourism and the leisure industries with their almost limitless prospects. When this happens, everything

that they had so merrily demolished during the belle époque is reconstituted at great expense. Where destruction has not been complete, "renovation" becomes the order of the day, or imitation, or replication, or neo-this or neo-that.'

Conservation policies and strategies came in four waves (see Table 9.1). The first involved the protection of individual buildings and historic/ancient monuments. Although this started in many countries during the nineteenth century, more consistent and comprehensive practice developed after 1945.

Realisation that the settings of historic buildings also needed protection led to a second wave of policies emerging during the 1960s and 1970s. These area-based policies were concerned with groups of historic buildings, townscape and the spaces between buildings. Such policies were also a reaction to the evident social, cultural and physical disruption caused by policies of clearance and comprehensive redevelopment and by road-building schemes. Rather than 'preservation' policies, these were 'conservation' policies: preservation being concerned with stopping or limiting change; conservation about the inevitability of change and the management of that change. Lynch (1972: 233), for example, argued that the key to conservation was to '... *disentangle it from the idea of preserving the past.'*

In most countries, the change from the protection of individual buildings to conservation areas rapidly developed from a straightforward and restrictive concern with preservation to a concern with the management of change and with revitalisation. The third and – more fragmentary – wave was thus the development of local revitalisation policies, which, in essence, stemmed from realisation that once historic buildings and areas were protected they needed to be in active and viable use. While the initial preservation policies had largely been concerned with the 'pastness of the past', the later conservation and revitalisation policies were increasingly about a 'future for the past' (Fawcett 1976).

TABLE 9.1 Four Waves of Conservation Policy

	Preservation	Conservation	Revitalisation	Stewardship
Rationale	Protection (preservation) of individual buildings and structures.	Management of change.	Economic development to enable buildings to be protected through being in active use.	Area management to protect and enhance sense- and quality-of-place.
Challenge	Protection of elite buildings.	Protection of many buildings – but too many to all be museums or to be protected at public expense.	Economic development that is sensitive to sense-of-place and to historic buildings.	Manage conflicts between different land uses. Social character. Physical changes.
Key Actors	Art historians.	Conservation planners.	Conservation planners. Experts in economic development.	Conservation planners. Urban managers and place management organisations.

While they had been saved *from* destruction, the next issue was to consider what they had been saved *for*. There was also a simultaneous broadening of the locus of professional concern from architects and art historians to planners, urban designers, economic development specialists and others, including notably cultural anthropologists, historians and geographers. The fourth wave was the stewardship and continuing care of the conserved and newly revitalised areas.

Continuity of Place — A Continuing Narrative

The emergence of conservation resulted in increased concern and respect for the uniqueness of places and their history and, in large part, was instrumental in the evolution of contemporary urban design. Many current approaches to urban design respond to the existing sense-of-place, stressing 'continuity with' rather than emphasising a 'break from' the past. In a world of rapid change, visual and tangible evidence of the past is valued for the sense-of-place and continuity it conveys. As the elements of the city change at different rates, some 'essence' of a city's identity is retained despite ongoing and constant change. In many cities, for example, street and plot patterns have seen and accommodated incremental change. As discussed in Chapter 4, Buchanan (1988a: 32) argued that the movement network, and the monuments and civic buildings within and adjacent to it, are the relatively permanent parts of the city. Within this more permanent framework, individual buildings come and go, but it is the parts that endure over time — including the buildings able to survive — that contribute to the sense of continuity, and provide evidence of the progression of time, within that place. 'Robust' patterns of development, therefore, provide stability and continuity of place.

The relative permanence of an urban space helps establish its qualities as a meaningful place, while its physicality provides tangible record of the passage of time and embodies 'social memory'. Focusing on the effect of time on the changing fabric of a city, Rossi (1982) discussed the idea of a city's 'collective memory', where urban form was a repository of culture from the past and for the future. Rossi argued that the fabric of the city consists of two elements: the general urban 'texture' of buildings lining streets and squares, which would change over time, and 'monuments' — large-scale buildings whose presence gave each city its particular character and embodied the 'memory' of the city (see also Boyer, 1994).

There are, however, alternative attitudes to the physical continuity of places and the value attributed to the sense-of-place. As well as a disdain for much of the built legacy of the past, Modernists embraced ideas about the 'impermanence' of buildings — ideas based on the potential of industrial production. Buildings, like cars, could be a mass-produced product with built-in

obsolescence, designed to be discarded once the immediate utility was exhausted (see, for example, MacCormac 1983: 741). Such attitudes are antithetical both to architecture's traditional place-making and place-defining qualities and to the importance attached to considerations of environmental sustainability.

Nonetheless, taken to extremes, extensive preservation and conservation can obstruct, frustrate, even halt a city's evolution and development. Emphasising the necessity of adaptability, Lynch (1972: 39) argued that environments that could not be changed 'invited their own destruction':

'We prefer a world that can be modified progressively against a background of valued remains, a world in which one can leave a personal mark alongside the marks of history. … The management of change and the active use of remains for present and future purposes are preferable to an inflexible reverence for a sacrosanct past.'

To preserve the capacity for change, environments must be capable of evolution — able to '… *welcome the future and accommodate the present without severing the thread of continuity with the past.*' (Burtenshaw *et al* 1991: 159) (Figure 9.3).

The issues are not black and white — total preservation is rarely completely right and total redevelopment completely wrong. Instead, it is usually a matter of balance. Lynch (1972: 236), for example, advocates exposing 'successive eras of history' and inserting new material that enhances the past by 'allusion and contrast', with the aim of producing '… *a setting more and more densely packed with references to the stream of time rather than a setting that never changed.*' Such approaches emphasise a need for new development to express or represent its own zeitgeist.

Pendlebury (1999) identified three conservationist paradigms — preservationist; visual management (heritage) and morpho-conservationist (see Figure 9.4 and Table 9.2). These paradigms can be illustrated through their different responses to the practice of facadism (see Box 9.1). In the preservationist paradigm, facadism is unacceptable; visual management has little difficulty with the practice; while the morpho-conservationist response is conflicted and nuanced.

More generally, to work within established contexts, urban designers need to understand how environments adapt to change and, more importantly, why some environments adapt better than others. The visual and physical continuity of valued places relates to issues of the 'obsolescence' of buildings and environments, the time frames of change, and the 'robustness' and 'resilience' of the built fabric and other physical attributes of that place. Going beyond narrower conceptions of 'conservation', these interrelated concepts are all aspects of the effects of time and change on buildings and environments.

FIGURE 9.3 City of London (*Image: Matthew Carmona*). Older buildings give both material and symbolic stability to an area. New interventions generally reflect progress and advancement. The protected views of St Paul's Cathedral in London are designed to maintain the city's sense of history, with Sir Christopher Wren's dome symbolising the city. This can be contrasted with the demand for new high-rise office development in the Square Mile, which reflects the city's contemporary role as a world financial centre

Obsolescence

Obsolescence is the reduction in the useful life of a capital good. There are several interrelated dimensions of obsolescence: some are attributes of the building and/or its functions, others relate to the area as a whole (see Table 9.3). Obsolescence is primary an outcome of the inability of 'fixed' urban structures and locations to adapt to change,

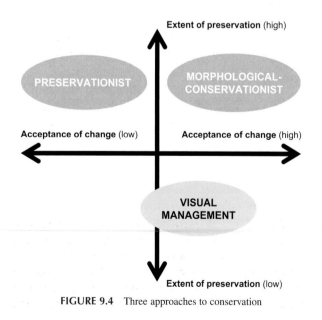

FIGURE 9.4 Three approaches to conservation

whether technological, economic, social or cultural. The typical life cycle of a building can be described as follows: when commissioned, it will be built to the contemporary standards of building construction, will usually be 'state-of-the-art' with regard to its function and appropriately located for that function. As the building ages and the world around it changes, factors relating to its profitability change and the building becomes increasingly obsolescent relative to newer buildings. Eventually it falls out of use and is abandoned and/or demolished and the site redeveloped.

As obsolescence is rarely absolute, an important consideration is *economic* or *relative obsolescence* — the degree of obsolescence with regard to the cost of alternative opportunities, which include competition from other buildings and areas, the cost of alternative development on the site and the cost of development on an alternative site.

When buildings are regarded as obsolescent, a distinction should also be made between obsolescence in their *current use* and that for *any use*. A warehouse located in or near the city centre might be obsolete in its current use but could be converted to residential use (i.e. the obsolescence is cured by the change of use). A further distinction should also be made between 'curable' obsolescence (that which is cost-efficient to cure) and non-curable obsolescence (that which is not cost-efficient to cure).

Conservation controls afford historic buildings an 'administrative layer of protection', which prolongs their

TABLE 9.2 Conservation Paradigms

	Preservationist	Morpho-conservationist	Visual Management
Rationale and ethos	'Purist' — single-minded concern for retention of authentic 'historic' fabric.	Evolving sense-of-place with past, present and future — a 'continuing narrative', in which sense-of-place is a product of development and evolution over time.	'Pragmatic — holistic concern including viability factors (but danger of expediency). Freezes/embalms historic sense-of-place.
Origins/evolution	Reaction to Victorian over-restoration. Debates about appropriate treatment of particularly important historic sites or monuments.	Based on study of settlement's historical development (process) — development of townscape seen as physical manifestation of the development of society and imbrued with cultural meaning, becoming spirit-of-place (genius loci).	Need for conservation of historic areas — response to opportunities for economic development through tourism and commodification of place/heritage.
Philosophy of intervention	Minimal intervention — leave it be. Change visible and preferably reversible.	Focus on processes of change — though intervention should be within grain/sense-of-place (i.e. importance given to maintaining sense-of-place). Change accommodated; becomes part of the continuing narrative.	Importance given to retention of external spatial and visual character. Change hidden to enable conformity with heritage theme corresponding to historic sense-of-place.
Significance of historic fabric (attitude to rehabilitation and facadism)	Retention of historic fabric is paramount, with high value placed on authenticity. Integrity of historic structure as a whole — thus facadism is unacceptable due to loss of integrity of buildings.	Retention of historic fabric is important — though not necessarily primary issue. Intervention must be based on detailed and sophisticated understanding of the evolution of urban form, particularly patterns, forms and motifs created. Acceptability of facadism depends on individual case (e.g. whether contained within original plot).	Less important. Least concerned with historic fabric — more oriented to aesthetic and urban design considerations. Facadism seen as legitimate.
New development: spatial character	Neutral.	Need to respect existing morphology, scale, massing, etc., as contribution to sense-of-place. Design should respect historic form (e.g. plot lines).	Need to respect scale, massing, etc., in principal locations.
New development: visual character	Buildings should be 'of-their-time'.	Neutral.	Generally historicist approach — new development should match historic sense-of-place.
Public realm design	Design should be contemporary.	Neutral	Generally historicist approach — new street furniture should match historic sense-of-place approach — e.g. 'period-style' street furniture.

Source: Adapted and extended from Pendlebury (1999: 425).

normal life cycle but increases the likelihood of obsolescence (Larkham 1996: 79). In effect, the extra layer of control/regulation creates a form of non-physical resilience (see below). While conservation controls may constrain or inhibit — or even deter — rehabilitation and new development, they do so to ensure the survival — conservation — of

the building or environment. Conservation of historic areas and buildings frequently entails keeping them in active use, which provides the necessary finance to maintain the historic fabric. In terms of economic activity, changes in occupation with new uses or activities replacing the former ones may give the building a new lease of life. The fabric

BOX 9.1 Facadism

It is often taken as axiomatic that buildings should have an 'honest' relationship between plan, facade and section (see Chapter 7). Instances where this relation is false or weak are usually known as facadism. Facadism refers to two distinct situations. The more general situation is a functional and structural 'dishonesty' between the interior and the exterior of a building. This principle can, however, be taken too far (see Watkin's *Morality and Architecture* 1984). Brolin (1980: 5–6), for example, argues that:

'… no virtue or higher morality is served by expressing interior uses "honestly" on the exterior. This is one moral preoccupation of Modernism which should be less important than the visual relationship between the building's exterior and its architectural context.'

The more specific situation is where a new building is built behind a retained facade. This type of facadism often raises questions about the value of retaining the facade of an older building.

Facadism in Philadelphia, Pennsylvania *(image, Matthew Carmona)*, despite being four stories, the retained facade is perceived as a dolls house

Richmond Riverside, London (*Image: Matthew Carmona*). Although the facade suggests a number of separate buildings, the development consists of a few large office buildings with open office floors extending across what from the outside seem to be party walls

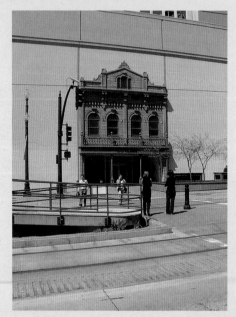

Facadism in Salt Lake City, Utah (*Image: Steve Tiesdell*). Where new buildings are placed behind retained facades, the new building's height generally needs to be similar to that of the building being replaced

Cambridge (*Image: Matthew Carmona*) Facadism is not new. Here a classical revival facade was placed on a Gothic building.

TABLE 9.3 Types of Obsolescence

Type	Occurrence/Cause	Consequence
Physical		
Building-specific	• Occurs as the building's fabric deteriorates through the effects of time, the weather, or through poor maintenance.	• Building needs repair over and above that offered by regular, ongoing maintenance. • Without refurbishment, building's physical condition interferes with its occupation — increases likelihood of demolition or abandonment.
Structural		
Building-specific	• Occurs as the building's structure deteriorates through the effects of time, the weather, earth movement, traffic vibration or through poor maintenance.	• Building needs repair over and above that offered by regular, ongoing maintenance. • Without repairs, building's structural condition interferes with its occupation — increases likelihood of demolition or abandonment.
Functional		
Building-specific Land-use specific Area-specific	• Occurs when the building is no longer suited for the function for which it was designed or is currently used. • Also arises from external factors on which the building's present use depends (e.g. difficulties of access as a result of narrow streets or traffic congestion).	• Curable by change of land use. • New technology may 'rescue' building/area.
Image/Style		
Building-specific Land-use specific	• Product of perceptions of a building or area. • Can apply to all possible uses of the building or be specific to a particular use (the present use).	• As a value judgement, may lack underlying substance. • Curable by change of land use.
Legal		
Building-specific Land-use specific Area-specific	• Occurs when a public agency determines certain minimum standards of functionality that the building does not or is not able to achieve. Also occurs where an area's zoning ordinance permits a larger building on the site.	• Building cannot be used for either its current use and/or for any use — increases likelihood of demolition or abandonment. • New technology may 'rescue' building/area.
Official		
Building-specific Area-specific	• Occurs when public authority designates an area to be acquired and cleared for (say) road building, road widening or comprehensive redevelopment.	• Increases likelihood of demolition or abandonment. • Designation may be overturned.
Location		
Land-use specific Area-specific	• Occurs due to its fixed location relative to changes in wider patterns of accessibility, labour costs, etc.	• Curable by change of land use.
Financial		
Building-specific	• Occurs through accounting and taxation procedures, which treat buildings as capital assets and assign them a depreciable life — building is regarded as a wasting asset.	• Once depreciable life has expired the building no longer appears on the balance sheet (i.e. its depreciable life has ended) — building still has an intrinsic value, but no longer has value for tax purposes.
Relative		
Building-specific Land-use specific Area-specific	• Obsolescence is always relative to the competing supply (stock) of buildings and locations.	• Buildings are rarely obsolete in an absolute sense.

Building-specific means that the obsolescence only affects specific buildings in an area.
Area-specific means that obsolescence affects all buildings in the area.
Source: adapted and extended from Lichfield (1988: 22–5; Tiesdell *et al* (1996).

may be adapted to contemporary requirements through various modes of intervention, which Fitch (1990: 46—7) lists as follows:

- *Preservation* involves maintaining a building in its current physical condition.
- *Restoration* is the process of returning the artefact to the physical condition it had at some previous stage of its life.
- *Refurbishment (conservation and consolidation)* entails physical intervention in the building's fabric to ensure its continued performance.
- *Reconstitution* entails a building's piece-by-piece re-assembly, either in situ or on a new site.
- *Conversion (adaptive re-use)* entails adapting a building to accommodate a new use.
- *Reconstruction* entails re-creating vanished buildings on their original site.
- *Replication* entails constructing an exact copy of an existing building.
- *Facadism* entails preserving the facade of an historic building with a new building built behind the retained facade.
- *Demolition and redevelopment* entails demolishing a building, clearing the site and undertaking new development.

While this illustrates the range of options, what is desirable or possible in any particular situation varies and, as Lowenthal (1981: 14) opines, '... *there is little point in "saving" the past if what is saved is debased or altered beyond recognition.*' Furthermore, dealing with existing or historic buildings and environments is no longer a case of 'new being better than old' or 'old better than new' but increasingly the nature of the vital relationship between the two (see Powell, 1999). In considering the character of existing buildings and environments, there are more permutations than fawning, restrictive reverence and simplistic — even contemptuous — dismissal. Furthermore, as discussed in Chapter 5, there are also issues concerning authenticity and 'reinvented places'.

Time Frames of Change

An essential element of urban design's time dimension is the need for urban designers to understand what stays the same and what changes over time. As discussed in Chapter 4, Conzen (1960) emphasised the difference in stability of the major morphological elements. While street and plot patterns survive a long time, buildings and, in particular, land uses are less resilient. In many places, however, buildings have lasted for hundreds of years, thereby helping to sustain and contributing to a sense of time within the place. Although the land uses within buildings have often changed, their exterior appearance and form have remained largely unchanged. Such buildings have qualities of robustness (see below).

Survival of now historic buildings and environments largely happened prior to the widespread practice of state intervention into the property market to conserve them: buildings from the past '... *survived fortuitously largely on their own merits, and chiefly because they continued to serve useful purposes.*' (Burke 1976: 117). While this may have been through simple economic necessity, it was also an expression of certain aesthetic and cultural values — the urban scene was considered sufficiently desirable, culturally or economically or both, to be retained rather than demolished.

For Duffy (1990), a building can be conceived of as a series of layers of longevities: the 'shell' or structure lasts the lifetime of the building; the 'services' (i.e. the cabling, plumbing, air conditioning, elevators, etc.) have to be replaced every 15 years or so; the 'scenery' (i.e. the layout of partitions, dropped ceilings, etc.) changes every five to seven years; while 'sets' (i.e. the layout of furniture) change over weeks and months. Brand (1994: 13—5) extends and develops Duffy's series of layers to create a series of six systems (see Table 9.4).

The systems are differently paced — 'site' and 'structure' are the slowest; 'stuff' and 'space plan' the quickest. The key to robust buildings — those able to accommodate change — is to allow the faster-paced systems to change without the need for change in the slower-paced systems

TABLE 9.4 Brand's Six Systems

Site	The legally defined lot, whose boundaries and context outlast generations of ephemeral buildings.
Structure	The foundation and load-bearing elements, the structural life of which ranges from 30 to 300 years and more.
Skin	The exterior surfaces, which — to keep up with fashion or technology, or for wholesale repair — may change every 20 years or so. (Note that, in load-bearing masonry structures, the skin is also the structure, while, in cladding systems, the skin is pure skin and can be unclipped and changed relatively easily.)
Services	The communications wiring, electrical wiring, plumbing, sprinkler system, heating, ventilation, and air conditioning, and moving parts such as lifts and escalators, which wear out or are replaced every seven to fifteen years.
Space plan	The interior layout (i.e. where walls, ceiling, floors and doors go) — the rate of change of which depends on the land use: commercial space will change more frequently than more spaces plans in a family house.
Stuff	Chairs, desks, phones, pictures, etc. — things that are moved around daily or weekly.

Source: Adapted from Brand (1994: 13—5).

(i.e. changing the services should not require change to the structure). The key issue is that, in robust buildings, the structure should not impose on and restrict the freedom of the more rapidly changing systems. Equally, it may be that the building's enduing character is embedded in the slower-moving systems.

Resilience and Robustness

'Resilience' and 'robustness' are sometimes used interchangeably. The distinction is that resilience is the ability to *resist* change without undue deformation (i.e. it resists the wearing effects of time and change — that is, physical and structural obsolescence), while robustness is the ability to *accommodate* change without significant change in the physical form (i.e. it resists functional obsolescence). Robustness is not just about form and function, however, because additional significance usually derives from the values, meanings and symbols associated with and embodied by that form. Robust buildings thus also need the elusive quality of 'charm': minor, and sometimes major, inconveniences in a building with charm are indulged; similar inconveniences in buildings lacking charm can often prove fatal (Figure 9.5).

One of the first explicit discussions of robustness was by Anderson in his book, *On Streets* (1978). Anderson drew on Gans' argument that physical settings can be interpreted as 'potential' environments providing a range of environmental possibilities and opportunities and that, at any moment in time, what is achieved is the 'resultant' or 'effective' environment (see Chapter 6). For Anderson, the 'latent' environment was the extent of the environmental possibilities not currently being exploited (whether or not those possibilities are recognised). For example, when

FIGURE 9.5 Warehouse conversions, Milwaukee (*Image: Steve Tiesdell*). As industrial lofts and warehouses converted to residential apartments connote 'artistic' and 'bohemian' qualities, the desire to convert such buildings is not just a consequence of the building's functionality but also its character

industrial lofts were first constructed, it was not anticipated that they would subsequently accommodate residential uses. Robustness is, thus, a function of the relationship between a building's form and the uses it can accommodate. Many land uses are relatively adaptable and can be accommodated within a variety of forms. Buildings, by contrast, are less flexible, and those that are overly specialised reduce the potential to accommodate changing land uses. Brand (1994: 192) makes the general point that, because technology changes faster than buildings and is usually more flexible than buildings, it is better to let the technology adapt to the building rather than vice versa.

Although Modernist functionalist doctrines espoused the concept of 'form follows function', the relationship between activities/land uses and spaces/forms is complex. Lynch (1972: 72), for example, observes that:

'Activities shift cyclically and progressively within their relatively unchanging spatial containers. The form of these containers cannot therefore "follow function" unless the use of a space is reduced to some single, invariant type of behaviour.'

Similarly, Tschumi (1983a: 31) identified three types of relationship between form and function: *indifference* — where 'space' and 'event' are functionally independent of one another; *reciprocity* — where spaces and events are totally interdependent and fully condition each other's existence; and *conflict* — where a space purposely designed for a particular function (subsequently) accommodates a completely different function. Additional meaning, and sometimes aesthetic richness, often derives from the latter relationship — a riverside power station converted to an art gallery, for example, can add new meaning to the artwork displayed (Figure 9.6).

Although robustness is the quality of averting, delaying or avoiding the loss of utility occasioned by the onset of functional obsolescence, functional obsolescence is not solely an attribute of the building and also relates to external factors, which can both create obsolescence and restore the utility of buildings without change to those buildings. The office stock of the City of London provides an interesting example. By the early 1980s, office buildings needed to handle the additional heat load resulting from the increased use of personal computers and the increasing cabling requirement related to the increased electronic and electrical servicing of workstations. New buildings would have larger floor-to-floor heights allowing for additional cooling equipment and a raised floor for cabling. The existing stock, however, faced the prospect of obsolescence. Accordingly, developers saw opportunities to redevelop sites in the City of London or for new development elsewhere, such as Canary Wharf. In practice, however, a new generation of personal computers with internal fans, together with the introduction of fibre-optic cables, extended the useful life of much of the City of London's

FIGURE 9.6 Bankside Power Station converted to the Tate Modern, London (*Image: Steve Tiesdell*)

office stock and the anticipated functional obsolescence did not materialise.

Robustness embodies the concept of 'long life/loose fit' — designing-in capacity for change so that buildings are able to adapt, alleviating the need or desire for redevelopment. Lynch (1972: 108–9) argues that 'environmental adaptivity' can be achieved by providing *excess capacity* at the outset; providing *generous communication facilities*; separating those elements likely to change from those unlikely to change; and allowing *space for growth* at the ends, sides or within sectors. For Brand (1994: 174) the evolution of both organisations and buildings is 'always and necessarily surprising'; adaptivity cannot be predicted or controlled and thus, in practice: '*All you can do is make room for it — room at the bottom.*'

The lifetime of buildings is unknowable: those intended for the short-term often only survive into what becomes the long-term; those intended for the long-term sometimes only survive the short-term. The choices are to design environments and buildings for the short-term — either through what Lawson (2001: 194–5) terms 'non-committal' design, which tends to result in bland, anonymous and neutral results, meant for the present only, with obsolescence built-in, and intended to be quickly thrown away and replaced with a more up-to-date version — or to design for the long-term. The former suggests a fundamental lack of

commitment to place — the light (and fleeting) touchdown of global capital as it arrives in a locality, while constantly looking for a better opportunity elsewhere. The sustainable option is to build resilient buildings with charm and character, designed to be robust (see Sustainability Insert 6).

Given the difficulty of predicating the likely changes that might occur during a building's expected life, there is value in learning from buildings that have successfully coped with changing uses. Studies by Duffy (1990), Bentley *et al* (1985), Moudon (1987) and Brand (1994) identify three key factors that influence the long-term robustness of buildings — cross-sectional depth, access and room shape (see Table 9.5). In Brand's hierarchy, these are all aspects of 'structure'. Building configurations that support robustness tend to be shallow in plan, relatively low-rise, and have many points of access, and generally to have regularly shaped rooms or spaces. While not all buildings can take this form, much of the building stock in any particular locality can. Few land uses have highly specialised requirements, and even those that do usually have less specialised parts.

Beyond the scale of the building, resilience should be a feature of both public space and the larger urban fabric. Robust and resilient urban space might be characterised by a number of key properties:

- *Open* — Not filled with 'paraphernalia' — un-movable hard and soft landscaping — or needlessly sub-divided into small single-use areas.
- *Flexible* — Capable of sub-division, but also offering the possibility for use as a large space to cater for a variety of uses/events.
- *Varied* — Not dominated by a single mode of travel (i.e. by roads) or infrastructure requirements, or by single uses. Many market squares, for example, cater for markets one day, festivities and special event the next, and quiet contemplation or car parking thereafter.
- *Comfortable* — Able to respond to different micro-climatic and weather needs — offering shelter from sun and rain, but also access to the sun when required (see Chapter 8).
- *Sociable* — Able to support different types and patterns of social activity (e.g. public display, privacy and collective and individual space).

Not only must sustainable environments be designed for robustness, they must also be designed to enable and facilitate maintenance. While high-quality materials help, the detailing of those materials and maintenance regimes are also important. The best strategies in terms of the physical fabric are either to prevent buildings from entering the spiral by 'preventative maintenance' — routinely servicing materials and systems in the building before they fail — and/or by designing and constructing the building to reduce the need for maintenance (Brand 1994: 112). The longer buildings and environments are expected to last, the

Sustainability Insert 6 – Robustness and Resilience

Building places with resilience and capacity-for-change (robustness) is profoundly sustainable because, once constructed, the built environment represents a considerable investment in energy and resources. The embodied energy in the infrastructure of a typical town or city, for example, typically represents many times more energy than ongoing processes of development and redevelopment will consume in many decades. For their part, buildings will continue to use energy once constructed – studies of conventional new houses indicate that, within five years, the accumulated energy costs in use exceed the embodied energy of the actual basic construction (Barton *et al* 1995: 133) – but, as more energy-efficient construction techniques are adopted, so the energy and resources invested in the construction process become more significant. Building to last also reduces the pressure on sources of construction materials, reduces the waste from, and energy used in, demolition, disposal and/or recycling and requires the construction of more resilient public spaces, urban patterns and infrastructure. This last concern is significant because, to be long-lasting, patterns of development need also to be adaptable

(robust) at the urban scale, as well as at the scale of individual buildings: public spaces need to cater for the many overlapping and sometimes incompatible functions; while settlement patterns need to be able to adapt over time to changing technologies, patterns of life and work and movement (Barton 2000: 130–2).

Research for the UK government suggests public spaces will have a key role in the future in delivering energy resilience – through hosting micro-generation technologies (wind, photo-voltaic and heat pump) –as countries search for ways to reduce their reliance on high-carbon fuel sources (GOS 2008: 148–50). Whatever measures are put in place to reduce climate change, it is still likely that the delayed effects of greenhouse gas emissions will be increasingly felt. In Western Europe, for example, more extreme weather conditions are anticipated, including hotter and drier summers, warmer and wetter winters, rising sea levels and flooding. This will require the design of buildings and spaces now that can adapt to these changed circumstances over time. For CABE (2009: 1) this requires working with the natural processes of the city:

Hammarby Sjöstad, Stockholm (*Image: Matthew Carmona*) integrates a robust urban block layout with its natural surroundings

'Spaces that are softer, greener, more organic and natural will store water and are critical to modifying urban temperatures. Green spaces with a generous planting of trees can link to form a network offering cooler, cleaner air.

Adaptation demands that we start really understanding how our towns and cities work naturally. How water courses through a town, for instance, and so how to manage it.' (see Sustainability Insert 4).

more that maintenance and other running costs will overwhelm the initial capital costs of construction and, hence, the greater the incentive for owners to invest in better construction to reduce future maintenance costs. This, however, relates to the distribution of costs between the developer and initial funders and subsequent owners, occupants, tenants and users (see Chapter 10). Nonetheless, as Tibbalds (1992: 72) warned: '*... unlike a landscape that*

will mature over time, a building, unless well cared for, will do the exact opposite – it will deteriorate.' In this respect, urban designers can learn from landscape designers, who recognise that design is a matter of directing a process of continuous change, where success depends on carefully managing what has been created.

Most of the world's great cities have proven adept at accommodating change. In such places the urban structures

TABLE 9.5 Key Physical Factors Affecting Robustness of Buildings

(i) Cross-sectional depth	Cross-sectional depth has a critical impact on the need for artificial lighting and ventilation, which in turn affects the variety of uses that can be accommodated. As most building uses require natural light and ventilation, buildings that are too deep cannot easily change use. Llewelyn-Davies (2000: 94) outlines the implications of different cross-sectional building depths: • Depths less than 9 m provide potential for good daylighting and ventilation but are usually too shallow for a central corridor and have limited flexibility in internal planning. • Depths between 9 and 13 m provide naturally lit and ventilated space and the opportunity for a central corridor (and, therefore, optimum robustness). • Depths between 14 and 15 m still facilitate sub-division, but some artificial ventilation and more artificial lighting are usually required. • Depths of greater than about 16 m require increasing amounts of mechanical ventilation and artificial lighting, and accordingly are more energy-intensive.
(ii) Access	As all buildings need some links to the outside world, the number of access points — and, as critically, egress points in the event of fire — governs how readily a building can adapt to a variety of uses. Building height is a particular constraint in this respect — in a tall building, the upper floors have restricted links to the outside, and, thus, are less suitable for a wide range of uses.
(iii) Room shape and size	In buildings intended to be robust, the rooms need to be sized to accommodate a broad range of activities, while also being capable of sub-division (which may relate to window positions) and/or being joined together to create larger spaces. In domestic buildings, rooms that are 10–13 m² in area, for example, can serve as bedrooms, kitchens, living rooms or dining rooms. Dwellings consisting of a series of rooms of this size have proved relatively robust during cycles of change between family houses and smaller flats (see Moudon 1987). Brand (1994: 192) also contends the rectangle is the only configuration of space that grows well, sub-divides well and is efficient to use.

Source: Adapted from Duffy (1990); Bentley *et al* (1985); Moudon (1987); Brand (1994); Llewelyn-Davies (2000).

allow incremental, and sometimes more fundamental, change to occur (see below) while retaining their essential character and functionality. This is often a function of their basic morphology (plot, block and public space structures), as well as how infrastructure supports growth and movement (see Chapter 4). Experience suggests that cities and neighbourhoods with a fine grain and a mix of uses, building types and shared public spaces are likely to be more accepting of change without the need for radical intervention to dismantle and retrofit inflexible buildings, spaces and infrastructure.

Nevertheless where environments have proven to be inflexible, Dunham-Jones & Williamson (2009) have demonstrated, through their studies of American suburbs, that radical retrofitting can be used retrospectively to insert the type of urban structure that will be more sustainable. They argue that by urbanising low-density residential suburbs, and suburban office, industrial and retail parks with a denser, more walkable, synergistic mix of uses '... *significant reductions in carbon emissions, gains in social capital and changes to systemic growth patterns can be achieved.*' (Dunham-Jones & Williamson 2009: 3). Moreover, the suburban market in the USA is already driving such change — though little of substance can be done where such developments are poorly located (e.g. where climate and the need for food and water can only be overcome by energy-intensive technological means).

Social Change and Gentrification

Place stability is often desirable in urban design, but this encompasses more than the physical structures alone. Chapter 6 discussed the social dimension of urban design, but a further social concern warrants mention here — that of gentrification. The discussion above has focused largely on how processes of change over time impact on the building stock and physical fabric of cities. Many of these changes stem from profound social and economic shifts that make particular buildings or parts of the city more (and less) desirable to users and investors, sometimes rendering them obsolescent.

These ongoing processes of change have implications for the communities that occupy areas subject to change. Sometimes these will be positive, for example, a run-down housing area being refurbished, or defective housing being demolished and re-built to improve conditions for existing residents. Sometimes the processes will be negative (at least for existing residents) when, for example, communities are broken up and re-housed elsewhere to make way for comprehensive redevelopment, or where physical changes price existing residents out of a particular locality.

In the former case, the balance between, and relative shortcomings of, comprehensive versus incremental change is discussed below — because this usually involves a choice between different forms and speeds of development, such processes are responsive to public policy and regulation (see Chapter 11).

In the latter case, the social changes brought about by trends in the second-hand housing market and by related trends in tenure, from rental to owner-occupier, will be more subtle, complex (in terms of the range of actors involved) and longer-term, and, as such, often go unnoticed by policy-makers.

Gentrification trends were first discussed by Ruth Glass in the 1960s following her observations of working-class neighbourhoods in London where everything from formerly modest terraced houses to large but dilapidated Victorian houses as being bought up by a growing middle class and turned into elegant and increasingly expensive residences. For her: *'Once this process of "gentrification" starts in a district, it goes on rapidly until all or most of the original working-class occupiers are displaced, and the whole social character of the district is changed.'* (Glass 1964: xviii).

The implications for the displaced communities can be profound. These trends are of particular concern for urban designers because, in recent years, urban design has been accused of facilitating gentrification through physical interventions in the built environment – trends seen by many commentators as socially divisive and undesirable.

Gentrification is a politically loaded term. The political right generally prefers less ideologically charged words such as regeneration, revitalisation and renaissance, which are seen as 'natural' processes of city development in which some displacement is inevitable and might even be desirable. For the political left, such terms are merely ciphers for 'gentrification'. Hackworth (2002: 815), for example, defines it as '… *the production of space for progressively more affluent uses.'* Gentrification thus involves the inevitable displacement of less affluent people and more marginal uses, and often the shifting, rather than solving, of social problems.

Discussing the roles of and challenges for urban design, Madanipour (2006) identifies gentrification as a potential by-product of urban design that can lead to social fragmentation. He argues it is the public sector's role to consider use value, not just exchange value, and as such to consider the social consequences of urban design.

Yet Smith (2002: 439) argues that it is precisely the actions of the state that, from the late 1990s onwards, led to a growth of gentrification from '… *a quaint urban sport of the hipper professional classes'* to a central goal of urban policy, driven forward by the desire to secure an urban renaissance – a movement that, in the UK at least, puts design quality at the heart of its agenda (Urban Task Force 1999; Punter 2009). For him, these processes are now universal, amounting to much more than the gradual transformation of run-down inner city and early suburban neighbourhoods, and extending to the transformation of '… *whole areas into new landscape complexes that pioneer a comprehensive class-infected urban remake.'* (Smith 2002: 443) – processes in which urban design is centrally implicated.

A counter argument is made by Andres Duany, who argues that we should give 'three cheers for gentrification' because there is 'nothing more unhealthy' for a city than a monoculture of poverty in its inner city neighbourhoods. Whether induced by public policy or spontaneous, he argues that once gentrification begins it is difficult to stop: *'Its motive force is great urbanism: well-proportioned streets, a good mix of activities in useful types of buildings, and a certain architectural quality.'* (Duany 2001: 2). By contrast, he argues, one proven technique that avoids gentrification and holds down prices is to give people bad design, because gentrification is essentially a process of real estate seeking its proper value. Thus, the places that revive are inherently attractive enough to be sought out by the affluent, while the places that resist gentrification are those where the housing is poorly designed or the quality of the urban space is mediocre: *'Thus the most surefire technique for permanently preventing gentrification is to provide dismal architectural and urban design.'* (Duany 2001: 3).

For Duany, the solution to gentrification is to build more new-traditional neighbourhoods, so that older neighbourhoods do not become over-valued through scarcity. Whether this would counter the effects of gentrification is doubtful given that such processes are typically spurred on by the initial low value of much dilapidated older housing stock and the attraction this holds for the types of urban pioneers required to instigate the process.

What are the alternatives? One might be to not invest in the types of public realm improvements that often proceed or at least encourage processes of gentrification. But this would condemn disadvantaged local communities to continue to live in poor-quality local environments. An alternative might be to recognise areas being, or likely to be, gentrified, and to 'inoculate' them so that they are receptive to the benefits of gentrification and more resistant to the negative side-effects. This might include the selective purchasing of units by the public sector for affordable housing in perpetuity, providing incentives to affordable housing providers to invest in areas (e.g. on publicly owned sites) and initiating equity-share schemes and other financial products that allow established communities to buy-in to, and benefit from, the rising value of their neighbourhoods.

MANAGING CHANGE OVER TIME

Urban design operates across numerous time frames – almost all of which necessitate a long-term perspective. While designers may have a relatively short-term involvement in particular development projects, created environments exist over what becomes the long-term and design decisions have long-lasting implications and effects. Furthermore, given the short-termism of markets and market behaviour, there is an imperative for urban designers to consider long-term issues relating to, for example, environment sustainability.

A key question is how urban change happens: change may come upon a place catastrophically and disastrously; it can also happen gradually, allowing for incremental adaptation and adjustment. Jacobs (1961: 307) wrote about the impacts of cataclysmic and gradual money. Cataclysmic money was destructive and '... *behaved like manifestations of malevolent climates beyond the control of man — affording either searing droughts or torrential, eroding floods.*' By contrast, gradual money behaved like '... *irrigation systems, bringing life-giving streams to feed steady continual growth.*'

As personal associations with our immediate environment are valued, and we draw comfort from its stability, the loss of familiar surroundings can be distressing, particularly when experienced over a short time period and on a large scale. But, when processes of change take place over a longer period of time and in an incremental manner through mixing the new and unfamiliar with the old and familiar, the changes may be seen as exciting, but also comfortable and acceptable: Lowenthal (1981: 16), for example, favoured 'anchoring' the 'excitement of the future' in the 'security of the past'. Hence, rather than change itself — which people expect, anticipate and often welcome — it is the pace and scale, and the sense that it is not amenable to local control, that presents problems.

Many urban design commentators thus advocate incremental and small-scale change. Lynch (1972), for example, argued that '*If change is inevitable, then it should be moderated and controlled so as to prevent violent dislocation and preserve a maximum of continuity with the past.*' Similarly, Tibbalds (1992: 77) recommended incremental development to ameliorate the 'pain of change': '*Blood transfusions, rather than organ transplants, are required. ... an approach characterised by a more contextual organic, incremental and sensitive way of thinking and designing.*'

Mechanist and Organicist Perspectives

Two recurring ways of looking at the 'control' of urban development consistently reoccur in the literature — the mechanist view (the city-as-machine) and the organicist view (the city-as-natural-process). In the mechanist view, society is, or can be, consciously planned, designed or otherwise created by human hand: it is a machine that is knowable and thus controllable. In this view, the market is primarily a relatively static machine for resource allocation. Largely a product of the twentieth century, the mechanist view has parallels with both modernisation and Modernism.

The organicist view, prevalent prior to the twentieth century, sees society as a self-organising process — that is, as a dynamic and adaptive process in that systems acquire and maintain structure and that no external agency controls. It defies human control and is, at best, moderately tameable. Adam Smith's metaphor of the invisible hand is itself derived from an organic conception, whereby the outcome of myriad individual actions is essentially benevolent:

'... *there is a harmony between the individual and the aggregate established by the "Invisible Hand" which is another name for deep structures of interconnectedness beneath the seemingly chaotic and uncoordinated individual actions.*'

(Desai 2002)

In this view, driven by an incessant search for profits, the market is a process of search and signalling, involving dynamic uncertainty, innovation and discovery.

An organicist view is evident in the writing of some of the great planning seers of the first half of the twentieth century, notably Geddes (1915), famously a botanist, and Mumford (1934, 1938, 1961). This tradition was continued by Jacobs (1961, 1969, 2000), Alexander (1965, 1979) and Alexander *et al* (1977, 1987). In the final chapter of *The Death and Life of Great American Cities* (1961), for example, Jane Jacobs was among the first in the urban design field to draw attention to organised complexity, while in 'A City is Not a Tree' (1965), Alexander's starting point was that 'artificial' cities did not have the complexity, life and vitality of 'natural' cities.

Within the contemporary organicist view there is a lot of interest both in natural systems and in processes of growth and change in such systems (see Jacobs 1969; Batty 2005; Healey 2006; Salingaros 2005). Complex system theory, for example, suggests that natural (and some other) systems both comprise a larger number of interacting elements and exhibit properties that are not those of the individual elements, but 'emerge' from the interactions between elements.

The organicist view has been further developed in the work of those highlighting key attributes of natural systems and organised complexity. In terms of natural systems, a key idea is that natural systems exhibit negative feedback, which serves to dampen the system and maintain it in a form of long-term stability, while artificial (man-made) systems exhibit positive feedback which amplifies and tends to deplete and exhaust the system. Kunstler (2005: 192) for example, explains how everything

'... *we identify with nature takes the form of inefficient systems. Biogenic or living systems are self-stabilising. They are self-buffered. Small differences are dampened out. Entropy is stalled within them. They exhibit negative feedback tending towards long-term stability. … Everything we identify with the man-made substitutes for natural bio-economies, that is, technologies, tends toward positive feedback, which is self-amplifying, self-reinforcing, and destabilising, featuring the removal of constraints to entropy flows and leading to the certain eventual destruction of that system.'*

Showing how complexity theory can embrace both deep structures of interconnectedness, which we can never truly understand let alone control, and a myriad of processes and elements that combine into organic wholes, Batty (2005) argues that bottom-up processes — in which the outcomes are always uncertain — can combine with new forms of geometry associated with fractal patterns and chaotic dynamics to provide theories readily applicable to highly complex systems such as cities.

Incremental Change

The essence of the organicist view is incremental change. Habraken (2000) discusses organic change in terms of multi-authored change, the cumulative outcome of incremental actions over time, often with the identity of particular authors lost over time. The author of an earlier action creates potential and opportunities for subsequent actors but cannot dictate or otherwise control what they might do. In *Design of Cities*, Bacon (1992: 109) refers to this as the 'rule of the second man': '… *it is the second man who determines whether the creation of the first man will be carried forward or destroyed.'* The pattern is always emergent but how it will develop remains unknown. Similarly, a core message from Rowe & Koetter (1978) was that cities could not be reshaped by a single designer, and, instead, designing cities is more like collage: '… *inventing a few things, but mostly arranging and reordering elements already at hand.'* (Barnett 2003: 44–5).

Small scale, incremental change relates to evolutionary change. Explaining the incremental nature of evolution, Dawkins (1996: 64) uses the parable of climbing Mount Improbable: *'The towering, vertical cliffs of Mount Improbable can never, it seems, be climbed. … thwarted mountaineers … shake their tiny, baffled heads and declare the brooding summit forever unscalable.'* But, 'so intent on the perpendicular drama of the cliffs', the mountaineers do not look around the other side of the mountain, where '… *they would find not vertical cliffs and echoing canyons but gently inclined meadows, graded steadily and easily towards the distant uplands.'* Evolution thus shows how radical change can happen through incremental change, as is also shown by the well-documented experience of Copenhagen's pedestrianisation (Gehl & Gemzoe 1996, 2000). Much of central Copenhagen became pedestrianised and car-free but it happened incrementally, at a pace that

allowed people to adapt and respond to the change (Box 9.2).

In small scale, incremental change, 'mistakes' are small and can be corrected relatively easily — the system could be thought of as self-correcting (homeostasis). In essence, this is how older urban environments developed. Garreau (1999: 239) describes how development follows the same basic (evolutionary) pattern:

'First there's a wild, enthusiastic wave of growth. Then there's a bank collapse. During the collapse, people figure out which were the horrible mistakes they made and promise to fix them if the banks ever open again. Sooner or later the gods relent and the banks reopen, and there's a second wave of growth that heads off in the newly enlightened mode. That is followed by another bank collapse, during which new wisdom is concocted. Seven or so cycles and several centuries into this process and you end up with Paris or Manhattan. The reason old cities look so good is that you see few of the preceding mistakes. They've been torn down or covered by ivy or marble.'

By contrast, in large-scale development, 'mistakes' have to be eliminated because they are much more difficult to correct later. Mistakes are inevitable, however, and often have to be lived with. In *The Oregon Experiment*, Alexander (1975: 77) argued that 'large-lump' development was based on the idea of *replacement*, while piecemeal growth was based on *repair*. As replacement meant consumption of resources, he argued that repair was better ecologically. There were, however, more practical differences:

'Large-lump development is based on the fallacy that it is possible to build perfect buildings. Piecemeal growth is based on the healthier and more realistic view that mistakes are inevitable … Piecemeal growth is based on the assumption that adaptation between buildings and their users is necessarily a slow and continuous business which cannot, under any circumstances, be achieved in a single leap.' (Alexander 1975: 77–9).

Arguing that urban development should be a process of sequential adaptation, Alexander and colleagues outlined a set of rules to replicate processes of organic growth. In *A New Theory of Urban Design* (Alexander *et al* 1987), they argue that the organic quality of older towns and cities does not, and cannot, exist in contemporary development because, while it might be piecemeal, the different elements remain fragmented and unrelated to a growing whole. Thus what is required is a process that creates 'wholeness in urban development':

'… it is the process above all which is responsible for wholeness … not merely the form. If we create a suitable process there is some hope that the city might become whole again. If we do not change the process, there is no hope at all.'

(Alexander *et al* 1987: 3).

They argue that, in any process of organic growth, certain fundamental rules exist:

- The whole grows piecemeal (bit by bit).
- The whole is unpredictable (when it starts coming into being, it is not clear how it will develop or where it will end).
- The whole is coherent (it is truly whole, not fragmented and its parts are whole).

- The whole inspires feeling (it has the power to move us) (Alexander *et al* 1987: 14).

From these, a single overriding rule was formulated: '*Every increment of construction must be made in such a way as to heal the city.*' (Alexander *et al* 1987: 22), with seven intermediate rules or principles developed to implement this rule (Table 9.6). These ideas were

---

BOX 9.2 Car-Free Streets and Squares in Copenhagen

The area of car-free streets and squares in Copenhagen has growm significantly in the last 40 years, increasing from 15 800 m² in 1962 to nearly 100 000 m² in 1996. The programme began in 1962 with the pedestrianisation of the city's main street, Stroget. By 1973, the pedestrianisation of streets had been completed and subsequent efforts concentrated on reclaiming and improving city squares.

Studies of the use of public space were undertaken in 1968, 1986 and 1995. The 1968 study showed the newly pedestrianised streets were popular as walking and shopping streets. The 1986 study showed the growth of a new and more active urban culture and informal public life, which the 1995 study showed had continued. An important contributory factor was the development of café culture. Largely unknown when the first streets were pedestrianised, the city now offers more than 5000 outdoor café chairs. Furthermore, although it was expected that the Danish climate would severely limit the potential to develop public life, the season for outdoor seating at cafés has gradually been extended from a summer season of

three or four months, to one lasting from April until November (Gehl & Gemzoe, 2000: 57).

Gradual expansion of the city's system of car-free and almost car-free spaces had three main advantages:
- City residents had time to develop a new city culture and to discover and exploit the opportunities.
- People had time to change their travel practices. Car owners, for example, gradually became accustomed to the idea of driving and parking in the city centre being more difficult: parking in the city centre was consistently reduced by 2–3% per year. Cycling and using public transport, however, became much easier.
- The success of earlier phases made it easier for politicians to take further incremental decisions about pedestrianisation schemes. (Gehl & Gemzoe 2000: 55–9).

The gradual transformation from 'car culture' to 'pedestrian culture' thus made possible an equally gradual development of city life and city culture. In short, radical change had happened gradually and with public consent and approval.

Pedestrianised space, Copenhagen
(*Image: Matthew Carmona*)

(continued)

BOX 9.2 Car-Free Streets and Squares in Copenhagen — Cont'd

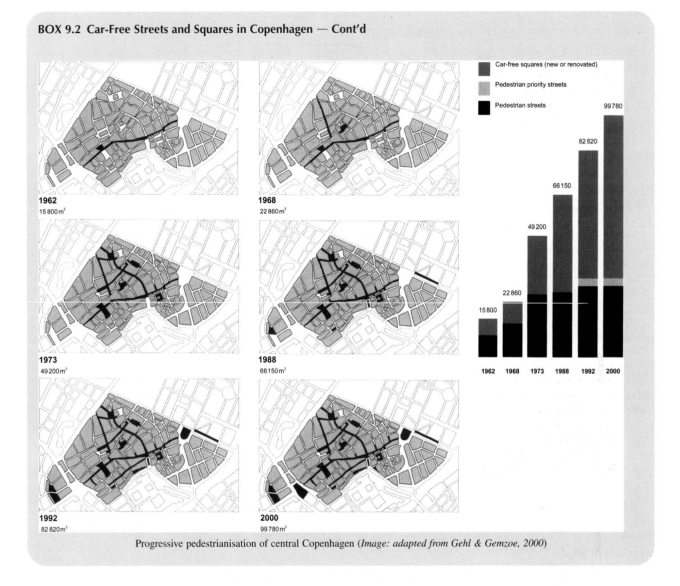

Progressive pedestrianisation of central Copenhagen (*Image: adapted from Gehl & Gemzoe, 2000*)

subsequently further developed by Alexander in his four-volume, *The Order of Nature* (Alexander 2004a, 2004b, 2004c, 2004d), in which he develops a comprehensive theory of how matter comes together to form coherent structures.

Marshall (2009: 288–9) also offers four key insights framing an evolutionary perspective on the growth of cities:

- First, cities are complex, dynamic, collective entities in which the parts are partly in cooperation, partly in competition.
- Second, over time, interactions between local components give rise to larger scale outcomes that were not anticipated. This concept of 'emergence' means that, as people react to local conditions and optimise their own location, then emergence can lead to a coherent structure even without conscious attempts to plan it.

- Third, environments constantly change over time and continue to adapt to local conditions and requirements — in other words, there is feedback from the environment to the emerging entity that is the city.
- Fourth, although the long-term effect of emergence may be unknown, this does not mean that the individual increments are not designed — thus,

'... urban planning and design can be part of urban evolution ... It also means that urban evolution is not only confined to some primitive historic phase of "unplanned" urbanism, that was supplanted and superseded by modern planning.'

(Marshall 2009: 289–9).

He argues that today's planned environment — at least those parts that survive — will, at some point, be part of tomorrow's 'traditional' environment.

TABLE 9.6 Alexander's Seven Rules of Organic Growth

Rule I	Piecemeal growth guarantees that no project is too large. There should be a mixed flow of small, medium and large projects in about equal quantities and a mix of uses.
Rule II	The growth of larger wholes should be a slow incremental process in which every building increment must help to form at least one larger whole in the city that is both larger and more significant than itself. Individual increments should initially hint at the creation of a larger whole and then subsequent increments will define and complete this whole.
Rule III	Visions should be the source of all increments so that every project is first experienced, and then expressed as a vision.
Rule IV	Every building should create coherent and well-shaped positive urban space in such a way that the space, rather than the building, becomes the main focus of attention. To achieve this, there should be a hierarchy of urban elements with pedestrian space prioritised, followed by buildings, then roads and finally parking.
Rule V	The layout of large buildings should be arranged so that the entrances, main circulation, main divisions, interior open space, daylight and movement within the building are all coherent and consistent with the position of the building in the street and in the neighbourhood.
Rule VI	The construction should be such that the structure of every building generates wholes in the physical fabric through the appearance of their structural bays, columns, walls, windows, building base, etc.
Rule VII	The formation of centres is the end result of making things 'whole'. Thus, every whole must be a centre in itself and must also produce a system of centres around it. In this context, a centre may be a building, a space, a garden, a wall, a road, a window or a complex of several of these at the same time.

Source: Adapted from Alexander *et al* (1987).

The seemingly organic continuity and incremental change of the pre-Modern period can be contrasted with Modernism's sense of a historical break. By designing *de novo* from first principles of essential urban functions, some contend that Modernist rational planning disrupted the natural evolution of the city. The general post-1945 programme of large-volume, large-scale innovation and experimentation was thus a case of 'big trial and big error' — magnifying the process of evolution in the form of cities, resembling a 'Cambrian explosion' and 'hopeful monsters' (Marshall 2009: 289). Ensuring only the fittest survives, an evolutionary perspective on urbanism views this as simply par for the course. Given that (as Garreau above suggests) all the poorly adapted traditional development has been lost, Marshall argues that, when modern planned environments are compared unfavourably with those parts of traditional environments that have survived, what is being compared is well-adapted traditional development and (mostly) poorly adapted modern development.

The continuing development of cities will, like natural evolution, require innovation, and sometimes novelty, if it is to continue adapting to new circumstances. Seeing it as the role of the planner and designer '… *to manage this adaptation, through sensitive generative and selective interventions.*' (Marshall 2009: 289), Marshall offers the following recommendations for an evolutionist approach to urban design:

- Make each step viable now — new interventions should be immediately adapted to their surroundings from day one, healing their edges as they go.
- Proceed by small steps — avoid 'monstrosity'.

- Avoid suppressing 'unsolicited novelty' — encourage innovative solutions to functional problems, but not novelty for its own sake.
- Discard moribund models — avoid clinging on to old forms and processes when human requirements have moved on.
- Devolve decision-making — empower people to encourage more apt, fit-for-purpose solutions (Marshall 2009: 270–6).

The Part and the Whole

While incremental change is desirable, there is a need to ensure that the incremental steps add up to larger wholes: natural systems are able to do this because they are (for the most part) self-correcting systems. But a potential weakness, and limitation of, incrementalist approaches is that there may be no innate/inherent capacity to coordinate actions across ownership or plot boundaries to create Alexander's desired, but rather nebulous, 'wholeness'.

Urban form arises from the interactions of many designers over time and thus one not only designs a building, landscape or infrastructure, but also contributes to the emergent character of streets, neighbourhoods, towns and centres. Drawing on the Latin term *concinnus* (meaning 'deftly joined'), Childs (2009: 131) advocates 'civic concinnity' to emphasise that the independent designers of the parts of a city or environment should also consider how those parts add to the larger whole: '*The beauty of a healthy meadow and the delight of a classic main street are the emergent products of the co-adaptation of independent actors.*'

Childs argues that 'civic concinnity' offers a route between three situations:

- 'Over-independence of individual built form', where individual built places fail to work together to make a compelling larger form and to create district synergies: *'Excessive independence causes inefficiencies such as duplicate parking, disconnected sidewalks and poorly defined interstitial spaces.'* (2009: 132).
- 'Totalising order', the 'lifeless order of single hand design', seen in tract housing and themed districts — where a monotony of repetition replaces the vibrancy of multiple designs — and big projects designed by a single designer.
- 'Hollow manners' of a mock or shallow contextualism, where regulatory control and technique triumph over content, resulting in a lack of depth and nuance: *'Narrow definitions of context miss or avoid the productive struggle with the complexities, multiple histories and nuances of place.'* (Child 2009: 134).

Civic concinnity is, in essence, a call for design sensibilities recognising and valuing context and the need to consider the whole ('the city') and the part ('the building'). Similar to chess — in which 'the meaning of a move is dependent on the location of the other pieces and on the characteristics of the piece' — it requires '... *that individual products be designed to engage their built and natural contexts in order to deftly create larger forms.'* (2009: 135, 138).

Civic concinnity attempts to address a collective action problem in which individual, independent and beneficial actions can produce a cumulative outcome that is detrimental to all (i.e. a version of the prisoners, dilemma, but also relating to the tragedy-of-the-commons, where individuals have no incentive to consider the impact of their action on the whole). Childs (2009: 140), for example, acknowledges the inevitability of tensions between the 'civic view' and the 'building view': *'Meadows and other ecosystems are not composed solely of happy symbiotic relationships. The balance of predators, prey and parasites are components of natural ecosystems and similar relationships may be part of a civic gestalt.'*

Voluntaristic adoption of particular design sensibility may not be sufficient to resolve these core tensions and, as is discussed in Chapter 10, collective action problems can be resolved through the coercive powers of a higher authority (the state or, in some circumstances, the landowner) or through co-operative action, but, in effect, what must happen is that the limits or rules that exist in a natural system have to be created in an artificial (man-made) system. The challenge is thus to find ways of coordinating the parts with the 'always-emergent' whole without stultifying its emergence — that is, for some form of 'control' that protects the integrity of the system, without stifling bottom-up vitality and adaptation.

Two levels of control are perhaps necessary — the first at a more strategic level, and involving the design of a framework or 'armature' (the 'whole') and the second at a more detailed level and involving the design of the 'parts'. Whole/part relations will change with spatial scale: at the city level, the city is the whole and each neighbourhood might be the part; at the neighbourhood scale, the neighbourhood is the whole and each street block might be the part; at the urban block scale, the block is the whole and the plot division the part. As Eliel Saarinen (cited in Frederick 2007) advocates: *'Always design a thing by considering it in its larger context — a chair in a room, a room in a house, a house in an environment, an environment in a city plan.'*

This also suggests urban design implementation as a process of guiding or steering incrementalism (see Carmona 2009a). Ellin (2006: 103), for example, argues for '... *a combination of large-scale and small-scale interventions, both systematic and serendipitous.'* She argues that:

'Like a good parent, a good plan nurtures healthy growth and change without being "over-involved", without determining everything, allowing the city to blossom and define itself. While providing some overall defining guidelines, these frameworks should not prescribe every land use and every architectural detail.'

(2006: 103).

A place vision or design framework can provide strategic coordination (see Chapter 10), but it must also retain sufficient flexibility to accommodate underlying and evolving processes of change, and also to allow incorporation of the (as yet unknown) 'better idea'. An important distinction thus exists between 'frameworks' and 'blueprints' — while blueprints *dictate*, frameworks *guide* (see Table 9.7) (see Chapter 11). Ellin's Integral Urbanism, for example, features

TABLE 9.7 Blueprints and Frameworks

Blueprint	Framework
A complete or total design	Codes/rules/principles
Deterministic	Flexible
Design everything — 'the city to the spoon'	Design enough — 'what matters'
Single outcome	Range of outcomes
Single author	Multiple authors
Single built-out (to completion)	Continuous build-out
Direct design/first-order design	Indirect design/second-order design
Artificial diversity	Authentic diversity
Scripted dialogue	Open conversation

'... *a willingness to relinquish control, to let things happen, and to play – a vulnerability. This translates into a shift from the all-inclusive masterplan ... to a more project-oriented, site- and client-specific, incremental, catalytic, and tentacular form of intervention.*'

(2006: 121).

This view of urbanism and urban development emphasises process rather than product; as Brain (2005: 229) explains:

'... *urbanism is defined not simply as a scenographic effect achieved by a designer but as a collaborative work of many hands, independently contributing to a cumulative effect that comes to life because of the way it combines elements of order, an orchestration of diverse aspirations, and a certain historical contingency.*'

Large Lump Developments

Although cycles of growth and decline still mark eras of investment and stagnation, the pace of change has quickened to such a degree that much of what was built in the 1960s and 1970s has already been redeveloped, with many of the most successful developments of the 1990s and 2000s representing clear reactions to the well-documented mistakes of the 1960s. While the era of widespread comprehensive redevelopment has passed, economic and political realities appear to make large-scale developments inevitable. The historical trend towards large-scale growth and away from smaller-scale, incremental growth has also led, in some places, to an increasingly controlled and monotonous urban fabric – lacking the diversity, character and experiential depth of places that have developed incrementally.

Asserting that piecemeal change is diminishing, Dovey (1990: 8) observes how the economic context often favours 'mega-projects' bringing massive one-off investments, jobs and political kudos. The flexibility of capital investment by multi-national corporations gives them power to play cities off against each other. Governments are induced to compete for such projects on an 'all-or-nothing' basis, and often to overrule, and undermine, regulatory and design processes to secure investment (see Chapter 11).

'Big Bang' and 'Big Ticket' developments are often presented as necessary to change the nature and economy of a place in ways that, it is argued, would not otherwise occur or would take too long to happen incrementally. Examining the spread of ground-scrapers (low-rise, deep-plan office buildings) in London, Carmona & Freeman (2005) show how these 'mega' forms of development represent a rational response by the market and public sector to the development context. For the funders of these developments they provide the necessary space for the increasing number of 'blue-chip' multi-national occupiers seeking to bring their disparate workforces together on fewer sites, and, in the context of terrorist threats and the desire for deep-plan trading floors and other work spaces, ground-scrapers are a viable and desirable alternative to tower buildings for these companies. For the public sector they help to avoid building high in historic city centres, and offer the potential to deliver public benefits without cost to the public purse, for example by incorporating new pseudo-public urban spaces. Often, however, these benefits are at the expense of local permeability, historic grain and mix, and the creation of potentially exclusionary environments.

Large lump developments in all their forms have the potential to address issues of place-making – at least initially – in a coherent and joined-up manner and, in particular, to fund the provision of major new elements of the capital web, including new urban spaces (see Chapter 10) (Figure 9.7). As larger sites enable developers and their designers to internalise many externalities, the related issues are whether projects are sufficiently connected and joined-up with their wider context (see Bacon *et al* 2008) and whether they can happen incrementally in the first instance, and subsequently evolve incrementally. Tibbalds (1992: 77), for example, argued for the need to '... *encourage the development of smaller sites, set limits on the extent of site assembly and break up the larger sites into more manageable components.*'

Larger developments are typically organised into a series of smaller development projects to be implemented over different time frames (i.e. short-, medium- and long-term), each by a different building developer and perhaps also by a different designer, thereby allowing a range of inputs and contributions, and, once built, a diversity of owners. Traditional urban block structures and plot divisions, for example, suggest ways of sub-dividing the larger development project (see Chapter 4).

Such development usually involves separating land and building development, and also design and development tasks, between a lead/master developer, who primarily undertakes land development and who employs a lead or master designer (i.e. a masterplanner) and a series of parcel developers and designers. The lead developer typically installs infrastructure and sub-divides the site into development parcels. Hence, there are also a number of parcel developers and designers. It thus also poses the challenge of coordinating the contributions of other (parcel) developers and their designers, while also allowing those designers (and perhaps developers) to also contribute something of their own. The required control could, in principle, be entrusted to normal public controls over design and development. More typically, lead developers exercise private control over design development, particularly if they have subsequent phases to develop and sell (and, thus, intend to benefit from an escalating asset) or intend to hold the development as an investment in the longer-term (see Chapter 11).

FIGURE 9.7 Liverpool One, Liverpool (*Image: Matthew Carmona*) Although a 'Big Bang' development, issues of place-making were addressed through a masterplan. The resulting development is highly commercial, but includes a new rooftop public park and once again connects the city centre to its waterfront

Love (2009: 215), for example, notes examples of successful single-authored, 'coordinated urbanism' — Louis Kahn's Salk Institute, Michelangelo's Campidoglio and the United Nations Buildings. But, rather than urban design, he considers these 'very large-scale architectural works' — that is, Big Architecture — requiring implementation by their initial authors to achieve the desired 'gesamtkunstwerk'. Distinctive (architectural) design by a single author also tends to reinforce an area's identity as an enclave with distinct boundaries rather than as an integrated and seamless part of the city: the complex has a distinctive identity, but one emphasising its separateness.

Love (2009: 215) postulates a 'tipping point' at which development projects become too large to be successfully designed and executed by a single designer, and where the need for variety and diversity of response kicks in: '*Once control by a single author exceeds this scale … the control borders on the megalomaniacal.*' A rough rule-of-thumb might put the upper limit at three or four typical city blocks.

Rather than an 'artificially induced variety conjured by compositional effort', the aim is that, as Love (2009: 215–6) suggests, '*… a phased project designed by many hands will result in true variety.*' Similarly Brain (2008:

253) advocates achieving variety, not by a single designer 'working stenographic effects by fiat', but '*… the cumulative effects of genuinely individual architectural statements — as an open conversation and not simply a scripted dialogue.*' (Figure 9.8).

Continuing Evolution

Once completed, large developments must be able to change incrementally; Jacobs (1961: 307) presciently warned that: '*All city building that retains staying power … requires that its locality be able to adapt, keep up-to-date, keep interesting, keep convenient, and this in turn requires a myriad of gradual constant, close-grained changes.*' The ongoing single control regime of large lump developments may be stultifying and — lacking the internal capacity and stimulus for creativity, innovation and development — may only be capable of (slow) managed decline. While large lump developments often need land ownership to be consolidated to allow development to proceed, to allow subsequent change to occur incrementally that land ownership may need to be broken down.

In *Urban Form: The Death and Life of the Urban Block* — a title consciously echoing Jane Jacobs' first book — Panerai *et al* (2004: 166) emphasise the capacity of urban block

FIGURE 9.8 Brindleyplace, Birmingham (*Image: Steve Tiesdell*). Consisting of a number of different buildings each designed by different firms of architects, this development is, in Leon Krier's analogy, a flotilla of ships rather than a single mega-liner

systems both to provide stability and to accommodate growth and change:

'The dialectical relationship between street and built plots creates the tissue and it is the continuation of this relationship — capable of modification, extension and the substitution of buildings — where resides the capacity of the city to adapt to the demographic, economic and cultural changes that mark its evolution.'

Similarly, studying change and stability in San Francisco neighbourhoods, Moudon (1987: 188) highlighted the importance of the pattern of land ownership in enabling incremental change. Small lots enabled constant fine-grain adaptation instead of the sudden and potentially devastating changes that came with large parcels. Small lots also give greater individual control and greater variety — the more owners, the more gradual and adaptive the ongoing change: *'... the place looks a little different every year, but the overall feel is the same from century to century.'* (Brand 1994: 75). It can also be argued that sustainability requires a capacity for organic development, rendering clean-sweep redevelopment unnecessary.

CONCLUSION

The temporal dimension of urban design focuses on understanding the implications and impact of time on places. As Lynch (1972: 240) argued, 'effective action' and 'inner well-being' depended on '... *a strong image of time: a vivid sense of the present, well connected to future and past, perceptive of change,* [and] *able to manage and enjoy it.'*

Time involves change — both that which happens in cycles and that which occurs in progressive, unfolding and irreversible ways. Change itself both responds to and shapes further change. Urban designers need an awareness of potential change; to understand how places change over time and be able to anticipate the impacts of actions, how and why development will occur and even how materials will weather; the series of opportunities and constraints that may arise; and how change can be managed. As discussed here, the visual and physical continuity of valued places relates to issues of the 'obsolescence' of buildings and environments, the time frames of change, and the 'robustness' and 'resilience' of the built fabric and other physical attributes of that place. Working within established contexts thus requires an understanding of how environments adapt to change and, more importantly, why some environments adapt better than others.

The final part of this chapter argued that, to be robust and sustainable, environments need to be capable of evolution and incremental change. It thus anticipates the discussion in Part III, which discusses the development, control and communication processes in urban design.

Implementing Urban Design

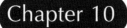

The Development Process

A disconnect often exists between urban designers and the real estate development process. Yet, awareness of this process, particularly the balance of risk and reward driving it, gives urban designers a deeper understanding of the context in which they operate and how their design policies, proposals and projects are either transformed, or can resist transformation, through implementation. Lacking such awareness, they are at the development industry's mercy. Furthermore, as they frequently need to argue the case for development and place quality, their arguments are more persuasive and effective when informed by this awareness.

This chapter is in three main sections. The first section outlines the process of real estate development utilizing the 'pipeline' model of the development process. The third section discusses roles and relationships in the development process and the fourth section discusses development quality. Although focusing on urban development design, the discussion necessarily overlaps with design guidance and control, which are the specific focus of Chapter 11.

REAL ESTATE DEVELOPMENT

Real estate development combines various inputs — land, labour, materials and finance (capital) — in order to achieve an output or product. Classically an 'entrepreneur' brings these together and adds value to them. In the case of real estate development, entrepreneurs are 'speculators' — their interest is short-term; entrepreneurs aim to start and operate firms in the long-term — and are usually known as developers. The product is a change of land use and/or a new or altered building that (hopefully) has higher value than the cost of undertaking the transformation. According to Ambrose (1986), the process can be thought of as a series of transformations: (i) capital is converted into supplies of raw materials and labour, brought as commodities in the marketplace; (ii) which are converted into some other saleable commodity (a building); and (iii) which, in turn, is then converted back into money (i.e. capital) by selling the commodity in the market place.

Successful real estate development requires sale or otherwise profitable disposal of the completed development. Indeed, realising capital has come to be seen as more significant in capitalist accumulation strategies than production. As Gottdiener (2001: 44) explains, the manufacturing process 'valorises' commodities by creating value through production. For capitalists to realise that extra value, they must sell the goods they produce — only *if* they are successful in making a profit on sales can they remain alive for the next cycle of accumulation. Because it is harder to realise capital than to produce goods, the contemporary economy places more emphasis on marketing and selling (Gottdiener 2001: 71).

For the real estate development process to be profitable, the amount received from sales has to be greater than the production costs. A calculus of reward, mediated by the risk of achieving that reward, thus, drives the process. Reward is easily understood, but considerations of risk are as important and instrumental as reward. As Leinberger (2008: 183) explains:

'Although many developers, personified by Donald Trump, have the image of being the ultimate gamblers, most are extremely cautious. The name of the game is to minimise all risks up front before any financial exposure is taken, such as, have national credit tenants, use other people's money, do not start a development unless you know your exit strategy, develop only proven conforming products, do not pioneer, have construction-cost guarantees with a bonded construction firm, etc.'

Rather than a one-off sequence of transformations, for most developers the process is a recurring cycle. There is also an important time dimension: the rapid turnover of capital in any particular development project allows it to be recycled more quickly, generating profits more rapidly and reducing risk. Tiesdell & Adams (2010) argue that, rather than 'location, location, location', what matters in real estate development is 'location, product, timing' — that is, the *right* product in the *right* place at the *right* time.

The process of designing and producing the built environment involves a variety of 'actors' or decision-makers, each with different goals and motivations. Hence, in any given instance, creating the built environment is the result of a variety of actors, each with different objectives, motivations, resources and constraints, and all connected with one another in different ways. As Ball *et al* (1998) has argued, rather than an anonymous and impersonal economic process, development is a function of social relations specific to time and place involving a variety of key actors — landowners, investors, financiers, developers, builders, various professionals, politicians, consumers, etc. The state — both local and national — is also an important actor in its own right and as a regulator of the other actors. These sets of relations represent what Ball terms the 'structures of building provision', which need to be seen in terms of their specific linkages — functional, historical, political, social and cultural — with the broader structural elements — economic and institutional — of the political economy.

To facilitate the study and understanding of the development process, several models have been devised and can be grouped as follows:

- *Equilibrium models* — derived from neo-classical economics, these assume that development activity is structured by economic signals about effective demand, as reflected in rents, yields, etc.
- *Event-sequence models* — derived from estate management, these focus on the management of stages in the development process.
- *Agency models* — derived from attempts to explain the development process from a behavioural or institutional point of view, these focus on the actors in the development process and their relationships.
- *Structure models* — grounded in political economy, these focus on the way markets are structured; the role of capital, labour and land in the development process; and the forces organising the relationships of the development process and driving its dynamics.
- *Institutional models* — these both describe events and agencies and explain how they relate to broader structural forces (see also Healey 1991a).

The outline of the development process presented below is based on an event-sequence model. Despite providing a good introduction to the development process, such models understate aspects that other models emphasise, such as the differential power of the various actors and institutions involved. Furthermore, they do not explain why urban development takes the form it does.

The Development Pipeline Model

Barrett, Stewart and Underwood's 'development pipeline' model — an event-sequence model — is shown in Figure 10.1. Their model divides the development process into three broad sets of events each forming one side of a triangular 'pipeline'. The three stages are discussed in more detail below (adapted from Adams 1994).

Although the discussion focuses principally on private sector development, the stages and principles are broadly similar regardless of whether the developer is a private, public or non-profit organisation. Two types of urban design practitioner are considered — those employed by the developer (in terms of urban development design) and those by the public sector (in terms of design policies, guidance and control). Table 10.1

summarises their roles at each stage — those working for the public sector are usually most influential and active at the initiation stage, and those working for the private sector at the feasibility stage.

Development Pressure and Prospects

External influences — economic growth, fiscal policies, the impact of long-term social and demographic trends, technological developments, market restructuring, etc. — create development pressure and prospects, which trigger activity within the pipeline. When development opportunities arise, appropriate sites are sought, with activity in the pipeline beginning as development actors seek to relate development proposals to suitable sites and *vice versa.*

Development may be initiated by a developer or a third party (including the public sector) anticipating a demand or need for a certain type of development and seeking an appropriate development site. Initiation may also come from the site-owner (or a third party) who anticipates or envisages a higher value use for the site. In both cases, urban designers may be involved in evaluating, exploring and demonstrating the site's potential. To direct or attract development to particular sites or areas (or to direct it away from other areas), a planning authority might establish, or have previously established, a planning policy framework. To stimulate (and subsequently to shape and coordinate) development, it might also prepare a development brief, masterplan or development framework for the site or area (see Chapter 11). These might be produced *proactively* to encourage interest in a development site, *reactively* following a developer's interest or by developers to expedite the approval process.

As well as identifying a site and a development proposal, this stage is also likely to include initial ideas about development form and an outline financial appraisal. In essence, this is a 'back of an envelope'-type analysis combining a broad assessment of the likely costs and subsequent value, with a more subjective judgement based upon experience and feel for the market. If the proposed development is worth pursuing further, the feasibility stage — the pipeline's second side — develops this initial assessment in more detail, which, in turn, determines whether it will proceed.

Development Feasibility

In the pipeline model, feasibility is tested in five specific ways, each related to a particular set of influences or constraints. If development is to occur, all five streams must be successfully negotiated. If the proposal is not feasible, it must be changed or abandoned. Successful developers are, nonetheless, skilled in confronting and overcoming constraints.

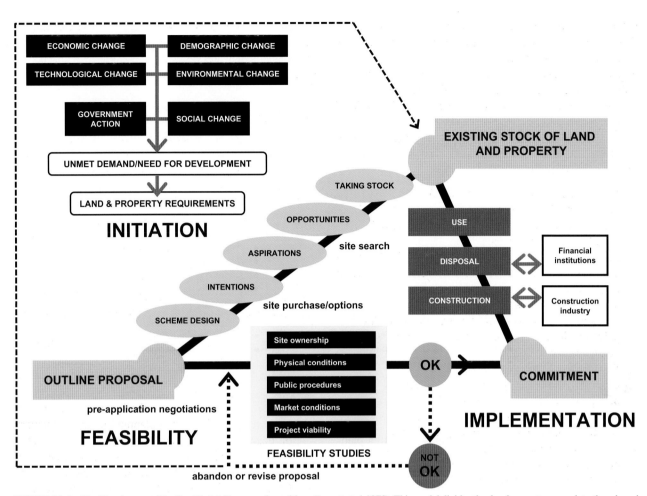

FIGURE 10.1 The Development Pipeline Model (*Image: adapted from Barrett* et al *1978*). This model divides the development process into three broad sets of events — development pressure and prospects, development feasibility and implementation and disposal — each forming one side of a triangular 'pipeline'. External factors generate development pressure and prospects along the first side, culminating in the identification of specific sites at the lower left hand angle. Development feasibility is tested along the second side. Construction and disposal — the third side — include both construction and transfer of the completed development into its new use. Sites move around the pipeline at varying speeds and, at any particular point in time, sites with development potential will be at different points. Operating as a spiral, producing a fresh pattern of land use at the end of each cycle, the model shows that the development process is dynamic and cyclical

(i) **Ownership constraints**

Prior to development, developers need to know whether they will be able to acquire either the site for the proposed development or rights over that site. The availability of land is often restricted by planning, physical, valuation or ownership constraints forming obstacles to development (see Adams *et al* 1999). A multiplicity of ownership rights, for example, often exists in a single piece of land and the developer must either acquire or respect all such rights. Land in multiple ownership may require land assembly or formation of a partnership or joint venture to carry out development. Public sector compulsory purchase powers may be used to facilitate land assembly.

(ii) **Physical conditions**

To determine whether the site can accommodate the proposed development, the site's physical conditions are assessed (e.g. ground levels, soil structure, levels of contamination, etc.). The site's capacity will also be assessed to determine whether, subject to criteria of 'good' urban form and environmental performance, the required or intended volume of development can be accommodated satisfactorily. The design proposals themselves will start as a concept sketch, getting progressively more detailed as the development proposal increases in certainty and ultimately in sufficient detail for the development to be built. Considerations of good urban form might limit or determine density, massing and/or height. These might be determined by the developer (e.g. guided by concern to build a certain quality of development). Most schemes have a client or project brief setting out the design parameters, the gross floor area (GFA) of different uses and the indicative budget.

TABLE 10.1 Development Process and Urban Designers

Stage	Urban Designer's Activities	
	Acting for developer	*Acting for public sector*
Development pressure and prospects	• Spots 'opportunity' • Identifies suitable sites • Provides 'vision' • Prepares brief/masterplan for site	• Anticipates development pressure/opportunities • Spots and promotes development opportunities • Prepares planning policy framework • Provides 'vision' • Prepares development framework/development code • Prepares development brief for site/masterplan for area • Directs/attracts development to suitable sites • Influences developer's brief for the site
Development feasibility	• Carries out feasibility study • Provides advice • Prepares design proposals • Negotiates with planning authority • Prepares and submits planning/development application	• Negotiates with developer • Provides advice • Comments on design proposals • Makes decision/recommendation on planning/development application
Implementation	• Scheme quality may seal commitment with funders • Ensures quality of development • Influences management of development	• Ensures quality of development • Influences management of development

Alternatively, limits might be imposed through planning policies, a zoning ordinance, a development brief, an urban design framework or masterplan. As physical constraints can normally be expressed in terms of extra costs (i.e. additional preparation, design or construction costs), they do not necessarily prevent development.

In the early stages of the development process, designs can be altered and amended with relatively little cost. As the development process progresses, however, the cost of design changes increases until the cost of making changes is greater than the benefit of those changes. The opportunity for municipalities to influence the design is thus greatest prior to this point.

(iii) Public procedures

All legal and other public procedure issues relating to the site and/or the proposed development must be assessed, including, as necessary, the likelihood of receiving planning/development consent (see Chapter 11). Permissions and consents may also be required for a range of other issues — for example, land and property ownership; conservation and/or historic preservation consents; diversion or closure of rights of way, light, and support; actions necessary to connect with all main service and infrastructure provisions; etc. — all of which may incur cost or delay to the process of development. While not always affecting the principle

of development, legal, planning and public policy constraints usually affect design and layout.

In those countries with zoning systems (e.g. the USA and many parts of Europe), provided the proposed development is in accordance with the zoning ordinance, there is automatic planning consent — although sometimes a 'development permit' is required. Zoning systems may also be supplemented by design review panels focusing specifically on design quality.

In the UK, a discretionary planning system operates, in which acts of development, including so-called material changes of use, require the planning authority's formal consent. Development also needs separate building regulation consent.

(iv) Market conditions

Appraising market conditions assesses whether there will be sufficient demand for the proposed development at the time of completion. Forecasting future demand involves risk and uncertainty. As market conditions may change rapidly during the development process, it is a matter of risk whether demand or completion will be strong enough to make the development viable. To reduce their exposure to risk, developers will often arrange a pre-let or pre-sale tying in a future occupier or purchaser to the development at an early stage. In a fragile market, development is unlikely to commence without a pre-let or pre-sale — which is often necessary to secure funding for development. In markets with strong demand, developers may be less concerned with securing a pre-let because it could reduce their overall return. Risk is thus traded-off against overall reward.

Market conditions are monitored throughout the development, so that, where possible, appropriate changes can be made to maximise return. In a difficult economic climate, design quality is often a casualty as developers try to cut costs and pare back their margins. Some developers, however, deliberately invest more in their design during such periods to differentiate their product. Conversely, in a developers' — as opposed to a buyers' — market, tenants and purchasers (investors) often have to take what is available and design issues may become less important in their decision-making.

(v) Project viability

While a market appraisal assesses whether there is an unsatisfied demand, project viability assesses whether it can be met at the desired rate of profit. For private sector development, assessment of project viability includes analysis of the market (i.e. the likely demand) for the proposed development and the potential returns in relation to development costs and risk. In the public sector, it assesses whether appropriate forms of cost recovery are available, whether the development constitutes an appropriate use for public money (relative to other purposes for which the money could be used), whether it provides value for money and whether it accords with cost yardsticks or benchmark costs for similar developments.

Several methods of development appraisal exist, but, in simple terms, appraisals consider four related factors:

- End or expected value of the development (development revenues).
- Land acquisition costs.
- Production costs (e.g. building costs, legal and agents' fees, professional fees, costs of borrowing, developer's profit).
- Developer's profit or required level of profit.

The latter is important because, if the developer cannot achieve the desired level of profit, other sites and developments may be more attractive or the developer may pursue alternative investment opportunities. For a development to be viable, its expected value must be greater (at least, to the extent of the developer's required profit) than the production and land acquisition costs.

A common method of appraisal is the 'residual method'. At it simplest, this involves subtracting the total projected development costs and the developer's 'reward' from the estimated end value to establish a residual value — that is, what the developer can afford

to pay for the land to enable a sufficient return. Alternatively, if the land price is held constant, the method can be used to determine whether a target rate of profit can be achieved.

Apart from shaving profit margins, developers cannot absorb additional or unexpected costs. If the additional costs create additional value, developers can pass those costs on to the end purchaser or occupier (provided they are willing and able to pay for the additional value); if the additional costs do not create additional value, then the developer must reduce the price offered to the landowner. As landowners will often refuse to sell their land at a lower price or the land price already agreed or paid, the developer often has to find development proposals offering a higher end value (for example a different mix of uses or higher density development); if they are unable to do so, then the project becomes unviable.

For a variety of reasons developers frequently overpay for land (which often means they seek to over-develop sites), and it can often be a case of 'lucky' landowners rather than 'greedy' developers. But, as Syms (2002: 7) points out, although landowners may appear to be intransigent by holding out for maximum payment for their land, they may in practice be trapped by historic valuations on the basis of which their land has been used for collateral against bank borrowings or other loans. Once a 'hope value' has been established, it becomes very difficult to shift.

The residual method has two basic weaknesses:

- By assuming costs are spread evenly over the development period, it is not sensitive to the timing of expenditure and revenues. Cash flow appraisals can overcome this.
- By relying on single figure 'best estimates', it hides uncertainty and risk. Sensitivity analysis, which looks at a range of possible outcomes and then narrows them down to probable outcomes, can remedy this.

The design and costing of development proposals occur in parallel and in increasing detail as a scheme progresses. Viability studies may highlight the need for design modification to, for example, increase the land uses likely to produce most revenue. To be financially viable, a site may require a greater volume or intensity of development than it would initially appear to be able to accommodate. Urban design skills may be required to put that volume of development onto the site in a manner that does not diminish development quality. Design is, however, intrinsically limited: disadvantages of location or lack of (effective) demand for the development cannot be totally overcome by design (Cadman *et al* 1991: 19).

Developers rarely fund development entirely — or even substantially — from their own resources and, if development appears viable, funding must be obtained. Project viability, thus, also assesses whether the developer can obtain the necessary funding and, if so, on what terms. The terms involve certain risks for the developer — for example, when funds are borrowed and interest charged, steep rises in interest rates may cause development projects to be postponed or abandoned.

Developers normally arrange two types of finance: short-term finance — *development funding* — to cover costs during the development period, and longer-term finance — *investment finance* — to cover the cost of holding the completed development as an investment (whereby the developer becomes an investor) or, alternatively, a buyer (or investor) for the completed scheme (see below).

To reduce exposure, help their cash flow and/or acquire greater operational flexibility, larger developments are often phased so that some parts are finished and earning income before the whole is complete. Developments may also be designed so that non-revenue-generating elements occupy the later phases. In a residential development, for example, the developer might build the houses first, leaving community facilities and open space until later. This logic can also be reversed where non-revenue-generating elements such as a high-quality public realm help sell or let the revenue-generating elements, in which case they may be built at the same time or before the other elements (Figure 10.2).

If the initial phases of a development prove unsuccessful, the decision may be taken to change the design of the later phases, or even to halt or abandon development. Equally, if the initial phases are successful, subsequent phases may be changed in order to maximise the more successful, and minimise less successful, elements. Phasing considerations also affect design: if the development is to be let or sold in phases, each must be designed to appear complete and tolerably self-sufficient.

Construction, Marketing and Disposal

If a development passes all five streams of feasibility tests, the decision will be taken to commence development, and the developer (and other parties) commits to the scheme. So begins the construction and disposal stage — the pipeline's third side. The developer's ultimate aim is to produce a marketable development — one for which occupiers and/or purchasers (investors) are willing and able to pay the rent and/or purchase price that at least covers the development costs. The implementation stage is thus the development process's final stage and includes the development's construction, marketing and sale or letting. If the developer retains the development for letting, then his/her role changes to that of investor (see below).

Once implementation starts, developers lose their flexibility of action. The main task is to ensure the development is carried out at the appropriate speed, cost and quality. Developers are particularly reliant on their builders and will also expect their professional team to monitor the builder's performance and be concerned simultaneously about time, cost and quality. In the short-term, time and cost can crowd out concern for quality; over the longer-term, time and cost recede in importance.

DEVELOPMENT ROLES

To more fully understand the development process, it is necessary to identify the key actors and their relationships with each other; to consider why they are involved in the development process; and, more generally, why they might pursue — or be persuaded to provide — higher quality. In this and the following section, therefore, the event-sequence model is extended by considerations of 'agency' and 'structure'. Agency refers to how development actors define and pursue their strategies, interests and actions (Adams 1994: 65). The behaviour of development actors is also set within a broader context — usually known as 'structure' — that consists of the organisation of economic and political activity and of prevailing value systems that frame individual decision-making.

Different actors perform different roles in the development process. For the purpose of analysis, these roles are considered individually, though, in practice, a single actor often performs several roles. Volume housing developers in the UK, for example, typically combine the roles of

FIGURE 10.2 Brindleyplace, Birmingham (*Image: Matthew Carmona*). Where non-revenue-generating elements enable early sales or lets of revenue-generating elements, they may be built at the same time or in advance of other elements. At Brindleyplace, the central public space was completed before the surrounding office blocks

developer, funder and builder. As well as identifying the actors and the roles they perform, it is also necessary to understand and appreciate why they are involved. Each development role can be considered in terms of five generalised criteria:

- *Financial objectives* — whether the actor has a primary concern for cost minimisation or for profit maximisation.
- *Time-span* — whether the actor's involvement and interest in the development is primarily short- or long-term.
- *Design: functionality* — whether an actor has a *specific* concern for the development's ability to serve its functional purpose (e.g. to be used as an office).
- *Design: external appearance* — whether an actor is *primarily* concerned with the development's external appearance.
- *Design: relation to context* — whether a development's relation to its context is a primary concern to the development actor (see Table 10.2).

While each actor will internally trade-off between these criteria, the interactions and differential power of the various actors will also mean criteria are traded-off *between* actors. Achieving high quality urban design may not be an objective shared by all the participants in the process — and, in any case, may mean something different to each actor. The objective can also be constrained by a wide variety of factors, many lying outside the designer's or developer's sphere of influence, such as:

- The requirements and preferences of clients/customers, which may conflict with those of the wider community.
- Market conditions.
- Limitations and costs imposed by the site.
- The need for various consents (legal, planning, development, highways adoption, etc.), and, more generally, by the public sector's regulatory and statutory requirements.
- Limits on the rents/values achievable in particular locations.
- The short-termism often inherent in investment decisions (longer-term exposure increases the risk involved).

The following sections discuss the main development roles and actors and are grouped into producers, consumers and regulators.

Producers

Developers

Developers are many and various. The term embraces a wide range of agencies, at a range of scales from, for example,

volume house builders to small local house builders and self-builders, and with various levels of profit motivation, from the most profit-driven private sector developers through central and local government and other public agencies to charities and non-profit organisations. Some developers specialise in particular sectors of the market, such as retail, office, industrial or residential, while others operate across a range of markets. Some developers have established a niche market, such as the conversion of historic buildings. Some are strongly embedded in particular places, concentrating on projects in or around a particular town or city, while others operate regionally, nationally and even internationally and have less allegiance to particular places.

Based on how they operate, Logan & Molotch (1987, from Knox & Ozolins 2000: 5–6) identified three different types of developer:

- *Serendipitous entrepreneurs* who acquire real estate in various ways (perhaps through inheritance or as a side line to their regular business) and then find that it would be more valuable sold or rented for some other use.
- *Active entrepreneurs* who anticipate changing patterns of land use and land values, and buy and sell land accordingly.
- *Structural speculators* who operate more strategically and, in addition to anticipating changing patterns, seek to influence or engineer change for their own benefit (e.g. by changing the zoning ordinance or development plan; influencing the route of a road or the location of a public transport stop; encouraging public expenditure in certain locations; etc.).

To these might be added social developers using charitable or public funding to meet particular social needs; for example, for social housing. Though not entrepreneurs in a profit-seeking sense, these actors are still developers in the sense that they develop, and need to compete within the market to secure land, labour, materials and often finance to secure their social ends. British Housing Associations are of this type and will often be particularly concerned with design quality as they have a long-term stake in managing their products (i.e. they are developers *and* investors).

Some developers operate primarily as land developers — they acquire land, clean it up as necessary, obtain necessary consents, install infrastructure, sub-divide (parcel) the land and then sell serviced plots (lots) to other (building) developers (or, more simply, builders). They may also exercise control over the building developers by means of covenants, design briefs or design codes (see Chapter 11). The separation of land development and building development is more common in some countries than in others. In northern European countries, for example, the state often plays a significant role in land development, while residential

TABLE 10.2 Motivation of Development Actors in the Place-Production Process

Development roles	Cost		Design Issues		
	Time scale	Financial strategy	Functionality	External appearance	Relation to context
Supply-Side Actors – *those who 'produce' development/places or contribute to their production*					
(Initial) Landowner	Transient	Profit maximisation	No	No	No
Land developer	Transient; to completion of project	Profit maximisation	Yes, but only to financial end	Yes, but only to financial end	Yes, to extent there are positive or negative externalities
Parcel/building developer	Transient; to completion of parcel	Profit maximisation	Yes, but only to financial end	Yes, but only to financial end	Yes, to extent there are positive or negative externalities
Development funders	Transient; to completion of project	Profit maximisation	No	No	No
Lenders of patient equity	Long-term	Profit-seeking	Yes	Yes	Yes
Builder	Transient	Profit maximisation	No	Yes	No
Designer	Transient	Profit maximisation/ seeking	Yes	Yes, to extent external appearance/design reflects on them and their future business	No
Demand-Side Actors – *those who 'consume' development/places*					
Investors (Investment funding)	Enduring	Profit maximisation	Yes, primarily as means to financial end	Yes, but primarily as means to financial end	Yes, to extent there are benefits to making positive connections
Occupiers	Enduring	Balance spaces cost against quality and contribution to business returns	Yes	Yes, to extent external appearance symbolises/ represents them	Yes, to extent there are benefits to making positive connections
Adjacent landowners	Enduring	Protect property values	No	Yes, to extent new development has positive or negative externalities	Yes, to extent new development has positive or negative externalities
(Local) Community	Enduring	Neutral in principle; practice may vary	Yes, to extent that buildings are used by general public	Yes, to extent it defines and forms part of public realm	Yes
Regulatory Actors – *those who 'regulate' development/place-production process*					
Public sector	Enduring	Neutral in principle; practice may vary	Yes	Yes, to extent it forms part of a greater whole	Yes, to extent it forms part of a greater whole

Source: Adapted and extended from Henneberry (1998).

development in North America often involves separation of land and building development. In the UK, volume house builders are typically both land and building developers.

Developers (and investors) also have differing operating characteristics — or, more formally, differing business strategies with respect to rates of return, project scale, areas of operation, attitudes to risk, etc. These behavioural differences may reflect structural and institutional differences (e.g. charities as developers usually have a more favourable tax status; larger developers can often borrow funds at lower interest rates; etc.), but they are *not* determined by such differences.

Some developers, however, seem to 'care' more about design than others, undertaking the development, for example, that is closely tailored to the location, and is respectful of, and enhances, the sense of place. Others undertake less respectful development. These developer types can be considered to be 'place' and 'non-place' entrepreneurs, respectively (Table 10.3). This distinction is best understood as a continuum from those entrepreneurs more sensitive to the intrinsic value and characteristics of the place, to those less sensitive.

In the private sector, as their primary concern is a marketable product, developers (the supply side) must necessarily consider and anticipate the needs and preferences of investors and occupiers (the demand side). In principle, occupiers make demands of building owners (investors), who make demands of developers, who — in turn — set the brief for building designers. The possibility of producer–consumer gaps, however, is discussed below. Responding to and balancing the needs of investors and occupiers, developers tend to see 'design' as essentially a means to a financial end rather than as an end in itself. Their general design concerns thus include:

- Investor and occupier requirements, preferences and tastes, and, in particular, the price they will pay for a product responding to these.
- Flexibility of building and site layout to meet changing circumstances.
- Buildability (including control over building costs).
- Cost efficiency and value for money.
- Visual impact (including image as an aid to sale or letting).
- Management implications (including running costs) (Rowley 1998: 163).

Madanipour (2003: 215–6) notes that, as development companies have grown in size and complexity, small locally based companies with links to local decision-makers have increasingly given way to companies whose centre of operations typically resides outside the locale. Similarly, the financing of projects and ownership of commercial properties are increasingly the responsibilities of national and multi-national companies. The result is a growing

TABLE 10.3 Typical Characteristics of Place and Non-place Entrepreneurs

'Place' Entrepreneurs

- Independent (non-corporate) operators — strong ties to particular localities and often locally embedded
- Use financial appraisals based on what will/might happen in the future (i.e. seek growth)
- Work on intuition and experience (i.e. risk-accepting)
- Value diversity — 'everywhere different'
- Use strategies of design differentiation (i.e. to address risk)
- Gain significant psychic benefits from investment/development (i.e. development of something to cherish) — strong personal associations
- Possess (mainly) local knowledge and expertise

'Non-place' Entrepreneurs

- Non-local (global), corporate (institutional) operators — often with weak ties to particular localities
- Use financial appraisals based on what has happened before (i.e. seek stability)
- Work on past 'evidence' (i.e. risk-averse)
- Value homogeneity — 'everywhere the same'
- Use strategies of standardisation of design (i.e. to reduce risk)
- Few psychic benefits from investment/development (i.e. development is merely a financial commodity) — weak personal associations with individual/firm
- Possess (mainly) global knowledge and expertise

disconnect between those responsible for development and the locality: *'If particular developments had some symbolic value for their developers in the past, it is now more the exchange value in the market that determines their interest.'* (Madanipour 2003: 216) — thus, the development becomes a mere commodity. In such a climate, a safe return (the investor's primary interest) will most readily be guaranteed by responding to the needs of occupiers, while those of the wider community will have a low priority. While investors and occupiers are interested parties in any development, they are not the only interested parties and there are others whose interests should be considered, including adjacent owners and the general public.

Developers' thinking is often broader than stereotypes may suggest. Individual developers are often very concerned with development quality, strongly supporting design guidelines where their value in maintaining place quality, and thereby property values, is clear (see Box 10.1). Some developers also look beyond immediate market pressures, and consider broader civic responsibilities and obligations. Many derive psychic benefits through their close association with buildings and developments. Furthermore, due to the discipline of operating in a market economy, they may often have a greater awareness of consumers' needs and preferences than many designers.

All developers are, nevertheless, motivated by the opportunity to appropriate the development value of

BOX 10.1 Canary Wharf, London

Canary Wharf, London (*Image: Matthew Carmona*)

Canary Wharf is of particular note because it helped to establish a new model of design-led (or at least design-aware) development. In the early 1980s, development in London's Docklands was jump started by the designation of an Enterprise Zone on the Isle of Dogs and the establishment of the London Docklands Development Corporation (LDDC). The wave of development that followed was characterised by a design and development free-for-all, with the LDDC almost entirely devoid of any serious design vision for the area beyond 'anything goes'.

With the arrival of Canary Wharf (10 million sq ft of commercial offices and ancillary uses) from the mid-1980s onwards everything changed. Design was seen not as a barrier to innovation and a cost on investment, but as a means to establish a marketable sense of place. The urban yet starkly private vision that resulted was fixed within a detailed masterplan and series of design codes designed to contrast dramatically with the surroundings — economically, physically and socially.

History shows that the developer, Olympia and York, over-stretched themselves and, when faced with a major economic downturn in the early 1990s, were unable to let enough space to service their spiralling debts. The scheme, however, demonstrated the importance of the certainly (up to a point) that goes hand-in-hand with a clear urban design framework — finding no such plan in place, the market sought to create one. During the economic recovery from the mid-1990s onwards and ever since, the masterplan has continued to deliver a robust place-based framework for Canary Wharf, helping to safeguard the massive investment that continues to be made in the area by the development's current owners, Canary Wharf Group (see Carmona 2009c).

or piece of land, development value often 'floats' over a wider area and may also 'shift' from one site to another. As Reade (1987: 16) notes, if a steadily expanding city is surrounded on all sides by agricultural land, all owners may hope to sell land at a price higher than its value in agricultural use (i.e. there is hope value). In practice, however, only a relatively small proportion of owners will (at this point in time) be able to sell their land for development. Thus, while development value floats over an extensive area, it settles on only a small part of it. Similarly, while there might be several possible sites for a multi-screen cinema complex within a particular city centre, the development value may largely be appropriated by the first development to be completed, with any subsequent developments having to compete with the first complex. New infrastructure or development also shifts value from one site to another. Planning controls also shift value by giving the land a particular designation (e.g. housing or agricultural) and, in discretionary planning systems, by decisions on planning applications (see Box 10.2).

In general, the developer aims to appropriate the development value by meeting unmet demand. For office development, for example, this might derive from shortages of certain sizes of office suites, shortages of office space in certain locations, or buildings able to accommodate state-of-the-art user requirements. Developers, therefore, orchestrate the assembly of inputs (sites, finance, professional advice, construction, etc.) and seek to make a profit by selling the completed development at a price greater than the cost of producing it. Given that a calculus of

BOX 10.2 The Origin of Land Value

Land value derives from two sources — the land itself and the capital improvements upon that land. The former results from the land being in a specific geographical position relative to infrastructure networks (roads, water and electricity supplies, sewers, etc.), physical amenities (schools, shops, hospitals, housing, etc.) and natural amenities (beaches, forests, open countryside, etc.). The latter results from buildings, roads, fences, etc., constructed and sited on the land itself. A key point is that through unilateral action the landowner can only change the value of the capital improvements; the value of the land itself can only be changed by the actions of the community at large.

Economic value in real estate thus derives from two sources — socially or 'community-created' value, which resides in the land, and 'owner-created' value, which resides in capital improvements upon that land. The former is often so extensive that Rypkema (2001: 210) argues the primary source of value in real estate is 'largely external to the property lines'. This also means that the value of a building derives in substantial part from its surroundings, which, in turn, explains why real estate owners are very concerned about what happens on neighbouring sites.

particular sites. This is a function of the gap between the value of the property and/or land in its existing use and its value in a 'higher-and-better' use, less site acquisition and production costs. Rather than being fixed to a particular site

reward mediated by the risk of achieving that reward drives the process, then, in the main, developer's objectives are short-term and financial.

Landowners

Land is power in the development process: development cannot happen without it and control over land development may be a more useful tool than public planning controls. Land (and property) is also heterogeneous. While other parcels may be similar, they are never identical, and every parcel of land is, thus, unique – at least by dint of its location if nothing else. As the location of land is fixed, its ownership is a source of power, particularly where spatial monopolies can be created. Housing developers, for example, compete for land in particular locations. In areas where readily developable land is in short supply, once a developer has acquired the land or purchased an 'option' – an agreement to buy the land at a specified price before some future specified date or upon some specified event occurring – and subsequently gained consent for development, they effectively have a local monopoly. Anyone wishing to buy a house in that location has to buy from them, thereby providing greater freedom to set quality levels and prices in their own interest.

As real estate is not physically moveable and property interests are tied to locations, this affects the behaviour of real estate owners. If they can move their investments from one property to another (or out of property altogether and into another asset class), their decisions in aggregate and when spatially concentrated can trigger a tipping point resulting in widespread abandonment. Conversely, if they cannot – or do not want to – move away, then they are likely to take actions to restore demand. As Beauregard (2005: 2434) observes:

'Property owners cannot easily move their investments nor do they always want to do so. As a result, any decline in demand for the property or in property values instigates attempts to reverse the blight. Without these frictions to spatial mobility, it is likely that many fewer downtown business coalitions would have formed.'

Landowners own land prior to the commencement of development; during the development process the developer holds the land. With the exception of those holding land with the expectation of subsequently developing it (e.g. builders or developers with land banks), landowners do not normally take an active role in the development process and simply release land for development when offered a sufficient price. Their objectives are, thus, usually short-term and financial.

Landowners (and developers holding land) influence the development process in four broad ways:

- *By releasing or not releasing land:* Adams (1994) makes a distinction between 'active' and 'passive' landowners. Active landowners are those who develop their own land (i.e. they become developers), enter into joint venture developments or make their land available for others to develop. They may also seek to overcome site constraints to make their land more marketable or suitable for development. Passive landowners, by contrast, take no particular steps to market or develop their land, rarely attempt to overcome site constraints and may – or may not – respond to offers from potential developers. Where public authorities are involved in or support the principle of development, powers of compulsory purchase or 'vesting' can be used to enable land assembly, though this is typically time-consuming and costly. When land for development is not freely available, it may result in 'scattered' growth, where – rather than incremental and generally outward growth from a centre – development leapfrogs or bypasses land not available for development. Shoup (2008) suggests a method of encouraging voluntary land assembly. Graduated density zoning allows higher density on larger sites and thus increases the incentive for owners to cooperate in land assembly that creates higher land values. It does not eliminate the incentive to hold out, but creates a fear of being left out because holdouts left with sites that cannot be combined with enough contiguous properties to trigger higher density lose a valuable economic opportunity. A consolidated land holding also enables the exercise of greater control over the development of the land.

- *Through the size and pattern of land parcels released:* Knox & Ozolins (2000: 5), for example, contrast the large ranchos and mission lands around Los Angeles that formed the basis of extensive tracts of uniform suburban development with East Coast cities where the early pattern of land holdings was fragmented and subsequent development more piecemeal. The land might also be sub-divided and then released for development. Platting or sub-division of land for the purpose of sale or development has a major influence on subsequent development. Simpler sub-division/land release strategies are where either the street blocks are the development parcels or the street blocks are sub-divided into development plots (Figure 10.3). More complex strategies may involve development parcels consisting of (say) two parcels facing one another across a street or a single parcel containing a street element (Figures 10.4 and 10.5).

- *Through conditions imposed on subsequent development:* Landowners can attach contractual provisions or restrictive covenants limiting the nature of subsequent development to land transfers (Knox & Ozolins 2000: 5). Landowners can also have an important role in setting down a site plan (in two dimensions) or a design framework (in three dimensions) to control the subsequent development of the land.

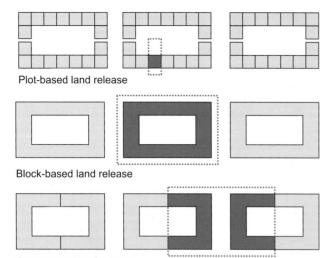

Plot-based land release

Block-based land release

Street parcel land release

FIGURE 10.3 Land release strategies. The upper part of this diagram shows a plot-based land release. This is common in some countries with regard to residential development, where a land developer provides house builders with serviced plots. House builders either commission bespoke designs for those plots or purchase standard plans. The plots might also be sold to investors who commission designers and employ house builders. To ensure variety in the street scene, limits may be placed on the total number of plots and/or the total number of contiguous plots on a single street block that a single house builder can purchase. The middle part illustrates land release on a block-by-block basis — each development parcel consists of an entire street block. The lower part shows land release on a street parcel basis, where each development parcel includes parts of two street blocks and the street space between them. The latter approach enables a single designer to design both sides of the street, thus enhancing visual coherence and a positive focus on the space as the centre rather than the edge of the development parcel

- *Through leasing rather than selling land:* Due to their long-term interest in the land, freeholders granting leases are concerned with the quality of what might be built on their land. As Sudjic (1992: 34—5) observes, in this sense development is closer to farming than trade. Aiming to

FIGURE 10.4 Block-by-block parcel sub-division — Hulme, Manchester (*Image: Steve Tiesdell*)

FIGURE 10.5 Plot-based development — Borneo Island, Amsterdam (*Image: Steve Tiesdell*)

produce a regular income, rather than to accumulate capital by selling assets, this entails taking a longer-term view on the economic health of the properties and the careful management of tenants and the uses to which they put their premises. The intention is also to build a continuing relationship rather than one-off transaction. Contractual provisions in leaseholds, for example, were responsible for the form of much of Georgian and Victorian London, Edinburgh and Glasgow.

Development funders (financial capital)

Rarely using their own capital to undertake development, developers arrange finance on the most favourable terms available with regard to cost and flexibility. When borrowing money, developers have to take lenders' concerns into consideration — in other words, the funds come with strings attached. Those investing in urban development do so for their own purposes, which are usually concerned with making profits. If acceptable profits are not achieved, they will invest elsewhere. Developers are normally concerned with arranging short-term finance (development funding), discussed here, and, in subsequently, longer-term finance (investment finance) (see below under investors).

Short-term finance — *development funding* — is needed to cover costs during the development period (i.e. the costs associated with land acquisition, construction and various professional services). The principal short-term funders are clearing and merchant banks. On completion, when long-term finance is raised, the development finance is repaid. Funding for a specific development is typically raised through a combination of equity and debt finance.

Debt involves loans, mortgages or bonds. Lenders of debt finance have the right to be repaid with interest but do not normally have a legal interest in the project (except as security in event of default) nor any entitlement to share in development profits. Debt is also first in line to be repaid by a project or company; due to this first position it involves the least risk and thus charges the lowest relative interest for the money invested (Leinberger 2008: 197).

Equity is cash, land, an existing building, professional fees, shares, etc., invested in the project. Paid off after debt is serviced on an annual basis, equity is at much greater risk and, as a result, has much higher return expectations than debt (Leinberger 2008: 197). Lenders of equity finance participate in the risks and rewards of development, are entitled to a share in development profits and have a legal interest in the project.

Patient equity (capital) is another name for long-term capital – that part of the development financing structure that does not have a defined payback period. With patient capital, the investor is willing to invest in a project with no expectation of turning a quick profit. Instead, the investor is willing to defer any return for an extended period of time. By foregoing any type of immediate return, the investor anticipates profits down-the-road being more substantial (Figure 10.6).

The terms on which development finance is made available reflect the characteristics of both the project (e.g. if the investor considers the development high risk, then funds will be made available on more exacting terms) and the borrower (e.g. developers with track records of successful development will be able to borrow funds on more favourable terms). As Leinberger (2005, 2008) explains, to enable it to more easily fund and trade developments, Wall Street commoditised US real estate into a small number of standard products (see Box 10.3 and Table 10.4). As Kelbaugh (2008b: 42) describes, the consequence of this 'sanctioning of diminished variety' coupled with a short-term investment mentality 'blind to financial returns beyond the first five to seven years' is an 'architectural dumbing down' of the built environment.

To assist their funding package, developers sometimes seek – or are offered – public subsidies. Public redevelopment and regeneration agencies may provide funding for development projects in the form of low-interest loans, grants or subsidies or – less commonly – through joint ventures. As grants and subsidies are typically used to make socially desirable but economically marginal projects viable, eligibility for support is usually couched in terms of various 'social' rather than 'economic' objectives. Providing subsidies also gives agencies leverage to seek design improvements. Although developers are often astute in making arguments that their projects are both socially desirable and would not be viable without gap funding, the intention is to provide just enough subsidy to make the project viable while not subsidising the developer's profit. Rather than reducing production costs, however, subsidies might simply be capitalised into higher land prices.

Development funders' objectives are typically short-term and financial. Their interest in design is primarily

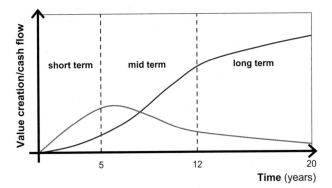

FIGURE 10.6 Hypothetical financial characteristics of walkable (blue) and drivable suburban (red) development (*Image: Redrawn from Leinberger 2005*). The graph shows a gap between the returns from driveable suburban and walkable urban development in the initial five to seven year period. Leinberger argues that a way to resolve this and to make driveable urbanism more viable is to increase the amount of equity investment in the project. He estimates that, in conventionally financed real estate development, equity represents about 20% of the total money invested in a project, while debt is about 80% (Leinberger 2008: 197). One of the reasons why drivable suburbanism loses value and walkable urbanism gains value in the longer term is that, in the former, more development is worse (i.e. it creates congestion and reduces privacy and exclusivity), while, in the latter, more is generally better (i.e. it creates greater demand and greater footfall, resulting in more amenities and facilities within walking distance). As developer of I'On (Charleston) and New Point (Beaufort), for example, Vince Graham argues, where people want 'exclusivity-and-privacy' then more is always worse, but where people want 'community-and-sociability' then more is better

a means towards a financial end. Lenders of equity finance will, however, have a greater interest in the totality of the development, including its design, than lenders of debt finance. Providers of patient equity will have a long-term interest in the development and a keen interest in its design quality.

Development agencies

Also active in the development process are various public sector development or regeneration agencies, which may include the municipality itself, arm's length companies formed by the municipality or companies and agencies formed by national, central or state/regional government. These may also be the executive body of various types of public–private partnership. These bodies seek to assist and support development either across the whole of a governmental district or within a designated target area. Some such bodies are executive and carry out physical development, such as building houses, factories and roads. Others are facilitative and operate by enabling development, through preparing land for others to develop, preparing development frameworks and masterplans, operating more 'relaxed', entrepreneurial planning and development controls, and/or by providing finance, advice, etc.

BOX 10.3 The Power of Finance

Leinberger (2005: 24) asserts that: *'The best design ideas are worthless unless money can be raised to build them.'* He explains how the American — and increasingly the worldwide — real estate finance system operates according to well-understood decision-making rules; rules that once produced older suburbs, but now produce lower-density development on the urban periphery (Leinberger 2005: 24). Ellin (1997) describes it as 'form follows financing'. As Leinberger (2005: 24) argues: *'Learning how this system works, and how it may be influenced to accept different models, should be one of the top concerns of advocates of change.'*

A major problem for investors has always been that real estate is an illiquid asset class, making it difficult and time-consuming to buy or sell. The emergence of real estate investment trusts (REITs) and Commercial Mortgage-backed Securities (CMBS) eased this problem. REITs owned large stocks of real estate properties, but, rather than buying and selling individual properties, investors bought and sold shares in the REIT through public stock exchanges, generally the New York Stock Exchange.

As Leinberger (2008: 48) observes, the public market prefers to trade 'like-for-like' and, for trading efficiency, real estate had to be commoditised (i.e. made identical). The industry did this with what it knew how to build then: drivable suburban products. Commoditisation resulted in what are known as the 'nineteen standard real estate product types' that Wall Street knows and understands, and that can be traded in large quantities. Any deviation created a 'non-conforming' product — which Leinberger (2008: 50) notes was a 'term-of-art' on Wall Street. Non-conforming products either did not get financing or did so on far more unfavourable terms, while developers, traders and financiers increasingly specialised in one product type only, with little interest in other types or in combinations of the individual products.

The following are the characteristics of one of the nineteen standard real estate products — those of a standard neighbourhood retail centre:

- Twelve to fifteen acres of land on the going-home side of a four- to eight-lane major arterial road with at least 25 000 cars per day.
- Market draw area of at least 25 000 customers within three miles, preferably with above-average incomes.
- Twenty percent of the site covered by one-storey buildings, set back from the street by 150 feet.
- Remainder of the site paved with asphalt for parking at the front and a drive at the rear where deliveries are made and trash is removed.
- A 50 000–60 000 sq ft grocery store with a superior credit rating at one end of the centre.
- A 20 000–25 000 sq ft drug store with a superior credit rating at the other end.
- In between national and regional chains or franchises, plus a couple of out parcels for fast-food chain restaurants or banks.
- Drug store, bank and fast-food restaurants will all have drive-up windows.
- Virtually everyone will get there by car.

Development advisors

Providing professional services to developers and to other development agents, development advisors include marketing consultants, estate agents, solicitors, planners, architects, landscape designers, engineers, facility managers, site agents, quantity surveyors, cost consultants, etc. As most advisers earn one-off profits in the form of fees paid for their services related to particular aspects of the project, their objectives are typically short-term and financial. Some advisers — such as management agents of investment properties — earn fees for continuing involvement and their objectives are typically long-term, financial and functional. Other advisers — architects, other designers, urban design practitioners — earn one-off profits in the form of fees paid for their services but may also use the completed project to advertise their services. They also derive significant psychic benefits from their involvement in the project. Their objectives are typically long-term, financial and design-related. Some designers also engage in development and thus operate as designer-developers, using their design skills to add value unhindered by the mediation of a developer.

Builders (industrial capital)

Builders — or contractors (and sub-contractors) — seek to make a profit by constructing the development at a cost lower than the price paid by the developer for the work and materials involved. Their objectives are, thus, primarily short-term and financial. As builders may also use the development as an advertisement for their services, they have an interest in its construction and design quality. Many

TABLE 10.4 The Nineteen Standard Real Estate Product Types (2006)

Office	Apartment
• Built to suit	• Suburban garden
• Mixed-use urban	• Urban high density
• Medical	Miscellaneous
Industrial	• Self storage
• Build to suit	• Mobile home park
• Warehouse	Housing
Retail	• Entry level
• Neighbourhood centre	• Move-up
• Lifestyle centre	• Luxury
• Big-box anchored	• Assisted living/
Hotel	retirement
• Business and luxury hotels	• Resort/second home

Source: Adapted from Leinberger (2008: 51).

builders also engage in development, thus operating as builder-developers.

Consumers

Investors

In contrast to short-term development funding, investment finance is longer-term and covers the cost of holding the completed development as an investment. Investors are, thus, the purchasers (and subsequently sellers) of completed schemes. As investment essentially requires foregoing the current use of resources for an enhanced benefit at a later date, investors in real estate are primarily interested in the (potential) income flow from user rents now, which is capitalised into the property's exchange or investment value, which may be realised at a future point in time. For commercial and industrial development, the principal investors are insurance companies and pension funds. For residential development, the principal investors are owner-occupiers, private and social landlords.

Investors generally look for investment opportunities satisfying the following criteria:

- *Security of capital and income* (low risk) — in general, the more secure an investment, the lower the risk that the capital invested will be lost or that the expected income will not arise. Investors may also look to diversify their investment through the development of portfolios that balance investment risk.
- *Potential growth of income and capital* (high returns) — although high returns may be achieved through either income or capital growth, or both combined, capital growth and high overall returns ultimately depend on the prospects for income growth (i.e. from user rents).
- *Flexibility* (high liquidity) — commercial investors (and to a much lesser extent residential ones) will look for the ability to change their investments to produce the best returns. Liquidity depends on such factors as the existence of potential purchasers, transfer costs, the investment's overall size and its capacity for sub-division. The more liquid an investment, the easier it is to sell, either in whole or in part (Adams 1994).

In practice, no single investment offers complete security, perfect liquidity and guaranteed profitability. Each investment thus represents a different combination of these attributes, with investors trading off among them and/or creating a portfolio of properties/investments. Higher expected returns are required from higher-risk investments — the investor sacrificing security in pursuit of greater return. Institutions have traditionally adopted a risk-averse approach to property investment and have concentrated their funds on the most secure, liquid and profitable types of property, usually termed 'prime property' — property in the best locations, let on long leases to tenants of 'unquestionable' covenant.

As a type of investment opportunity, real estate has particular characteristics distinguishing it from other forms of investment, such as stocks, shares and government bonds. Real estate investments are, for example, fixed in their location (not moveable), heterogeneous, generally indivisible and entail inherent responsibilities for management (e.g. collecting rents, dealing with repairs and renewals, and lease negotiations). The total supply of land (and property) is also fixed, and although the supply in a particular land use can change, it is relatively fixed in the short-term. It takes a large amount of capital to buy a small amount of real estate and there also tend to be high transaction costs involved in the transfer of real estate holdings. Real estate investments are, nevertheless, generally durable and typically provide a source of income.

Investors often use yield to gauge investment performance and to balance risk with return. In markets exhibiting significant uncertainties, investors will generally seek developments delivering a high yield and a quicker turn around on their investments. In buoyant markets, however, where there is significant competition between investors for investment opportunities, yields will generally fall. A low yield thus indicates a healthy investment market and high capital values, and that profits will increase in the near future as rents rise to reflect new capital valuations.

As their return takes the form of present and future rental income and capital appreciation, investors' objectives are typically long-term and financial, and their interests in design are as a means to a financial end. Acquisition policies of large property investment companies, for example, tend to be risk-averse — that is, they seek properties that will minimise their risk (i.e. the risk of not being able to dispose of a property at a target price and/or not being able to let a building at a target rental level) by focusing on properties acceptable to a large number of similar institutions. The properties they seek therefore need to produce an increasing rental income over a long period of time; be flexible and easily adapted to alternative occupiers; be acceptable to tenants with sound credit ratings; and be acceptable to other investing institutions (Rowley 1998: 164).

Adjacent landowners

Owners of sites adjoining or within the immediate area of a development site will seek to ensure development on that site does not reduce, and hopefully increases, their property values. Similarly, as landowners may sell only part of their holding at a time while retaining adjacent sites, they have a strong interest in what happens to the land they sell. A building's relation to its context — and, indeed, its external appearance — can be considered a spill-over effect. As the potential use and value of any parcel of land are directly affected by activity taking place on neighbouring land, buildings are interdependent assets: their value is in part a function of the value of the neighbourhood, while the value of the neighbourhood derives — again, in part — from the value of that particular building. All developments contribute to a neighbourhood's composite value. As there can be positive neighbourhood effects (i.e. where the value of neighbouring buildings increases the value of a property) and negative neighbourhood effects (i.e. where it reduces the value of a property), new developments either enhance or detract from the neighbourhood's composite value. Adjacent owners' objectives are, thus, long-term, financial and design-related in terms of external appearance and relation to context.

Occupiers and users

Occupiers or users — those who rent or buy space in the user market — derive direct use and benefit from buildings. They are primarily interested in a building's use value, especially in matters affecting business productivity and operating costs, such as appearance, comfort, convenience and efficiency. Their objectives are typically long-term, financial and design-related with respect to functionality and perhaps also to external appearance (see below).

As the use of buildings depends on both price and physical qualities, occupiers trade-off between financial (rent levels) and physical (the quality of the space, its character, its location, etc.) attributes. Although occupiers normally treat the space they rent as one of the factors necessary for the production or delivery of their goods or services and assess its contribution to this wider aim, they may also be concerned with what the building symbolises to consumers and the general public (i.e. status, solidity, quality, etc.). To communicate certain messages, companies may commission 'trophy' or iconic buildings. Certain companies will also seek out existing buildings and/or locations based on the image of their firms and the self-images of their staff and potential staff. While the development's image (as principally connoted by its external appearance) might be important to a particular occupier or investor, its value is relatively intangible and difficult to price. Furthermore, although a company's buildings might at one time have been an element of its marketing strategy, as the scale of markets increase, that element becomes less important.

Although a company's buildings may be considered less important than its website, major firms continue to invest in high-quality buildings, often by commissioning their own buildings, which in turn gives them a more commanding role in the development process (see Box 10.4 below). While, in part, this is a strategy to reinforce brand identity, it is also a means of attracting and retaining key workers by providing working environments that inspire creativity and reduce absenteeism. This suggests recognition of building quality as a contribution to employee satisfaction and performance, and reductions in absenteeism and sick leave — that is, concern for the building's functionality. The concern may also extend to the spaces surrounding the building. Research by Carmona *et al* (2001), for example, identified strong occupier-driven demand for better-quality environments.

The general public — the community

The general public — in the form of households, industrialists, retailers, etc. — consumes the products of the development process directly and indirectly (i.e. to the extent that the development is visible from, or is itself part of, the public realm). The general public thus represents a further part of the demand side of the development process. As it consumes developments in aggregate (i.e. across property lines), its concern is with each individual development's contribution to a greater whole. The general public's objectives are, thus, typically long-term and design-related in terms of external appearance and contribution to context.

As well as being (passive) recipients of the products of the development process, the general public may also actively affect the development process through, for example, protests over specific development projects, participation or consultation on particular projects (see Chapter 12), and/or involvement in amenity and conservation groups and pro- or anti-growth organisations. Through the democratic process, they also — indirectly, in aggregate and perhaps in principle only — control the regulatory side of the development process.

Regulators

The Public Sector

The public sector (in the form of government bodies, regulatory agencies and planning authorities) seeks to regulate the development and use of land through the planning or zoning system, and through other means of regulation. This regulatory role complements its development role outlined above — though, because regulation and development stimulation functions may be undertaken by different public agencies or different departments within the same municipality, developers may seek to play one off against the other.

In general, the public sector does not act directly on private sector actors: in most circumstances, for example, it cannot compel a private sector developer to undertake development. It does, however, establish the public policy and regulatory framework, which, in turn, provide the context for private sector decision-making, especially

BOX 10.4 Consumer–Producer Gaps in the Development Process

Example One

A company builds an office building from its own resources for its own occupation. A single actor performs the roles of developer, funder, owner and occupier. The costs and benefits of higher-quality features/higher-quality design thus fall on a single actor. Hence, as a single actor combines several development roles — developer/funder/owner/user — the conflict between different objectives and motivations is *internalised* and traded-off to produce the most optimal outcome subject to budget constraints.

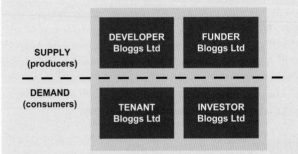

Example Two

A developer builds an office, funded by and pre-sold to an investor (i.e. funder and investor) who intends to rent it to — as yet unknown — tenants (i.e. occupiers). The funding/sale arrangement reduces the developer's risk, while the funder's long-term outlook/preferences influence the building's design. Although the costs and benefits are distributed among the developer, investor and future occupier, the future occupier is unknown and does not have a direct influence on building design and specification. While the developer and the investor/owner must anticipate and provide for the occupiers' needs, the likelihood of more costly features beneficial to the occupier being included is reduced. Hence, while a single actor combines the roles of funder and owner/investor, there are gaps between this actor, the developer and the occupiers and another gap between the developer and the occupiers. Development quality falls through these gaps.

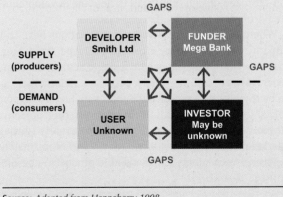

Source: *Adapted from Henneberry 1998.*

private sector investment decisions (i.e. the decision environment).

As well as meeting the planning authority's basic requirements (i.e. those that are non-negotiable), there will often be scope for negotiation and perhaps bargaining. The planning authority might require certain 'planning gains' (public open space, contributions to infrastructure, etc. — though strictly these are not gains and are means of offsetting or redressing the public costs imposed by the development). The developer may also offer certain incentives to make the scheme more acceptable to the planning authority and/or the local community. In some countries such planning gains are a legal requirement (e.g. through exaction fees), the intention being to compensate the local community for the proposed development's negative spill-over effects, to recover the cost of public infrastructure that benefits the development, and sometimes to provide a fund for future infrastructure of benefit to the development and/or community.

As refusal of planning/development consent and the probable need to go to appeal costs the developer time and money, it is extremely undesirable. If the system allows (see Chapter 11), developers will thus negotiate with the planning authority to ensure consent is likely. Similarly, the planning authority is able to encourage developers to make changes to the scheme at risk of not receiving planning consent — this empowers the planning authority's development controllers and urban designers in their negotiations with developers. The negotiation process thus provides opportunities for urban designers on both sides of the development process to influence the design and quality of the proposed development — by, for example, encouraging and/or requiring the developer to invest more time or money in improving development quality.

Planning and design controls are often seen as unnecessary constraints on development — more is heard, for example, about the cost of regulations and much less about the benefits (Van Doren 2005): the costs, however, are often immediate, tangible and imposed directly on the developer; and the benefits are less tangible, will occur at some future time and will benefit a wider range of people. Nevertheless, while controls and restrictions may reduce the return from development of any particular site, they protect the composite property values and amenity of the area or neighbourhood, and thus provide a more secure investment environment. Typically developers favour planning controls but, to reduce their development risk, often want greater certainty and clarity in their operation. As Barnett (2003: 44) explains:

'The real estate marketplace, far from being an uncontrollable force, is made up of conservative institutions that look for as much certainty as possible. Developers may argue against a specific rule that applies to their individual project, but they favour a system of ground rules that apply to others.'

The advantages of masterplans, frameworks, codes, etc. to developers are to ensure and hopefully enhance the composite value of all investments in the area, to reduce development risk and to create a more secure investment environment. These also provide incentives for developers to accept the necessary constraints on their freedom of operation. These are necessary but not sufficient conditions, however: 'good' urban design frameworks are also needed, together with sufficient consensus about what constitutes a 'good' place and 'positive context', and commitment to achieving it. This also provides a justification for public intervention into the private development process. The role of the public sector is discussed more fully in Chapter 11, but, in relation to any particular scheme, the public sector's objectives are typically long-term, functional and design-related.

DEVELOPMENT AND PLACE QUALITY

The quality of contemporary development, and the associated challenge for developers, is an important policy issue. There is nonetheless a conceptual problem relating to what is meant by 'higher quality' and 'better design' (see Carmona *et al* 2002). Three interrelated notions of design quality can be identified and, while criticisms of a lack of design quality may be directed at any or all, for analytic tractability it is important to see them as conceptually distinct:

- *Physical/construction quality* — this refers to the quality of materials used and how well these are assembled. Achieving higher quality here will usually directly increase production costs, but *should* be recompensed by increased development revenues (where these can be achieved).
- *Intrinsic building/architectural design* — this relates, in essence, to the familiar triad of 'firmness, commodity and delight' (plus economy) (see Chapter 7). In the short-term, this includes such considerations as 'kerb appeal' and, in the longer-term, the development's overall functionality and appeal. Improving building design quality will generally increase design costs (at least in terms of professional fees), but increased development revenues *or* reduced production costs *should* offset this.
- *Place quality* — that is, the overall quality of the development within its wider context. This includes, *inter alia*, the design quality of the public realm and the provision and quality of amenity spaces and facilities. More fundamentally, however, it is about synergy and the individual components of development contributing to a larger, more integrated whole. Improving overall place quality may, but frequently does not, increase production costs and *should* also be offset by increased development revenues.

Developments actors are each more, and less, concerned with each of these aspects of quality and, in considering development quality, it is important to consider the relationships between different actors. In most economies they are related through market processes and structures. Given the discipline of a market economy, development actors only become involved in the development process to the extent that it contributes to the achievement of their basic objectives. Two issues follow from this: (i) the characteristics of a proposed development will be assessed according to the degree to which they contribute to each actor's objectives and (ii) as the various actors may have different objectives for the same development, there will inevitably be conflict and negotiation between them (Henneberry 1998). From these, three key issues arise: (i) a gap — and, indeed, gaps — between the producer and consumer sides of the development process; (ii) the role of the urban designer within the producer side of the development process; and (iii) considerations of place quality over and above those of construction or architectural/design quality.

Producer–Consumer Gaps

The costs and benefits of any particular feature or element of a development project are not neutral in their (perceived) impact on the different development actors. Thus, for example, while high-quality, low-maintenance materials increase initial development costs, reduce long-term occupation costs and enhance long-term functionality, the costs are borne by the developers but the benefits accrue to the occupier. To the extent that increased costs are passed on in the purchase price, investors bear higher costs, which they recoup from occupiers through higher rental levels. To the extent that lower occupation costs and greater functionality increase rental and capital value, higher returns are achieved. What is significant in Table 10.2 is that supply-side actors tend to have short-term and financial objectives (where the development is simply a financial commodity) (the notable and significant exceptions are lenders of patient equity), while demand-side actors tend to have long-term and design objectives (where the development is an environment to be used).

Where differing objectives and motivations have to be traded-off between roles effectively played by a single actor or organisation (i.e. where a single actor is developer, funder, investor and occupier), conflict is internalised and can be traded-off to produce the most satisfactory outcome subject to budget constraints. Where differing objectives and motivations have to be reconciled externally (through a market process), there is scope for a series of mismatches or gaps between supply and demand (a producer–consumer gap) (see Box 10.4).

As the user/owners are unknown and unable to directly inform the design and development process, a producer—consumer/user gap is a structural feature of speculative development. The lack of direct consumer input, combined with situations where consumers effectively have to buy what is offered for sale (e.g. where demand exceeds supply), means producers are able to produce 'poorer-quality' development serving narrower financial purposes only. Thus, although the supply side (the developer) has to anticipate the demand side's needs and requirements (the needs of the consumer or user), it also tends to produce, where and if at all possible, a product that suits its own objectives. In general, better-quality development is more likely to occur when development roles are combined in ways bridging the producer—consumer gap. Although professionals, such as real estate agents, often act as proxies for the real occupiers, this may present problems because the interests of the proxy can never correlate exactly with those of the actual occupants.

Where producer—consumer gaps occur, the balancing of costs and benefits among all actors is critically dependent on supply-side actors being convinced — and acting on that conviction — that providing benefits will result in higher prices/values or, at least, enable cost recovery. If occupiers do not recognise the benefits of including particular features in buildings by being prepared to pay higher prices/rents (paying more for buildings with these features than for those without), then developers (especially) and funders/investors (generally) are unlikely to provide or fund them. Furthermore, developers tend to prefer the 'certainty' of reduced production costs now to the 'promise' of enhanced — but uncertain (and thus risky) — development revenues later.

This issue can also be considered in terms of 'appropriate quality' and 'sustainable quality'. In theory, 'good' design should add value to real estate development, but, as Rowley (1998: 172) argues, in the UK at least, the notion that 'better buildings mean better business' has been a matter of debate:

'The dominant attitude in private-property decision making is still the "appropriate" quality view: this holds that high-quality development, however defined, is unnecessary so long as there is some sort of market for the development at a lower standard; which may be easier to maintain, at least in the short-term; which may demand less skill and care to produce;

and which, it is assumed, can be delivered at a lower initial cost. ... The opposing attitude is that high quality helps generate long-term commercial success: this is termed the "sustainable" quality view.'

If a developer creates a higher quality building than occupiers and investors require — and, more importantly, are prepared to pay for — then the extra costs (i.e. of producing the level of quality over and above that which consumers are prepared to pay) have to be met by the developer. In short, there is an over-specification. Prudent (profit-maximising) developers, therefore, attempt to match closely the quality sought by the consumer with the quality of the product supplied: in other words, they build developments at sufficient or appropriate levels of quality, where 'sufficient' and 'appropriate' are judged against short-term criteria. Developing buildings with higher specifications — and, therefore, higher costs — increases the risk that buyers cannot be found at the higher price required to cover the additional costs. The aim of achieving 'appropriate quality' persists, therefore, on the basis that higher-quality development is unnecessary provided there is a market for the development at a lower standard (Rowley *et al* 1996).

This argument, however, assumes additional costs are involved in producing higher-quality developments. This may be true where better 'design' is seen primarily as a function of higher specification or better-quality materials (see Sustainability Insert 7), but is less true where better design relates to place quality — for example, different layouts and configurations of buildings and spaces providing better connections with the surrounding context. In these respects, better urban design may involve no additional costs (see Carmona *et al* 2001b).

Producer—consumer gaps can be closed or narrowed by coercive means (i.e. through regulation, developers *have to* provide better quality development), through remunerative means (i.e. developers calculate that it is *worth it* (financially beneficial) to provide better quality development) and through normative means (i.e. developers *want to* provide better quality development).

Sustainability Insert 7 — Resource Efficiency

Prudent use of finite resources underpins all notions of environmental sustainability, implying care in the use of energy and care in the use of non-renewable or environmentally destructive materials. For urban design this implies concern for the use of both energy and resources in and by the fabric of the built environment, and, at the larger scale, an increasing concern for energy use by preventing unsustainable spatial patterns of

building and their implications on energy consumption through travel demands (Thorne & Filmer-Sankey 2003).

Mainstream technological means now exist to reduce much of the current resource profligacy — in the use of more sustainable building materials; in designing for natural light, sun and air and for solar gain; in more efficient heating and power systems; and in more efficient use of existing infrastructure (Mandix 1996). Many of

(Continued)

Sustainability Insert 7 – Resource Efficiency—cont'd

these technologies can be applied immediately across the various design scales to retrofit established environments as well as in building more resource-efficient new environments (Terence O'Rourke plc 1998).

Active technologies such as micro-generation of power through wind turbines and installation of photovoltaic cells are increasingly cost-effective and widespread, with, for example, savings in energy consumption of up to 80% achievable when combined with passive technologies (Power 2008). Even modest programmes of wall insulation and the fitting of modern boilers in homes can reduce energy use by 50% at relatively modest cost (Lowe & Oreszczyn 2008).

Reviewing take-up of energy efficient technologies in the residential sector in the USA, however, Sathaye & Murtishaw (2004) identify both market failure and consumer preferences as decisive factors limiting take-up. The latter (consumer preference) stems from ignorance among consumers about the resource choices they make, including, for example, disconnect between their use of – and the price paid for – energy (GOS 2009: 90–1). The former (market failure) follows from this and reveals itself in the resistance of market actors to adopt design innovations that are seen as costly to produce and for which there is no corresponding up-lift in value, leading to potential market disadvantage.

In this area, until the economic imperative is reconciled with the sustainable one, by either market, fiscal or regulatory means, the fact that it is cheaper over the short-term to build and live unsustainably with destructive use of resources – particularly high energy consumption – reduces the incentive to look

long-term and to reduce resource consumption (Hatherway 2000). The challenge for urban designers is to persuade their clients – as consumers and regulators – that the long-term benefits outweigh the short-term costs.

Street shading, Izmir, Turkey (*Image: Mathew Carmona*) Low-tech street shading reduces the need for air-conditioning

The Developer–Designer Gap

Given the prevalence of producer–consumer gaps and the structural estrangement of developers (producers) and users (consumers), it is necessary to look more closely at the producer side, particularly at the designer's role. The 'producer' side typically consists of a number of actors each with differing sets of objectives. While Tables 10.2 and 10.3 summarise how development actors' motivations vary, Sue McGlynn's powergram illustrates the power of the various actors (see Figure 10.7). McGlynn (1993) draws basic distinctions between actors who exercise *power* to initiate or control development, those with a legal or contractual *responsibility* towards some aspect of development, and those with an interest or *influence* in the process.

The powergram graphically illustrates how power is concentrated on the matrix's left-hand side among those actors (i.e. developers and funders) able to initiate and control development in a very direct way. It also shows the wide-ranging interest of designers (but also their lack of any real power to either initiate or control design), and the lack of power wielded by the users of development

(including the local community). Actors on the right-hand side (i.e. designers and users) rely primarily on argumentation, alliances and participation to influence the process.

The powergram also shows the apparent correspondence between the designer's objectives and those of users and the general public. Designers are thus indirectly charged with representing users' and the general public's views within the producer side of the development process. Bentley (1999) conceptualises the interaction of different development actors, particularly the developer and the designer, and suggests a series of metaphors – 'heroic form-giver', 'master and servant', 'market signals' and 'battlefield' (see Table 10.5). Due to principal-agent problems, Bentley favours the battlefield metaphor in which actors negotiate, scheme and plot with and against other development actors to achieve the design/built form they want and in which the character, personality and interpersonal skills of the various actors are crucially important.

The opportunity space for negotiation (scheming and plotting) is set by various considerations and constraints – or 'rules' – on the various development actors. Drawing on

BUILT ENVIRONMENT ELEMENTS \ ACTORS	SUPPLIERS		PRODUCERS					CONSUMERS
	Land owner	Funder	Developer	Planners	Highway engineers	Architects	Urban designers	Everyday users
STREET PATTERN	-	-	○	○	●	-	○	○
BLOCKS	-	-	-	-	-	-	○	-
PLOTS – sub-division & amalgamation	●	●	●	○	-	-	○	-
LAND/BUILDING USE	●	●	●	●	◉	○	○	○
BUILDING FORM – height/mass	-	●	●	●	-	◉	○	○
BUILDING FORM – orientation to public space	-	-	○	◉	-	-	○	○
BUILDING FORM - elevations	-	○	○	●	-	◉	○	○
BUILDING FORM – elements of building construction	-	○	●	◉	-	◉	○	○

KEY
● Power – either to initiate or control   ○ Interest/influence – by argument or participation only
◉ Responsibility – legislative or contractual   – No obvious interest

FIGURE 10.7 The powergram *(Image: McGlynn & Murrain 1994)*

TABLE 10.5 Metaphors of the Developer–Designer Relation

Metaphor	Theme	Commentary
Heroic form-giver	Development form is generated through the creative efforts of particular development actors (e.g. architects). More generally, built environment professionals are the main agents in shaping urban space.	Bentley (1999: 30) argues this is a 'powerful myth', overstating the role of designers.
Master and servant	Development form is determined by powerplays between various development actors, whereby those with most power issue orders to those with less — that is, developers make the main decisions, with designers merely providing 'packaging' for those decisions.	Understates the role of designers and other built environment professions. Bentley (1999: 32) suggests the prevalence of the idea may be because it enables less powerful actors to adopt positions of resignation or compliance, whereby they simply do the developer's bidding and do not struggle too hard to achieve better outcomes.
Market signals	Rather than being forced into line, resource-poor actors passively respond to market signals — that is, they may disagree, but they appreciate who is paying their salaries/ fees.	Clients/developers do not have the knowledge to design buildings themselves, while their professional advisers are difficult to control.
Battlefield	Actors negotiate, plot and scheme to achieve the development form they want.	For Bentley (1999: 36), this is the most convincing metaphor.

Source: Adapted from (Bentley 1999).

Giddens' structuration, Bentley (1999) argues that all development actors have 'resources' (finance, expertise, ideas, interpersonal skills, etc.), which the other actors want and need, and 'rules' by which they operate. For private sector developers, the 'rules' relate to budget constraints, appropriate rewards and the amount of risk to be incurred. Externally enforced through sanctions of bankruptcy, such rules are not arbitrary or optional. The various webs of rules create 'fields of opportunity' — or opportunity space — within which all actors necessarily operate.

Developing the concept of opportunity space, Tiesdell & Adams (2004) set out a model of the potential for better design. The developer's opportunity space is the scope or potential to create a viable development — the larger it is, the easier it is to create a viable development. Within this opportunity space, developers devise strategies to achieve their objectives. Tiesdell & Adams argue that the developer's opportunity space is framed by three structures or contexts — the development site and its local context; the market context; and the regulatory context (Figure 10.8).

The boundaries or 'frontiers' of the opportunity space are best conceived as fuzzy and ambiguous rather than hard-edged and clear-cut — they ultimately depend on the respective negotiating abilities of development actors and on the social dynamics of their relations. Furthermore, while they are relatively fixed at any particular moment in time, they are dynamic and open to transformation over time as, for example, the policy context and the property market(s) change over time. Hence, as well as opportunity space, there are changing 'windows of opportunity'. Certain public policy actions can enlarge the developer's opportunity space — financial subsidies and grants, for example, give the developer more scope to respond to a particular market context; a less constraining regulatory context might encourage development; while infrastructure

improvements on or near the development site can make the site easier to develop (e.g. by reducing risk).

Within the developer's opportunity space, various other development actors (typically members of the developer's consultant team, such as surveyors, architects, engineers, etc.) compete for their own opportunity space and devise strategies to achieve their objectives. For the present purposes, the critical relationship is that between the developer and the designer (Figure 10.9). 'Designer' denotes an actor possessing the resource of design expertise.

Internally, the developer's brief sets the initial agenda and broad parameters for design. Discussing the phenomenon of 'the developer's vernacular', Rabinowitz (1996: 34) observes how significant design decisions are often made before projects reach the designer. He further notes, however, that the more prescriptive parameters in the client's brief are neither 'arbitrary nor capricious', because they have been shown to 'work' and are based on the 'needs of the marketplace' (1996: 36).

Such briefs are rarely cast in stone and usually provide the starting point for discussion and negotiation about design. There will, nevertheless, be elements that are negotiable and those that are not. In some circumstances, designers will have great freedom to interpret the brief. In others the opportunity space for design will be severely constrained, with designers merely providing packaging or styling — because, for example, the design exercise consists of laying out standard units on a site, or because all the fundamental design decisions have already been made according to a pre-set formula or design brief (e.g. it is a standard real estate product). Such approaches, however, limit the opportunity for designers to bring design intelligence to bear and frequently result in designs unresponsive and unrelated to the local context.

To further their own interests and, *inter alia*, the opportunity for better design, designers seek to enlarge their

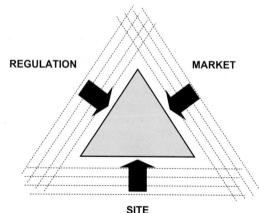

FIGURE 10.8 Developer's opportunity space. Three forces (structures/contexts) frame the developer's opportunity space in which to carry out viable development:

- *Site/context* — moving towards the centre represents a more difficult or constrained site/context.
- *Market context* (e.g. the need to create a saleable product) — moving towards the centre represents a more demanding/competitive market (i.e. less producer sovereignty).
- *Regulatory context* (e.g. the need for planning/development consent) — moving towards the centre represents a more exacting regulatory context.

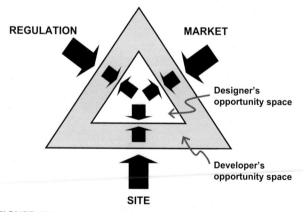

FIGURE 10.9 The designer's opportunity space. The designer's opportunity space lies within the developer's opportunity space, and is constrained by the same forces but also by how the developer filters those forces (the developer's agency becomes a structure for the designer) and the agency of the other development actors

opportunity space by negotiating with developers. In general, the more challenging the design task, the greater the developer's need for a skilled designer to achieve viable development, and so, in turn, the more space the developer is compelled to yield to the designer. In general, when developers yield opportunity space to designers, the opportunity for better design arises. For developers, a key issue is the freedom (opportunity) they choose – and the freedom they have – to give to designers; for designers, it may involve knowing how far developers can be pushed (Bentley 1999).

Opportunity space for design can also be enlarged by external forces/actions. Through the need for planning/development consent, the developer's opportunity space is constrained by public sector requirements. Design control can reduce the developer's opportunity space from the outside but also compel the developer to yield opportunity space to the designer, thus enlarging the opportunity space for design. Some designers, for example, acknowledge the support from planning and public authorities as means of changing developer attitudes to design. Relaxing regulation does not *ipso facto* enlarge the opportunity space for design, nor does it necessarily allow the designer to design, because, first, the enlarged opportunity may be claimed by the developer and, second, the designer is still the developer's employee (agent). Although reducing or alleviating constraints may enlarge the opportunity space for development (and thereby encourage development), a policy dilemma arises with regard to development quality. Higher development quality may require a tightening of regulatory control so that the developer is compelled to yield opportunity space to the designer (see Chapter 11). Provided the development remains sufficiently profitable, developers will generally follow the path of least resistance in terms of regulation; if that path is made more difficult then developers either have to up their game in design terms or find a new path.

The larger the designer's opportunity space the more scope there is for the designer to influence or determine development design. While this presupposes the designer's ability to respond to identified needs (and reconcile competing needs), such ability is at the heart of design as a problem-solving process. It is also the case that, without the constraints provided by the context, the budget, the policy framework, etc., there is little for designers to respond to in generating design ideas (nor reason for the developer to employ a designer).

However, a larger opportunity space for the designer does not inevitably translate into better design – it merely provides the opportunity for better design. More skilled and talented designers will be able to exploit the opportunity more than less skilled designers – though, equally, all designers could use the opportunity to impose their own 'heroic' view.

Discussing how designers negotiate with clients/developers about design – and thus also design quality –

Bentley (1999: 37) identifies three types of power that designers deploy:

- Through *knowledge and expertise,* which is a product of their learning, research, professional experience and, more generally, their awareness of precedents.
- Through *taking the design initiative,* because it is usually only 'designers' who make proposals for physical designs.
- Through their *reputation* and thus through the designer's commitment to maintaining a particular reputation for (say) design quality, which in part is why they have been hired now and why they will be hired again in the future. The developer will also incur costs in changing designers.

In each case, it is a power to influence, rather than compel, a particular outcome. In essence, designers argue that good design is in a developer's self-interest and that providing a high-quality development has direct financial (or other) benefits for the developer. It may, for example, enable higher returns – the design of a higher-quality housing development for the same cost will improve the development cost/value balance and will mean that the developer can sell the houses for a higher price or sell them more quickly. Anticipating higher returns involves greater risk and developers may be more persuaded by potential savings in immediate production costs. Good design might also exploit the site's positive features or minimise the effect of any detrimental or negative features. It may also convince the planning authority to accept a greater volume or density of development than had previously been envisaged (Table 10.6).

Research has sought to identify the value premium added by good/better design (Carmona *et al* 2001b). To some degree, this represents a holy grail for designers and policy-makers, because, if it can be shown that design adds value, and in what circumstances, then it is more likely developers (and the public sector) will be willing to invest in it. Research also needs to examine the salience of design as a factor in developers' business strategies and especially in their appraisal of risk and reward (see Tiesdell & Adams 2004).

Place Quality

Improvements in the design quality of individual developments are a necessary but not sufficient condition of 'good' urban design and better places. Developers responding to the needs of occupiers and investors can exclude the needs of the general public and of society at large. Segregated housing estates – in extreme form, gated communities – and inward-focused developments provide what purchasers and occupiers purportedly want, but lacking connections to and integration with the public realm, contribute little to it.

TABLE 10.6 Beneficiaries of Value in Urban Design

Stakeholders	Short-Term Value	Long-Term Value
Landowners	• Potential for increased land values	–
Funders (short-term)	• Potential for greater security of investment depending on market	–
Developers	• Swifter permissions • Increased public support • Higher sales values • Distinctiveness • Increased funding potential • Allows difficult sites to be tackled	• Better reputation • Future collaborations more likely
Design professionals	• Increased workload and repeat commissions from high-quality, stable clients	• Enhanced professional reputation
Investors (long-term)	• Higher rental returns • Increased asset value • Reduced running costs • Competitive investment edge	• Maintenance of value/income • Reduced maintenance costs • Better re-sale values • Higher-quality, longer-term tenants
Managing agents	–	• Easy maintenance if high-quality materials
Occupiers	–	• Happier workforce • Better productivity • Increased business confidence • Fewer disruptive moves • Greater accessibility to other uses/facilities • Reduced security expenditure • Increased occupier prestige • Reduced running costs
Public interests	• Regeneration potential • Reduced public/private discord	• Reduced public expenditure • More time for positive planning • Increased economic viability for neighbouring uses/development opportunities • Increased local tax revenue • More sustainable environment
Community interests	–	• Better security and less crime • Increased cultural vitality • Less pollution • Less stress • Better quality of life • More inclusive public space • More equitable environment • Greater civic pride • Reinforced sense of place • Higher property prices

Source: Adapted from Carmona *et al* (2001b: 29).

There is also a general disparity between how we invest in buildings as objects (seen as a private responsibility) and how we invest in the spaces between them (seen as a public responsibility).

From a design perspective, the process and product of development are often flawed because they are essentially concerned with individual developments rather than creating places. The Project for Public Spaces (www.pps. org) considers the typical development process focuses on 'projects' and 'disciplines', and that, as a result:

- Its goals are narrowly defined.
- It is only capable of addressing superficial design and superficial political issues.
- Its scope and assessment are defined by the boundaries of disciplines.

- It imposes an external value system.
- It relies on professionals and 'experts'.
- It is expensive and is funded by government, developers, corporations, etc.
- It sets up the community to resist changes.
- Its solutions are centred around static design and are unresponsive to use.
- It results in a limited experience of place and limited civic engagement in the public realm.

Sudjic (1993: 44–5) observes how developers are considered to have no interests in the public realm and, instead, concentrate on 'creating manageable chucks of development' — an office building, shopping centre, or an industrial park. In Christopher Alexander's terms, the developments are 'objects' rather than 'relationships'. This could be seen as an inevitable outcome of market-driven development: Sternberg (2000: 275), for example, argues that: '*Operating according to an impersonal and autonomous logic, real estate markets slice up and sub-divide the urban environment into self-contained compartments, generating cities that are incoherent and fragmented.*'

The essential need is for ways of encouraging — or compelling — developers to contribute to making places, by, for example, looking beyond site boundaries at their development's contribution to the larger whole (see Chapter 9). The Project for Public Spaces (2001) suggests recasting the development process to focus on 'places' and 'communities', claiming that such a development process would:

- Grow out of a place and its potential for civic engagement;
- Allow communities to articulate their aspirations, needs and priorities;
- Provide a compelling shared vision that would attract partners, money and creative solutions;
- Encourage communities to work collaboratively and also effectively with professionals;
- Make design become a secondary tool to support the desired uses;
- Make solutions flexible, building on existing successes; and
- Make commitment grow as citizens are empowered to actively shape their public realm.

Managing, guiding and enabling the development process can be undertaken in ways that both recognise the collective interest and exploit the self-interest of developers. Buildings are interdependent assets, and developers typically attempt to benefit from the context or neighbourhood's positive externalities (e.g. pedestrian flows, particular views, etc.) and avoid negative ones (e.g. poor views, noise, etc.). In practice, however, they have often been more concerned about the negative externalities,

creating inward-focused developments, where the milieu is more amenable to control. Such developments detract from the surrounding context and reduce its value, thereby justifying further inward-focused developments and engendering a vicious spiral, where each succeeding increment of development fails to contribute to the context. If urban design is to be a process of making better places, this spiral has to be arrested and reversed.

For a virtuous circle, each successive increment of development must contribute to a greater whole. For this to come about, developers have to respect and have confidence in the context, in the rules and regulations that control development in that area, or in some form of self-binding 'rule system'. This has happened to a degree in the past through the limitations of available building materials and construction techniques and the limited power to initiate development. It is also what Alexander *et al* (1987) proposed in *A New Theory of Urban Design* (see Chapter 9).

Despite the collective benefits in creating a positive context and in developers creating outward-oriented developments benefiting from and enhancing that context, individual developers may be unwilling to do this. The neighbourhood effect works in both directions: it does not benefit individual property owners to improve their property (and, thereby, the context), unless all other property owners will do the same. In essence, there is a collective action problem, whereby individuals acting in what they perceive to be their own self-interest produce an outcome that is worse for everyone.

Collective action problems can be addressed in different ways, through, for example, the coercive powers of a higher authority (the state or, in some circumstances, the landowner) or, alternatively, through co-operative action. There are several different ways to achieve the necessary co-ordination and ensure — in principle — all increments of development contribute to a larger whole:

- Where there is a single overarching land ownership or where land has been consolidated into a single holding, the landowner can create a masterplan or framework to be followed by developers purchasing interests in the land. This would typically deal with issues of place-making, overall coherence and the relation between the parts and the whole, and with the transition and connections between development and the wider local context.
- A public authority can perform the same role in terms of establishing a masterplan or framework, which would — by private agreement or through statutory powers — be binding on all developers operating in the locality. In this instance, the public authority has a leading and co-ordinating role and, in principle, acts in the collective interest. It may also develop the control mechanism in consultation or collaboration with local stakeholders.

- Rather than 'command-and-control' models, a third model is more collaborative and voluntary. Various developers, landowners, community groups and other stakeholders come together and agree a 'vision', masterplan, framework, etc., and the method of realising it, which would be binding on all — though the means of ensuring compliance are less obvious than in the first two ways.
- Rather than a masterplan or framework, the 'community' could agree upon a set of rules or codes. This is the essence of what is termed 'generative urbanism' (see Alexander *et al* 2008; Mehaffy 2008; Talen 2009b). Generative codes are, as Talen (2009b: 152) explains, '… *rules guiding construction decisions, rather than rules designed to achieve specific physical forms. They allow certain freedoms, but only within a framework of prohibitions focused on preventing damage to neighbours.*' They are, as Hakim (2001: 22, cited in Talen 2009b: 152) suggests, '… *a bottom-up system of self-regulation, and thus democratic.*' 'Situational architecture', where buildings are expressly designed to respond to their immediate situation, could also be considered a form of generative urbanism (see Kaliski 2008b).
- Similarly, given some agreement about rules of good place-making, integration/joining-up can derive from a small number of developers owning multiple sites within an area (and being prepared to work together); the same designer being employed by different developers within an area (with the designer providing the necessary co-ordination); and/or by partnerships between developers and/or between developers and public agencies.

Because it may rarely be possible to get all (potential) developers and (potential) stakeholders together at the same time, or to achieve a universally beneficial consensus, these may be somewhat ideal situations. A 'community' plan or vision is, nevertheless, not intended to be immutable: it will be made at one point in time and subsequently reviewed and/or revised later.

Public agencies can also undertake various actions to help develop a sense of confidence and certainty in a locality, and to which *quid pro quo* 'design strings' can be attached. Public agencies, for example, could:

- *Invest in pioneering demonstration (catalytic) projects* — Considerable risks are associated with being the 'first-mover' developer in an area and, thus, publicly sponsored demonstration projects are intended to pioneer areas or new types of development within areas and to demonstrate, for example, the commercial success and risk profile of that use in that location or, more generally, of the location itself (see Weiler 2000).

- *Invest in flagship projects and/or subsidising development* — Flagship projects are usually large-scale development schemes and generally have three overlapping purposes: to act as pioneering demonstration projects as above; to act as exemplar projects setting standards for subsequent developments; and/or by their scale to create a critical mass of development (or of a particular type of development) within the area.
- *Invest in infrastructure improvements* — Environmental and public realm improvements might be crucially important in changing the area's image. Signifying commitment to the area, they often form the basis for place marketing and other promotional campaigns (see Chapter 5). The design of new infrastructure can often be used to establish design intentions, principles and standards (Figure 10.10).
- *Investing in area-based improvements* — Although key initial and demonstration projects are necessary, redevelopment frequently needs to be encouraged on a wider basis with measures to improve the area on a comprehensive rather than piecemeal basis — the intention being to create a widespread positive neighbourhood effect.
- *Provide dedicated area management* — Place management organisations seek to reduce risk by express management of the area and of development within the area. An important aspect of maintaining a secure investment environment is to manage, where possible, the process and pace of development. Embryonic and emerging markets are more susceptible to boom-and-bust cycles than more established markets (see Jones & Watkins 1996). Place managers may thus seek to exercise control the flow of investment capital into the area and control over the availability of property — too much available stock may flood the market, with real estate

FIGURE 10.10 Erasmus Bridge ('The Swan'), Rotterdam (*Image: Matthew Carmona*). New infrastructure elements can enhance local character and identity, and set design standards

prices falling; too little stock may mean a market struggles to become established because it does not have sufficient critical mass.

CONCLUSION

This chapter has discussed the real estate development process; development roles and actors and their interrelation; and the issue of development quality. In the absence of mechanisms compelling better-quality urban design, developers (and, more generally, the producer side of the development process) will only be convinced to act where it can be demonstrated that investment in quality will be compensated by enhanced development revenues and/or reduced costs — in other words, tangible evidence of the design premium. As argued above, in contrast to higher architectural quality and better-quality materials, better urban design and better places may involve no additional costs.

Research in the UK has shown, albeit tentatively, a link between better urban design and higher value and investment returns (Carmona *et al* 2001b). Research in the USA (Eppli & Tu 1997) and Australia (Property Council of Australia 1999) supports this finding. The UK research, for example, indicated 10 ways in which better-quality design added value:

- In higher returns on investments (good rental returns and enhanced capital values).
- As a means of establishing new markets (e.g. for city-centre living) and opening up new areas by differentiating products and raising their profile.
- By responding to a clear occupier demand that also makes developments attractive for long-term investment.
- By helping to deliver more lettable area (higher densities) on sites, while maintaining quality levels.
- By reducing management, maintenance, energy and security costs.
- In more productive and contended workforces.
- By supporting the 'life-giving' mixed-use elements in developments.
- By opening up new investment opportunities, raising confidence in development opportunities and attracting public sector grant funding.
- By creating an economic regeneration and place-marketing dividend.
- By delivering viable planning gain and reducing the burden on the public purse of improving poor-quality urban design (Carmona *et al* 2001).

Complementing the discussion here, the next chapter discusses the public sector role in securing and maintaining high-quality places.

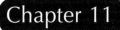

The Control Process

The public sector plays a major role in securing and maintaining high-quality environments. This chapter explores how public agencies use a range of statutory powers not only to provide a quality threshold over which development proposals must pass, but also to guide, encourage and enable appropriate development and to enhance the public realm. The public sector's role is, however, much more than one of 'controlling' or 'guiding' design and development. It also acts in a more corporate manner and, in its various forms, has the potential to influence place-making and design quality through a wide range of statutory and non-statutory functions (see Table 11.1). Through these mechanisms, it is an important contributor to the quality of the built environment both in its own right (in a direct 'hands-on' manner) and by influencing and requiring (in a more indirect 'hands-off' manner) high quality development from the private sector. A study of London's urban environment illustrates the diversity of these public sector activities, organising them into 'policies and processes', 'maintaining influences' and 'enabling factors' (Figure 11.1).

Lynch (1976: 41–55) identified four modes of action for public authorities: 'diagnosis' (appraisal); 'policy'; 'design'; and 'regulation'. Rowley (1994: 189) adds two further modes — 'education and participation' and 'management'. As participation is dealt with in Chapter 12, Lynch's four modes together with education and management provide the organising structure for this chapter. The modes relate particularly well to public sector actions in urban design; most also relate to private sector activity. Before discussing the detail of the public sector's role, it is necessary first to consider the public sector's legitimacy in seeking to intervene.

PUBLIC INTERVENTION

Ellin (2006: 102) poses a core question about public intervention, asking whether we should '... *step aside and allow the city to grow and change without any guidance whatsoever?*' She answers her own question:

'*No, that would simply allow market forces to drive urban development. Markets are only designed to allocate resources in the short term and without regard for things that do not have obvious financial value like the purity of our air and water or the quality of our communities.*'

Although public intervention and regulation of development might be seen as an appropriate response to the dysfunction of (real estate) markets that results in poor development design and place-making, this presumption is susceptible to the fallacy that the solution to imperfect markets is (perfect) government. Just as markets fail, so do governments. Hence, the presumption that 'good' design guidance and control will, *ipso facto*, create good places must be treated with some scepticism. The situation is complex and raises fundamental questions about the state's role in a market economy.

Some argue that often there is no market failure in the first place, and the expensive and time-consuming bureaucracies put in place to correct presumed failure often have worse side-effects than the problems they seek to address. Arguing against zoning, for example, Siegan (2005) suggests zoning increases the price of homes by limiting supply; encourages sprawl by imposing restrictions on uses, densities and height; and is exclusionary because it acts against the needs of disadvantaged groups by distorting the market from meeting their needs (e.g. discount shopping or an auto repair shop in a residential area). It may be, however, that rather than a fault of intervention per se, this is the fault of poor public intervention that has, first, failed to allocate enough land for development, and, second, as Leinberger (2008) argues, is based on a drivable suburban model of development, rather than a walkable neighbourhood model. Clearly, just as there is good and bad development, so there is good and bad regulation.

As land — and the power and resources to develop it — is in large part vested in private hands, public sector intervention and regulation is in some form inevitable to (i) protect the property rights of other landowners and (ii) protect the rights of society at large against inappropriate development. There is no such thing as a 'free' market, as, even in the least regulated places, controls of some form or other on the use of space can be found. In Houston, for example, the only major US city without zoning controls, ordinances have been adopted to alleviate particular land use problems including banning nuisances, imposing off-street parking, and regulating minimum lot, density and land use requirements (Siegan 2005: 227).

Rather than a debate about whether to intervene, the debate is about what *type* of intervention and *how* that intervention occurs. It is vital, for example, for urban

Public Places – Urban Spaces. DOI: **10.1016/B978-1-85617-827-3.10011-2**

TABLE 11.1 Public Actions

- Advertisement control
- Building/development permits/control
- Building public facilities
- Conservation activity/controls
- Cultural events and public art
- Design control/review
- Design guidance, policy and briefing
- Furnishing and lighting public spaces
- Image-building and promotion
- Local environmental action such as Local Agenda 21
- Land assembly and sub-division
- Land reclamation
- Land disposal
- Land use allocation (zoning)
- Open space and recreational resources
- Parking control
- Partnership and joint venture schemes
- Pedestrianisation, pavement widening and traffic calming
- Public involvement and participation
- Public order management and crime control
- Public building and demonstration projects
- Public education
- Social housing funding and/or provision, and management
- Town centre management
- Transport management, investment and planning
- Urban management and maintenance
- Urban regeneration and grant making

designers to understand where public sector interventions into the private sector development process can be most effective — typically before or during the development design stage rather than after it, namely as proactive rather than reactive intervention.

Guidance, Incentive and Control

Control — the title of this chapter — is itself a problematic term, suggestive of coercive imposition. In fact the public sector has a range of possible 'tools' at their disposal with which to intervene in the design process (see Chapter 3). Schuster & Monchaux (1997 in Schuster 2005: 337–8) have categorised these as:

- Ownership and operation: the public sector may choose direct provision by owning land and building itself (the state will do X).
- Regulation, by intervening directly in the actions of others who seek to develop (you must or must not do X).
- Incentives (and disincentives), offered to encourage certain behaviours, for example grants, land transfer or enhanced development rights (if you do X the state will do Y).
- Establishment, allocation and enforcement of property rights, for example through zoning or re-zoning land uses (you have the right to do X, which the state will enforce).

- Information, by collecting and distributing information intended to influence the actions of other actors, such as the production of guidance on desirable design attributes (you should do X or you need to know Y in order to do X).

For urban designers acting in the public sector seeking to influence the design of development, these can be reduced to three key processes of 'guidance', 'incentive' and 'control':

- *Guidance* equates to the 'positive' encouraging of appropriate development by producing a range of plans and guides. These will have more (or less) authority depending on the statutory powers under which they are prepared. They range from simple 'information' tools to 'establishment, allocation and enforcement' devices guiding the distribution and redistribution of land uses. Ultimately, however, it will typically be for landowners to determine whether they wish to develop (or not). The power to make positive proposals is thus limited by it typically being the private sector that has access to resources.
- *Incentive processes*, by contrast, equate to more proactive processes of enabling development that is in the public interest, through actively contributing public sector land or resources to the development process (perhaps to fill a funding gap), or otherwise making the prospect of development more attractive to landowners, perhaps by providing public amenities or development bonuses, altering land allocations or providing a high-quality public realm.
- *Control processes* give public authorities the power over the development process through the 'negative' ability to refuse development. For this reason this chapter is named 'control' because, if guidance and incentive fail, then control offers the ultimate sanction for municipalities to ensure the public interest is being met via a series of overlapping regulatory regimes — planning, conservation, highways adoption, environmental protection, building permits, etc. Although denying relevant development consents is a negative act, control processes often involve negotiation, advocacy, persuasion, even bluff (threatening to deny permission). Controlling development is thus often a complex and highly skilled process involving a weighing and balancing of public and private needs and aspirations.

Rather than a top-down, command-and-control activity, a better way of understanding the role of urban design in the public sector is thus as means of encouraging and enabling the production of higher design quality and better places, where processes of control are shaped by allied processes of guidance and incentives, which should, ideally, precede the act of control. Punter (1998: 138) highlights how public sector control has changed from an inherently negative

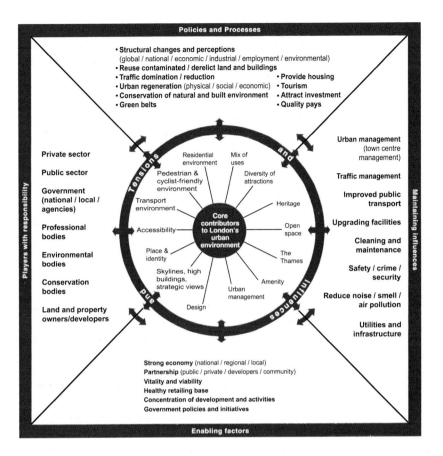

FIGURE 11.1 Core contributors to the quality of London's urban environment (*Image: Government Office for London 1996*). The diagram highlights the relationships between public agencies and the private sector, as well as the core qualities each aims to influence

concern with *design control* to a more positive concern for *design quality*. He argues that the traditional view of design has been a static one of an 'end product' — a particular piece of built form — rather than a dynamic one of a process — a creative problem-solving process — through which development is produced. The need, therefore, is for interventions in the design and development processes that understand and appreciate the potentially positive and proactive role of the public sector in shaping places, backed up by the ultimate sanction of control.

Design Quality, But Whose?

Design quality is also problematic, not least because it may mean different things to different actors and stakeholders. Furthermore, within any particular community or society, there may not be consensus about what is higher design quality, nor about what makes a good place. Indeed, a primary task of stakeholder consultation and engagement is often to build consensus about what constitutes design quality (see Chapters 10 and 12).

Based on restrictions of private property rights, systems of controlling design and development invariably arouse great passions and sometimes controversy. Those who perceive themselves to be most directly affected —

designers and developers — often make the most strident case against such forms of control. As Walters (2007: 132–3) argues: '*Many architects are guilty of knee-jerk reactions to design standards, preferring the "freedom" to produce poor buildings rather than be required to improve standards of design to meet mandated criteria.*' Not uncommonly, however, some designers hold the inherently contradictory attitude that design controls should apply to everyone but themselves.

Writing in a US context, Scheer (1994: 3–9) articulated many of the perceived problems with public sector attempts to control design. She suggests such processes are:

- Time-consuming and expensive.
- Easy to manipulate through persuasion, 'pretty pictures' and politics.
- Performed by overworked and inexperienced staff.
- Inefficient at improving the quality of the built environment.
- The only field where lay people are allowed to rule over professionals directly in their area of expertise.
- Grounded in issues of personal rather than public interest, particularly in maintaining property values.
- Violating rights to free speech.
- Rewarding ordinary performance and discouraging extraordinary performance.

- Arbitrary, vague and superficial.
- Encouraging judgements that go beyond issues outlined in adopted guidelines.
- Lacking in due process (because of the sheer variety of issues and processes of control).
- Failing to acknowledge there are no rules to create beauty.
- Promoting principles that are abstract and universal, not specific, site-related or meaningful at the community scale.
- Encouraging mimicry and the dilution of the 'authenticity' of place.
- The 'poor cousin' of urban design because of the focus on individual projects at the expense of a broader vision.

Addressing these criticisms, Rybczynski (1994: 210–1) outlines why, despite their perceived faults, processes of controlling design continue to command significant commitment within public authorities. Given the frequency and ferocity of debates on the issue, he argues such processes can be considered to be 'extremely effective'. Furthermore, the processes reflect both public dissatisfaction with the idea of professional expertise and an apparent lack of consensus in the architectural profession about what constitutes good design. He, therefore, suggests such processes should be seen as tools to guarantee at least a minimum compatibility between 'new' and 'old', and are of particular value because they reflect and promote deeply held public values. Moreover, noting that, by the end of the twentieth century, such values had a 'nostalgic' rather than 'visionary' flavour, he argues this is entirely understandable in an era when the explosion in building techniques and materials has unleashed a multiplicity of design styles and possibilities, many of which contrast unhappily with established contexts (1994: 210). He concludes that historic experiences of state intervention in design:

'...in cities as disparate as Sienna, Jerusalem, Berlin, and Washington DC, suggest that public discipline of building design does not necessarily inhibit the creativity of architects – far from it. What it does have the potential to achieve ... is a greater quality in the urban environment as a whole. Less emphasis on the soloist and more on ensemble playing will not be a bad thing.'

(1994: 211).

Although debates will undoubtedly continue, the processes increasingly carry political commitment and widespread public endorsement. This is critical because, before there can be guidance, incentive or control, urban design practitioners – and perhaps some politicians – operating inside and around the public sector must persuade politicians and other decision-makers that concern for design quality is necessary and worthwhile. Equally, if they are to have any impact, they also need to persuade those with the power to make a difference – developers, investors,

occupiers – of the benefits of investing in place quality (see Chapter 10). Given their role in influencing place quality, practitioners working in the public sector and politicians need both a better-developed understanding of place-making, and to move from being unknowing to become knowing urban designers. Urban design practitioners, thus, have an important role not just as advocates but also as educators.

Carmona (2001: 132) argues that the priority given to design by public authorities is evident in four key ways: through the development of design criteria developed through public consultation and considered relevant to the public interest; through the responses to, and concern for, local context; through the value placed on the different mechanisms used to control design; and through the resources devoted to design and securing better places. Taken together, these factors largely define a municipality's approach to design. A range of factors can, nevertheless, act to undermine local initiative, including:

- the political will to engage in design concerns (nationally and locally);
- the strength of local investment and property markets;
- the 'conservatism' and anti-development attitudes of local communities and politicians;
- the capacity of the historic fabric to accommodate change;
- the availability of skilled designers (particularly those with urban design expertise);
- the willingness of developers and investors to consider issues of, and invest in, design quality; and
- the lack of flexibility of some regulatory systems to work outside their own technocratic processes and narrowly defined design standards.

Conflict or Productive Negotiation?

In Chapter 1, the notion of three professional tyrannies was introduced – the creative, market and regulatory tyrannies (see Carmona 2009a). An epitome of the latter might be the reactionary local politician proclaiming 'we know what we like and we like what we know', or the unbending council technocrat determined that 'rules are rules'. In other words, a public sector characterised by a concern for conformity rather than good design. Such a narrow and technocratic view of the public sector rapidly erodes its legitimacy in the eyes of those who come up against its precepts, and eventually of the system itself. It will certainly prove ill-equipped to meet creative and market as well as regulatory aspirations.

At the heart of each tyranny is a different and overriding imperative, respectively to achieve an innovative design solution (within the constraints of site, budget, brief, etc.), to make a good return on investment (e.g. to sustain a viable

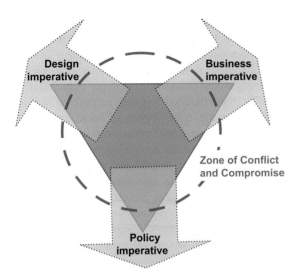

FIGURE 11.2   Three tyrannies: zone of conflict and compromise (*Image: Matthew Carmona 2009b*)

business) and to satisfy a broad range of public policy objectives. As these are often in opposition to each other, the result can easily be a three-way tug of war, with the central ground stretched thinly over what can be characterised as a zone of conflict and compromise (Figure 11.2). This caricature has long typified development processes around the world.

Yet, alternatives exist that see the public sector role as one of building consensus between creative, market and

regulatory imperatives within a zone of productive negotiation (see Figure 11.15 below). Carmona (2001: 132–66) argues more sophisticated municipalities typically achieve this through:

- *A broad conception of design*, extending beyond 'aesthetics' and basic 'amenity' considerations to include concern for environmental quality that encompasses urban design and sustainability – economic, social and environmental.
- *An approach to design informed by context*, based on appraisal of areas and sites and on public consultation and/or participation (see Chapter 12).
- *An integrated hierarchy of design guidance* extending from the strategic city/district-wide scale (or beyond), to area-specific guidance for large-scale regeneration, conservation or development projects, to design guidance for particular sites and development opportunities.
- *An urban design team* with the means and capabilities to engage in the design process by preparing proactive policy/guidance frameworks and design briefs to identify, incentivise and guide development opportunities and to respond positively to development proposals.

A number of international exemplar cities – Birmingham (see Box 11.1), Portland, Barcelona, Amsterdam, Friedberg, Vancouver and Singapore – have long had such approaches; many others are catching up fast. The main part of this chapter thus sets out and discusses some of the key elements.

BOX 11.1 Birmingham, UK: Re-inventing Through Urban Design

Victoria Square, Birmingham (*Image: Matthew Carmona*)

Birmingham has long been the UK's exemplary urban design case study. Post-war re-building of the city centre in the 1950s and 1960s made it Britain's first 'car city'. Urban decay in the 1970s and 1980s, exacerbated by the strangulation of the city centre inside its ring roads, led to the first serious attempt in the

UK to consider a city from an urban design perspective. The urban design strategy that emerged in the early 1990s prioritised making connections across the city (for pedestrians), understanding how people used and read the city from a ground-level perspective, exploiting the city's heritage and distinctive qualities, and, once again, creating a city for people rather than cars.

In the subsequent 20 years, the city stuck determinedly to this strategy, investing its own resources in the public ream, but, more importantly, and with increasing success, attracting private sector developers to once again invest in the city centre. These investments include the Brindleyplace business quarter and, more recently, the Bull Ring shopping centre and numerous residential schemes.

Throughout this period the city has shown considerable leadership, driving the transformation forward through proactive and often visionary design guidance, and by maintaining the UK's largest local authority in-house urban design team. In the period 2000–2008, the city experienced a major investment boom as perceptions of the city transformed, while in the post-2007 downturn the city has used its own resources to fill the gap and continue the vision with, for example, plans to deliver the city's first new park for over a century.

DIAGNOSIS/APPRAISAL

Chapter 3 discussed the nature of urban design as a process and related it to the key stages of a 'universal' model of design process: setting goals; analysis; visioning; synthesis and prediction; decision-making; and evaluation. By setting out the initial parameters from which design proposals (or policies) are developed, and feeding back into the process as outcomes are evaluated, appraisal — the first of Lynch's modes of action — can be considered as both a start (as analysis) and an end (as evaluation) of the design process.

Universal or meta-principles of urban design merely provide a framework — each site or locality possesses its own unique set of qualities, opportunities and threats — through which to focus urban design action. Private sector developments and public sector interventions, whether project- or policy-based, begin with appraisal as the starting point. For the public sector, however, a systematic analysis of context has an extra dimension because the range of scales across which public authorities operate — district/region-wide, area-wide and site-specific — necessitates different types of analysis to inform appropriate design responses. For all but the largest private sector developments, analysis generally remains at the site-specific scale.

In most countries, public authorities emphasise the importance of respecting the local context. Central government design advice in the UK, for example, has consistently emphasised the need to evaluate development proposals by reference to their surroundings. As means both to develop clear indications of public design expectations and to make judgements about particular design proposals, municipalities are encouraged to understand and appreciate the character and nature of the context over which they have jurisdiction. The intangible as well as the more tangible qualities of place should — where possible — be the subject of appraisal at the district/region-wide, area-wide and site-specific scales.

City/Region-Wide Scale Appraisal

Appraisal at this scale ranges from evaluating the broad character of the underlying natural landscape through identifying distinctive areas of towns and cities (e.g. neighbourhoods or quarters) to understanding the capital web and movement patterns. These provide means to understand urban growth patterns and to relate new development to existing urban areas in a sustainable fashion (Figure 11.3).

Large-scale spatial analysis happens most frequently and with greatest sophistication with regard to natural (rural) landscapes. One of the largest identified 181 landscape character zones in England, each with a detailed nature conservation, landscape character and ecological character description (Countryside Commission & English Nature 1997). On a smaller, but still regional, scale, such analysis

has been advocated by a number of influential urban design researchers (e.g. Lynch 1976; Hough 1984). In many parts of Europe — Germany and Sweden in particular — landscape/ecological analysis now forms the basis for strategic design and planning decision-making (Lundgren Alm 2003). Such analysis is often directed towards identifying the area's 'landscape capacity' (the degree of modification before unacceptable damage would occur), the landscape's sensitivity and the potential for new development to strengthen positive attributes and ameliorate negative ones. The capacity of settlements to accommodate development in a manner that both enhances the established character and ensures growth occurs in a sustainable manner should also be a fundamental part of strategic design.

Tensions between new development and the preservation of established character occur most acutely in historic urban contexts, and it is here that work on urban capacity points a possible new direction for large-scale spatial analysis. In Chester (UK), for example, much of the city and its surrounding landscape are of significant conservation importance, making provision for new development extremely challenging and necessitating a strategic conservation-led approach to growth. Linking this strategy to broader sustainable objectives highlighted the need to examine the city's carrying capacity, and led to a city-wide environmental capacity assessment (Arup Economics & Planning 1995: 14—8) (Figure 11.4). The analysis formed part of a broader drive to develop strategic development guidelines.

For Southworth (2003b) the question of large-scale appraisal of the natural and built environment is integral to considerations of 'quality' and how the problem of defining quality might be resolved. He notes that huge quantities of data are now available at the city-wide or regional scale, much of which reflects directly on perceptions of quality, and which can be manipulated through GIS technologies (see Chapter 12). For him: *'Traditional measures used by city planners such as land use patterns, density, floor area ratio (FAR), or circulation patterns have limited proven value in measuring or predicting the quality of the built environment as experienced by users.'* (Southworth 2003b: 345). Instead, he highlights our ability to measure with 'some degree of reliability' many sensory aspects of the built environment 'more closely related to perceived quality', such as views, topography, sun and shadow, microclimate, street definition, scale and pattern, noise levels, building footprints, public and green open spaces, public facilities, infrastructure, special landscape features such as street trees or urban wilds, and recognised hazards. Observing 'few technical limitations in measuring and managing many qualitative aspects of the built environment', he notes a lack of political will to do so. Without such information, qualitative dimensions will continue to be undervalued in city-wide design processes.

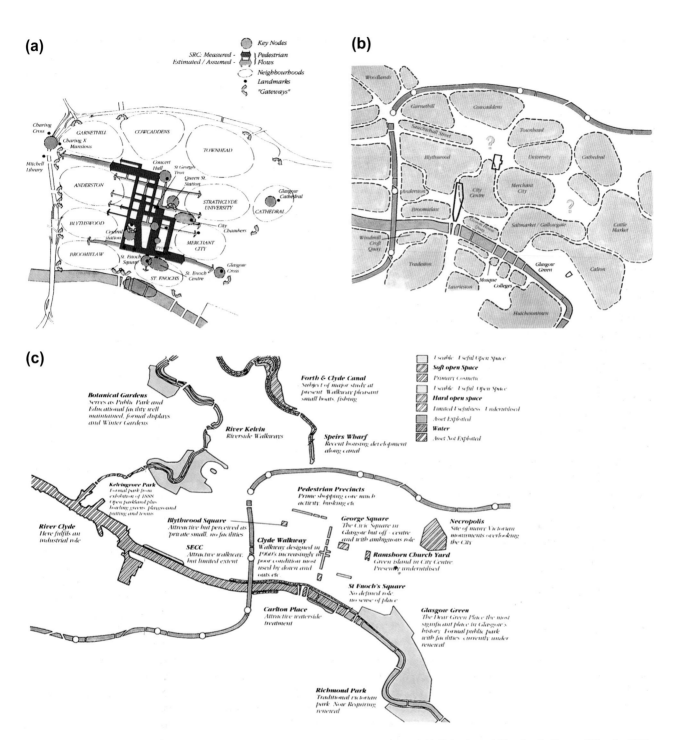

FIGURE 11.3   (a–c) Glasgow city centre: (a) movement patterns, (b) open space structure and (c) distinctive neighbourhoods (*Image: Gillespies 1995*). As the basis for a design-based regeneration strategy, Glasgow city centre's spatial character was mapped in a variety of ways

Area-Wide Appraisal

At the area-wide scale, appraisal is often a precursor to formulating design policies and guidance. Appraisal at this scale, however, is frequently expensive, time-consuming and dependent on skilled manpower (often in short supply in the public sector), and frequently remains generalised in nature. Most comprehensively undertaken in historic (designated) areas, this reflects both the increased scope for public sector intervention in such areas and the more comprehensive guidance available to practitioners.

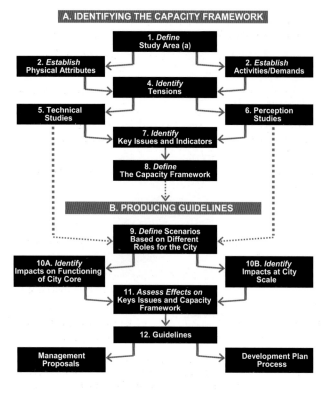

A. IDENTIFYING THE CAPACITY FRAMEWORK

1. *Define* Study Area (a)

2. *Establish* Physical Attributes

2. *Establish* Activities/Demands

4. *Identify* Tensions

5. Technical Studies

6. Perception Studies

7. *Identify* Key Issues and Indicators

8. *Define* The Capacity Framework

B. PRODUCING GUIDELINES

9. *Define* Scenarios Based on Different Roles for the City

10A. *Identify* Impacts on Functioning of City Core

10B. *Identify* Impacts at City Scale

11. *Assess Effects on* Keys Issues and Capacity Framework

12. Guidelines

Management Proposals

Development Plan Process

English Heritage (1997, 2005) — a body charged with guiding and administering much of the conservation legislation in England — regards appraisal as the basis for conservation and planning action and offers a framework for such analysis (Table 11.2). Despite approaching appraisal from a historic and predominantly visual perspective, the framework enables a clear and concise articulation of character. The objective for urban designers is to develop their own conception based on knowledge of both the range of issues pertinent to an area and the skills and resources available to undertake analysis. At whichever scale, the approach used should include analysis of morphological, visual, perceptual, social and functional characters, plus the prevailing environmental, political and economic contexts.

To provide a more systematic approach to area appraisal, the UK's Urban Design Alliance created 'Placecheck' (www.placecheck.info) — a method of assessing the qualities of a place, identifying what improvements are needed and focusing on local people and organisations, including the local municipality, working together to achieve those improvements. It does this by encouraging these groups to come together to ask a series of questions about their city, neighbourhood or street and to record the answers by a variety of methods including photographs, maps, plans, diagrams, notes, sketches and even video. The aim is not only to develop a better understanding and appreciation

of places, but also to provide a prompt for the production of positive forms of guidance, such as design frameworks, codes, briefs, etc.

Three key questions are asked initially: (i) what do you like about this place?; (ii) what do you dislike about it?; and (iii) what needs to be improved? Fifteen more specific questions then focus on who needs to be involved in, and how people use and experience; the place.

The People

- Who needs to be involved in changing the place for the better?
- What resources are available locally to help get involved?
- What other methods might we use to develop our ideas about how to improve the place?
- How can we make the most of other programmes and resources?
- How can we raise our sights?
- What other initiatives could improve the place?

The Place

- How can we make this a special place?
- How can we make this a greener place?
- How can the streets and other public spaces be made safer and more pleasant for people on foot?
- How else can public spaces be improved?
- How can the place be made adaptable to change in the future?
- How can better use be made of resources?
- What can be done to make the most of public transport?
- How can routes be made better connected? (Cowan 2001b: 11).

To provide additional prompts to thinking, these questions are broken down into more than one hundred further questions. The approach is intended to be used in a variety of ways, and has been widely tested through a series of pilot projects. The Project for Public Spaces provides an equally useful approach through their Place Diagram (www.pps. org). In this, users evaluate a specific place in term of four key criteria — comfort and image; access and linkage; uses and activities; and sociability — in terms of a number of intuitive or qualitative aspects ('intangibles'); quantitative aspects can then be measured by statistics or research (see Table 8.1).

A less sophisticated but (because of its simplicity) particularly effective form of analysis — the SWOT (Strengths, Weaknesses, Opportunities, Threats) analysis — can be used to similar effect. SWOTs involve brainstorming and recording a place's strengths and weaknesses, the opportunities that could be exploited and the likely threats. The value of Placecheck, Place Diagram and SWOT techniques is to move beyond

TABLE 11.2 Checklist for Assessing Character

Location and population	To set the area within the context of the wider settlement and to understand how the area's social profile informs its character.
Landscape setting	To understand the relationship of the development to the landscape and topography of the area.
Origins and development of area	To establish how the area has grown and evolved, particularly to trace its morphological lineage.
Prevailing and former uses and activities within area	To understand how uses have shaped the area's character, both with regard to the form and layout of the buildings and spaces and the public realm's social characteristics.
Key views and vistas	To recognise important views into and out of the area and the role of any landmark buildings.
Definition of character areas or zones	To identify any sub-areas as derived from landscape or architectural character.
Area's archaeological significance	Expert assessment may be required to ensure proper regard is paid to underlying archaeology.
Architectural and historic qualities of buildings	To make reference to any dominant architectural styles or building traditions, any groups of buildings making a special contribution to character or the contribution of roofscape.
Contribution of unlisted buildings	To ensure buildings without statutory protection in their own right are still recognised for their contribution to the area's character.
Character and relationship of spaces within area	To ensure particular regard is given to the relationship between public and private spaces in an area, but also as a means to define townscape and visual characteristics of space (particularly means of enclosure) and the ways in which spaces function and are used.
Prevalent and traditional building materials, textures, colours and details	Detail on buildings, floorscape street furniture often provides much of the visual interest in an area and therefore makes a major contribution to establishing local distinctiveness.
Contribution of green spaces, trees, ecology and biodiversity	To recognise the vital part the natural and man-made green environment makes to the character of urban areas.
Area's setting and relation to its surroundings	To have regard for the wider landscape/townscape context and particularly for the topography, views and vistas to any countryside or landmarks.
Extent of loss, intrusion or damage to area	Negative features or significant threats will often have as great an impact on character as positive ones.
Existence of neutral areas	To ensure all opportunities for enhancement are recognised, including opportunities for contemporary design.
Problems, pressures and capacity for change	To establish how the area is changing, positively or negatively, and the capacity to shape this.

Source: Adapted from English Heritage (1997, 2005).

analysis to identify potential courses of action. These techniques are also appropriate at the site-specific scale.

Site-Specific Appraisal

For designers and developers, site-specific appraisal is a prerequisite for development. Similarly, for the public sector, the production of context-specific site-based design guidance generally relies on a comprehensive site-specific appraisal. At this scale, Kevin Lynch (in Lynch & Hack 1984) argued that each context and study requires its own approach to appraisal in order to develop concepts based on its distinctive characteristics, coherent patterns and equilibrium, including negative as well as positive characteristics. Site-specific appraisal should aim to identify both those features worthy of protection and the potential for improvement, and, thereafter, to define principles and proposals that respect or ameliorate these qualities.

Chapman & Larkham (1994: 44) provide a useful appraisal checklist (Table 11.3). A comprehensive list and discussion of appraisal techniques can also be found in the third edition of New Zealand's Urban Design Toolkit (Ministry for the Environment 2006) (see Table 11.4).

Where ensuring development respects its context is a key objective of design policy, Punter & Carmona (1997: 351) assert that understanding context is critical. Appraisal is an expensive and time-consuming process, but also an unavoidable process if high-quality places are to be secured. Municipalities in particular should ensure adequate appraisal across strategic and area-wide scales inform their policies and guidance on design. They also have a vital role to play in ensuring adequate site-specific appraisal informs development proposals, and may themselves provide such analysis for key sites as part of a development briefing process (see below) and to incentivise good design.

POLICY, DESIGN AND REGULATION

Reflecting emphasis, in the public sector context, on guiding and controlling the design of development, the next three modes of action — 'policy', 'design' and 'regulation' — will be discussed in this section. As direct public sector investment in creating complete new environments ('Total Design', see Chapter 1) is less common, the public sector's role in securing high quality development is often limited to these functions. Nevertheless, through a variety of public institutions, most systems of governance have extensive powers to ensure private sector design proposals serve the public/collective interest.

Such systems usually operated through interrelated processes of planning, conservation and building control. In many countries these are related but separate regulatory systems, though they may also be combined in different configurations, for example planning and conservation may be a single system, and grant of planning consent may also include a building permit. Each is established through a policy (legislative) context that may be elaborated further through various forms of design (guidance) tools, which provide the context within which actual regulation (control) occurs. This then provides the structure for the discussion below.

Design Policy

For a long time, design quality was either given lip-service, only prioritised in sensitive historic contexts, or actively excluded from the political agenda, as was the case in the UK in the 1980s. This resulted in open inter-professional conflict, substandard design outcomes, and a gradual decline in public sector design skills. More recently, driven by the global movement of design up the political agenda, local and national administrations have increasingly been searching for appropriate tools both to overcome critiques of public sector intervention in design and, more importantly, to deliver better places.

In part, this reflects the new positions of architecture and urban design as weapons in the battle of global and local inter-city competition (Smyth 1994; Fainstein & Gladstone 1997; Hall 2000) but also the rise of sustainability, as a result of which national and local governments have been reviewing their policies on design. For some, the

---

TABLE 11.3 Checklist for Site-Specific Appraisal

- *Record general impressions of the site* – e.g. the existing sense-of-place; use notes, sketches, plans, photographs to record information including legibility.
- *Record site's physical characteristics* – e.g. site dimensions/area, features, boundaries, slopes, ground conditions, drainage and water resources, trees and vegetation, ecology, buildings and other features.
- *Examine relationships between site and surroundings* – e.g. land uses, roads and footpaths, public transport nodes and routes, local facilities and services and other infrastructure.
- *Consider environmental factors affecting the site* – e.g. orientation, sunlight/daylight, climate, microclimate, prevailing winds, shade/shelter, exposure, pollution, noise, fumes, smells.
- *Assess visual and spatial characteristics* – e.g. views or vistas, panoramas, attractive features or buildings, eyesores, quality of townscapes and surrounding spaces, landmarks, edges, nodes, gateways, spatial sequences.
- *Note any danger signals* – e.g. subsidence, land-slips, poorly drained or marshy ground, fly-tipping, vandalism, incompatible activities or adjacent uses, sense of security.
- *Observe human behaviour* – e.g. desire lines, behaviour settings, general atmosphere, gathering places and activity centres.
- *Consider area's background and history* – e.g. local and regional materials, traditions, styles, details, prevailing architectural and urban design context, urban grain and archaeological significance.
- *Assess existing mix of uses* – e.g. variety, on site, around site, contribution to vitality.
- *Research statutory and legal constraints* – e.g. ownership, rights of way, planning status (policies and guidelines), planning conditions, covenants, statutory undertakers services.
- *Use a SWOT analysis* – e.g. SWOT analyses are sometimes used to good effect as the starting point for design appraisal and brief writing, and have the advantage of focusing attention on prescription as well as description.

Source: Adapted from Chapman & Larkham (1994: 44).

TABLE 11.4 Appraisal Techniques

- Accessibility Assessment
    - Accessibility audit
    - Accessibility option appraisal
    - Accessibility action plan
- Archive Research
- Assessment of Environmental Effects
- Behaviour Observation
    - Behaviour mapping
    - Activity mapping
    - Physical trace observation
- Building Age Profile
- Character Appraisal
- Crime Prevention Through Environmental Design Safety Audit
- Crime Prevention Through Environmental Design Safety Site Assessment
- Health Impact Assessment – Urban Design and Health/Well-being
- Legibility Analysis
    - Cognitive mapping
    - Mental mapping
- Mapping
    - Overlay mapping
    - GIS mapping
    - Aerial photographs
    - Digital elevation model
    - Digital terrain model
- Ped-shed Analysis
- Social Impact Assessment
- Space Syntax Analysis
- Surveys
    - Public satisfaction surveys
    - 3+, 3− surveys
    - Three questions surveys
    - Visual preference survey
    - Placecheck
    - Post-occupancy evaluation
    - Design quality indicators
    - Benchmarking
- Tissue Analysis
    - Urban tissue
- Transport Impact Assessment
- Transportation and Traffic Modelling
    - Multi-modal transport modelling
    - Traffic flow modelling
- Urban Design Audit
- Urban Morphology
    - Figure-ground mapping
    - Typological analysis
    - Materials and components analysis
- Walk-Through Analysis

Source: New Zealand's Urban Design Toolkit, Ministry for the Environment (2006).

recently, Italy's Legge-Quadro Sulla Qualita Architettonica (2008). For others, the role and rights of the state to control design have emerged through legal interpretations of more generic legislation or constitutional rights. In the USA, for example, such processes have been tested through the courts refining the First Amendment guarantee of free speech; the courts' finding in favour of municipal rights on the basis of the 'general welfare' of the population at large (the same basis on which police powers are guaranteed) (Lai 1994).

Yet, despite the seemingly robust statutory basis on which design regulation occurs, the policy through which it is enacted remains a source of tension and dispute. The most persistent challenge to public attempts to influence design through statutory processes has been the charge that design is essentially subjective, and thus attempts to control it are inevitably highly value-laden and prejudiced – or, in Case Scheer's (1994) analysis (see above), 'arbitrary, vague and superficial'. In the UK, such charges of subjectivity have long been the focus of debate on the validity of policy-based attempts to control or influence design quality:

- In 1980, government guidance for England argued that: *'Planning authorities should recognise that aesthetics is an extremely subjective matter. They should not therefore impose their tastes on developers simply because they believe them to be superior.'* (Circular 22/80 para19).
- In 1992, this became: *'Planning authorities should reject obviously poor designs which are out of scale or character with their surroundings. But aesthetic judgements are to some extent subjective and authorities should not impose their taste on applicants simply because they believe it to be superior.'* (PPG1 1992: para A3).
- By 1997, the reference to subjectivity had disappeared: *'Local planning authorities should reject poor design, particularly where their decisions are supported by clear plan policies or supplementary design guidance which has been subjected to public consultation and adopted by the local planning authority.'* (PPG1 1997: para 17).
- In 2005 the importance of design was recognised as a central concern: *'Good design ensures attractive usable, durable and adaptable places and is a key element in achieving sustainable development. Good design is indivisible from good planning'* (PPS1 2005: para 33).

This change of approach epitomises the evolution of government thinking on design premised on an acknowledgement that design issues can be addressed objectively but only on the basis of pre-conceived policy and guidance, preferably based on a systematic assessment of character. At the same time, it has demonstrated a move away from

context for engaging with design begins in specific state legislation, which sets out specific obligations for and responsibilities of the state – for example France's Loi 77–2 sur l'architecture, dating back to 1977, or, more

a primary emphasis on detailed architectural design (i.e. aesthetics), and towards urban design and place-making. Recently, the importance of good design in delivering sustainability has also come to the fore.

Nonetheless, the UK government's attempt to treat design on a more objective basis lags behind practice in other parts of Europe and the USA. Systems employed in Germany, France, and some American cities, for example, are based on a mixture of legally binding zoning provisions and design guidance through development plans or design codes supplemented by design review procedures. In the USA, the Supreme Court affirmed the principle of 'fair certainty', requiring that the administrative discretion of municipalities to determine design quality is tempered by the publication of clear standards or guidelines on which those decisions are to be based (Lai 1994: 31–2). As a consequence, where published, zoning controls carry entitlement rights to those wishing to develop, and confer on local municipalities legally guaranteed means to control development.

Zoning controls have significant impact on the urban and architectural design of areas – albeit primarily through controlling the mix of uses, morphological characteristics (e.g. building line, plot depth and width, etc.) and the three-dimensional form of development (e.g. height, setbacks, density, etc.). Other urban design criteria and more detailed architectural controls requiring more interpretation are rarely the subject of zoning.

As a supplement to zoning, and as a means to extract greater public benefits from the development process, systems of incentive zoning are widespread in the USA. In exchange for extra floor space, developers can provide public amenities such as better design features, landscaping or public spaces. In New York, for example, by 2000, 503 new public spaces had been obtained through this route, most attached to office, residential and institutional buildings that, in exchange for the new pseudo-public spaces (see Chapter 6), had been built higher or larger than originally intended (Kayden 2000).

Although effective at delivering public amenities, the limitations and abuses of such bonus systems have discredited them as means to achieve better design (Cullingworth 1997: 94–9). These problems include the tendency for developers to see bonuses as 'as-of-right' entitlements; the tendency to increase floor space (and building heights and volumes, regardless of impact); failure to deliver the public amenities after bonuses had been taken; the inequitable and time-consuming nature of a system lacking clear ground rules; and the poor quality of the public amenities provided (Loukaitou-Sideris & Banerjee 1998). In New York, for example, despite the impressive quantity of new public spaces and some exemplars of quality, new public spaces were often barren, hostile and highly controlled (Kayden 2000). Furthermore, bonuses are only provided where developers want to build rather than where public spaces are needed.

By itself, zoning can be a blunt instrument for influencing development and place quality and many municipalities now produce additional design guidance. A particularly well-known and sophisticated example is Portland, which has a reputation as one of America's best-planned and -designed cities (see Punter 1999). In part, this reputation is derived from its clear – and highly effective – policy framework, which combines a spatial design strategy for the city with a set of 'Central City Fundamental Design Guidelines' (Figure 11.5). The latter

Project: ______
Case File No.: ______
Date: ______

Applicable	Does Comply	Does not Comply	
			A. PORTLAND PERSONALITY
☐	☐	☐	A1 Integrate the River
☐	☐	☐	A2 Emphasize Portland Themes
☐	☐	☐	A3 Respect the Portland Block Structures
☐	☐	☐	A4 Use Unifying Elements
☐	☐	☐	A5 Enhance, Embelish, and Identify Areas
☐	☐	☐	A6 Re-use/Rehabilitate/Restore Buildings
☐	☐	☐	A7 Establish & Maintain a Sense of Urban Enclosure
☐	☐	☐	A8 Contribute to the Cityscape, The Stage, & the Action
☐	☐	☐	A9 Strengthen Gateways
			B. PEDESTRIAN EMPHASIS
☐	☐	☐	B1 Reinforce & Enhance the Pedestrian System
☐	☐	☐	B2 Protect the Pedestrian
☐	☐	☐	B3 Bridge Pedestrian Obstacles
☐	☐	☐	B4 Provide Shopping & Viewing Places
☐	☐	☐	B5 Make Plazas, Parks, & Open Space Successful
☐	☐	☐	B6 Consider Sunlight, Shadow, Glare, Reflection, Wind & Rain
☐	☐	☐	B7 Integrate Barrier-Free Design
			C. PROJECT DESIGN
☐	☐	☐	C1 Respect Architectural Integrity
☐	☐	☐	C2 Consider View Opportunities
☐	☐	☐	C3 Design for Compatibility
☐	☐	☐	C4 Establish a Graceful Transition between Buildings & Public Spaces
☐	☐	☐	C5 Design Corners that Build Active Intersections
☐	☐	☐	C6 Differentiate the Sidewalk Level of Buildings
☐	☐	☐	C7 Create Flexible Sidewalk Level Spaces
☐	☐	☐	C8 Give Special Attention to Encroachments
☐	☐	☐	C9 Integrate Roofs & Use Rooftops
☐	☐	☐	C10 Promote Permanence & Quality in Development

FIGURE 11.5 Central City Fundamental Design Guidelines, Portland, Oregon

are condensed into a design checklist used to assess all projects in the city centre (Portland Bureau of Planning 1992). The aims are:

- To encourage urban design excellence in the central city;
- To integrate urban design and preservation of heritage into the process of central city development;
- To enhance the character of Portland's central districts;
- To promote the development of diversity and areas of special character within the central city;
- To establish an urban design relationship between the central city districts and the central city as a whole;
- To provide for a pleasant, rich and diverse pedestrian experience in the central city;
- To provide for the humanisation of the central city through promotion of the arts;
- To assist in creating a 24-hour central city that is safe, humane and prosperous; and
- To ensure new development is at a human scale and relates to the character and scale of the area and the central city.

The German and French planning systems provide for a strategic plan — *Flächennutzungsplan* in Germany and *Schéma Directeur* in France — to guide large-scale spatial planning and design decisions, including key open space, landscape, conservation and infrastructure provisions. This is often supplemented at the local scale by more detailed plans — *Bebauungsplan (B-Plan)* in Germany and *Plan d'Occupation des Sols* in France. These are akin to zoning ordinances, in which detailed codes covering layout, height, density, landscaping, parking, building line and external appearance can be laid out for each zone or plot. Detailed design guidance is also now common in both countries (Figure 11.6).

Experience in Europe and parts of the USA demonstrates the value of well-conceived policy and guidance mechanisms as the basis for objective public sector intervention in design (see Hillman 1990). In Germany — although the degree of detail and control is up to local discretion — the content of B-Plans is regulated by law. A common notation is prescribed in terms of scale, symbols, colours and hatchings for land uses, and for particular 'line' types (e.g. where building lines 'must' or 'may' be located). The approach ensures both consistency across the country and that B-Plans are easily understood. In the UK, the most important local policy tool is the development plan (in England known as the Local Development Framework),

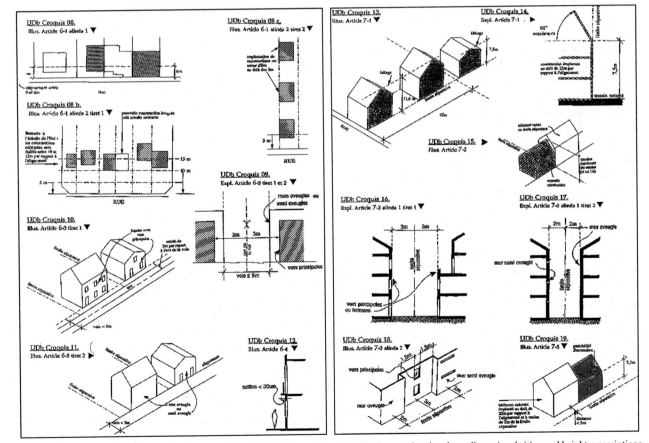

FIGURE 11.6   Ville de Montreuil, Plan d'Occupation des Sols *(Image: Trache 2001)*. Extract showing three-dimensional siting and height prescriptions

which – in principle – sets out design principles against which development proposals will be assessed.

Earlier research on design policies in England (Punter & Carmona 1997), however, found that development plan policies were often vague and ill-conceived and inadequately based on a clear understanding and appreciation of the local context. The American experience has also shown the difficulty of legally prescribing robust design standards when even apparently scrupulously constructed attempts to determine design criteria have been struck down by the courts as 'void for vagueness' and violating reasonable certainty (Lai 1994: 35). To overcome problems of vagueness, UK government guidance on design and the planning system relates seven policy objectives to the physical form of development. This approach seeks to ensure policy moves beyond generalised aspirations and explains how the principles can be interpreted in the light of particular circumstances. Its authors boldly claim that:

'Any policy, guidance or design that cannot be seen clearly as a response to one or more of the urban design objectives will contribute nothing to good urban design. Equally, any policy, guidance or design that is not expressed clearly in terms of one or more aspects of development form will be too vague to have any effect.'

(Campbell & Cowan 1999).

Although not included in the final guidance, the authors developed a 'thinking machine' (or matrix) as a means to link objectives to form (Figure 11.7).

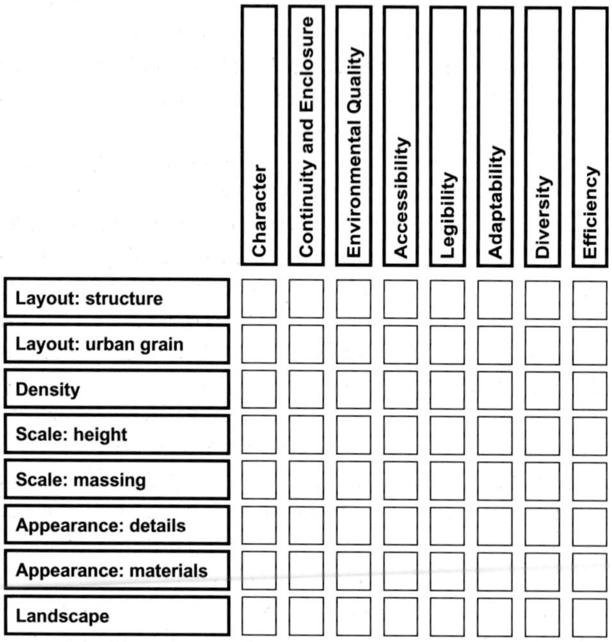

	Character	Continuity and Enclosure	Environmental Quality	Accessibility	Legibility	Adaptability	Diversity	Efficiency
Layout: structure	☐	☐	☐	☐	☐	☐	☐	☐
Layout: urban grain	☐	☐	☐	☐	☐	☐	☐	☐
Density	☐	☐	☐	☐	☐	☐	☐	☐
Scale: height	☐	☐	☐	☐	☐	☐	☐	☐
Scale: massing	☐	☐	☐	☐	☐	☐	☐	☐
Appearance: details	☐	☐	☐	☐	☐	☐	☐	☐
Appearance: materials	☐	☐	☐	☐	☐	☐	☐	☐
Landscape	☐	☐	☐	☐	☐	☐	☐	☐

FIGURE 11.7 Thinking matrix (*Image: redrawn from Campbell & Cowan 1999*). Although not included in the final version of *By Design*, this 'thinking machine' (or matrix) was developed to relate policy objectives to the physical form of development

The art of writing policies is discussed in Chapter 12; guidance based on the experience of writing policies in England is offered in Table 11.5. While well-conceived and -articulated policies should provide a key means for the public sector to influence and direct design policy, the extent of influence is limited: no matter how well-conceived, they will never adequately substitute for the willingness to invest in design quality from the development industry and in the public realm from government (local and/or national). Arguments for high – and higher – quality urban design must be won in all arenas.

TABLE 11.5 Writing Robust Design Policies

The process of design policy writing
1. Design aspirations should be embedded across the hierarchy of design policy and guidance.
2. Pursuit of design quality should infuse other policy areas (e.g. housing or transport).
3. Use previous implementation experience in writing new policies.
4. Appropriate design process should be covered in policy.
5. Analytical area appraisals and public consultation should underpin policy formulation.

The fundamentals of design policy
6. Design policy represents an opportunity to establish a positive vision for future change.
7. Ensure development responds appropriately to its context.
8. Policies should be based on a broad concept of sustainable urban design.
9. Municipalities should develop a clear spatial design strategy at strategic and area scales.

Key aspects of design policy coverage
10. Policies covering the different dimensions of urban design are the cornerstone of design policies.
11. Considerations of landscape should pervade policies at all scales.
12. Encourage the use of architectural skills and the development of contemporary designs.
13. Encourage the co-ordination and positive management of the urban environment.
14. Conservation policies should emphasise design opportunities as well as constraints.
15. Policies should encourage special attention to the settings of historic buildings.

Writing, implementing and monitoring design policies
16. Policies should respond to the most commonly encountered design problems and inadequacies.
17. Policies should be written with the means of implementation in mind.
18. Area- and site-specific guidance should be cross-referenced to generic design policies.
19. Design policies should be implemented through appropriately skilled regulatory processes.
20. Design policies should be monitored to assess and improve their effectiveness.

Source: Adapted from Carmona *et al* (2002: 11).

Design (Guidance)

The process of policy writing for development plans or zoning ordinances is part of the wider design process and is, in itself, a creative problem-solving process. Design here is what was described in Chapter 1 as a 'second-order' design activity (George 1997), where, rather than directly designing buildings and spaces or settlements, it shapes the decision environments of key development and design actors. As they relate to future development proposals, which at the time of writing are usually unknown, and often for large areas, most design policies and ordinances are abstract in nature. To ensure design principles are considered and can be applied at a more local level, many municipalities provide design guidance for particular areas and sites. These forms of guidance are the next stage in a hierarchy that starts with strategic policy and ends at the site-specific scale. Although resource-intensive to prepare, such guidance is widely regarded as effective both in making public design aspirations explicit and in securing better design (Carmona 2001: 284–8).

At its most basic, design guidance can be defined as a generic term for a range of tools that set out design parameters with the intention of better directing development design. Different countries have different traditions and use different forms of guidance to greater and lesser degrees. In France, typo-morphological guidance is commonly used to understand and respond to the character of larger historic areas. In Australia, Victoria's Rescode provides a state-level design guide for residential developments, while, in the USA, the New Urbanists' Transect (see below) offers a generic design guidance for all types of development along a continuum from city core to countryside.

In the UK, if one asked 'what is design guidance?', the detailed and unwieldy residential design guides produced by municipalities up and down the country since the 1970s would come to mind — the *Essex Design Guide* being the best known. These forms of guidance were, and still are, produced by the public sector to guide the design of (predominantly) housing developments across entire municipalities. Yet design guidance does not have to take this form; it does not have to be produced by the public sector; it can relate to all types of development; and, rather than generic guidance for all areas within an administrative jurisdiction, it can be customised to guide development for specific areas or sites.

Reflecting this diversity, there has been a proliferation of types of design guidance, among which are local design guides, design strategies, design frameworks, design briefs, development standards, spatial masterplans, design codes, design protocols and design charters. These terms are often confusing, poorly defined and overlapping. Despite attempts to classify them in relation to one another (e.g. Carmona 1998b), their sheer variety merely illustrates the ambiguity of design guidance as a design/development tool, and the confusion that easily results.

Distinguishing design guidance from ordinance or policy is, first, the fact that guidance is not legally defined and binding — the latter suggests an enforceability that 'guidance' does not possess. Instead, guidance suggests advice rather than compulsion. Second, it cannot be a 'blueprint', because 'guidance' equally suggests a sense of direction for, but not an end solution to, a design problem. Finally, guidance cannot simply be analysis, such as site or character appraisals, as analysis in isolation does not suggest a design direction at all, merely information that might be useful in establishing one. As such, it is not always apparent how design guidance fits into the range of tools available. Lynch's (1976: 41–55) four modes of action for public authorities, for example, make no reference to guidance. In fact, aspects of design guidance will often have a role in each of Lynch's modes, and the boundaries between them are not clear. For the purposes of this discussion, Lynch's third mode — design — can be modified to 'design guidance' because the public sector role rarely extends to scheme design.

Despite the ambiguity and surfeit of labels for different forms of design guidance, design guidance can be classified through its core characteristics (see Table 11.6). Unfortunately, knowing that a great variety of design guidance exists is of little value unless users understand, first, why different forms of guidance are used and, second, their problems and potentials. The answer to the first question is simple: all forms of design guidance exist for a single purpose — to inform the process of design so that it is more likely to achieve specified ends. Thus, guidance can be deemed successful when outcomes are better than would otherwise have been achieved.

Depending on the aspirations of guidance designers and the nature of the development context, the goals envisaged for design guidance vary. The intention might, for example, be to establish minimum thresholds for quality or, alternatively, to raise the bar by striving for superior design. The former — 'a 'safety net' approach — may be the limited ambition of a generic local design guide or a guide in areas beset by poor-quality development. The latter — a 'springboard to excellence' — should be the case for site-specific guidance or for guidance in areas where stakeholders are already committed to achieving better quality. While not mutually exclusive, these aspirations depend on the nature of likely users, the extent to which they are receptive to the content of guidance, and on the balance of power between stakeholders (particularly between public and private sectors). More generally, it emphasises that the development process, and how design guidance is used within it, must be fully understood (see Chapter 10). A number of types of design guidance are discussed below, while

TABLE 11.6 Design Guidance: Classification by Distinguishing Characteristics

Subject matter	Classifying by land use, location (suburban, urban, rural), or development issue (e.g. infill sites, shop fronts, building additions, etc.). Some forms of design guidance may deal with more than one of these.
Context type	The context to which guidance relates, and its relative sensitivity, whether extensive new-build sites, infill development in established urban areas, or change within a historic setting.
Scale of application	Whether dealing with strategic design concerns such as infrastructure provision, urban design issues (space networks, public realm, mix of uses, etc.) or questions of architecture and detailed landscape design.
Governance level	From central government and its various agencies, to state/regional and sub-regional authorities, to local municipalities
Generic versus specific	Whether relating to specific sites or generic, relating to large areas (e.g. a whole municipality) and undefined sites. Generally, the smaller the scale of application and the lower the governance level, the greater the degree of specificity.
Level of detail	From broad aspirational principles of 'good' design, to very detailed guidance on particular aspects of a design problem.
Level of prescription	Although advisory, some aspects may be expressed with a greater (or lesser) degree of conviction than others: 'developers must …'; 'developers should normally …'; 'developers might consider …'.
Ownership	Typically design guidance is produced by the public sector agencies to improve the design of private sector development, but can also be produced by the private sector to shape the inputs of different corporate partners into a common project.
Process or product	The relative emphasis in guidance on the design, development and regulatory processes as opposed to the desired products or outcomes.
Medium of representation	Traditional printed form, or more interactive electronic and web-based means. This will not necessarily change the content of guidance, but will determine its style, and how and by whom it is used.

Table 11.7 demonstrates the distinctions in Table 11.6 for three historically influential examples of design guidance.

Design/Development Briefs

Design briefs are common means of providing site-specific design guidance. Depending on local circumstances, briefs may emphasise design concerns, broad planning issues or development/management issues. 'Development brief' is thus a generic term for briefs focusing on design, planning or development issues (Figure 11.8). They are of particular value for a number of reasons, including:

- Providing a positive and proactive approach to planning and design.
- Ensuring that important design issues are considered.
- Offering a basis from which to promote sites and negotiate on development proposals; encouraging collaborative approaches to design.
- Ensuring that the public interest is considered alongside private interests (particularly the levering of public amenities from developments).
- Offering a straightforward means of providing greater certainty and transparency in the design decision-making process.

Hall (2007: 13) argues that briefs are '… *the foundation of the proactive approach and the physical vehicle for setting*

out design expectations for a site.' Because they set out design principles (preferably) in advance of development interest for particular sites, they can help to unlock complex urban sites, by establishing core principles around which negotiation can occur. However, as briefs bring public design guidance to a highly prescriptive level, municipalities must be aware that — to avoid stifling innovation or creativity — such guidance should be market-aware and flexible. Hall (2007: 13) nevertheless argues that they should provide unambiguous guidance on physical form, including specification of blocks and frontages. In practice, formats vary widely depending on the site's nature and sensitivity, the range of issues to be addressed, political considerations, and the past practice of municipalities. Depending on the resources available for their preparation: for example, some use bespoke site-specific formats; others use standardised checklists for all sites.

Briefs generally include a mix of 'descriptive' elements (information on site characteristics and context), 'procedural' elements (outlining the application procedures) and 'prescriptive' elements (spelling out the municipality's intentions). They also generally cover the following areas:

- *Background and statement of purpose* — e.g. the circumstances under which the guidance has been

TABLE 11.7 Comparison of Design Guidance

	Canary Wharf Design Guidelines (1987)	Hulme Guide to Development (1994)	Essex Design Guide (2005)
Generic 'type'	Design code	Design strategy/code	Local design guide
Subject matter	Commercial office and public realm	Residential development and public realm	Residential and mixed-use areas
Context type	New-build brownfield	Clearance and regeneration	Infill and new-build greenfield
Scale of application	Architecture and landscape	Urban design	Urban design, architecture, landscape
Governance level	n/a (enterprise zone)	Local	Sub-regional
Generic versus specific	Specific	Specific	Generic
Level of detail	Highly detailed	Broad principles	Comprehensive coverage
Level of prescription	Highly prescriptive	Advisory	Advisory
Ownership	Private	Public, quango	Public, local government
Process- or product-oriented	Product	Product	Process and product
Goals	Higher quality	Threshold quality	Threshold quality

prepared, its relation to wider design policy and to spatial strategies, and any planning gain requirements.

- *Survey and analysis* — e.g. of the built and natural environment, including identification of any specific constraints or opportunities for development.
- *Planning and design requirements* — e.g. spelling out in policy form the key criteria against which any proposals will be assessed.
- *Engineering and construction requirements* — e.g. highways and other infrastructure specifications.
- *Procedures for application* — e.g. outlining how the guidance is to be used to evaluate schemes and any procedures or additional presentational and survey requirements.
- *Indicative design proposals* — e.g. outlining development possibilities for the site, including phasing requirements, but without providing unnecessary detail or stifling innovation.

Design briefs are typically produced in-house by municipal planning or urban design teams, and less commonly by external consultants.

Design strategies, frameworks, regulating plans and masterplans

The terms 'design strategies', 'frameworks', 'regulating plans' and 'masterplans' are often used interchangeably. The exact terminology is less important than why they are produced in the first place — that is, as proactive means to guide the development process and achieve a range of enhanced design outcomes. While all provide a clear

two- or three-dimensional vision of future development form (albeit with different degrees of prescription), Table 11.8 puts these tools into a hierarchy.

Design strategies generally provide a spatial design vision for a large area such as a town or city centre. They are conceptual and flexible in nature and focus on establishing and coordinating the potential of key sites and infrastructure projects within an area to realise a wider design-based vision (see Biddulph & Punter 1999) (Figure 11.9). Design frameworks, by contrast, are used to guide major

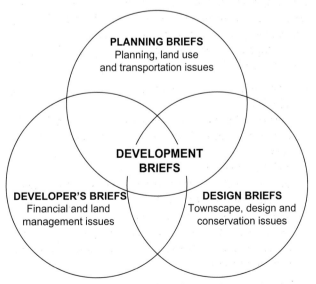

FIGURE 11.8 Types of development briefs (*Image: redrawn from Chapman & Larkham 1994: 63*)

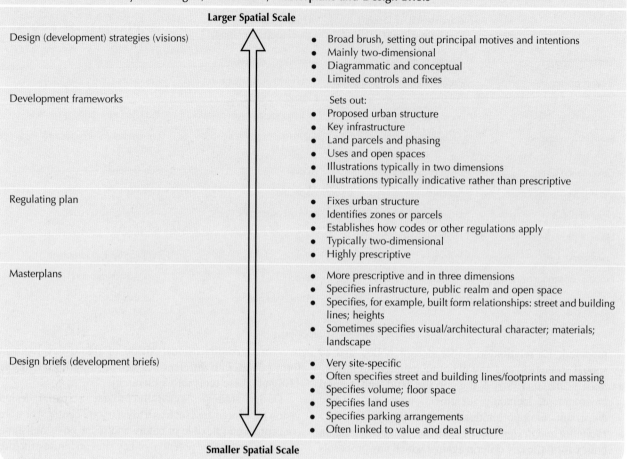

TABLE 11.8 — Hierarchy of Strategies, Framework, Masterplans and Design Briefs

Larger Spatial Scale

Design (development) strategies (visions)	• Broad brush, setting out principal motives and intentions • Mainly two-dimensional • Diagrammatic and conceptual • Limited controls and fixes
Development frameworks	Sets out: • Proposed urban structure • Key infrastructure • Land parcels and phasing • Uses and open spaces • Illustrations typically in two dimensions • Illustrations typically indicative rather than prescriptive
Regulating plan	• Fixes urban structure • Identifies zones or parcels • Establishes how codes or other regulations apply • Typically two-dimensional • Highly prescriptive
Masterplans	• More prescriptive and in three dimensions • Specifies infrastructure, public realm and open space • Specifies, for example, built form relationships: street and building lines; heights • Sometimes specifies visual/architectural character; materials; landscape
Design briefs (development briefs)	• Very site-specific • Often specifies street and building lines/footprints and massing • Specifies volume; floor space • Specifies land uses • Specifies parking arrangements • Often linked to value and deal structure

Smaller Spatial Scale

development on large sites, by coordinating the key design features and by setting out a spatial framework for infrastructure, urban structure, development parcels, landscape and the distribution of land uses. They are often used instead of a masterplan where greater flexibility is required for sites that will be built-out over considerable periods of time, and as such much of the illustration may be two- rather than three- dimensional (see Cowan 2002).

Masterplans and especially regulating plans are more detailed and prescriptive in terms of the physical layout and form of proposed development. Regulating plans equate broadly to what are known in Germany as B-Plans, and are typically used in the USA in conjunction with form-based coding (see below). Parolek *et al* (2008: 17) describe three functions for them:

• Administrative, by identifying on a plan the boundaries or areas to which different regulations apply, for example different elements of a code.
• Layout design, by establishing the two-dimensional layout of the urban form in terms of street layout and frontages, ground floor uses, building types, etc.

• Zone character, through identifying the form and character of the different development zones and thereby also establishing the public realm.

In a code-based approach, the regulating plan will often be created alongside the code as a means to relate its provisions to particular plots or development parcels. As its name suggests, its role is primarily regulatory, and it will typically involve the evolution of a previously established vision for the site contained in an urban design framework, or more likely a masterplan.

Masterplan is a much misused and misunderstood term, and thus further clarity is required. Masterplans are often criticised as overly rigid and inflexible, and for suggesting or proposing a greater degree of control than is actually desirable, necessary or possible. Garreau (1991: 453, from Brand 1994: 78), for example, defines masterplanning as:

'… *that attribute of a development in which so many rigid controls are put in place, to defeat every imaginable future problem, that any possibility of life, spontaneity, or flexible response to unanticipated events is eliminated.*'

FIGURE 11.9 Urban Design Strategy, Nottingham (*Image: URBED 2009*). Nottingham's new City Centre Masterplan 2005-15 — more precisely, an urban design strategy — synthesises ambitious public realm initiatives and provides guidance for key sites. The city also has a longstanding practice of using design briefs to maintain a proactive approach to planning

This statement, however, refers to what is best described as a 'blueprint' masterplan — for example, that associated with a big architecture project, rather than an urban design plan per se. A less rigid form is a 'framework' masterplan. As discussed in Chapter 9, the key difference is that, while blueprint masterplans specify a single intended outcome, framework masterplans generally set out broad urban design aspirations and principles, providing scope for interpretation and development within the framework's parameters — the final outcome is also typically multi-

authored. Given this confusion, the term 'development framework' is often preferred to masterplan.

In the UK, the use of masterplans has become far more widespread as national policy has increasingly highlighted the importance of design. For Bell (2005) this reflects enhanced appreciation among promoters of development of the economic benefits of such masterplans, but also raises questions about the dominance of private interests (who produce the majority of masterplans) in the production and planning of the built environment, and about the quality of the masterplans produced. To improve both the process and content of masterplanning, guidance from CABE (2004a) suggests they should define:

- Layout and connections of the streets, squares and open spaces of a neighbourhood;
- Height, bulk and massing of buildings;
- Relationships between buildings and public spaces;
- Activities and uses in the area;
- Movement patterns for pedestrians, cyclists, cars, public transport, service and refuse vehicles;
- Provision of utilities and other elements of infrastructure;
- Relationship of physical form to the social, economic and cultural contexts; and
- Integration of new development into existing communities, and the built and natural environments.

Strategies, frameworks, regulating plans and masterplans generally:

- Provide an overall 'vision' or concept to guide development;
- Set standards and expectations of quality;
- Ensure minimum levels of quality (i.e. it may prevent reduction in potential development value by prohibiting poor-quality development);
- Provide (degrees of) certainty for all parties (investors, developers, occupiers and the local community); and
- Provide co-ordination and ensure that the component parts contribute to a greater whole (i.e. seek to avoid 'bad neighbour' developments that reduce amenity, and seek to create a better place) (see Chapter 10).

Unlike design briefs, these forms of guidance are often produced by external urban design consultancies, commissioned by municipal authorities, but also, particularly in the case of masterplans and regulating plans, frequently commissioned by developers. Like design briefs, and with the exception of regulating plans, they are usually presented in a report format, with numerous plans and illustrations. In common with all design policy instruments, they should be promotional, be comprehensive, encourage innovative design and be presented in easily understandable and usable formats. In such formats they combine policy-based information with indicative/prescriptive design ideas.

Design standards and codes

This final category of design guidance is also the most prescriptive. Different forms of design guidance have existed throughout recorded history, with types of coding used as far back as Roman times. This can be seen in Roman street standards (Southworth & Ben-Joseph 1997), or by reference to Vitruvius, whose *Ten Books on Architecture* covered such issues as the layout of cities (including

the choice of a healthy site, construction of city walls, orientation and public spaces), public and private buildings and the use of building materials (Rowland & Howe 1999).

Today, a wide range of development standards are used to guide the design of buildings and the urban environment at large, controlling almost every aspect of the built environment:

- National building codes or regulations dictate the internal and (to some degree) the external design of buildings — for example, the US-based International Building Code.
- Highway design standards (national and local) control a good part of the public realm through their impact on road and footpath design and layout.
- Planning standards (national and local) dictate density levels, space between buildings, parking requirements, open space requirements, etc.
- 'Secured by design' or CPTED precepts (see Chapter 6) determine lines of sight, permeability, access points, etc.
- Emergency service access guidelines dictate distances between buildings and points of access.
- Health and safety standards are increasingly pervasive, right across the built environment.

Sometimes these standards are found within other forms of design guidance, such as the types of area of site-based guidance described above, but more often they are adopted by municipalities as generic standards to control development irrespective of context. Tracing the evolution of the 'hidden codes' that dictate much of the form and function of urban space around the world, Ben-Joseph (2005) argues that the original purpose and value of the codes are often forgotten as the bureaucracies put in place to implement them do so with little regard to their actual rationale, and even less to their knock-on effects. Furthermore, most of these are limited in their scope and technical in their aspirations, and are not generated from a physical vision or understanding of a particular place or site (DCLG 2006a: 11).

Instead, these forms of standards are about achieving minimum requirements across the board. In many cases, slavish adherence to such standards creates bland and unattractive places — a critique of the use of such standards goes back at least as far as the 1950s to the emergence of the townscape movement in the UK and its critique of 'prairie planning' (see Cullen 1961: 133–7 and Chapter 7). This represents a classic case of regulatory (rather than market) failure, so much so that Ben-Joseph (2005: xxi) concludes that even today we may excel at making codes but fail to make good places.

Design codes — or what are known in the USA as form-based codes — are, by contrast, a distinct form of detailed design guidance that stipulates the three-dimensional components of a particular development and how these relate to one another, without establishing the shape of the intended outcome (Carmona *et al* 2006: 240–2). Such codes aim to clarify what constitutes acceptable design quality for a particular site or area, providing certainty for developers and the local community. Used in this way, and in contrast to development standards, they provide a positive statement about the intended qualities of a particular place. As such, they focus on design principles such as the requirements for streets, blocks, massing, etc., but may also cover landscape, architectural and building performance issues (e.g. energy efficiency).

Codes have reached their greatest degree of sophistication – and simplicity – in New Urbanist developments in the USA, where the design code typically consists of a small number of diagrams and charts, often presenting urban, architectural, public realm and landscape elements in a series of separate but related codes – as, for example, at Kentlands in Maryland (see Chapter 4) (Figure 11.10).

Typically regulating elements such as roof pitch and the use of materials, the architectural code is the most controversial and (arguably) the least important. Duany *et al* (2000: 211) nevertheless highlight contradictions in the criticism of such codes:

'Colleagues who complain to us about Seaside usually have two criticisms. The first is the restrictiveness of the architectural code, and the second is the significant number of over-decorated "gingerbread" cottages there. They are usually surprised to learn that the gingerbread houses at Seaside demonstrate not the requirements of the (largely style-neutral) code but the code's inability to overcome the traditional tastes of the American housing consumer. The only way to have wiped out the hated architecture would have been to tighten the hated code.'

Depending on what level of control is desired, the architectural codes can be made more or less prescriptive. Some architectural codes have exemptions for designs of intrinsic merit or for certain building types (such as public buildings), while others have an urban code but no architectural code. A recent innovation is the Transect, a kind of 'regulatory code' developed by Duany Plater-Zyberk's architects that has been codified into a 'model zoning ordinance' known as the Smart Code (see Box 11.2).

In the UK, design codes have been extensively tested through a government-funded pilot programme (DCLG 2006b), which identified a range of potential benefits of coding, including:

- Establishing high-quality design aspirations in a manner that allows their consistent application across successive phases of large developments.
- Providing a robust form of design guidance that, because of its relative prescription, is enforceable and difficult to challenge.
- Testing, developing and delivering the vision contained in the masterplan or other site-based vision, by

designing and fixing the 'must-have' design parameters of a scheme.
- Creating greater certainty and a 'level playing field' for development interests, based on their willingness and ability to deliver high-quality design.

Of these, the key strength of design codes is their ability to co-ordinate design across successive development phases of large sites to deliver a coherent design vision. As such, they are most valuable when sites are either large (or multiple smaller adjacent sites) that will be developed in phases over an extended period of time; in multiple ownership; or likely to be developed by multiple development and design teams. The UK pilot programme (DCLG 2006a) identified seven fundamental factors for the success of coding projects:

- *Urban design first* – the achievement of sustainable urban design should be the primary focus of design codes.
- *Setting quality thresholds* – design codes should establish the essential unifying elements of 'place' by setting clear minimum quality thresholds while encouraging designers to do better.
- *Investing up-front* – preparation of design codes involves a significant up-front commitment of time and resources by all parties, paid for over time by enhanced sales values and reduced friction within the development process.
- *Rules for delivery that build upon a spatial vision* – design codes need to build on the firm foundation of a robust site-based design vision, typically in the form of a masterplan.
- *A collaborative environment and a partnership of interests* – between the public sector, development and design stakeholders is a prerequisite for successful and efficient coding.
- *Clear and effective leadership* – leadership is critical to effective code preparation and use, and can come from landowners, developers, planners, politicians or code designers.
- *No substitute for skills* – a multi-disciplinary approach is required but also the exercise of advanced design skills throughout the process of code preparation and use.

These seven fundamentals not only relate directly to design coding, but also to the all forms of design guidance. Design codes are not the only tool with a role to play in enhancing design quality, and are certainly not appropriate for all forms of development. However, where they are, the evidence suggests they can make a real contribution to raising the bar and to delivering a better place. For the public sector the lessons are clear: the need to establish quality aspirations early in the development process and to

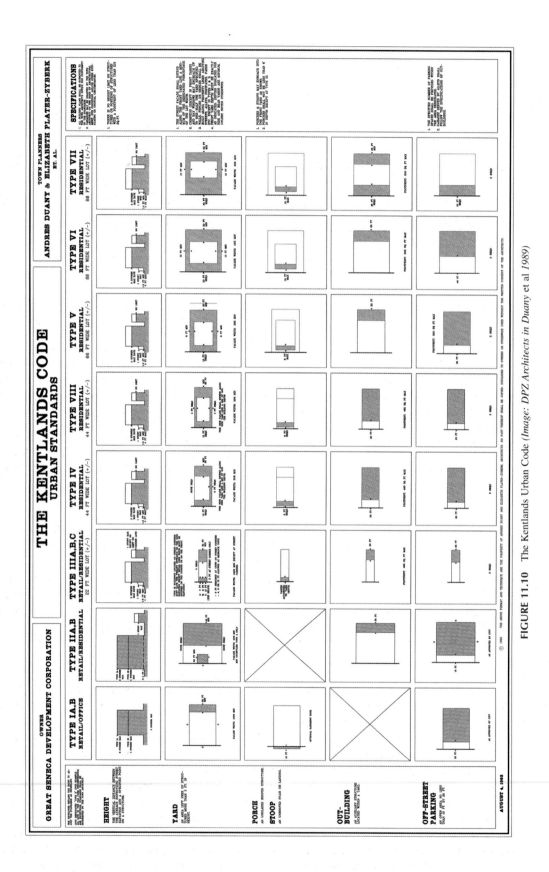

FIGURE 11.10   The Kentlands Urban Code (*Image: DPZ Architects in Duany et al 1989*)

BOX 11.2 The Transect

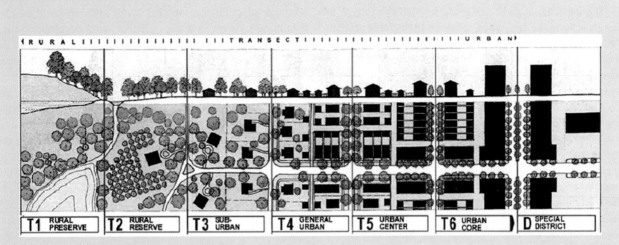

| T1 | RURAL PRESERVE | T2 | RURAL RESERVE | T3 | SUB-URBAN | T4 | GENERAL URBAN | T5 | URBAN CENTER | T6 | URBAN CORE | D | SPECIAL DISTRICT |

The transect's definitive feature is the relation of coded character to the position in a notional transect or cross-section through an archetypal settlement, from urban centre (T6) to wilderness (T1). The idea of a transect dates back at least to the work of Sir Patrick Geddes a century earlier, and more recently has been extensively re-worked by typo-morphologists in their historical studies of city development (see Chapter 4). The innovation of the New Urbanists, however, is the transect's use as a regulatory tool in which six types of environmental zone are defined by their morphological character and which, if followed, would create a type of 'idealised' city form (see Parolek *et al* 2008: 18−22; Walters 2007: 110−5; Duany & Talen 2002a, 2002b).

The concept has critics. Brower (2002), for example, criticises it as an essentially physical model of an ideal city that fails to adequately recognise the social context for building communities. Southworth (2003a), by contrast, criticises it for its rigidity in assuming cities are (or should be) monocentric, when polycentric forms are increasingly the norm, and that, once created, the smooth transition from core to periphery will remain forever static.

Despite these criticisms, the transect's impact, through the gradual adoption of Smart Code across the USA, has been profound, and it is playing a significant role in the shift from single-use car-based zoning to traditional neighbourhood development (TND).

relate these clearly to real places through well-conceived design guidance (see Carmona *et al* 2006: 283−5).

Design Regulation

Regulation is the primary means by which design policy and guidance are implemented. Regulation does not *ipso facto* produce high-quality design, and its function should more correctly be understood as increasing the *probability* of creating better places.

Regulatory processes themselves reflect one of two major types − either they are based on fixed legal frameworks with unquestioning administrative decision-making, or they are discretionary, where a distinction is drawn between law and policy − the latter enacted through 'guiding' plans, skilled professional interpretation in the light of local circumstances, and political decision-making (Reade 1987: 11). The former is based on a system of fixed constraints (e.g. a zoning system); the latter requires formal permission to be granted before certain defined actions can be undertaken. Typically, most regulatory regimes represent a mix of the two. In the UK, for example, planning,

conservation and environmental protection are discretionary (although a shortage of key skills among the professionals charged with their interpretation can lead municipalities back to adopting fixed standards (Carmona 2001: 225−7), while building control and highways adoption processes are fixed technical processes, not open to interpretation or challenge at appeal.

Punter (2007a) argues that, in recent years, the two types of system have converged through the overlay of design review procedures in fixed legal systems to give more flexibility by seeing design in the round and through the addition of more detailed design guidance to increase certainty in discretionary systems.

Both forms of decision-making can contribute to the perception of a regulatory tyranny − discretionary decision-making because of its perceived arbitrary, inconsistent and potentially subjective nature; fixed legal systems because of their lack of flexibility or inability to consider non-standard approaches (Booth in Cullingworth 1999: 43). Moreover, the diversity of regulatory process and systems (even in a single place), and their often disjointed, uncoordinated and even contradictory nature, adds to a perception that '*... a marathon of red tape needs to be run.*' (Imrie & Street 2006: 7).

The key challenge in designing regulatory systems for design is to make the 'good' easy and the 'bad' arduous. This presupposes being able to distinguish good from bad and having a system of incentives or sanctions in place to encourage it. As the ultimate sanction of regulatory processes is to deny permission to do something (to build in the case of urban design) the prime incentive will be to grant timely consent for a proposal, while the main sanction will be to withhold it. However, to encourage standards of design that go beyond the basic level required to receive the relevant permissions, municipalities might offer development bonuses (see above), streamlined consent processes (avoiding the torture of slow consents), direct financial assistance in the form of grants to secure key public objectives (e.g. the retention of historic buildings), prizes, awards and publicity for good design, or even direct investment in schemes (e.g. public/private partnerships).

In the prevailing neo-liberalist era, there are frequently calls to relax regulation in order to reduce the 'burdens' on business and to facilitate economic development (usually by attracting inward investment). This is sometimes associated with a call to relax design control, with the mantra of allowing 'designers to design'. The notion that deregulation attracts development, however, is challenged by the argument that tighter (more predictable) policy frameworks offer developers greater certainty. Observing US cities, Duany *et al* (2000: 177) describe how some cities '*... abdicated initiative to market forces rather than providing a predictable environment for the market to thrive in.*'

Similarly, the argument that looser regulatory frameworks offer freedom for the 'designer to design', which *ipso facto* facilitates better design, is false — the practical reality is that designers are employed by and answerable to developers, and, without appropriate public sector safeguards, development will be directed solely at meeting their ends. A well-conceived design policy framework, by contrast, ensures developers are compelled both to employ skilled designers and to yield opportunity space to them (see Chapter 10).

There is thus a tension between the deregulatory impulse (characteristic of neo-liberalism) and the design quality impulse of public regulation, and a spectrum ranging from encouraging development regardless of design quality to encouraging development *with* design quality. The former is a short-termist concern merely with the fact and volume of development; and the latter takes a longer-term perspective but requires development be refused if design quality is not sufficient.

Nonetheless, many cities have chosen — or been forced — to run down their forward planning function. Many cities are also reluctant to impose more stringent design policies for fear of deterring development. The consequence is that,

rather than through proactive plan policies, strategies and frameworks, issues of design quality are often addressed through reactive development control/management and by planning officers actively working with developers once designs have been developed — the latter is frequently described as a 'rescue job' or, alternatively and more graphically, as 'putting lipstick on a gorilla'.

Even when development management involves bargaining and negotiation, proactive design policies give development controllers something to bargain with. The absence of such policies puts planning authorities on the back foot — reliant on the design and persuasive skills of development managers to improve design quality at the eleventh hour. The scope to improve development proposals at this late stage is, however, limited, as key design decisions will already be made and development 'hope values' established. At this stage the city effectively has the choice of giving consent, tinkering at the edges, or refusing consent, as it stands. Refusal requires political will and the development having reached this stage, proposals are rarely refused on design grounds, which — in turn — exposes the limitations of relying on reactive control.

Design review and evaluation

Those proposing and implementing urban design controls or guidelines need a positive vision of the intended outcomes otherwise policies and guidelines simply operate in a vacuum. This is either a *vision* of what good urban form/urban design is or — alternatively — the *means* (i.e. cognitive skills/principles) to recognise it when it is presented. Furthermore, rather than controls for the sake of controls, as noted above, controls need to be informed by a vision of desired place. An example of this is the use of build-behind lines rather than build-to lines; the former is a negative regulation — it states what cannot be done; the latter is a positive regulation — it states what you must do (e.g. contribute to the spatial definition of a street). Understanding the difference between these ways of regulating, and where and when to use them, has major effects on the built outcome.

The forms of guidance discussed above provide means of moving broad policy objectives closer to realisation. These instruments — and the policies on which they build — ultimately fulfil the same function: offering a basis against which to evaluate development proposals. The process of their preparation is characterised in Figure 11.11).

Once prepared, they provide the means to operate regulatory processes — design review/control — on the basis of clearly identified and publicly available policy and guidance. In the USA, regulation of this nature began with the perceived need to control the aesthetic impact of billboard advertising. The aim was to control the potential for offence to the visual sensibilities of the average

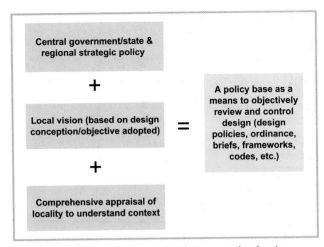

FIGURE 11.11   Policy base for design control and review

person — 'safety, morality and decency' were controllable within the constitution, though, at that time, pure aesthetics were not (Cullingworth 1997: 103). In Europe, powers to control design typically developed out of the need to improve basic health and amenity standards in urban housing, usually as the forerunner to comprehensive planning systems.

In most countries, design review/control processes are tied to broader planning process, successful negotiation of which is necessary to secure planning consent or a permit to build. Design review is typically dealt with either as an integral part of planning processes (as part of the wider regulatory process) or as a separate but linked process (see Box 11.3).

In some systems, processes of development and/or design control are tied to a further public regulatory function of the public sector — building control, which typically deals with the detailed health and safety aspects of construction standards and the design realisation of the private realm (space standards, ventilation requirements, structural stability, etc.). In the UK, these aspects are separated from broader urban design and planning processes, and handled through different statutory instruments and procedures. In Germany, although legislation distinguishes between planning and building law, the latter is open to local amendment and can have a much greater impact on architectural design through, for example, control of building form and materials.

Whatever the relationship, the interface between such micro-design regulation and the macro-design concerns typically dealt with through planning processes requires careful co-ordination, particularly for issues crossing the administrative divide, such as disabled access, energy use/conservation and the control of pollution from buildings (in construction and use). Encompassed in the sustainability agenda (see Sustainability Inserts 3, 7 and 8), these concerns illustrate how the scope of urban design is becoming wider and more complex — a complexity that needs to be matched by the sophistication of the regulatory processes.

Sustainability Insert 8 — Pollution Reduction

If settlements are viewed as living organisms, which ingest resources and eject waste products, then reducing waste emissions is a key aspect of sustainable urban design — to use resources more efficiently, to reduce the impact of development on its surroundings and to reduce the energy expended in waste removal and disposal (Ritchie 2003). Pollution reduction also plays an important role in improving quality of life in urban areas. Some of the most negative collective perceptions about urban areas and a major factor driving migration out of cities to more suburban and rural areas concerns, the pollution, dirt and noise that is characteristic of central areas (Mulholland Research Associates Ltd 1995).

Across all spatial scales, the key objective is to tackle pollution by reducing it in the first place — insulating against noise; ventilating against fumes; designing-out light pollution; designing-in filtration by trees; and investing in public transport while (as far as possible) controlling private car use. Supporting reduction efforts, the reuse and recycling of waste products (energy, water, materials, etc.) should form a second objective (Edwards 2000:12—29). Where possible, this should occur on site — for example, through the filtration of foul water through sustainable urban drainage (SUDS) schemes — or in the local neighbourhood, through collecting and incinerating waste as a fuel source for local combined heat and power stations. Removal of waste from sites should be a last resort.

Taking one example: the purification of water is an expensive, energy-intensive process, yet only 7% of purified water provided to homes in England is used for drinking and cooking — a third is simply flushed down the toilet; at the same time, most storm water is washed into sewers (CABE 2009: 18). Pollution reduction therefore requires urban designers attuned to the first three Rs: 'reduce', 'reuse' and 'recycle' — and 'remove' only when necessary.

Non-polluting transit (*Image: Matthew Carmona*) electric trams in Hammarby Sjöstad, Stockholm

BOX 11.3 Integrated and Separated Design Review Processes

(**1**) Integrated Design Control/Review Process

INTEGRATED SYSTEM

In this model, design is treated as an integral part of wider planning processes. Connections between design and other planning issues — economic development, land uses, social infrastructure, etc. — can be made, understood and weighed one against the other, and informed and balanced judgements made. The danger, however, is that design objectives can be, and often are, sacrificed in the pursuit of short-term economic and social objectives. The UK's process of design control provides an example of an integrated approach. Procedures,

however, exist to isolate design where necessary from other planning concerns by giving outline — rather than full — planning permission for development, with design issues held back as 'reserved matters' for further consideration at a later date. Some municipalities convene non-statutory (third-party) design review panels to advise planning committees on matters of design. In England, The Commission for Architecture and the Built Environment (CABE) provides independent design review for major schemes of national importance.

(**2**) Separated Design Control/Review Process

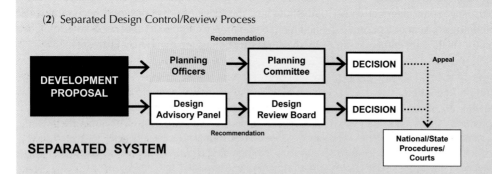

SEPARATED SYSTEM

In this model, decisions on design are isolated from other planning/development concerns, with a separate body responsible for reviewing and controlling design. Design issues consistently receive an appropriate weighting before development consents are granted or refused, usually by staff with well-developed design awareness: this is frequently not the case in the integrated model. A shortcoming of this model is the difficulty of making the necessary connections between design and other planning

issues, some of which — for example decisions on land use zoning, density, and transport/infrastructure provision — will have a major impact on design outcomes. In these circumstances, design is often reduced to 'mere' aesthetics. Many municipalities in the USA have separated models, with the review boards frequently only having an advisory role to the planning commission. In some instances, the review board has delegated powers to make final decisions on matters of design.

Source: *adapted from Blaesser in Case Scheer & Preiser 1994*

Whatever administrative procedures are adopted for design review/control, design proposals go through similar processes of design evaluation. These include not only formal procedures of application presentation and public consultation, but also less formal procedures of appraisal,

consultation with specialists, and negotiation with controllers (Punter & Carmona 1997: 303). As such, procedures rely on a coherent and comprehensive policy and guidance base already being in place, Table 11.9 sets out procedures at key stages of the design review process.

TABLE 11.9 Good Practice Procedures for Design Review

Those making review decisions about a proposed development should:

Before an application is received:
- Enable potential developers to consult the municipality about design proposals;
- As necessary, instigate design briefing (see above) procedures;
- As appropriate, initiate collaborative and/or participative arrangements (see Chapter 12).

After an application has been received:
- Appraise the site and its surroundings to establish the design context;
- Review established design policies and guidance for the site;
- Review the application to ensure design aspects have been clearly and appropriately presented;
- Instigate public consultation procedures;
- Obtain skilled/specialist advice (i.e. design panel procedures, historic building specialists, landscape specialists, etc.);
- On the basis of information gathered/received, negotiate design improvements;
- Consider and negotiate implementation requirements (phasing, planning gain requirements, reserved matters, etc.);
- On the basis of information gathered/received, make a reasoned recommendation or decision (i.e. to grant, grant with conditions or refuse consent).

After a negative decision has been made:
- Where necessary, use the information gathered/received to fight any appeal;
- Use the appeal decision to monitor evaluation procedures, but also – where necessary – to revise design policy and guidance.

After a positive decision has been made (or an appeal successfully made):
- Carefully monitor the implementation of the design (and if necessary enforce decisions/conditions);
- Evaluate design outcomes;
- Use the information collected to monitor wider evaluation procedures and, where necessary, revise design policy and guidance.

Source: Adapted from Carmona (2001: 159).

Evaluations undertaken by project teams (whether in the public or private sectors) of their own projects follow a similar process. Such evaluations include:

- Ongoing gathering of information to inform designing and decision-making.
- Seeking additional specialist expertise as and when required.
- Evaluating design proposals against the original objectives/brief and any new information.
- Making the decision to proceed with the scheme to presentation/implementation; retain certain aspects of the design for refinement and reject others for redesign; or reject the scheme in its entirety and redesign.

- Ongoing learning as schemes are completed and implemented and new schemes begun that draw from the experience of the design process itself; and, feedback on the scheme's performance.

The greater the degree of discretion within the regulatory systems, the greater the extent of interpretation and negotiation that may occur, which, in turn, requires highly skilled individuals to apply their discretion to evaluating submitted proposals. Hall (2007: 62) argues that this is typically a process of teamwork, which requires time to get right: '… *it is necessary to be prescriptive, to scrutinise, to challenge, to keep negotiating and to spend time on the public realm … Quality developers will be supportive of this process.*' He considers this to be a process requiring a dedicated professional team with good urban design skills and a commitment to the place, able to work with and beyond the statutory control processes and able to develop good working relationships with developers and other statutory authorities. Critically, it also involves changing the emphasis of regulation, from a focus on legalistic, procedure concerns to a focus on outcomes, and from silo-thinking to collaboration and partnership (Hall 2007: 175–6).

As well as standard public sector project evaluation techniques – assessing schemes against site appraisals, established policy and guidance, skilled advice and the results of any consultation activity – other techniques are used to evaluate the economic and socio-environmental impact of schemes. Cost–benefit analysis and environmental impact assessment techniques are commonly used for such purposes (see Moughtin *et al* 1999: 139–49). By including aspects that are readily quantified (e.g. employment, traffic impacts or levels of pollution), however, such assessments may neglect other impacts. For example, less tangible impacts – the loss of culturally important buildings or the positive impact of a well-designed public realm – are more difficult to quantify, and their value can be underestimated or ignored. Due to the resources required, such methods also tend only to be used on larger schemes, such as those associated with major infrastructure projects.

Government guidance in the UK (DETR/CABE 2000) argues that the 'art of urban design' lies in applying good practice principles to the particular conditions of an area or site. Design principles should also be capable of being expressed as performance criteria, permitting assessment of the extent to which they have been achieved (see Chapter 12). Despite strongly supporting the need for collaborative approaches to urban design, the guidance also notes that such proactive approaches are not a substitute for having good designers and are essentially '… *a way of making space for them to design creatively, and helping them avoid later finding themselves tripped up by matters of public policy, economics or local context which they failed to take into account.'* (Campbell & Cowan 1999). Those charged with writing and implementing design policy must, therefore, recognise that policy and regulation of any type will never be a sufficient substitute for good design proposals. Municipalities can be explicit about encouraging the use of good designers in policy, but, most crucially, by setting high aspirations in policy and guidance; insisting on the submission of high-quality, comprehensive illustrative materials supported by written justification of the proposals; and consistently seeking high standards through design review, employing appropriately skilled designers will become an essential prerequisite for gaining the necessary consents.

Monitoring and Review

The final stage in the design process is the feedback loop that involves learning from past experience and using the lessons to inform future practice. Arguing that growth and learning are essential parts of design, Zeisel (1981: 16) suggests it is '... *a process that, once started, feeds itself both by drawing on outside information and by generating additional insight and information from within.'* As much of this insight comes from past experience of what has worked and what has not, the more urban designers learn from past experiences, the more likely they are to repeat successes and avoid mistakes. This also applies at the organisational level, and reiterates the importance of public authorities and consultancies systematically monitoring their work and using the results to review both their design/management processes and subsequent design outcomes.

At its most basic, all design policy and guidance should be regularly monitored to assess how effectively it meets its objectives. The outcomes from such exercises can then be used to improve the effectiveness of policy and guidance frameworks (Punter & Carmona 1997: 311–4). Monitoring should also include assessing completed projects against the original brief and/or policy objectives, and post-occupancy evaluations. In the public sector, assessments of the results of appeals against planning/design review decisions (i.e. proportion allowed/disallowed and why) and the quality of planning applications received can also be monitored. Monitoring should involve all the actors involved in making decisions — municipal officers and elected planning committee/board members — as well as the users of the service and final scheme — architects, developers, civic and amenity societies and the wider community.

As an optional, post-implementation activity — and because staff, resources and energies are usually re-directed to new projects — systematic monitoring is rarely undertaken. Nevertheless, increasingly sophisticated methods are being employed to monitor public services and audit service quality. In the UK, the development of a series of performance indicators across local government services offers a means to compare some aspects of performance (Carmona & Sieh 2005). In the USA, performance indicators are a well-established part of the zoning process (Porter *et al* 1988). Performance indicators, however, often rely on quantitative measures of performance — the speed of processing planning consents; the number of applications submitted by architects; or the number of design-related planning appeals won — that only indirectly measure the qualitative dimensions of urban design.

By focusing only on aspects amenable to quantitative measurement, decision-making processes can be distorted. More fundamental approaches to monitoring include quality audit processes (DETR/ CABE 2000: 81), which involve systematic review of the practices and policies — and preferably also the outcomes — of public sector services to evaluate their success in meeting clearly defined objectives. Audits of this nature, however, tend to focus on processes rather than outcomes.

Other approaches to monitoring design quality include:

- Design awards schemes, which, in principle, also provide incentives for developers and designers to strive for better design (see Biddulph *et al* 2006).
- Design advisory panels, which reflect on completed schemes as well as schemes seeking planning approvals.
- Inspections of and visits to completed projects by elected councillors and officers, both to highlight and illustrate design issues and to make decision-makers aware of the impact of their decisions.

As well as formal approaches to monitoring, informal practices might be established. These include monitoring and review processes as a routine component of working arrangements. Such practices can be as simple as making time before beginning a project to research what has worked elsewhere, or simply recording personal impressions or informal discussions with colleagues to feed views back into formal policy review procedures or ongoing design and decision-making processes. In examining the conundrum of monitoring and measuring quality, Carmona & Sieh (2004: 309) conclude that holistic assessment of the impact of a public sector planning or urban design service requires measures of:

- Service quality (efficiency, effectiveness, economy and equity) across the key stages of the planning/development process and against clearly defined quality thresholds.
- The organisational-level leadership, skills, resources and integration processes deployed in order to deliver a high-quality service.
- The products or outcomes of the processes, both (and where possible) as a direct result of definable actions (e.g. design improvements through design review), but,

where this is not possible, by measuring what might be defined as the wider organisational product of the municipality as a whole (e.g. indicators of sustainable development).

All this requires significant time and resources, however, and smaller organisations need to judge where to focus their limited resources to obtain the information required to improve the services offered. One answer will be in evaluating their skills. Capacitycheck.co.uk (Urban Design Alliance 2008) is intended for this purpose, and aims to establish awareness, understanding and professional competence in urban design, as a means for organisations to focus on filling the gaps.

EDUCATION AND MANAGEMENT

The time-scale over which such concerns operate connects the final two modes of action – 'education' and 'management'. Over the long-term, education potentially provides the means to inspire greater commitment to environmental quality among the population at large, while management represents the ongoing stewardship of the urban environment, which helps stimulate identification with place.

Despite issues of environmental quality having moved up the political agenda, long-term commitment to place quality by the public sector and the local community remains essential because such issues are often sacrificed when perceived to conflict with economic and social goals. This long-term commitment is epitomised by how the built environment is managed. Nevertheless, as awareness of the link between environmental quality and economic prosperity and social well-being grows, so does the demand for better quality environments from across the range of stakeholders. This demand stems from a variety of factors, including:

- Companies and many individuals having a direct financial stake in the environment or property they own (for many householders their primary financial asset is their house).
- More people being better travelled and being more aware of high quality environments to compare with their own.
- The link between environment, health and contemporary lifestyles being clearly accepted and regularly debated (see Chapter 8).
- Built environment issues being newsworthy, both nationally and locally.

Dissatisfaction with how the built environment is managed is a consistent concern of local populations, and has been a particularly important factor in educating politicians to keep issues of quality high on the political agenda (Carmona & de Magalhaes 2006).

Education

The perception that the general public lack taste and visual literacy has long been considered a barrier to achieving better places (Punter & Carmona 1997: 338–40), as has a sense that the great industrial and business patrons of the past have gone (Figure 11.12).

Research in the UK and the USA has consistently shown that lay and professional tastes on design differ substantially (see Nasar 1998). In any one place, architects' tastes often differ from those of planners, which differ from those of local politicians and those of the general public. Nevertheless, as the design disasters of the post-war period remind us, professionals should be extremely wary of dismissing lay taste. Taking local public opinion on board in design proposals represents a means of ensuring design proposals will be supported by those most affected by them (see Chapter 12). Moreover, rather than assuming public taste is necessarily poor, it is best, first, to try to understand it, and then, as part of such engagement processes, to inform, educate and raise awareness about alternatives.

Although proactive design and regulation (rather than education) might be seen as the primary roles of the state in helping to shape better places, education is an important additional tool, which Schuster (2005: 353) argues might be used as an alternative to regulation. Taking the example of design review, he argues that '... *a design review board's most important role may be to sensitise those engaged in the development process as well as the public more generally to the needs of the public realm and the importance of good design.*' Over time, such processes amass invaluable information about how a community views design, helping to educate controllers and to shape their

FIGURE 11.12 Contemporary patterns of patronage *(Image: Louis Hellman)*

decision-making processes. As Schuster (2005: 354) correctly warns, '… *regulation is not the only mode of governmental intervention to consider when implementing policy to take account of the conflicts between social and private value or to internalise externalities';* information and thereby education might equally '… *represent an important tool in the public sector's design intervention toolbox.'*

Education should question, challenge and perhaps alter the 'mindsets' of key development and design actors — that is, encourage, provoke or otherwise cause mindshifts. For Landry (2000: 52), a mindset is '… *the order within which people structure their worlds, and how they make choices, both practical and idealistic, based on values, philosophy, traditions and aspirations.'* Mindsets are also a function of our social interaction within, and socialisation into, different behavioural settings. Thus, there are 'professional cultures' and 'house views' (i.e. within particular firms and organisations). Mindsets, however, are partial and may inhibit seeing the world in a more holistic, or even simply a different, fashion. They may also establish an unquestioned 'conventional wisdom', which inhibits the development and exploitation of new ideas — J K Galbraith defined the conventional wisdom as 'a commonly held set of ideas, frequently wrong' (Figure 11.13).

Laudry (2000: 52) defines a mindshift as '… *the process whereby the way one thinks of one's position, function and core ideas is dramatically re-assessed and changed.'* Challenging established or conventional cultural mindsets and encouraging mindshifts is about creativity and encouraging actors to think outside the box (i.e. outside normal cultural frames). It may involve enlarging the stock/ supply of ideas and concepts (e.g. encouraging decision-makers to commission design studies, design strategies,

FIGURE 11.13 Loft living, Shad Thames, London (*Image: Steve Tiesdell*). Loft living challenged the development industry's conventional wisdom that people did not want to live in former industrial buildings with open places, exposed pipework and brickwork walls

masterplans, etc.) but, as importantly, may also increase awareness of and receptivity to those ideas and concepts. Design champions in municipalities, for example, can be instrumental in changing the mindsets of key city actors, especially those of politicians, about the value and importance of design (CABE 2004b).

Management

The final element to be dealt with in this chapter concerns the everyday management and stewardship of the urban environment. Management processes are central to any conception of urban design, and particularly to public sector regulatory functions. In a more circumscribed role, however, management processes can be viewed as the day-to-day stewardship of already existing environments as a means to maintain and enhance place quality. In this role, the public sector has a key part to play, particularly through its management of transport, urban regeneration, conservation, and cleaning and maintenance processes — all key contributors to place quality.

Transport

Issues of transportation dominate debates about the sustainability of urban living patterns. Easily thought of as someone else's problem (at least at the macro scale), for urban design practitioners they are fundamental to decisions taken about — at one end of the urban design remit — the spatial design of settlements and — at the other end — the comfort and liveability of urban space. At the macro scale, much of the debate focuses on political issues of private versus public transport provision, on means to efficiently move people around urban areas, and on means to restrict car use. Decisions at the macro scale and within the political arena eventually feed through to the micro scale.

Urban design practitioners have an important role to play when designing new environments to ensure that vehicular needs are balanced with other users of urban space — pedestrians, cyclists and public transport (see Chapters 4 and 8). Most of the day-to-day decisions concerning transport provision, however, concern managing existing urban space — a role central to securing and maintaining a high-quality public realm. For the public sector, the aim should be to encourage equitable access for all sections of society by, for example, taming private car use; freeing space for pedestrians and cyclists; reducing situations of auto-dependency by providing a choice of travel modes; and integrating public transport at local and spatial scales.

Jones *et al* (2007) argue that part of the difficulty in designing streets as successful movement arteries (their 'link' potential) and people places (their 'place' potential) is the range of professionals involved in their creation and management, each with different skills, interests and objectives. As a minimum, this involves traffic planners (concerned with planning links), urban planners (concerned with spatial planning), traffic engineers (concerned with designing roads) and urban designers (concerned with designing places). Thus, a transport plan focuses on the strategic network, an urban plan on the land uses, a highway project on the carriageway, and urban design on the bits that are left.

What is required, they argue, is a 'Street Plan' that takes the planning and design of the street as an integrated whole and considers its link (movement) and place potential together. Street Plans would be like a conventional land use plan for a neighbourhood or city, with the future of streets positively considered and laid out as an expression of future intention. The link status would be determined by transport planners advised by traffic engineers, and the place status by urban planners with advice from urban designers. Hence, a street with higher link status would pay greater attention to the requirements of through-movement, while greater place status requires more attention to accommodating place-related uses such as street stalls, seating, pavement space and so on. The advantages of this approach are in making such trade-offs explicit, in giving planners and urban designers an equal stake to traffic engineers in the future planning of street space, and, most importantly, in ensuring that place quality is considered in street design.

Regeneration

Urban design also has an important contribution to make to urban regeneration. Ongoing processes of adaptation and change presuppose development as well as decline — the former is often dependant on the latter before reinvestment and renewal occurs. Again, the public sector has a key role to play in managing these processes through planning activity, but also through urban regeneration policy, including land reclamation, place promotion, direct investment (e.g. in infrastructure), and in providing subsidies or starting capital for revolving funds. Many of these roles are incentive-based activities, providing critical opportunities to use public resources to lever better design.

To manage and guide the regeneration and revitalisation of particular areas, ad hoc agencies or partnerships are often created. These may take many forms and are often termed 'growth coalitions', 'growth machines' or public/private partnerships (e.g. Logan & Molotch 1987). Many are three-way partnerships and include the private, public and voluntary/community sectors, with the various partners contributing different resources, powers and abilities, such as finance (both in the form of public subsidies and development finance), planning and legal powers (including, in particular, the ability to acquire development land) and what might be regarded as community consent or approval.

Whatever the particular mechanisms used to deliver regeneration activity — local government, public/private partnerships, voluntary agencies or government quangos such as urban development corporations — during the 1990s it was increasingly accepted that effective regeneration required the creation of sustainable social and economic structures alongside investment in physical design (see Urban Task Force 1999).

Positive actions by local authorities, revitalisation agencies and partnerships or others committed to an area can also be taken on the supply side to stimulate demand. The methods employed typically include encouraging or subsidising flagship (catalytic) projects; subsidising development; area-based improvements; provision of infrastructure; restricting opportunities for competitive supply; and/or developing urban design frameworks or masterplans. As development involves calculation of reward and risk, these actions are generally intended to reduce risk and to provide a more secure investment environment. Better-quality design helps ensure regeneration is sustainable, while poor-quality design might reduce the speed at which regeneration impacts propagate through local economies (Carmona et al 2001b: 76–7).

Many cities are simultaneously stimulating/attracting investment, while also regulating the resulting development. One potential consequence of this is that design criteria may be relaxed or compromised to ensure investment happens (see Chapter 10). However, high-quality investment in the public realm by municipalities can be rapidly undermined when regulatory processes permit sub-standard development schemes. This is often further complicated by institutional fragmentation, whereby one municipal department (or an arm's length public agency) is concerned with stimulating development (e.g. an economic development or regeneration agency) and another is regulating it (e.g. the planning department/ agency). This will be particularly so if policy and practices of the various agencies are not adequately 'joined-up', creating the opportunity for developers to exploit the gaps.

Conservation

Cities such as Boston in the USA and Barcelona and Sheffield in Europe have used high-quality design as a means of establishing a new image for, and confidence in, their central areas and, in doing so, have helped sustain wider regeneration activity. In each location, the built heritage and the city's existing character and history were used as a starting point for regeneration activity. Used positively, conservation activity can offer a powerful tool to deliver urban regeneration objectives (see English Heritage 2000b: 8–10).

Although inextricably linked to wider planning and regeneration activity, and in large part reliant on private sector investment to achieve its aims, conservation represents a further area of public sector activity. It is also a key means to deliver contextually respectful urban design that builds on established patterns of development and associations with place. In most regulatory and planning systems, conservation mechanisms operate through a separate legislative base; look to the past as a means to provide reference points to anchor and inform the present; look to the future by accepting the inevitability and desirability of change; and link these by 'capturing' and developing what is locally distinctive in the environment to inform contemporary development. By such means, conservation activity can reflect the widespread public support for preserving familiar and cherished local scenes. It also avoids the recurrent criticism that such activity merely panders to an unhealthy obsession with the past (particularly in the English-speaking world), to an associated desire to preserve and 'theme park' heritage, and to a desire to preserve physical artefacts as traces of bygone patterns of life, without the activities that gave rise to them in the first place (see Chapter 9).

Interpreted broadly, conservation encompasses a wider and forward-looking agenda encapsulated by such concepts as diversity, identity, place, community, distinctiveness and sustainability (Figure 11.14). In essence, this broader notion of conservation can be considered to represent a more forceful application of urban design principles. In this regard, conservation could be included under most of Lynch's modes of action. It is included here because conservation controls represent an overarching management regime applicable to certain environments that benefit

from additional policy and regulatory mechanisms. English Heritage's checklist for assessing character (Table 11.2) illustrates the scope of the conservation concern.

The tensions between economic forces for redevelopment and a widespread desire to maintain established social and physical structures are at their greatest in sensitive historic contexts, as are tensions between desires for innovation and continuity in design (see Chapters 7 and 9). To control these tensions, most conservation controls create a two-tier system of regulation with designated buildings and areas subject to an additional regime of control operating beyond that of the statutory planning processes operating elsewhere — for example: listed buildings and 'conservation areas' in the UK; the 'National Register of Historic Places' in the USA; and *'buildings inscrit'* or *'classés'* and *'Zones de Protection du Patrimonies Architectural et Urbain'* in France.

Cleaning and Maintenance

A lack of proper maintenance can easily precipitate a spiral of decline. As Wilson & Kelling's broken windows theory of crime prevention contends, when a window in a building is broken and left unrepaired, the rest of the windows will soon be broken. Wilson & Kelling (1982) explain that:

'Window-breaking does not necessarily occur on a large scale because some areas are inhabited by determined window-breakers, whereas others are populated by window-lovers. Rather, one unrepaired window is a signal that no one cares, and so breaking more windows costs nothing.'

They also argued that failure to deal promptly with minor signs of decay in a community, such as graffiti or soliciting by prostitutes, can result in a rapidly deteriorating situation as hardened offenders move into the area to exploit the breakdown in control.

A high-quality public realm requires a clean, healthy, safe and well-maintained environment. While the public sector will often have ultimate responsibility for this, contributions — either positive or negative — are likely to come from a range of public and private sources including refuse and environmental health services, transport authorities, planning authorities, parks and recreation departments, police authorities, statutory undertakers, private businesses, community organisations and the public. Indeed, this diversity of interests and the incremental changes for which they are responsible makes the process of urban management difficult (Carmona & de Magalhaes 2008: 20–1).

The sense of a deterioration in the public realm in the 1980s and 1990s (Hillman 1988) explained — in part — the dramatic growth in the development of out-of-town shopping malls (and other more pseudo-public spaces), where the environment is maintained, designed, policed and regulated by a single, clearly identifiable private

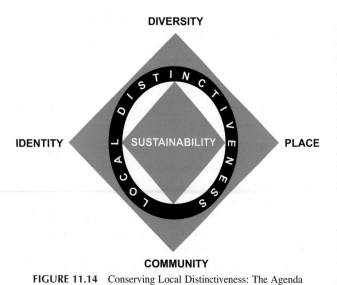

DIVERSITY

IDENTITY · DISTINCTIVENESS · SUSTAINABILITY · LOCAL DISTINCTIVENESS · PLACE

COMMUNITY

FIGURE 11.14 Conserving Local Distinctiveness: The Agenda

interest. In the UK, recognition of the competitive threat of out-of-town retail developments and their effect on the 'vitality and viability' of traditional town and city centres during this period led to a rethink of urban management and to the emergence of integrated Town Centre Management (TCM) (URBED 1994). In places as diverse as the centres of major urban conurbations and small country market towns, town centre managers have been employed to co-ordinate actions, to monitor changes and act as town centre janitors, to promote and market town centres and to advocate and enable programmes of improvement.

In the USA, and subsequently around the world, Business Improvement Districts (BIDS) emerged as a semi-private solution to the problems of urban management. Unlike publicly funded TCM, BIDS are funded by a supplementary charge on local businesses who directly fund an additional layer of management (maintenance, cleansing and, typically, security) that, by its very nature, is focused on meeting their business needs, namely attracting more customers to their shops and higher rentals for their properties, rather than wider community needs. In essence, however, both TCM and BIDS reflect recognition of the public sector's failure to adequately care for the urban environment, and thus attempt to cut through the mire of complex overlapping responsibilities for public space to deliver basic public space management.

Based on a review of international public space management regimes and practices, Carmona *et al* (2008: 209) suggest that the aspiration shuold be a system that involves all stakeholders in caring for the quality of public space, particularly where, left to its own devices, the public sector has done a poor job. They see

'... no moral or practical superiority of one model (state, market or community-centred) over another, each, and different combinations of them, can provide the right solutions in particular contexts. The key is to recognise the advantages and disadvantages of each and from there decide where and how they should be appropriately used.'

The aim should be to deliver the 'public good', while avoiding unintended consequences, perhaps through safeguards offered by tight legal agreements, planning conditions, strong enforcement, co-ordinated partnerships, and the checks and balances provided by an overview role for the public sector for all public space.

Davis (1997) proposes a specific programme of action to enhance character and improve convenience and, thereby, to breathe new life into urban centres. His checklist illustrates not only the diversity of public sector action required, but also the extent of co-ordination required between public sector agencies and between public and private sector interests to procure and maintain high-quality urban design (Table 11.10).

TABLE 11.10 Improving the High Street Environment

Convenience	Improvement Actions
Welcome	• Tidy up car park entrances • Make car park interiors welcoming • Integrate paths to the high street • Clarify pedestrian direction signs
A cared-for place	• Eliminate flyposters and graffiti • Clear litter and rubbish • Position waste recycling bins
Comfort and safety	• Calm traffic

Character	Enhancement Actions
Pavements	• Specify quality pavements • Reduce street furniture clutter • Rationalise traffic street furniture
Shops	• Improve shop fronts • Reduce impact of vacant shop fronts • Relate shop signs
Urban space	• Design infill development • Create incidental urban space • Plant street trees • Introduce seasonal colour
Street life	• Encourage market stalls and kiosks • Vary activities in urban spaces • Establish special events
Local landmarks	• Accentuate landmarks • Design paving for special places • Install public lighting • Place art in public places

Source: Adapted from Davis (1997).

CONCLUSION

In this chapter, the public sector's contribution to encouraging, securing and maintaining high-quality urban design has been discussed. Diverse, all-pervasive and potentially highly positive, this role can be encompassed in the six modes of action:

- *Appraisal/diagnosis* — analysing context to understand the qualities and meanings of place.
- *Policy* — providing policy instruments to guide, encourage and control appropriate design in particular places.
- *Regulation* — implementing policy objectives through negotiation, review and statutory processes.
- *Design* — developing and promoting specific design and development solutions, from large-scale infrastructure to site-specific solutions.
- *Education and participation* — 'spreading the word' and involving potential users in the process.

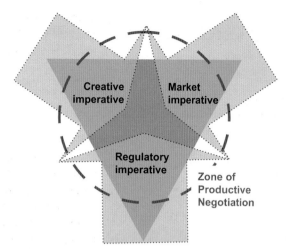

FIGURE 11.15 Three tyrannies: The zone of productive negotiation *(Source: Matthew Carmona 2009b)*

- *Management* — ongoing management and maintenance of the urban fabric.

Nevertheless, as the public sector — like the private sector — rarely operates in isolation, it is the successful partnership between public and private that, over time, offers the greatest potential for successful, sustainable urban design. In essence, this requires forms of public intervention that deliver public goals while enhancing creativity and value generation as critical contributions to place-making. In other words, allowing the essentials of good urbanism to be defined and regulated at the start of the process, raising market value in the process and allowing room for design creativity. As Elizabeth Plater-Zyberk (in Case Sheer & Preiser 1994: vii) argues

'... *control and freedom can co-exist most effectively when incorporated in regulations that precede the act of design, framing parameters of a given programme, rather than conflicting in judgement exerted on the completed design.*'

As the experience with piloting design coding in the UK suggests (Carmona 2009a), whether in creative, market or regulative roles, stakeholders benefit profoundly from positive engagement with each other. Done well, the preparation of proactive policy and guidance provides a medium through which to shake off narrow sectoral perspectives — the tyrannies — and to compel the creators of the built environment to see the process as a collective endeavour. In the final analysis, 'control' may be necessary, but seeing processes of regulation as an opportunity for consensus building within a zone of productive negotiation will produce better places than the conflict and compromise of the past (see Figure 11.15).

Chapter 12

The Communication Process

As design is a process of exploration and discovery, drawing and other forms of representation and communication are integral parts of this process. The fate of design ideas and projects is significantly affected by the designer's abilities to convey ideas effectively, whether to other members of the design team, to clients, or to community and other stakeholder groups. Urban designers thus need to represent and communicate ideas – both visually and verbally – clearly and logically to a variety of audiences. Ideas and principles are of little value if urban designers are unable to communicate them effectively. Highlighting the role of graphic material in joint thinking, Condon (2008), for example, stresses the designer's role in articulating the ideas coming from stakeholders and the wider community, through the use of drawings not just showing the end result of discussion, but, more importantly, where creating drawings *is* the discussion.

This chapter discusses communication in urban design, focusing on four main issues. The first is the act of communication. The second is community engagement as a form of communication. The third is the means and methods of presentation. The fourth is written communication.

COMMUNICATION, PERSUASION AND MANIPULATION

When urban designers seek to secure a commission, gain support and/or acceptance for a project, obtain funding and/or secure permission for a development or proposal, communication processes come to the fore. Urban designers need to market their services and promote their ideas to potential clients whether these are private individuals, companies, government organisations or politicians. Equally, every urban design project has to be presented to an audience, the nature and type of which varies from other members of the design team to client representatives, other professionals, representatives from the public sector, funding institutions, the local community, the media, etc. Communication requires oral and graphic presentation skills tailored to the particular audience, with presentations being a means to an end, rather than an end in themselves – the end being to achieve something worthwhile on the ground.

Communication is not a straightforward process and there are significant issues of power, manipulation, seduction and misinformation involved. In his book, *Representation of Places: Reality and Realism in City Design*, Bosselmann (1998: 202), for example, notes how proponents show a proposal to its best advantage, with negative impacts being played down or omitted from the presentation, while opponents are equally selective in highlighting the negative and acknowledging few, if any, of the benefits.

In principle, there are two fundamental types of communication. The first is *informative communication* where the main objective is to furnish the audience with information to enable a better understanding of the project. The second is *persuasive communication,* aimed at securing acceptance, approval, consent or funding. The distinction can be academic – in practice, all forms of communication are both persuasive and informative. A more important distinction is between communications that are intentionally persuasive, those that are accidentally or unconsciously persuasive and those that are deliberately manipulative. While various techniques can be used to represent the 'reality' of schemes, because images can be manipulated, it is the communicator's choice whether – or, more precisely, to what extent – to manipulate 'reality'.

Persuasion and manipulation are closely related. Manipulation operates primarily by keeping the audience ignorant. Dovey (1999: 11) suggests a common practice is where the representation of design projects is distorted to produce a form of 'manipulated consent' from ignorant participants. 'Seduction' is a different form of manipulation – a highly sophisticated practice that manipulates the interest and desires of the subject and entails '… *the constructions of desire and self-identity and with significant implications for the built environment.'* (Dovey 1999: 11). While seduction is usually positive and manipulation usually negative, both involve the exercise, and perhaps abuse, of power. The dangers of such manipulation are ever-present.

Commenting on the 'sometimes miraculous images' used to illustrate development proposals, Biddulph (1999: 126) notes the difficulty of differentiating between 'future environment' and 'advertisement'. Carmona (2006: 122) comments on the massive amounts of specialist communications talent and technology increasingly lavished on presenting major schemes in order to give developers (and their design teams) an edge. For the highest profile international commissions and competitions, the resources required to be competitive limit the field to a small number of international consultancies and signature architects (see Chapter 5); teams thoroughly immersed in the art of visual seduction. McNeill (2009: 47, 72–6) argues that for the highest profile architects – the 'star-chitects' – huge attention is paid to how to represent their brand, which is built up through how they present themselves; how they are represented in the press, publications and via their formidable publicity machines; in the choice of competitions and awards to enter; through the carefully vetted visual outputs from their offices; and, of course, in their buildings (see Chapter 5).

Rather than to confuse, seduce or manipulate an audience, communications might be used to challenge it, and to expose and reveal new insights. Designers frequently want to show an audience something that they had not previously considered. To communicate schemes and ideas, designers may employ metaphors and/or evoke precedents. Precedents can be an effective tool for communication: *'By demonstrating the intention of a design through example, a designer can provide an immediately recognisable image, a familiar ambience that explains the goal of the proposal.'* (Trancik 1986: 60).

Precedents and metaphors should be used with caution, however. Images of Italian hill top towns were used, for example, to sell the concept of Cumbernauld new town, sited on an exposed and windswept hill top north of Glasgow. Rather than just visual and oral presentations, client groups can make visits to precedent developments to experience them firsthand and to talk with residents and users – if so, they should also be encouraged to be critical and to reflect on their experiences, impression and observations.

Power is an inevitable part of communication – the first speaker, for example, has the power of initiation and agenda-setting, which subsequent speakers must challenge. To be effective, communicators need credibility based on criteria such as trust and respect. An audience may be neither seduced nor deceived by manipulation, but obviously manipulative communicators lose credibility and what they are communicating will be treated with suspicion. Forester (1989) has discussed communication in planning. Transposing 'urban designers' for planners, his points and arguments remain appropriate:

'If they fail to recognise how their ordinary actions have subtle communicative effects, they will be counterproductive, even though they may mean well. They may be sincere but mistrusted, rigorous but unappreciated, reassuring but resented. Where they intend to help, [urban designers] may instead create dependency and where they intend to express good faith, they may raise expectations unrealistically with disastrous consequences. But these problems are hardly inevitable. When [urban designers] recognise the practical and communicative nature of their actions,

they can devise strategies to avoid these problems and to improve their practice as well.'

(Forester 1989: 138–9).

In discussing his concept of the 'ideal speech situation', Habermas (1979) argued that we expect speech to be comprehensible, sincere, legitimate and truthful. Interpreting Habermas' ideas, Forester (1989: 144) argued that mutual understanding depends on satisfying these four criteria:

'Without comprehensibility in interaction, we have not meaning but confusion. Without a measure of sincerity, we have manipulation or deceit rather than trust. When a speaker's claims are illegitimately made, we have the abuse rather than the exercise of authority. And when we cannot gauge the truth of what is claimed, we will be unable to tell the difference between reality and propaganda and fact.'

These are 'ideal' conditions and, in practice, their value is to measure how far real speech falls short of these conditions.

Communication Gaps

Effective communication is a two-way process of both speaking *and* hearing, which involves some form of connection between a communicator and an audience. Although communication is a means to empower people so that they can contribute positively and constructively, its efficacy may be adversely affected by gaps in this connection. Urban designers must appreciate where communication gaps are likely to arise and be aware of how to overcome them. There is, for example, typically a gap between the producers and consumers of the urban environment (see Chapter 10). There are also communication and social gaps between the designer and the user and the professional and the layperson. If their desire is to make places for people, urban designers need to narrow rather than exacerbate these gaps.

(i) **The professional–layperson gap**

Through their training and education, urban design practitioners acquire the skills necessary to represent both what exists and what might become reality. This is simultaneously a strength and weakness. Lang (1987), for example, argues that environmental design professionals remain overwhelmingly locked into a pictorial mode of urban design that treats the city as a work of art rather than as a setting for everyday life. Hubbard (1996: 31) observes how

'... design training and socialisation inculcates a professional perspective which emphasises the objective, physical qualities of the environment and discourages a more personal, subjective response. ... one can comfortably assume that such disparities reflect fundamental differences in the ways in which designers and non-designers think

about their surroundings, not simply differences in the way they express themselves.'

Not simply a matter of training and professional perspective, the problem is inherent in any representation. As Bosselmann (1998: xiii) recognises, because the real world's 'richness and complexity' cannot be completely represented, designers inevitably select from reality an 'abstraction of actual conditions':

'For them the process of representation is a complex form of reasoning. What they choose to represent influences their view of reality and very significantly defines the outcome of designs and plans, and thus the future form of cities.'

This raises issues regarding the nature of professional expertise, and potential gaps between professionals and laypeople. Rather than considerations of 'experts' and 'non-experts', it is better to conceptualise this in terms of different types of expertise. While easy to understand in terms of communication between different types of professional expert, the expertise of supposed non-experts is less obvious. This is of particular note in situations where urban design practitioners are dealing with communities and users. Bentley (1999) suggests distinguishing between 'local' and 'global' expertise, arguing professionals have global expertise, while local people have local expertise. Each needs to be respected in the design process and in making places that are responsive, meaningful and valued by their users.

A key challenge for global experts is to tease out the knowledge of local experts. A variety of innovative techniques have been used to achieve this, such as asking local people to write a postcard or to make a short film. In some cases, local people explore the life experiences of a hypothetical group of people representing a range of age, gender and ethnic groups. In other cases, local people are encouraged to tell stories in which the speakers can remove themselves from the narrative and speak of their experiences indirectly.

As well as through pictures and images, the professional–layperson gap may be exacerbated through the use of words and language. Just as urban design practitioners need to think spatially, they also need to describe spatial concepts in words and to express spatial concepts, ideas and principles in written policy and codes. Similarly, for the purpose of securing permissions and consents, and as a means of supporting and explaining graphic submissions, urban designers may also need to write design statements. Language, words, phrases, slang and shorthand versions of common concepts, however, can create communication gaps. Duany *et al* (2000: 213), for example, observe how some architects have tried to regain a 'sense of power' through what they describe

as 'mysticism': '*… by developing illegible techniques of representation, and by shrouding their work in inscrutable jargon, designers are creating increasingly smaller realms of communication.'*

(ii) The designer–non-designer gap

A gap exists between designers and non-designers. Non-designers and those with little design aptitude or appreciation tend to see shapes and lines on a piece of paper as just that. Some volume house builders, for example, employ technicians (rather than designers) to 'design' housing layouts, using standardised layouts and house types. This may happen without the technician ever having visited the site and, thereby, without appreciating its qualities and attributes. All the technician sees is a two-dimensional site plan, and design becomes a process of pattern-making.

By contrast, designers tend to read drawings spatially and to understand that the shapes and lines represent three-dimensional objects that both define and are defined by space. The act of drawing – and, indeed, of design – involves a vital connection between hand, eye and brain. Other media change the nature of this connection and relationship. Mechanical and computer-aided forms of drawing, for example, reduce the fluency of this connection. It may simply be different, but designers need to appreciate how it is different, and what impact this has on the design process.

(iii) The reality–representation gap

In general, greater realism in the representational image of a scheme increases the likelihood of viewers understanding the project in the same way as they would in the real world. A common problem encountered, however, is that perception cannot be fully represented graphically. A crucial limitation of many representations is that they present a primarily visual experience of place that fails to portray its wider perceptual and social experiences. As we move through space, our view and perception of the environment – through sight, touch, hearing, smells and sensitivity to climate – around us changes (see Chapter 5).

As techniques for representation increase in their sophistication and realism, we increasingly confront the problems arising from the confusion of realism in representations – the realism–reality gap. The problem is not that forms of presentation can be realistic or not, or distorting and misleading or not, but the need to recognise the potential for this and, where possible, correct for it. Representations must, nevertheless, not be confused with reality, while audiences may need to be educated to appreciate the limitations, including both strengths and weaknesses, of representation techniques. As is discussed later, scale models can be particularly misleading.

(iv) The powerful–powerless gap

Although the gap between the powerful and the less powerful in urban design manifests itself in many ways, it is often a function of gaps between the 'paying' and 'non-paying' clients of urban design (see Chapters 1 and 3) and between producers and consumers (see Chapter 10). In economic theory, where markets work well the consumer has sovereignty and the producer provides what the consumer wants. In practice, this rarely prevails and imbalances in economic power are sometimes corrected through the use of governmental and regulatory power.

In 1969, Sherry Arnstein developed her ladder of citizen participation to illustrate eight levels of citizen involvement (Figure 12.1). While the lower levels of Arnstein's ladder are generally tokenistic, processes further up the ladder involve greater transfers of power to citizens. Arnstein (1969: 216) argued that 'participation of the governed in their government' is – in principle – 'the cornerstone of democracy'. For Arnstein (1969: 216), this is a 'revered idea' that is 'vigorously applauded by virtually everyone', but that applause is '... *reduced to polite handclaps ... when this principle is advocated by the have-not*[s] ... *And when the have-nots define participation as redistribution of power.'*

Arnstein's ladder has been extensively re-written and adapted since its original publication. Barton *et al* (2003: 53) re-frame it as a journey from spin and bluster, through tokenism, two-way information, genuine consultation, partnership and delegated

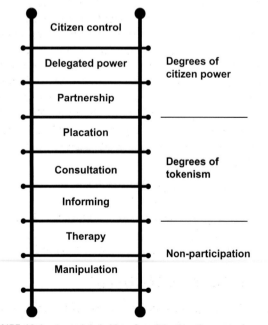

FIGURE 12.1   Arnstein's ladder of participation (*Image: redrawn from Arnstein 1969*)

powers, to autonomous powers. Each step reflects a change in the public authority's attitude to involvement, starting from autocratic and journeying through manipulative, technical, enabling, and collaborative, to confrontational; the last because an alternative seat of decision-making and power is suggested by devolving powers to an autonomous body.

In this respect, design is no different to any other area of public policy. Assuming a zero-sum game, the more power transferred to local populations, the less power resides in the hands of those financing, developing, designing and politically sanctioning the project. More generally, this may also mean empowering those on the right-hand side of McGlynn's powergram (see Chapter 10). Power is a complex phenomenon and has been extensively theorised (see Lukes 1975), but is best considered to be multi- rather than uni-dimensional. Rather than some actors having power and other actors having none (which is how it is conceived in Arnstein's model), all actors have some power and they interact in complex ways.

Partnerships are – in principle – a form of power-broking (and trust-building) in which conflicts of interest are resolved within the partnership. Revised power relationships may be justified by the increased potential for early resolution of conflicts, collaborative and supportive arrangements leading to more sustainable outcomes, added value through more considered design policies and proposals, and greater commitment to development/design proposals through broader ownership of the processes that led to them. As well as executive agencies and support coalitions, partnerships in urban design may also operate as pressure/lobby groups, usually to defend the amenity of an area.

In the absence of trust, the sense of ownership of the environment by local populations and economic interests can be undermined, along with the willingness to invest in an area. In such circumstances, the public sector is frequently left to cope with the social, economic and environmental fallout.

(v) The designer–user gap

A perennial problem in design is that the designer's priorities and aspirations may not accord with those of users. During the 1960s and 1970s, designers looked to the social sciences for useable information, advice and guidance about behaviour and human needs. Social research offered the specious ability to make predictions about human behaviour derived from their environmental settings. Although designers often treated these as scientific data, this was a 'misplaced certainty'. It is questionable who, if anyone, was to blame for this – researchers who were extravagant in their claims and who did not adequately qualify their research, or designers who ignored the qualifications. Heavily qualified information, however, is unlikely to be welcome to practitioners. Jenks (1988: 54), for example, notes how,

'... tentative guidelines may be edited and summarised, and recommendations made upon which action can be taken. In turn, recommendations may be translated into guidelines, design principles or standards to facilitate the designer's task. There is nothing inherently wrong with this, and it is undeniably useful. However, once turned into that epitome of certainty, a standard or guideline, the rationale, the reasoning and the careful qualifications tend to get lost. At that stage it may not even be clear whether the standard or recommendation is authoritative, or whether it is based on research or supposition.'

More fundamentally, Vischer (1985) advocates changing from a 'needs and preferences' model of user research to an 'adaptation and control' model concerned with developing users' abilities to adapt to and control their environment. The conceptual shift is from users as passive expressers of needs and preferences to users as active agents of change. Adaptation refers to users' ability to change themselves and their behaviour in response to different environmental contexts. Control refers to users' ability to change the physical dimensions of their environment that they are not motivated to adapt.

Research into the needs and preferences of users often assumes that, because people cannot make their voice heard, project sponsors should advocate or at least advance the users' perspective to designers. Implied here is the idea that more of users' needs could be met if more information was available (Vischer 1985: 289). There are at least three questionable assumptions here:

- That questioning can identify users' needs and preferences. As users are often unable to formulate exhaustive lists of their requirements in rank order of need and preference, researchers have to make assumptions and, in so doing, introduce their own values.
- That appropriate design can result in users' needs being met.
- That users inevitably have a relatively passive role. As Vischer (1985: 291) notes, identifying and responding to users' needs places the users

'... in a passive, recipient role in terms of their behavioural relationship to the environment and also places the researcher (who identifies needs) and the designer (who responds to needs) in key roles of responsibility regarding the ultimate fit between users and environments.'

The model thus fails to recognise users' active role as both agents in the operation of the environment and instigators of environmental change.

Vischer (1985: 293–4) concludes that giving users some control over their environment may be more effective than trying to design a direct response to users' needs as they express them: 'Users are not passive and inert entities ... they take an active role in their environments, interacting with it and adjusting it to suit changing situations.'

What is also important in considering designer–user gaps are issues of values and of power. As is discussed below, community engagement techniques and practices are increasingly interactive, involving exchange, debate and the development and exploration of ideas and options. Action research, for example, through such techniques as 'enquiry by design', is a reflective process of progressive problem solving, usually led by individuals working with others in teams, and intended to improve the way they address issues and solve problems. Community engagement of this type not only challenges the traditional twentieth century model of disinterested professionals, requiring them to be much more engaged and committed; it also entails a conflict between the more 'descriptive' sciences and engineering, which collect data on issues, and the more 'interpretative' arts, which involve feelings, emotions, values and worldviews (Newman *et al* 2009: 116).

In *Making Social Science Matter* (2001), Flyvbjerg offers a new form of social science to address this apparent conflict. Based on the classical Greek concept *phronesis* (i.e. practical wisdom or common sense), he presents a concept of phronetic social science as an alternative to traditional, 'epistemic' social science. Going beyond analytical, scientific knowledge ('episteme') and technical knowledge ('techne'), phronetic social science involves deliberations about values and power, and about which social actions are good or bad for humans. Hence, for Flyvbjerg, community engagement, and other forms of social action, must explicitly address four values related questions:

- Where are we going?
- Is this development desirable?
- Who gains and who loses, and by which mechanisms of power?
- What, if anything, should we do about it?

COMMUNITY ENGAGEMENT

Community engagement in the process of urban design is increasingly promoted as a means to overcome — or, at least, reduce — the professional–layperson, powerful–powerless and designer—user gaps. Forms of participation take many different forms, but can be broadly conceptualised as top-down or bottom-up approaches.

- *Top-down approaches* tend to be instigated by public authorities and/or developers, usually as a means to gauge public opinion and gain public support for proposals. Development options or policy proposals will already be prepared as the focus for an arranged participation exercise. The danger of such approaches is that the agenda may already be largely set, leading to a manipulation of local opinion, or simple acquiescence, rather than genuine involvement and engagement. More positively, such approaches may offer an effective use of resources by using professional expertise to mobilise, co-ordinate and interpret community opinions.
- *Bottom-up approaches* are instigated and led from the grassroots level, usually in response to some perceived opportunity or threat. While these exercises offer highly effective means to influence political decision-making processes, they suffer from their time-consuming nature, the time and commitment required to develop appropriate expertise and from the frequent failure to connect aspirations with the resources needed to put them into effect.

Ideally, whatever approach is adopted, the aim — over either the short or longer term — should be to develop a mutually advantageous dialogue and partnership between public, private and voluntary stakeholders. To stimulate dialogue, community and stakeholder groups might be presented with a range of design and development options, showing, for example, extremes of development densities or different development forms or typologies. This allows the community and stakeholder groups to react to these proposals and to explore ideas between the proffered options (Figure 12.2). A range of games — traditional and computer-based — have been developed by consultancies and others, simulating the development process and thereby allowing players to engage more fully to understand these complex design decision-making processes and the pros and cons and trade-offs involved in different development scenarios (Arias *et al* 1997). These can be a particularly valuable precursor to formal design processes.

In the context of Manchester City Council's design guide for the city's Hulme area (Hulme Regeneration Limited 1994), Rudlin & Falk (1999: 213) discuss the need to create, and subsequently to maintain, a support coalition for design ideas, principles and proposals. The design guide initially met with intense opposition from private and social housing developers, police, traffic engineers and institutional investors and it was a struggle to maintain the principles and ideas contained within it. What helped was the strong support coalition established between the consultant professionals and the local politicians.

An essential part of the support coalition comes from the local community and those directly affected by proposals. Research by the Urban Design Group (1998: 17) identified a high level of demand by local communities for involvement in the planning and management of their local environment. By involving communities, a sense of ownership of the resulting decision may be engendered, the eventual urban design quality of the scheme may be improved, and benefits may be more equitably distributed. Involving those affected by development in its production is also essentially sustainable, helping to give communities control over their local environment and encouraging a greater sense of self-sufficiency (see Sustainable Insert 9).

Sustainability Insert 9 — Self-sufficiency

Development of the built environment prior to the twentieth century was slow with most lives centred on local areas and using local resources — both human and natural. With increasing internationalisation and greater ease of communications, patterns of living and development processes take place on an ever-expanding stage. The implications are unsustainable due, in larger part, to the increasing distances populations and resources need to travel to cater for everyday needs (Hopkins 2005: 28–9). Once established, patterns of living become embedded in, and perpetuated through, the built environment's spatial arrangement and thus unsustainable patterns of living are difficult to change. If the nearest shop from which to buy bread and milk is a 15-minute walk away across busy highways, the tendency will be to take the car.

Although patterns of life will be difficult to change over the short term, design has an important role to play in providing people with the choice to lead more self-sufficient lifestyles in the future. This may include physical measures such as providing for cyclists to encourage greater self-sufficiency in travel, providing fast Internet connections to allow home working or simply allowing space for local food production in less dense urban areas (Hopkins 2000). More fundamentally, it will require key stakeholders and local populations to have a greater active involvement in developing a vision for their locality and in its ongoing management (Stewart 2000). Active participation thus represents a key tenet both of self-sufficiency and of sustainable development more widely. It extends to the notion that, in a democratic society, the actions of the few should not impact adversely on the amenities enjoyed by the many. This implies that, through its design, development should be environmentally benign, or that recompense should be made locally to redress the balance (Dunster 2006).

Sustainability Insert 9 — Self-sufficiency—cont'd

Inevitably, not all members of the community will be engaged to the same degree in environmentally supportive behaviours, but it may be that urban design processes can encourage greater participation. A 4Es model (DEFRA 2006) can be used to increase the likelihood of enduring behavioural change:

1. *Engaging* — by providing opportunities for the public to participate in debates, through community and social networks and marketing.
2. *Encouraging* — by rewarding certain behaviours and discouraging others, for example through local award schemes, fiscal incentives or legislative controls such as on parking.
3. *Enabling* — by delivering the infrastructure that allows sustainable behaviours to occur, for example the provision of safe, attractive routes to key local destinations, or space to store recycling bins.
4. *Exemplifying* — by actively demonstrating through exemplar schemes and local leadership.

Cultivated urban space, Nicosia Cyprus (*Image: Matthew Carmona*)

Public involvement and consultation can thus be an important means of brokering trust and building support for design principles. This is clearly seen in the redevelopment of public sector housing estates where tenant involvement in designing the masterplan or development framework helps develop a sense of ownership. Successful initial actions and projects ('early wins') are also important in terms of holding the support coalition together.

In any consultation/participation exercise, three distinct activities should be recognised — dispersing information; gathering information; and promoting dialogue. The first two are essentially one-way (monological) forms of communication. Although communities have frequently been involved as part of a consultation exercise on development proposals, such approaches have often tended merely to inform rather than to actively solicit their views. They have also been indirect rather than hands-on and take place after rather than during the design process. Consequently, the community's engagement has been slight, and the benefits of their involvement minimal.

In an attempt to bring communities more fully into the design process, a range of more active participatory mechanisms has been developed seeking to promote dialogue and two-way interaction. Such approaches work most effectively when initiated from the bottom up (run and 'owned' by the local community) and less effectively when imposed from above — although some initial encouragement and support may be required. Some of the more common methods are:

- *'Planning-for-real' exercises*, which use large-scale models to encourage non-confrontational community involvement in identifying and addressing problems.

Participants are encouraged to make suggestions by filling out suggestion cards and attaching these to a model, the outcomes of which can be pursued in detail at follow-up group meetings. The process relies on members of the community trying out different ideas, with the professionals recording the results, arbitrating and acting as enablers and facilitators.

- *Action planning events*, which are collaborative events, structured to enable different sections of local communities to work with independent specialists from a variety of disciplines to produce proposals for action. Events are usually staged over several days and involve processes of briefing from key stakeholders, analysing the physical context, workshops and brainstorming sessions, synthesis and presentation of proposals, and finally reporting back and the dissemination of results.

- *Urban design assistance teams (UDATs)* that represent a variation on action planning where multidisciplinary teams from outside the area 'parachute in' to facilitate an event and, with the local community, 'brainstorm' an approach to a problem and, thereby, help the local community devise recommendations for action. UDATs should be community-inspired and -led (i.e. from the bottom up) (Figure 12.3 and Box 12.1).

A number of publications list the array of participation approaches available. Examples include the New Economics Foundation's *Participation Works! 21 Techniques of Community Participation for the 21st Century* (1998) and the Urban Design Group's *Involving Local Communities in Urban Design* (UDG 1998). These reports identified a total of 78 separate techniques (Table 12.1),

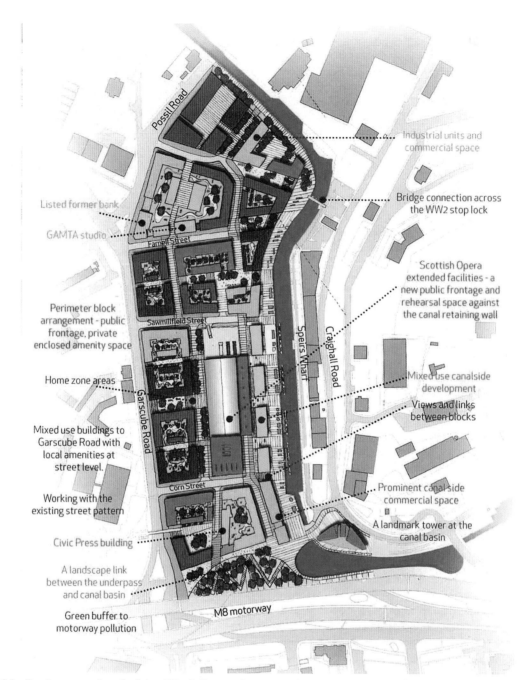

FIGURE 12.2 Development options for Spiers Wharf, Glasgow (*Image: Isis Waterside Development*). To stimulate discussion and debate about development options, community groups were presented with three development configurations – 'courtyards', 'fingers' and 'terraces'

many of which use design as a means to explore issues and options that communities face in a manner that allows solutions to emerge rather than being simply a re-statement of problems.

For a successful collaborative approach, Barton *et al* (2003: 47) suggest five golden rules:

1. *Clarity of purpose*
   - What are you trying to achieve?
   - Why is consultation or collaboration needed?
   - Who are you targeting?

2. *Fitness for purpose*
   - Are the participatory approaches suited to the task?
   - Will the approaches help deliver a co-ordinate plan?
   - Does the approach fulfil statutory requirements?
   - Have you got capacity to see it through?
   - Have the other participants got the capacity to see it through?

3. *Avoiding false expectations*
   - Are you clear about your 'bottom line'?
   - Are the project boundaries explicit?

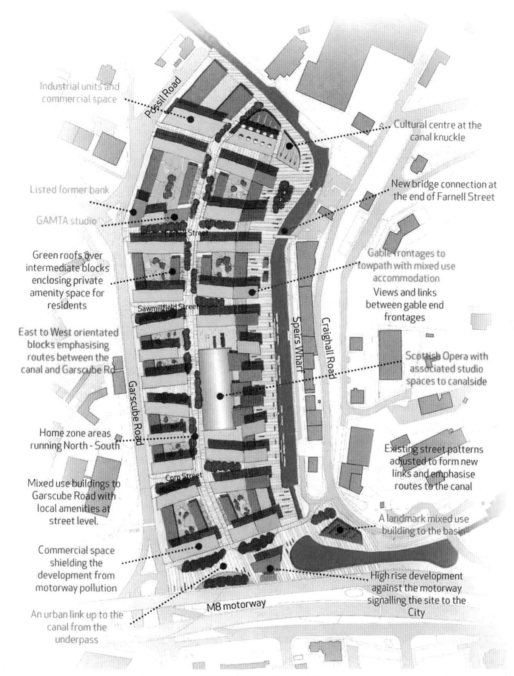

Industrial units and commercial space

Listed former bank

GAMTA studio

Green roofs over intermediate blocks enclosing private amenity space for residents

East to West orientated blocks emphasising routes between the canal and Garscube Rd

Home zone areas running North - South

Mixed use buildings to Garscube Road with local amenities at street level.

Commercial space shielding the development from motorway pollution

An urban link up to the canal from the underpass

Possil Road

Sawmillfield Street

Garscube Road

Corn Street

M8 motorway

Speirs Wharf

Craighall Road

Cultural centre at the canal knuckle

New bridge connection at the end of Farnell Street

Gable frontages to towpath with mixed use accommodation

Views and links between gable end frontages

Scottish Opera with associated studio spaces to canalside

Existing street patterns adjusted to form new links and emphasise routes to the canal

A landmark mixed use building to the basin

High rise development against the motorway signalling the site to the City

FIGURE 12.2 (*continued*)

- Have you got something of value to offer the participants?
- Have you got on board key agencies that can deliver improvements?

4. *An open, inclusive process*
  - Can you give leadership without patronising participants?
  - Can you share ownership of the process with the other participants?

- Are the channels for involvement clear and inviting?
- Is information about the process as it evolves available for scrutiny?

5. *A positive process*
  - Have you a programme for developing a shared vision?
  - Can you orientate the process towards problem solving and win—win solutions?

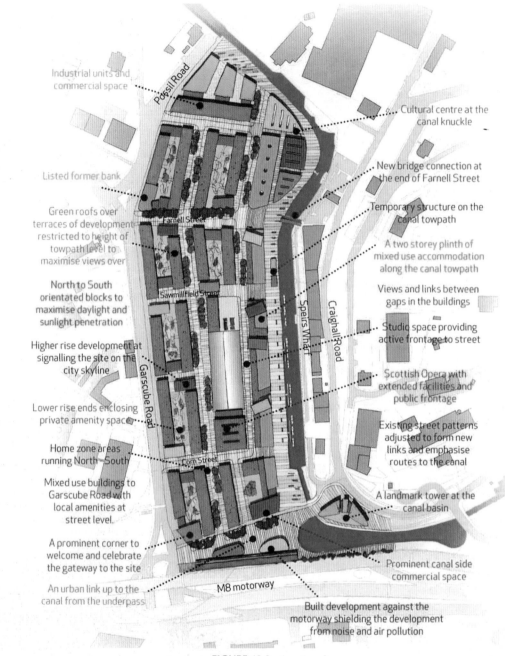

Industrial units and commercial space

Listed former bank

Green roofs over terraces of development restricted to height of towpath level to maximise views over

North to South orientated blocks to maximise daylight and sunlight penetration

Higher rise development at signalling the site on the city skyline

Lower rise ends enclosing private amenity space

Home zone areas running North–South

Mixed use buildings to Garscube Road with local amenities at street level.

A prominent corner to welcome and celebrate the gateway to the site

An urban link up to the canal from the underpass

Cultural centre at the canal knuckle

New bridge connection at the end of Farnell Street

Temporary structure on the canal towpath

A two storey plinth of mixed use accommodation along the canal towpath

Views and links between gaps in the buildings

Studio space providing active frontage to street

Scottish Opera with extended facilities and public frontage

Existing street patterns adjusted to form new links and emphasise routes to the canal

A landmark tower at the canal basin

Prominent canal side commercial space

Built development against the motorway shielding the development from noise and air pollution

Pogsil Road · Farnell Street · Sawmillfield Street · Speirs Wharf · Craighall Road · Garscube Road · Corn Street · M8 motorway

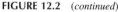

FIGURE 12.2   *(continued)*

- Can you avoid the dangers of polarisation and entrenched views?

In addition, when choosing the appropriate approach, urban designers should ask:

- What are the values of the main stakeholders, and how can these be reflected in the adopted approach?
- What resources exist and what is the time scale?
- What level of participation is required?

- How can quality of participation be balanced with quantity?
- How can disenfranchised groups be involved?
- What role (if any) should experts play?
- How can momentum be maintained?

Each question poses challenges that, to a greater or lesser extent, different processes address. The different approaches available also indicate the effort required to move beyond tokenistic consultation procedures. Most

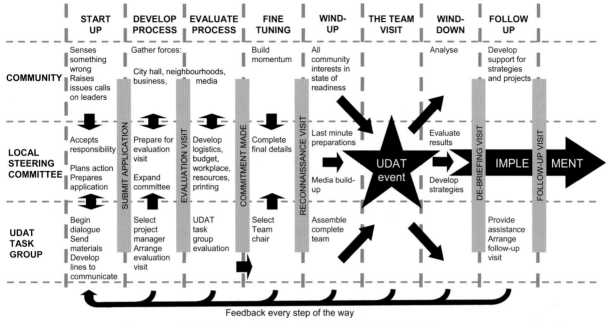

	START UP	DEVELOP PROCESS	EVALUATE PROCESS	FINE TUNING	WIND-UP	THE TEAM VISIT	WIND-DOWN	FOLLOW UP
COMMUNITY	Senses something wrong Raises issues calls on leaders	Gather forces: City hall, neighbourhoods, business, media		Build momentum	All community interests in state of readiness		Analyse	Develop support for strategies and projects
LOCAL STEERING COMMITTEE	Accepts responsibility Plans action Prepares application	Prepare for evaluation visit Expand committee	Develop logistics, budget, workplace, resources, printing	Complete final details	Last minute preparations Media build-up	UDAT event	Evaluate results Develop strategies	IMPLE MENT
UDAT TASK GROUP	Begin dialogue Send materials Develop lines to communicate	Select project manager Arrange evaluation visit	UDAT task group evaluation	Select Team chair	Assemble complete team			Provide assistance Arrange follow-up visit

SUBMIT APPLICATION · EVALUATION VISIT · COMMITMENT MADE · RECONNAISSANCE VISIT · DE-BRIEFING VISIT · FOLLOW-UP VISIT

Feedback every step of the way

FIGURE 12.3   The Urban Design Assistance Team process

BOX 12.1 Charettes

The term *charette* derives from the little cart used to collect students' quick architectural exercises (*esquisses*) at the Ecole Des Beaux Arts in Paris. In more recent practice, charettes are a development from UDATs, which had originally been developed in the USA by the American Institute of Architects. Since the late 1960s the approach has gradually been refined, though in essence charettes and UDATs remain large-scale workshops involving stakeholders, communities and professionals in the planning and design of an area during intensive sessions lasting at least a few days and sometimes, though rarely, up to two weeks.

There are two basic types of charrette – visioning charrettes and implementation charrettes (Condon 2008). The former are intended to involve anyone with an interest in how an area should develop; the latter those stakeholders, agencies and others who might be able to deliver the plan.

As with most forms of community and stakeholder engagement, charettes can be expensive – Condon (2008) quotes around GB£80000 (US$120000) to run a three-day event, while, for more extensive charrettes, the figures may run to several hundred thousand. The benefits, however, are that the concentration of technical, political and community effort during the charette – provided all the key decision makers and stakeholders are present – allows the short-circuiting of what might otherwise be years of work. Furthermore, involving local people in an inspirational event can produce support where previously there was opposition.

Based on his extensive experience of participating in charrettes, Walters (2007: 167) argues that charettes need to involve all key stakeholders to establish a shared community vision; work in a cross-disciplinary manner to maximise group learning and productivity; use short feedback loops as means to test ideas and stimulate participation; and work in detail

where required to test the feasibility of alternative concepts. All this requires a carefully managed process to build trust and ensure the process remains on track. Providing a wealth of guidance on conducting charettes, Walters (2007: 168) concludes that:

'Charettes are fun … Through this process of collaborative design and public input occurring over several consecutive days, everyone – from city planner to local business owner to local resident – becomes aware of the complexities of development and design issues, and this knowledge helps participants work together to arrive at the nest possible solution.'

Community Charette, Cirencester, UK (*Image: John Thompson and Partners*)

TABLE 12.1 Approaches to Participation

Action Planning	Design Workshop	Participatory Strategic Planning
Activity Mapping	Development Trust	Participatory Theatre
Act Create Experience (ACE)	Elevation Montage	Planning Aid
Adaptable Model	Enspirited envisioning	Planning Day
Appreciative Inquiry	Environment Shop	Planning for Real
Architecture Centre	Finding Home — Visualising our	Planning Weekend
Architecture Week	Future by Making Maps	Process-Planning Session
Awareness-Raising Day	Fish Bowl	Real-Time Strategic Change
Beo	Forum	Resource Centre
Best Fit Slide Rule	From Vision to Action	Roadshow
Briefing Workshop	Future Search Conference	Round-Table Workshops
Broad-Based Organisation	Guided Visualisation	Social Audit
Capacity-Building Workshop	Imagine!	Street Stall
Choices Method	Interactive Display	Table Scheme Display
Citizen Advocacy	Issues, Aims, Expectations,	TalkWorks
Citizens' Juries	Challenges & Dialogues in a Day	Task Force
Community Appraisals	Local Sustainability Model	Team Syntegrity
Community Design Centre	Mobile Planning Unit	Time Dollars
Community Indicators	Mock-Up	Topic Workshop
Community Plan	Neighbourhood Planning Office	Trail
Community Planning Forum	Open Design Competition	Urban Design Game
Community Projects Fund	Open House Event	Urban Design Soapbox
Community Site Management Plans	Open Space Workshop	Urban Design Studio
Community Strategic Planning	Parish Maps	Urban Studies Centre
Consensus Building	Participatory Appraisal	Visual Simulation
Design Assistance Team	Participatory Building Appraisal	Web Site
Design Day		
Design Game		

Sources: UDG (1998) and New Economics Foundation (1998).

community consultation strategies use a range of engagement methods for different social groups — a meeting in a town hall will attract a different social group to an online bulletin board. Innovative techniques are often needed to engage with hard-to-reach groups, such as teenagers. Provision of support, such as assistance with transport and childcare, is also often necessary to enable people to attend engagement sessions.

Where different publics/societal groups exist, different types of public participation and information exchange — public meetings, exhibitions, focus groups, technical reports, etc. — can be employed to create a matrix of possibilities, whereby different techniques are used to engage with different groups. Using such matrices helps urban designers to devise programmes of participation and consultation that are both sensitive and tailored to local needs and circumstances (Figure 12.4).

Personal computers provide opportunities for greater public participation in the design and development process. Methods of participation and involvement are also likely to be improved by the Internet through which Information such as text, illustrations, video, audio and computer files can be readily communicated to any number of different sources. As a result, virtual design studios and digital design on the Internet will inevitably increase. As

collaborative design projects become increasingly prominent, the World Wide Web provides a medium for communicating and storing design information. These new technologies also facilitate integrated working. High-quality videos and digital photographs can be viewed and shared through the Internet and comments made in real-time discussion groups.

It is, of course, easy to evangelise and even romanticise the potential of engaging the public in design and

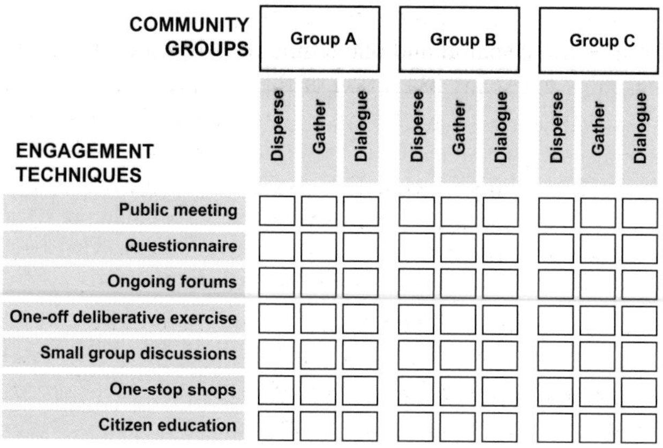

FIGURE 12.4 Matrix of community groups and engagement techniques (*Image: redrawn and adapted from Darke 2000*)

development processes. Undoubtedly, as Walters (2007: 170) suggests, a good professional must strive to garner public support, and the best way to educate the public is to allow them into the design process, to witness the complex and often difficult choices that need to be made. He nevertheless cites Holden & Iveson (2003: 68), who question why we should necessarily assume local people know what is best for their community. They argue that there can be a lot of negativity in communities, particularly when faced with major development proposals on their doorsteps and, as such, public opinion can be firmly set against good planning or urban design. In such circumstances a major role of a participatory process may be in simply making the case for development per se, which may, in turn, require an educational process relating to the fundamentals of environmental sustainability and social equity, before questions of the type and quality of development can be considered (Walters 2007: 170).

REPRESENTATION

Urban designers typically develop and present ideas, concepts and proposals through sketches, diagrams and other forms of graphic representation. For Baker (1996: 66), diagrams are the 'essential tool' of both analyst and designer, their use stimulating: '… *thought patterns capable of considerable dexterity. This dexterity — the ability to grasp the essence of a concept — and through this understanding to fully develop an idea, is central to the act of design.*'

Bosselmann (1998: xiii) offers a cautionary reminder, however, that, while urban design practitioners know the power and limitations of representation, '… *they may take for granted how representation influences design thinking.*' Thus, as well as being mechanisms through which to communicate the qualities of the final design to others, modes of representation employed while designing inevitably frame our thinking.

Representation techniques range from elementary two-dimensional maps and diagrams to highly sophisticated, interactive visualisations representing all four dimensions — three spatial and one temporal. All representations are, in essence, an abstraction of reality in a form that can be easily communicated and understood. Bosselmann (1998: 3) argues that 'pictures do not mimic what we see' and, while we might assume photography truthfully records the world around us, '… *no optical system exists to mimic the task performed by our eyes.*' In common with film, television recording, and eye-level drawings rendered by hand or computer, photography relies on a 'convenient geometric fiction' called 'central projection' or linear perspective: '… *a technique that offers a somewhat limited representation of reality.*' (Bosselmann 1998: 3).

The conventional methods of graphic representation are the perspective and the plan view (see Bosselmann 1988:

3—18). These are now so commonplace it is difficult to conceive of a time when they did not exist. Filippo Brunelleschi (1377—1466) is usually credited with discovering — or rediscovering — linear perspective. Thirty years after Brunelleschi's death, a second method of representing the world was developed, when Leonardo da Vinci drew the first known example of a plan view based on an actual survey for the small town of Imola in Italy's Emilia Romagna. In 1502, Leonardo had been commissioned to design repairs for the town's fortifications, ruined during a siege in 1499. Late medieval plans represented cities iconically — a single perspective, with selected buildings chosen to symbolise the city drawn in elevation and distinguished in size according to their religious significance (Bosselmann 1998: 14). New methods of warfare involving cannons required attention to a fortification's plan dimensions and the accurate measurement of angles, rendering such representations of little use. Leonardo, therefore, required a method showing the actual dimensions of streets and city blocks. Leonardo's lead was followed by Giambattista Nolli, who between 1736 and 1748 undertook a famous survey of Rome (see Figure 4.22).

Bosselmann (1998: 18) argues that these two methods — 'map' and 'perspective' — represent distinct ways of looking at and understanding the world: Brunelleschi's represents the earlier view, an understanding of the world based on visual experience, while Leonardo's map '… *symbolises our need to go beyond direct experience, to explain the structure of things, the theory behind the phenomena we can see.*' Bosselmann argues that these two methods of representation introduced a division in professional thinking between the 'clarity of abstractions' (the view from above) and 'befuddling richness and confusion' (the ground-level view). Although the former could be considered to be the 'architect's view' and the latter the 'planner's view', adequately representing a place requires both methods. While the map and the perspective are both abstractions, the latter is more closely related to our actual experience.

Graphic representations of urban design proposals need to reflect two sides of the communication process — information and vision. Representations intended for 'internal' purposes (to facilitate the design team's own decision-making and its decision-making with others) will be primarily information-focused. Those intended for 'external' purposes (for promotional and/or regulatory purposes) will focus more on communicating the vision. As noted earlier, although design-related professionals readily understand graphic presentations, others are less fluent and able. Bosselmann (1998: xiii), for example, notes that:

'… *professionals understand conceptual representations — or claim to — but few people outside the professions can read the information, let alone understand what it would be like to walk through the streets or neighbourhoods described in such representations.*'

As discussed above, those without a design sensibility and appreciation typically draw or read drawings (or other representations) without properly understanding what it is that they are drawing or seeing. This can be considered to be analogous to writing words in a language that one does not understand: the writer does not know whether she/he is making sense or writing gobbledygook. As a result, it is important to facilitate the process by, for example, representing the views that people will actually experience — those that people can imagine looking at, moving through and/or sitting in.

In general, representations of three and four dimensions, such as animations, photomontage, computer-generated models and artists' impressions, are more easily understood by laypeople than plans and conceptual diagrams. As such, urban designers need to represent both that which exists but also, more importantly, what might become reality. The inherent richness and complexity of real environments, however, means that this will only ever be an abstraction of reality with the aim being to create visual representations that can be readily understood as substitutes for reality.

The method by which urban design proposals are presented is of considerable importance. Meeda *et al* (2007) distinguish four key techniques: conceptual, analytical, measurable and perceptual. Typically, though not always, the first three of these are abstract, usually two-dimensional representations of reality. The fourth is often three- and increasingly four-dimensional in character.

More detailed discussions can be found in *Graphics for Urban Design* (Meeda *et al* 2007) or within in-house design handbooks, such as Urban Design Associates' (2003) *Urban Design Handbook*.

Analytical and Conceptual Representations

Analytical and conceptual diagrams are essential tools for urban designers. Representations enable analysis and evaluation — and the communication of that analysis and evaluation — for example; of the existing urban and townscape context. Such diagrams include site analyses, townscape notations and pedestrian activity maps. In discussing the role they play in design analysis and in communicating design, Baker (1996: 66) observes that diagrams:

- Are selective;
- Are about clarity and communication;
- Reveal the essence;
- Are often simple;
- Separate out issues so as to better comprehend the complex;
- Allow a degree of artistic licence;
- Can have a vitality of their own; and
- Can explain form and space better than words or photographs.

Analytical diagrams are important to enable the identification and understanding of constraints that could influence the design. These are usually carried out at the initial stage of a project as part of a site survey, analysis and appraisal. Such diagrams consist of the graphic representation of a site together with contextual information that aids understanding of both the opportunities and the potential problems. Other graphic methods of analysing a site include sun-path, daylight and shadow diagrams together with wind-flow assessments, which enable understanding of some of the environmental factors.

As discussed in Chapter 11, the site analysis forms an important resource for the design process. Meeda *et al* (2007: 16—26) suggest the following will nearly always be required: contextual appraisal of a site's immediate hinterland; an opportunities and constraints plan; urban form analysis; landscape/open space analysis; and a movement plan. Analytical graphics are likely to also include charts, graphs and tables as means to illustrate the statistical data describing the socio-economic context.

Conceptual drawings or diagrams often represent initial or embryonic ideas in an abstract form and are often used to explain the key principles of an urban design project and how it functions. Throughout the design process, however, they can remain powerful means to express the essence of an idea: '*At its simplest it may be a cartoon, an ideogram or a visual sound bite. More complex means include painted artworks or mood boards which convey atmosphere or precedent without committing to form.*' (Meeda *et al* 2007: 6). By this means, unresolved ideas can be presented in a way that encourages debate without committing to particular solutions or familiar concrete images.

Analytical and conceptual diagrams are often highly abstract drawings, using symbols and annotations, images and words to represent the relationship between a particular quality or idea and reality. Such diagrams convey ideas and principles rather than the intended reality of the scheme or site (Figure 12.5). They often aid a viewer's understanding of the context and/or design proposal and can also enable designers to keep sight of their original intent — the 'vision' — during the design development stages of a project. As such, they are an aid to the decision-making process. Forming part of the thought process in the initial design stages, schematic, functional and flow diagrams are similar to concept drawings in that they emphasise relationships between different parts of a project and/or add the fourth dimension of time by identifying movement, direction, intensity and potential conflicts.

Ahlava & Edelman (2009: 191) distinguish between static and dynamic diagrams, both of which, they argue, are valuable at the start of projects as part of the analytical process. Static diagrams illustrate immobile and separate elements — for example a figure-ground diagram that illustrates the relationship between built and unbuilt spaces.

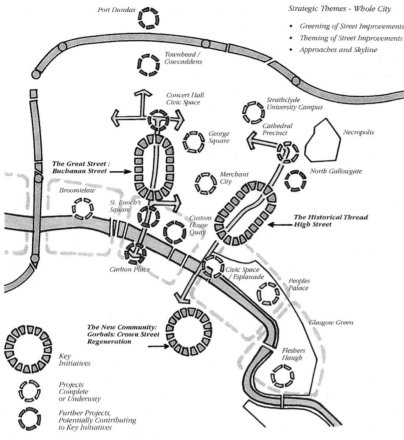

Dynamic diagrams, by contrast, illustrate a process of change, and include topological diagrams in which different elements intertwine to describe the dynamic state of the city in flux.

Urban designers often use Kevin Lynch's elements of imageability — paths, nodes, edges, districts and landmarks — as means of analysing areas and sites, usually by recording the incidence of these elements on a plan view. This is a common and useful technique. It does, however, as Lynch (1984: 251) warned, misunderstand the purpose of his original study, which was to remind designers of the necessity of consulting users and residents. Lynch, for example, lamented that, while plans had been 'fashionably decked out' with nodes, etc., there had been few attempts to reach out to the actual inhabitants. Thus, for Lynch, instead of his 'new jargon' '... *opening a channel by which citizens might influence design, the new words became another means of distancing them from it.*' Rather than designers recording their own assumptions about city images, a more meaningful record of imageability can be obtained by returning to Lynch's own methods of undertaking mental-mapping exercises with users (see Chapter 5).

Some urban designers have developed notational systems to represent urban design qualities or features such as Lynch's five elements. Lynch's elements are, for example, often used to communicate schematic and indicative ideas about built form and spaces without having to consider the specificities of buildings. Notations can be an important and effective means of communication between urban designers and the communities with which they are working. Various forms of notation are now used as key methodologies for appraising and conveying the character of context.

Cullen (1967) developed his 'notation' to represent townscape, and included denotations for the broad types and perceptions of environment encountered. Four primary divisions were defined:

- *Humanity* — the study of people.
- *Artefacts* — buildings and objects.
- *Mood* — the character of place.
- *Space* — the physical space.

In addition, four secondary parameters categorise the primary divisions:

- The range of the category;
- Its usefulness;
- Its behaviour; and
- Its relationships.

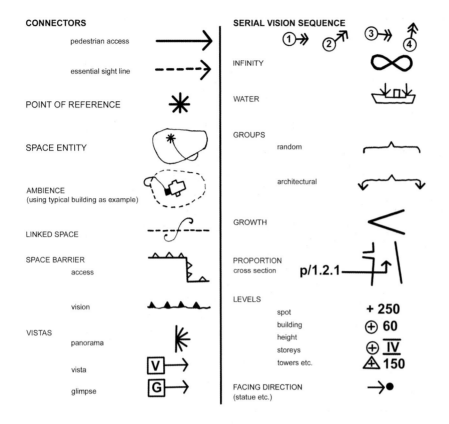

FIGURE 12.6 Cullen's notation (*Image: Cullen 1967*)

Indicators, the most frequently emulated part of the system, denoted isolated qualities that exist in their own right, such as levels and heights; boundaries; spatial types; connections; views and vistas; etc. (see Figure 12.6).

While a number of other systems of notation have been developed since Cullen's, no definitive system exists. Systems might vary from project to project, but they should all be capable of easy interpretation, adaptation and addition. In Portland, Oregon, for example, city planners developed a coherent notation for conveying design ideas in order to communicate the design frameworks established in the 1988 *Central City Plan* (Figure 12.7).

A further graphic means of analysing places is through the use of pedestrian activity maps (Figure 12.8). These record observations about where people gather, sit, stand or hurry through spaces. Recording the times of day and climatic conditions, they enable analysis of how people use urban spaces. They can also be used to plot and analyse movement patterns, as in Appleyard's (1981) famous study of how traffic volumes affect pedestrian movement patterns in residential streets (see Chapter 4). Alternatively, the Project for Public Spaces (2000) has used time-lapse photography and video techniques to compress periods of street activity into a few minutes of screen action, giving a stronger impression of movement and activity patterns within a space.

Figure-ground studies, space syntax analysis (see Chapter 8) and the analysis of the cross-sections of spaces provide means to undertake and communicate morphological analyses. Figure-ground techniques derive from Giambattista Nolli's survey of Rome (1736–1748), in which he used white to represent publicly accessible space and black to represent the coverage of buildings (see Figure 4.22 – note that the interiors of churches and other public buildings are also white). These drawings highlight the relationships between solids or mass (black) and voids (white). Such drawings enable a better understanding of relationships and patterns, revealing what is not immediately apparent and perhaps changing how an area or project is perceived. They can also reveal the urban grain of an area and highlight aspects of the relationship of new development to its surrounding context.

'Tissue' studies are used as a means to evaluate urban form and the size and scale of spaces against well-known and/or successful precedents (see Hayward, in Hayward & McGlynn 1993: 24–9). The technique involves overlaying a site plan with another plan view showing a selected piece of urban form (at the same scale), enabling an appreciation of the size and scale of different urban areas. In the regard, a valuable book is *To Scale* (Jenkins 2008), which depicts one hundred city environments in figure-ground form and at a consistent scale (see Chapter 4).

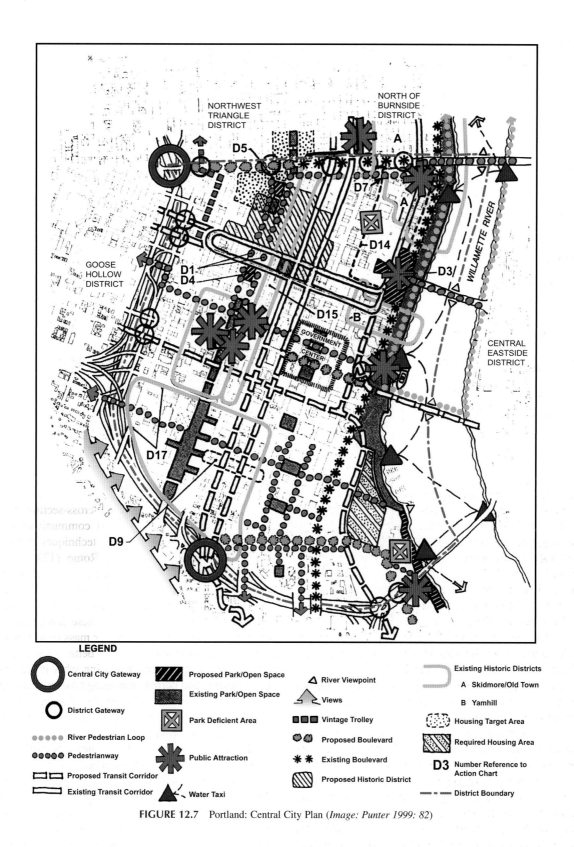

LEGEND

⭕	Central City Gateway
◯	District Gateway
●●●●●	River Pedestrian Loop
●●●●●	Pedestrianway
▭▭	Proposed Transit Corridor
▭▭	Existing Transit Corridor

▨	Proposed Park/Open Space
▨	Existing Park/Open Space
⊠	Park Deficient Area
✳	Public Attraction
▲	Water Taxi

△	River Viewpoint
⬆	Views
▪▪▪	Vintage Trolley
✳✳	Existing Boulevard
▨	Proposed Historic District
◌◌	Proposed Boulevard

▭	Existing Historic Districts
	A Skidmore/Old Town
	B Yamhill
▨	Housing Target Area
▨	Required Housing Area
D3	Number Reference to Action Chart
▬ ▬ ▬	District Boundary

FIGURE 12.7   Portland: Central City Plan (*Image: Punter 1999: 82*)

FIGURE 12.8   Pedestrian activity map for the same street in Copenhagen on Wednesday 19 July 1995 and Monday 23 July 1968 (*Image: Bosselmann 1998: 44*)

Sieve maps can also be used to overlay different layers of spatial information. In their simplest form, tracing paper overlays are used on an ordnance survey map base, with each overlay mapping different constraints. This can help identify parts of an area or site that present difficulties for development because of one or a combination of constraints (Moughtin *et al* 1999: 70). When undertaken using Geographic Information Systems (GISs) or similar mapping systems, many layers of socio-economic and physical data can be combined and compared (see below). Public authorities often collect and maintain extensive

GIS-based data on issues as diverse as population statistics, social deprivation patterns, traffic levels, pollution levels, environmental resources and existing land uses. Combined with site studies, such data provide a powerful analytical tool for design.

Representations of Two Dimensions

This section discusses two means of representing design in a two-dimensional form — orthographic projections and GISs.

(i) Orthographic projections

Orthographic projections represent three dimensions in two-dimensional drawings by means of views called plans, sections and elevations. They usually require a series of vantage points to illustrate a scheme. The plan view does not represent urban form in the way in which it is experienced; it is an abstracted view from above and is drawn as if seen from infinity so that there are no distortions due to perspective. Sections are strategic drawings, which complement the plan – which on its own rarely provides sufficient information – by showing the vertical dimension relative to the horizontal dimension (Figure 12.9). They can also show and, thereby, enable exploration of the relationship between inside and outside spaces and the relationship between different levels. In urban settings, sections can often be more informative and valuable in communicating the character of an area than a plan view. Orthographic projections are important means of communicating design projects particularly as part of a package of working or construction drawings displaying the scheme at a true scale.

(ii) Geographic information systems

More recent additions to the range of tools available to urban designers are Geographic Information Systems (GIS). These are computer-based systems for geographically referenced information. Initially GIS was associated with any number of data sets related to a two-dimensional digitised map of an area. Contemporary systems, however, can contain information on utilities and services, schedules of spaces and accommodation and transportation routes. In addition, visual and audio information – such as photographic and video images – can be stored, viewed and manipulated in association with more traditional forms of data. This multi-layered approach takes GIS beyond the realms of two-dimensional representation. Urban designers can use GIS to aid their understanding and analysis of urban areas. Extensive amounts of information related to an area can be stored within the system, including data related to both the buildings and spaces, and the way they are used. Traditionally the domain of geographers and urban planners, GISs are increasingly used in design analysis and in the design process.

The main disadvantage of two-dimensional representations is that non-designers find it difficult to interpret such drawings, which often bear little resemblance to real views of spaces or townscapes. They are, however, a key means of communicating design information between professionals, and are also relatively quick and inexpensive to produce.

Representations of Three Dimensions

Three-dimensional representations communicate proposals in a widely understandable form, but their production generally requires more skill, is time-consuming and is more costly than two-dimensional graphics. Despite their additional realism, these diagrams – with the exception of physical models – are still communicated through a two-dimensional medium such as paper or a computer screen. The most commonly used means of representing urban design are perspective drawings; sketches; paraline drawings; computer-aided design; and physical models.

(i) Perspective drawings

Brunelleschi's experiments with linear perspective as a technique for representing realism and defining the location of objects in space marked a turning point in visual representation (Figure 12.10). Perspectives represent the optical effect where the eye perceives parallel lines as converging with distance. Perspective drawings are useful both to convey finalised design proposals and as quick sketch aids at the project's concept stage. Abstract qualities such as mood, character and atmosphere can be conveyed more effectively

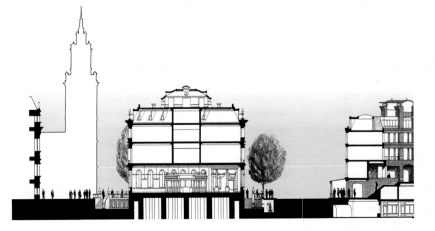

FIGURE 12.9 The cross-section (*Image: Papadakis 1993: 102*). Sections are particularly useful in communicating the relationship between internal and external spaces. Plan views tend to communicate information about the logic of the spatial organisation, while sections convey the emotional mood of the space or environment (Frederick 2007)

FIGURE 12.10 Vredeman de Vries' *On Perspective* 1599 (*Image: Hans Vredeman de Vries 1599*)

than through orthogonal drawings, and thus perspectives are of value in enabling non-professionals to understand design proposals. They are, however, only useful when they represent views that are seen — the artistic license used on perspectives may mean the view illustrated is not that experienced in reality. Aerial perspectives, for example, are increasingly common because of the 'wow' factor they generate. Such drawings are of little value in representing the likely lived experience on the ground, and thus their primary purpose is promotional.

Another potential pitfall is that rendering any new development in the same technique as the existing context on an illustration can make a design appear to 'fit-in', when this may not be the case. Conversely, without full rendering, a perspective gives little sense of materials, texture or colour.

(ii) Sketches and photomontages

By helping to portray an idea quickly while aiding the observation and analysis of the environment, sketches are important communication devices, useful as an investigation of an early design idea, to test visual effects or to set a design in context. Rather than as ends in themselves, they should be considered as part of the process of understanding. Although sketch-type drawings can be produced on computers, hand-drawn sketches suggest a level of quality, personality and atmosphere that it is difficult to reproduce electronically. They are also quick to produce and can encourage participation in the design process, for example through sketching at a participative event (Meeda *et al* 2007: 14).

Superimposing an illustration of the design onto a photographic image can provide a realistic impression, giving a good idea of whether it integrates with the existing context. Although a realistic effect,

attention needs to be paid to details such as shadows. Such presentations are popular with clients, local planning authorities and the general public who can quickly understand and react to proposals. Increasingly the technology of Accurate Visual Representation (AVR) which superimposes a three-dimensional computer model onto a photographic image, after which it can be manipulated, means that care needs to be taken to ensure images remain both accurate and honest (Meeda *et al* 2007: 51).

(iii) Paraline drawings

Based upon orthographic projections, paraline drawings convey a third dimension through the representation of length, breadth and height in a single drawing using axonometric or isometric projections (Figure 12.11). They enable space to be organised by volume rather than by area, as with orthographic views. They aid visual perception but only to a limited degree because perspective effects are ignored.

(iv) Computer-aided design

The use of computer-aided design (CAD) enables ideas to be presented quickly and alternatives generated (Figure 12.12). The designer is encouraged to think in three dimensions from the initial stages of a project. Software packages can also calculate and simulate artificial and daylight conditions, materials, etc., through the application of textures and realistic colours. Computer models can take on an extra dimension of realism through animation (see below) and the addition of people, vehicles, landscaping, street furniture, etc. A debate in modelling, however, focuses on the level of desirable detail for urban design decision-making. Some argue that highly detailed models obscure the fundamental urban form issues such as setbacks and massing because questions

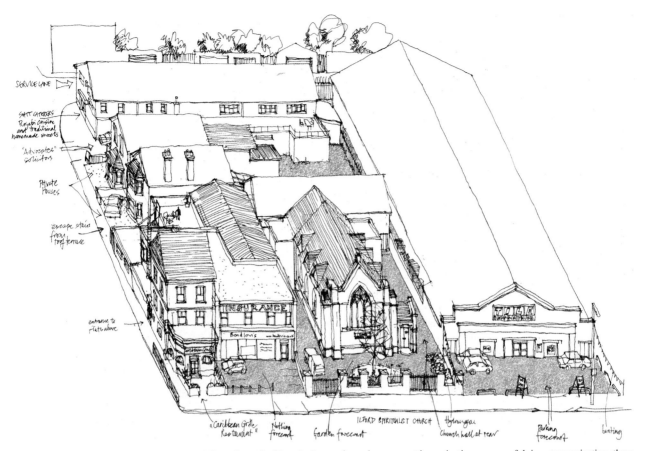

Service lane
Satt caterers
Punjabi cuisine
and traditional
homemade sweets
"Advocates"
solicitors
Private
houses
escape stairs
from
roof terrace
entrance to
flats above

INSURANCE
Bond Lewis

"Caribbean Girdle   Nothing
Restaurant"   forecourt
              Garden forecourt
                        ILFORD SPIRITUALIST CHURCH   Hydrangea
                                              Church hall at rear
                                                            Parking
                                                            forecourt   bunting

FIGURE 12.11 Paraline drawings (*Image: Gort Scott Architects*). Isometric and axonometric projections are useful in communicating three-dimensional form. They can also be used as analytical tools, as in this analysis of an urban block

of style and surface materials inevitably captivate viewers' attention and become the focus for discussion. Others argue that, without architectural detail, it is difficult for viewers to relate the representation to the reality in their minds. It may be that different levels of detail are required for different audiences, with professionals able to comprehend and make use of more technical and less 'real' images more easily than lay audiences (Levy 1998: 67). Once detail has been modelled, it is easy to add and remove it in order to prepare a range of drawings focusing on different design aspects: block and street layout, three-dimensional modelling, architectural treatment, etc.

Computer-generated three-dimensional models of urban areas help in assessing the impact of new buildings and alterations to existing townscape, allowing different development/design proposals to be 'slotted' into the existing computer model and viewed from any angle (see Bosselmann 1998: 100–9) (Figures 12.12 and 12.13). Options such as colour schemes, materials, roof pitches, heights and fenestration can then be tested and appraised. Design issues can, therefore, be explored and resolved quickly and efficiently with almost instant revisions. Computer

technology can also be used to supplement freehand techniques by scanning in images and enhancing them with computer techniques (adding daylighting, shadows, etc.). The possibility of the technology's presentational 'gloss' overshadowing the scheme's attributes must, however, be guarded against, as well as any tendency for the technology to dictate the design.

The production of three-dimensional models is particularly useful for communicating the consequences and impacts of urban design decisions. Bosselmann (1998: 100–9) describes an instance where planners defined an air rights policy without necessarily appreciating how it might affect the experience of the place. Once a computer model had been generated of possible development scenarios, the impacts became much clearer. Using simulations, politicians, planners and others can walk through the places they are responsible for, thereby acquiring a better understanding of whether their policy would deliver the desired outcomes.

(v) Models

To enable better understanding and communication of a project, physical models can complement or replace traditional drawings (Figure 12.14). Depending upon

FIGURES 12.12 AND 12.13 Digital model of central Glasgow (*Images: Glasgow City Council*). Glasgow City Council commissioned an interactive three-dimensional digital model of the city centre and River Clyde (www.glasgow.gov.uk/urbanmodel). The model allows the public greater access to and understanding of the development of the city. The intended benefits include enhancing public understanding; assisting regeneration; improving the participation and consultation process for future development proposals; providing a visual aid to help explain the impact of a development to the public, elected members and developers; providing a promotional tool to showcase development; and improving development quality

its application and the stage of the project at which it is constructed, the role of a model varies:

- *Conceptual models* used in the initial design stages are essentially three-dimensional diagrams, expressing and exploring the designer's initial ideas.
- *Consultation models* are used as a tool for community engagement and typically consist of a site model on which blocks representing building and other forms of development can be moved around to suggest and explore alternative layouts.

- *Working models* used during design development enhance the understanding of spatial and sequential relationships and may also be used for simulating lighting and climatic conditions.
- *Presentation models* represent the final design solution. Suitably embellished with 'entourage' (people, landscape, vehicles, etc.), they usually form important aids for communication and marketing rather than decision-making purposes.

FIGURE 12.14 Physical model for development on the Isle of Dogs, London (*Image: Matthew Carmona*)

While a well-established method of representing architectural and urban form, models raise particular issues concerning the realism—reality gap. Presenting a three-dimensional version of a proposed development may seem more 'truthful' than drawings, but problems frequently arise in trying to understand what the full-sized building and its environment will be like. This is a means—ends confusion – the observer is seduced into seeing the model as an end rather than as a means to another end. Models have the characteristic of miniaturising objects and space, creating difficulties with perception of scale. Conway & Roenisch (1994: 200), for example, note how models can be seductive, representing an ideal world:

'Beautifully made … they remind us of the doll's houses, model frames and railways that we played with as children. The seductiveness … is not only to do with their size and the materials used, it is also to do with their clarity and cleanliness of the forms, the way they are lit and the way shadows fall. They represent pure, ideal buildings that are removed from their context and are not subject to the wear and tear of weather and time.'

A certain idealisation – or abstraction – of models is often deliberate. It helps to highlight certain features, while emphasising that it is only a model (a representation of reality). Grey and white models tend to show form better because the shadows are sharper. Such models also allow designers and clients to keep their options open regarding the materials, finish and colour. Equally, however, such models tend to abstract buildings from their surroundings. Some urban designers consider the most appropriate scale for models showing urban form to be 1—300 – their function being to explore and communicate the intended massing of the development and spaces created rather than

to show the buildings in detail. Larger-scale models (e.g. 1—200) usually require architectural detail, which distracts from urban space design issues.

Representations of Four Dimensions

Experiencing an urban environment is a dynamic activity involving movement and time (see Chapter 9). Adding a time dimension to graphic representations can thus enhance understanding and communication. For centuries, designers and artists have tried to capture some of these experiences in graphic and visual terms. Early Modernist artists, such as the Cubists, attempted this through works such as Duchamp's *Lady Descending the Stair*. Several techniques of spatial representation have been developed to record and communicate the experience of complex interacting three-dimensional events through the sequential description of space and time.

(i) Serial vision

Serial vision is a method of communicating townscape in a realistic manner by introducing movement through a series of sequential illustrations. Cullen's sketches in *The Concise Townscape* (1971) and Bacon's diagrams in *Design of Cities* (1967) embody the concept that movement can be read and understood as a pictorial sequence. As discussed in Chapter 7, Cullen used serial vision as a tool for visual analysis and creative design. Whereas traditional static images illustrate space at a certain moment in time, serial vision shows the temporal unfolding of movement as a dynamic activity. However, as Bosselmann (1998) observes, serial vision graphics do not provide a sense of how we actually experience and interpret places, nor how we generate a sense of structure and location in space. They are best used as an analytical tool.

(ii) Video animations

Accustomed to television and video technology, people can increasingly understand projects presented through video images. Computer-generated video presentations and 'fly-throughs' are increasingly used to communicate projects to clients, planning authorities, funding institutions and communities. Video technology has a great ability to engage viewers by involving visual, aural, kinaesthetic, spatial and temporal senses, allowing them to make more accurate judgements regarding dimensions and proportions than from still pictures. Viewers, however, are restricted to a predetermined and scripted route, which restricts perception of the environment and, thus, to an extent, predetermines feedback. As in serial vision, the field of vision is too narrow to truly represent and capture what human eyes can see and other senses perceive. Representations also inevitably eliminate some information available to peripheral vision that might otherwise attract attention. Moreover, though fly-throughs are now ubiquitous in promotional presentations, projects will rarely, if ever, be experienced in this way, raising questions regarding their legitimacy for regulatory and other decision-making purposes.

(iii) Computer imaging and animation

Whereas traditional representations are static, fixed viewpoints in space, computers enable the perception of movement through space — though presentation is still confined to the two-dimensional abstraction of the computer screen or hard copy in the form of printed material. A range of new technologies, such as virtual reality, will have a significant impact upon urban design. Indeed, few new computer technologies have captured the imagination in the way that virtual reality has. Previously, the only way to walk through a project in real-time was to construct a full-scale mock-up of the design. Sophisticated, high-speed computer power with images, sound and other effects can now create an interactive system so fast and intuitive that the computer disappears from the user's mind, leaving the computer-generated environment as the reality. Viewers can perceive and understand an environment in their own way, and at their own pace, enabling better-informed feedback and participation.

Representations of urban environments and design proposals in four dimensions are increasingly important in the communication, promotion and selling of projects. Nonetheless, this evolving technology continues to be harnessed to enhance the understanding of proposals for both the designer and lay person. New techniques offer a highly realistic and interactive environment with choice of movement giving freedom to viewers to choose their own routes as opposed to the pre-programmed walk-through of traditional manual and computer presentations. As part of the creative process, and as a decision-making, presentational and evaluation tool, its importance will increase. Despite its evident potential to bridge the gap between what you see and what you get in urban design, designers need to be aware of the dangers in the persuasiveness of virtual reality.

Many visual and graphic techniques exist to communicate the experience of places. As communication technology becomes increasingly familiar to both professionals and the public, this will offer new opportunities to experience urban design proposals. The previous sections have shown the increasingly important role that technology is playing in the representation and communication of urban design. As a means of representation, computer-aided design has superseded all previous methods.

The use of technology could help to create an increased awareness of design and facilitate the ability for everyone to react to, and interact with, development proposals. Although new technology has offered the opportunity to make information more accessible and comprehensible, designers need to appreciate the many roles that a computer can play in the design process, as well as the advantages and disadvantages of the computer for each task. The ability to communicate design more persuasively raises important issues regarding the ethics of communication. New, highly specialised technology associated with state-of-the-art visualisations of projects means that — except for a few specialists — few people understand precisely how the data is manipulated. As a consequence, few can access the information to verify the simulation's accuracy. It is important, nevertheless, that these developments in technology are harnessed to enable better understanding and involvement of the public in decisions affecting their environment.

WRITTEN COMMUNICATION AND DESIGN

As well as graphic communication, urban designers need to communicate urban design concepts in written forms, in ordinances, policies and analysis and guidance of all types; as well as in reports, design statements, articles and a wide range of other publicity and official material. The purpose and use of some of these tools in regulatory processes were discussed in Chapter 11; here the presentation and expression of design concepts in written formats are discussed both as an end in itself, and as a supplement to graphic forms of communication.

The professional–layperson gap discussed above is often exacerbated as much through written forms of design-based communication as through graphic ones. Duany *et al* (2000: 213) cite an example from the Harvard Graduate School of Design News (Winter/Spring 1993: 13) describing the plan for a single family house:

'These distortions elicit decipherment in terms of several constructs that allow the house to analogise discourse and call for further elucidation. These constructs are continually motivated and frustrated by conflicts in their underlying schemata and the concrete form in which they are inscribed. They refer to the ideal or real objects, organisations, processes and histories which the house approximately analogises or opposes.'

Using text to confound and complicate has little value in aiding the understanding of, or garnering support for, design proposals. A more positive example of the use of language in urban design concerns the improvements in Birmingham (UK) during the 1990s (see Wright 1999: 298). Prior to the late 1980s, there had been very little concept of a physical vision for the city and it was considered important to communicate design ideas and principles so that people could understand what was intended. Key phrases — 'mending our city'; 'breaking the concrete collar'; 'a good environment is good business'; 'streets and squares'; 'city living'; and 'giving the streets back to the people' — captured the essence of important urban design principles without unnecessary jargon.

Perhaps the most comprehensive study in this area is the study of English local plan policies conduced by Punter & Carmona (1997) in the 1990s. A survey of regional government offices undertaken as part of this work identified a set of pointers for writing design policies (Punter & Carmona 1997: 62–6) and with adaptation relates equally to the range of tools through which design concepts need to be expressed in writing:

- *Balance prescription with flexibility* — the exact balance will depend on the nature of the urban design tool chosen, its purpose and whether it is part of a discretionary or regulatory system (see Chapter 11). Legally binding tools will need to be appropriately prescriptive to avoid inaccurate interpretation and legal challenge, but discretionary policy and forms of guidance may need to be more flexible to allow appropriate professional interpretation and leeway in the design process.
- *Balance detail with clarity* — more can be less in this regard. Overly detailed policy and guidance documents may simply obscure in a sea of detail the critical dimensions of design that need to be taken on board by designers, regulators or other audiences.

- *Be analytical, not descriptive* — highly descriptive analysis or guidance is typically of limited value to users. Instead it is important to interpret the material being presented for the audience, being analytical and propositional rather than woolly and overly descriptive.
- *Be relevant and precise* — in all forms of design-based writing, it is vital to consider the audience, and to express text appropriately, avoiding unnecessary and unexplained jargon and either overly poetic or overly legal language, restricting content to what is specifically relevant to the document's intended purpose.
- *Distinguish advice from legal requirement* — even in legally binding documents, policy or ordinance is often interspersed with guidance of a more advisory nature. In all such cases, and to avoid confusion, it is critical to distinguish optional from mandatory requirements.
- *Be encouraging and positive* — documents produced for regulatory purposes can be overly negative and restricting, focusing on what is not acceptable, rather than on what is encouraged. Urban design is a proactive and visionary discipline, and ideally written (like graphic) communication should reflect something of this positive nature, being encouraging and supportive of good practice, while also identifying what is not acceptable.
- *Demonstrate reasoning and rationale* — where space and format allow, it is valuable to justify prescriptions contained in policy and guidance so that users can fully understand and appropriately respond to advice and design requirements from an informed point of view.
- *Balance written with graphic communication* — 'a picture tells a thousand words'; thus, in all forms of ordinance, policy and guidance, it is worth thinking about the balance between graphic and written content. If a design intention can be expressed graphically, it is likely to be clearer and more accessible to do so.

On this last point, extensive work on both sides of the Atlantic has focused on the use of form-based/design codes (see Chapter 11). Commenting specifically on form-based codes in the USA (but relevant to most urban design tools, Parolek *et al* (2008: 172) stress the importance of 'knowing your users' (audience):

'Critical to this understanding is recognizing the wide variety of people who will be using the code. These include staff planners, property owners, developers, architects, planners, business owners, local politicians, potential property owners and residents, general citizens, and, last but not least, attorneys and judges. Each of these people will be looking at the code for answers to a multitude of different questions, all of which should be easy to find and understand from each person's point of view.'

(Parolek *et al* 2008: 174).

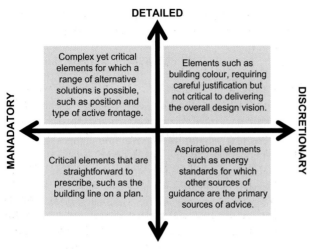

FIGURE 12.15 Positioning coded elements, prescription versus flexibility (*Image: adapted from DCLG 2006: 77*)

For lay users, the text accompanying images may be particularly important to interpret the graphics and to place them in context. They emphasise that, for both graphics and text, the mantra: 'keep it simple'.

Government guidance on the preparation of design codes in the UK advises that: '… *it is not necessarily the case that a good masterplanner will translate his or her skills into an effective writer of codes, and the project team should be clear about the distinctive set of skills that will be needed to write a code.*' (DCLG 2006: 76). In codes, as in other forms of design policy or guidance, the relative balance between prescription and flexibility will need consideration for the document as a whole, as well as for each element within the code. A four-quadrant framework is offered in the UK

guidance to help designers determine whether a particular element should be discretionary or mandatory, detailed or not detailed (see Figure 12.15). Urged '… *never to use words when an illustration will do*' (DCLG 2006: 73), code writers are advised that mandatory requirements should generally be characterised by the verb forms 'will', 'shall' or 'must', while discretionary requirements more commonly use 'should', 'may', or 'can'.

Punter & Carmona (1997: 114) conclude:

'There will always be difficult trade-offs to be made between clarity and conciseness, between precision and generality, between policy and justification and application of advice, between technical precision and readability for the lay person, but it is always important to tailor policies to local circumstances. Policy-writing is a delicate art of balancing both competing interests and opposing objectives, and where the line is drawn is both a political and a practical judgement.'

Trade-offs need to be made in any form of policy, ordinance or guidance, and to be effective communicators urban designers increasingly need to be skilled communicators in written as well as graphic/pictorial forms.

CONCLUSION

Communication in urban design covers all aspects of verbal and non-verbal presentation as well as the ability to listen to, appreciate and respect the views, values and aspirations of others. Communication is an important tool that can influence decision-making (Figure 12.16). Communicating any urban design project should require as true a representation of the project as is possible to all interested parties — deceit, mistrust and manipulation of images will cause problems and difficulties downstream.

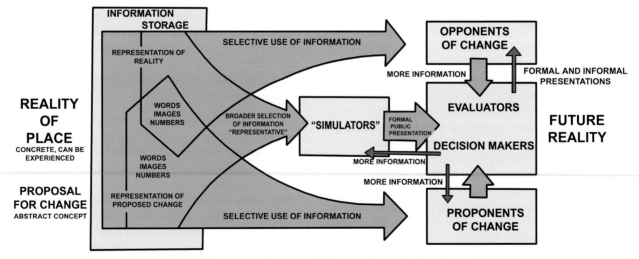

FIGURE 12.16 Design communication model (*Image: redrawn from Bosselmann 1998: 202*)

There are a number of implications of the media chosen, including appropriateness, cost, time and designers' skill. It is important, though, to design the project rather than the presentation. Given the influence of presentational technique on how designers perceive their creations, the mode of representation has a strong influence on the scheme's design — designers need to be wary of designing for the representational medium rather than for the real world. There is also an increasing trend for some designers to use presentation methods that are so abstract and complex that only other designers can understand them. This form of professional elitism may do little to persuade an audience of the merits of high-quality design and undermines effective communication of design ideas. Meeda *et al* (2007:10) offer the following watch-points:

- Ensure all involved understand the purpose of the illustration;
- Clearly communicate the level of precision or impression to the audience;
- Use the appropriate technique to convey information — analytical, conceptual, perceptual or measurable;
- Understand the strengths and limitations of hand-drawn and computer-generated techniques before deciding which to use; and
- Avoid using graphics to mislead the audience.

Everyone views and perceives the urban environment in a different way, as we each respond to the particular phenomenon that attracts or interests us. How the environment is seen is conditioned by our background, familiarity with the place, purpose within it and/or mode of travel (see Chapter 5). In communicating design projects, the aim should be to enable viewers to perceive a scheme in ways similar to reality. Good visual images should provide legible and understandable information for a wide and varied audience, enabling evaluation by those affected by the design. Presenters need to understand the context of the the communication process and thus to understand the audience. They should also be aware of potential barriers to the communication process, including social, psychological, technical, the use of language, and non-verbal modes of communication such as body language.

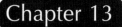

Holistic Urban Design

This book has broadly moved from theory through to practice. Part One began by discussing the nature of urban design and the role of the urban designer. Discussion moved on to review the evolution of urban design and its impact on urban form and to review a number of over-arching contexts — local, global, market and regulatory. In Part Two, key areas of urban design thought were reviewed in the form of six dimensions — morphological, perceptual, social, visual, functional and temporal. In Part Three, the nature and roles of the public and private sectors in delivering and sustaining high-quality urban design were explored. The overarching definition used throughout has been that urban design is about making places for people. This definition asserts the importance of four themes: urban design being concerned with people; valuing 'place'; operating in the 'real' world such that the urban designer's field of opportunity is constrained and bounded by market and regulatory forces; and urban design as a design process.

In this final chapter, we stress and reiterate the fourth and final point in this definition: urban design as a design process, and in particular the challenges designers face in addressing perhaps the key context discussed in Chapter 3 — the global consequences of what we design.

'QUESTIONING' URBAN DESIGN

This book should be understood as a discussion of how to make 'places' out of 'spaces'. As noted previously, this is done not so much by urban designers as by the people who inhabit space with their activities. To focus this discussion, the book is structured into key areas of urban design action. Within this structure the key contributions to urban design thought have been accommodated and related. Though it can be debated where to place individual contributions — particularly since, due to the integrative nature of urban design, most writers and commentators range across the different dimensions — the book's structure attempts to emphasise urban design's multi-dimensional and multi-layered nature. While it is structured for convenience, our experience is not. Our experience of urban environments is an integrative one. To understand it better, however, it is necessary to analyse the constituent parts. Designing new places and making positive contributions and interventions into existing places, however, requires those constituent parts to be drawn together and considered as a whole.

In making the case for urban design, this book has not sought to produce a 'new' theory of urban design in a prescriptive fashion. Neither has it sought to offer a new definition nor to provide a formulaic 'solution' to urban design. Chapter 1, for example, showed that, while most definitions of urban design are appropriate and valuable, they are also limiting and contestable. Although some useful frameworks from distinguished urban designers were presented, they were accompanied by the caveat that they should not be treated as inflexible dogma, nor reduced to mechanical formulas. Application of a formula negates the active process of design and downgrades the role of the designer and of design intelligence. No single set of rules (or objectives) can capture the scope and complexity of urban design, nor offer a step by step formula for successful place-making. It is an exploratory, intuitive and deductive process involving research into the problem posed and into the variable and specific conditions of time and place. The complex interactions between the variety of processes and elements in a place can, however, be examined and these can give generic clues to why some places succeed while others fail.

It is thus necessary to have a continually questioning and inquisitive approach to urban design. As in any design process, there are no 'right' or 'wrong' answers in urban design — there are only 'better' and 'worse' answers, the quality of which may only be known in time. Lawson (2001: 247), for example, argues that design typically

'... requires action in the form of decisions, even in the face of inadequate time and knowledge. For these reasons sometimes it is useful to oversimplify in order to structure thought enough to make design decisions slightly less arbitrary. We cannot hope to make them perfect.'

The necessary attitude is encapsulated in Frank Lloyd Wright's response to a question asked near the end of his career regarding what he thought was his best building. Wright replied: 'The next one'.

A number of organisations set out a series of questions to establish an agenda for improving the quality of place. Building for Life, for example, sets out 20 questions to determine 'What makes a great place to live?' (see www.buildingforlife); The Project for Public Spaces sets out 36 questions seeking to answer 'What makes a successful place' (see www.pps.org); and the Urban Design Alliance sets out over 100 detailed questions for users to assess the 'Qualities of Place' (see www.placecheck).

Public Places – Urban Spaces. DOI: 10.1016/B978-1-85617-827-3.10013-6

Box 13.1. Questioning Urban Design

Defining urban design

- Will the project have an impact — no matter how small — on the public realm?
- Will the project contribute to the creation or enhancement of a meaningful place?

The contexts

- Does the project respect, understand, learn from and integrate with the existing context?
- Are the proposals environmentally supportive or, at least, environmentally benign?
- Are the proposals economically viable and designed to provide sustainable quality?
- Has the proposal involved and garnered the support of stakeholders?

Morphological

- Have morphological patterns been understood and positively extended-to-create distinct urban blocks and coherent networks of well-connected, fine-grained streets and spaces?

Perceptual

- Will the project contribute to the creation of an established or new sense-of-place?
- Will the project create a legible and meaningful public realm?

Social

- Will the development encourage an accessible and safe use of the public realm?
- Will the development provide opportunities for social interaction, social mix and diversity?

Visual

- Have buildings, streets and spaces, hard and soft landscaping and street furniture been considered together to create drama and visual interest and to reinforce or enhance the sense-of-place?

Functional

- Will the mix and distribution of uses animate the public realm and support necessary, optional and social activities?
- Does the planned infrastructure integrate with and, where necessary, extend the established capital web?

Temporal

- Have the proposals been considered across different time horizons — day and night, summer and winter, long and short term?
- Will the project enable an incremental mix of old with new, avoid comprehensive redevelopment as far as is appropriate, and be 'whole' at each stage, repairing its edges as it goes?
- Have long-term management and maintenance issues been considered?

Developing urban design

- Is the scheme financially feasible and able to offer security to developers, investors and occupiers over short-, medium- and long-term horizons?

Controlling urban design

- How have public aspirations been expressed and reflected in the proposed development?

Communicating urban design

- Are the vision and/or the proposals clearly communicated to, understandable by and owned by stakeholders?

To bring together some of the various contributions and dimensions discussed in this book, Box 13.1 offers a series of questions. Rather than a complete conceptualisation of, or prescriptive agenda for, urban design and place-making, the intention is to provide a reminder of key issues. The questions can be used to evaluate proposed schemes, but, equally appropriately, can also be used to ask why some places succeed, while others fail.

THE CHALLENGE

The day-to-day problems of achieving high-quality urban design are real and are illustrated by the difficulty of finding high-quality examples of contemporary urban design. A wide range of barriers can be highlighted that militate against the delivery of better-quality urban design and better places (Carmona *et al* 2001b: 32–3), many of which have been discussed in earlier chapters, including:

- *Lack of awareness* — There is a variable awareness of urban design issues among investors and occupiers concerning the value given to environmental quality in its broadest sense to the success of their operations. Research, however, suggests different sub-markets have

different levels of concern and sophistication as regards design: retailers, for example, tend to be more aware of the contribution of design than office occupiers.

- *Poor information* — The scarcity of reliable information about the preferences of prospective occupiers and investors adds to the risk of departing from conventional and 'safe' standards of design quality.
- *Unpredictable markets* — The timing of a development in relation to the fluctuations of the property and investment market often dictates attitudes towards investing in urban design quality as perceived risk changes. The cyclical behaviour of property markets can, therefore, be a barrier to good urban design.
- *High land costs* — High land costs can reduce profit margins and leave little room for any extra investment in quality, especially since real estate prices adjust only slowly and imperfectly.
- *Fragmented land ownership* — Fragmented patterns of land ownership can increase the time and uncertainty of the development process, and lead to fragmented and uncoordinated developments.
- *Uncoordinated development* — Individual acts of development are often uncoordinated and do not

aggregate into a greater whole. In general, larger sites (once assembled into a single land ownership) are more likely to address issues of 'place-making' and make it easier for investors to capture beneficial externalities in the form of rents and capital values. It is also necessary to acknowledge the possibility and potential of enlightened management and control that derives from a development within a single land ownership. Equally, small-scale and incremental development, particularly when co-ordinated in some (perhaps unconscious) way, will often produce 'better' places.

- *Combative relationships* — Confrontational relationships between developers and the public sector increase the time taken to develop, consequently increasing uncertainty and risk.
- *Economic conditions* — Uncertainty and instability in the general economic climate can often lead to shorter-term investment decisions and to less investment in design.
- *Lack of choice* — Constraints in the supply of the right quality of property in the desired location reduce the contribution of design considerations in occupier decision-making — if the right location does not have good-quality space on offer, occupiers will often trade poorer development for an alternative location.
- *Short-termism* — The structure of capital markets with planning horizons of three to five years makes it difficult for many businesses to engage in the long-term planning necessary for the investments perceived necessary for better design. This is also shown by the preference for short-term and one-off transactions rather than a continuing, potentially long-term relationship involving repeat custom.
- *Perceptions of cost* — The perception among occupiers that, while many of the benefits of good design accrue to the wider community (i.e. they are social benefits), it is the occupiers who pay for it in the form of higher rent, running costs and commercial rates (i.e. they involve private costs).
- *Decision-making patterns* — Many of the most important urban design decisions being taken not by planners, developers or designers, but by people who may not think of themselves as being involved in urban design (i.e. unknowing urban designers). Such actors often lack appreciation of the wider impacts and consequences of the decisions they make, particularly their impact on the urban environment.
- *Negative planning* — Largely reactionary as opposed to 'positive' and proactive approaches to urban design across many local authorities, and a general failure to link concerns for urban regeneration with those for better urban design.
- *Skills deficit* — The low levels of urban design skills on both sides of the development process represent a significant and consistent impediment to the effective delivery of better design.

Such constraints should be seen as challenges — successful urban designers are skilled in confronting and overcoming constraints and in creating good places.

Urban design is not simply a passive reaction to change, but also a positive attempt to shape change and to make better places. To succeed, however, urban designers also need political and operational skills. Tibbalds (1988a: 12–3), for example, identified a set of personal skills required by successful urban designers:

- Being able to operate at a high level — being a force to be reckoned with and appreciated by politicians, administrators, industrialists, developers, etc.
- Being passionately concerned with achievability — putting all manner of design ideas to practical effect.
- Being outward-looking and able to show deference and humility to the other professions and to the community.
- Being able to argue cogently and convincingly for the necessary resources of finance, land and manpower to see ideas through.
- Possessing astute financial awareness.
- Being idealistic but realistic — able to recognise why things go wrong.
- Having an unfettered imagination and a commitment to quality and to finishing the job.

As Tibbalds (1988a: 13) notes, these skills are only means to an end — the real end is to achieve something worthwhile on the ground. In this regard Lang (2005: 393) has observed that urban design is no longer a composite activity encompassing all those parts of the established built environment professions that focus on 'the bit in-between' — the urbanism (see Chapter 1) — and instead '… *it has developed its own areas of expertise and has become what it should never have become — a discipline in it own right.*' If this continues, he suggests, it will not remain a collaborative discipline, drawing on expertise from across the built environment professions, but differing from them '… *in that it has become more development oriented, more socially oriented and more conscious of the politically volatile nature of decision-making at the urban level.*' (Lang 2005: 394).

The barriers listed above highlight the importance of the public sector in establishing a political and regulatory climate within which good design can flourish. In cities demonstrating the best examples of urban design such as Barcelona, Copenhagen, Vancouver, Birmingham, Portland and San Francisco, the barriers have, to a greater or lesser extent, been overcome. In such places, while recognising the proactive role of public authorities in establishing a supportive climate for design, the positive role played by

FIGURE 13.1 Aker Brygge, Oslo (*Image: Matthew Carmona*). Establishing a new city centre quarter, Aker Brygge's success as a place derives from:

- *Diverse range of uses* — cafes, restaurants, retail, festival shopping, offices, two theatres, theatrical academy, residential, cinemas, health centre, kindergarten
- *Morphological form* — positive relationship to its waterside setting, sequence of spaces lined with active uses, pedestrian-friendly car-free status, good pubic transport connections and high permeability (visually and physically) without compromising the intimacy of the key space
- *Architectural mix* — a rich mix of bold contemporary architecture with revitalised historic buildings
- *Response to climate* — with protected pockets, interior walkways and spaces for the winter and uses that spill out into the external spaces in good weather
- *Size and density* — 64 ha of high-density development but with relatively small buildings and with a good resident and working population

FIGURE 13.2 The South Bank, London (*Image: Matthew Carmona*). The South Bank is a major success story of urban design in London. The diversity of its attractions and dramatic nature of its context with views across the Thames to the cities of London and Westminster make the experience a major draw for tourists and Londoners. Rather than a conventional piece of urban design in the form of a new development, it is a rejuvenated — and still evolving — riverside walk stretching from east of Tower Bridge to Westminster Bridge and taking in London's Design Museum, Southwark Cathedral, the historic Borough Market, the Globe Theatre, the Tate Modern (art gallery), and the National Theatre, along with a host of other entertainment, arts, residential, commercial, retail and restaurant/café uses. Dominated by the pedestrian route, along which most of the attractions are arranged, the urban form is a mix of high-density traditional space and contemporary commercial developments. The historic public realm has been the subject of considerable public sector investment, and includes high-quality public art and landscaping. It also includes a number of successful contemporary interventions such as Tower Bridge Piazza and the Coin Street social housing development. Architecturally, a number of iconic set pieces add to the area's appeal — Tower Bridge, the London Assembly Building, the converted Bankside power station, the Millennium Bridge, the London Eye and the Royal Festival Hall. The quantity and quality of visual and social stimuli make Bankside a memorable place. Its success is all the more significant because of the diversity of players responsible for its creation, including a proactive local authority regeneration team and a host of voluntary, community and commercial interests. In large part, the area has been revitalised through managed incremental development (rather than through any grand masterplan), and through a concern for quality around the unifying theme of the Thames Path

private sector developers and investors to ensure a shared commitment to quality across different stakeholder groups has been equally significant. When commitment from all sectors is present, then there is the opportunity to create contemporary public places and urban space to rival the best in any century. Figures 13.1–13.4 illustrate five examples where this has been the case.

If many of the barriers to delivering better-quality urban design relate to processes of design, development and public regulation, then (like sustainable development) so do many of the solutions. Certain process-related barriers — local market conditions, the macro-economy, etc. — are almost impossible for urban designers, or indeed any built environment professionals, to influence. Other factors are only amenable to influence over extended periods of time and as a consequence of national/state or regional action. They include the awareness of urban design and place-making among key actors, established patterns of decision-making, the cost of land and the nature of the planning system and other regulatory mechanisms. These were discussed in Chapter 3 as the market and regulatory contexts for urban design, which, for practical purposes, urban designers often have to accept as givens.

There are, nevertheless, a series of constraints that urban designers, their clients and local communities can influence: the availability of information on demand and public preferences; the consolidation of land and development opportunities; the operation of the planning process as a positive force for change; education about the value of better design; the availability of appropriately skilled individuals in both public and private sectors; and the formulation and adoption of a coherent local vision. Most of all, urban design practitioners can move beyond short-sighted, hard-edged professional approaches and adopt more collaborative working relationships focused on the creation of good places.

FIGURE 13.4 Community event, Vauban, Freiberg, Germany (*Image: Iqbal Hamiduddin*). Begun in the mid-1990s, Vauban is a new neighbourhood of 5000 inhabitants and 600 jobs, 4 km to the south of Freiburg city centre. Built on a former military barracks, this urban extension is designed as a sustainable model district, with excellent public transport links to the city, 40% car-free housing, shared street space with 5 km/hour speed limits, houses built to a low-energy standard with estimated carbon dioxide savings through good insulation and efficient heat supply of 60%, and 65% of the development's electricity produced on-site through a combined heat and power (CHP) plant and photovoltaics. The development has equally challenging social aspirations with far-reaching participation processes designed to engage residents directly in the process of shaping their own environments, as well as in the on-going management of the community. Some larger building companies have been involved in the development, but much of the housing has been built by a combination of small private builders and 'Baugruppen', or groups of owners that collectively build their own schemes within the parameters set out in detailed plan and codes. The result is small-scale variety within a coherent urban fabric and high-quality liveable built environment (http://www.vauban.de/info/)

FIGURE 13.3 Pioneer Courthouse Square, Portland, Oregon, USA (*Image: Steve Tiesdell*). Located in the centre of Portland's downtown, Pioneer Courthouse Square is a successful piece of urban design. The square's long gestation period contributed both to its character and to the sense of ownership felt for it by the city's citizens. In 1952, the former grand Portland Hotel was demolished and a two-storey garage structure constructed. In the early 1960s, it was proposed to replace the garage with a public square, but it was not until 1972 that the Downtown Plan for Portland designated the block for future use as a public square. The city eventually purchased the land in 1979 and, in 1980, an international competition was held to select a design for the square. A citizen jury chose a scheme by a local firm of architects, but a change of mayor and the formation of the Downtown Business Association for Portland Process halted plans. A grassroots action group − Friends of Pioneer Square − fought to retain the project, raising $1.6 million by selling sponsorship of the square's benches, trees and lights, plus more than 60 000 paving bricks. Opened in 1984, the square offers a variety of spaces providing varying degrees of refuge and exposure, opportunities for people-watching and a variety of sitting locations. Its centre is palpably pregnant with opportunity and hosts 300 events annually. The square has also played a significant role in restoring Portland's downtown as the region's social and economic centre, while an enlightened transport policy has made it the main terminal of a regional light-rail system.

A HOLISTIC APPROACH

Place-Making + Sustainability

We conclude this book by stressing the holistic nature of urban design. As discussed in Chapter 3, the criteria of good design − 'firmness', 'commodity', and 'delight' − have to be satisfied simultaneously. In any design process, there is a danger of narrowly prioritising a particular dimension − aesthetic, functional, technical or economic − and of isolating it from its context and from its contribution to the greater whole. Much of the so-called 'functionalism' of Modernist architecture suffered from this problem. According to the functionalist approach, functional requirements were primary and would generate building layout, form and visual expression. Reacting to the overcrowded and unhealthy conditions of the industrial cities, Modernists argued that people needed fresh air, more

daylight, sunlight and greenery. Hence, new housing, for example, could be designed following certain key criteria such as a rigid application of daylighting standards, which lead to the spreading out of buildings. Such an approach inappropriately emphasises one aspect of design to the probable detriment of other considerations, such as integrating development into its local context and existing movement patterns, and the preferences and choices of those likely to live there.

Chapter 3 added a fourth criterion − economy − to the well-established trinity of 'firmness, commodity and delight'. Economy is to be interpreted not only in the narrower financial sense of respecting budget constraints, but also, more importantly, in its widest sense − reflecting the imperative of minimising environmental costs. The need to address complex sustainability issues represents perhaps the greatest challenge of the twenty-first century. Those engaged in designing and managing urban areas will play an important role in addressing this challenge.

In different ways, sustainability impacts on each of the dimensions of urban design as it does throughout the development process, as the Sustainability Inserts in Parts II and III have shown. Discussion of the 10 sustainable design principles at their different scales (see Chapter 3) highlights the complexities inherent in developing – let alone delivering – a sustainable urban design strategy. It also reveals the agenda's aspirational nature and the inevitability of internal contradictions only resolvable through practice. For example, the desire for more concentrated patterns of development might unintentionally design-out opportunities for increasing bio-diversity or for sustainable drainage; design for optimum passive solar gain may require more south-facing development, while human needs for a more sociable environment may necessitate a permeable grid. The principles outlined in this book represent only the start of a design process, with a development's impact on the global context also needing to be reconciled with its place in the local context and in governmental and market contexts.

However, fundamental questions have also arisen about whether this new imperative for the design agenda can be addressed within the 'making places' tradition that now dominates the theory and practice of urban design, and to which this book broadly subscribes (see Chapter 1), or whether an entirely new orthodoxy is required – one placing sustainability, rather than place-making, at its heart.

Beddington Zero Energy Development (BedZED) in London (Figure 13.5) – a well-known 'sustainability exemplar' – for example, deliberately eschews its suburban context and establishes itself as a self-contained zero-carbon enclave based on a continuous structure of south-facing terraces. Other models are increasingly being put forward by high-profile architects that either see sustainable urban

design as a return to object-architecture – for example Ken Yeang's vertical 'green' skyscrapers – or as technology-driven settlements on a 'total design' model (see Chapter 1) with designed lifestyles to match – for example Arups' proposed zero-carbon city in Dongtan, Shanghai (see Chapter 8). Foster & Partners' Masdar City in Abu Dhabi combines both – the whole city is viewed as a single object in which technology enables residents to live carbon-neutral lives in the middle of a desert.

These examples suggest a break with urban design as place-making, at least to the extent that form and impact rather than people and place are the priority. However, none of the sustainable urban design principles outlined in this book necessarily imply that concerns for place-making cannot also be met. Ritchie (in Ritchie & Thomas 2009: 92), for example, concludes that:

'… we need to analyse the ingredients that make a successful "place" and work with them once again … [while recognising that] … we are now dealing with modern issues that affect the recipe: a changing climate and the need for more people to live in a more humane city environment.'

The authors of the *Urban Design Compendium 2* (Roger Evans Associates 2007: 72) conclude that: '*There is a common misconception that a conflict exists between principles of good urban design … and an optimal approach to environmental sustainability.*' They argue that it is perfectly possible to engage with street-based design while also achieving optimal thermal performance.

What may be required, however, is a more sophisticated and multi-functional view about urban environments and their constituent elements: people using their own homes to generate power; green open spaces used for water recycling; neighbourhoods accommodating multiple land uses; public spaces supporting wildlife; etc. (Thwaites *et al* 2007). Moreover, with climate change now impacting on and changing local environments around the world, there will be a need for flexibility and to learn the lessons from history about what characteristics of urban form can be used in different climatic circumstances to modify local climates without reliance on energy-intensive technologies.

Golany (1996), for example, argues that urban morphology can be designed to cool or warm temperatures in urban areas as appropriate, without need for active, energy-intensive technologies. He argues that, while in stressed climates (which climate change are making more widespread) compact city forms will be generally desirable, continuous street grid systems will better suit hot climates by encouraging air penetration deep into the city, with closed irregular street systems more suitable in cooler climates. Golany (1996: 464) concludes that we need to combine innovation born through research with in-depth knowledge of how our ancestors coped with climate. These

FIGURE 13.5 Beddington Zero Energy Development (BedZED) (*Image: Matthew Carmona*). Deliberately eschewing its suburban context, BedZED establishes itself as a self-contained zero-carbon enclave based on a continuous structure of south-facing terraces

arguments support the case made in this book that sustainability does not require reinventing the wheel, but, instead, is an overarching lens through which the dimensions (morphological, perceptual, social, visual, functional, temporal) and processes (development, control, communication) of good place-making should be seen — that is, a holistic view.

An Even Greater Challenge

Any conceptualisation of sustainable urban design is of little value unless it can be implemented. The drivers encouraging more active approaches to delivering sustainable design are well accepted and relate to the potential for lasting damage wreaked by increasingly unsustainable patterns of life and development, and to recognition that mankind holds the potential both to irreversibly damage the natural environment and to repair and enhance it. The decisions are essentially moral ones to be debated through international, national and local political processes for delivery through associated processes of development and governance. Frey (1999: 144), for example, argues that:

'… to achieve sustainable city regions requires the rethinking not only of the city and city region but also of current policies, approaches and professional responsibilities as well as education. What is needed is a strong political will to act upon this commitment by implementing strong, co-ordinated policies, approaches and strategies; and this equates with a kind of gentle and friendly revolution. Half-heartedness will not achieve sustainable city regions.'

Barriers to delivery are formidable and may sometimes seem impossible to overcome, not least because they sit alongside and reinforce the generic barriers to good design discussed above. They encompass:

- *Established patterns of living* — which are frequently ingrained and difficult to change; for example, reliance on car-based travel and the layout of the urban environment based on that premise.
- *Public awareness and aspirations* — which often aspire to unsustainable, high-consumption modes of living, including aspirations (particularly in the Anglo-Saxon world) for low-density housing and to own a car (sometimes two or three).
- *Economic and governance systems* — which rarely reflect the true environmental costs of development.
- *Lack of political will* — to influence development processes because of the over-riding pressures to deliver, first, economic goals, second, social ones, but only a poor third, environmental objectives.
- *Lack of vision* — in either the public sector or the private sector to innovate new solutions and think beyond tried-

and-tested — but often unsustainable — development processes.
- *Selfishness* — because too many stakeholders see the environment as 'someone else's problem' and thus fail to consider (and sometimes actively dismiss) their own role.
- *Lack of choice* — because many individuals have little or no choice in the way they lead their lives because of cultural, economic, educational and physical constraints.
- *The scale of the problem* — in that turning around unsustainable patterns of living and development is a massive long-term process dependent on fundamental changes to attitudes and on co-operation between many different stakeholders across spatial scales. In such a context, it is easy to think that individual contributions will have little impact and that positive action can be put off for another day (Carmona 2009b: 69–70).

The European Union Working Group on Urban Design for Sustainability (EU 2004: 41) agreed with this assessment, concluding that obstacles commonly relate to a

'… lack of political will and awareness; difficulties with planning and administration systems, legislation and procedures; the need for appropriate training and education; lack of appropriate knowledge sharing systems; the persistence of the traditional, sector-based approach to urban planning and design; the complexity of the holistic vision of sustainable development and planner's reluctance to accept it.'

Clearly, the barriers are both international and endemic and extend across public and private spheres of responsibility.

Yet, a wide range of means exist through which the public and private stakeholders discussed in Part Three of this book can influence the delivery of a more holistic, sustainable urban design. Table 13.1 identifies the range of stakeholders who need to be engaged in the delivery of sustainable urban design, as well as the diversity of means across spatial scales through which to influence its delivery. The table demonstrates the wide range of public sector agencies and potential influences on sustainable design, as well as the diverse interests of public, private and community sectors across four spatial scales. It emphasises the need for 'joined-up' approaches to governance in this area (perhaps above all others) where responsibility is thinly spread. It also emphasises the important role of agencies with plan-making and grant-making powers — planning authorities, highways authorities and regeneration agencies — in central leadership and stewardship roles to coordinate public sector contributions and deliver a partnership of public and private interests focused on delivering sustainable places (see Sustainability Insert 10).

Sustainability Insert 10 — Stewardship

Sustainable places are those where, at all scales of development, on-going processes of adaptation and change are positively channelled in an integrated manner towards achieving a better-quality built environment. This requires governance regimes to establish clear and measurable targets for each aspect of sustainability, while maintaining a sense of how each target contributes to greater, integrated, economic, social and environmental goals (Roger Evans Associates 2007: 33).

Policy agendas around the world have catching up with this new agenda. New Zealand's *Urban Design Protocol* (Ministry for the Environment 2005), for example, situates urban design within the country's Sustainable Development Programme of Action, calling for towns and cities to be competitive, thriving, creative and innovative, but also liveable and environmentally responsible. Similarly, the UK's national planning policy now stipulates: *'Good design ensures attractive, useable, durable and adaptable places and is a key element in achieving sustainable development.'* (ODPM 2005: para.33).

In the latter case, the design principles discussed in the previous Sustainability Inserts are reflected in the national benchmark for well-designed housing and neighbourhoods — Building-for-Life (2008). This sets 20 questions that developers can use to write development briefs, or local authorities to demand higher design standards.

Reflecting this approach, and supplementing Box 13.1, planners, designers, developers and other stakeholders might usefully ask:

1. Do proposals support diversity and choice in movement, access and land use mix?
2. Do proposals respect what is distinctive about their environment and help to build or preserve local sense-of-place?
3. Do proposals support human needs for security, social contact, comfort and artistic fulfilment?

4. Do proposals support the biotic environment through the careful integration of built and natural resources?
5. Are proposals concentrated to reduce land take and energy use and increase urban vitality and viability?
6. Are proposals resilient enough to withstand and robust enough to adapt to change over time?
7. Are proposals efficient in their consumption and long-term use of energy and natural resources?
8. Are proposals likely to support the establishment of more self-sufficient, involved local communities?
9. Do proposals minimise pollution of the wider environment both in their construction and long-term management?
10. Do proposals enhance their context, effectively join-up the range of contributions and therefore help to carefully steward in change over time?

Chicago Farmers' Market (*Image: Matthew Carmona*) meeting human and environmental needs

Of greatest importance to delivering more sustainable urban design, however, is the need to establish an impetus for change. International, national and local government agendas increasingly recognise that change is not only desirable, but both necessary and inevitable (EU 2004: 30–8). Though delivery is undoubtedly a shared public/private responsibility, the impetus may first need to come from the public sector if something more than tokenism is to be achieved. Initiatives such as the US Green Building Council's LEED for Neighborhood Development rating system, the UK government's Sustainable Building Code, and CABE's www.sustainablecities.org.uk provide tools to deliver on the challenge.

CONCLUSION

Good urban design is sustainable, but, as discussion of sustainability throughout this book has shown, this involves much more than simply reducing energy use and carbon emissions. Instead it involves a much more profound basis on which to make decisions that impact on the social, economic and environmental sustainability of the built environment. It requires a holistic — sustainable place-making — view that considers each dimension of urban design in terms of its impact on local and global contexts, and through associated delivery processes.

At the same time it is important to recognise that urban design is one part of the broader sustainable development

TABLE 13.1 Delivering Sustainable Design — Stakeholders and Influences (Carmona, 2009b)

	Buildings	Spaces	Quarters	Settlements
Private Sector				
Design professionals	Building design Urban design Design vision	Urban design Landscape design Design vision	Urban design Landscape design Design vision	Urban design Design vision
Developers	Building developments	Urban developments Public/private partnerships	Urban developments Public/private partnerships	New settlements Public/private partnerships
Investors	Project financing Long-term investment	Project financing Long-term investment	Project financing Long-term investment	Project financing
Public Sector				
Planning authorities	Local plan policy Design guidance Design briefs Development control	Local plan policy Design guidance Design briefs Development control Planning gain	Local plan policy Design guidance Design frameworks Development control Planning gain	Strategic planning policy Local plan policy Design strategies
Highways authorities		Road construction standards Road adoption procedure	Highways layout standards Road adoption procedure	Transport plans Traffic management
Building control/permits	Building controls			
Fire authorities	Fire spread standards	Fire spread standards	Fire prevention access standards	
Environmental health	Noise control	Refuse disposal/ control	Vehicle emissions control	Pollution control
Housing authorities/ providers	Social housing provision/subsidy Design standards	Design standards/ quality indices		Housing strategies
Parks and recreation departments		Open space maintenance	Open space provision/ preservation	Landscape/open space strategies
Police authorities	Architectural liaison	Architectural liaison Public order Traffic control	Public order bylaws	
Regeneration agencies/ authorities	Design guidelines	Design guidelines Gap-funding/grants Public/private partnerships	Land reclamation Gap-funding/grants Public/private partnerships	Public/private partnerships
Conservation agencies	Gap-funding/grants Listed building designations/controls	Enhancement schemes/ funds Conservation area designations/controls	Enhancement schemes/ funds Conservation area designations/controls	
Urban managers		Urban streetscape management/ co-ordination	Urban promotion/ management/ co-ordination	
Public/Private				
Utility providers		Road/pavement repair standards		Infrastructure provision
Public transport providers		Public transport management	Public transport provision	Public transport integration

(Continued)

TABLE 13.1 Delivering Sustainable Design — Stakeholders and Influences (Carmona, 2009b)—cont'd

	Buildings	Spaces	Quarters	Settlements
Educational institutions/sector			Local engagement	Raising environmental awareness
Community-Based				
Voluntary groups/ communities	Consultation response	Actively engaging (participation, urban management)	Campaigning Actively engaging (design, appraisal, participation)	Campaigning
Local politicians	Statutory powers	Statutory powers Spending priorities	Statutory powers Spending priorities Lobbying	Statutory powers Spending priorities Lobbying
Private individuals/ companies	Home/building maintenance	Lifestyle choices Civic responsibility	Civic responsibility	

agenda that seeks to create sustainable places: economically, socially and environmentally. Allmendinger & Tiesdell (2004) have suggested this requires getting right the 'people factors' — skills, resources and commitment, social infrastructure, economic infrastructure — and 'place factors' — communication, physical resources, economic structure, location, quality of life opportunities, local governance. As urban design relates to all of these, it is thus a vital part of this wider agenda.

Despite this important role — and unlike, for example, the field of architecture — there are very few 'big names' in urban design. In part, this is because good urban design is often unobtrusive. It blends in and 'disappears' — we do not notice that it is there. Conversely, poor urban design often stands out. Indeed, it may only be noticed when it does not work. Good urban design is often like the referee in a soccer match who has a 'good' game by not being noticed. In delivering good urban design, the contribution of the individual is almost always eclipsed by that of the team. This, in turn, reflects the nature of sustainable urban design as a process of joining-up — both joining-up environments and places and joining-up professionals and other actors with each other, with communities and with those who wish to invest.

To achieve its full potential, however, urban design and place-making considerations need to figure more centrally in the decision-making processes of public and private actors (all those in Table 13.1), and, furthermore, in educational programmes in built environment and related fields. There also needs to be a more general cultural shift towards perspectives more appreciative and mindful of urban design. It is hoped that this book will make a contribution on both these fronts.

If urban design is about making public places for people, the challenge is to design the sorts of spaces that people will want to use and to live in. In his conclusion to *Cities and Civilisation*, Hall (1998: 989) writes that the greatest cities have never been 'earthly utopias' but rather

'... places of stress and conflict and sometimes actual misery ... places where the adrenalin pumps through the bodies of the people and through the streets on which they work, messy places, sordid places sometimes, but places nonetheless superbly worth living in ...'

This is the real motivation for urban design — creating places superbly worth living in.

A

Abbott, C (1997) Portland: Gateway to the North-West, American Historical Press, Washington

Abramson, D; Birch, E; Dunham-Jones, E; Hack, G; Laurance, P; Leatherbarrow, D; Pizarro, R; Sommer, R & Strickland, R (2008) Educating Urban Designers for Post Carbon Cities, http://www.upenn.edu/penniur/afteroil/manifesto.html

Adams, D; Allmendinger, P; Dunse, N; Tiesdell, S; Turok, I; & White, M (2003) Assessing the Impact of ODPM Policies on Land Pricing, research report for the Office of the Deputy Prime Minister (ODPM), London

Adams, D & Tiesdell, S (2008) The vital city, Town Planning Review, 78(6), 671–680

Adams, D (1994) Urban Planning and the Development Process, UCL Press, London

Agrawal, A W; Schlossberg, M & Irvin, K (2008) How far, by which route and why? A spatial analysis of pedestrian preference, Journal of Urban Design, 13(1), 81–98

Ahlava A & Edelman H (2009) Urban Design Management: A Guide to Good Practice, Taylor & Francis, Abingdon

Aldous, T (1992) Urban Villages: A Concept for Creating Mixed-Use Developments on a Sustainable Scale, Urban Villages Group, London

Alexander, C (2004a) The Phenomenon of Life: The Nature of Order (Book 1), Centre for Environmental Structure, Berkeley, CA

Alexander, C (2004b) Process of Creating Life: The Nature of Order (Book 2), Centre for Environmental Structure, Berkeley, CA

Alexander, C (2004c) Vision of a Living World: The Nature of Order (Book 3), Centre for Environmental Structure, Berkeley, CA

Alexander, C (2004d) The Luminous Ground: The Nature of Order (Book 4), Centre for Environmental Structure, Berkeley, CA

Alexander, C (1965) A city is not a tree', Architectural Forum, 122 (1 & 2), April/May, also in Bell, G & Tyrwhitt, R (1992) (Editors) Human Identity in the Urban Environment, Penguin, London

Alexander, C (1987) A New Theory of Urban Design, Oxford University Press, Oxford

Alexander, C (1979) The Timeless Way of Building, Oxford University Press, Oxford

Alexander, C (1975) The Oregon Experiment, Oxford University Press, Oxford

Alexander, C; Ishikawa, S & Silverstein, M (1977) A Pattern Language: Towns, Buildings, Construction, Oxford University Press, Oxford

Alexander, C; Neis, H; Anninou, A & King, I (1987) A New Theory of Urban Design, Oxford University Press, New York

Alexander, C; with Schmidt, R; Hanson, B; Alexander, M M & Mehafy, M (2008) Generative codes: The path to building welcoming, beautiful, sustainable neighbourhoods', in Haas, T New Urbanism and Beyond: Designing Cities for the Future, Rizzoli International, New York, 14–29

Alfonzo, M; Boarnet, M G; Day, K; McMillan, T; & Anderson, C L (2008) The relationship of neighbourhood built environment features and adult parent walking, Journal of Urban Design, 13(1), 29–52

Allen, J (2006) Ambient power: Berlin's Potsdamer Platz and the seductive logic of public spaces, Urban Studies 43(2), 411–455

Allen, S (no date) - http://www.stanallenarchitect.com/v1/infrastructure/ accessed 01/08/2009 20:16)

Allen, S (2001) 'Mat urbanism: The thick 2-D in Sarkis, H., CASE: Le Corbusier's Venice Hospital and the Mat Building Revival, Prestel, Harvard Design School, Munich, 118–126

Allmendinger, P & Tiesdell S (2004) Making sense of sustainable communities', Town & Country Planning, November, 313–316

Almy, D. (2007) (editor) On Landscape Urbanism, Center 14, Centre for American Architecture and Design, University of Texas at Austin, Austin

Ambrose, P (1986) Whatever Happened to Planning, Meuthen, London

Amin, A & Graham, S (1997) The ordinary city, Transactions of the Institute of British Geographers 22, 411–429

Anderson, S (1978) (editor) On Streets, MIT Press, Cambridge, Mass

Appignanesi, R & Garratt, C (1999) Introducing postmodernism, Icon Books, London

Appleyard, D (1991) Foreword', from Moudon, AV Public Streets for Public Use, Columbia University Press, New York, 5–8

Appleyard, D (1982) Three kinds of urban design practice, in Ferebee, A (Editor) Education for Urban Design, Institute for Urban Design, New York

Appleyard, D (1981) Liveable Streets, University of California Press, Berkeley

Appleyard, D (1980) Why buildings are known: A predictive tool for architects and planners, in Broadbent, G; Bunt, R & Llorens, T Meaning and Behaviour in the Built Environment, John Wiley & Sons, Chichester

Appleyard, D (1976) Planning a Pluralist City: Conflicting Realities in Ciudad Guyana, MIT Press, Cambridge, Mass

Appleyard, D & Lintell, M (1972) The environmental quality of city streets: The residents' viewpoint Journal of the American Institute of Planners, 38, 84–101

Appleyard, D; Lynch, K; & Myer, J (1964) The View from the Road, MIT Press, Cambridge, Mass

Ardrey, R (1967) The Territorial Imperative: A Personal Inquiry into the Animal Origins of Property and Nations, Collins, London

Arefi, M (1999) Non-place and placelessness as narratives of loss: Rethinking the notion of place, Journal of Urban Design, 4(2), 179–193

Arendt, H (1958) The Human Condition, University of Chicago Press, Chicago

Arias, E; Eden, H & Gerhard, F (1997) Enhancing Communication, Facilitating Shared Understanding, and Creating Better Artifacts by Integrating Physical and Computational Media for Design, University of Colorado, Boulder

Arnheim, R (1977) The Dynamics of Architectural Form, University of California Press, Berkeley

Arnstein S (1969) A ladder of citizen participation, American Institute of Planners Journal, July, 216–224

Arup Economics & Planning (2000) Survey of Urban Design Skills in Local Government, DETR, London

Ashworth, G J (1998) The conserved European city as cultural symbol: The meaning of the text in Graham, B (editor) Modern Europe: Place, Culture, Identity, Arnold, London, 261–286

Ashworth, G J (1997) Conservation as preservation or as heritage: Two paradigms and two answers, Built Environment, 23(2), 92–102

Ashworth, G J & Tunbridge, J E (1990) The Touristic-Historic City, Belhaven Press, London

Atkinson, R (2003) Domestication by cappuccino or a revenge on urban space? Control and empowerment on the management of public spaces, Urban Studies 40 (9), 1829–1843

Attoe, W & Logan, D (1989) American Urban Architecture: Catalysts in the Design of Cities, University of California Press, Berkeley

Auge, M (1995) Non-places: An Introduction to an Anthropology of Supermodernity, Verso, London

Aurigi A (2005) Making the Digital City: The Early Shaping of Urban Internet Space, Ashgate, London

B

Bacon, E (1992) Design of Cities, Thames & Hudson, London (first published in 1967)

Bacon, K L; Dagenhart, R; Leigh, N G; & Skach, J (2008) The economic development – Urban design link in brownfield redevelopment Economic Development Journal, Spring, 30–39

Badland, H & Schofield, G (2005) Transport, urban design and physical activity: An evidence-based update Transportation Research Part D: Transport and the Environment, 177–196

Baker, G (1996) Design Strategies in Architecture: An Approach to the Analysis of Form, second edition, London: E & FN Spon

Balfour, J & Kaplan, G (2002) Neighbourhood environment and loss of physical function in older adults: Evidence from the Alameda County Study, American Journal of Epidemiology, 155(6): 507–515

Ball, M (1998) Institutions in British property research: A review Urban Studies, 35(9) 1501–1517

Ball, M (1986) The built environment and the urban question Environment & Planning D: Society & Space, 4, 447–464

Banerjee, T (2001) The future of public space: Beyond invented streets and reinvented places, APA Journal, 67(1) 9–24

Banerjee, T & Southworth, M (1991) (editors) City Sense and City Design: Writings and Projects of Kevin Lynch, MIT Press, Cambridge, Mass

Banerjee, T & Baer, W C (1984) Beyond the Neighbourhood Unit, Plenum Press, New York

Banister, C & Gallent, N (1998) Trends in commuting in England and Wales – Becoming less sustainable? Area, 30, 331–341

Bannister, J; Fyfe, N & Kearns, A (2006) Respectable or respectful? (In) civility and the city, Urban Studies, 43(5–6) 919–938

Baran, P K; Rodriquez, D A & Khattak, A J (2008), space syntax and walking in a New Urbanist and suburban neighbourhoods, Journal of Urban Design, 13(1), 5–28

Barnett, J (2003) Redesigning Cities: Principles, Practices, Implementation, Planners Press, Chicago, IL

Barnett, J (1982) An Introduction to Urban Design, Harper & Row, New York

Barnett, J (1974) Urban Design as Public Policy, Harper & Row, New York

Barrett, S; Stewart, M & Underwood, J (1978) The Land Market and the Development Process, Occasional paper 2, SAUS, University of Bristol, Bristol

Barthes, R (1967) Elements of Semiology, Hill & Wang, New York

Barthes, R (1968) The death of the author, in Barthes, R (1977) Image–Music–Text, Flamingo, London, 142–148

Bartlett, K (2003) Testing the "Popsicle Test": Realities of retail shopping in New "Traditional Neighbourhood" Development, Urban Studies 140(8), 1471–1485

Barton, H & Tsourou, C (2000) Healthy Urban Planning, Spon Press, London

Barton, H; Davis, G & Guise, R (1995) Sustainable Settlements: A Guide for Planners, Designers, and Developers, Local Government Management Board, Luton

Barton H; Grant, M & Guise, R (2003) Shaping Neighbourhoods, A Guide for Health, Sustainability and Vitality, Spon Press, London

Barton, H (1996) Going green by design, Urban Design Quarterly, 57, January, 13–18

Barton, H; Davis, G; & Guise, R (1994) Sustainable Settlements: A Guide for Planners, Designers, and Developers, Local Government Management Board, Luton

Batty, M (2008) Hierarchy, scale and complexity in urban design in Haas, T New Urbanism and Beyond: Designing Cities for the Future, Rizzoli International, New York, 258–261

Batty, M (2005) Cities and Complexity Understanding Cities with Cellular Automata, Agent-Based Models, and Fractals, MIT Press, Cambridge, Mass

Baudrillard, J (1994; in French 1981) Simulacra and Simulation, University of Michigan, Ann Arbor

Baudrillard, J (1983; in French 1981) Simulations, Semiotext, New York

Beauregard, R A (2005) The textures of property markets: Downtown Housing and Office Conversions in New York City, Urban Studies 42 (13) 2431–2445

Beck U (1992) Risk Society: Towards a New Modernity, Sage, London

Bell D (2005) The emergence of contemporary masterplans: Property markets and the value of urban design, Journal of Urban Design, 10 (1): 81–110

Bell, P A; Fisher, J D; Baum, A & Greene, T C (1990) Environmental Psychology (third edition) Holt, Rinehart & Winston, Inc., London

Bemelmans-Videc, M-L (2007) Introduction: Policy instrument choice and evaluation, in Bemelmans-Videc, M-L Rist, R; & Vedung, E (2007) (editors) Carrots, Sticks and Sermons: Policy Instruments and Their Evaluation, Transaction Publishers, London, 1–20

Ben-Joseph E (2005) The Code of the City: Standards and the Hidden Language of Place Making, MIT Press, Cambridge Mass

Ben-Joseph, E (1995) Changing the residential street scene: Adopting the shared street (Woonerf) concept to the suburban environment, Journal of the American Planning Association, 61(4) 504–515

Bentley, I (1999) Urban Transformations: Power, People and Urban Design, Routledge, London

Bentley, I (1998) Urban design as an anti-profession, Urban Design Quarterly, 65, 15

Bentley, I (1990) Ecological urban design, Architects' Journal, 192, 24 October, 69–71

Bentley, I (1976) What is urban design? Towards a definition, Urban Design Forum, 1

Bentley, I; Alcock, A; Murrain, P; McGlynn, S & Smith, G (1985) Responsive Environments: A Manual for Designers, Architectural Press, London

Beunderman, J; Hannon, C; & Bradwell, P (2007) Seen and Heard, Reclaiming the Public Realm with Children and Young People, DEMOS, London

Bianchini, F (1994) Night cultures, night economies, Town & Country Planning, 63, 308–310

Biddulph, M; Punter, J & Hooper, A (2006) Awards, patronage and design preference: An analysis of English awards for housing design, Urban Design International, 11(1), 49–61

Biddulph, M, Franklin, B & Tait, M (2003) From concept to completion: A critical analysis of the urban village, Town Planning Review 74(2): 165–193

Biddulph, M & Punter, J (1999) (editors) Urban design strategies in practice Built Environment, 25(4)

Biddulph, M (2007) Introduction to Residential Layout, Architectural Press, Oxford

Biddulph, M (2001) Home Zones, A Planning and Design Handbook, The Policy Press, Bristol

Biddulph, M (2000) Villages don't make a city, Journal of Urban Design, 5(1) 65–82

Biddulph, M (1999) Book review of Bosselmann, P (1998) Representation of place: Reality and realism in city design, Journal of Urban Design, 4(1) 125–127

Biddulph, M (1995) The value of manipulated meanings in urban design and architecture', Environment & Planning B: Planning & Design, 22, 739–762

Biffault, R (1999) A government for our time? Business improvement districts and urban governance, Columbia Law Review, XCIX (2) 365–477

Birmingham City Council (1994) Convention Centre Quarter, Planning & Urban Design Framework, Birmingham City Council, Birmingham

Blake, P (1974) Form Follows Fiasco, Little & Brown, Boston

Blakely, EJ & Snyder, MG (1997) Fortress America: Gated Communities in the United States, Brookings Institution Press, Washington DC & Lincoln Institute of Land Policy, Cambridge, Mass

Blowers, A (1993) Planning for a Sustainable Environment, Earthscan Publications Ltd, London

Blowers, A (1973) The City as a Social System: Unit 7: The Neighbourhood: Exploration of a Concept, Open University, Milton Keynes

Boarnet, M G & Crane, R (2001) Travel by Design: The Influence of Urban Form on Travel, Oxford University Press, Oxford

Boddy, T (1992) Underground and overhead: Building the analogous city, in Sorkin, M (1992) (Editor) Variations on a Theme Park, Noonday Press, New York, 123–153

Boorstein, D (1961) The Image: A Guide to Pseudo-Events in America, Atheneum, New York

Bonamoni, L (1990) NonEn Le Temps des Rues: Vers un Mouvel Amenagement de l'Espace Rue, Institute for Built Environment, Lausanne

Booth, K; Pinkston, M; & Carlos Poston, W (2005) Obesity and the built environment, Journal of the American Dietetic Association, 105(5) supplement: 110–117

Booth, NK (1983) Basic Elements of Landscape Architectural Design, Elsevier, Oxford

Borchert, J (1991) Future of American cities, in Hart, JF (Editor) Our Changing Cities, John Hopkins Press, Baltimore

Bosselmann, P (2009) Urban Transformation: Understanding City Design and Form, Island Press, Washington DC

Bosselmann, P (1998) Representation of Places: Reality and Realism in City Design, University of California Press, Berkeley

Boudon, P (1969) Lived-in Architecture: Le Corbusier's 'Pessac' Revisited, MIT Press, Cambridge, Mass

Boyd, R (2006) The value of civility? Urban Studies, 43(5–6) 863–878

Boyer, M C (1996) Cybercities, MIT Press, Cambridge, Mass

Boyer, M C (1994) The City of Collective Memory, MIT Press, Cambridge, Mass

Boyer, M C (1993) The city of illusion: New York's public places', in Knox, P (1993) (Editor) The Restless Urban Landscape, Prentice Hall, Eaglewood, California, 111-126

Boyle, D (2004) Authenticity: Brands, Fakes, Spin and the Lust for Real Life, Harper, London

Brain, D (2008) Beyond the neighhbourhood: New Urbanism as civic renewal in Haas, T (2008) (editor), New Urbanism and Beyond: Designing cities for the future, Rizzoli International, New York, 249–254

Brain, D (2005) From good neighbours to sustainable cities: Social science and the social agenda of New Urbanism, International Regional Science Review, 28(2), 217–238

Brand, S (1994) How Buildings Learn: What Happens after They Are Built, Penguin Books, Harmondsworth

Braunfels, W (1988) Urban Design in Western Europe: Regime and Architecture 900-1900, University of Chicago Press, Chicago

Breheny, M (1997) Centrists, decentrists and compromisers: Views on the future of urban form', in Jenks, M; Burton, E & Williams, K (1997) (Editors) Compact Cities and Sustainability, E & F N Spon, London, 13–35

Breheny, M (1995) The compact city and transport energy consumption, Transactions of the Institute of British Geographers, 20(1) 81–101

Brenheny, M (1992a) (Editor) Sustainable Urban Development and Urban Form, Pion, London

Breheny, M (1992b) The contradictions of the compact city: A review, in Brenheny, M (1992) (Editor) Sustainable Urban Development and Urban Form, Pion, London

Brenner, N. & Theodore, N (2002) Cities and the geographies of "Actually Existing Neoliberalism", Antipode, 34(3), 349–379

Brill, M (1989) Transformation, nostalgia, and illusion in public life and public space, in Altman & Zube (1989) (editors) Public Places and Spaces, Plenum, New York, 7–29

Broadbent, G (1990) Emerging Concepts of Urban Space Design, Van Nostrand Reinhold, New York

Brolin, B C (1980) Architecture in Context: Fitting New Buildings with Old, Van Nostrand Reinhold, New York

Brower, S (2002) The sectors of the transect, Journal of Urban Design, 7 (3): 313–320

Brown, L, Dixon, D & Gillham, O (2009) Urban Design for an Urban Century, New Jersey, John Wiley & Sons

Bruegmann, R (2005) Sprawl: A Compact History, University of Chicago Press, Chicago

Buchanan, P (1988a) What city? A plea for place in the public realm, Architectural Review, No 1101 (November) 31–41

Buchanan, P (1988b) Facing up to facades, Architects Journal, 188(50) 21–56

Building Design Partnership (2002) Urban Design for Retail Environments, British Council of Shopping Centres, London

Building for Life (2008) Evaluating housing principles step by step, http://www.buildingforlife.org/

Building Research Establishment (BRE) (1999) An Assessment of the Police's Secured by Design Project, BRE, Watford

Building Research Establishment (BRE) (1990) BRE Digest 350: Climate and Site Development, BRE, Watford

Burton, E & Mitchell, L (2006) Inclusive Urban Design: Streets for Life, Architectural Pre Baird, G (2008) The New Urbanism and public space, in Haas, T (2008) (editor), New Urbanism and Beyond: Designing Cities for the Future, Rizzoli International, New York, 120–123

Biddulph, M; Franklin, B & Tait, M (2003) From concept to completion: A critical analysis of the urban village, Town Planning Review, 74(2), 165–193

Brain, D (2008) Beyond the neighbourhood: New Urbanism as civic renewal, in Haas, T (2008) (editor), New Urbanism and Beyond: Designing Cities for the Future, Rizzoli International, New York, 249–254

Butina Watson, G & Bentley, I (2007) Identity by Design, Architectural Press, Oxford

C

CABE (2009) Hallmarks of a Sustainable City, CABE, London

CABE Space (2008) Public Space Lessons: Designing and Planning Play, CABE, London

CABE (2008) Inclusion by Design: Equality, Diversity and the Built Environment CABE, London

CABE Space (2007) Living with Risk: Promoting Better Public Space Design, CABE, London

CABE (2006) The Principles of Inclusive Design (They Include You) CABE, London

CABE (2005) Design Coding: Testing Its in Use in England, CABE, London

CABE (2004a) Creating Successful Masterplans: A Guide for Clients, CABE, London

CABE (2004b) Local Authority Design Champions, CABE, London

CABE (2003a) Protecting Design Quality in Planning, CABE, London

CABE (2003b) The Councillor's Guide to Urban Design, CABE, London

CABE (2002) Paving the Way: How we can achieve clean, safe and attractive streets CABE, London (commissioned by CABE and ODPM, produced by Alan Baxter & Associates in association with EDAW)

Calthorpe, P (2005) New Urbanism: Principles or style? Fishamn, R (editor), Michigan Debates on Urbanism Volume II: New Urbanism, University of Michigan/Distributed Arts Press, New York, 15–38

Cadman, D & Topping, R (1995) Property Development (fourth edition) E & F N Spon, London

Cadman, D & Austin-Crowe, L (1991) Property Development (third edition edited by Topping, R & Avis, M) London, Chapman & Hall

CAG Consultants (1997) Sustainability in Development Control, a Research Report, Local Government Association, London

Calthorpe, P (1993) The Next American Metropolis: Ecology, Community and the American Dream, Princeton Architectural Press, New York

Calthorpe, P (1989) Pedestrian pockets: New strategies for suburban growth, in Kelbaugh, D (editor) The Pedestrian Pocket Book: A New Suburban Design Strategy, Princeton University Press, Princeton, 7–20

Campbell, H & Marshall, R (2002) Utilitarianism's bad breath? A re-evaluation of the public interest justification for Planning Theory, 1(2) 163–187

Campbell, K & Cowan, R (1999) Finding the Tools for Better Design, Planning, 1305, 12 February, 16–17

Caniggia, G & Maffel, G L (1984) NonEnComposizione Architettonica e Tipologia Edilizia: 2, Il Oprogettonell'Edilizia di Basi, Marsilio Editori, Venice

Caniggia, G & Maffel, G L (1979) NonEnComposizione Architettonica e Tipologia Edilizia: 1, Lettura dell'Edilizia di Base, Marsilio Editori, Venice

Cantacuzino, S (1994) What Makes a Good Building? An Inquiry by the Royal Fine Arts Commission, RFAC, London

Canter, D (1977) The Psychology of Place, Architectural Press, London

Carmona, M & Tiesdell, S (2007) (editors) Urban Design Reader, Architectural Press, Oxford

Carmona, M; Marshall S; & Stevens, Q (2006) Design codes, their use and potential, Progress in Planning, 65(4), 209–289

Carmona, M & Freeman, J (2005) The groundscraper: Exploring the contemporary reinterpretation, Journal of Urban Design, 10(3), 309–330

Carmona M; de Magalhaes C; Hammond, L; Blum, R & Yang L (2004) Living Places: Caring for Quality, Office of the Deputy Prime Minister, London

Carmona, M; Carmona, S; & Gallent, N (2001a) Working Together: A Guide for Planners and Housing Providers, Thomas Telford, London

Carmona, M; de Magalhaes, C & Edwards, M (2001b) The Value of Urban Design, CABE, London

Carmona, M & de Magalhaes, C (2008) Public Space: The Management Dimension, Routledge, London

Carmona, M & de Magalhaes, C (2006) Public space management – Present and potential, Journal of Environmental Planning & Management, 49(1), 75–99

Carmona, M; Marshall, S & Stevens, Q (2006) Design codes, their use and potential, Progress in Planning 65, (4)

Carmona, M; Punter, J & Chapman, D (2002) From Design Policy to Design Quality, the Treatment of Design in Community Strategies, Local Development Frameworks and Action Plans, Thomas Telford, London

Carmona, M & Sieh, L (2004) Measuring Quality in Planning, Managing the Performance Process, Spon Press, London

Carmona, M & Sieh, L (2005) Performance measurement innovation in English planning authorities, Planning Theory & Practice, 6(3), 303–333

Carmona, M (2009a) Design coding and the creative, market and regulatory tyrannies of practice Urban Studies, 46(12), 1–25

Carmona, M (2009b) Sustainable urban design: Definitions and delivery, International Journal for Sustainable Development, 12(1), 48–71

Carmona, M (2009c) The Isle of Dogs: Four waves, twelve plans, 30+ years, and a renaissance … of sorts, Progress in Planning, 71(3), 87–151

Carmona, M (2006) Designing mega-projects in Hong Kong: Reflections from an academic accomplice, Journal of Urban Design, 11(1), 105–124

Carmona, M (2001) Housing Design Quality: Through Policy, Guidance and Review, Spon Press, London

Carmona, M (1998a) Design control-bridging the professional divide, part 2: A new consensus Journal of Urban Design, 3(3), 331–358

Carmona, M (1998b) Urban design and planning practice Greed, C & Roberts, M Introducing Urban Design: Interventions and Responses, Harlow, Longman

Carmona, M (1996) Sustainable urban design: The local plan agenda, Urban Design Quarterly 57, 18–22

Carr, S; Francis, M; Rivlin, L G; & Stone, A M (1992) Public Space, Cambridge University Press, Cambridge

Carter, S L (1998) Civility: Manners, Morals and the Etiquette of Democracy, Harper Perennial, London

Castells, M (1977) The Urban Question – A Marxist Approach, Edwin Arnold, London

Castells, M (1991) The Informational City, Blackwell, Oxford

Cavanagh, S (1998) Women and the urban environment in Greed C and Roberts M, (1998) (editors) Introducing Urban Design: Interventions and Responses, Longman, Harlow

Centre for Livable Communities (1999) Street Design Guidelines for Healthy Neighbourhoods, Local Government Commission, Sacramento

CERTU (2001) NonEnAccidents en Milieu Urbain: Sorties de chaussée et chocs contre obstacles latéraux, Centre d'études sure les réseaux, les transports, l'urbanisme et les constructions publiques, Lyon

Chase, JL; Crawford, M & Kaliski, J (2008) Everyday Urbanism (second edition), The Monacelli Press, New York

Chaplin, S (2007) Places, in Evans B & McDonald F (Editors) Learning from Place 1, RIBA Publishing, London, 104–121

Chapman, D & Larkham, P (1994) Understanding Urban Design, an Introduction to the Process of Urban Change, University of Central England, Birmingham

Chase, JL; Crawford, M & Kaliski, J (1999) Everyday Urbanism, The Monacelli Press, New York

Chase, J L (2008) The space formerly known as parking, in Chase, JL; Crawford, M & Kaliski, J (2008) Everyday Urbanism (second edition), The Monacelli Press, New York, 194–199

Chatterton, P & Hollands, R (2002) Theorising urban playscapes: Producing, regulating and consuming youthful nightlife city spaces, Urban Studies, 39(1) 95–116

Chase, J; Crawford, M & Kaliski, J (2008) Everyday Urbanism (second edition), Monacelli Press, New York

Chaven, A; Peralta, C & Steins, C (2007) (editors) Planetizen Contemporary Debates in Urban Planning, Island Press, Washington

Chermayeff, S & Alexander, C (1963) Community and Privacy, Pelican, Harmondsworth

Cheshire, P (2006) Resurgent cities: Urban myths and policy hubris: What we need to know, Urban Studies 43(8), 1231–1246

Chih-Feng Shu, S (2000) Housing layout and crime vulnerability, Urban Design International, 5(2), 177–188

Childs, M C (2009) Civic concinnity Journal of Urban Design, 14(2), 131–145

Childs, M C (2004) Squares: A Public Place Design Guide for Urbanists, University of New Mexico Press, Albuquerque

Clarke, P (2009) Urban planning and design', in Ritchie A Thomas R (2009) Sustainable Urban Design – An Environmental Approach (second edition) Taylor & Francis, London, 12–20

Clarke, RVG (Editor) (1992) Situational Crime Prevention: Successful Case Studies, Harrow & Heston, New York

Clifford, S & King, A (1993) Local Distinctiveness: Place, Particularity and Identity, Common Ground, London

Cohen, E (1988) Authenticity and commoditisation in tourism, Annals of Tourism Research, 15(3), 371–386

Coleman, A (1985) Utopia on Trial: Vision and Reality in Planned Housing, Shipman, London

Collins, G R & Collins, C C (1965) Translators' Preface', in Sitte, C (1889) City Planning According to Artistic Principles, (translated by Collins, G R & Collins, C C, 1965) Phaidon Press, London, ix-xiv

Colomb, C (2007) Unpacking new labour's 'Urban Renaissance' agenda: Towards a socially sustainable reurbanization of British cities? Planning Practice & Research, 22(1), 1–24

Commission of the European Communities (CEC) (1990) Green Paper on the Urban Environment, EUR 12902, CEC, Brussels

Condon, PM (2008) Design Charrettes for Sustainable Communities, Island Press, Washington DC

Congress for the New Urbanism (no date) Charter for the New Urbanism, <http://www.cnu org/charter html>

Conrads, U (1964) Programmes and Manifestos of Twentieth Century Architecture, Lund Humphries, London

Conway, H & Roenisch, R (1994) Understanding Architecture: An Introduction to Architecture and Architectural History, Routledge, London

Conzen, M P (1960) Alnwick: A study in town plan analysis', Transactions of the Institute of British Geographers, 27(1), 1−122

Cook, R (1980) Zoning for Downtown Urban Design, Lexington Books, New York

Corner, J (2009) Terra fluxus, in Waldheim, C (2009) (editor) The Landscape Urbanism Reader, Princeton Architectural Press, New York, 21−34

Cornish, D B & Clarke, R V G (2003) Opportunities, precipitators and criminal decisions: A reply to Wortley's criticism of situational crime prevention', Crime Prevention Studies, 16, 41−96

Council for the Protection of Rural England (CPRE) (2001) Compact Sustainable Communities, CPRE, London

Countryside Commission & English Nature (1997) The Character of England: Landscape, Wildlife & Natural Features, English Nature, Peterborough

Cowan, R (2004) A Dictionary of Urbanism, Streetwise, London

Cowan, R (2002) Urban Design Guidance: Urban Design Frameworks, Development Briefs and Masterplans, Thomas Telford, London

Cowan, R (2001a) Responding to the challenge, Planning, 1413, 6th April, p 9

Cowan, R (2001b) Arm Yourself with a Placecheck: A Users' Guide, Urban Design Alliance, London

Cowan, R (2000) Beyond the myths on urban design', The Planner, 17 November, p24

Cowan, R (1997) The Connected City, Urban Initiatives, London

Cowan, R (1995) The Cities Design Forgot, Urban Initiatives, London

Crane, P (2000) Young People and Public Space: Developing Inclusive Policy and Practice, School of Human Services, Queensland University of Technology

Crang, M (1998) Cultural Geography, Routledge, London

Crawford, M (2008a) Introduction, in Chase, J L; Crawford, M & Kaliski, J (2008) Everyday Urbanism (second edition), The Monacelli Press, New York, 6−11

Crawford, M (2008b) Preface: The current state of everyday urbanism', in Chase, J L; Crawford, M & Kaliski, J (2008) Everyday Urbanism (second edition), The Monacelli Press, New York, 12−15

Cullen, G (1971) The Concise Townscape, Architectural Press, London

Cullen, G (1967) Notation, Alcan, London

Cullen, G (1961) Townscape, Architectural Press, London

Cullingworth, B (1999) British Planning, 50 Years of Urban and Regional Policy, The Athlone Press, London

Cullingworth, B (1997) Planning in the USA: Policies, Issues and Processes, Routledge, London

Curdes, G (1993) Spatial organisation of towns at the level of the smallest urban unit: plots and buildings', in Montanari, A; Curdes, G & Forsyth, L (Editors) Urban Landscape Dynamics: A Multi-level Innovation Process, Avebury, Aldershot, 281−294

Cunningham, C & Jones, M (1999) The playground: A Confession of failure?' Built Environment, 25(1), 11−17

Cuthbert, A R (2007) Urban design: Requiem for an era − Review and critique of the last 50 years, Urban Design International, 12, 177−223

Cuthbert, A R (2006) The Form of Cities: Political Economy and Urban Design, Blackwell, Oxford

Cuthbert, A R (2003) (editor) Designing Cities: Critical Readings in Urban Design, Blackwell, Oxford

D

Dagenhart, R & Sawicki, D (1994) If urban design is everything, maybe it's nothing, Journal of Planning Education & Research, 13(2), 143−146

Dagenhart, R & Sawicki, D (1992) Architecture and planning: The divergence of two fields, Journal of Planning Education & Research, 21, 1−16

Darke, R (2000) Public participation, equal opportunities, planning policies and decisions, Allmendinger, P; Prior, A & Raemaekers, J (2000) (editors) Introduction to Planning Practice, Wiley, London, 385−412

Davis, CJ (2002) Street clutter: What can be done? Municipal Engineer, 151, 231−240

Davis, C (1997) Improving Design in the High Street, Architectural Press, Oxford

Davis, M (1998) Ecology of Fear: Los Angeles and the Imagination of Disaster, Picador, London

Davis, M (1990) City of Quartz: Excavating the Future in Los Angeles, Verso, London

Davison I (1995) Viewpoint: Do we need cities any more? Town Planning Review, 66(1) iii-vi

Dawkins, R (1996) Climbing Mount Improbable, Viking, London

Day, K (1999) Introducing gender to the critique of privatised public space, Journal of Urban Design, 4(2), 155−178

DCLG/DoT (Department for Communities and Local Government/ Department for Transport)(2007) Manual for Streets, London, Thomas Telford − available from http://www.dft.gov.uk/pgr/ sustainable/manforstreets/

Dear, M (1995) Prolegomena to a postmodern urbanism, In Healey, P; Cameron, S; Davoudi, S; Graham, S; & Mandanipour, A (Editors) Managing Cities: The New Urban Context, John Wiley, Chichester, 27−44

Dear, M & Flusty, S (1999) The postmodern urban condition, in Featherstone, M & Lash, S (1999) (Editors) Spaces of Culture: City-Nation-World, Sage Publications, London, 64−85

Dear, M & Wolch, J (1989) How territory shapes social life, in Wolch, J & Dear, M (editors) The Power of Geography: How Territory Shapes Social Life, Unwin Hyman, Boston

Del Cerro Santamaria, G (2007) Bilbao: Basque Pathways to Globalisation, Elsevier, Oxford

Denby, E (1956) Oversprawl', Architectural Review, December, 424−430

Dennis, K & Urry, J (2009), After the Car, Polity Press, Cambridge

Denton-Thompson, M (2005) The environmental agenda: A personal view Harvey, S & Fieldhouse, K (Editors) The Cultured Landscape, Designing the Environment in the 21st Century, Routledge, London, 125−146

Department for Communities & Local Government (DCLG) (2006a) Preparing Design Codes: A Practice Manual, DCLG, London

Department for Communities & Local Government (DCLG) (2006b) Design Coding in Practice: An Evaluation, DCLG, London

Department for Environment, Food & Rural Affairs (DEFRA) (2006) An Environmental Behaviours Strategy for DEFRA, DEFRA, London

Department of Environment, Transport & Regions/Commission for Architecture & the Built Environment (DETR/CABE) (2000) By Design: Urban Design in the Planning System: Towards Better Practice, DETR, London

Department of Environment, Transport & Regions (DETR) (2000a) Best Value Performance Indicators 2001/2002, DETR, London

Department of Environment, Transport & Regions (DETR) (2000b) Survey of Urban Design Skills in Local Government, DETR, London

Department of Environment, Transport & Regions (DETR) (1999) Good Practice Guidance on Design in the Planning System, DETR, London

Department of Environment, Transport & Regions (DETR) (1998) Places, Streets and Movement: A Companion Guide to Design Bulletin 32 Residential Roads and Footpaths, DETR, London

Department of Environment (DoE) (1997) Planning Policy Guidance: General Policy and Principles (PPG1) The Stationary Office, London

Department of Environment (DoE) (1996) Analysis of Responses to the Discussion Document 'Quality in Town and Country', HMSO, London

Department of Environment (DoE) (1994) Quality in Town and Country: A Discussion Document, DoE, London

Department of Environment (DoE) (1992) Planning Policy Guidance Note 12: Development Plans and Regional Planning Guidance, HMSO, London

Department for Transport (DfT) (2007) Manual for Streets, Thomas Telford Publishing, London

Desai, M (2002) Marx's Revenge: The Resurgence of Capitalism and the Death of Statist Socialism, Verso, London

Desai, M (2000) Globalisation: Neither ideology nor utopia', Cambridge Review of International Affairs 14 (1), 16−31

Dickens, P G (1980) Social sciences and design theory Environment & Planning B: Planning & Design, 7, 353−360

Dines, N & Cattell, V (2006) Public Spaces, Social Relations and Well-being in East London, The Policy Press, Bristol

Dittmar, H & Ohland, G (2004) (editors) The New Transit Town: Best Practices in Transit-Oriented Development, Island Press, Washington DC

Dobbins, M (2009) Urban Design and People, John Wiley & Sons, New Jersey

Docherty, I & Shaw, J (2008) Traffic Jam: Ten Years of 'Sustainable' Transport in the UK, Policy Press, Bristol

Dovey, K (2010) Becoming Places, Urbanism/Architecture/Identity/Power, Routledge, London

Duany, A (2001) Three Cheers for Gentrification, American Enterprise, Washington DC

Dovey, K (1999) Framing Places: Mediating Power in Built Form, Routledge, London

Dovey, K (1990) The Pattern Language and its enemies, Design Studies, 11(1), 3−9

Downs, A (2001) What does "Smart Growth" really mean? Planning (American Planning Association) April

Duany, A & Brain, D (2005) Regulating as if humans matter: The transect and post-suburban planning, in Ben-Jospeh, E & Szold, T (editors) Regulating Places: Standards and the SHAPING of urban America, Routledge, London

Duany, A & Talen, E (2002) Transect planning, Journal of the American Planning Association, 68(3), 245−266

Duany, A & Plater-Zyberk, E with Speck, J (2000) Suburban Nation: The rise of Sprawl and the Decline of the American Dream, North Point Press, New York

Duany, A; Plater-Zyberk, E & Chellman, C (1989) New town ordinances and codes, Architectural Design, 59(5/6), 71−75

Duany, A & Plater-Zyberk, E (1991) Towns and Town-Making Principles, Rizzoli, New York

Duany, A & Talen, E (2002a) (editors) Special Issue: The transect Journal of Urban Design, 7(3)

Duany, A & Talen, E (2002b) Transect planning, Journal of the American Planning Association, 68(3), 245−266

Duffy, F (1990) Measuring building performance, Facilities, May

Dunham-Jones, E & Williamson, J (2009) Retrofitting Suburbia: Urban Design Solutions for Redesigning Suburbs, Wiley, New Jersey

Dunham-Jones, E (2008) New Urbanism: A forum, not a formula', in Haas, T (2008), New Urbanism and Beyond: Designing Cities for the Future, Rizzoli International, New York, 70-73

Dunphy, R T; Cervero, R; Dock, F C; McAvey, M; Porter, D R & Swenson, C J (2004) Developing Around Transit: Strategies and Solutions that Work, Urban Land Institute, Washington DC

Dunster, B; Simmons, C & Gilbert, B (2008) The ZED Book, Taylor & Francis, London

Dunster B (2006) What is the "New Ordinary"? Moor M & Rowland J (Editors) (2006) Urban Design Futures, Routledge, London, 122−134

Dutton, J A (2000) New American Urbanism: Re-forming the suburban Metropolis, Skira, Milan

Dyckman, J W (1962) The European motherland of American urban romanticism, Journal of the American Institute of Planners, 28(2), 277−281

E

EDAW (1998) Croydon 2020: The Thinking and the Vision Ideas Competition, London Borough of Croydon, London

Edwards, B (2000) Sustainable Housing, Principles & Practice, E & F N Spon, London

Edwards, B (1994) Understanding Architecture through Drawing, E & F N Spon, London

Elkin, T; McLaren, D & Hillman, M (1991) Reviving the City: Towards Sustainable Urban Development, Friends of the Earth, London

Ellin, N (2006) Integral Urbanism, Routledge, London

Ellin, N (2000) The postmodern built environment', in Knox, P & Ozolins, P (2000) (Editors) Design Professionals and the Built Environment: An Introduction, Wiley, London, 99-106

Ellin, N (1999) postmodern Urbanism (Revised edition) Blackwell, Oxford

Ellin, N (1997) (Editor) The Architecture of Fear, Princeton Architectural Press, London

Ellin, N (1996) postmodern Urbanism, Blackwell, Oxford

Ellis, C (2002) The New Urbanism: Critiques and rebuttals, Journal of Urban Design, 7(3), 261−291

English Heritage (2005) Guidance on Conservation Area Appraisals, English Heritage: London

English Heritage (2000a) Streets for All: A Guide to the Management of London's Streets, English Heritage, London

English Heritage (2000b) Power of Place: The Future of the Historic Environment, English Heritage, London

English Heritage (1998) Conservation-led Regeneration: The Work of English Heritage, English Heritage, London

English Heritage (1997) Sustaining the Historic Environment: New Perspectives in the Future, English Heritage, London

English Partnership/The Housing Corporation/Roger Evans Associates (2000), Urban Design Compendium Volume 2: Delivering Quality Places, EP/HC, London. Available from: http://www.englishpartnerships.co.uk/qualityandinnovationpublications.htm

English Partnerships (1998) Time for Design 2, English Partnerships, London

Engwicht, D (1999) Street Reclaiming, Creating Liveable Streets and Vibrant Communities, New Society Publishers, British Columbia

Entrikin, J N (1991) The Betweenness of Place: Towards a Geography of Modernity, John Hopkins University Press, Baltimore

Environmental Protection Agency (EPA) (2001) What is smart growth? EPA Fact Sheet, Environmental Protection Agency (United States) April 2001

Eppli, M & Tu, C (1997) Valuing the New Urbanism: The impact of New Urbanism on Prices of Single Family Houses, Urban Land Institute, Washington DC

Essex County Council (1973) A Guide to Residential Design, Colchester: Essex County Council

Essex Planning Officers Association (EPOS) (1997) A Design Guide for Residential and Mixed Use Areas, EPOA, Essex

Ewing R, Handy S, Brownson R, Clemente O & Winston E (2006) Identifying and measuring urban design qualities related to walk-ability, Journal of Physical Activity & Health, 3(1), 223−240

European Union Working Group on Urban Design for Sustainability (2004) Urban Design for Sustainability, <www.lebensministerium at>

Evans, G (2003), Hard-banding the cultural city − From Prado to Prada, Journal of Urban & Regional Research, 27, 417−440

Evans, G; Lercher, P; Meis, M; Ising, H; & Kofler, W (2001) Community noise exposure and stress in children, Journal of Acoustical Society of America, 109(3), 1023−1027

Ewing, R; Schmid, T; Killingsworth, R; Zlot, A & Raudenbush, S (2008) Relationship between urban sprawl and physical activity, obesity and morbidity', in Marzluff, J; Shulenberger, E; Endlicher, W; Alberti, M; Bradley, G; Ryan, C; Simon, U & ZumBrunnen (2008) (editors) Urban Ecology: An International Perspective on the Interaction Between Humans and Nature, Springer, New York

Ewing, R & Handy, S (2009) Measuring the unmeasurable: Urban design qualities related to walkability, Journal of Urban Design, 14(1), 65−84

F

Fainstein, S (1994) The City Builders: Property, Politics and Planning in London and New York, Oxford, Blackwell

Farr, D (2008) Sustainable Urbanism, Urban Design with Nature, New Jersey, John Wiley & Sons

Featherstone, M (1998) The Flaneur, the city and the virtual public realm, Urban Studies, 35(5/6), 909–925

Featherstone, M (1995) Undoing Culture: Globalisation, postmodernism and Identity, Sage Publications, London

Featherstone, M (1991) postmodernism and Consumer Culture, Sage Publications, London

Featherstone, M & Lash, S (1999) (Editors) Spaces of Culture: City-Nation-World, Sage Publications, London

Federal Highways Administration (1997) Flexibility in Highway Design, US Department of Transportation, Federal Highway Administration, Washington DC

Felson, M & Clarke, RV (1998, p 25) Opportunity makes the thief: Practical theory for crime prevention, Police Research Series Paper 98, Home Office, London

Field, F (2003) Neighbours from Hell: The Politics of Behaviour, Politico's Publishing, London

Fishman, R (2008a) New Urbanism in the age of re-urbanism', in Haas, T (2008), New Urbanism and Beyond: Designing Cities for the Future, Rizzoli International, New York, 296-298

Fishman, R (2008b) Foreword, in Kelbaugh, D & McCullough (2008) (editors), Writing Urbanism: A Design Reader, Routledge, London

Fishman, R (2005) (editor) Michigan Debates on Urbanism Volume II: New Urbanism, University of Michigan/Distributed Arts Press, New York

Fishman, R (1987) Bourgeois Utopias: The Rise and Fall of Suburbia, Basic Books, New York

Fitch, R (1990) Historic Preservation: Curatorial Management of the Built Environment, University Press of Virginia, Charlottesville

Fitzpatrick, T (1997) A tall of tall cities', The Guardian On-Line, 6 February p 9

Florida R (2002) The Rise of the Creative Class, Basic Books, New York

Flusty, S (2000) Thrashing downtown: Play as resistance to the spatial and representational regulation of Los Angeles, Cities, 17(2), 149–158

Flusty, S (1997) Building paranoia in Ellin, N (1997) (editor) Architecture of Fear, Princeton Architectural Press, New York, 47–59

Flusty, S (1994) Building Paranoia: The Proliferation of Interdictory Space and the Erosion of Spatial Justice, Los Angeles Forum for Architecture & urban Design, West Hollywood, CA

Flyvbjerg, B (2001) Making Social Science Matter: Why Social Inquiry Fails and How It Can Succeed Again, Cambridge University Press, Cambridge

Ford, L (2000) The Spaces Between Buildings, The John Hopkins University Press, London

Forester, J (1989) Planning in the Face of Power, University of California Press, Berkeley

Forsyth, A & Southworth, M (2008) Guest Editorial: Cities Afoot – Pedestrians, walkability and urban design, Journal of Urban Design, 13(1), 1–4

Francescato, D & Mebane, W (1973) How citizens view two great cities, in Downs, R & Stea, D (1973) (Editors) Image and Environment, Aldine, Chicago

Franck, K & Stevens, Q (2007) (editors) Loose Space: Diversity and Possibility in Urban Life, Routledge, London

Franck, KA (1984) Exorcising the ghost of physical determinism, Environment & Behaviour, 16, 411–435

Franco Suglia, S; Gryparis, A; Wright, R & Schwartz, J (2008) Association of black carbon with cognition among children in a prospective birth cohort study', American Journal of Epidemiology 167(3), 280–286

Frank, L & Engelke, P (2001) The built environment and human health activity patterns: Exploring the impacts of urban form on public health, Journal of Planning Literature, 16(2), 202–218

Frank, L; Andresen, M & Schmid, T (2004) Obesity relationships with community design, physical activity, and time spent in cars, American Journal of Preventive Medicine, 27(2), 87–96

Fraser, W (1993) Principles of Property Investment and Pricing (second edition) Palgrave Macmillan, Basingstoke

Frederick, M (2007) 101 Things I Learned in Architecture School, MIT Press, Cambridge, Mass

Frey H (1999) Designing the City, Towards a More Sustainable Urban Form, E & F N Spon, London

Frieden, B J & Sagalyn, L (1989) Downtown Inc.: How America Rebuilds Cities, MIT Press, Cambridge, Mass

Friedmann, J (1998) Planning theory revisited, European Planning Studies, 6(3), 245–253

Friedson, E (1994) Professionalism Reborn, University of Chicago, Chicago

Frumkin, H (2001) Urban Sprawl and Public Health, Public Health Reports, 117, May–June, 201–217

Futuyma, DJ (1997) Evolutionary Biology, Sinauer Associates, Inc., Publishers, Sunderland, MA

Fyfe, N; Bannister, J & Kearns, A (2006) (In)civily and the city, Urban Studies, 43(5–6), 853–862

Fyfe, N (1998) (editor) Images of the Street: Planning, Identity and Control in Public Space, Routledge, London

G

Galbraith, J K (1992) The Culture of Contentment, Penguin Books, London

Gallo, K; Owen, T; Easterling, D & Jamason, P (1999) Temperature trends of the US historical climatology network based on satellite-designated land use/land cover, Climate, 12, 1344–1348

Gans, H J (1968) People and Planning: Essays on Urban Problems and Solutions, Penguin, London

Gans, H J (1967) The Levittowners: Ways of Life and Politics in a New Suburban Community, Allen Lane & The Penguin Press, London

Gans, H J (1961) Planning and social life: friendship and neighbour relations in suburban communities Journal of the American Institute of Planners, 27(2), 134–40

Gans, H J (1962) The balanced community: Homogeneity or heterogeneity in residential areas? Journal of the American Institute of Planners, 27(3), 176–84

Garcia Almerall, P, Burns, M C, Roca Cladera, J (1999). An economics evolution model of the environmental quality of the city. In: Paper presented at the 6th European Real Estate Society (ERES) Conference, Athens, Greece, 23–25 June

Garreau J, (1999) Book review of Kay, J H (1997) Asphalt nation: How the automobile took over America and how we can take it back, in Journal of Urban Design, 4(2) 238–240

Garreau, J (1991) Edge City: Life on the New Frontier, Doubleday, London

Geddes, P (1915) Cities in Evolution, Williams & Norgate, London

Gehl, J (2000). There is much more to walking than walking. In: Keynote address to the first Walk21 international walking conference, London

Gehl, J (2008) Lively, attractive and safe cities – But how?' in Haas, T (2008), New Urbanism and Beyond: Designing Cities for the Future, Rizzoli International, New York, 106–108

Gehl, J (1996, (first published 1971) Life Between Buildings: Using Public Space (third edition) Arkitektens Forlag, Skive

Gehl, J & Gemozoe, L (1996) Public Spaces – Public Life, The Danish Architectural Press, Copenhagen

Gehl, J & Gemozoe, L (2000) New City Spaces, The Danish Architectural Press, Copenhagen

George, R V (1997) A procedural explanation for contemporary urban design, Journal of Urban Design, 2(2), 143–161

Gibberd, F (1953a; 1969) Town Design, Architectural Press, London

Gibberd, F (1953b) The design of residential areas', in Ministry of Housing & Local Government (MHLG) (1953) Design in Town & Village, HMSO, London

Giddens, A (2001) The Global Third Way Debate, Polity Press, Bristol

Giedion, S (1971) Space, Time and Architecture, fifth edition, Cambridge, Mass.: Harvard University Press

Gillespies (1995) Glasgow Public Realm, Strategy and Guidelines, Strathclyde Regional Council, Glasgow

Girardet, H (2004) Cities, People, Planet, Wiley-Academy, Chichester

Glass, R (1964) London: Aspects of Change, Centre for Urban Studies and MacGibbon & Kee, London

Golany, G (1996) Urban design morphology and thermal performance', Atmospheric Environment, 30(3), 455–465

Goodman, R (2001) 'A traveller in time: Understanding deterrents to walking to work', World Transport Policy & Practice, 7, 50–54

Gordon, I & Buck, N. (2005) Introduction: Cities in the new conventional wisdom, in Buck, N; Gordon, I, Harding, A & Turok, I (2005) (editors) Changing Cities: Rethinking Urban Competitiveness, Cohesion and Governance, Palgrave Macmillan, Basingstoke

Gordon, P & Richardson, H (1991) The commuting paradox – Evidence from the top twenty, Journal of the American Planning Association, 57(4), 416–420

Gordon, P; Richardson, H & Lue, M (1989) Gasoline consumption and cities – A reply, Journal of the American Planning Association, 55(3), 342–345

Gore, T & Nicholson, D (1991) Models of the land development process: A critical review, Environment & Planning A, 23, 705–730

Gosling D (2003) The Evolution of American Urban Design, Wiley-Academy, Chichester

Gosling, D (1996) Gordon Cullen: Visions of Urban Design, Academy Editions, London

Gosling, D & Maitland, B (1984) Concepts of Urban Design, Academy, London

Gospodini, A (2004) Urban morphology and place identity in European cities: Built heritage and innovative design', Journal of Urban Design, 9(2), 225–248

Gospodini, A (2002) European cities in competition and the new "uses" of urban design, Journal of Urban Design, 7(1), 59–73

Gottdiener, M (2001) The Theming of America: American Dreams, Media Fantasies, and Themed Environments, Westview Inc., New York

Gottdiener, M (1995) postmodern Semiotics: Material Culture and Forms of postmodern Life, Blackwell, Oxford

Government Office for London (1996) London's Urban Environment, Planning for Quality, HMSO, London

Government Office for Science (GOS) (2008) Powering Our Lives: Sustainable Energy and the Built Environment, GOS, London

Graham, S (2001) The spectre of the splintering metropolis, Cities, 18(6), 365–368

Graham, S & Marvin, S (2001) Splintering Urbanism: Networked Infrastructures, Technological Mobilities and the Urban Condition, Routledge, London

Graham, S (2008) Urban network architectures and the structuring of future cities, in Haas, T (2008), New Urbanism and Beyond: Designing Cities for the Future, Rizzoli International, New York, 212–218

Graham, S & Marvin, S (1999) Planning cybercities? Integrating telecommunications into urban planning? Town Planning Review, 70(1), 89–114

Graham, S & Marvin, S (1996) Telecommunications and the City: Electronic Spaces, Urban Places, Routledge, London

Greed, C & Roberts, M (editors) (1998) Introducing Urban Design: Interventions and Responses, Addison Wesley Longman, Harlow

Greed, C (2003) Inclusive Urban Design: Public Toilets, Architectural Press, Oxford

Greed, C (2007) A Place for Everyone? Gender Equality and Urban Planning A ReGender Briefing Paper, Oxfam, London

Gummer, J (1994) More Quality in Town and Country, Department of the Environment News Release 713, DoE, London

H

Haas, T (2008), New Urbanism and Beyond: Designing Cities for the Future, Rizzoli International, New York

Habermas, J (1979) Communication and the Evolution of Society (translated by McCarthy, T) Beacon Press, Boston

Habermas, J (1962) The Structural Transformation of the Public Sphere (translated by Burger, T & Lawrence, F), MIT Press, Cambridge, Mass

Habraken, NJ (2000) (edited by Teicher, J) The Structure of the Ordinary: Form and Control in the Built Environment, MIT Press, Cambridge, MA

Hague, R & Harrop, M (2004) Comparative Government and Politics: An introduction (sixth edition) Palgrave Macmillan, Basingstoke

Hajer, M & Reijndorp, A (2001) In Search of New Public Domain, NAI Publishers, Rotterdam

Hall, D (1991) Altogether misguided and dangerous – A review of Newman & Kenworthy (1989), Town & Country Planning, 60(11/12), 350–351

Hall, P (1998) Cities in Civilisations: Culture, Innovation and Urban Order, Weidenfeld & Nicolson, London

Hall P (1995) Planning and urban design in the 1990s Urban Design Quarterly, 56, 14–21

Hall, P & Imrie, R (1999) Architectural practices and disabling design in the built environment', Environment & Planning B: Planning & Design, 26, 409–425

Hall, P (1973) Great Planning Disasters, Weidenfeld, London

Hall, T (2008) Turning a Town Around: A Proactive Approach to Urban Design, Blackwell Publishing, Oxford

Hall, T (1998) Urban Geography, Routledge, London

Hancock, T & Duhl, L (1988) Promoting Health in the Urban Context, WHO Healthy Cities Papers No 1, Copenhagen, FADL

Hannigan, J (1998) Fantasy City: Pleasure and Profit in the postmodern Metropolis, Routledge, London

Harcourt, B E (2001) Illusion of Order: The false Promise of Broken Windows Policing, Harvard University Press, Cambridge, Mass

Hardy D (2005) Poundbury, the Town that Charles Built, Town & Country Planning Association, London

Hargroves, K C & Smith, MH (2005) The Natural Advantage of Nations, Earthscan Publications, London

Hart, S I & Spivak, A L (1993) The Elephant in the Bedroom: Automobile Dependence and Denial: Impacts on the Economy and Environment, New Paradigm Books, Pasadena

Harvey, D (2005) A Brief History of Neo-liberalism, Oxford University Press, Oxford

Harvey, D (1997) The New Urbanism and the communitarian trap, Harvard Design Magazine (Winter/Spring) 68–69

Harvey, D (1989a) From managerialism to entrepreneurialism: The transformation in urban governance in late capitalism', Geografiska Annaler Series B: Human Geography, 71(1), 3–17

Harvey, D (1990) The Condition of Postmodernity: An Enquiry into the Origins of Cultural Change, Basil Blackwell, Oxford

Harvey, D (1989b) The Urban Experience, Blackwell, Oxford

Hass-Klau, C (1990) The Pedestrian and City Traffic, Belhaven Press, London

Hass-Klau, C; Crampton, G; Dowland, C; & Nold, I (1999) Streets as Living Space: Helping public Spaces Play Their Proper Role, Landor, London

Hatherway, T (2000) Planning local movement systems' in Barton H (2000) (editor) Sustainable Communities – The Potential for Eco-Neighbourhoods, Earthscan, London, 216-229

Hawkes, D (2003) Civic dimensions: Public places, urban spaces: The dimensions of urban design – Book Review', Architectural Review, August

Haworth, G (2009) Coin street housing: The architecture of engagement, in Ritchie & Thomas (Editors)Sustainable Urban Design – An Environmental Approach, second edition, Taylor & Francis, London, 116–131

Haughton, G & Hunter, C (1994) Sustainable Cities, Jessica Kingsley Publishers, London

Hayden, D (2004) A Field Guide to Sprawl, WW Norton & Company, London

Hayden, D (1995) The Power of Place: Urban Landscapes as Public History, MIT Press, Cambridge, Mass

Hayden, D (1980) What would a non-sexist city be like? speculations on housing, urban design and human work', in Stimpson, S; Dixler, E; Nelson, M; & Yatrakis, K (1980) (editors) Women and the American City, Chicago University Press, Chicago, 266–281

Hayward, R (1993), Talking tissues, in Hayward, R & McGlynn, S (1993) (editors) Making Better Places: Urban Design Now, Architectural Press, Oxford, 24–29

Hayward, R & McGlynn, S (1993) (Editors) Making Better Places, Urban Design Now, Butterworths Architectural Press, Oxford

Healey, P (2006) Urban Complexity and Spatial Strategies: Towards a Relational Planning for Our Times, Routledge, London

Healey, P (1997) Collaborative Planning, Macmillan, London

Healey, P (1999) Institutionalist Analysis, communicative planning and shaping places', Journal of Planning Education & Research 19, 111–121

Healey, P (1992) An institutional model of the development process, Journal of Property Research, 9, 33–44

Healey, P (1991a) Models of the development process: A review Journal of Property Research, 8, 219–238

Healey, P & Barrett, S (1990) Structure and agency in land and property development processes: Some ideas for research, Urban Studies, 27, 89–104

Heath, G; Brownson, R; Kruger, J; Miles, R; Powell, K; Ramsey, L & the Task Force on Community Preventive Services (2006) The effectiveness of urban design and land use and transport policies and practices to increase physical activity: A systematic review', Journal of Physical Activity & Health, 3, Supplement 1, s55–s76

Heath, T (1997) The twenty-four hour city concept: A review of initiatives in British cities', Journal of Urban Design, 2(2), 193–204

Heath, T & Stickland, R (1997) Safer Cities: The twenty-four hour concept, in Oc, T & Tiesdell, S Safer City Centres: Reviving the Public Realm, Paul Chapman, London, 170-183

Hebbert, M (2008) Re-enclosure of the urban picturesque: Green space transformations in post modern urbanism, Town Planning Review, 79(1), 31–59

Hebbert, M (2006) Town planning versus urbanismo, Planning Perspectives, 21, 233–251

Hebbert, M (2005) Engineering, urbanism and the struggle for street design, Journal of Urban Design, 10(1), 39–59

Hebbert, M (2003) New Urbanism – The movement in Context, Built Environment 29(3), 193–209

Hebbert, M (1998) London: More by Fortune than Design, Chichester, John Wiley & Son

Hedges, C (2009) Empire of Illusion: The End of Literacy and the Triumph of the Spectacle, Nation Books, New York

Henneberry, J (1998) Development Process', course taught at the Department of Town and Regional Planning, University of Sheffield

Hess, P M (2009) Avenues or arterials: The struggle to change street building practices in Toronto, Canada', Journal of Urban Design 14(1), 1–28

Hiedegger, M (1969) Identity and Difference, Harper & Row, New York

Hiedegger, M (1962) Being and Time, Harper & Row, New York

Hillman, J (1990) Planning for Beauty, RFAC, London

Hillman, J (1988) A New Look for London, HMSO, London

Hillier B & Sahbaz O (2009) Crime and Urban Design: An Evidence-based Approach' in Cooper R, Evans G& Boyko C (2009) (editors) Designing Sustainable Cities, Wiley-Blackwell, Chichester

Hillier, B & Penn, A (2004a) Response to rejoinder to Hillier and Penn', Environment & Planning B: Planning & Design, 31(4), 501–511

Hillier, B (1996a) Space is the Machine, Cambridge University Press, Cambridge

Hillier, B (1996b) Cities as movement systems, Urban Design International, 1(1), 47–60

Hillier, B (1988) Against enclosure, in Teymur, N; Markus, T & Wooley, T (1988) (editors) Rehumanising Housing, Butterworths, London, 63–88

Hillier, B (1973) In defence of space, RIBA Journal, November, 539–544

Hillier, B; Penn, A; Hanson, J; Gajewski, T & Xu, J (1993) Natural movement: Or configuration and attraction in urban pedestrian movement', Environment & Planning B: Planning & Design, 20, 29–66

Hillier, B; Leaman, A; Stansall, P & Bedford, M (1986) space syntax, Environment & Planning B: Planning & Design, 13, 147–185

Hillier, B & Hanson, J (1984) The Social Logic of Space, Cambridge University Press, Cambridge

Hitchcock, H R & Johnson, P (1922) The International Style: Architecture Since 1922, W W Norton & Company, New York

Hobbs, D; Hall, S; Winlow, S; Lister, S; & Hadfield, P (2000) Bouncers: The Art and Economics of Intimidation, final report to ESRC Research Programme: Violence, University of Durham, Durham

Holden, A & Iveson, K (2003) Designs on the urban: New labour's urban renaissance and the spaces of citizenship, City, 7(1), 57–72

Holford, W G (1953) Design in town centres', in Ministry of Housing & Local Government (MHLG) (1953) Design in Town & Village, HMSO, London

Hollyoak, K (2002) Difficulties in providing access to brownfield sites and urban extensions, Municipal Engineer, 151, 117–124

Hont, I & Ignatieff, M (1983) Needs and justice in the wealth of nations: An introductory essay', in Hont, I & Ignatieff, M (1983) (editors) Wealth and Virtue: The Shaping of Political Economy in Scottish Enlightenment, Cambridge University Press, Cambridge, 1–44

Hope, T (1986) Crime, community and environment Journal of Environmental Psychology, 6(1) 65–78

Hopkins J (2005) Music-makers and the Dreamers of Dreams, in Harvey S & Hopkins R (2000) 'The food producing neighbourhood', in Barton H (Editor) (2000) Sustainable Communities – The Potential for Eco-Neighbourhoods, Earthscan, London, 199–215

Horan, T A (2000) Digital Places: Building Our City of Bits, Urban Land Institute, Washington

Hough, M (1984) City Form and Natural Process: Towards a new Urban Vernacular, Routledge, London

Howard E (1889) Tomorrow: A Peaceful Path to Real Reform, Swan Sonnenschein, London

Hubbard, P J (1992) Environment-behaviour studies and city design: A new agenda for research? Journal of Environmental Psychology, 12, 269–277

Hulme Regeneration Limited (1994) Rebuilding the City: A Guide to Development, Manchester City Council, Manchester

Huo, N (2001) The Effectiveness of Design Control in China, Unpublished PhD thesis, Glasgow, University of Strathclyde

Huxtable, AL (1997) The Unreal America: Architecture and Illusion, The New Press, New York

I

Imrie, R & Street, E (2006) Papers in 'The Codification and Regulation of Architects' Practices', Project Paper 3, The Attitudes of Architects Towards Planning Regulation and Control, Kings College London, London

Imrie, R & Hall, P (2001) Inclusive Design: Designing and Developing Accessible Environments, Spon Press, London

Isaac, D (1998) Property Investment, Macmillan, Basingstoke

Isaacs, R (2001) The subjective duration of time, Journal of Urban Design, 6(2), 109–127

Ittelson, WH (1978) Environmental perception and urban experience, Environment & Behaviour, 10, 193–213

Iveson, K (1998) Putting the public back into public space', Urban Policy & Research 16(1), 21–33

J

de Jonge, D (1962) Images of urban areas: Their structure and psychological foundations, Journal of the American Institute of Planners, 28, 266–276

Jackson, JB (1994) A Sense of Place, a Sense of Time, Yale University Press, New Haven

Jackson, K T (1985) Crabgrass Frontier: The Suburbanization of the United States. Oxford University Press, Oxford

Jackson, L (2003) The relationship of urban design to human health and condition, Landscape & Urban Planning, 64, 191–200

Jackson, R (2003) The impact of the built environment on health: An emerging field, American Journal of Public Health, 93(9), 1382–1383

Jacobs, A (1995) Great Streets, MIT Press, Cambridge, Mass

Jacobs, A; Macdonald, E & Rofé, Y (2002) The Boulevard Book, MIT Press, Cambridge, Mass

Jacobs, J (2000) The Nature of Economies, Random House, New York

Jacobs, J (1969) The Economy of Cities, Random House, New York

Jacobs, A B (1993) Great Streets, MIT Press, Cambridge, Mass

Jacobs, A & Appleyard, D (1987) Towards an urban design manifesto: A prologue Journal of the American Planning Association, 53(1), 112–120

Jacobs, J (1961, (1984 edition) The Death and Life of Great American Cities: The Failure of Modern Town Planning, Peregrine Books, London

Jabareen, YR (2006) Sustainable urban forms: Their typologies, models and concepts', Journal of Planning Education & Research 26(1), 38–52

Jackson, M (2004) Malt Whisky Companion (fifth edition), Dorling Kindersley, London

Jameson, F (1984) postmodernism or the cultural logic of late capitalism', New Left Review,146, 53–92

Jarvis, R (1994) Townscape revisited', Urban Design Quarterly, No 52, October, 15–30

Jarvis, R (1980) Urban environments as visual art or social setting, Town Planning Review, 51(1), 50–66

Jencks, C (2005) The Iconic Building: The Power of Enigma, Frances Lincoln, London

Jenkins, E J (2008) To Scale: One Hundred Urban Plans, Routledge, New York

Jencks, C (1990) The New Moderns: From Late to Neo-modernism, Academy Editions, London

Jencks, C (1986) What is postmodernism? St Martins Press, London

Jencks, C (1984) Late Modern Architecture, Rizzoli, London

Jencks, C (1980) The architectural sign, in Broadbent, G; Bunt, R & Jencks, C (1983) (editors) Signs, Symbols and Architecture, John Wiley, Chichester, 71–118

Jencks, C (1977) The Language of Post Modern Architecture, Rizzoli, London

Jencks, C (1969) (Editor) Meaning in Architecture, The Cresset Press, London

Jenks, M; Burton, E & Williams, K(1997) (Editors) Compact Cities and Sustainability, E & F N Spon, London

Jenks, M; Burton, E & Williams, K (1997) Compact cities and sustainability: An introduction', in Jenks, M; Burton, E & Williams, K (1997) (Editors) Compact Cities and Sustainability, E & F N Spon, London, 3–8

Jenks, M; Burton, E & Williams, K (1996) The Compact City: A Sustainable Urban Form? E & F N Spon, London

Jenks, M (1988) Housing problems and the dangers of certainty, in Teymur, N; Markus, T A; & Woolley, T (editors) Rehumanising Housing, Butterworth, London, 53–60

Jessop, B (1999) Reflections on globalisation and its (il)logics in Dicken, P; Olds, K; Kelly, P; & Yeung, H. (1999) Globalisation and the Asia-Pacifica: Contested Territories, Routledge, London, 19-37

Jiven, G & Larkham, P J (2003) Sense of place, authenticity and character: A commentary, Journal of Urban Design, 8(1), 67–82

JMP Consultants (1995) Travel to Food Superstores, JMP Consultants, London

Johns, R (2001) Skateboard city', Landscape Design, The Compact City, A Sustainable Urban Form? 303, 42–44

Johnston, B D (2008) Planning for child pedestrians: Issues of health, safety and social justice, Journal of Urban Design, 13(1), 141–146

Jones, C & Watson, C (1996) Urban regeneration and sustainable markets, Urban Studies, 33(7), 1129–1140

Jones, M (2003) Safe streets – Challenging the principles, Municipal Engineer, 156, 191–195

Jones, M (2001) Promoting cycling in the UK – Problems experienced by the practitioners, World Transport Policy & Practice, 7(2), 7–12

Jones, P; Boujenko N; & Marshall, S (2007) Link and Place: A Guide to Street Planning and Design, Landor Books, London

Jones, T & Newburn, T (2002) The transformation of policing? Understanding current trends in policing systems', British Journal of Criminology 42(1), 129–146

K

Kashef, M (2008) Architects and planners approaches to urban form and design in the Toronto region: A comparative analysis Geoforum 39, 414–437

Kaliski, J (2008a) The present city and the practice of city design', in Chase, J L; Crawford, M & Kaliski, J (2008) Everyday Urbanism (second edition), The Monacelli Press, New York, 88-109

Kaliski, J (2008b) Everyday urban design: Towards default urbanism and/ or urbanism by design', in Chase, J L; Crawford, M & Kaliski, J (2008) Everyday Urbanism (second edition), The Monacelli Press, New York, 216-220

Katz, P (1994) The New Urbanism: Towards an Architecture of Community, McGraw-Hill, New York

Kaplan, S (1987) Aesthetics, affect and cognition: Environmental preferences from an evolutionary perspective, Environment & Behaviour, 191(1), 12

Kaplan, S & Kaplan, R (1982) Cognition and Environment: Functioning in an Uncertain World, Praeger, New York

Kay, J H (1997) Asphalt Nation: How the Automobile Took Over America and How We Can Take It Back, Crown, New York

Kayden, J S (2000) Privately Owned Public Space: The New York Experience, John Wiley & Sons, London

Keates, S & Clarkson J (2004) Countering Design Exclusion: An Introduction to Inclusive Design, Springer, London

Keating, M (1988) The City That Refused to Die: Glasgow – The Politics of Urban Regeneration, Mercat Press, Glasgow

Kelbaugh, D & McCullough (2008) (editors), Writing Urbanism: A Design Reader, Routledge, London

Kelbaugh, D (2008a) Further thoughts on the three urbanisms in Kelbaugh, D and McCullough, K K (2008) (editors) Writing Urbanism: A Design Reader, Routledge, London, 105–114

Kelbaugh, D (2008b) Three urbanisms: New, everyday and post', in Haas, T (2008) (editor) New Urbanism and Beyond, Rizzoli, New York, 40–47

Kelbaugh, D (2002) Repairing the American Metropolis: Common Place Revisited, University of Washington Press, Seattle, WA

Kelbaugh, D (1997) Common Place: Toward Neighbourhood and Regional Design, University of Washington, Seattle

Kelling, G L (1987) Acquiring a taste for order: The community and the police Crime & Delinquency, 33(1) 90–102

Kidder, R M (1995) How Good People Make Tough Choices: Resolving the Dilemmas of Ethical Living, Simon & Schuster, New York

Kindsvatter, D & Van Grossman, G (1994) What is urban design? Urban Design Quarterly, Spring/Autumn, 9–12

King, R in Knox, P & Ozolins, P (2000) The built environment', in Knox, P & Ozolins, P (2000) (Editors) Design Professionals and the Built Environment: An Introduction, Wiley, London

King, A (2004) Spaces of Global Culture: Architecture Urbanism Identity, Routledge, London

Kintrea, K J & Atkinson, R (2000) Owner-occupation, social mix and neighbourhood impacts, Policy & Politics, 28(1), 93–108

Klosterman, R E (1985) Arguments for and against planning, Town Planning Review, 56, 5–20

Knox, P & McCarthy, L (2005) Urbanization: An Introduction to Urban Geography (second edition), Pearson/Prentice Hall,Upper Saddle River, New Jersey

Knox, P & Marston, S A (1998) Places and Regions in a Global Context: Human Geography, Prentice Hall, New York

Knox, P & Ozolins, P (2000) The built environment', in Knox, P & Ozolins, P (2000) (Editors) Design Professionals and the Built Environment: An Introduction, Wiley, London, 3–10

Knox, P & Pinch, S (2000) Urban Social Geography: An Introduction, Prentice Hall, Harlow

Knox, P (2005) Creating ordinary places: Slow cities in a fast world, Journal of Urban Design, 10(1), 1–12

Knox, P (1994) Urbanisation, Prentice Hall, Englewood Cliffs, New Jersey

Knox, P (1993) The Restless Urban Landscape, Prentice Hall, Eaglewood Cliffs, New Jersey

Knox, P (1987) The social production of the built environment: Architects, architecture and the post-Modern city, Progress in Human Geography, 11, 354–378

Kohn, M (2004) Brave New Neighbourhoods: The Privatisation of Public Space, Routledge, London

Komossa, S; Meyer, H; Risselada, M; Thomaes, S; & Jutten, N (2005) Atlas of the Dutch Urban Block, Thoth Uitgeverij, Netherlands

Koolhaas, R (1995) Whatever happened to urbanism? Koolhaas, R & Mau, B (1995) (editors), S, M, L, X L, Monacelli, New York

Kostof, S (1992) The City Assembled: The Elements of Urban Form Through History, Thames & Hudson, London

Kostof, S (1991) The City Shaped: Urban Patterns and Meanings Throughout History, Thames & Hudson, London

Kotkin, J (2001) The New Geography: How the Digital Revolution is Reshaping the American Landscape, Random House, New York

Kreitzman, L (1999) The 24 Hour Society, Profile Books, London

Krieger, A & Saunders, W S (2009) (editors) Urban Design, University of Minnesota Press, Minneapolis

Krieger, A (2009a) Introduction: A frame of mind, in Krieger, A & Saunders, WS (2009) (editors) Urban Design, University of Minnesota Press, Minneapolis & London, vii-xix

Krieger, A (2009b) Where and how does urban design happen? in Krieger, A & Saunders, WS (2009) (editors) Urban Design, University of Minnesota Press, Minneapolis & London, 113–130

Krieger, A (1995) Reinventing public space', Architectural Record 183 (6), 76–77

Krier, L (2009) The Architecture of Community (edited by Thadani, D A & Hetzel, P J), Island Press, Washington DC

Krier, L (1990) Urban components, in Papadakis, A & Watson, H (1990) (editors) New Classicism: Omnibus Edition, Academy Editions, London, 196–211

Krier, L (1987) 'Tradition–Modernity–Modernism: Some necessary explanations, Architectural Design, 57(1/2), 38–43

Krier, L (1984) Houses, places, cities', Architectural Design, 54(7/8), 43–49

Krier, L (1979) The cities within a city, Architectural Design, 49(1), 19–32

Krier, L (1978a) The reconstruction of the city', in Deleroy, R L (1978) Rational Architecture, Archives d'Architecture Moderne, Brussels, 38–44

Krier, L (1978b) Urban transformations Architectural Design, 48(4), 219–266

Krier, R (1990) Typological elements of the concept of urban space, in Papadakis, A & Watson, H (1990) (editors) New Classicism: Omnibus Edition, Academy Editions, London, 212–219

Krier, R 1979; (first published in German in 1975) Urban Space, Academy Editions, London

Kropf, K (2006) Against the perimeter block: A morphological critique', Urban Design, Winter, 97, 12–13

Kropf, K S (1996) An alternative approach to zoning in France: Typology, historical character and development control, European Planning Studies, 4(6), 717–737

Kuh, D J L & Cooper, C (1992) Physical activity at 36 years: Patterns and childhood predictors in a longitudinal study, Journal of Epidemiology & Community Health, 46, 114–119

Kunstler, J H (2005) The Long Emergency: Surviving the End of Oil, Climate Change and Other Converging Catastrophes of the Twenty-First Century, Grove Press, New York

Kunstler, J H (1996) Home from Nowhere: Remaking our Everyday World for the 21st Century, Simon & Schuster, New York

Kunstler, JH (1993) The Geography of Nowhere: The Rise and Decline of America's Man-Made Landscape, Simon & Schuster, New York

L

LaFrage, A (2000) (editor) The Essential William H Whyte, Fordham University Press, New York

Lagopoulos, AP (1993) Psotmodernism, geography and the social semiotics of space', Environment & Planning D: Society & Space, 11, 255–278

Lai, R (1994) Can the process of architectural design review withstand constitutional scrutiny? in Case Scheer B & Preiser W (1994) (editors) Design Review, Challenging Urban Aesthetic Control, New York, Chapman & Hall

Lai, R T (1988) Law in Urban Design and Planning, Van Nostrand Reinhold, New York

Lane, R J (2000) Jean Baudrillard, Routledge, London

Lang, J (2005) Urban Design – A Typology of Procedures and Products, Oxford, Architectural Press

Lang, J (1996) Implementing urban design in America: Project types and methodological implications, Journal of Urban Design, 1(1), 7–22

Lang, J (1994) Urban Design: The American Experience, Van Nostrand Reinhold, New York

Lang, J (1989) Psychology and Architecture', Penn in Ink Newsletter of Graduate School of Fine Arts, University of Pennsylvania, Fall, 10–11

Lang, J (1987) Creating Architectural Theory: The Role of the Behavioural Sciences in Environmental Theory, Van Nostrand Reinhold, New York

Lang, R E (2003a) Edgeless Cities: Exploring the Elusive Metropolis, Brookings Institution Press, Washington DC

Lang, R (2003b) Are the Boomburbs Still Booming? Fannie Mae Foundation Census Note 15, Fannie Mae, Washington DC

Lang, R E & LeFurgy, J B (2003) Edgeless cities: Examining the non-centered metropolis, Housing Policy Debate 14(3), 427–460

Lang, R E & LeFurgy, J B (2007) Boomburbs: The Rise of America's Accidental Cities, Brookings Institution Press, Washington DC

Lang, R & Simmons, P (2001) Boomburbs: The Emergence of Large, Fast-Growing Suburban Cities in the United States' Fannie Mae Foundation Census Note 06, Fannie Mae, Washington DC

Langdon, P (1994) A Better Place to Live: Reshaping the American Suburb, The University of Massachusetts Press, Amherst

Langdon, P (1992) How Portland does it: A city that protects its thriving, civil core Atlantic Monthly, 270(5) 134–141

Lange, B (1997) The Colours of Copenhagen, Danish Architectural Press, Copenhagen

Larice, M & Macdonald, E (2006) (editors) The Urban Design Reader, Routledge, London

Larkham, P (1996a) Settlements and growth', in Chapman, D (1996) (editor) Neighbourhoods and Places, E & F N Spon, London, 30–59

Larkham, P (1996b) Conservation and the City, Routledge, London

Lash, S & Urry, J (1994) Economies of Signs and Space, Sage, London

Laurie, M (1986) An Introduction to Landscape Architecture (second edition) Elsevier, Oxford

Lawrence, RJ (1987) Houses, Dwellings and Homes: Design, Theory, Research and Practice, Wiley, New York

Lawson, B (2001) The Language of Space, Architectural Press, London

Lawson, B (1994) How Designers Think: The Design Process Demystified, (second edition) Butterworth Architecture, Oxford

Lawson, B (1980) How Designers Think: The Design Process Demystified, Butterworth Architecture, Oxford

Layard, A; Davoudi, S; & Batty, S (2001) Planning for a Sustainable Future, Spon Press, London

Le Corbusier, (1927) Towards a New Architecture (1970 edition) Architectural Press, London

Ledrut, R (1986) Speech and the silence of the city', in Gottdiener, M & Langopoulos, A (1986) The City and the Sign: An Introduction to Urban Semiotics, Columbia University Press, New York

Ledrut, R (1973) NonEnLes images de la ville, Anthropos, Paris

Lee, T (1965) Urban neighbourhood as a socio-spatial schema', from Proshansky, H M; Ittleson, W H; & Rivlin, L G (Editors) (1970) Environmental Psychology: Man and His Physical Setting, Holt Rinehart & Winston, New York, 349–370

Lefebvre, H (2004) Rhythmanalysis: Space, Time and Everyday Life, Continuum, London

Lefebvre, H (1991) The Production of Space, Basil Blackwell, London

Lefebrve, H (1968) The Right to the City', in Lefebrve, H (1996) (edited and translated by Kofman, E & Lebas, E) Writing on Cities, Blackwell, Oxford, 63–181

Leinberger, C (2008) The Option of Urbanism: Investing in a New American Dream, Island Press, Washington DC

Leinberger, C B (2005) The need for alternatives to the nineteen standard real estate product types, Places 17(2), 24–29

Leinberger, C B (1998) The market and metropolitanism', The Brookings Review, Fall, 1–25

Levy, R (1998) The visualisation of the street, computer modelling and urban design, in Fyfe N (1998) (editor) Images of the Street, Planning, Identity and Control in Public Space, Routledge, London

Lewis, R K (1998) Architect? A Candid Guide to the Profession (Revised edition) MIT Press, Cambridge, Mass

Llewelyn-Davies (2000) Urban Design Compendium, English Partnerships/The Housing Corporation, London

Lichfield, N (1988) Economics in Urban Conservation, Cambridge University Press, Cambridge

Linden, A & Billingham, J (1998) History of the Urban design group, in Urban Design Group (1998) Urban Design Source Book, UDG, Oxford, 40–43

Lindsey, G; Wilson, J; Yang, J A; & Alexa, C (2008) Urban greenways, trail characteristics and trail use: Implications for design', Journal of Urban Design, 13(1), 53–80

Littlefair, P J; Santamouris, M; Alvarez, S; Dupagne, A; Hall, D; Teller, J; Coronel, J F & Papanikolaou, N (2000) Environmental Site Layout Planning: Solar Access, Microclimate and Passive Cooling in Urban Areas, BRE/European Commission JOULE/DETR, London

Littlefair, PJ (1991) Site Layout Planning for Daylight and Sunlight: A Guide to Good Practice, Building Research Establishment, Watford

Llewelyn-Davies (2007) Urban Design Compendium 1 (second edition), English Partnerships & The Housing Corporation, London

Llewelyn-Davies, Weekes, Forestier-Walker & Bor, W (1976) Design Guidance Survey: Report on a Survey of Local Authority Guidance for Private Residential Development, DoE & Housing Research Federation, HMSO, London

Lloyd-Jones, T (1998) The scope of urban design', in Greed, C & Roberts, M (1998) Introducing Urban Design: Intervention and Responses, Longman, Harlow

Lofland, L (1973) A World of Strangers: Order and Action in Urban Public Space, Basic Books, New York

Logan, J R & Molotch, H L (1987) Urban Fortunes: The Political Economy of Place, Berkeley, California, University of California Press

London Docklands Development Corporation (1982) Isle of Dogs Development and Design Guide, LDDC Publications, London

Loukaitou-Sideris, A & Banerjee, T (1998) Urban Design Downtown: Poetics and Politics of Form, University of California Press, Berkeley, CA

Loukaitou-Sideris, A (2010) A new found popularity for TODs? Lessons from southern California, Journal of Urban Design, 15(1), 105–124

Loukaitou-Sideris, A (1996) Cracks in the city: Addressing the constraints and potentials of urban design' Journal of Urban Design, 1(1), 91–106

Loukaitou-Sideris, A (1995) Urban form and social context: Cultural differentiation in the uses of urban parks, Journal of Planning Education & Research, 14(1), 89–102

Lovatt, A & O'Connor, J (1995) Cities and the night time economy, Planning Practice & Research, 10 (2 May), 127–134

Love, T (2009) Urban design after Battery Park City: Opportunities for variety and vitality, in Krieger, A & Saunders, WS (2009) (editors) Urban Design, University of Minnesota Press, Minneapolis, 208–226

Low, S & Smith, N (2006) Introduction: The imperative of public space', in Low, S & Smith, N (2006) (editors) The Politics of Public Space, Routledge, London, 1–16

Low, S & Smith, N (2006) (editors) The Politics of Public Space, Routledge, New York

Lowe, R & Oreszczyn, T (2008) Regulatory standards and barriers to improved performance for housing', Energy Policy (special issue), 36(12), 4475–4481

Lowenthal, D (1981) Introduction', from Lowenthal, D & Binney, M (1981) Our Past Before Us – Why do We Save It, Temple Smith, London, 9–16

Loyer, F (1988) Paris Nineteenth Century: Architecture and Urbanism, New York

Lucan, J (1990) OMA – Rem Koolhaas: Architecture 1970–1990, Princeton Architectural Press, New York

Lukes, S (1975) Power: A Radical View, Macmillan, Basingstoke

Lundgren Alm E (2003) Visualizing urban green qualities in Sweden: A way of raising the quality of the regional landscape, Built Environment 29(4), 296–305

Lynch, K (1984) Reconsidering the image of the city, in Banjeree, T & Southworth, M (1991) (Editors) City Sense and City Design: Writings and Projects of Kevin Lynch, MIT Press, Cambridge, Mass., 247–256

Lynch, K (1981) A Theory of Good City Form, MIT Press, Cambridge, Mass

Lynch, K (1976) Managing the Sense of a Region, MIT Press, Cambridge, Mass

Lynch, K (1972) What Time is This Place? MIT Press, Cambridge, Mass

Lynch, K (1965) The openness of open space, in Banerjee, T & Southworth, M (1991) (Editors) City Sense and City Design: Writings and Projects of Kevin Lynch, MIT Press, Cambridge, Mass., 396–412

Lynch, K (1960) The Image of the City, MIT Press, Cambridge, Mass

Lynch, K & Carr, S (1979) Open space: Freedom and control, in Banerjee, T & Southworth, M (1991) (Editors) City Sense and City Design: Writings and Projects of Kevin Lynch, MIT Press, Cambridge, Mass., 413–417

Lynch, K & Hack, G 1994, (first published 1984) Site Planning, MIT Press, Cambridge Mass

M

MacCormac, R (1987) Fitting in offices', Architectural Review, May 1987, 62–67

MacCormac, R (1983) Urban reform: MacCormac's manifesto, Architects Journal, 15 June, 59–72

MacCormac, R (1978) Housing and the Dilemma of Style', Architectural Review, 163, April, 203–6

McGlynn, S & Murrain, P (1994) The politics of urban design, Planning Practice & Research, 9, 311–320

McGuckin, N & Murakami, E (1999) Examining Trip-chaining behaviour: Comparison of travel by men and women, Transportation Research Record, Journal of the Transportation Research Board, 1693, 79–85

McHarg, I (1969) Design with Nature, Doubleday & Company, New York

McKendrick, J; Fielder, A & Bradford, M (1999) Privatization of collective play spaces in the UK, Built Environment, 25(1), 44–57

McKendrick, J (1999) Not just a playground: Rethinking children's place in the built environment, Built Environment, 25(1), 75–78

McNeill, D (2009) The Global Architect: Firms, Fame and Urban Form, Routledge, London

Macek, S (2008) Gated communities', in St James Encyclopedia of Pop Culture 20020129, FindArticles com http://findarticles.com/p/articles/mi_g1epc/is_tov/ai_2419100492 (accessed 07 May 2008)

Madanipour, A (2006) Roles and challenges of urban design Journal of Urban Design, 11(2), 173–193

Madanipour, A (2003) Public and Private Spaces of the City Routledge, London

Madanipour, A (1996) Design of Urban Space: An Inquiry into a Socio-Spatial Process, John Wiley & Sons, Chichester

Malmburg, T (1980) Human Territoriality, Mouton Publishers, New York

Malone, K (2002) Street life: Youth, culture and competing uses of public space, Environment & Urbanization, 14(2), 157—168

Manchester City Council (1994) Rebuilding the City: A Guide to Development in Hulme, Manchester City Council Manchester

Mandix (1996) Energy Planning: A Guide for Practitioners, Royal Town Planning Institute, London

Mantownhuman (2008) Manifesto: Towards a New Humanism in Architecture, www.mantownhuman.org

Marcuse, P (2005) The "threat of terrorism" and the right to the city, Fordham Urban Law Journal, 23, 767—785

Marcuss, C C & Sarkissian, W (1986) Housing As If People Mattered: Site Design Guidelines for Medium-Density Family Housing, University of California Press, Berkeley

Marsh, C (1997) Mixed use development and the property market' in Coupland, A (1997) Reclaiming the City: Mixed use development, London, E & F N Spon, 117—148

Marsh, D; Richards, D; & Smith, MJ (2003) Unequal plurality: Towards an asymmetric power model of British politics, Government & Opposition, 38(3), 306—332

Marshall S (2009) Cities Design and Evolution, Routledge, London

Marshall, S (2005) Streets and Patterns, Routledge, London

Marshall, T (2004) (editor) Transforming Barcelona, Routledge, London

Martin, L & March, L (1972) Urban Space and Structures, Cambridge University Press, Cambridge

Maslow, A (1968) Towards a Psychology of Being, Van Nostrand, New York

Massey, D (2005) For Space, Sage, London

Maxwell, R (1976) An Eye for an I: The failure of the townscape tradition', Architectural Design, September, 534—536

Mayo, J (1979) Suburban neighbouring and the cul-de-sac street', Journal of Architectural Research, 7(1), 22—27

Mazumdar, S (2000) People and the built environment', in in Knox, P & Ozolins, P (2000) (editors) Design Professionals and the Built Environment: An Introduction, Wiley, London, 157—168

Mean, M & Tims, C (2005) People Makes Places: Growing the Public Life of Cities, Demos, London

Meeda, B; Parkyn, N & Walton, D S (2007), Graphics for Urban Design, Institution of Civil Engineers, London

Mehaffy, M (2008) Generative methods in urban design: A progress assessment Journal of Urbanism, 1(1), 57—75

Mehrotra, R (2005) (editor) Everyday Urbanism: Margaret Crawford v. Michael Speaks, Michigan Debates on Urbanism Volume 1, Disturbed Arts Press, Michigan

Meiss, P Von (1990) Elements of Architecture: From Form to Place, E & F N Spon, London

Mensch, J (2007) Public space, in Continental Philosophy Review, 40, 31—47

Meyrowitz, J (1985) No Sense of Place, Oxford University Press, Oxford

Michell, G (1986) Design in the High Street, Architectural Press, London

Middleton, R (1983) The architect and tradition: 1: The use and abuse of tradition in architecture', Journal of the Royal Society of Arts, November, 729—739

Miao, P (2003) Deserted streets in a jammed town: The gated community in Chinese cities and its solution Journal of Urban Design, 8(1), 45—66

Milgram, S (1977) The Individual in a Social World: Essays and Experiments, Addison Wesley, Reading, Mass

Ministry for the Environment (2005) New Zealand Urban Design Protocol, http://www.mfe.govt.nz/issues/urban/design-protocol/index.html

Ministry for the Environment (2006) Urban Design Toolkit (third edition), Ministry for the Environment, Wellington

Minton, A (2006) What Kind of World Are We Building? The Privatisation of Public Space, RICS, London

Mitchell, D (2003) The Right to the City: Social Justice and the Fight for Public Space, The Guildford Press, New York

Mitchell, D (1995) The end of public space? People's Park, definitions of the public, and democracy, Annals of the Association of American Geographers, 85, 108—133

Mitchell, W J (2008) Connectivity and urban space', in Haas, T (2008), New Urbanism and Beyond: Designing Cities for the Future, Rizzoli International, New York, 208—211

Mitchell, W J (2002) City past and future', Urban Design Quarterly, Winter, 81, 18—21

Mitchell, W J (2001) Rewiring the city, Building Design, September 10, p 10

Mitchell, W J (2000) Foreword: The electronic Agora', in Horan, TA (2000) Digital Places: Building Our City of Bits, Urban Land Institute, Washington, DC, p ix-xii

Mitchell, W J (1999) E-Topia: 'Urban Life, Jim — But Not As We Know It', MIT Press, Cambridge, Mass

Mitchell, W J (1994) City of Bits: Space, Place and the Infobahn, MIT Press, Cambridge, Mass

Mohney, D & Easterling, K (1991) Seaside: Making a Town in America, Princeton Architectural Press, New Haven

Montgomery, J (2008) The New Wealth of Cities: Urban Dynamics and the Fifth Wave, Ashgate, Aldershot

Montgomery, J (1998) Making a city: Urbanity, vitality and urban design, Journal of Urban Design, 3(1), 93—116

Montgomery, J (1995) Animation: A plea for activity in urban places', Urban Design Quarterly, No 53 (January) 15—17

Montgomery, R (1989) Architecture invents new people, in Ellis, R & Cuff, D (editors) Architects' People, Oxford University Press, Oxford, 260—281

Moos M; Whitfield J; Johnson L; & Andrey J (2006) Does design matter? The ecological footprint as a planning tool at the local level Journal of Urban Design, 11(2), 195—224

Morris, E W (1996) Community in theory and practice: A framework for intellectual renewal Journal of Planning Literature, 11(1), 127—150

Morris, A E G (1994) A History of Urban Form before the Industrial Revolution, Longman, Harlow (first published 1972)

Mostafavi, M; Najle, C. & Architectural Association (2003) Landscape Urbanism: A Manual for the Machinic Landscape, Architectural Association, London

Moudon, A V (1994) Getting to know the built environment: Typo-morphology in France', in Franck, K & Scneekloth, L (1994) (Editors) Ordering Space: Types in Architecture and Design, Van Nostrand Reinhold, New York, 289—311

Moudon, A V (1992) The evolution of twentieth-century residential forms: An American case study, in Whitehead, J W R & Larkham, P J (1992) (Editors) Urban Landscapes: International Perspectives, Routledge, London, 170—206

Moudon, AV (1987) Public Streets for Public Use, Columbia University Press, New York

Moudon, AV (1986) Built for Change: Neighbourhood Architecture in San Francisco, MIT Press, Cambridge, Mass

Moughtin, C (1992) Urban Design, Street and Square, Butterworth Architecture, Oxford

Moughtin, C; Cuesta, R; Sarris, C & Signoretta, P (1999) Urban Design, Method and Techniques, Architectural Press, Oxford

Moughtin, J C; Oc, T; & Tiesdell, S A (1995) Urban Design: Ornament and Decoration, Butterworth-Heinemann, Oxford

Mulholland Research Associates Ltd (1995) Towns or Leafier Environments? A Survey of Family Home Buying Choices, House Builders Federation, London

Mumford, L (1961) The City in History: Its Origins, Its Transformations and Its Prospects, Harcourt Brace Jovanovich, New York

Mumford, L (1938) The Culture of Cities, Harcourt Brace, New York

Mumford, L (1934) Technics and Civilisation, Harvest, New York

Mumford, L (1925)The fourth migration, Survey Graphics, 7, 130—133

Murphy, C (2001) Customised quarantine', Atlantic Monthly, July–August, 22–24

Murrain, P (2002) Understand urbanism and get off its back, Urban Design International, 7(3–4), 131–142

N

Naser, J L & Evans-Cowley, J (2007) (editors) Universal Design and Visitability: From accessibility to zoning, The John Glenn School of Public Affairs/National Endowment for the Arts, Columbus, Ohio

Nasar J L (1999) 'Visual Preferences in Urban Signscapes', Environment & Behavior, 31(5), 671–691

Nasar, J L (1998) The Evaluative Image of the City, Sage, London

National Playing Fields Association (NPFA) (1992) The Six Acre Standard: Minimum Standards for Outdoor Playing Space, NPFA, London

Neal P & Hopkins J (2005) The Future: Landscape design in the 21st century, in Harvey S & Fieldhouse K (2005) (editors) The Cultured Landscape: Designing the Environment in the 21st Century, Routledge, London

Nemeth, J & Schmidt, S (2007) Towards a methodology for measuring the security of publicly accessible spaces', Journal of the American Planning Association, 73(3), 283–297

New Economics Foundation (2004) Clone Town Britain: The Loss of Local Identity on the Nation's High Streets, New Economics Foundation, London

New Economics Foundation (1998) Participation Works! 21 Techniques of Community Participation for the 21st Century, New Economics Foundation, London

Newman, O (1995) Defensible space – A new physical planning tool for urban revitalisation, Journal of the American Planning Association, 61(2), 149–155

Newman, O (1973) Defensible Space: People and Design in the Violent City, Architectural Press, London

Newman, P; Beatley, T & Boyer, H (2009) Resilient Cities: Responding to Peak Oil and Climate Change, Island Press, Washington DC

Newman P (2006) The environmental impact of cities, Environment & Urbanization, 18, 275–295

Newman, P & Kenworthy, J (2000) Sustainable urban form: The big picture, in Williams, K; Burton, E & Jenks, M (2000)(Editors) Achieving Sustainable Urban Form, E & F N Spon, London, 109–120

Newman, P & Kenworthy, J (1989) Gasoline consumption and cities: A comparison of US cities with a global survey Journal of the American Planning Association, 55(1), 24–37

Noland, R B (2000) Traffic fatalities and injuries: Are reductions the result of 'improvements' in highway design standards? (www.cts.cv.ic.ac.uk/staff/wp5-noladn.pdf) Paper to January 20001 Annual Meeting of the Transportation Research Board

Norberg-Schulz, C (1980) Genius Loci: Towards a Phenomenological Approach to Architecture, Rizzoli, New York

Norberg-Schulz, C (1969) Meaning in architecture, In Jencks, (Editor) Meaning in Architecture, The Cresset Press, London

Norberg-Schulz, C (1965) Intentions in Architecture, MIT Press, Cambridge, Mass

O

Oc, T & Tiesdell, S (2000) Urban design approaches to safer city centres: The fortress, the panoptic, the regulatory and the animated', in Gold, J R & Revill, G (2000) (Editor) Landscapes of Defence, Prentice Hall, Harlow, 188–208

Oc, T & Tiesdell, S (1999) The fortress, the panoptic, the regulatory and the animated: Planning and urban design approaches to safer city centres, Landscape Research, 24(3), 265–286

Oc, T & Tiesdell, S (1997) Safer City Centres: Reviving the Public Realm, Paul Chapman Publishing, London

Office of the Deputy Prime Minister (ODPM) (2005) Planning Policy Statement (PPS) 1: Delivering Sustainable Development, The Stationery Office, London

ODPM (2002) Better Streets, Better Places: Delivering Sustainable Residential Environments, ODPM, London

Oldenburg, R (1999) The Great Good Place: Cafes, coffee Shops, Bookstores, Bars, Hair Salons and the Other Hangouts at the Heart of a Community (third edition) Marlowe & Company, New York

Osbourne & Gaebler (1992) Reinventing Government: How the Entrepreneurial Spirit is Transforming the Public Sector, Plume Publishing, New York

Osborne F 1918; (second edition 1942) New Towns After the War, J M Dent Publishers, London

Oswalt, P (2006) (editor) Atlas of the Shrinking City, Hatje Cantz, Netherlands

Oswalt, P; Misselwitz, P; & Overmeyer, K (Urban Catalyst) (2007) Patterns of the unplanned, in Franck K & Stevens Q (2007) (editors) Loose Space: Possibility and Diversity in Urban Life, Routledge, London, 271–288

Owens, S (1992) Energy, environmental sustainability and land-use planning, in Breheny, M (1992) (editor) Sustainable Urban Development and Urban Form, Pion, London

P

Panerai, P; Castex, J; Depaule, J C; & Samuels, I (2004) Urban Forms: The Death and Life of the Urban Block, Architectural Press, Oxford

Papadakis, A (1993) (Editor) Terry Farrell: Urban Design, Academy Editions, London

Papadakis, A & Watson, H (1990) (Editors) New Classicism, Academy Editions, London

Papadakis, A & Toy, M (1990) Deconstruction: A Pocket Guide, Academy Editions, London

Parfect, M & Power, G (1997) Planning for Urban Quality, Urban Design in Towns and Cities, Routledge, London

Parolek, D; Parolek, K & Crawford, P (2008) Form-Based Codes: A Guide for Planners, Urban Designers, Municipalities and Developers, Wiley, New Jersey

Peck, J (2001) Neoliberalising states: Thin policies/hard outcomes, Progress in Human Geography, 25(3), 445–455

Pendlebury, J (1999) The conservation of historic areas in the UK: A case study of 'Grainger Town', Newcastle upon Tyne Cities, 16(6), 423–433

Pendlebury, J. (2000) Conservation and regeneration: Complementary or conflicting processes? The case of Grainger Town, Newcastle upon Tyne', Planning Practice & Research 17 (2), 145–158

Penn, A; Hillier, B; Banister, D; & Xu, J (1998), Configurational modelling of the urban movement networks Environment & Planning B: Planning & Design, 25, 59–84

Peponis, J; Hadjinikolaou, E; Liveieratis, C; & Fatourous, D A (1989) The spatial core of urban culture, Ekistics, 334/335, 43–55

Percy-Smith, J (2000) Policy Responses to Social Exclusion: Towards Inclusion? Open University Press, Milton Keynes

Perry, C (1929) The Neighbourhood Unit, in Lewis, H M (Editor) Regional Plan for New York and its Environs, Volume 7, Neighbourhood and Community Planning, New York

Pharoah T (2008) Streets past and future, Urban Design, Issue 105, 15–18

Pharoah, T (1992) Less Traffic, Better Towns, Friends of the Earth, London

Phillips, T & Smith, P (2006) Rethinking urban incivility research: Strangers, bodies and circulations, Urban Studies, 43(5–6), 878–902

Philips, C (2003) Sustainable Place, Wiley-Academy, Chichester

Piccinato, G (1987) NonEnLas teories del Urbanismo; un intento de analisis, Urbana, 7, 9–14

Pisarski, A E (1987) Commuting in America: A National Report on Commuting Patterns and Trends, ENO Foundation for Transportation, Westport, Connecticut

Pitts, A (1999) 'Technologies and Techniques', presentation given at Education for the Next Millennium: Environmental Workshop, University of Sheffield, January, 1999

Pocock, D & Hudson, R (1978) Images of the Urban Environment, Macmillan, London

Pope, A (1996) Ladders, Princeton Architectural Press, New York

Popper, K (1972) Objective Knowledge, Oxford University Press, London

Porta, S & Latora, V (2008) Centrality and cities: Multiple centrality assessment as a tool for urban analysis and design, in Haas, T (2008), New Urbanism and Beyond: Designing Cities for the Future, Rizzoli International, New York, 140—145

Porteous, J D (1996) Environmental Aesthetics: Ideas, Politics and Planning, Routledge, London

Porteous, L (1977) Environment and Behaviour, Addison-Wesley, London

Porter, D; Phillips, P & Lassar, T (1988) Flexible Zoning, How it Works, Urban Land Institute, Washington, DC

Porter, L & Shaw, K (2009) (editors) Whose Urban Renaissance? An International Comparison of Urban Renaissance Policies, Routledge, London

Porter, ME (1995) The competitive advantage of the inner city, Harvard Business Report, 73(3), 55—71

Porter, T (1997) The Architect's Eye: Visualisation and Depiction of Space in Architecture, E & F N Spon, London

Porter, T (1982) Colour Outside, Architectural Press, London

Porter, T & Goodman, S (1985) Manual of Graphic Techniques 4, Butterworth Architecture, Oxford

Porter, T & Goodman, S (1983)Manual of Graphic Techniques 3, Butterworth Architecture, Oxford

Porter, T & Goodman, S (1982) Manual of Graphic Techniques 2, Butterworth Architecture, Oxford

Porter, T & Greenstreet, B (1980) Manual of Graphic Techniques 1, Butterworth Architecture, Oxford

Portland Bureau of Planning (1992) Central City Developer's Handbook, Portland Bureau of Planning, Portland

Powell, K (1999) Architecture Reborn: The Conversion and Reconstruction of Old Buildings, Lawrence King Publishing, London

Power, A (2008) Does demolition or refurbishment of old and inefficient homes help to increase our environmental, social and economic viability? Energy Policy (special issue), 36(12), 4487—4501

Prince's Foundation (2007) Valuing Sustainable Urbanism: Measuring and valuing New Approaches to Residentially Led Growth, Princes Trust, London — summary available online at http://www.princes-foundation.org/files/0707vsuoverview.pdf

Project for Public Spaces (PPS) (2000) How to Turn a Place Around: A Handbook for Creating Successful Public Spaces, Project for Public Spaces, Inc., New York

Property Council of Australia (1999) The Design Dividend, PCA National Office, Canberra

Proshansky, H M; Ittelson, W H; & Rivlin, L G (1970) (editors) Environmental Psychology: Man and His Physical Setting, Holt Rinehart & Winston, New York

Punter, J (2009) (editor) Urban Design and the British Urban Renaissance, Routledge, London

Punter, J (2007a) Developing urban design as public policy: best practice principles for design review and development management', Journal of Urban Design 12(2), 167—202

Punter, J (2007b) Design-led Regeneration? Evaluating the design outcomes of Cardiff Bay and their implications for future regeneration and design', Journal of Urban Design 12(3), 375—405

Punter, J (2005) Urban design in Central Sydney, 1945—2002: Laissez-faire and discretionary traditions in the Accidental City, Progress in Planning, 63(1), 1—160

Punter, J (2004) From the ill mannered to the iconic: Design regulation in Central Sydney 1947—2002, Town Planning Review, 75(3), 405—445

Punter, J (2003a) The Vancouver Achievement: Urban Planning and Design, University of British Columbia Press, Vancouver

Punter, J (2003b) From design advice to peer review: The role of the Urban Design Panel in Vancouver, Journal of Urban Design 8(1), 113—136

Punter, J (2002) Urban design as public policy: Evaluating the design dimension of Vancouver's planning system, International Planning Studies 7(4), 265—282

Punter, J (1999) Design Guidelines in American Cities, Liverpool University Press, Liverpool

Punter, J (1998) Design', from Cullingworth, JB (1998) (editor) British Planning: 50 Years of Urban & Regional Policy, The Athlone Press, London, 137—155

Punter J (1995) Portland cements reputation for design awareness, Planning, 1114

Punter, J & Carmona, M (1997) The Design Dimension of Planning: Theory, Content and Best Practice for Design Policies, E & F N Spon, London

Putnam, R (2000) Bowling Alone: The Collapse and Revival of the American Community, New York, Simon and Schuster

R

Rabinowitz, H (1996) The developer's vernacular: The owners influence on building design, Journal of Architectural & Planning Research, 13(1), 34—42

Rapoport, A (1977) Human Aspects of Urban Form: Towards a Man-Environment Approach to Urban Form and Design, Pergamon Press, Oxford

Ratti, C (2004a) space syntax: Some inconsistencies, Environment & Planning B: Planning & Design, 31(4), 487—499

Ratti, C (2004a) Rejoinder to Hiller and Penn', Environment & Planning B: Planning & Design, 31(4), 513—516

Read, J (1982) Looking backwards, Built Environment, 7(2), 68—81

Reade E (1987) British Town and Country Planning, Open University Press, Milton Keynes

Read, S (1999) space syntax and the Dutch city', Environment & Planning B: Planning & Design, 26(3), 251—264

Reekie, R F (1946) Draughtsmanship, Edward Arnold, London

Rees, W & Wackernagle, M (1994) Urban ecological footprints: Why cities can not be sustainable — And why they are the key to sustainability, Environmental Impact Assessment Review, 16, 223—248

Relph, E (1987) The Modern Urban Landscape, John Hopkins University Press, Baltimore

Relph, E (1981) Rational Landscape and Humanistic Geography, Croom Helm, London

Relph, E (1976) Place and Placelessness, Pion, London

Reps, J W (1965) The Making of Urban America, Princeton University Press, New Haven

Rhodes, R A W (1994) The hollowing out of the state: The changing nature of the public service in Britain Political Quarterly, 65, 138—151

Rhodes, R A W (1996) The new governance: Governing without government, Political Studies, 44, 652—667

Rhodes, R A W (1997) Understanding Governance: Policy Networks, Governance, Reflectivity and Accountability, Open University Press, Buckingham

RIBA (Royal Institute of British Architects) (2006) Practice Bulletin, no 339, 2 March

Richards, B (2001) Future Transport in Cities, Spon, London

Richards, J (1994) Facadism, Routledge, London

Rishbeth, C (2001) Ethnic minority groups and the design of public open space: An inclusive landscape?' Landscape Research, 26(4), 351—366

Ritchie, A (2009) Summary' in Ritchie & Thomas (2009) (editors) Sustainable Urban Design — An Environmental Approach (second edition), Taylor & Francis, London, 92—94

Ritchie, A (2003) Waste and resources' in Thomas, R (Editor) Sustainable Urban Design — An Environmental Approach, Spon Press, London, 100—108

Ritter, P (1964) Planning for Man and Motor, Pergamon Press, Oxford

Robbins, K (1991) Tradition and translation: National culture in its global context, in Corner, J & Harvey, S (1991) (Editors) Enterprise and Heritage: Crosscurrents of National Culture, Routledge, London

Roberts, M & Eldridge, A (2009) Planning the Night-Time City, Routledge, London

Roberts, M & Turner, C (2005) Conflicts of liveability in the 24-hour city: Learning from 48 hours in the life of London's Soho, Journal of Urban Design, 10(2), 171–193

Roberts, P (2004) The End of Oil: The Decline of the Petroleum Economy and the Rise of a New Energy Order, Bloomsbury, London

Robinson, N (1992) The Planting Design Handbook, Gower, Aldershot

Roger Evans Associates (2007) Delivering Quality Places -Urban Design Compendium 2, English Partnerships & The Housing Corporation, London

Rogers, R (1997) Cities for a Small Planet, Faber & Faber, London

Rogers, R (1988) Belief in the future is rooted in memory of the past', Royal Society of Arts Journal, November, 873–884

Rojek, C (2001) Celebrity, Reaktion Books, London

Romaya, S & Rakodi, C (2002) Building Sustainable Urban Settlements, Approaches and Case Studies in the Developing World, ITDG Publishing, London

Rossi, A (1982; (first published in Italian, 1966) The Architecture of the City, MIT Press, Cambridge, Mass

Rouse, J (1998) The seven clamps of urban design, Planning No 1293, 6 November, 18–19

Rowe, C & Koetter, K (1978) Collage City, MIT Press, Cambridge, Mass

Rowe, C & Koetter, K (1975) Collage city', Architectural Review, August, 203–212

Rowland, I & Howe, T (1999) (editors) Vitruvius: Ten Books on Architecture, Cambridge University Press, Cambridge

Rowley, A; Gibson, V; & Ward, C (1996) Quality of Urban Design: A Study of the Involvement of Private Property Decision-makers in Urban Design, Royal Institution of Chartered Surveyors, London

Rowley, A (1998) Private-property decision makers and the quality of urban design, Journal of Urban Design, 3(2), 151–173

Rowley, A (1996) Mixed use development: ambiguous concept, simplistic analysis and wishful thinking?', Planning, Practice & Research, 11(1), 85–98

Rowley, A (1994) Definitions of urban design: The nature and concerns of urban design', Planning Practice & Research, 9(3), 179–197

Royal Society (2008) Ground-Level Ozone in the 21st Century: Future Trends, Impacts and Policy Implications, The Royal Society, London

Rudlin, D (2000) The Hulme and Manchester design guides, Built Environment, 25(2), 317–324

Rudlin, D & Falk, N (1999) Building the 21st Century Home: The Sustainable Urban Neighbourhood, Architectural Press, Oxford

Rugare, S & Schwarz, T (2008) Urban Infill No 1: Cities Growing Smaller, Cleveland Urban Design Collaborative, Cleveland

Rybczynski, W (1997) The Pasteboard Past', New York Times Book Review, 6 April, 13

Rybczynski, W (1995) City Life, Simon & Schuster, London

Rybczynski, W (1994) Epilogue', in Scheer, B C & Preiser, W (1994) (editors) Design Review: Challenging Urban Aesthetic Control, Chapman & Hall, New York, 210–212

Rypkema, D.D. (2001) Property Rights and Public Values, paper to the Georgetown Environmental Law & Policy Institute, June 13-www.law.georgetown.edu/gelp/takingsprypkema.html (accessed 24 January 2005)

S

Sabatier, P A (1988) An Advocacy Coalition Framework of policy change and the role of policy-oriented learning therein Policy Science 21(2), 129–168

Saegert, S (1980) Masculine cities and feminine suburbs: Polarised ideas, contradictory realities', Signs 5 (3 supplement) 93–108

Salamon, L (2002) The Tools of Government: A Guide to the New Governance, Oxford University Press, Oxford

Salingaros, N A (2005) Principles of Urban Structure, Techne Press, Amsterdam

Sandercock, L & Forsyth, A (1992) A gender agenda: New directions for planning theory, Journal of the American Planning Association, 58(1), 49–59

Sandercock, L (1997) Towards Cosmopolis, Academy Editions, London

Saoud, R (1995) Political influences on urban form, Paper Presented to the New Academics in Planning Conference, Oxford Brookes University

Sathaye, J & Murtishaw, S (2004) Market Failures, Consumer Preferences, and Transaction Costs in Energy Efficiency Purchase Decisions, California Energy Commission, Sacramento

Sawyer, A & Bright K (2007) The Access Manual, Auditing and Managing Inclusive Built Environments, Blackwell Publishing, Oxford

SceneSusTech (1998) Car-Systems in the City: Report 1, Department of Sociology, Trinity College, Dublin

Scheer, B C (1994) Introduction: The debate on design review, in Scheer B C & Preiser W (Editors) Design Review: Challenging Urban Aesthetic Control, Chapman & Hall, New York, 3–9

Scheer B C & Preiser, W (Editors) (1994) Design Review: Challenging Urban Aesthetic Control, Chapman & Hall, New York

Schon, D (1991) The Reflective Practitioner: How Professionals Think in Action, Ashgate, Aldershot

Schuster M (2005) Substituting information for regulation, In search of an alternative approach to shaping urban design', in Ben-Joseph E & Szold T Regulating Place, Standards and the Shaping of Urban America, Routledge, New York

Schuster, M & de Monchaux, J (1997) (editors) Preserving the Built Heritage: Tools for Implementation, Salzburg Seminar/University Press of New England, Hanover

Schwarz, T & Rugare, S (2009) Urban Infill No 2: Pop Up City, Cleveland Urban Design Collaborative, Cleveland

Schwarzer, M (2000) The contemporary city in four movements, Journal of Urban Design, 5(2) 127–144

Scoffham, E R (1984) The Shape of British Housing, George Godwin, London

Scott, A (2001) Capitalism, cities and the production of symbolic forms, The Royal Geographical Society, 26(1), 11–23

Scottish Office (1994) Planning Advice Note 44: Fitting New Housing Development into the Landscape, Scottish Office, Edinburgh

Scruton, R (1982) A Dictionary of Political Thought, Pan, London

Sebba, R & Churchman, A (1983) Territories and territoriality in the home, Environment and Behaviour, 15(2), 191–210

Sennett, R (1994) Flesh and Stone: The Body and the City in Western Civilisation, Faber & Faber, London

Sennett, R (1990) The Conscience of the Eye: The Design and Social Life of Cities, Faber & Faber, London

Sennett, R (1977) The Fall of Public Man, Faber & Faber, London

Sennett, R (1970) The Uses of Disorder, Faber & Faber, London

Sert, J L (1944) Can Our Cities Survive? MIT Press, Cambridge, Mass

Shane, D G (2009) The emergence of landscape urbanism, in Waldheim, C (2009) (editor) The Landscape Urbanism Reader, Princeton Architectural Press, New York, 69–86

Shane, D G (2005) Recombinant Urbanism: Conceptual Modelling in Architecture, Urban Design and City Theory, Wiley, Chichester

Sharp, T (1953) The English Village', in Ministry of Housing & Local Government (MHLG) (1953) Design in Town & Village, HMSO, London

Shearing, C D & Stenning, P C (1987) Say cheese: The Disney order that is not so Micky Mouse, in Shearing, C D & Stenning, P C (1987) (editors) Private Policing, Sage, London

Shields, R (1991) Places on the Margin, Routledge, London

Sheller, M & Urry, J (2000) The city and the car, International Journal of Urban & Regional Research, 24(4), 737–757

Shelton, B (1999) Learning from the Japanese City: West Meets East in Urban Design, E & F N Spon, London

Sherman, B (1988) Cities Fit to Live in, Channel Four Book, London

Sherman, L; Gottfredson, D; MacKenzie, D; Eck, J; Reuter, P & Busways, S (2001) Preventing Crime: What Works, What Doesn't, What's Promising, USA National Institute of Justice, Washington

Shields, R (1989) 'Social spatialisation and the built environment: The West Edmonton Mall', Environment & Planning D: Society & Space, 7, 147–164

Shoup, D (2008) Graduated density zoning' Journal of Planning Education & Research, 28(2), 161–179

Shoup, D (2005) The High Cost of Free Parking, American Planning Association, Chicago

Siegan B (2005) The benefits of non-zoning in Ben-Joseph E & Szold T (2005) (editors) Regulating Place, Standards and the Shaping of Urban America, Routledge, New York

Siksna, A (1998) City centre blocks and their evolution: A comparative study of eight American and Australian CBDs Journal of Urban Design, 3(3), 253–283

Silber, J (2007) Architecture of the Absurd: How 'Genius' Disfigures a Practical Art, Quantuck Lane Press, New York

Sircus, J (2001) Invented places', Prospect, 81, Sept/Oct, 30–35

Sitte, C (1889) City Planning According to Artistic Principles, (translated by Collins, G R & Collins, C C, 1965) Phaidon Press, London

Sklair, L (2006a) Iconic architecture and capitalist globalisation', City 10(1), 21–47

Sklair, L (2006b) Do cities need architectural icons? Urban Studies 43(10), 1899–1907

Smith, N (2002) New globalism, New Urbanism: Gentrification as global urban strategy, Antipode, 34(3), 427–450

Smith, P F (1980) Urban aesthetics, in Mikellides, B (1980) (Editor) Architecture and People, Studio Vista, London, 74–86

Sohmer, R R & Lang, R E (2000) From seaside to southside: New Urbanism's quest to save the inner city Housing Policy Debate, 11(4), 751–760

Soja, E (1996) Los Angeles, 1965–1992: The six geographies of urban restructuring, in Scott, A J & Soja, E (1996) (Editors) The City: Los Angeles and Urban Theory at the End of the Twentieth Century, University of California Press, Los Angeles, 426–462

Soja, E (1995) postmodern urbanisation: The six restructurings of Los Angeles, in Watson, S & Gibson, K (editors) postmodern Cities and Spaces, Blackwell, Oxford, 125–137

Soja, E (1980) The socio-spatial dialectic', Annals, Association of American Geographers, 70, 207–225

Sommer, R M (2009) Beyond centres, fabrics, and cultures, in Krieger, A & Saunders, W S (editors) Urban Design, University of Minnesota Press, Minneapolis & London, 135–152

Sommer, R M (2006) Beyond centres, "fabric" and the culture of congestion: Urban design as metropolitan enterprise, Harvard Design Magazine Fall/Winter, 50–59

Sorkin, M (Editor) (1992) Variations on a Theme Park: The New American City and the End of Public Space, Hill & Wang, New York

Southworth, M (2003a) New Urbanism and the American metropolis, Built Environment, 29(3), 210–226

Southworth M (2003b) Measuring the liveable city, Built Environment 29(4), 343–354

Southworth, M & Ben-Joseph, E (1997) Streets and the Shaping of Towns and Cities, McGraw-Hill, New York

Southworth, M & Ben-Joseph, E (1995) Street standards and the shaping of suburbia, Journal of the American Planning Association, 61(1), 65–81

Southworth, M & Owens, P M (1993) Studies of community, neighbourhood and street form at the urban edge, Journal of the American Planning Association, 59, 271–287

Southworth, M (1997) Walkable Suburbs? An evaluation of neotraditional communities at the urban edge, Journal of the American Planning Association, 63(1), 28–44

Speaks, M (2005) Everyday is not enough, in Mehrotra, R (2005) (editor) Everyday Urbanism: Margaret Crawford v. Michael Speaks, Michigan Debates on Urbanism Volume 1, Disturbed Arts Press, Michigan, 34–44

Spreiregen, P D (1981) Urban Design: The Architecture of Towns and Cities, Robert E Krieger, Malabar, Florida

Steadman, P (2004) 'Guest editorial: Developments in space syntax', Environment & Planning B: Planning & Design, 31(4), 483–486

Steel, C (2009) Hungry City: How Food Shapes Our Lives, Vintage, London

Stemmet (2002) The engineer: Key enabler in urban design, Municipal Engineer, 151, 101–119

Stevens Q (2007) The Ludic City: Exploring the Potential of Public Spaces, Routledge, London

Stern, N (2009) A Blueprint for a Safer Planet: How to Manage Climate Change and Create a New Era of Progress and Prosperity, The Bodley Head, London

Stern, N (2007) The Economics of Climate Change, Cambridge University Press, Cambridge

Stern, N (2006) Stern Review: The Economics of Climate Change, House of Commons, London

Sternberg, E (2000) An Integrative theory of urban design, Journal of the American Planning Association, 66(3), 265–278

Sternberg, E (1996) Recuperating from market failure: Planning for biodiversity and technological competitiveness, Public Administration Review, 56(1), 21–29

Steuteville, R, Langdon, P & Special Contributors (2009) New Urbanism: Best Practices Guide, (fourth edition), New Urban News Publications, Ithaca, NY

Stewart M (2000) Community governance in Barton H (Editor) Sustainable Communities: The Potential for Eco-Neighbourhoods, Earthscan, London, 176–186

Strickland, R (2005)(editor) Michigan Debates on Urbanism Volume III: Post Urbanism and Re-Urbanism, University of Michigan/Distributed Arts Press, New York

Sudjic, D (1996) Can we fix this hole at the heart of our cities?', The Guardian, Saturday January 13, p 27

Sudjic, D (1993) The 100 Mile City, Flamingo, London

Syms, P (2002) Land, Development & Design, Blackwell Publishing, Oxford

T

Tahrani, S & Moreau, G (2008), Integration of immersive walking to analyse urban daylighting ambiences, Journal of Urban Design, 13(1), 99–124

Talen, E (2009a) Bad parenting, in Krieger, A & Saunders, W S (2009) (editors) Urban Design, University of Minnesota Press, Minneapolis, 183–185

Talen, E (2009b) Design by the rules: The historical underpinnings of form-based codes Journal of the American Planning Association, 75(2), 144–160

Talen, E (2009c) Urban Design Reclaimed: Tools, Techniques, and Strategies for Planners, American Planning Association, Washington DC

Talen, E (2008a) The Design of Diversity: Exploring Socially Mixed Neighbourhoods, Architectural Press, Oxford

Talen, E (2008b) The unbearable lightness of New Urbanism', in Haas, T (2008), New Urbanism and Beyond: Designing Cities for the Future, Rizzoli International, New York, 77–79

Talen E (2005) New Urbanism and American Planning, Routledge, London

Talen, E (2002) Help for planning: The transect strategy Journal of Urban Design, 7(3), 293–312

Talen, E (2000) The problem with community in planning, Journal of Planning Literature, 15(2), 171–183

Talen, E (1999) Sense of community and neighbourhood form: An assessment of the social doctrine of New Urbanism, Urban Studies, 36(8) 1361–1379

Taylor, A F; Wiley, A; Kuo, F E & Sullivan, W C (1998) Growing up in the inner city – Green spaces as places to grow, Environment and Behaviour, 30(1), 2–27

Taylor, D & Filmer-Sankey, W (2003) DB32 and the design of good urban streets, Municipal Engineer, 151, 111–116

Taylor, D (2002) Highway Rules', Urban Design Quarterly, 81, 27–29

Terence O'Rourke plc (1998) Planning for Passive Solar Design, BRECSU, Watford

Thiel, P (1961) A sequence-experience notation for architectural and urban space, Town Planning Review, 32, 33–52

Thorne, R & Filmer-Sankey, W (2003) 'Transportation' in Thomas, R (2003) (editor) Sustainable Urban Design – An Environmental Approach, Spon Press, London, 25–32

Thwaites, K; Porta, S; Romice, O; & Greaves, M (2007) (editors) Urban Sustainability Through Environmental Design: Approaches to Time-People-Place Responsive Urban Spaces, Routledge, London

Tibbalds, F (1992) Making People Friendly Towns: Improving the Public Environment in Towns and Cities, Longman, Harlow

Tibbalds, F (1988a) Ten commandments of urban design, The Planner, 74(12), 1

Tibbalds, F (1988b) Mind the Gap!', The Planner, March, 11–15

Tibbalds Colbourne Karski Williams (TCKW) (1990) City Centre Design Strategy (Birmingham Urban Design Strategy) City of Birmingham, Birmingham

Tibbalds Colbourne Karski Williams Monro (TCKWM) (1993) London's Urban Environmental Quality, London Planning Advisory Committee, Romford Tiesdell, S; Oc, T & Heath, T Revitalising Historic Urban Quarters, Architectural Press, Oxford

Tiesdell, S; Oc, T & Heath, P (1995) Revitalising Historic Urban Quarters, Architectural Press, Oxford

Tiesdell, S & Adams, D (2010) (editors) Urban Design in the Real Estate Development Process, Blackwell, Oxford

Tiesdell, S & Adams, D (2004) Design matters: Major house builders and the design challenge of brownfield development contexts', Journal of Urban Design, 9(1), 23–45

Tiesdell, S & Allmendinger, P (2005) Planning tools and markets: Towards an extended conceptualisation', in Adams, D Watkins, C & White, M (2005) (editors) Planning, Public Policy and Property Markets, Blackwell Publishing, Oxford, 56–76

Tiesdell, S & Macfarlane, G (2007) The part and the whole: Implementing masterplans in Glasgow's New Gorbals, Journal of Urban Design 12(4), 407–433

Tiesdell, S & Oc, T (1998) Beyond fortress and panoptic cities – Towards a safer urban public realm', Environment & Planning B: Planning & Design, 25, 639–655

Tiesdell, S & Slater, A-M (2006) Calling time: Managing activities in space and time in the evening/night-time economy, Planning Theory & Practice, 7(2), 137–157

Tiesdell, S (2002) New Urbanism and English residential design guidance, Journal of Urban Design, 7(3), 353–376

Toffler, A (1970) Future Shock, Random House, New York

Tolley, R (2008) Walking and cycling: Easy wins for a sustainable transport policy? in Docherty, I & Shaw, J (2008) (editors) Traffic Jam: Ten Years of 'Sustainable' Transport in the UK, Policy Press, Bristol, 117–138

Tomsen, S (1997) A top night: Social protest, masculinity and the culture of drinking violence, British Journal of Criminology, 37(1), 90–102

Town, S & O'Toole, R (2005) Crime-friendly neighbourhoods: How "New Urbanist" Planners Sacrifice Safety in the Name of "Openess" and "Accessibility" Reason, 36(9), 30–36

Trache, H (2001) Promoting urban design in development plans: Typomorphological approaches in Montreuil, France, Urban Design International, 6(3/4), 157–172

Trancik, R (1986) Finding Lost Space: Theories of Urban Design, Van Nostrand Reinhold, New York

Tripp, HA (1942) Town Planning and Traffic, Arnold, London

Tripp, HA (1938) Road Traffic and Its Control, Arnold, London

Tschumi, B (1983) Sequences, Princeton Journal, 1, 29–32

Tuan, Y-F (1975) Place: An experiential perspective', The Geographical Review, LXV (2), 151–165

Tugnutt, A & Robertson, M (1987) Making Townscape: A Contextual Approach to Building in an Urban Setting, Michell, London

Tunbridge, J E (1998) The question of heritage in European cultural conflict, in Graham, B (editor) (1998) Modern Europe: Place, Culture, Identity, Arnold, London, 236–260

Turok I (2009) The distinctive city: Pitfalls in the pursuit of differential advantage, Environment & Planning A, 41(1), 13–30

U

University of Reading (2001) Training for Urban Design, DETR, London

Unwin, R (1909) Town Planning in Practice: An Introduction to Artistic City Planning, T Fisher Unwin, London

Urban Design Alliance (UDAL) (1997) The Urban Design Alliance Manifesto, UDAL, London

Urban Design Alliance (2008) Capacitycheck: Urban Design Skills Appraisal, available at www.capacitycheck.co.uk

Urban Design Associates (2003) The Urban Design Handbook, Techniques and Working Methods, WW Norton & Company, New York

Urban Design Group (2008) Design and Access Statements Explained, Thomas Telford Publishing, London

Urban Design Group (UDG) (1998a) Involving Local communities in urban design, promoting good practice, Urban Design Quarterly, Special Report 67, July, 15–38

Urban Design Group (UDG) (1998b) Urban Design Sourcebook, Urban Design Group, Oxon

Urban Design Group (UDG) (1994) Urban Design Sourcebook, Urban Design Group, Oxon

Urban Task Force (1999) Towards an Urban Renaissance, Urban Task Force, London

Urban Villages Forum/English Partnerships (1999) Making Places: A Guide to Good Practice in Undertaking Mixed Development Schemes, Urban Villages Forum/English Partnerships, London

Urban Villages Forum (1995) Economics of Urban Villages, Urban Villages Forum, London

URBED (1997) The model sustainable urban neighbourhood? Sun Dial, 4, 2–5

Urry, J (1999) Automobility, car culture and weightless travel: A discussion paper, available at http://www.comp.lancs.ac.uk/sociology/soc008ju html

V

Van Doren P (2005) The political economy of urban design standards, in Ben-Joseph E & Szold T (2005) (editors) Regulating Place, Standards and the Shaping of Urban America, Routledge, London 45–66

Von Borcke, C (2003) Landscape and nature in the city' in Thomas R (Editor) (2003) Sustainable Urban Design – An Environmental Approach, Spon Press, London, 33–45

Vakkri George, R (1997) A procedural explanation for contemporary urban design, Journal of Urban Design, 2(2), 143–161

Van Doren, P (2005) The political economy of urban design standards, in Ben-Joseph E & Szold T (2005)(editors) Regulating Place, Standards and the Shaping of Urban America, Routledge, London, 45–66

Vandell, K & Lane, J (1989) The economics of architecture and urban design: Some preliminary findings, Journal of the American Real Estate and Urban Economics Association, 17(2), 235–260

Varoufakis, Y (1998) Foundations of Economics: A Beginner's Companion, Routledge, London

Venturi, R (1966) Complexity and Contradiction in Architecture, MOMA, New York

Venturi, R; Scott Brown, D & Izenour, S (1972) Learning from Los Vegas: The Forgotten Symbolism of Architectural Form, MIT Press, Cambridge, Mass

Vischer, J C (1985) The adaptation and control mode of user needs: A new direction for housing research Journal of Environmental Psychology, 19(5), 287–298

W

Waldheim, C (2009) The Other '56', in Krieger, A & Saunders, W S (2009) (editors) Urban Design, University of Minnesota Press, Minneapolis & London, 227–236

Waldheim, C (2006a) (editor) The Landscape Urbanism Reader, Princeton Architectural Press, New York

Waldheim, C (2006b) Landscape as urbanism, in Waldheim, C (2006) (editor) The Landscape Urbanism Reader, Princeton Architectural Press, New York, 55–68

Walters, D (2007) Designing Community: Charettes, Masterplans and Form-Based Codes, Architectural Press, Oxford

Ward, G (1997) postmodernism, Hodder & Stoughton, London

Warren, J; Worthington, J & Taylor, S (1998) (editors) Context: New Buildings in Historic Settings, Architectural Press, Oxford

Watkin, D (1984) Morality and Architecture, University of Chicago Press, Chicago

Webber, M M (1964) The urban place and the non-place urban realm', in Webber, M M; Dyckman, J W; Foley, D L; et al (1964) Explorations into Urban Structure, University of Pennsylvania, Philadelphia, 79–153

Webber, M M (1963) Order, diversity: Community without propinquity', in Wingo, L (1963) (editor) Cities and Space: The Future Use of Urban Land, John Hopkins University Press, Baltimore, 23–54

Webster, C J (2002) 'Property rights and the public realm: gates, green belts and gemeinschaft'. Environment & Planning B, 29(3), 397–412

Webster, C J (2001) 'Gated cities of tomorrow', Town Planning Review, 72(2), 149–170

Weiler, S (2000) 'Pioneers and settlers in Lo-Do, Denver: Private risk and public benefits in urban redevelopment', Urban Studies 37(1), 167–179

Weintraub, J (1995) 'Varieties and vicissitudes of public space', in Kasinitz, P (1995) (editor) Metropolis: Centre and Symbol of Our Times, Macmillan, London, 280–319

Weller, R (2007) 'Global theory, local practice', Journal of Landscape Architecture, RERB 15, 66–71

Welsh, B & Farrington, D (2002) Crime Prevention Effects of Closed Circuit Television: A Systematic Review, Home Office, London

White, E (1999) Path – Portal – Place, Appreciating Public Space in Urban Environments, Architectural Media Ltd, Tallahassee

Whitehead, J W R (1992) The Making of the Urban Landscape, Blackwell, Oxford

Whitehead, J W R & Larkham, P (1992) (Editors) Urban Landscapes: International Perspectives, Routledge, London

Whitzman, C (2007) 'Stuck at the front door: Gender, fear of crime and the challenge of creating safer space', Environment & Planning A, 39(11), 2715–2732

Whyte, W H (1980) The Social Life of Small Urban Spaces, Conservation Foundation, Washington DC

Whyte, W H (1988) City: Rediscovering the Centre, Doubleday, New York

Wiggington, M (1993) 'Architecture: The rewards of excellence', in Better Buildings Mean Better Business, Report of Symposium, London, Royal Society of Arts, 4–7

Wilford, M (1984) 'Off to the races or going to the dogs', Architectural Review/Design, 8–15

Williams, J (2005) 'Designing neighbourhoods for social interaction: The case of co-housing', Journal of Urban Design, 10(2), 195–227

Williams, K; Burton, E & Jenks, M (2000a) (Editors) Achieving Sustainable Urban Form, E & F N Spon, London

Williams, K; Burton, E & Jenks, M (2000b) 'Achieving sustainable urban form: An introduction', in Williams, K; Burton, E & Jenks, M (2000) (Editors) Achieving Sustainable Urban Form, E & F N Spon, London, 1–5

Williams, R (1973) The Country and the City, Chatto & Windus, London

Williams, R (1961) The Long Revolution, Penguin Books, London

Willmott, P (1962) 'Housing density and town design in a new town: A pilot study at Stevenage', Town Planning Review, 33(2), 115–127

Wilson, E (1991) The Sphinx in the City: The Control of Disorder and Women, Virago, London

Wolf, C (1994) Markets or Government? Choosing Between Imperfect Alternatives (second edition) MIT Press, Cambridge, Mass

Wolfe, T (1981) From Bauhaus to Our House, Penguin Books, Harmondsworth

Woolley, H (2003) Urban Open Spaces, Spon Press, London

Woolley, H; Carmona, M; Rose, S & Freedman, J (2004) The Value of Public Space, How High Quality Parks and Public Spaces Create Economic, Social and Environmental Value, CABE Space, London

Worpole K (1999) 'Open all hours, like it or not', New Statesman, 26 April, xxvi–xxvii

Worpole K & Knox K (2007) The Social Value of Public Spaces, Joseph Rowntree Foundation, York

Worskett, R (1969) The Character of Towns: An Approach to Conservation, Architectural Press, London

Wortley, R (2001) 'A classification of techniques for controlling situational precipitators of crime', Security Journal 14(1), 63–82

Wortley, R (1998) 'A two-stage model of situational crime prevention', Studies on Crime & Crime Prevention 7, 173–188

Wright, G (1999) 'Urban design 12 years on: The Birmingham experience', Built Environment, 25(4), 289–299

Wunderlich, F (2008) 'Walking and rhythmicity: Sensing urban space', Journal of Urban Design, 13(1), 125–139

Wunderlich, F (2010) 'The aesthetics of place-temporality in everyday urban space: The Case of Fitzroy Square', in Edensor, T (2010) (editor) Geographies of Rhythm: Nature, Place, Mobilities and Bodies, Ashgate, London

X

Xu, M & Yang, Z (2009) 'Design history of China's gated cities and neighbourhoods: Prototype and evolution', Urban Design International, 14(2), 99–117

Y

Yang, D (2006) Waterfronts: Spatial Composition and Cultural Use, unpublished PhD thesis, UCL, London

Yeang, K (2009) Eco Master Planning, Wiley Chichester

Young, J (1992) 'Ten points of realism', in Jewkes, Y & Letherby, G (2002: 44) Criminology: A Reader, Sage, London, 42–55

Young, IM (1990) Justice and the Politics of Difference, University Press, Princeton

Z

Zeisel, J (2006) Inquiry by Design: Tools for Environment-Behaviour Research, Cambridge University Press, Cambridge

Zeisel, J (1981) Inquiry by Design: Tools for Environment-Behaviour Research, Cambridge University Press, Cambridge

Zeisel, J (1975) Sociology and Architectural Design, Russell Sage Foundation, New York

Zucker, P (1959) Town and Square: From the Agora to Village Green, Columbia University Press, New York

Zukin, S (1995) The Cultures of Cities, Basil Blackwell, Oxford

Zukin, S (1991) Landscapes of Power: From Detroit to Disney World, University of California Press, Berkeley

Zukin, S (1989) Loft Living: Culture and Capital in Urban Change, Rutgers University Press, New Brunswick, NJ

Websites

http://agentsofurbanism com/2008/04/16/sustainable-city-race-part-3-dongtan
http://www.bestpractices.org
http://www.buildingforlife
http://www china org.cn/english/environment
http://www.cittaslow.blogspot.com
http://www.cnu.org
http://www.completestreets.org
http://www.dieoff.com
http://www.english.donga.com/srv/service
http://www.lifeaftertheoilcrash.net
http://www.livingstreets.org.uk
http://www.mfe.govt.nz/issues/urban/design-protocol/index.html
http://www.buildingforlife.org/publications/delivering-great-places-to-live
http://www.placecheck.info
http://www.pps.org

http://www.pps.org/info/placemakingtools/casesforplaces/gr_place_feat
http://www.princes-foundation.org
http://www.slowmovement.com
http://www.smartgrowth.org

http://www.sustainablecities.org.uk
http://www.the-edi.co.uk/?section=publications_EDG
http://www.transitorienteddevelopment.org
http://vancouver.ca/commsvcs/currentplanning/urbandesign/index.htm